"The brilliance of the *International Critical Pedagogy Reader* is its audacity to de-colonize the taken for granted 'Center-Periphery' exporting model of critical pedagogy—creating, instead, a powerful place for subaltern voices to be heard. This comprehensive, illuminating, and timely edited book re-inserts the centrality of both the 'critical' and political coherence, remaining loyal to principles of liberation and emancipation. The *International Critical Pedagogy Reader* makes it powerfully clear that critical pedagogy is a way of life that does not require courage to be critical but simply demands coherence, humility, and ethics."

Donaldo Macedo, Distinguished Professor of Arts and Education,
University of Massachusetts Boston

"Intellectually engaging and emotionally inspiring. Relevant global coverage to inform reflective practitioners, and a scholarly companion for educators motivated by social and pedagogical justice."

Juliana McLaughlin, Senior Lecturer, Queensland University of Technology, Australia
and Past President, Australian and New Zealand Comparative and
International Education Society

"With such a comprehensive blend of particulars and universals, local and global, this reader assumes an inimitable encyclopedic significance. Indispensable for educational professionals, researchers, and students, it will engender innumerable milestones in educational research across the globe."

Dev Pathak, Assistant Professor of Sociology, South Asian University, India

"Curating essays from over 20 countries around the world, the *International Critical Pedagogy Reader* shows how critical pedagogy is being reframed and reinvented philosophically, politically, and pedagogically in relation to contextual, cultural, social, and economic sensibilities and specificities. Widening the critical pedagogical lens beyond Western countries, this reader is an essential reference source for all students, academics, social activists, and researchers who subscribe to the view that the 'struggle for freedom, equality, and social justice is never an act of courage, but an act of intellectual honesty.'"

Juliet Perumal, Faculty of Education, University of Johannesburg, South Africa

"This reader is destined to become a pivotal book in critical pedagogy. It will reshape the field by extending critical pedagogy's geography and issues. A must-read for educators committed to decolonizing pedagogy."

Carmel Borg, Faculty of Education, University of Malta, Malta

"Paulo Freire has said that critical pedagogy can transform the world for the benefit of humanity. This volume shows the extent to which critical pedagogy has itself now become a global phenomenon and the impact it has made on the theory and practice of radical education around the world."

Mike Neary, University of Lincoln, United Kingdom

"The *International Critical Pedagogy Reader* holds the keys to the forthcoming evolution of this discipline in the near future. Indispensable not only for professors, students, and researchers of critical pedagogy but also for critical sociology, cultural theory, and cultural studies professionals."

Eugenio-Enrique Cortés-Ramírez, Universidad de Castilla – La Mancha, Spain

"This book brings us a powerful discussion on critical pedagogy from around the world. All concerns exposed in this collection are the same concerns held by many critical scholars to empower public education and teachers. It is a crucial book for graduate and undergraduate students in education, as well as for public school teachers."

Alvaro Moreira Hypolito, Associate Professor, Federal University of Pelotas, Brazil

International Critical Pedagogy Reader

Carefully curated to highlight research from more than twenty countries, the *International Critical Pedagogy Reader* introduces the ways in which the educational phenomenon that is critical pedagogy is being reinvented and reframed around the world. A collection of essays from both historical and contemporary thinkers coupled with original essays introduce this school of thought and approach it from a wide variety of cultural, social, and political perspectives. Academics from South America, Europe, Africa, the Middle East, Asia, and North America describe critical pedagogy's political, ideological, and intellectual foundations, tracing its international evolution and unveiling how key scholars address similar educational challenges in diverse national contexts. Each section links theory to critical classroom practices and includes a list of sources for further reading to expand upon the selections offered in this volume. A robust collection, this reader is a crucial text for teaching and understanding critical pedagogy on a truly international level.

Antonia Darder holds the Leavey Presidential Endowed Chair in Ethics and Moral Leadership in the School of Education at Loyola Marymount University and is also Professor Emerita of Educational Policy, Organization, and Leadership at the University of Illinois at Urbana-Champaign.

Peter Mayo is Professor of Education Studies at the University of Malta and a member of the Collegio Docenti for the doctoral research program in Educational Sciences and Continuing Education at the Università degli Studi di Verona.

João Paraskeva is Chair of the Department of Education Leadership and Director of the EdD/PhD in Education Leadership and Policy Studies at the University of Massachusetts, Dartmouth.

International Critical Pedagogy Reader

Antonia Darder, Peter Mayo,
and João Paraskeva

EDITORS

Routledge
Taylor & Francis Group

NEW YORK AND LONDON

First published 2016
by Routledge
711 Third Avenue, New York, NY 10017

and by Routledge
2 Park Square, Milton Park, Abingdon, Oxon, OX14 4RN

Routledge is an imprint of the Taylor & Francis Group, an informa business

Library of Congress Cataloging in Publication Data
Darder, Antonia.
The international critical pedagogy reader / by Antonia Darder, Peter Mayo, and João Paraskeva.
pages cm
Includes bibliographical references and index.
1. Critical pedagogy. I. Paraskeva, João M. II. Mayo, Peter, 1955- III. Title.
LC196.D37 2015
370.11'5--dc23
2015002429

ISBN: 978-1-138-01788-7 (hbk)
ISBN: 978-1-138-01789-4 (pbk)

Typeset in Minion
by Saxon Graphics Ltd, Derby

Printed and bound in the United States of America by Publishers Graphics, LLC on sustainably sourced paper.

Contents

28   The University at a Crossroads (Portugal)   295
      BOAVENTURA DE SOUSA SANTOS (2012)

29   Higher Education and Class: Production or Reproduction (Greece)   303
      PANAGIOTIS SOTIRIS (2013)

30   Local Struggles: Women in the Home and Critical Feminist
      Pedagogy in Ireland   310
      G. HONOR FAGAN (1991)

31   Say You Want a Revolution: Suggestions for the Impossible Future
      of Critical Pedagogy (Luxembourg)   317
      GERT J.J. BIESTA (1998)

      Further Readings   327

      Contributors   329

      Permissions   332

      Index   334

The Internationalization of Critical Pedagogy
An Introduction

Antonia Darder, Peter Mayo, and João Paraskeva

Since the early eighties scholars in the English-speaking world have been exposed to a heterogeneous corpus of literature from the United States under the rubric of critical pedagogy, an educational literature. Peter McLaren, a central figure in this U.S. tradition, describes critical pedagogy as "fundamentally concerned with the centrality of politics and power in our understanding of how schools work" (McLaren 1994: 167). For this volume, 'schools' with 'education' is conceived in its broadest context, to do justice to the various provisions and manifestations of the field, formal, non-formal and informal. This definition is particularly significant and necessary to an international reading of critical pedagogy, which also applies to the domain of emancipatory adult learning. Paulo Freire and U.S. neo-Gramscian scholars such as Henry Giroux, Michael Apple, and others helped to frame this field of study with respect to new theoretical avenues, anchored in key critical principles, including cultural politics, political economy, oppressor-oppressed dialectic, hegemony, ideology, critique, resistance, dialogue, consciousness, and hope and possibility (Darder, Baltodano, & Torres 2008).[1] Most importantly and worth repeating, critical pedagogy unapologetically engages education as a significant political arena in the struggle for democracy.

Critical pedagogy is fundamentally concerned with the relationship between education and power in society and, thus, uncompromisingly committed to the amelioration of inequalities and social exclusions in the classroom and society at large. Conceptually and in practice, this radical educational view contends forthrightly with the inextricability of power/knowledge relations. Critical pedagogy in the U.S. has drawn inspiration from a host of radical Western intellectuals of the 20th century. Most notably are the writings of Karl Marx, Antonio Gramsci, the Frankfurt school, Jürgen Harbermas, Michel Foucault, and others. These works were most formidably developed and expanded into a critical theory of education by U.S. intellectuals such as Henry Giroux, Peter McLaren, Michael Apple, Donaldo Macedo, bell hooks, Joe Kincheloe, Ira Shor, Antonia Darder, Douglas Kellner, Shirley Steinberg, and others.

While the theorists involved in the evolution of the field utilize a variety of analytical approaches, one common element underscored is the political foundation of education. Education, hence, is not viewed as a neutral enterprise, but rather as a contested terrain. Heuristically speaking, education is perceived as serving one of two purposes in society. It either serves to 'domesticate' and strengthen the existing relations of power and therefore perpetuates the ills—economic, social, and environmental—critiqued throughout its corpus of literature, rendering conditions of oppression as non-existent (Sousa Santos 2014); or else it serves to 'liberate' in contributing to the ushering in of a new world in which principles of social justice and ecological sustainability are held uppermost.

1

Of course, this dialectic of oppression and liberation comprises ends of a non-linear continuum, with critical educators striving assiduously to move towards the latter end, while being buffeted by a variety of forces, towards the other. Odd as it might be, in a world with such deeply entrenched inequalities, critical educators face tough challenges and uphill battles, in their efforts to make "the critical" a truly dominant tradition (Sousa Santos 1999). Needless to say, contending with the resulting tensions and contradictions is often tantamount to living and acting critically. Conceptually and politically, it is this notion that fundamentally connects critical pedagogy to the work of Paulo Freire in *Pedagogy of the Oppressed*, although he is clearly not the only educational philosopher to speak to these pedagogical concerns, as will become most apparent by this collection of international authors writing, directly or indirectly, about many of the critical principles that have informed the tradition of U.S. critical pedagogy.

Beyond a North American Context

Despite attributions made to Paulo Freire's work by major exponents of the field, the field in general has been presented with a decidedly North American ring to it. Stretched further, it incorporates insights from an Anglo-dominated world, which includes USA, Canada, Australia, New Zealand, and the United Kingdom. The southern voices incorporated, although important voices in the majority world, still are those ensconced in the intellectual traditions dominated by Western North American scholarship. And yet we would argue that there is an international dimension to the field that extends well beyond these limited geographical contours. It includes radical intellectuals from different parts of the world, some of whom make no bones about subscribing to critical pedagogy; while others, including historical revolutionary figures and social movements, who have addressed similar issues concerning education and power, would not have called themselves so, particularly since they anticipated 'critical pedagogy' by several years, and, in certain cases, a century or more.

What renders their work germane to and in sync with a critical pedagogy is their basic pedagogical and philosophical vision, which embraces a non-negotiable utopia, as well as directly counters historical *epistemicides* produced by Western hegemonic assumptions of the world (Paraskeva 2014; Sousa Santos 2007). What enhances their suitability to be included in the field is the fact that texts concerning critical pedagogy, such as the basic foundational one by McLaren (1994), as well as contemporary critical pedagogy websites (see the Paulo-Nita Freire International Critical pedagogy website),[2] list mostly male historical figures such as W. E. B. Dubois, John Dewey and Antonio Gramsci (who along with Paulo Freire is one of the few non North-Americans who constantly make it into the list) among major exponents of the field. Although, it makes sense for critical pedagogy to acknowledge these sources of inspiration; once they are listed among the pantheon of critical pedagogy scholars, then it makes equal sense to draw on a larger body of thinking, deriving from historical individuals and movements situated beyond the constraints of a Western North American context. In so doing, we argue for the need to interrupt an unintentional fallacy of a U.S. driven critical pedagogical canon, whose modern Western thinking, as Boaventura de Sousa Santos claims (2007), produces an "abyssal thinking," in that it consists

> …of a system of visible and invisible distinctions, the invisible ones being the foundation of the visible ones. The invisible distinctions are established through radical lines that divide social reality into two realms, the realm of "this side of the line" and the realm of "the other side of the line." The division is such that "the other side of the line" vanishes as reality, becomes nonexistent, and is indeed produced as nonexistent. Nonexistent means not existing in any relevant or comprehensible way of being. Whatever is produced as nonexistent is radically excluded because it lies beyond the realm of what the accepted conception of inclusion considers to be its other. What most fundamentally characterizes

abyssal thinking is thus the impossibility of the co-presence of the two sides of the line. To the extent that it prevails, this side of the line only prevails by exhausting the field of relevant reality. Beyond it, there is only nonexistence, invisibility, non-dialectical absence.

(45).

With all this in mind, we turn now to a brief discussion of some key international influences; some that, although generally absent from the critical pedagogical literature, also bring decisively distinct and useful insights to our international understanding of critical pedagogy.

Paulo Freire

Outside Western North American influences, Paulo Freire stands out as one of the most formidable intellectual forces in critical pedagogy. Freire's ideas, grounded in his adult literacy work in the rural countryside of Brazil, gained prominence in the 1970's, as a direct outcome of both the historical moment and the release of the English translation of *Pedagogy of the Oppressed* in the United States. As in France, Mexico, and other parts of the world, student unrests of the late 1960s and early 1970s resulted in significant political movements for emancipatory struggles, where Freire's writings, along with those of Frantz Fanon, Albert Memmi, Amilcar Cabral, Julius Nyerere, Ernesto (Che) Guevara, and others provided impetus for rethinking conditions of material and political oppression beyond dominant Western assumptions of the other. Among these, Freire's work, at the time, provided some of the most focused and systematic arguments related to question of oppression and the education of oppressed populations.

A central concept of Freire's pedagogy is that of *liberating praxis*, which entails a process of teaching and learning that supports the evolution of conscientização or social consciousness (Mayo 2004).[3] For Freire, pedagogy should enable students to read not only the word but also their world; and to do so critically without avoiding unsettling questions that unveil the complexities of asymmetrical power relations and hegemonic social arrangements. The focus here is placed upon students moving from 'object' to 'subject' of history, in the sense of individuals becoming active social actors, as opposed to passive producers and consumers. As social actors, students become capable of learning and acting collectively to advocate for change and contribute to the renegotiation of hegemonic social relations.

The key entry point to learning for Freire, then, is the learners' existential situation or lived experience. Moreover, Freire's view deeply counters the fatalism of banking education, which indulges in the *mythification* of the world (Freire 1994; 1970) and, by so doing, conserves the objectification of students and the reification of knowledge. As such, the learning process should be one that enables students to contend with their actual conditions, in order to move towards greater critical consciousness and a critical literacy that prepares them to engage effectively with complex forms of knowledge and to enact practices in their lives in sync with a more just world. This also clearly entails a humanizing pedagogy for the radicalization of oppressed populations, which is fundamentally grounded in an integral dialogical process fueled by a radical love for the world and a deep commitment to social and material liberation (Darder 2015; 2002).

It is also worth noting here that beyond the historical influence of Freire's ideas internationally, his ideas continue to be expanded and reinvented by intellectuals and educators in Brazil and beyond, including his widow, Ana Maria Araujo Freire who has authored numerous publications and edited several volumes that aim to conserve the integrity of Paulo Freire's humanizing vision of education (Borg & Mayo 2000). Along the same lines, the existence of hundreds of Freirian-inspired institutes, schools, educational projects, and publications bear witness to the saliency and power of Freire's ideas within the international arena of critical pedagogy.

Don Lorenzo Milani

An important international figure in the critical pedagogy field is Don Lorenzo Milani. Milani, an Italian Catholic priest from Florence, is a household name in his native Italy and has a following in other countries such as Spain, inspiring a movement of educators there. He is best associated with an important text, *Letter to a Teacher* (Borg, Cardona and Caruana 2013), written by his students at the School of Barbiana, in the locality of Sant'Andrea in Barbiana, Tuscany. The text, inspired by the teachings of Milani, anticipated many of the salient ideas associated with the 'new sociology of education' and the North American-driven critical pedagogy (Mayo 2013). Its political impact was so strong that it became a rallying text for social movements in Italy engaged in the much-documented 1968 period of turmoil and activism that swept across Europe. Written in the form of a narrative by eight boys who were school 'dropouts,' the text provides a strong illustration of the way social class politics conditions students' life chances, mediating the process of success or failure of a bourgeois-oriented public education system.

Issues addressed by the text, yet familiar in our contemporary context, include 'cultural capital' and 'habitus' (Bourdieu 1986), political misrepresentation of the oppressed in parliament, selectivity and tracking, private tuition, indirect taxation and cultural alienation. These are offset against aspects of the Barbiana experience. This experience includes dialogic and collective learning and writing, utilizing different learning pathways for different students, peer tutoring involving senior students teaching younger ones, reading history to counter 'sanitized' chronicles, and critical media literacy that included reading and responding to daily national newspapers. Milani's pedagogy also combined academic with technical education, humanistic with scientific learning, and the study of foreign languages at home and abroad.

Don Milani was also instructive in his teaching and reading of history *against the grain* as part of the struggle to exercise the right to conscientious objection regarding the military draft. This draft was compulsory for young men until just a few years ago. His writings provided grist for the mill in this regard, as written responses to the military chaplains who chided conscientious objectors and to the judges contending with the case that was filed against him. Milani's writings are most relevant for a critical pedagogy against the 'culture of militarization,' a salient topic in the field today (Batini, Mayo and Surian 2014); and for a culture of peace (Borg and Grech 2014). Milani's writings are also most relevant to contemporary discourses about working class solidarity. Lastly, one can indeed detect parallels between Freire and Milani's pedagogical approaches (Mayo 2007), in that both offered a humanizing understanding of education, where faith in students' capacity to learn is paramount and the liberation of the most vulnerable populations is an intentional pedagogical purpose.

Other Intellectual Influences

Theorists writing in the critical pedagogical tradition are also heavily indebted to other intellectual influences. Martin Buber, for example, exerted an important influence on the emergence of the Freirean concept of 'authentic dialogue' through his writings on interpersonal communication as captured in such works as *I and Thou* (Buber 1958). Buber, who originally hailed from Central Europe, moved to the Middle East to what was then Palestine. He left a tremendous legacy, especially in the state of Israel, where an Institute at the Hebrew University of Jerusalem bears his name. His intellectual legacy among Israelis and Jews in general is probably as great and far-reaching as that of Nikolaj Frederik Severin Grundtvig among Danes and other Scandinavians.

If we remain within the region, a turbulent region where people need little reminding that *education is political*, we come across the ideas of a leading Palestinian intellectual, Ibrahim Abu-Loghod, especially with regard to critical curricular issues. Abu-Loghod lived and taught for many years in the USA but spent the last years of his life in Ramallah, Palestine, where he served as Rector of Bir Zeit University, and spearheaded the development of a Palestinian curriculum that replaced the Jordanian one for schools on the West Bank and the Egyptian one for schools in Gaza. He developed important curricular ideas for a beleaguered people, when involved in the process of Palestinian curriculum development. His writings and those of his daughter Lila Abu-Loghod and Edward Said, both having lived in the USA but with constant contact with their own homeland, have inspired Palestinian and non-Palestinian writers in the field of critical pedagogy. Nahla Abdo (in Borg and Mayo 2007), a sociologist, activist, and writer constitutes yet another Palestinian example. Abdo, whose writings engage critical issues related to gender, has worked in Palestine helping to set up the Palestinian Ministry for Women Affairs, a 'first' for governments in the region.

Moving from the Middle East to Africa, we also find important experiences and insights for an international critical pedagogy. Without overlooking persistent forms of indigenous education in Africa, well documented also within the context of critical pedagogy (Dei 2011), we highlight noteworthy initiatives in the same continent undertaken by visionary state officials such as Kwame Nkrumah, Gamal Abdel Nasser Hussein, Julius Nyerere (Nyerere 1968; 1979), and freedom fighters and leaders such as Amilcar Cabral—who, in particular, had an important influence on Paulo Freire's thinking (Freire 1978)—in promoting an anti-colonial public education with its efforts to Africanize education, without throwing out the (knowledge) baby with the (colonial) bathwater. In an article that João Paraskeva helped translate into English, Freire not only acknowledges his intellectual admiration for Cabral, but also establishes a dialogue between Cabral and Antonio Gramsci, arguing Cabral as the conceptualizer of a specific critical organic intellectuality (see Freire 2009).

Some of the revolutionary writings and insights of Martinican, Frantz Fanon and Tunisian-Jew, Albert Memmi are most pertinent to this discussion. Both of these radical authors worked tirelessly to articulate a critical understanding of the destructive impact of colonialism to racialized populations, both as individuals and social beings. Given Fanon and Memmi's unapologetic anticolonial stances, their contributions have provided significant foundational insights in positing a postcolonial education—viewed here in a wider context. An example of this is evident in the last chapter of *Pedagogy of the Oppressed*, where Freire employs important ideas by both Fanon and Memmi in developing his ideas related to revolutionary leadership (Freire 1970; 1993). Hence, these also fall within the purview of an international critical pedagogy, especially critical pedagogy that incorporates postcolonial sensibilities. In South Africa, critical pedagogical forms emerged through important educational social movements such as the People's Education, Workers' Education, and Education with Production. In addition, individuals such as I. B. Tabata, Rick Turner, Ruth First, Steve Biko, Mathew Goniwe, Abu Asvat, Neville Alexander, and others have contributed to the formation of an emancipatory educational tradition in the region. More recently, the writings of scholar-activists such as Salim Vally and Juliet Perumal continue to expand on this tradition.

Historical moments in different parts of the globe also have furnished us with pedagogical strategies that fall easily within the context of an all-embracing critical pedagogy. Many of these ideas have emanated from Latin America, Mexico and the Caribbean, within the context of the revolutionary movements of Cuba, Nicaragua, and Grenada; and, most recently, the Zapatista struggles in Chiapas and the Bolivarian revolution in Venezuela (Marquez 2005). One can argue that these experiences have not been short of exposure in the international education literature. They have featured prominently in critical pedagogy, mainly because of the Freirean connection, and also in comparative and international education. Although not always noted in critical pedagogical discussion, Freire's exposure to the liberation theology movement of the 1950s and 60s in Latin America—particularly through the writings of Gustavo Gutierrez and others—as well as Freire's time in Chile also supported his emancipatory vision of education. In addition, the contribution to critical pedagogy by one of Freire's Brazilian contemporaries Augusto Boal, whose *theatre of the oppressed* has inspired radical popular education movements around the globe, is also noteworthy.

In India, several forms of critical pedagogy have evolved, inspired by the historical writings and practices of two significant public figures, Mahatma Gandhi and Rabindranath Tagore, who contributed to the evolution of an anti-colonial public discourse across the country, which also extended into the arena of education (Bhattacharya 2013). Although neither would be considered explicitly anti-capitalists, their ideas have been garnered by critical educators in India to support a liberating pedagogy and a critique of neoliberal capitalism. For instance, Gandhi's view on linking work to education—although misinterpreted by the post-independence Indian bourgeoisie as vocationalization of education—essentially spoke to an emancipatory pedagogy that could instill social agency in the dignity of labor among students, particularly in a country where the oppressed have contended with a hardened caste system of discrimination and the ravages of its colonial past (Kumar 2012). He is also indirectly connected, via associates such as Mira Behn and Vinoba Bhave, with concepts such as environmental activism and learning, through the Chipko movement and *Nai Talim* (New Learning).[4]

Tagore, on the other hand, founded one of the greatest critical humanistic educational experiments in India, at the turn of last century. In his works *Nationalism* (1918), and *Religion of Man* (1931), Tagore argues for the need for global critical learning processes that can channel humanity toward sustainable progress. He considered connections with nature to be every bit as important to learning as those forged among teachers and students within a school and believed that the curriculum had to be kept flexible and geared upon the particular proclivities of students, with a clear intercultural focus on history, art and literature (Mukherjee 2014). Although profoundly influenced by Socrates and Rousseau as well, Tagore was able to implement an indigenous educational project that placed arts, ethics, and creativity at the very core of a permanent self-criticism, a humanizing pedagogical process that conceived of the world as holistic.

On a more academic terrain, Gayatri Chakravorty Spivak's post-colonial discourses on *subaltern* populations and Homi Bhabha's articulations on *hybridity* and *the third space* have challenged hegemonic assumptions of Indian identity and oppressive social conditions that impact the everyday lives of economically and politically marginalized students in India. Drawing on Gramsci's work, notably his notes on Italian history and interrupted writing on the 'Southern Question,' Ranajit Guha and his colleagues in the *Subaltern Studies* group promoted readings of history against the grain of conventional interpretations, seeing post-British Raj history within the context of caste and social class politics, using Gandhi's dictum of 'colonization without the English.' Lastly, we would also like to bring attention to the contributions of Jotirao Phule and Savitri Phule, who were also important educators and thinkers in the 19th century, given that they belonged to the marginalized class and caste. Their views on education were refreshingly distinct from more affluent Indian thinkers, in that they brought their experiences as subaltern subjects to their writings on education.[5]

Europe, too, has contributed to significant upsurges in critical pedagogical thinking, primarily in reaction to its Western authoritarian legacies of the state. Take for example Spain, or, more accurately, the various regions with their specific identities, some aspiring to nationhood, others falling under control of the state. The 'second republic,' brutally dismantled following the Spanish civil war and its popular democratic legacies destroyed during the Franco years, furnished us with a broad array of anti-dogmatic (there were persisting legacies of the 'Inquisition' which extended well beyond its established historical period) and anti-oppressive educational and cultural initiatives. This involved recognition and re-evaluation of different forms of popular culture (e.g. Flamenco music and dancing) and communal theatre (e.g. the work of Lorca and his University troupe, *La Barraca* [the Shed]: see Flecha 1992*)*, an attempt at mass public education of the formal and non-formal type, and programs of teacher education. Many of these teachers, education leaders and cultural organizers subsequently paid for their efforts with their life. Federico Garcia Lorca features prominently among these victims.

When we look at Europe, we discover critical pedagogues who anticipated many of the themes later foregrounded in critical pedagogy. And we are not referring here to the 'mini-revolution' in educational thought brought about in the early seventies by the 'new sociology of education' in England, spearheaded by an introduction to a compendium of writings penned by Michael Young (Young 1971). We are referring to a wide breadth of ideas, experiences, and struggles, which included the phenomenon of 'independent working class education' that spread throughout the continent and also as far as Canada and Australia (Waugh 2009). We also note here ideas and educational experiments by a few figures from the Frenchman, Celestine Freinet; to the Catalans, Francesc Ferrer I Guardia and later Rosa Sensat i Vilà; to the efforts of Pep Aparicio Guadas and associates at the Instituto Paulo Freire de España; to the Italians, Maria Montessori, Danilo Dolci, Aldo Capitini and the late Mario Lodi.

Ferrer I Guardia left a mark with his *Escuela Moderna* (Modern School) and its anarchist undertones (the Modern School also had a following in the form of a movement in the U.S.). One can also consider his fellow Catalan, Rosa Sensat i Vilà with her *Institut de Cultura i Biblioteca Popular de la Dona* (Woman's Cultural Institute and Popular Library). Her pedagogical philosophy differed considerably from that of Ferrer I Guardia and she was less politically committed, more of a Catalan equivalent to Montessori.[6] However, she has the merit of having given rise to Europe's first women's cultural and working educational centre. Freinet's cooperative learning experiences and reconstruction of the media are well documented. The cooperative learning experiment was taken up and reinvented by Lodi in Italy.

Maria Montessori also deserves her due recognition in critical pedagogy not least for her different forms of peer tutoring as well as her principled stance in relation to the Fascist government of the time. Then there is Danilo Dolci with his learning through collective community action (involving hunger and 'reverse' strikes) in a Mafia dominated Sicily, with its high levels of unemployment, poverty and total neglect by the country's authorities, even in the immediate aftermath of catastrophic earthquakes. In Northern Italy, we come across the Umbrian, anti-Fascist peace activist and educator, Aldo Capitini with his adult education initiatives for peace and grassroots democracy (omnicrazia), mainly through his contribution to setting up throughout Umbria and beyond centres for social orientation (COS).

Political Conflict, Social Movement, & Critical Pedagogy

Most relevant for a critical pedagogy are issues emerging from different sites of struggle, involving military and other political conflicts, resulting in perennial losses of life, as in the Middle East, Africa, and other regions. Then there is the issue of the constantly hazardous and life threatening task of migrants, victims of a globally ravaging neoliberal and imperial process, crossing the Sahara and the Mediterranean sea to reach Europe, with its constructed image of the 'good life' and the 'Eldorado'—constructions which often prove illusory. Both of these are important topics in a genuinely international critical pedagogy. Equally important and pertinent are recent mass struggles such as those in Greece and Spain, involving movements known as the *indignados* and Turkey with respect to the *Gezi Park Revolt*. The general thrust of all these manifestations, each involving learning dimensions and critical educational dimensions, is a strong anti-neoliberal stance.

As might be expected, critical pedagogy has quite a following in these countries. One comes across scholars and activists in Greece who are fully committed to a critical pedagogy, drawing insights from many of the critical scholars discussed earlier. Greek activist scholars, such as Maria Nikolakaki (University of the Peloponnese), and those of a decidedly Marxist bent, such as Panagiotis Sotiris (University of the Aegean), or Kostas Skordoulis (University of Athens), who contributed to the establishment of the critical education conference, have been active in the field. Critical pedagogy in Greece gains particular resonance in view of the quite recent experience of totalitarianism (1967–1974) and its scars, beyond the current situation of *debtocracy*, which has led to demonstrations in globalised public spaces such as Syntagma Square. The same would apply to Spain, which has witnessed similar events, in the context of the quest for a *¡Democracia Real YA! (Real Democracy Now!)*. It boasts centres of critical pedagogy such as CREA at the University of Barcelona, involving Ramon Flecha, Marta Soler, Lidia Puigvert Mallart, Lena de Botton, and the late Jesus Pato Gomes, among others. Spain also hosts a Paulo Freire Institute comprising of critical pedagogues from the Valencia and Seville areas. These include Emilio Lucio, very active in education among social movements and with respect to the participatory budget and Manolo Reyes collective memory project (unearthing repressed memories of the Franco years), Dolores Monferrer, Paqui Borox and Pep Aparicio Guadas. The last three have been responsible for popular education initiatives, of Freirean and critical pedagogical inspiration, within the Valencia area and for the publication of numerous texts in Castilian and Valencian / Catalan some of which being translations of established critical pedagogy texts.

Also in Spain, we need to highlight the role of intellectuals, such as José Gimeno Sacristán (1988), Jurjo Torres Santomé (2001; 2012), Mariano Fernández Enguita, Ángel I. Pérez Gómez (2004), and Julia Varela (2007; 2011), as the engines of the *Movimientos de Renovación Pedagógica e da Pedagogía Crítica*. At the very end of General Franco's dictatorship and at the emergence of the current Spanish democratic representative liberal matrix, such groups of organic intellectuals engaged in the production and reproduction of powerful critical analysis, having a huge impact within the educational system. They challenged strong mechanisms of oppression in universities framed by ideological and discursive control mechanisms, such as Opus Dei, which was quite towering during General Franco's regime. These groups of intellectuals were also responsible for promoting some of the most radical and critical thought from the UK, the US, and France.

A good example of this was the *Congreso Internacional de Didáctica, "Volver a pensar la educación,"* organized by Jurjo Torres Santomé held in Corunha in 1993, a landmark in critical theory and pedagogy in Spain and in Portugal as well. World-renowned critical theorists and pedagogues as well as Spanish left intellectuals participated in this crucial meeting. Such a group of intellectuals from different autonomic regions of Spain showed an impressive record of publications, working with teachers and public schools, defending public education as well as examining and promoting liberatory educational practices. It is within this context that Spanish critical intellectuals connected with the most important progressive educational publisher in Spain *Ediciones Morata*. One cannot understand accurately the history of the democratization of education in Spain without the massive impact of the titles published by *Morata*. This group of intellectuals together with Jaume Carbonell and many teachers connected with the different *Movimentos de Renovação Pedagógico* (MRPs) would end up promoting the countless educational experiences as well as analysis of social mobilization that were published in the Journal *Cuadernos de Pedagogia* that just celebrated 40 years. These intellectuals organized debates, social forums, general assemblies, challenging the mainstream media the neoliberal and ultra-conservative policies imposed by conservative governments, such as LOMCE (Ley Organica de Melhora da Qualidade Educativa 2013). This group of intellectuals has been on the front line in national massive strikes, challenging the conservative austerity policies imposed both by PSOE and Partido Popular.

In Portugal, profoundly influenced by a wrangle between southern European critical perspectives and US approaches, critical pedagogues tried to conquer a space and time within the complex terrain of educational leadership. The works of Steven Stoer, Antonio Magalhães, Luisa Cortesão, and more recently Paraskeva, are graphic examples of the strengths and limitations of the critical pedagogical project in Portugal, as a semi-peripheral nation. Seminal debates such as *Orgulhosamente Filhos de Rousseau*, led by Stoer, Cortesao and others, as well the heated debates on *Abordagens Criticas e Pos-Estruturais* and *Marxismo e Educacao – Educacao Publica em Debate* championed by Paraskeva at the University of Minho have moved critical pedagogy to a more productive terrain, despite conservative challenges.

Odd as it might be the challenge in Portugal came, not only from dominant groups but also from within the very core of specific progressive intellectuals circles profoundly concerned with the way radical critical theory and pedagogues were occupying a substantive space. The volume, *Marxismo e Educacao,* edited by Paraskeva, Ross, and Hursh *(2005)* was the first comprehensive Marxist/neo Marxist examination of education and ideological production published in Portugal. Paraskeva was also responsible for the translation into Portuguese of countless seminal work of critical theorists and pedagogues that were never translated in Portugal before, namely Michael Apple, Henry Giroux, Donaldo Macedo, and Peter McLaren. Quite recently *Pedagogia da Autonomia* was published in Portugal as well. In 2001, Paraskeva together with Hypolito and Gandin founded the first open access journal *Curriculo sem Fronteiras* (CsF) a publication that aims at being a forum for discussion on critical and emancipatory education and for advancing the dialogue among the Portuguese-speaking countries. In a CsF manifesto, Paraskeva, Hypolito and Gandin (2001) argued,

> contemporary education enters the new millennium immersed in a set of extremely complex challenges, especially if we consider the social and economic asymmetries that are being multiplied by the subtleties of the strategies imposed by the dynamics of capitalism, in which the mechanisms and the policies that constitute the foundation of globalization are diffused. Nevertheless, the overwhelming majority of countries that contribute to the consubstantiation of this social project is largely excluded from the benefits of this hegemonic process. Among these countries – with different levels of inclusion/exclusion – are Angola, Brazil, Cape Verde, Guinea-Bissau, Mozambique, Portugal, S. Tomé and Príncipe, and Timor-Leste, expressing together a specific unity in diversity. In spite of their particular identities, underpinned by a common and intertwined past – as the historic will of these peoples in the plastic arts, literature, music, and cinema expresses –, we believe that these distinct realities can constitute a specific political project. This project could allow not only for the construction of a specific set of actions but also for the development of dynamics that, as a whole, can participate in an ample counter-hegemonic political movement, one that represents an opposition to the social policies imposed by the neo-liberal and neo-conservative strategies.
>
> (1)

With respect to critical theory and pedagogy in Portugal, we need also to highlight two other seminal pieces. Michael Apple and Antonio Novoa's *Paulo Freire Politica e Pedagogia* and Boaventura de Sousa Santos' *Porque é tão difícil construir uma teoria crítica?* While in the former Apple and Nóvoa (2002) challenge the impact of neoliberal policies and the role of critical pedagogues in challenging such nefarious policies, on the latter, Sousa Santos (1999) questions how and why in a world, with so much to criticize, it has been so difficult to produce a robust critical theory.

Critical pedagogy has also been finding fertile ground in Turkey, where a vibrant left has made its mark in a variety of ways, through manifestations, academic conferences, publications, and through the presence in such centres as Istanbul and Ankara of a thriving leftist book culture, comprising publications in Turkish of texts considered to be critical pedagogy classics. Kalkedon, Dipnot, Notabene, Ayrıntı, Metis, Yordam, Tan, Sol and Utopya feature among these publishing houses, in addition to left wing national newspapers such as *Bir-Gün* and *Sol* which often carry articles focusing on different aspects of critical pedagogy. As a consequence, critical pedagogy is making its mark among university teachers and students, in centres such as the University of

Ankara, Gazi University in Ankara and Boğazici University in Istanbul, some of whom reach out to various communities including the various branches of the leading and left oriented-teachers union, Eğitim Sen[7]. This union also promotes critical pedagogy through the many seminars it funds, activities it carries out, and its academic and professional journals. Kemal Inal (Gazi University), Fatma Gök (Boğazici University) and Hasan Aksoy (University of Ankara) are very active in critical pedagogy, with Inal serving as editor of the journal *Elestirel pedagoji* (Critical Pedagogy).

The work of critical pedagogy in many contexts often occurs against a turbulent background characterised by State-perpetrated violence. Still vivid are memories of the 1973 military coup instigated by the CIA in Chile, to ensure the country's transition to Neoliberalism, and the 1977 May Day massacre at Taksim Square Istanbul, which led to a long suspension of this annual inter-ethnic workers' manifestation. A mothers' movement meets persistently every Saturday afternoon at Galatasaray Square in Istanbul to protest the disappearance of loved ones during the 1980 coup, when even leftist editors lost their life. This echoes Latin America struggles, in Chile and in Argentina, where mothers of the disappeared launched the *Madres de Plaza de Mayo* movement.

In 2013, students and academics in Istanbul joined forces in events such as protest marches and the occupation of Gezi Park, in defence of a public space against a neoliberal encroachment and privatization onslaught (Inal 2013; Gezgin, *et al* 2014). It constituted a defence against a form of 'primitive accumulation.' Critical pedagogy is carried out here in the context of opposition to the current Turkish regime that embraces old Islamic, anti-secularist values alongside large scale US based Neoliberal capitalism. Enacting critical pedagogy in these circumstances often results in facing a police backlash with alleged use of pepper spray, pressured water, plastic bullets and beatings from the police. Tear gas is frequently used, as participants at a recent critical education conference in Ankara (May 2013) found out, when they joined a protest in Ankara against the purported Government induced explosions, on Saturday May 11 2013 in Reyhanli, next to the Syrian border, which left 51 people dead. In an era paced by a state of exception (Agamben 2005) that creates the conditions not for a strong state, but for a violent state, critical pedagogues are expected, in these scenarios, to 'walk the talk,' at the risk of being bruised and battered, or possibly suffering a worse fate at the hands of the state's repressive forces.

Again, Turkish struggles are reminiscent of political conditions and struggles in the Caribbean, Mexico, Central America, and South America, where there has existed a long history of popular uprisings and struggles against repressive forces of the military and the impunity of the state. Within these contexts, emancipatory political actions, literacy campaigns, and popular education efforts have drawn inspiration from the historical writings of Simon Bolívar, José Martí, Enrique Dussel, Pablo Neruda, José Carlos Mariátegui, Emiliano Zapata, Aimé Césaire, Marcus Garvey, and many others who wrestled with questions of politics, justice, human rights, cultural identity, and societal inequalities, particularly with respect to the southern region's colonial past.

Critical pedagogy, however, is also about hope and possibility (see Giroux 1981). Just recently and as an example, Joao Paraskeva hosted Captain Otelo Saraiva de Carvalho at the University of Massachusetts Dartmouth. At the age of 37, Captain Otelo Saraiva de Carvalho masterminded and implemented a revolution—that would end up being called the 'carnation revolution'—which overthrew the Portuguese dictatorship modeled after Mussolini and that lasted 49 years. Captain Carvalho became a world renowned political figure who not only put an end to the Portuguese totalitarian dictatorship, but who was also instrumental in helping liberate the last bastion of colonialism in Africa with the independence of Angola, Cape Verde, Guinéa-Bissau, Mozambique, and São Tomé and Príncipe. When confronted after his keynote address about his courage to do the revolution, Captain Carvalho straightforwardly quoted Amilcar Cabral and said 'the struggle for freedom, equality and social justice is never an act of courage. It is an act of intellectual honesty.' This is what is asked of critical education theorists and pedagogues. This is precisely what many are doing internationally, in the name of emancipatory education and democratic life.

In light of oppression in the world, however, critical pedagogy must also be understood as a form of 'leaving'—a leaving behind of the destructive, degrading, and disabling educational attitudes and practices that rob us of our humanity.

[margin note: critical pedagogy involves leaving behind destructive, degrading, disabling educational attitudes + practices]

Critical Pedagogy Reader as an International Project

Unfortunately, this brief discussion can only skim the surface of the international foundations and the movements that are evolving within the arena of critical pedagogy. There are areas of the globe (particularly non-English-speaking regions) where writings on critical pedagogy are just emerging or, perhaps, not yet fully reinvented or translated with respect to the cultural sensibilities and historical contributions of, for example, Chinese, Japanese, Korean, Thai, Pilipino, or Indonesian intellectuals. Yet, potential contributors to an international critical pedagogy, from past and present, are legion. It is for this reason that formal spaces are needed, in which authors from different parts of the globe can divulge and analyze, as well as excavate and resurrect experiences and writings that can provide grist for the mill of a truly and genuinely international critical pedagogy. Constructing this reader, to complement existing, predominantly North American-oriented, readers in critical pedagogy was, indeed, our intent here, in order to provide an initial, albeit modest, contribution to the task of appreciating and acknowledging critical pedagogy as a genuinely international phenomenon.

There is no doubt that critical pedagogy has become an established school of thought in the field of education. Donaldo Macedo (2006) and Antonia Darder (2012; 2002; 1991), among others, have framed critical pedagogy within the matrix of the political economy of cultural theory and politics, bringing culture, language, and power to the core of the analysis and the struggle against a Western politics of cultural eugenics, where the worldviews of subaltern populations are expected to give way to the alleged superiority of Western ideals and the consuming dictates of advanced capitalism. Given the current *quasi* totalitarian cult that dominates public education, framed in assimilative pedagogies, standards, high stakes tests, and the myth that there are only three solutions to the crises of public schools—convert schools into charters, fully privatize them, or close them down—critical pedagogy and educators around the world have become epistemological lightening rods in challenging dominant pedagogical forms.

This dialectic of struggle and possibility is powerfully reflected throughout the articles included in the seven sections that comprise this collection; including discussion of critical pedagogy and the politics of education; globalization, democracy and education; history, knowledge and power; society, politics and curriculum; critical praxis and literacy, critical pedagogy and the classroom; and critical higher education and activism. It is also apparent by the growing number of critical educational scholars and the flourishing of scholarly articles dedicated to the subject. Moreover, the steadily increasing flow of international writings on critical pedagogy that have emerged in just the last decade also substantiate the need for rethinking—philosophically, politically, and pedagogically—the larger radical educational project. All this, again, points to the pressing need for an *International Critical Pedagogy Reader* that can provide an introductory compilation of some of the most salient articles from around the world, in order to fill the current gap in the literature for an accessible international text that can provide depth and breadth to the field, as well as help us to extend, complement and, at times, challenge the discourse of North American-centric formulations of critical pedagogy; in order that we might more accurately unveil how critical educators around the world are addressing similar or different challenges and possibilities.

Nevertheless, we recognize that no one volume can possibly provide a fully comprehensive and unitary snapshot of the ways in which critical pedagogies are being produced, reinvented, and reframed, particularly outside of English-speaking contexts. This volume, then, is but one modest effort to bring to light this burgeoning phenomenon—a phenomenon that may also signal a growing political dissatisfaction around the world with oppressive educational and state practices, as well as a growing international yearning for greater emancipatory life within schools and society. Critical Pedagogy, hence, is conceived within this volume as a large political-pedagogical movement embodying insights from past and present, from different sides of the colonial divide, from South and North, and from individuals and other specific movements.

In the struggle for human liberation, we contend that human beings everywhere express yearning for the freedom of expression and justice, but through their own cultural, historical, and material forms. If we are to embrace a quest for the genuine globalization of human rights and economic democracy, then we must also open ourselves to learn from the cultural and intellectual traditions of those who historically have been afforded too little room, if any at all, to participate at the center of the praxis. Most importantly, this collection does not pretend to comprise an authoritative volume; in that, true to a critical pedagogy, we acknowledge both the multidimensionality and absences that persist in the field. Thus, it is truly impossible to do so, given limitations of knowledge, space, resources, and the unfortunate lack of English translation of important works. Nevertheless, the writings compiled in this book are meant to arouse and whet the intellectual, political, and pedagogical appetite of critical researchers, educators, students, and activists who seek to better understand critical pedagogy as an international political project for liberation.

Notes

1. See *The Critical Pedagogy Reader* (Routledge) edited by Antonia Darder, Marta Baltodano, and Rodolfo D. Torres (2008) for a concise introduction and discussion of the major principles, generally speaking, associated with critical pedagogy.
2. See website http://freireproject.org/ Accessed 23 September 2014.
3. See Peter Mayo's (2004) *Liberating Praxis* (Praeger) for a well-grounded and in-depth discussion of Paulo Freire's articulation of praxis as a liberating pedagogical phenomenon.
4. See *The Story of Nai Talim: Fifty Years of Education at Sevagrram* by Majorie Sykes at: http://www.swaraj.org/shikshantar/naitalimmarjoriesykes.htm for a concise discussion of Nai Talim that sought to connect physical work, indigenous craft traditions and formal education.
5. See O'Hanlon, R. (2002) (1985). *Caste Conflict and Ideology: Mathama Jotirao Phule and Low Caste Protest in Nineteenth Century Western India* (Revised ed.). Cambridge: Cambridge University Press for an extensive discussion of Jotirao Phule and Savitri Phule contributions.
6. We are indebted to Professor Angel Marzo from the University of Barcelona for this clarification.
7. Not to be confused with the AKP-government oriented Eğitim bir Sen.

References

Apple, M. & Novoa, A. (2002) *Paulo Freire, Politica e Pedagogia*. Porto: Porto Editora.

Agamben, G. (2005) *The State of Exception*. Chicago: University of Chicago Press.

Batini, F, Mayo, P and Surian, A (2014) *Lorenzo Milani, The School of Barbiana and the Struggle for Social Justice*, New York, Frankfurt and Vienna: Peter Lang.

Borg, C. and Mayo, P. (2000). Reflections from a "Third Age" Marriage: Paulo Freire's Pedagogy of Reason, Hope and Passion. In *McGill Journal of Education*, V. 35. N. 2, Spring (105–120).

Borg, C and Mayo, P (2007) *Public Intellectuals, Radical Democracy and Social Movements. A Book of Interviews*, New York, Frankfurt and Vienna: Peter Lang.

Borg, C and Grech, M (eds.) *Lorenzo Milani's Culture of Peace: Essays on Religion, Education and Democratic Life*, New York and London: Palgrave-Macmillan.

Borg, C, Cardona, M and Caruana, S (2013) *Social Class, Language and Power. 'Letter to a Teacher': Lorenzo Milani and the School of Barbiana*, Rotterdam, Boston and Taipei: Sense Publishers.

Bourdieu, P. (1986) The forms of capital. In J. Richardson (Ed.) *Handbook of Theory and Research for the Sociology of Education*. New York, Greenwood (241–58).

Buber, M (1958) *I and Thou*, R. G. Smith (trans.), New York: Charles Scribner's Sons.

Burtchaell, J. T., ed. (1988). *A Just War No Longer Exists. The Teaching and Trial of Don Lorenzo Milani*, Indiana: University of Notre Dame Press.

Corradi, A. 2012. *Non so se don Lorenzo* (I don't know if Don Lorenzo)

Darder, A. (1991). *Culture and Power in the Classroom*. Westport, CT: Bergin & Garvey.

Darder, A. (2002). *Reinventing Paulo Freire: A Pedagogy of Love*. Boulder, CO: Westview.

Darder, A. (2011). *A Dissident Voice: Essays on Culture, Pedagogy, and Power*. New York: Peter Lang.

Darder, A. (2012) *Culture and Power in the Classroom: Educational Foundations for the Schooling of Bicultural Students*. Boulder: Paradigm Publishers

Darder, A. (2015), *Freire and Education*. New York: Routledge.

Darder, A., M. Baltodano, & R.D. Torres (2008). *Critical Pedagogy Reader*. New York: Routledge.

Dei, G. S (Ed.) (2011) *Indigenous Philosophies and Critical Education*, New York, Frankfurt and Vienna: Peter Lang.

Enguita, M. (1999) *La profesión docente y la comunidad*. Madrid: Morata.

Flecha, R. (1992). Spain. In P. Jarvis (Ed.), *Perspectives on Adult Education and Training in Europe* (pp. 190–203). Leicester, UK: NIACE.

Fondazione Laboratorio Mediterraneo (Ed.). (1997). *Obiettivi e Mezzi per IL Parternariato Euromediterraneo. Il Forum Civile EuroMed*. (Objectives and Means of the Euro-Mediterranean Partnership. The EuroMed Civil Forum). Naples: Magma.

Freire, P. (1970/1993). *Pedagogy of the Oppressed* (30th Anniversary Edition). New York: Continuum.

Freire, P. (1978). *Pedagogy in Process. The Letters to Guinea Bissau*. New York: Continuum.

Freire, P (1994) *Pedagogy of Hope*. New York: Continuum.

Freire, P. (2009) Amilcar Cabral. Pedagogue of the Revolution vs. Revolutionary Pedagogue. In Sh. Macrine (ed). *Critical pedagogy in uncertain times: hope and possibilities*. New York: Palgrave.

Gezgin, U. B, Inal, K and Hill, D (2014) *The Gezi Revolt: People's Revolutionary Resistance against Neoliberal Capitalism in Turkey*, Brighton: The Institute for Education Policy Studies (www.ieps.org.uk)

Giroux, H. (1981). *Ideology, Culture and the Process of Schooling*. Philadelphia: Temple University Press.

Gomez, A. (2004) *La cultura escolar en la sociedad neoliberal*. Madrid: Morata.

Inal, K (2014). *Gezi, Isyan, Özgürlük. Sokağın Şenlikli Muhalefeti*, Ankara: Ayrinti Yayinlari.

Kumar, R. (2012). *Education and the Reproduction of Capital*. New York: Palgrave Macmillan.

Macedo, D. (2006). *Literacies of Power*. Westview Press.

Marquez, H. (2005). Venezuela declares itself illiteracy-free. *Global Exchange*, http://www.globalexchange.org/countries/americas/venezuela/3558.html Accessed 17th January 2011

McLaren, P (1994). *Life in Schools: An Introduction to Critical Pedagogy in the Foundations of Education*. New York & London: Longman.

Mayo, P. (2004). *Liberating Praxis*. Santa Barbara, CA: Praeger.

Mayo, P. (2007). "Critical Approaches to Education in the Work of Lorenzo Milani and Paulo Freire." *Studies in Philosophy and Education* 26 (6): 525–44.

Mayo, P (2013). 'Italian signposts for a sociologically and critically engaged pedagogy. Don Lorenzo Milani (1923–1967) and the schools of San Donato and Barbiana revisited'. *British Journal of Sociology of Education*, published online 16 December DOI:10.1080/01425692.2013.848781.

Mukherjee, M (2014). Tagore's Humanist Philosophy and its Relevance in the Contemporary World in *Comparative and International Education Society* website. http://cies2015.org/response-mukherjee.html.

Nyerere, J.K. (1968) *Freedom and Socialism*. Oxford: Oxford University Press.

Nyerere, J.K. (1979). Adult education and development (H. Hinzen & V.J. Hundsdorfer, authors/ eds.), *The Tanzanian Experience. Education for Liberation and Development* (49–55) Hamburg, Germany: UNESCO Institute for Education; London: Evans Brothers.

O'Hanlon, R. (2002) (1985). *Caste Conflict and Ideology: Mathama Jotirao Phule and Low Caste Protest in Nineteenth Century Western India* (Revised ed.). Cambridge: Cambridge University Press

Paraskeva, J. (2014). *Conflicts in Curriculum Theory: Challenging Hegemonic Epistemologies*. New York: Palgrave Macmillan.

Paraskeva, J., E. W. Ross, & D. Hursh (2006). *Marxismo & Educacao*. Porto: Profedicoes.

Paraskeva, J. Hypolito, A. & Gandin, L. (2001) Manifesto. *Journal Curriculo sem Fronteiras*. www.curriculosemfronteiras.org.

Sacristan, J. G. (1988). *Currículum: una reflexión sobre la práctica*. Madrid: Morata.

Scuola di Barbiana (1996). *Lettera a una Professoressa* (Letter To A Teacher), Florence: Libreria Editrice Fiorentina.

Sousa Santos, B. (1999). 'Porque é tão Difícil Construir uma Teoria Crítica?' *Revista Crítica de Ciências Sociais*, 54, pp. 197–215.

Sousa Santos, B. (2007). *Another Knowledge is Possible*. London: Verso.

Sousa Santos, B. (2014). *Epistemologies of the South*. Boulder: Paradigm.

Tagore, R. (1918). *Nationalism*. London: MacMillan and Co.

Tagore, R. (1949). *The Religion of Man*. London: MacMillan and Co.

Torres C.A. (1998a) *Education, Power, and Personal Biography: Dialogues with Critical Educators.* New York and London: Routledge.

Torres Santome, J. (2001) *Educacion en Tiempos de Neoliberalismo.* Madrid: Morata.

Torres Santome, J. (2012) (6 edicion) *Globalización e interdisciplinariedad: El curriculum integrado.* Madrid: Morata.

Varela, J. (2007) *Las Reformas educativas a debate (1982–2006).* Madrid: Morata.

Varela, J. (2011) *Mujeres con voz propia.* Madrid: Morata.

Waugh, C. (2009). *Plebs. The Lost Legacy of Independent Working Class Education.* Occasional paper. Sheffield, UK: Post 16 Educator.

Young MFD (ed.) (1971). *Knowledge and Control: New Directions for the Sociology of Education.* London: Collier-Macmillan.

Section 1
Critical Pedagogy and the Politics of Education

As for their lives as sovereign young men and women tomorrow, I cannot tell my pupils that the only way to revere the law is to obey it. I can only tell them that they should hold mankind's laws in such esteem as to observe them when they are fair (that is, when they uphold the weak). When they see that they are not fair (that is, when the laws sanction abuse of power by the strong) they should fight to change them.

Don Lorenzo Milani, *Letters to the Judges* (1965)

Education is part and parcel of the very nature of education…It does not matter where or when it has taken place, whether it is more or less complex, education has always been a political act.

Paulo Freire, *Pedagogy of the City* (1993)

1

Critical Pedagogy and Postcolonial Education

Ayman Abu-Shomar

King Saud University, Saudi Arabia

A growing body of literature on education explores the potentials of the post-colonial theoretical perspective in myriad domains ranging from global relations to the localities of classroom practices. Post-colonial theoretical tenets have drawn attention to previously under-researched areas and have provided an epistemological challenge to existing theoretical 'frameworks' that normally guide educational studies. Post-colonial forms of analysis, for example, are used "to provide an account of the construction of racialised and stereotyped identities through the colonial curriculum and how these were implicated in the maintenance of a colonial world view and ultimately of colonial power itself" (Crossley and Tikly, 2004, p. 149).

More importantly, post-colonialism's contentions surrounding the relationship between knowledge and power are linked directly to education, both as an institution, where people are inculcated into hegemonic systems of reasoning, and as a site where it is possible to resist dominant discursive practices (Rizvi *et al.* 2006).

A consistent theme in post-colonial literature in education is its work towards a critical review of relations of power, and its attempts to unfold the bitter insinuations regarding claims of homogeneity, universality as well as the Euro-centricity of canons.[1]

Post-colonialism's major interest in this regard is to offer a reappraisal and exploration of the pervasive impact of colonial power over colonised people in cultural, political, social, economic, educational, and intellectual domains. Currently, the fundamental assumptions of the post-colonial theory are grounded in its interest in the histories of the European colonialist and institutional practices and responses, whether resistant or otherwise, to these practices on the colonised societies. In this vein, three strands of the theory are identified: literal description of formerly colonised societies, description of global relations after the colonisation period, and a description of discourse informed by epistemological orientations (Kumar, 2000).

Post-colonialism has informed research into critical reviews of the taken-for-granted narratives in both global and local educational contexts as well as the relational flow from the 'centre' to the 'margin'. Rizvi (2005) views post-colonialism as a forceful means to question and deconstruct the notion of globalisation as 'a global context' and its implications for education. He claims that the hegemonic role it plays in organising a 'particular way of interpreting the world' is often unnoticed and accepted as if unproblematic. The basic idea which Rizvi argues against is the seemingly 'ubiquitous' notion of 'the global context'. He points out that the hegemonic nature of the idea of 'the global context' becomes obvious when applying the concept to developing countries, since it basically means the global spread of Western ideas. Therefore, when thinking of education as becoming almost universal, 'the global context' means the domination of a set of imperial assumptions entrenched on these contexts. Such policies, whether borrowed or imposed on developing countries, misinterpret cultural and political globalisation and tend to steer national policies into the 'same neo-liberal direction'. Rizvi reasons: "institutional disciplinary definitions and hierarchies, legitimizing publications, and institutional authority reside mostly within the core, with 'the periphery' left simply to mimic the core's dominant discourses and practices" (p. 11).

As such, it could be maintained that discourses of globalisation reiterate the former colonial ones that claimed that they were spreading civilisation to people around the world. As Said (1978) reminds us, colonial discourse and the production of 'knowledge' about 'the Orient' was an ideological accompaniment of colonial power, which aimed to justify the colonisers' desire to perpetually subjugate colonised societies. He applied the concept of 'discourse' to examine how the formal study of the 'Orient' in key literary and cultural works to create 'objective' knowledge supported by various disciplines, such as philology, history, anthropology, philosophy, archaeology, and literature. Said asserts that these works were accredited by Western academic consensus. Therefore, "the authority of academic institutions and governments" can create

> ... not only knowledge but the very reality they appear to describe. In time, such knowledge and reality produce a tradition, or what Michel Foucault calls a discourse, whose material presence or weight, not the originality of a given author, is really responsible for the texts produced out of it.
>
> (Said, 1978, p. 94)

Within this understanding, post-colonialism reveals how discourses of former colonialism and the current phenomenon of globalisation intersect with power, language, and knowledge to create an understanding of the world, and embody the values by which one lives, either willingly or by force. Thus, post-colonial repertoires draw attention to how meanings and discourses such as 'global context' or 'international community' are demystified in a way that blurs the lines between ideological and objective. This is, according to Said, is a 'political vision of reality' that incorporates informed assumptions that legitimise its practice over the colonised. In sum, this analysis opens further possibilities to trace connections between the visible and the hidden, ideas and institutions, and the dominant and marginalised in the context of globalised educational contexts. It also shows how power works through language, literature, culture, and the institutions that demonstrate authoritative assumptions about 'other cultures'.

In addition to offering an alternative understanding of the colonial discourse, post-colonialism provides compelling interventionist approaches to address concrete educational problems. Crowley and Matthews (2006) use post-colonialism to establish reconciliation and anti-racism in the classrooms of South African schools. They deem their 'pedagogical intervention' of anti-racism, especially when connected to post-colonial thoughts, a workable model for establishing trust between the white inhabitants and indigenous black Africans. Similarly, Smith (1999) explores the issue of representation of Maori students in New Zealand to assist them in their struggle as subaltern subjects to speak for themselves. Adopting Freire's 'pedagogy of hope' and post-colonialism, Lavia (2006, 2007) examines issues of identity, subalternity and representation in the academic settings. She argues that to enable the teachers, as subaltern professionals, there is a need to promote social awareness of teaching as a form of 'critical professionalism'. However, she insists that "post-colonial aspirations for education require consideration of practice as the convergence of philosophical and methodological endeavours in which the personal, collective and professional can be understood" (p. 328).

Furthermore, post-colonialism adapts miscellaneous theoretical frameworks, such as new historicism, subaltern studies, and feminist theory. The notion of 'discursive practice' (see below) is central to post-colonialism where eclecticism as a discursive epistemological position presents the theory, "rather than a coherent project of proposition, [but as a critical stance that] offers a persistent questioning of power, knowledge, culture and identity that de-universalises the project of the Enlightenment and displaces the mythologies and discourses of modernity and development that shaped these practices" (Andreotti, 2006, p. 10). Young (2003) perceives this eclecticism by maintaining that

> [p]ost-colonial theory, so called, is not in fact a theory in the scientific sense [...] It comprises instead a related set of perspectives, which are juxtaposed against one another, on occasion contradictory. ... Above all, post-colonialism seeks to intervene, to force its alternative knowledges into the power structures of the west as well as the way they behave, to produce a more just and equitable relation between the different people of the world.
>
> (p. 6–7)

In a similar vein, the theory expands its theoretical perspectives to affiliate with other similar theories including feminism, subaltern studies and deconstructionism to respond to various social and cultural problems including education. From a feminist-deconstructivist standpoint, Spivak (1985) explores how to recover the voices of those who have been made subjects of colonial representations, particularly women, and read them as potentially disruptive and subversive. She uses the concept of imperialism to emphasise that colonialism is still at work in different forms. Her interest is in examining "not just imperialism in the nineteenth-century sense, but as it was displaced into neo-colonialism and the international division of labour" (Spivak, 1985, p. 7). In her analysis of colonial discourse, she problematises the speech act between the speaker and the listener on the grounds that it is determined by the relational conditions of their interaction. She argues that voices seen as unworthy of circulation (the subaltern) do not exist in isolation from the systems of representation, but are conditioned by them. The listeners are also conditioned by these systems, which determine how they listen (Spivak, 1988).

Employing a self-reflexive approach, Spivak (1988, 1993) analyses the practices of representing women in once-colonised societies. Reflecting on her position as a privileged academic woman living in the West, she problematises the relationship between 'Third World' women and their representation via 'First World' scholarship. Her basic assumption is that Western scholarship, ignoring the diversity, heterogeneity, and the overlapping nature of subaltern groups, follows fundamentally essentialist premises. And any elitist position aiming to voice these groups cannot avoid this essentialism, since the very act of defining them as a subaltern group, differentiates them from the elite.

In her analysis of the position of Indian women, Spivak concludes that the 'subaltern cannot speak'. She contends that there is no way in which an oppressed or politically marginalised group can voice their resistance. Her argument is that "no act of dissent or resistance occurs on behalf of an essential subaltern subject entirely separate from the dominant discourse that provides the language and the conceptual categories with which the subaltern voice speaks" (Ashcroft *et al.*, 1995, p. 219).

As can be observed from this quick survey, educational inquiry informed by post-colonialism has acknowledged the 'gaps' and 'discontinuities' that unified theories fail to notice. The discursive and the multi-trajectory nature of the theory enabled research to examine the 'shifts', 'developments' and omissions' that, in their pleas for coherence, positivistic theoretical frameworks discount. The proliferation of epistemologies that the theory affords is not simply academic in fashion; it is rather a response to substantive changes in the way we perceive what it means to provide a claim for knowledge and meaning-making, from the most private and intimate to the most exoteric and global.

Analysing 'post-colonial' educational systems

Having this quick review of educational research informed by post-colonialism, I utilise this section to review the current educational systems in countries with former experience of colonialism. I discuss how these systems still, to a large extent, adhere to colonial legacies through cleaving to Western educational models. I argue that 'neo-colonial' metaphors still largely prevail in our policies where education remains one of the areas where colonial legacies are mostly still at play. As I pointed out above, the 'colonial discourse' or, more precisely, 'regime of truth' is a system of knowledge and beliefs through which the relationship between the coloniser and colonised is recognized; it still reiterates in our current times. It, however, regenerates a new language that in turn replicates the former 'colonial discourse'. As Ashcroft *et al.* (1999) insist, "education is the most insidious and in some ways the most cryptic of colonialist survivals, older systems now passing, sometimes imperceptibly, into neo-colonialist configurations" (p. 426).

The current discourses of development and modernisation surrounding issues of education, I argue, still incorporate the landmarks of colonial ideologies. Notions such as 'national integration' and 'nation building' bear the genealogy of European 18th century imperial ideologies. As Spivak (1993) contends, the role of education in 'Third World' countries marks a continuation of colonial ideologies. She argues that as power shifts from the centre to the margin, the margins simply replicate the colonial systems, creating 'neo-colonial' educational systems. She asks: "does not participation in such a privileged and authoritative apparatus require the greatest vigilance?" (p. 85), calling for vigilance to ensure neocolonialism does not prevent decolonisation. Thus, she recognises the difficulty inherent in conceptualising a post-colonial space without an adequate historical referent but stresses the importance of advancing the decolonising agenda and identifies the central issues:

> the political claims that are most urgent in decolonised space are tacitly recognised as coded within the legacy of imperialism: nationhood, constitutionality, citizenship, democracy, even culturalism.
>
> (p. 60)

The most underprivileged category in these educational systems are the learners who lack voice to express their real interests and are thus excluded from decision-making regarding their own education. It seems that the three decades that separate our contemporary times from the work of Freire regarding the promotion of the '*Pedagogy of Hope*' have left us with traditional and oppressive models of education that continue to adopt totalising and static approaches to knowledge, and espouse rehearsal approaches to normalise and subdue voices of learners.

As Freire (1985) observes, learners are the most disadvantaged and oppressed category as they are excluded and made invisible in mainstream education. By adhering to the ideology of colonialism that nurtures the class division and widens the gap between those in power and those who lack it, policy makers have privileged their own interests at the expense of the majority of the society, including the learners. They fail to inculcate their 'enlightening' education to a class of powerless and voiceless learners. Consequently, most educational systems in these countries are dysfunctional and weak in organisation, pedagogy, curriculum, policy making, and planning (Hickling-Hudson *et al.*, 2004).

The banking model of education, for example, sees students as empty vessels that teachers fill with 'appropriate' knowledge without consideration of their needs, which projects education as a practice of domination (Freire, 1989). Currently, Fiedler (2007) perceives these models as persistent in the 'Third World's' educational sites claiming that they adopt "a notion of knowledge that can be compartmentalised into different academic subjects with clearly defined boundaries and power relations between them" (p. 50). Such a notion, he contends, fails to prepare the learner for the diversity of the modern world:

> for a learner this means that learning is mainly about taking in and storing what has been taught [...] in order to be assessed at a later stage by standardised tests. Education in other words is ultimately not about how we learn but what we learn and as such it is failing to prepare learners to live in a diverse and globalised society.
>
> (p. 50)

He argues that in the so called 'knowledge societies', knowledge is seen as a 'thing', a 'product' introduced as a factual outcome that is stored in learners' minds. Conversely, Apple (2000) maintains that "knowledge is never neutral; it never exists in an empiricist, objective relationship to the real. Knowledge is power, and the circulation of knowledge is part of the social distribution of power" (p. 42). The means and ends involved in educational policy and practice are the results of struggles between powerful groups and social movements. Both attempt to make their knowledge legitimate, to defend or increase their patterns of social mobility, and to increase their power in the larger social arena. Hence, "it is naïve to think of school curriculum as neutral knowledge" (ibid, p. 43). Foucault (1983) warns that, in its distribution, education, in what it permits and in what it prevents, follows the well-trodden paths of social conflict. To him, every educational system is a political means of maintaining or modifying the appropriation of discourse, with the knowledge and the powers that carry it.

Indeed, such arguments are robustly relevant to present educational discourses and practices. In their adoption of post-colonial analytical frameworks, those writers draw out attention to culture, power and discourses of teaching and learning, and call us to engage with views of education that contest the modernist globalised or neo-colonised paradigm of education.

An enduring hegemony of English literature

English literary education in post-colonial settings, I argue, revolves around two traditions: avoidance of political and cultural issues, and/or adopting Eurocentric models of textual interpretations; both of which project the Anglo-American literary canon as a colonising agent. Hall (2005) contends that "the strict 'Beowulf to Virginia Woolf' approach of old-style Oxbridge English study was uncritically exported to the colonies and beyond" including Egypt, Jordan and the West Bank (Palestine) (p. 146). He claims that the literary curriculum in these contexts tends to be "conservative, over-specified in terms of excessive reading loads of prescribed canonical works, but under-specified in terms of educational aims, as if the value of literature was obvious" (p. 146). Similarly, Kouritzin (2004) observes in the context of the British Columbian context, "the study of English literature, as traditionally conceived in high schools and universities, reinforces Eurocentrism, racism, [and] elitism" (p. 185).

In the era of colonisation, colonial education was principally dependant on English literature to 'educate' colonised subjects in the norms, values and cultures of the coloniser. In addition to using the power of English literature as a vehicle for imperial authority, and vital process of socio-political control, English literature itself is propagated as having a unique universal human value, and perpetuates "the humanistic functions, traditionally associated with the study of literature, for example, the shaping of character or the development of the aesthetic sense or the disciplines of ethical thinking" (Viswanathan, 1987, p. 2). Other World literatures or literatures of non-White people written in English are often referred to as lacking these universal values, and of being unable to meet the literary 'standards' of those of the centre, and are, therefore, often marginalised or excluded. As Viswanathan reminds us, "in the colonies, English studies substituted for prestigious Latin and Greek studies, setting in place a form of British culture to which colonials might aspire" (p. 20). If British literature took the place of the classics in the colonies, then 'other literatures' became what English literature was to England, "a less prestigious variant of English studies" (p. 22). This has created a hierarchy of cultural capital with classical European literature as the most respectable and colonial literature as the least.

In addition to its role as a colonising agent by means of text selection, the study of English literature provides ways of reading and interpreting texts to nurture Eurocentric ideals and to mute the voice of those on the margins from being heard. Analysing the educational systems in the countries with history of colonialism, Viswanathan (1989) concludes that teaching English literature in the colonies is complicit with the maintenance of colonial power. She reasons that English in colonial institutions has gained a particular importance as it "took on a more moralistic, humanistic function" (p. 85). She points out that the study of literature as an expression of the culture has led to a historical approach to literature which served two purposes: "first, to develop a historical awareness of the cultural moments in which those usages, precedents, and conventions are especially strong and second, to reclaim those moments as exemplary instances of truth, coherence, and value" (p. 119).

In her experience of studying English literature, Kincaid (quoted in McLeod, 2000) recalls that "the Brontës, Hardy, Shakespeare, Milton, Keats ... were read to us while we sat under a tree". McLeod contends that "[t]he teaching of English literature in the colonies must be understood as part of the many ways in which Western colonial powers such as Britain asserted their cultural and moral superiority while at the same time devaluing indigenous cultural products" (p. 140). Christian morality, furthermore, was indirectly taught in these settings through English literature.

McLeod points out that "English literary texts were presented in profoundly moral terms, with students invited to consider how texts conveyed 'truths' at once universal and timeless, yet entirely correspondent with Christian morality" (p. 142). Loomba (2005) believes that even those texts which are arguably seen to be distant from colonial ideologies, can be made so through the educational systems that devalue other literatures, "and by Eurocentric critical practices which insist on certain Western texts being the markers of superior culture and value" (p. 75).

Currently, such colonial ideologies have found currency among educators in the once colonised countries who, according to Ghandi (1998) have enabled a hierarchy of literary value that established the English literary canon as the normative embodiment of beauty, truth, and morality and as a textual standard that enforces the marginality and the inferiority of other literatures compared with the great English tradition. University English departments in the 'Middle East' have developed the habit to construct a particular brand of 'standards', not by teaching literature written in English, but rather by insisting on teaching the 'best' works represented by the 'classics' of English literature (Zughoul, 2003; Hall, 2005; Balzer, 2006; Abu-Shomar, 2012).

In addition to canonical selections, the process of reading English literature provides ways of interpreting and understanding literary texts that nurture Eurocentric ideals. Since theory regulates how literary meanings are derived, current literary theories, with Western genealogy, construct Eurocentric views of knowledge and discourse. Therefore, literary interpretations governed by literary theory are not neutral and objective (Eagleton, 2008); but socially and culturally constructed. As Balzer (2006) contends, Western literary theory is embedded within power/knowledge/ culture configurations. When literature is established as an academic subject, theories developed to guide readers' interpretations of texts turned the study of literature into a search for meaning using theories shaped by European philosophies and epistemologies. Thus, the production of criticism became "the central activity of the culture industries of the imperial centres, especially those in institutions of higher education" (Mitchell, 1995, p. 476).

Towards the mid-twentieth century, modernism has been used almost exclusively in the teaching of literature until the introduction of reader-response theory in the 1980s. Both of these however deny students the opportunity to read with other than Western eyes (Ghandi, 1998). Other diverse critical theories including New Criticism or Formalism, which also occupy a large place in the literature-classroom, have practiced a remarkable role in reinforcing the power of the English literary canon.

As Ghandi (1998) points out, "New Critics postulated the text as a sacrosanct object, hermetically sealed from the contaminations of both rational enquiry and materialistic world which occasioned such enquiry" (p.160). One result of this monolithic methodological approach to textual analysis has projected an interpretation tradition that preserves the creation of a putative 'universal' reader. As Mukherjee (1995) observes, students focusing on the universality of human experience erase "the ambiguities and the unpleasant truths that lie in the crevices" and forget that "society is not a homogenous grouping but an assortment of groups" (p. 450).

Mukherjee speaks of his disappointment by his Canadian students' responses to a short story by Margaret Laurence entitled 'The Perfume Sea'; a story that aims at exposing "the nature of colonialism as well as its aftermath" (449). He expected his students to criticise the hairdresser salon owner in Ghana after independence for making "the African Bourgeoisie slavishly imitate the values of its former colonial masters" in beauty and fashion (p. 448). The students' analysis digressed and focused on how 'believable' or 'likable' the main characters are and on how they found happiness at the end by accepting change. He blames the 'source' of his students' 'universal' vocabulary, the 'literary critics and editors of literature anthologies' who rather than facing the realities of power, class culture, social order and disorder, hide behind the universalist vocabulary that only mystifies the true nature of reality.

Literary theory that is founded in the imperial centre, and critical theory that aims to invite post-colonial readers to challenge the notions of European modernism and universalism, should consider the cultural particularities of those readers. To achieve this aim, there should be a need to develop and promote other alternative ways to empower readers beyond the Eurocentric traditions. Post-colonialism, according to Mukherjee (1995), is the world's theory that pronounces these voices. He believes that post-colonialism "makes us interrogate many aspects of the study of literature that we were made to take for granted, enabling us … to re-interpret some of the old canonical texts from Europe from the perspective of our specific historical and geographical location" (pp. 2–4).

Since, post-colonial approaches to reading and writing are primarily concerned with geography, the promotion of learners' voices in the 'peripheries' becomes possible. Said (1993) reminds us to consider: "the geographical notation, the theoretical mapping and charting of territory that underlies Western fiction, historical writing, and philosophical discourses of the time" while engaging in a process of reading and writing (p. 6). As Said urges us to do, individually or together, we (educators) need to offer to our learners "a kind of geographical inquiry into human experience" (p. 6). In brief, the act of reading of literature should in post-colonial contexts create conditions for readers to broaden their understanding of social and cultural diversity, and develop reading approaches around Critical Pedagogy and post-colonial repertoires. These beliefs about learners' education and literary experiences would help transform the decision-making map to include a wide variety of stakeholders including learners in a process of emancipation and liberation.

Critical pedagogy and signs of hope

In these post-colonial times, when at least some of the earth's humans struggle to undo the material and symbolic harm rendered in the era of European imperialism and continued in the present era of neo-colonialism, educators have a great deal of searching to do if they hope to rid their ethical, political and educational principles of colonial legacies. Yet, new languages or critical discourses are not inevitably the ideal ones to remedy inherent problems in 'post-colonial' educational contexts.

Perhaps a re-conceptualisation and a re-contextualisation of old ones might provide us with workable solutions. For many of us, educators concerning ourselves with regaining the sovereignty of our educational systems and overthrowing the colonial heritage, the incredible work of Paulo Freire and Henry Giroux continue to offer hope, for their work might be viewed as early post-colonial arguments. In their seminal texts, *Pedagogy of the Oppressed* (1989), *Pedagogy of Hope* (1994) and *Border Crossing* (1992), Freire and Giroux have provided us with a lifetime of practice and theory devoted to helping formerly colonised peoples throw off the yoke of oppression and determine the direction of their own lives.

In critical educational studies, the word 'hope' is often associated with the work of Paulo Freire. In fact, the entire philosophy of education for Freire was established on the 'ontology of hope'. For him, "Hope is rooted in men's incompleteness from which they move out in constant search" (Freire, 1972b, p. 64). At the same time, "it is in our incompleteness, of which we are aware, that education as a permanent process is grounded" (Freire, 1998a, p. 58). Both education and hope share the same root and feed each other both ontologically and epistemologically. Yet, the meaning of hope, which Freire talks about, is one that is associated with action, struggle and the desire for change.

At the same time, actions without hope are pessimistic and fatal or constitute a 'pure scientific approach'; "the attempt to do with hope, in the struggle to improve the world, as if that struggle could be reduced to calculated acts alone, or purely scientific approach, is a frivolous illusion" (p. 52). For Freire, the very possibility of the act of education is grounded in this understanding of hope as a constant search born of the human consciousness of its own incompleteness. Webb (2010) argues that what is important is not only the possibility of education that is grounded in hope but also its purpose, for if hope is characterised as a constant search then the purpose of education is to act as its permanent guide" (p.327). It is for this reason that Freire perceives the need for a 'kind of education in hope' that is so "important for our existence, individual and social, that we must take every care not to experience it in a mistaken form" (Freire, 1994, p. 3).

Elsewhere, (1989) he argues that viewing education as a neutral entity is a contradiction in terms since whether at the university, high school, primary school, or adult literacy classroom, the very nature of education has the inherent qualities to be political, as indeed politics has educational aspects. In other words, an educational act has a political nature and a political act has an educational nature. Dominant groups in society create situations, where, even if there are compromises and accords to include the less powerful, they are ones who benefit from such concessions. Freire argues that education and politics feed on each other. The way the curriculum is designed is political in the sense that certain material is selected that has to be taught to preserve the values and interests of certain groups.

In a similar vein, Giroux (1992) calls for the development of a Critical Pedagogy, "through which educators and students can think critically about how knowledge is produced and transformed in relation to the construction of social experiences informed by a particular relationship between the self, others, and the larger world" (pp. 98–99). He refers to the conditions in which "both educators and students can rethink the relations between the centres and margins of power structures in their lives" (p. 99). '*Border Pedagogy*' creates conditions for teachers and students to respect and understand their differences while working towards a common goal. It calls for shifting borders that undermine and re-territorialize different configurations of culture, power and knowledge. It also links the notions of schooling and the broader category of education to a more meaningful struggle for a just society. In order to achieve this goal, he contends that a number of theoretical considerations need to be unpacked.

For him, the category of border "signals a recognition of those epistemological, political, cultural, and social margins that structure the language of history, power, and difference" (p. 28). It also "speaks to the need to create pedagogical conditions in which students become border crossers in order to understand otherness in its own terms, and to further create borderlands in which diverse cultural resources allow for the fashioning of new identities within the existing configuration of power" (p. 28).

Giroux recognizes Bourdieu's notion of 'cultural capital' and hopes to counter culture as 'an object of unquestioning reverence' by calling for a new notion of culture as a "set of lived experiences and social practices developed within asymmetrical relations of power" (p. 99). The pedagogical approach that enables teachers and students to critique and challenge the notions of cultural capital is political and begins with liberation and empowerment. His notion of critical pedagogy calls for a critique of canons to acknowledge the colonising of differences through the representations of the 'other'.

He contends that canonical literatures typically represent the 'other' from a deficit perspective; in which the humanity of the 'other' is posited either as cynically problematic or ruthlessly denied. For emancipation to occur, Giroux's *pedagogy of difference* unravels "the ways in which the voices of the Other are colonised and repressed by the principal of identity that runs through the discourse of dominant groups and enables the Others to reclaim "their own histories, voices and visions" (pp. 103-104).

Both Freire and Giroux view education as a setting where a genuine dialogue must be established between those who '*offer*' knowledge and those who '*receive*' it. Yet, for this dialogue to take place, it has to acknowledge education as a site of political powers, to work on the deconstruction of these matrices of relations of power, and to reconfigure positions of its parties so that the once powerless category could gain voice. Failing to liberate the marginalised, it would not be possible to free these contexts from their problems and dysfunctionality.

Freire (1989) suggests that cultural invasion can be reversed if the educator "asks himself what he will dialogue with the later [students] about" (p. 82) and begins to consider education as liberating by inviting learners to recognise and unveil real criticality (Freire, 1985). The dialogical relationship between the educator and the learner encourages a more just and liberating education that alters the relationship between the invaders and the oppressed, the coloniser and the colonised, in an effort to work toward a more equitable society.

Note

1. The notion of canons could be optimised as authoritative texts (whether literary or otherwise) holding unique and everlasting moral, aesthetic, and trusting value.

References

Abu-Shomar, A. and MacDonald, M. (2012). 'Dialogic Spaces': diasporic negotiation of difference. *Journal of Post-colonial Cultures & Societies*, 3 (3 and 4): 1–36.

Andreotti, V. (2006). *A postcolonial reading of contemporary discourses related to the global dimension in education in England*. PhD Thesis, University of Nottingham.

Apple, M. (2000). *Official knowledge: Democratic education in a conservative age*. New York: Routledge.

Ashcroft, B., Griffiths, G. Tiffin, H. (eds.) (1999). *The postcolonial studies reader*. London: Routledge.

Balzer, G. (2006). *Decolonizing the classroom: Reading aboriginal literature through the lenses of contemporary literary theories*. PhD Thesis, University of Sakatchewan.

Carter, L (2006). Postcolonial interventions within science education: Using postcolonial ideas to reconsider cultural diversity scholarship. *Educational Philosophy and Theory, 38* (5): 677–91.

Crossley, M. and Tikly, L. (2004). Postcolonial perspectives and comparative and international research in education: A critical introduction. *Comparative Education, 40* (2) 147–56.

Crowley, V. & Matthews, J. (2006). Museum, memorial and mall: Postcolonialism, pedagogies, racism and reconciliation, *Pedagogy, Culture & Society, 14* (3): 263–277.

Eagleton, T. (2008). *Literary theory: An introduction* (anniversary edition) London: Blackwell.

Fiedler, M. (2007). Postcolonial learning spaces for global citizenship. *Critical Literacy: Theories and Practices, 1* (2): 50–58.

Foucault, M. (1983/1986). *The Foucault reader*. London: Penguin.

Freire, P. (1972). *Pedagogy of the oppressed*. Hammondsworth: Penguin.

Freire, P. (1985). *The politics of education: Culture, power, and liberation*. South Hadley, MA: Bergin & Garvey.

Freire, P. (1989). *Pedagogy of Freedom*. New York: Continuum.

Freire, P. (1994). *Pedagogy of hope*. New York: Continuum.

Ghandi, L (1998). *Postcolonial theory: A critical introduction*. New York: Colombia University Press.

Giroux, H. (1992). *Border crossing: Cultural workers and the politics of education*. New York: Routledge.

Gowan, B., Panitch, L. and Shaw, M. (2001). The state, globalisation and the new imperialism: a roundtable discussion. *Historical Materialism, 9* (1) :3–38.

Hall, G. (2005). *Literature in language education*. London: Palgrave Macmillan.

Hickling-Hudson, A., Matthews, J and Woods, A. (2004). Education, postcolonialism and disruption. In Hickling-Hudson, A., Matthews, J and Woods, A. (eds.), *Disrupting Preconceptions: Postcolonialism and Education* (pp. 1–16). Brisbane: Post-Pressed.

Kouritzin, A. (2004). The British Columbia literature 12 curriculum and I: A soliloquy. *Curriculum Inquiry, 34* (2): 185–212.

Kumar, M. (2000). Postcolonial theory and cross-cultural: Collective 'signposts' of discursive practices. *Journal of Educational Enquiry, 1* (2): 82–92.

Lavia, J. (2007). Repositioning Postcoloniality and Pedagogies: theories, contradictions and possibilities. *International Journal of Inclusive Education, 11* (3): 283-300.

Lavia, J. (2006). The practice of postcoloniality: A pedagogy of hope, *Pedagogy, Culture & Society,14* (3): 279–93.

Loomba, A (2005). *Colonialism/postcolonialism* (second edition), London: Routledge.

McLeod, J. (2000). *Beginning postcolonialism*. Manchester: Manchester.

Mitchell, W. (1995). Postcolonial culture, postimperial criticsm. In Ashcroft, B., Griffiths, G., and Tiffin, H. (eds.), *The Postcolonial Studies Reader* (pp. 475–79). New York: Routledge.

Mukherjee, A. (1995). Ideology in the classroom: A case study in the teaching literature in Canadian universities. In Ashcroft, B. and Tiffin, H. (eds.), *The Postcolonial Studies Reader* (pp. 447–51). New York: Routledge.

Mulenga, D. (2001). Mwalimu Julius Nyerere: A critical review of his contribution to adult education and postcolonialism. *International Journal of Lifelong Education, 20* (6): 446–470.

Rizvi, F (2006). Postcolonialism and education: Negotiating a contested terrain. *Pedagogy, Culture & Society, 14* (3): 249–62.

Rizvi, F (2005). Globalization and policy research education, In Ryan, K. and Cousins, J. (eds.), *The SAGE International Handbook of Educational Evaluation* (pp. 3-18). Thousand Oaks, CA: Sage.

Sadiq, E (2007). Postmodernism in Second, Third and Fourth World literatures: Postcolonial literary theory. In Mursi, W. & Batouk, L. (eds.), *Post-colonial readings: Essays in literature and language* (pp. 2–29). King Saud University: Al Mutanbbi Library.

Said, E (1978). *Orientalism*. Harmondsworth, London: Penguin.

Said, E (1993). *Culture and imperialism*. London: Chatto & Windus.

Smith, L (1999). *Decolonizing methodologies. Research and indigenous peoples*. London: Zed Books.

Spivak, G (1985). Strategies of vigilance: An interview conducted by Angela McRobbie, *Block*: 105–9.

Spivak, G (1988). Can the subaltern speak? In Nelson, C. & Grossberg, L. (eds.), *Marxism and the Interpretation of Culture* (pp. 271–313). Chicago: University of Illinois Press.

Spivak, G (1993). *Outside in the teaching machine*. London: Routledge.

Viswanathan, G (1989). *Masks of the Conquest: Literary study and British rule in India*. London: Faber and Faber.

Viswanathan, F (1987). The beginnings of the English literary study in India. In Donald, J. and Rattansi, A. (eds.), *'Race', culture and difference* (pp. 149–65). London: Sage.

Webb, B. (2010). Paulo Freire and 'the need for a kind of education in hope'. Cambridge Journal of Education, *40* (4): 327–39.

Young, R. (2008). What is discursive practice? *Language Learning. 58* (2): 1–8.

Zughoul, M. (2003). Globalisation and EFL/ESL pedagogy in the Arab World. *Journal of Language & Learning, I* (2): 106–46.

2

From Critical Theories to a Critique of the Theories

Dialogues between Social Thought and Its Appropriations through Educational Debates in Brazil

Inês Barbosa de Oliveira and Maria Luiza Süssekind

The development of critical social theories during Cold War years led to the emergence of critical thought in the field of education in Europe and North America, which excelled and influenced Brazilian left-wing intellectuals during the sixties and seventies. Prior to that time Brazilian left-wing intellectuals and educators had relied on Marxist analyses of society to undergird their opposition to the military dictatorship (1964–1985), as well as to produce educational theories and to understand social-educational phenomena. The relationship between capitalism and educational policies was debated and analyzed by left-wing authors according to the model of understanding as if schools were conceived to perpetuate the status quo. Some of the most influential texts were particularly based on works such as Bourdieu and Passeron, "The Reproduction"[1] and Baudelot and Establet, *The Capitalist School in France*, as well as Bowles and Gintis, *Schooling in Capitalistic America*. Less influential, but still relevant is the critical theory [CT] related to the work of authors of The Frankfurt School [FS], who have made their presence felt on debates remarkably up through Habermas's neo-Marxist thought.

Surveying the work of 1970s Brazilian scholars, a diversity of approaches and emphasis can be identified. Although not all of the studies were directly concerned with curricular thinking and educational policies, they are relevant to the study of the influence of critical theories in a kind of debate not always in an explicit dialogue with the more traditional theories. Prior to that decade, there had been an active debate on these topics, a debate marked by a progressivist outlook. What made the 1970s special was that many works inspired by critical thinking and reflecting on Brazilian educational issues were published, and the risk of criticizing capitalism and its institutions from a Marxist point of view under a military dictatorship was present. Nevertheless, Luiz Antônio Cunha, Jamil Cury, Vanilda Paiva, Maurício Tratenberg, Wagner Rossi and other authors wrote works that would become iconic for the next generation of critical thinkers. Besides European and American ideas Paulo Freire's work has also influenced those authors.

A necessary aside: Freire and his educative actions, beginning at the end of the 1950s and continuing on through the 1960s, could be characterized by his political commitment to the poor rural workers and working class and intellectual autonomy, which could make him the first prominent Brazilian author whose ideas can be related to critical educational theories. His books *Pedagogy of the Oppressed* and *Education as the Practice of Liberty* [EPL], still iconic, were both written during the 1960s and were based on real educational experiences. In the poorest illiterate wilderness he developed emancipatory experiences[2] in teaching, helping working class people to achieve self-appropriation of formal content, always acknowledging what they already knew. Freire was looking to surmount people's alienation by a proposition of education focused on "conscientization" or a kind of political self-awareness. He faced the third-world decolonization via education, enunciating a crystal-clear critique of the bourgeois model of school that has sustained the oppression of the masses, as he clarifies in *EPL* (Freire 1982, 35–36). He had a huge influence on the critical thinkers who have succeeded him, notably Henry Giroux and Michael Apple.

One of the most important subjects in the field of education and curriculum in Brazil, for at least the last 50 years, has been the linkage between politics and education. Freire's example and influence as both a thinker and a high-ranking official in the government, in the early 1960s and later in 1982, are remarkable. This was just one of a large number of emancipatory experiences in politics concerning education in that era that were erased by the dictatorship.

This understanding leads us to consider the hypothesis that, some of the important critical theorists who mark the field of curriculum origins in Brazil were also influenced by Freirean ideas and experiences that the dictatorial government attempted to silence, but which were alive in the minds of those who were implicated in thinking about and making connections to what came to us from overseas. So, Cunha's (1977) framing the debate as early as 1972, understood that it has to be not-ingenuity in thinking educational policies. From 1973 on he has influenced Brazilian educational thinking by reflecting on the relationship of social inequality of opportunities available to students of the bourgeois and the popular classes through sociological analyses of liberal thought and the school system structure (Cunha 1979).

Working over famous works of liberalism—from the fields of economy, sociology and even philosophy—to critique their thinking, Cunha uses numerous left-wing references into his critique of the Brazilian educational system and to the social reproduction to which it gave rise. Not by chance, on the back cover of Cunha's 1979 book (reprinted ten times in eight years), listed in the same collection named "Education in Question" is the precursor book *The Reproduction*, presented side-by-side with others related to no-directive pedagogies and some discussion that extrapolates the hegemony of technicism and the liberal thought that supports it. Cunha's work shows the almost immediate penetration of critical theories in the field of Brazilian education and has been widely divulgated and used in universities. Nowadays, he is acknowledged as one of the forerunners of left-leaning educational reflection in the country.

Albeit going further into the debate with those authors above could be more revealing as to the conflicts and nuances than to who is effectively critical, democratic, and/or progressivist, according to João Paraskeva (2011), we claim that in the Brazilian trajectory those distinctions seemed to be much clearer. Considering the primacy of Freire's work and the socio-political context at that time, it will be viable to assign that in the field of curriculum, the political recrudescence encouraged a clear dichotomy between the critical theorists and capitalists, relegating to secondary status their insider debates. This dichotomy clearly splits the uses of terms like progress and efficiency, to one side, and democracy, autonomy, and political commitment to the other, as Guiomar Namo de Mello's classic *Basic School Teaching: From Technical Competence to Political Commitment* [*BST*], first published in1982, explains and dialogues with. This is also the focus of the even more important *Education: From Common Sense to Philosophical Conscience* by Dermeval Saviani, first published in 1981. It is remarkable that both visions acknowledge the role of school and school knowledges, although from distinctive perspectives.

There were other authors that have been important to the building of subsequent generations of critiques and the critical theorists, who took part in educational debates then and above all since the emergence of the new lefts during the redemocratization years, the late 80s. Jürgen Habermas's thought begins to filter into the field and The *Reconstruction of Historic Materialism* (1981) complexifies the variety of critical approaches that have been in conversation and developed in Brazil. His defense of the existence of a "life-world" replete with more than the structural constraints of social reality implies the impossibility of making an immediate nexus of determination between reality and social and economic structure. This impossibility definitely contributes to the fight against structuralism that overrides the specificities of the different social "spacetimes," keeping up the Frankfurtian critical tradition. Many thinkers have followed this critical trend and its debates that have greatly evolved since the postcritical reflections began to be unfolded, many of them situated in the debate with poststructuralism (Silva 1999).

Back to 1978, *Ideology and Brazilian Education: Catholics and Liberals* by Cury is another remarkable book. The foreword written by Amoroso Lima (1978), an important Catholic progressive thinker[3] and opponent of the dictatorship, brings up the unequivocal link between the book and CT. Referring to Cury's critique and accusation that both groups—Catholics and liberals—support the interests of the dominant classes, ends to puts him in a third group:

> Neither the spiritualist viewpoint assumed by "catholics" nor the pragmatism assumed by the "pilgrims." His position is marxiologist, according to that the quintessential fact of human society up to the present day is to be divided in two antagonist plans: oppressors and oppressed.
>
> (p. x)

The book is based on a dissertation that has been done under the aegis of the development of graduate programs in Brazil at that time. An important variable for understanding the arrival and spread of critical theories is the big investment made to expand and consolidate the graduate programs in Brazil by the dictatorship, which inadvertently led to the building of a net of intellectuals all over the world united by the discussion about the relationship of education and society.

As early as 1977, Paiva published two articles in which she accuses educational thought of being ideological. While she relies on the ideas of Freire and Pierre Furter—Freire's colleague that has written the forewords to Freire's books—to criticize some authors who have espoused educational policies, specially those proffered by UNESCO, for being "idealists" and dislocating the central point of the educational debate which is: the relationship between the economy and the education of the laboring class.

Republished in a book in 1985, Paiva's articles together with those of Henrique Rattner are committed to the critical perspective opposing the technocrats and the naïves (noncritical theorists[4]) (Paiva & Rattner 1985). Relevant about Rattner's discussion is the early presence of the critique of the Theory of Human Capital that would be a main theme in the beginning of the 80s and in the context of which Gaudêncio Frigotto's work would be canonized. *The Productivity of the Unproductive School*, first published in 1984, analyzes "the roots of the bourgeois economism thought that has influenced Education in the last decades" as the cover vaticinates. In a way equally critical of liberal ideology thought and the technocracy that underlies it during the military dictatorship years, Baía Horta (1983) also claims that CT is the way to overcome the political and sociological naïveté of technocratic propositions and thinking.

Among the many emblematic works that follow this same line of argumentation is Wagner Rossi's *Capitalism and Education* (1980). Besides the title, which plainly announces the author's allegiance to the group of "criticals," the foreword is illuminating as an epoch ideal which can be summarized by the subtitle not shown on the cover: A Contribution to the Critical Study of the Capitalist Educational Economy. It should be included in the list of works critical of institutional education that, in the second half of the 1980s, have been presenting different perspectives in the debates about the Brazilian educational reality. In a way, the book complements and develops the field of studies in which the works by Cunha, Manfredo Berger, and Barbara Freitag and Miriam Jorge Warde, among others, are pioneers.

Criticizing the "pedagogism" by "those who to seek to solve social problems through school" Rossi (1980) announces that his critique goes further than the understanding that education reproduces the present society. He unveils, beyond the function of reproducing, the contradictions that invade school and other social institutions under capitalism and that derive radically from the conditions inherent to the structures of production of the society that opposes the ownership class to the working force. On one side there is the role of capitalist education as embedding the hegemonic ideology of the dominated and socialization and as a means to expand the capacity of the workforce which demystifies the illusory character of "democratization" of education and other "liberal" proposals while it offers a shattering counterfeit of all the traditional conceptions of the "economics of education," and its theoretical creation of "human capital."

(p. 8)

With those debates being in the foreground, the curricular issue appears as secondary in this set of works, in part, because of the majoritarian understanding that the reproductive structure was pedagogically inevitable and unavoidable. Specific knowledges acting in the educational practices are considered as a superstructure, fully dependent and conditioned by the infrastructure. We consider Maria Tereza Nidelcoff's classic *A School for People*, published in 1978, an exception to this "rule" in that it brings up some specific school issues such as the subjects and contents of teaching. In 1981, another work appeared, one dedicated to the investigation and reflection about what happens inside schools and the problematizing of teaching, which also deserves the spotlight: *BST* by Namo de Mello, already cited.

In the early 1980s, however, the level of discussion around curricular issues in Brazil began to increase sharply, and the publication of *Curriculum and Ideology* by Apple is exemplary in this regard. A more detailed examination of American and European theoretical production shows that, an immense field of specific curricular discussion had already opened up by the 1970s; the same occurred in Brazil, somewhat later—the mid-1980s—yet the discussion was just as vigorous, notably in the hands of Antônio Flávio Moreira and Tomaz Tadeu da Silva. For more than ten years these two precursor scholars stood out because of their scholarly production that updated the curriculum field in relation to what had been produced abroad while at the same time seeking dialogue with the specificities of our education.

A wide noisy propagation of the critical ideals followed, during the political redemocratization at the end of the 1980s. Although quite mainstream, the critical perspective on education had not yet narrowed its focus to economic and economism-based analyses during the decade of the 1980s. Gadotti[5], an assumed Freirean and Marxist, in his best-known works[6] highlights the influence of both Gramsci's thought and the social class battles in his own thinking—yet at the same time he deviates from critical orthodoxy. In the introduction to *Education and Commitment* he takes up the discussion around the questions of school itself, in addition to economic and even political and social determinations. He restores the importance of the school and the active role of educators from within the escolanovista theories[7] about effecting societal change inspired by progressivism and liberal ideas for the most part. He declares that educators "tired of listening to an inconsequent criticism of school" (Gadotti 1985, p. 12) should seek less-ambitious projects that can bring them some immediate satisfaction. He points out how difficult it is to "overcome the dichotomy between knowledge and power, between expertise and political commitment" (p. 13), by way of emphasizing the depth of the resolve needed to bridge the divide between critical theorists and conservative "naïves."

Many other Brazilian and foreign authors have advocated transcending the idea of the school as a mere reproductive institution of infrastructural relationships. The New Sociology of Education [NSE] emerged in England, for example, while elsewhere the critiques of the critical theories were flourishing. In this sense we take the risk of claiming that those critiques also engender the postcriticism and the perspectives on poststructuralism and can also be related to Hall's "cultural turn"[8].

Towards the end of the 1980s *Participant Research* by Justa Ezpeleta and Elsie Rockwell (1989) was published in Brazil. It became iconic because it fostered understanding of the "need to seek a new kind of knowledge about school reality out of the dominant models [available to study it]" (p. 8). This book can be considered the "keystone" of ELS in Brazil, and this "seeking" remains an important and innovative perspective on the field of curriculum in the country (Pinar 2011).

In other words, since the beginning of the 1980s with a democratic overture and the redemocratization in the end of this decade, the ideals professed by groups related to the social and cultural movements silenced during the dictatorship years, especially Freirean thinking have reemerged and begun to share with critical studies a space in educational and curriculum discussions specifically. The visualization of political and social ideals that served as basis for a critique of the economism and hegemonic structuralism created and gave substance to studies and interpretations of Brazilian educational issues in the debate with CT itself in the following years. This deep perspective widely investigates the bases of support for the structures of power and also the production and maintenance of social inequalities in Brazil. Leading authors such as Apple, Young, Pinar, Giroux, and McLaren became references in this scenario (ones more than others), typically secondhand, because only a few translations were available to Brazilian readers. These are authors associated with critical theories, but which far outweigh the reproductivists perspectives from the 1970s.

We can affirm that in the field of study of curriculum in Brazil, the notion of the "hidden curriculum" pedagogically traces the "presence" in the classroom of issues raised by critical theorists and by the curriculum reconceptualization movement. Those issues were prominent to the very constitution of the field in Brazil from the 1980s on to the extent that contributed to the field's avoidance of the purely formalistic discussions of traditional perspectives or the "metodologisms" linked to escolanovism and other non-directive pedagogical perspectives, or those based on analyses and proposals coming from psychology, such as the "Piagetian schools" in vogue in the late 1970s and early 1980s.

Although a minority, intellectuals and educators who criticized CT started the debates and bring up educational proposals during the post-dictatorship period. Using theories and questionings built particularly under the influence of cultural studies, by social movements from diverse minorities, and by the debates around the anthropology of the complex societies' works and other trends in contemporary, political, and social thought, those critiques of criticism inscribed themselves in a postcritical perspective that drew attention to the salient features of the current educational scenario, as understood by Silva (1999) and others.

In the beginning of the 1990s the series "Social Sciences in Education" brought critical reflections and shades to educational debates that valued this lingering conversation with the social sciences. In his introduction to Bruno Pucci's (1994) *Critical Theory and Education*, Silva offers the following summary:

> It is possible to affirm that critical theorization in education has now reached a respectable stage of maturity and development. This has contributed to the building of what today can even be considered a tradition in the educational and pedagogic thinking that was made gradually by a whole generation of educators, social theorists, historians and philosophers of education. (...) "Banking education"[9] "hidden curriculum" "cultural reproduction," "code," "cultural capital," "state ideological apparatus" are expressions, which are mandatory parts of the current critical analyses. The notion of critique by itself is integrant and primal of this "tradition."
>
> (p. 7)

Moreira and Silva coauthored two books that became emblematic: *Curriculum, Culture and Society* and *Contested Territories: The Curriculum and New Political and Cultural Maps* (1995). Both books point out the supremacy of CT and, in a sense, set the tone for the field's debates during the 1980s and 1990s. In addition, Moreira published *Currículos e Programas no Brasil* in

1997, a reference work that discusses the constitution of the field and the influences it has felt in its earliest days of establishment, growing out of the need he felt to incorporate the critical literature into his courses after reading *Ideology and Curriculum* by Apple and *Knowledge and Control*, edited by Young. In the 1990s Silva continued to organize and publish collective works with the participation of several countries' thinkers; both Silva and Moreira assumed important positions in Brazilian academic studies and in the dialogue with foreign production, which expanded curricular debates and contributed to the development of the field.

Silva's *Identity Documents: One Introduction to the Theories of Curriculum*, has been considered since its publication in 1999 one of the basal references for initiates into the field of curriculum studies. He proposes a classification of curricular thinking in three major trends: the traditional theories, critical, and postcritical. Practically a bible for teacher education courses, this book presents CT as a better way—or even the only way—to understand the challenges facing *curriculum* in the 1970s, certainly, but also beyond, and that "classification" has become the paradigm for curriculum studies in Brazil. At the time of the book's publication, the main authors in the field were a group of scholars who understood curriculum as a dialogue with culture, power and politics—and yet Silva (1999) deliberately goes so far as to justify the silencing of others' *not-so-important theories*. In this book (which has been reprinted ten times) he points out that theories are worldviews and there is one that is better than *the others* (p. 3). Elucidating the Reconceptualization in the U.S., he explains that the consequence of confronting of "traditional curricular thought" is antagonism between those who were concerned with criticizing the established school and curricula, obviously emphasizing the role of the economy, power, and politics, and *the others*. Torres (1998), honoring Paulo Freire as one of the main critical inspirations and points of reference in the field in Brazil, states that critical studies provide "the necessary tools to fully understand and combat the relationship between education and unequal cultural, political and economic power" (p. 15).

Moreira (2007) accepts Silva's characterization of the history of curriculum studies noting the dominance of CT during the 1980s and the 1990s, when the field was being consolidated. When he mentions the influence of North American debates on the "new" themes raised by the poststructuralist approach to curricular ideas, he points to the continued influence of Apple and Giroux in particular.

In a 2002 article Moreira analyzed the Reconceptualization movement in the U.S., underlining in all tendencies of postcritical theorists their common objections to curriculum as a prescription; the nonpolitical character of the studies in the field until the Reconceptualization; the lack of historicity; the excessive concern with improving school outcomes; and the indefiniteness of the field's object of study. All of those "rejections" and the subsequent polarization of curriculum studies between the "politics and power" and "experience" camps were also prominent features of the field in Brazil back then. The influence by FS and French EL sociology has been significant; however the work of a range of scholars has gained space in the curriculum scene since that time. Both the Reconceptualist neo-Marxist trend, represented in Brazil by scholars strongly influenced by Apple and Giroux, and the NSE, represented by Young and his adherents in Brazil, will be well published and canonized. The later dialogue with the more humanist and autobiographic and with other non-Marxist tendencies of Reconceptualization has opened up a wide space for the post-structuralist questionings and for "new" authors such as Ivor Goodson, with his historicity and narratives of identities.

Mapping the field's debates at the end of the 1990s, Moreira (2001) opened the big discussion on *multiculturalism*. Investigating the notions of curriculum as the main subject of forty-six articles presented at the Anped (National Association of Educational Research) annual meeting, Moreira maintains that scholars approach the debate by discussing curriculum and racial relations; curriculum and cultural diversity; multiculturalism and curriculum policies; multiculturalism and teachers' education; and curriculum and gender. Only one article took up the topic of curriculum and social class. Based on his analysis, Moreira identifies only one author as a major influence on the field—McLaren (p. 73)—although he recognizes the impact of other authors, notably from Gimeno Sacristán and Jurjo Torres Santomé, the author of *El Curriculum Oculto* (1994). Moreira voices his disquietude with the secondary role of "social classes" as a potential topic within curricular studies. He argues that the field's *raison d'être* means that social class absolutely cannot be overlooked when it comes to debating curriculum in a country with so many social inequalities (Moreira 2002).

However, in *Curriculum in Contemporaneity: Incertitudes and Challenges* (2003), coedited with Garcia, Moreira brings together the scholarship authors who discuss issues of the field of curriculum without necessarily focusing on class inequality. Judging from the diversity of approaches represented, it seems clear that the interest in making the debate publicized between scholars in Brazil and international production assumes a high-priority role in relation to this or that particular trend.

Within the ongoing debate with Silva, Paraskeva (2011) has argued that critical scholars of curriculum do make the claim for social justice and equality. They bring to the forefront the concepts of ideology, hegemony, common sense, hidden curriculum, power, reproduction and resistance among others, which reshaped the field in the 1990s. He points out that the main goals for some of the critical (progressive) educators in the field today are social justice and real democracy, which cannot be realized without cognitive justice.

Contradictorily, the building of democracy in Brazilian society and the widening of access at all levels of schooling[10] have arrived hand-in-hand with a new positivistic wave. That wave, in spite of all the achievements that curriculum scholars have made in the form of critical and postcritical studies in education, crushes the work of teachers by blaming them for the terrible results achieved by their students. The spread of evidence-based politics and standardized tests implemented by governments at various levels are traces of this positivistic view (Hypolito 2010). Apparently, this new positivism also gives a new strength to critical studies and its economic and political statements.

So, it is understandable that Marxist ideas would inspire social critiques and the critical theorists would dominate the field of curriculum for so long. In a way, they wrote the history of the field. For Pinar (2011), the field in Brazil "is so theoretically sophisticated" that to know about it opens possibilities of

> the provocation of a myriad exchanges, most of which will not occur in English or be published in North America but will be acknowledged in the disciplinary histories future curriculum scholars will be compelled to write.
>
> (3–4)

In 2002 appeared *Creating Curriculum within Everyday Life*, a revolutionary book in the history of the field. Talking with teachers, treating the writing of the book as a conversation among teachers, Nilda Alves, Elizabeth Macedo, Inês Barbosa de Oliveira, and Luiz Carlos Manhães drew a new epistemological proposal, one weaving terms like "nets to knowledge" and "curriculum to creation." Dialoguing with the critical theorists, the liberals, and the naïves but going much further, they confronted the hegemony of the paradigms, inaugurating something like the criticism of the critique. They used cunning words and did not just discuss poststructuralist notions but literally applied a deconstructive strategy to the epistemological and methodological doing of curricula research and theorizing within the field of curriculum. Consequently, the confrontation with the critical theorists and the dominant scientific positivistic paradigm concerning curricular knowledge and invention and the protagonism of schools and teachers was inevitable.

From the 1990s and the readings of Ezpeleta and Rockwell's already cited book and feeling uncomfortable with the hegemony of the studies that considered the school as being only a spacetime of ignorance and repetition, Alves and Garcia (2008), both professors at Fluminense

Federal University[11] and in parallel Geraldi at Campinas State University[12] claimed more and more that everyday life (EL) was a spacetime in which to create knowledges and curricula, and they started to adopt "EL" as a research locus and premise. The deepening of these studies, as well as the growth of research conducted on this basis (Alves & Oliveira 2008) have been promoting the development of the field and have given rise to what is being done today by various groups throughout Brazil and scholars researching groups from UFES[13] and UERJ,[14] of which numerous researchers are a part, even some who, without defining themselves as "EL scholars," incorporate and use much of the knowledge that has been produced and disseminated as EL studies [ELS].

Alves and Oliveira (2008) have woven together a strong (and international) net of scholars; teachers from all over the country have been working on ESL in education. This network of researchers acts in an effort to broaden reflections around the idea that *EL is more than a spacetime common sense* and therefore the absence of political and epistemological reflection on reality is attributed to its actions, their constraints and processes. They understand EL as a spacetime of are creation and originality, in which the different dimensions of social life are presented and are entangled by virtue of the dynamism intrinsic to those proper social nets in which practitioners of EL (Certeau 1994) live and create culture, society, and curricula. In these networks there are teachers and researchers working in EL within schools, acknowledging the production of singular knowledges and curricula.

After a fruitful collaboration with Moreira during the early 2000s,[15] Macedo turned to the development of her own theory about policies, curriculum, and practices, building the concept of "curriculum as enunciation" (Pinar 2011, p. 16). She is among the leading figures in the trend in curriculum studies in Brazil that questions "the usual separation between formal curriculum and curriculum in action" (Lopes & Macedo 2011, p. 2) by improving and expanding curriculum research under the theme of curriculum and policies.

Alice Lopes (2013) recently contextualized the state of the field in the 2000s by noting that critical studies are still in *vogue* (p. 13). Furthermore, she argued that in Brazilian curriculum studies, debates between critical and postcritical scholars persist. In this work, she remarks on the influence of Silva, as a theorist, translator, publisher, and an intellectual primarily concerned with politics has succeeded in tilting the field in favor of the critical theorists. An adherent of poststructuralism, Lopes makes use of Derrida's concept of *différance*[16] in her discussion of curriculum theory and curriculum policies.

Some important features of the current debates are the strong presence of Bourdieu's habitus and the EL epistemology of Certeau, Morin's complexity paradigm, Hall's identity, and an important discussion about "place and space" that acknowledges the in-betweens and seems to dialogue mostly with Bhabha's hybridism as explored by Ferraço. Additionally, original and unfolding readings of Deleuze and of Derrida's architecture of the self, as well as Maffesoli's ontology, are permeating debates among some curriculum scholars that go further with the building of notions as "curriculum as disfiguration" by Amorim and as "the aesthetic of school daily practices" by Aldo Victorio Filho, which rams Baudrillard's simulacrum. Those deep readings and multiple senses of curriculum and ways of doing curriculum research proliferate in many "native" theories, which enrich our epistemological diversity even more (All authors in: Pinar 2011, 55–69).

Asserting the primacy of "learning from the South," Oliveira "reiterates her (and her colleagues') commitment to surpass the simplifications that … science reinforces" by focusing on the "complexity of action" and "the researchers' presence within it" (Pinar 2011, 188, 189). And, after one year of interviews Pinar's conclusion about Brazilian curriculum studies is that "[r]esearch is thereby 'in-dissociable' from theory" and follows Barreto in saying that the most representative line of curriculum studies is centered in school knowledge (188, 193). The uniqueness of ELS within curriculum of schools in Brazil based on the displacement of practice–theory relationship has also been emphasized by Süssekind (2012).

In a recent work, Oliveira (2012) briefly presented one understanding of the state of field and how we tweak the inception of ELS within Curriculum in it:

> Thus the current studies in the field of curriculum in Brazil dialogue with different both theoretical and social fields and sociological and philosophical approaches, inscribing themselves in the different trends identified by Silva (1999), or creating new references, as attested by many works recently presented or books and journals published.[17] Beyond possible framings and classifications of this production, this proliferation attests the richness of the debates and the relevance that the field, in its plurality of possibilities, is taking on from a growing group of educators. [...] It is in this context that the reflections about everyday life within schools and specifically the notion of "curriculum as everyday life creation within schools" are inscribed.
>
> (81)

What we do realize and expect that you, the reader, also realizes, related to the trajectory of the field of curriculum in Brazil, is that even when the CT perspective is no longer majoritarian, its influence is still immense and maybe even hegemonic, which obligates other authors associated with all the other trends and shades from having an explanatory dialogue with it, even if in a subliminal way. Our comprehensive hypothesis concerns the intrinsic importance of the critical debate shaping the field in Brazil, considering that even the current majoritarian postcritical theories in vogue are mostly left-oriented, linked to emancipatory and democratic thought. On the other hand, we believe the fact that critical theories are epistemologically closer to modern thinking and its Scientificism with which CT dialogues under dualistic oppositions and arguments that oppose true and false, based on objective rules of understanding the world, makes them at the same time more comprehensible and sadly means they approach the logic of the dominant ones, allowing them to occupy, as a complementary opposite, the same side of the abyssal line.[18] The abyssal line excludes by its strategies of invisibility, throwing into the abyss other epistemological forms of understanding and explaining the world, the questions on education and curricula—but this is a future conversation.

Notes

1. Originally named "The Reproduction: Elements for a Theory of School System" was translated to English by the title: "Reproduction in Education, Society, and Culture."
2. One could say a complicated conversation (Pinar 2012) about experience was already quite alive in education theory circles; however, it always seems much more important for the majority of Brazilian thinkers in the field of education and above all, the Gramscian and Marxist intelligentsia, to focus on the economy, power, and social relationships.
3. Although an important power supporting oligarchies and conservative politics it was inside, along, within and sometimes with the support of the Catholic Brazilian Church that a teleological Marxism under an influence attributed to Paulo Freire has been highly developed, especially during the dictatorial years, also noted by Pinar and Kumar (2011).
4. The naïves are the noncritical theorists who believe that the potential of education to change society will neglect the very economic and political aspects to which that changing is linked and within which it is related.
5. Saviani, Frigotto, and Gadotti are just a few who marked the period.
6. "Education and Power: introduction to conflict pedagogy" [Educação e poder: introdução à pedagogia do conflito] 1980; "Education and commitment" [Educação e compromisso] 1985; and "Dialectic concept of education" [Concepção dialética da educação] 1983.
7. The 1930's had Anisio Teixeira as a major reference that dialogues directly with John Dewey.
8. Hall, S. (1992) *A identidade cultural na pós-modernidade [Cultural identity in post-modernity]*, DP&A Editora. Translated and published by: Tomaz Tadeu da Silva and Guacira Lopes Louro.
9. Educação bancária.

10. To understand Brazilian education and its numbers see: http://portal.unesco.org/geography/es/ files/13662/12960781625TOM_-_Brazil's_Ed_System_EN.pdf/TOM%2B-%2BBrazil's%2BEd %2BSystem_EN.pdf.
11. Universidade Federal Fluminense-UFF, Niterói-RJ, Brazil.
12. Unicamp, Campinas-SP, Brazil.
13. Federal University of Espirito Santo-UFES, Vitória-ES, Brazil.
14. Rio de Janeiro State University-UERJ, Rio de Janeiro-RJ, Brazil.
15. Notably in the book *Curriculum, Pedagogical Practices and Identities*.
16. Although usually translated to English as Difference, we kept the French word understanding that Derrida constructs the noun différance, a new word, a "non-word" that is a "non-concept" precisely because it cannot be either "narrowed-down" or "fixed" to a single part of both of its meanings.
17. It is worthwhile to highlight the recent production of the GT–Currículo of Anped (the curriculum working group of the National Association for Educational Research and Graduation) that since 2005 has been publishing e-books from an annual thematic call. The plurality of approaches, authors and epistemological and political references of the articles, although not exhaustive since there is curricular reflection outside of the GT, underlines the richness of the field.
18. According to Boaventura de Sousa Santos the abyssal thinking "consists of a system of visible and invisible distinctions, the invisible ones being the foundation of the visible ones. The invisible distinctions are established through radical lines that divide social reality into two realms, the realm of 'this side of the line' and the realm of 'the other side of the line.' This division is such that 'the other side of the line' vanishes as reality, becomes nonexistent. Nonexistent means not existing in any relevant comprehensible way of being. Whatever is produced as nonexistent is radically excluded because it lies beyond the realm of what the accepted condition of inclusion considers to be its other" (Santos 2010, 31–32; published in English in 2007, 45).

References

Alves, N. (Ed.) (2001), Macedo, E. Oliveira, I. B. and Manhães, L. C. *Criar currículo no cotidiano* [Create curriculum in everyday life]. São Paulo: Cortez.
Alves, N.; Oliveira, Inês B. (Comps.). (2008) *Pesquisa nos/dos/com os cotidianos das escolas: sobre redes de saberes*. [Everyday Life studies within schools: about nets and knowledges] Petrópolis, RJ: DP et Alii 2008.
Alves, N.; Garcia, R. L. (Eds.) (2008) *O sentido da escola*. [The meaning of school] Petrópolis, RJ: DP et Alii.
Apple, M. (1982) *Ideologia e currículo*. [Ideology and curriculum] São Paulo: Brasiliense.
Baudelot, C.; Establet, R. (1971) *L'école capitaliste en France*. [Capitalist school in Frace] Paris: Maspéro.
Bourdieu, P.; Passeron, J. C. *La reproduction*. (1971) [The Reproduction: Elements for a Theory of school system] Paris: Les Éditions de Minuit.
Bowles, S.; Gintis, H. (1981) *La instrucción escolar en la América capitalista*. [Schooling in Capitalistic America] Madrid: Siglo XXI.
Certeau, M. (1994). *The spectacle of everyday life*. Berkeley, CA: University of California Press.
Cunha, L. A. (1977) *Política educacional no Brasil: a profissionalização no ensino médio*. [Educational politics in Brazil: the vocational education in high school] Rio de Janeiro: Eldorado, 2. Ed.
Cunha, L. A. (1979) *Educação e desenvolvimento social no Brasil*. [Education and social development in Brazil] Rio de Janeiro: Francisco Alves, 2.Ed.
Cury, C. R. J. (1978) *Ideologia e educação brasileira: católicos e liberais*. [*Ideology and Brazilian Education: Catholics and Liberals*] São Paulo: Cortez & Moraes.
Ezpeleta, J.; Rockwell, E. (1986) *Pesquisa participante*. [Participant research] São Paulo: Cortez/Autores Associados.
Freire, Paulo. (1982) *Educação como prática de liberdade*. [Education as the Practice of Liberty] São Paulo: Paz e Terra, 13. Ed.
Freire, P. (1970/2000). *Pedagogy of the oppressed*. New York: Continuum International Publishing Group.
Frigotto, G. (1994) *A produtividade da escola improdutiva*. [The Productivity of the Unproductive School] São Paulo: Cortez/Autores Associados.
Garcia, R. L., & Moreira, A. F. B. (Eds.) (2003). Currículo na contemporaneidade: Incertezas e desafios. [Curriculum in contemporarity: Incertitudes and challenges.]. São Paulo: Cortez.
Gadotti, M. (1985) Educação e compromisso. [*Education and Commitment*] Campinas-SP: Papirus.
Gadotti, M. (1987) *Concepção dialética da educação: um estudo introdutório*. [The dialectical concept of education: a introductory study] São Paulo: Cortez/Autores Associados.
Giroux, H. (1986) *Teoria crítica e resistência em educação*. [Critical theory and resistence in education] Petrópolis, RJ: Vozes.

Goodson, Ivor. (1995) *Currículo: teoria e história*. [Curriculum: theory and history] Petrópolis, RJ: Vozes.

Habermas, J. (1981) *Para a reconstrução do materialismo histórico*. [The reconstruction of the historical materialism] São Paulo: Brasiliense.

Habermas, J.; Adorno, T.; Benjamin, W.; Horkheimer, M. (1983) *Os Pensadores*. [The Thinkers] São Paulo: Abril Cultural.

Horta, J. S. B. (1983) Planejamento educacional.[Educational planning] In MENDES, Dermeval Trigueiro (Coord.). *Filosofia da educação no Brasil*. Rio de Janeiro, Civilização Brasileira, p. 195–239.

Hypolito, A. (2010). *Curricular policies, state and regulation*. Campinas: *Revista Educação e Sociedade*, *31*(113), 1337–1354, out.-dez. 2010 1337. Retrieved from http://www.cedes.unicamp.br.

Khumar, A. (2011). Curriculum studies in Brazil: An overview. In W. F. Pinar (Ed.) *Curriculum studies in Brazil: Intellectual histories, present circumstances*. New York: Palgrave Macmillan.

Lopes, A. (2013). *Teorias pós-críticas, política e currículo*. [Postcritical theories, politics and curriculum] In: *Revista Educação, Sociedade e Cultura*, *39*, 7–23.

Lopes, A., & Macedo, E. (2011). Curriculum, policy, practice. *Transnational Curriculum Inquiry*, *8*(2). Retrieved from http://nitinat.library.ubc.ca/ojs/index.php/tci.

de Mello, G. N. (1982) *Magistério de 1º grau: da competência técnica ao compromisso político*. [Basic School Teaching: From Technical Competence to Political Commitment] São Paulo: Cortez/Autores Associados, 3. Ed.

Moreira, A. F. B. (2001). *A recente produção científica sobre currículo e multiculturalismo no Brasil (1995–2000): Avanços, desafios e tensões*. [Recent scientific production on curriculum and multiculturalism in Brazil (1995–2000): Advances, challenges and tensions.]. *Revista Brasileira de Educação*, *18*, 65–81. Retrieved from http://www.scielo.br/scielo.php?script=sci_arttext&pid=S1413-24782001000300007&lng=es&tlng=pt. 10.1590/S1413-24782001000300007.

Moreira, A. F. B. (2002). *O campo do currículo no Brasil: Construção no contexto da Anped*. [The field of curriculum in Brazil: A constructo in Anped's context.]. *Cadernos de Pesquisa*, *117*, 81–101. Retrieved from http://www.scielo.br/pdf/cp/n117/15553.pdf.

Moreira, A. F. B. (2007). *Apresentação*. [Forewords] In: *Educação em Revista*, *45*,109–117. Retrieved from: http://www.scielo.br/scielo.php?script=sci_arttext&pid=S0102-46982007000100006&lng=en&tlng=pt. 10.1590/S0102-46982007000100006.

Moreira, A. F. B. (2012) *Currículos e programas no Brasil*. [Curriculum and graduate programs in Brazil] Campinas, SP: Papirus, 18. Ed.

Moreira, A. F. B.; Macedo, E. (Eds.). (2002) *Currículo, práticas pedagógicas e identidades*. [Curriculum, pedagogical practices and identities] Porto: Porto Editora.

Nidelcoff, M. T. (1978) *Uma escola para o povo*. [A School for People] São Paulo: Brasiliense.

de Oliveira, I. B. (2003) *Currículos praticados: entre a regulação e a emancipação [Practices within curriculum: in-between regulation and emancipation.*] Rio de Janeiro: DP&A.

de Oliveira, I. B. (2012) O Currículo com criação cotidiana. [Curriculum as everyday life creation] Rio de Janeiro: DP et Alii.

Paiva, V.; Rattner, H. (1985) *Educação permanente e capitalismo tardio*. [Permanent education and late capitalism] São Paulo: Cortez/Autores Associados.

Paraskeva, João (2011) Conflicts in Curriculum Theory: Challenging Hegemonic Epistemologies. New York: Palgrave/MacMillan.

Pinar, W. F. (2003). A equivocada educação do publico nos Estados Unidos. [The misguided education of the public in United Stated]. In R. L. Garcia & A. F. B. Moreira, (Eds.), *Currículo na contemporaneidade: Incertezas e desafios*. [*Curriculum in Contemporaneity: Incertitudes and Challenges*] São Paulo: Cortez.

Pinar, W. F. (2011). *Curriculum studies in Brazil: Intellectual histories, present circumstances*. New York: Palgrave Macmillan.

Pinar, W. F. (2012). *What is curriculum theory?* (2nd ed.). New York: Routledge.

Pucci, B. (Ed.). (1994). *Teoria crítica e educação*. [Critical theory and education] Petrópolis,RJ: Vozes 1994.

Rossi, W. G. (1980). *Capitalismo e educação*. [Capitalism and Education] São Paulo: Editora Moraes, 2. Ed.

Santomé, J. T. (1994). *El curriculum oculto*. [The hidden curriculum] 4. ed. Madrid: Morata.

Saviani, D. (1986). *Educação: do senso comum à consciência filosófica* [Education: From Common Sense to Philosophical Conscience]. São Paulo: Cortez/Autores Associados, 4. Ed.

Santos, B. S. (2010). Para além do pensamento abissal. [Beyond abyssal thinking.] In: Santos, B. S. & Meneses, M. P. (Eds.). *Epistemologias do Sul*, [Epistemologies of the South.] São Paulo: Cortez.

Silva, T. T. (1995) *Alienígenas na sala de aula: uma introdução aos estudos culturais em educação*. [Aliens within the classroom: one introduction to cultural studies in education] Petrópolis, RJ: Vozes.

Silva, T. T. (1999). Documentos de identidade: *Uma introdução às teorias do currículo*. [Identity documents: One introduction to the theories of curriculum.]. Belo Horizonte: Autêntica.

Silva, T. T., & Moreira, A. F. B. (1994). *Currículo, cultura e sociedade*. [Curriculum, culture, and society.]. São Paulo: Cortez.

Silva, T. T., & Moreira, A. F. B. (Comps.). (1995). *Territórios contestados: O currículo e os novos mapas culturais.* [Contested territories: The curriculum and the new cultural maps]. Petropolis-RJ: Vozes.

Süssekind, M. L. (2012) *O Ineditismo dos Estudos nosdoscom os Cotidianos: Currículos e Formação De Professores, Relatos e Conversas em uma Escola Pública no Rio de Janeiro*, Brasil. [The uniqueness of everyday life studies: curricula and teachers education among a public school in Rio de Janeiro–Brazil] Revista e-Curriculum (PUCSP), v.9, p.1–21.

Torres, C. A. (Ed.). (1998). *Education, power and personal biography. Dialogues with critical educators.* New York/London: Routledge.

3

Gender Studies in Spain

From Theory to Educational Practice

Ana Sánchez Bello

Gender studies in Spain have traditionally been closely linked to the historical context of the struggle for democracy, which amongst many other aspects meant recognition of the right of social groups that until then had been excluded from social debate to participate fully in public life. As was also the case in other European countries, these groups initially gained recognition as a result of the public presence and voting power (Hobson 2003) granted to them by a non-dictatorial system.

It was in this context, during the late 1970s, that the first groups devoted to women's studies began to appear in Spanish universities. They were to be the seed of the first research projects, doctoral theses, research institutes and so on that would later be behind the widespread development of gender studies that began in the 1980s (Maquieira 2005; Rodríguez 2001). One of the consequences of the incorporation of gender theory in social sciences has been the materialisation of the link between private life and scientific knowledge.

In the case of Spain, gender studies with a specific focus on the world of education came to the fore in the 1980s, largely as a result of the growing importance of the feminist movement during those years. This movement, after forty years of a dictatorship led by General Franco and characterised by a strong patriarchal element in the educational system, since the latter was the prime factor of socialisation open to the victors of the Civil War (Sánchez-Bello 2012), was to remain dormant until the 1970s (prior to the dictator's death), when a new General Education Act was passed, constituting a legal framework that prevented discrimination against the female sex in terms of access both to centres of education and to the courses they could choose to study (Pilar Ballarín 2001; Canales 2012).

The 1980s saw a veritable explosion of gender studies, brought about by two significant facts that played a decisive role in the situation at the time, the first of these being the creation in 1983 of the Institute for Women's Affairs, which implemented specific measures to promote equal opportunities in the educational realm (Astelarra 2005). The second came in 1996, when the National Research and Development Plan decided to fund research in this field, giving it full scientific status (Page 2005; Rodríguez 2011).

The first systematic studies took place in this decade, and focused on the analysis of textbooks in order to describe degree of visibility of girls and women and the social role allotted to each of the sexes, either through images or through the concepts employed in the materials used in schools, examples being those published Garreta and Careaga (1987). Other prominent studies looked at classroom interaction, analysing the level of student intervention on the basis of gender, the different ways in which teachers related to boys and girls or the way in which their vocabulary varied according to the gender of their pupils: one of the pioneering studies in this field, which proved highly influential in the field of educational sociology, was that published by Marina Subirats and Cristina Brullet (1988).

With the coming of the 1990s research studies began to specialise in areas such as the analysis of coeducational schooling (Ballarín 1992); prospective studies of the status of female teachers and students in the various levels of the educational system (Grañeras 1999; Muñoz-Repiso 1993); studies on the glass ceiling (García de Cortázar and García de León 1997). One area in which studies abounded during this period was that of the relationship between academic and career choice and gender, a case in point being Carmen Alemany's monograph (1992).

The new century brought with it a change of focus, with studies starting to examine the question of identity from the standpoint of cultural diversity (CREA 2003; Ioé group 2003). At the same time there was an increase in the number of studies on the prevention of gender violence (Díaz-Aguado 2001; Montoya and Salguero 2004). More recently, as has been shown by the Instituto de la Mujer (2013), research has focused on the analysis of teenagers' conceptions of gender violence (Bonilla 2012; Leal 2009) or on the analysis of teacher training with regard to gender violence (Puigvert 2012).

The enormous diversity of research lines within the general field of gender studies in education have their origins in different theoretical proposals from within the feminist movement, but have all had a profound influence on everyday practice in schools. In this article we will analyse this relationship between the diversity of theoretical approaches and their reflection in educational practice. In order to do so, we will first analyze the way in which the most widely acknowledged perspectives in feminist theory have been interpreted in the Spanish context, and then look at how they have been implemented in the classroom.

The Theoretical Perspectives Embraced by the Feminist Movement in Spain

Gender studies in the educational field in Spain have been influenced by the different tendencies within the world of feminist theory, traditionally classified, as Alison Jaggar pointed out in her book *Feminist Politics and Human Nature* (1983), into four typologies: liberal, socialist, Marxist and radical. This classification was subsequently reduced to three kinds as a result of the confluence between the socialist and Marxist tendencies. More recently, the arrival of the postmodern, difference and queer tendencies have expanded the range of theoretical proposals that agglutinate the multiplicity of types of feminism with which we now find ourselves facing (Lorber 2010).

In Spain, the greatest success of the liberal perspective has been in the area of the formal barriers to women accessing the educational system. Those who represent the liberal tendency consider that the educational sphere is one of the most effective platforms for solving the problems of social disadvantage that beset women; to do so, it is necessary to ensure that girls enjoy the same opportunities as boys and that there is no obstacle to prevent them from choosing any kind of course or subject at any level of education.

The defenders of liberal feminism hold that in order to guarantee gender equality it is first necessary to abolish the laws and policies that discriminate on the basis of gender, and subsequently to modify the role differentiation that currently occurs in society and can be seen in the sexual dichotomisation of the different spheres occupied by humankind (Friedan 1974; Okin 1979).

The major criticism leveled against the liberal tendency is that it fails to question the reigning model of society, based on values constructed from a masculine standpoint, such as competitiveness or the individualism of the "every man for himself" philosophy. The consequence of this is that girls have to learn the masculine model if they want to succeed, instead of questioning the kind of model defended by schools and asking if it should be modified to give greater prominence to other kinds of values that have historically been attributed to women.

The socialist-cum-Marxist perspective argues that schools are at the service of the capitalist system, which is in itself patriarchal. Schools and colleges thus contribute to promoting gender inequality because girls choose typically feminine courses, which enjoy the added advantages of costing the State less whilst at the same serving to ensure that the women who graduate from them also do the work in the home. It can thus be said that the educational system encourages the association of certain post-school courses with the role of mother, of the person who looks after the family. The sexual division of labour was used to explain the identification of the teaching profession as an essentially female activity, by symbolically establishing the relationship between primary-school teaching and care-giving, a relationship that has generated negative effects by inferring that the activities carried out in this sphere should not be classified as professional (Acker 1989; De Lyon & Migniuolo 1989; Wharton 2005).

In order to solve this problem, the defenders of this standpoint say that is necessary to modify the roles of student and teacher: female pupils should play an active role in the teaching-learning process and be more than mere receivers of information, contributing to the learning of the other people in the classroom through the sharing of their experiences. Putting it another way, the idea is to convert female students into generators of knowledge, making it possible to modify preconceptions as to what women themselves are, feel and think. Such a theoretical perspective is eminently political, leading it to borrow from authors such as Michael Apple, Henry Giroux, Peter McLaren, Paulo Freire or Ira Shor (Totten y Pedersen 2012). The latter two in particular have placed great importance on matters of social oppression, although not specifically gender-based, unlike the view held by what are known as socialist feminist theories. What writers of both sexes on socialist critical feminist pedagogical thought have in common is their undeniable neo-Marxist grounding, which they have modified and reinterpreted in order to achieve a better understanding of the educational system and its interactions with other spheres of society.

The socialist-Marxist perspective, as has been pointed out by some of its foremost representatives, such as Sheyla Rowbotham (Rowbotham 1971), Roberta Hamilton (Hamilton 1978), Zillah Eisenstein (Eisenstein 1980) and Juliet Michell (Michell 1971), states that eradicating the oppression of women would mean modification of the existing social structure, with the ensuing economic, political, cultural and ideological consequences, amongst others.

The proposals put forward by "radical feminism" in the educational arena are linked to two wider actions: the work done in the sphere of feelings and promoting positive self-worth amongst women. In the case of the former, it is a matter of using the care extended to others not only as a part of what women learn but extrapolating it to the whole of humankind, since this tendency considers that if males were to learn about care and care-giving it would lessen the level of violence they exercise, thus promoting a type of masculinity more closely related to life and more distant from violent acts (Connell 1989 1995). This same standpoint also calls for the need for boys to work on their feelings, developing the ability to express sadness, frustration, unhappiness and the like (Askew & Ross 1991; Miedzian 1995) on the basis that exploring these areas will achieve the dual goal of reducing the level of male violence and constructing a more equal society.

Referring now to the importance of women's self-worth, work in schools focuses on modifying the oppression caused by a sexist culture, with particular emphasis being placed on self-awareness processes (Weiner 1999). This involves giving women the emotional and methodological tools they need to reconstruct their own personal history, to positively reconstruct their female identity and to empower them with the goal of changing society through the introduction of new social values.

Hand in hand with the women's liberation movement of the 1960s, as represented by, for example, Kate Millet (Millet 1970), Catharine MacKinnon (MacKinnon 1979) and Sulamit Firestone (Firestone 1970), there arose the conviction that the cause of the oppression of women lies in the development of a society based on patriarchy.

The radical perspective fights to modify a model of socialisation based on learning a type of female identity in which pride of place is occupied by the cult of beauty and fashion, idealised models of motherhood or the idealisation of the family. The social legitimacy of these models makes it hard to break away from the patriarchal instruments that support them, such as physical or psychological violence against women or sexual harassment, where the blame for such actions is laid on women for not following the models imposed on them by society.

In the early 1980s, following the publication of Jean-François Lyotard's book *La Condition postmoderne: Rapport sur le savoir* (Lyotard 1979), a new theoretical approach to the analysis of female inequality appeared on the scene: feminist post-modernism, which was critical of the fundamental tenets of the modern age, based on the ideas of the Age of Enlightenment. With respect to this guiding principle of post-modernist theory, it must be said that authors as representative of universalism as Seyla Benhabib (Benhabib 2006) assert that post-modernist thought is not to be despised, since it puts the legacy of the Enlightenment project to the test, helping to improve its postulates in order to solve those problems for which theories of a universal nature have been unable to find a solution.

Lacanian thought and the French post-structuralist school provide the foundations that have given birth to the theory of difference (Cavana 1995; Cirillo 2002), which represents a move away from post-modern theories (Piussi and Mañeru 2006). The postulates of this theory have been widely developed in France, above all through the works of Luce Irigaray (Irigaray 1974), Julia Kristeva (Kristeva 1981) or Hélène Cixous (Cixous 1995) and in Italy, taken up by the Milan Bookshop movement (1996), Luisa Muraro (Muraro 1987) and Anna María Piussi (Piussi 1989), the pillars on which the gender difference school of thought has been built.

The educational objective of this perspective is to highlight and positively appraise those characteristics its followers consider to be ontologically female. The first step is to elevate the status of everything related to what is "female": one of the goals highlighted by Luce Irigaray (1997) is for the education system to teach the difference between the sexes from earliest childhood.

The basis of all educational practice is the "relationship" as the starting point for any kind of educational process (Mañeru 2001). They consider that the practice of relationship is a fundamentally female one, since the fact that women are biologically capable of giving birth endows them with a body that "is itself open and available to be home to such a relationship" (Arnaus 2001, p. 231; Rivera 1996).

Following on from the post-structuralism postulated by Foucault and Derrida, the various forms of queer theory also propose the reinterpretation of feminist theory, based on the elimination of heteronormativity, which, according to authors such as Judith Butler (Butler 2001, 2002), is the social norm that rules the collective identity of our societies. This perspective is currently fostering a large number of research projects in schools into sexuality and the way it creates and re-creates identity in childhood and youth.

The Educational Actions Implemented by the Different Perspectives

Although there appears to be common ground on which the various feminist perspectives can base their efforts to achieve the best possible conditions for women within the educational system, it should not be forgotten that each one has given priority to certain educational actions over others, according to the *a priori* ideas they hold on gender inequality, and which we will now examine in greater detail.

The liberal perspective has mostly operated through the relationship between schools and institutional bodies such as Centres for Equality, local authorities, provincial authorities and the like. Although it would be untrue to say that every institution has implemented its activities from the liberal standpoint, it cannot be denied that this perspective has flourished above all within the institutional realm. The support provided by a variety of official bodies has led to the liberal perspective becoming the most widely extended in terms of educational action, deploying a wide range of proposals aimed at encouraging students and/or teaching staff to reject gender-based discriminatory attitudes. Particular emphasis has been placed on attempting to eliminate those stereotypes that implicitly deny the possibility of girls accessing areas of education traditionally occupied by boys. In this regard, the 1980s saw the beginning of a series of awareness-raising proposals in schools to encourage girls to opt for traditionally male courses of study, explicitly conveying the message of equal abilities or the importance of using non-sexist language. A variety of resources are brought into play, such as the holding of exhibitions showcasing women working in the realm of science or in traditionally male-oriented occupations, or reviving the memory of women who have established historical milestones. It is also worth mentioning the large volume of posters distributed amongst schools referring to girls' rights, to encouraging the reporting of any abuse of the latter, or promoting involvement in activities that are socially linked to boys, such as physical activity or new technologies. At the same time workshops have been organised, generally as part of teacher training courses, to raise teachers' awareness of the importance of gender equality.

The influence of the socialist perspective on educational action has been more indirect than direct (although this has by no means reduced its worth), due to the fact that its principal area of interest has been the inequalities that female teachers have had to put up with in their dual role: that of women and that of teachers. The result has been a significant awareness-raising process that has expanded through teacher associations, unions and the like, leading many female teachers to introduce a new slant to their class content regarding women's role in society. This has been done by groups of women teachers who have produced extremely valuable research that they have then put into practice in the classroom, promoting teacher networks that have carried out a multitude of activities of great constancy and efficacy despite their low profile. The great majority of these research projects have never been published, although that is not to refute their existence in fields such as women's contribution to society throughout history, where they provide a new vision that includes the female perspective by introducing a significant degree of criticism of the way in which historical events are taught and learnt. Such criticism aims to modify the prevailing approach of educational content, focusing as it does on the deeds performed by men and their consequences for the conceptualisation of the way we understand social power, which revolves around territorial gains, the conquest of power or the amassing of riches and excludes events occurring behind the front line, and highlighting an alternative form of social organisation in which women play a prominent role.

The radical approach is amongst those that attach the greatest importance to education, carrying out activities designed to modify a gender-based culture of inequality and placing girls at the centre of its educational proposals in order to achieve this. Such projects are based on the introduction of a change in the male model and work to modify aspects that have historically been absent from a boy's upbringing, such as the fact that they too are allowed to cry, that force should not be seen as the way of solving a problem, or the need to find new relationship strategies that see both sexes as equals and are not based on violence. At the same time other activities have been used to encourage the positive appraisal of girls, taking their needs into account and empowering them, such as incentives for girls to interact in technology and science classes with a higher level of involvement; forcing girls to say what they think or to assume a greater share of group leadership, not only within their classes but also in the school as a whole; or favouring a more equal distribution of playground space so that girls can have more room to carry out their playground activities. Parallel to all this, greater emphasis is placed on the female point of view in all aspects of the school syllabus, such as history, philosophy, literature, science and the like, and greater visibility is given to women in classroom content.

Turning now to the proposals put forward by the post-modern approach, the most relevant factor has been the introduction of proposals based on the idea of *gender difference*, since they have been widely incorporated into the theoretical debates on gender and education that have arisen in Spain. The educational goal of the difference theory is to highlight and positively appraise those characteristics that are considered to be ontologically female. For this reason they consider that any female value is intrinsically positive, that there are no negative values that need to be eradicated, and that the first step in any educational action should therefore be to extol everything related to what is "female." One of the most widely implemented educational practices in the gender difference approach is to encourage same-sex groups within the classroom to prevent girls from feeling intimidated or overshadowed by their male counterparts, thereby enabling them to enjoy greater freedom of thought and action.

The queer theory perspective is also proving successful due to the fact that it includes gender identity as a principle that questions the male-female tandem and provides a way for all those who do not feel represented by any of the heteronormative figures of this tandem to express themselves. In order to achieve a critical revision of our normative cultural construct the need is put forward to include, in both primary and secondary education, actions that help children and adolescents to review a variety of presuppositions concerning sexuality, seen as an act of relationship linked to aspects such as the concept of love, relationships within the couple or the level of affective and emotional bonding. With this end in mind a variety of teachers have been working, individually or in small groups, to develop projects to fight against homophobia or explore subjects such as pleasure. These projects seek to improve the way in which homosexuality is represented in classroom textbooks and to introduce activities that help pupils to rethink the model of homosexuality currently transmitted in TV series, comics or films.

We conclude that a variety of actions have been implemented in educational practice in Spanish schools with the aim of achieving gender equality. This has been done from a holistic perspective, integrating the diverse perspectives referred to in this article in an all-encompassing approach to classroom practice.

References

Acker, S.1989. *Teachers, gender and careers*. London: Lewes Falmer,
Alemany, C. 1992. *Yo nunca he jugado con electro-L*. Madrid: Instituto de la Mujer.
Arnaus, R. 2001. Aprender a lo largo de la vida desde el amor a la madre. In *Educación, Nombre Común Femenino*, A. Piussi and A. Mañeru, 210–31. Barcelona: Octaedro.
Askew, S. and Ross, C., 1991. *Los chicos no lloran. el sexismo en educación*. Buenos Aires: Paidós.
Astelarra, J. 2005. *Veinte años de políticas de igualdad*. Valencia: Universitat de Valencia.
Ballarín, P. 1992. *Desde las mujeres. Modelos coeducativos: coeducar-segregar*. Granada: Universidad de Granada.
Ballarín, P. 2001. La coeducación hoy. In *Educar En Femenino y En Masculino*. N. Blanco, *31–40*. Madrid: Akal.
Benhabib, S. 2006. *El ser y el otro en la ética contemporánea*. Barcelona: Paidós.
Bonilla, A. 2012. Superando Discriminaciones y Violencias: propuesta participativa para la igualdad entre los sexos en la adolescencia. Madrid: Instituto de la Mujer.
Butler, J. 2001. *El género en disputa*. Barcelona: Paidós.
Butler, J. 2002. *Cuerpos que importan. sobre los límites materiales y discursivos del sexo*. Barcelona: Paidós.
Canales, A. 2012. Little intellectuals. Girls' academic secondary education under Francoism: projects, realities and paradoxes, *Gender and Education*, 24, no: 4, 375–91.
Cavana, M. 1995. Diferencia. In *Diez Palabras Clave Sobre Mujer*. C. Amorós (Ed.), 85–119. Navarra: Verbo Divino.
Cirillo, L. 2002. *Mejor huérfanas. Por una crítica feminista al pensamiento de la diferencia*. Barcelona: Anthropos.
Cixous, H. 1995. *La risa de la medusa. ensayos sobre la escritura*. Barcelona: Anthropos.
Connell, R. W. 1989. Cool guys, swots and wimps: The interplay of masculinity and education. *Oxford Review of Education, 15,* 3: 291–312.
Connell, R. W. 1995. *Masculinities*. Berkeley: University of California Press.
CREA. 2003. *Proyecto BRUDILLA CALLÍ: Las mujeres gitanas contra la exclusion*. Madrid: Instituto de la Mujer.
DeLyin, H. And Migniuolo, F. (Eds). 1989. *Women Teachers*. Milton Keynes: Open University Press.
Díaz-Aguado, M. J. 2001. *La construcción de la igualdad y la prevención de la violencia contra la mujer desde la educación secundaria*. Madrid: Instituto de la Mujer.

Eisenstein, Z. 1980. *Patriarcado capitalista y feminismo socialista*. Madrid: Siglo XXI.

Firestones, S. 1970. *The Dialectic of Sex: The Case for Feminist Revolution*. New York: William Morrow.

Flax, J. 1967. *Building Feminist Theory*. New York: Longman.

Friedan, B. 1974. *La mística de la feminidad*. Madrid: Júcar.

García de Cortázar M. L. and García de León, A. 1997. *Mujeres en minoría: una investigación sociológica sobre las catedráticas de Universidad en España*. Madrid: Centro de Investigaciones sociológicas.

Garreta, N. And Careaga, P. 1987. *Modelos masculino y femenino en los textos de EGB*. Madrid: Ministerio de cultura.

Grañeras, M. 1999. *Las desigualdades de la educación en España*. Madrid: CIDE.

Hamilton, R. 1978. *Liberation of Women: A Study of Patriarchy and Capitalism. Controversies in Sociology*. London: Unwin Hyman.

Harding, S. 1996. *Ciencia y feminismo*. Madrid: Morata.

Hobson, B. 2003. *Recognition Struggles and Social Movements*. Cambridge: Cambridge University Press.

Colectivo IOÉ. 2003. *La escolarización de hijas de familias inmigrantes*. Madrid: Instituto de la Mujer.

Irigaray, L. 1974. *Speculum. de l'autre femme*. Paris: Minuit.

Irigaray, L. 1997. Progetto di formazíone alia cítadínaza per ragazze e ragazzí perdonne e oumíní. commissione per la realizzazione parita fra uomo e donna della régleme emllla-romagna.

Jaggar, A. 1983. *Feminist Politics and Human Nature*. Totowa: N. J. Rowman and Allanheld.

Kristeva, J. 1981. Woman can never be defined. In *New French Feminisms*, E. Marks & I. Courtivon, 114–37.

Leal, A. 2009. *Concepciones acerca de las relaciones de amor y el conocimiento de las necesidades del otro u otra: un studio con adolescents y jóvenes con objeto de entender y prevenir el maltrato en las relaciones de pareja*. Madrid: Instituto de la Mujer.

Librería de Mujeres de Milán. 1996. El final del patriarcado. Ha ocurrido y no por casualidad. *El Viejo Topo*, 96, 46–59.

Lorber, J. 2010. *Gender Inequality*. New York: Oxford University Press.

Lyotard, J. F. 1979. *La condition postmoderne: Rapport sur le savoir*. Paris: Minuit.

Mackinnon, C. 1979. *Sexual Harassment of Working Women*. New Haven: Yale University Press.

Mañeru, A. 2001. La diferencia sexual en la educación. In *Educar En Femenino y En Masculino*. N. Blanco, 131–43. Madrid: Akal.

Maquieira, V. 2005. *Democracia, feminismo y universidad en el siglo XXI*. Madrid: Universidad Autónoma.

Miedzian, M. 1995. *Chicos son, hombres serán. Cómo romper los lazos entre masculinidad y violencia*. Madrid: Horas y Horas.

Millet, K. 1970. *Sexual Politics*. New York: Doubleday.

Montoya, M.M. and Salguero, J.M. 2004. *Orientación educativa y prevención de la violencia: la diferencia sexual en la resolución de conflictos*. Madrid: MEC.

Muñoz-Repiso, M. 1993. *Las desigualdades de la educación en España*. Madrid: CIDE.

Muraro, l. 1987. Diotima: *Il pensiero della differenza sessuale*. Milan: La Tartaruga.

Okin, S. 1979. *Women in Western Political Thought*. Princeton, N.J.: Princeton University Press.

Page, A. 2005. Los estudios de género y de las mujeres: concepto, neesidad y vigencia. Su vinculación con el movimiento feminist. In *Democracia, feminismo y Universidad en el Siglo XXI*. V. Maquieira el al, 209–14. Madrid: Instituto de la Mujer.

Piussi, A. and Mañeru, A. 2006. *Educación, nombre común femenino*. Barcelona: Octaedro.

Piussi, A. 1989. *Educare nella differenza*. Turin: Rosenberg & Sellier.

Puigver, Lidia. 2012. *Incidencia de la Ley integral contra la violencia de género en la formación inicial del profesorado*. Madrid: Instituto de la Mujer.

Rivera, M.M. 1996. *El cuerpo indispensable. significados del cuerpo de mujer*. Madrid: Horas y Horas.

Rodríguez, C. 2001. Investigaciones sobre las desigualdades de género en el sistema educativo. In *Un Acercamiento a Los Estudios De Género*. A.A.V.V., 121–54. Valencia: Germania.

Rowbotham, R. 1971. *Women's Liberation and New Politics. Pamphlet, 17*, 5–10.

Rubin, G. 1975. The traffic in women: Notes on the political economy of sex. In *Toward an Anthropology of Women*. R. Reiter, Comp.157–210. New York: Monthy Review Press.

Sánchez-Bello, A. 2012. Gendered Agenda in Education. In *Globalism and Power: Iberian education and curriculum policies*. New York: Peter Lang. P. 221–35.

Subirat, M. And Brullet, C. 1988. *Rosa y azul: la transmisión de los géneros en la escuela mixta*. Madrid: Ministerio de cultura.

Totten, Samuel y Pedersen Jon (2012), *Educating about Social Issues in the 20th and 21st Centuries*, Washington, DC: Library of Congress

Weiner, G. 1999. *Los feminismos en la educación*. Morón: Kikiriki.

Wharton, A. 2005. *The Sociology of Gender. an Introduction to Theory and Research*. Singapore: Blackwell.

4

Genesis and Structure of Critical Pedagogy in Italy

Domenica Maviglia

In Italy, critical pedagogy arose as product of the events that took place in 1968, a historical turning point for Italian culture. The year 1968 became a symbol of deep cultural transformation that brought to life a wide protest movement led by young people manifesting against the existing ideological-political system. This student protest – fuelled by expectations and hopes for a better future – focused on the issues of anti-authoritarianism and participation, the ideology of knowledge and its dependence from the economic-political system, the free exercise of critical thinking and its social building power, and the realisation of the right to an active, critical, and participatory citizenship.

The significance and value of 1968 was therefore based on the window of opportunity that it provided to survey and analyse critically, thoroughly, and radically the renewal of the social role played by culture. By aiming at renewing knowledge, this culture led to the emergence of a movement of anti-authoritarian ideas that played a proactive role against alienation through the relaunch of democratic practices in society. By struggling to free itself from the existing dominant models and structures, this culture opened up to the most fundamental needs of individuals, with the goal of laying the foundations for rebuilding social life through the renewal of mentalities in all institutions and, in particular, through a change in the model and use of culture in every sector and field of knowledge. Therefore, as suggested by Tolomelli (2008, 127–29): "1968 left a remarkable and substantial hallmark characterised by 'forms of agitated democracy', the need of developing socio-political involvement and 'non-conventional forms of associative life', and a radical re-elaboration of cultural symbols in every field." In the academic community, the scholars of the Universities of Turin, Milan, Trento, Pisa, and Rome tabled a series of issues that had to be tackled by re-examining the identities of knowledge and, in a broad sense, the structured knowledge existing in Universities. They thus prompted a process of radical criticism on culture. Through this process, these scholars started a critical-structural analysis to expose, demystify, and question the certainties of traditional knowledge, with the aim of renewing the identity and role of institutions, especially the educational ones, and disciplines like pedagogy "which more than any other discipline is vulnerable to ideology, it has a diffused social power, and it is built on ancient (discursive and axiological) orders that are binding and functional to the political-social system" (Cambi 2009, 30).

The student protest placed in the spotlight educational institutions like school and family, thoroughly evaluating their structure and their function by analysing them through a critical lens linked to critical sociology, psychoanalysis, Marxism, and deconstructionist structuralism. The social educational institutions and their internal dynamics were therefore re-evaluated from this perspective by applying the principle of "suspicion" and by adopting a critical procedure aimed at exposing their true nature. This process led to the identification of school as the first state ideological apparatus (Althusser 1974); a place where skills, values, and ideologies were reproduced (Bourdieu & Passeron 1972); a selective system (Scuola di Barbiana 1967); and an institution devoted to the control of bodies, minds, and knowledge (Foucault 1977). On the other hand, the institution of family was accused of being the generator of authoritarian and conformist individuals and an institution structured around the father, a figure of control, authority, and at the centre of family dynamics. For these reasons, this process triggered an upheaval against the figure of the father, causing *de facto* the "death of the family" (Cooper 1970).

The cultural atmosphere of 1968 encouraged therefore the use of critical pedagogy as a fundamental tool to unhinge the structure of educational institutions, initiating a radical review of educational processes, teaching methods, and theoretical research, and providing also a series of innovative pedagogical insights. In other words:

> by promoting non-authoritarian, anti-institutional, and progressivist practices, pedagogy was "stripped away" of its conditioning factors, interests, and hegemonic forms [...] reclaiming an educational knowledge with a strong scientific power (= independent) which was able to expose the "social duplication" promoted by educational institutions, fight against the "myths of adults," recover and enhance infancy, denounce the "pernicious" forms of teaching and the "impossible" procedures of pedagogy, and relaunch the role of the educational relationship.
>
> (Mariani 2006: 30)

From this point of view, critical pedagogy stood out as a paradigm that deconstructed and is still deconstructing the fundamental aspects of pedagogy and education, critically defending the human being and its meanings. By using this paradigm, the individuals – as human beings endowed with a stubborn ability to self-realise themselves and dissent from others – became able to resist the ideology of consumption and conformism, freeing themselves from social and institutional conditioning factors and from a socially-defined "conservative" sub-conscious, while paving the way to a reinforcement of the individuals' ability to plan themselves and open up to the world.

Yet, it is clear that since 1968, pedagogy started interpreting and analysing in a critical and radical way both its knowledge and education. The discipline was hence reviewed, reoriented, and re-questioned, and it focused on the conditioning elements imposed by ideology, tradition, and societal trends; its scientific and critical vocation; and its theoretical infrastructure. The development of this critical perspective in pedagogy triggered an activity of reflexive re-interpretation of all educational practices and the links existing between theory and practice, paying particular attention to the "categories of reflexivity"[1] (Cambi 2009) on which was consolidated and developed the critical and theoretical research that inquired into the structure, the meaning, the object, and the set of rules concerning pedagogy.

Figures, models, function, and topicality

As previously described, in Italy critical pedagogy was shaped and developed between the 1960s and the 1990s in order to become a critical form of knowledge in the philosophical reflection on the issues concerning education. During the 1960s, critical pedagogy vigorously resurfaced on the Italian cultural scene with the aim of deconstructing and reorienting the educational action and the pedagogical thought, devising its epistemology, the reflexivity of its methodology, and the structure of the educational discourse. Yet, it was only at the crossroads of the 1970s that the die of critical pedagogy was cast. Why? Firstly, because of the decisive and reconstructive metamorphosis that turned pedagogics into the "sciences of education," a transformation that empowered pedagogy from its theoretical influences and allowed it to critically review the relationship between science and the structure of pedagogy. Secondly, because of the crisis suffered by pedagogy as a result of the theoretical practices that had the aim of exposing, deconstructing, and radically criticising the existing order in order to unhinge the social and epistemic status of the discipline and show how much it was enmeshed in ideology, prejudice, and institutions, a condition that strongly limited its critical power. All this created the need of developing a form of critical pedagogy explicitly suited to understand and self-regulate itself. Thirdly, there was the return of (critical) philosophy as a self-understanding tool for pedagogy and self-regulating device of its complex and articulated knowledge (Mariani 2006, 67). The combination of all these factors led to the emergence of a model of critical pedagogy that represented a form of pedagogy that was post-scientific, post-ideological, and in particular critical-radical, interpretative, and hence manageable only by using the philosophical discourse provided by "criticism," following the principles of neocriticism or Marxism, empiricism or phenomenology, existentialism or hermeneutics, and deconstructionism.

In Italy, several pedagogues and philosophers decided to follow the principles of this model, taking an explicit stand in their work and establishing a paradigm that gradually developed according to different and heterogeneous criteria with the same "critical objective." Compared to what happened in other countries, in Italy this model was characterised for a longer period by a strong philosophical character that had different orientations and took as reference point several specific philosophical models like Marxism, personalism, pragmatism, critical rationalism, structuralism, problematicism, phenomenology, hermeneutics, deconstructionism, and the critical theory of society. Each of these philosophical models implicated different interpretations of the "pedagogical discourse device" (Metelli di Lallo 1996), establishing its features and outlining its intrinsic complexity (Granese 1990). This device was then used as basis and means to refine the critical perspective employed in pedagogical theory and educational practice. As a matter of fact:

> following these stages, critical pedagogy became stronger and stronger: this process provided a logical and theoretical basis to the discipline; a tradition, even if only recent; it highlighted its de- and re-constructive function (critical-regulatory following the criteria of Kant); it established its meta identity (placed beyond pedagogy, because it was product and means of an integrated and rigorous reflection on pedagogy that had to re-interpret it in the light of its fundamental principles, i.e. according to its identity and the general criteria that its discourses had to respect, embed, and take as rule to become genuinely pedagogic).
>
> (Cambi 2009, 11)

In Italy, this model had eclectic and dialectic foundations which were declined in different variations. Indeed, as many as three generations of pedagogues elaborated a critical perspective of pedagogy: the pre-war generation (Visalberghi, Laporta, Cives), the post-war generation (most active in the 1960s and 1970s with Granese, Broccoli, Laeng and many others), and the post-1968 generation (the third generation of academics born in the years between 1940–1960 or later). Antonio Banfi, Massimo Baldacci, Giovanni Maria Bertin, Piero Bertolini, Lamberto Borghi, Angelo Broccoli, Giacomo Cives, Franco Cambi, Enza Colicchi, Maria Grazia Contini, Rita Fadda, Giuseppe Flores D'Arcais, Remo Fornaca, Franco Frabboni, Elisa Frauenfelder, Mario Gennari, Alberto Granese, Mauro Laeng, Raffaele Laporta, Mario Manno, Riccardo Massa, Carmela Metelli Di Lallo, Marielisa Muzi, Carlo Nanni, Alba Porcheddu, Luisa Santelli Beccegato, Giuseppe Spadafora, Aldo Visalberghi, Carla Xodo Cegolon are all names of researchers in critical pedagogy who – working with different methodologies, using different theories, or taking as starting point different philosophical assumptions – moved towards common ground and a partly shared idea advocating for the creation of models where "critics" cooperated to make their positions converge.

As a discipline, critical pedagogy became therefore linked to different social and cultural models and critical-radical forms of philosophic and scientific knowledge, while from a practical point of view it intertwined with social institutions like family and school. In other words, "today critical pedagogy is a global model declined in different forms related to traditions and views which might even be asymmetrical. This is what highlights the value of critical pedagogy and require it to rethink and review itself in a renovated and innovative way that simultaneously must also be structured and rigorous" (Cambi 2009, 10). The development of this paradigm on a European and international level was achieved by creating a wide range of profiles and samples in synergic or asymmetrical position, creating a general image of pluralism and a high level of complexity due to the multifaceted nature of criticism and philosophical schools. The bond between philosophy and pedagogy is based on the principle of "criticality," since it defines the relation between two forms of knowledge that, in this way, become synergic and interactive. "Philosophy turns into a critical tool to interpret *in toto* the wide range and identity of pedagogy as theory of education, playing therefore a meta-theoretical and meta-critical role" (Cambi 2009, 13). Considering all this, critical pedagogy becomes a critical regulatory device to evaluate the existing models: it is the product of an act of reflection on the meaning and the task of pedagogy that shows its circular and integrative function.

> It's both an epistemic and educational paradigm; an educational project that does not distinguish itself only for its epistemic and structural reflexivity on and in the field of educational knowledge. It is a type of knowledge that develops pedagogy both as science (by simultaneously reviewing the reflexive and purposive bond with science and establishing its epistemic model), and as general discipline (as a critical reflection open to all educational issues, emergencies, and institutions). It is the form of pedagogy of our time: it becomes critical because it goes beyond the existing educational practices; because it fixes new and open models that are questioned and criticised by pedagogy itself; because it cherishes a noble concept of education (individual and social) that is liberal, responsible, open, and flexible.
>
> (Cambi 2009, 18)

In other words, critical pedagogy tackles pedagogy by reviewing the entire discursive and functional apparatus of pedagogy and education, in order to rebuild its cultural, anthropological, and political meaning, with a particular emphasis on "what is worthy" and "what must become" in future. "This paradigm represents, therefore, a must that also recognises how much it needs to provide itself the tools to develop a series of operative strategies that might spur change and concretisation according to a perspective of empowerment of the individual and the community, re-obtaining in this way a more radical anthropological perspective – of individual and gender – framed in the 'malaise of civilisation,' in the condition of 'exploitation and domination,' in the will/need to unleash potential and fulfill expectations that have been suffocated, silenced, and alienated" (Cambi 2009, 25–26). Therefore, if we consider pedagogy as a reflexive knowledge on education, its processes, and its issues, it is always critical pedagogy. It refers to a methodology of work that embraces all the discursive complexity of pedagogy, its internal tensions, and its articulation at different levels, interpreting and organising them in the light of a reflexive cognitive activity based on the philosophical thought. It becomes an act of reflection oriented to safeguard the *proprium* of pedagogy and its interpretative status.

From this point of view, critical pedagogy is a "style" of pedagogy that creates (different) models sharing a reflexive ability and focusing on problems and/or arguments of pedagogical nature that pursue the re-establishment of a more specific order and meaning to pedagogy. The order is linked to the planning role of pedagogy; while the meaning refers to its anthropological-educational vocation. This kind of pedagogy is critical because of two main reasons. Firstly, it interprets pedagogy against every intrinsic form of reductionism; secondly, it recomposes its complete, ideal, regulatory "framework." Furthermore, from a philosophical perspective, it is critical because it draws its ideas and principles from the wide and heterogeneous tradition of criticism (from Kant to the "school of suspicion" and hermeneutics), keeping the typical self-reflexive and limiting ability of the transcendental conditions of this tradition.

To summarise, this "style" of pedagogy results is sophisticated and complex, with a scope that covers all forms of knowledge existing in the field of education but re-interpreting them by using new insights stemming from the *proprium* (or specific proprieties) of pedagogy, hence reuniting different forms of knowledge in a unique core. This is how critical pedagogy developed in Italy: as an act of reflection influenced by a series of scientific, ideological, pragmatic, dogmatic-metaphysical deviations that cut across (and often dominated) the entire scope of action of the discipline. From this point of view, critical pedagogy equals reflexive pedagogy, but with philosophy involved in order to play a strictly critical (post-Kantian) role (Cambi 2009).

Closing considerations

As outlined in the previous paragraphs, if we compare the development of critical pedagogy in Italy with the development of this discipline in other countries and particularly in the United States, it is possible to find several similarities. For example, the fact that critical pedagogy created strong links with different philosophical traditions, while keeping at the same time a clear distance from them in order to respect its own identity and peculiarities, aspects that Cambi (2009) labels as "categories of reflexivity" and which concern the epistemological, axiological, ontological structure of the pedagogical thought and the educational practice.

In the Italian scenario, this form of pedagogy becomes therefore a paradigm that without any doubt embraces the essence of its meaning and its value thanks to what Mariani (2006) defines a "virtuous circle" between reflexive theory and (open) educational issues. Nevertheless, this circle seems to be subject to a series of limitations, since it often risks to get lost in the hermeneutic white noise filled with positive ideals about mankind and its education in the current and future situation. In other words, the development of theories in the Italian paradigm of critical pedagogy – which, as already mentioned, can refer to a wide variety of philosophical traditions in order to give voice to the richness and axiological-semantic consistency of the polysemic term critical – seems to limit itself solely to a refined and thorough critical-philosophical theorisation both in pedagogical theory and educational practice, deemphasising the role of the real confrontation and exchange created by the interactive relation that should *de facto* exist between pedagogical theory (developed at an academic level) and educational practice (implemented in educational institutions).

Even though the current situation of pedagogy is complex and multifaceted, it is also true that the philosophical legacy in pedagogy has a wide scope that allows it to be functional to the "critical problematisation" and the act of self-reflection that must inspire the "pedagogical action" when facing the new challenges of education (Mariani 2006, 23). Considering all this, it becomes necessary to evaluate the etymological and hermeneutic richness of the term critical. In order to clarify the true meaning of the term critical in combination with the word pedagogy, it is useful to analyse the origins of the term. The first step requires therefore to understand the Greek verb *krinein*, which means to distinguish, to divide, to discriminate, to judge, to take a shrewd decision, and in a wider sense to the action of denoting, finding meaning in a new way, questioning. Criticism takes shape when individuals face an object that they need to investigate, and it requires an open and enquiring attitude. In other words, a critical procedure entails questions. It requires a space open to criticism, i.e. a space where everything is in doubt, which is the perfect place to expose and recognise the essence and the character of what is currently under scrutiny.

All this seems to depict criticism as the defining characteristic of pedagogical research, where not only researchers have to deal with an object - the education of individuals – but also with the dilemma of choosing between what might fairly and rightly be considered as educational – since it can lead individuals in the right direction towards their original destination – and what is not. Yet, in Italy as well as in other countries, critical pedagogy is also interested in preserving the delicate balance between social change and the acquisition of an individual critical spirit leading to the development of an educational practice suited to reach both goals. Therefore, the aim of critical pedagogy is:

> to enable individuals to take charge of the task of questioning a specific form of reality and contributing to redefine and change it through a thinking process that should not only be productive, constructive, and utopian, but also – and much more importantly – a process that could lead to expose, free, and criticise in the fullest meaning of the term. A constantly open attitude is what makes criticism and critical pedagogy so special: it corresponds to a permanent inquiring status that aims at receiving answers that are not necessarily true but yet represent a step forward on the road leading to the truth, because each answer is open to a new question and because the words and arguments used to ask something contain an infinite space for meaning.
>
> (Fadda 2009, 22)

Besides, even Freire (2005) has always contended that pedagogy cannot avoid the task of changing the world through the development of rigorous forms of analysis. In other words, critical pedagogy is not only interested in changing society, but also in nurturing the development of a critical sense of awareness among all members of society. At the same time, critical pedagogy is the first place where it is necessary to exercise freedom, which represents a responsibility and even a moral obligation in order to acquire (critical) awareness about all conditioning factors influencing our theories and our practical choices, representing therefore an opportunity to expose, suspect, research, and recognise the essence and character of these conditioning factors (Fadda 2009, 23).

Critical pedagogy represents therefore a well-defined style in Italian and international pedagogy that brought about a series of models sharing a reflexive status. In Italy, the development of this style tried to re-establish the epistemological order and the anthropological vocation of pedagogy. This process emphasised the fundamental role played by philosophy in pedagogy not at a metaphysical level but rather as a reflexive methodology, a continuously developing *forma mentis* that expands the limits of Italian critical pedagogy and provides a perfect tool for its theoretical and practical work in the era of globalisation and post-modernity. Without considering specific philosophical schools and traditions, in Italy critical pedagogy represents a sort of hermeneutic and epistemological filter that – by using a critical–radical principle – interprets the fundamental structures of the pedagogical discourse, asking at the same time for a stronger democratic participation in the educational institutions and pushing the individuals away from the edge of the cliff of conformism to move instead towards the light of critical reason.

Critical pedagogy therefore is a metatheoretical paradigm that in the era of globalisation and interculture acquires an increasingly global, topical, and fundamental role, requiring at the same time to be strengthened in order to become meta-analysis, meta-reflection, and meta-commitment. The complex multicultural society of our age represents something completely new in our history. Currently, we live in a diversified tangle of cultural models and beliefs which in its turn creates new models, mental habits, and *modus vivendi* that demand a change in mentality, or in better words the acquisition of a new mentality ready to go beyond appearance and open to the value of dialogue, exchange, and understanding. This paradigm is characterised by laicity, pluralism, encounter, and dialogue, universal emergencies that critical pedagogy proposes to turn into possibilities that we must learn to recognise, consider, adopt, enhance, and build in *interiore homine* and in social life. This is what confers on critical pedagogy the role of tool to go beyond appearance, prejudice, selfishness, and closure, in order to enter a space of pluralism and integrated, dialectic coexistence (Cambi 2006).

Therefore, the genuine resource of this pedagogical perspective is its strong appeal to a responsible participation to the life of the community, which requires a concrete involvement by the individual in a dimension of solidarity and respect for the "Other." This allows individuals to reduce their dependence from factors like culture, religious belief, sexual preference, gender, or social status. At the same time, this pedagogical perspective is a remarkable invitation – particularly for those people exercising educational responsibilities – to reflect, express their opinions, doubt, and openly question themselves, wearing the hat of "critical researchers" (Kincheloe 2008) to enhance the value of every aspect and dimension that is considered "different" or "divergent."

Notes

1. Franco Cambi (2009, 123–25) classifies the "categories of reflexivity" in "constitutive categories" and "historical categories." The former group refers to the epistemology, axiology, and ontology of pedagogy. The latter group is divided instead in "formal categories" (dialectics, change, bet, ideology), which highlight the character of tensional structure and dynamics of education/training in itself and in its individual and social phenomenology; and "content categories" (alienation, complexity, individual, and democracy), which involve anthropological and socio-political categories.

References

Althusser, L. (1974) *Ideologia e apparati ideologici di stato*. In: Barbagli, M. (ed.). *Scuola, potere e ideologia*. Bologna: Il Mulino.
Banfi, A. (1961) *La problematicità dell'educazione*. Florence: La Nuova Italia.
Baldacci, M. (2003) *Il problematicismo*. Lecce: Milella.
Bertin, G. M. (1968) *Educare alla ragione: lezioni di pedagogia generale*. Rome: Armando.
Bertolini, P. (1988) *L'esistere pedagogico*. Florence: La Nuova Italia.
Borghi, L. (1951) *Educazione e autorità nell'Italia moderna*. Florence: La Nuova Italia.
Borrelli, m. (2004) *Pedagogia critica*. Cosenza: Luigi Pellegrini Editore.
Bourdieu, P., Passeron, J. L. (1972) *La riproduzione del sistema scolastico*. Translated from the French by G. Mughini. Rimini: Guaraldi.
Broccoli, A. (1974) *Ideologia e educazione*. Florence: La Nuova Italia.
Cambi, F. (1986) *Il congegno del discorso pedagogico*. Bologna: Clueb.
Cambi, F. (2006) *Incontro e dialogo. Prospettive della pedagogia interculturale*. Rome: Carocci.
Cambi, F. (2009) *Pedagogie critiche in Europa*. Rome: Carocci.
Cives, G. (1978) *La filosofia dell'educazione oggi*. Florence: La Nuova Italia.
Colicchi, E. (ed.) (2009) *Per una pedagogia critica*. Rome: Carocci.
Contini, M. G. (1980) *Comunicazione e educazione*. Florence: La Nuova Italia.
Cooper, D. (1970) *The Death of the Family*. New York: Vintage Books.
Fadda, R. (2002) *Sentieri della formazione*. Rome: Armando.
Fadda, R. (2009) *Un modello di pedagogia critica. Presupposti, sviluppi, problemi aperti*. In: FLORES D'ARCAIS, G. (ed.). *Intervista alla pedagogia*. Brescia: La Scuola.
Fornaca, R. (1992) *Analisi critica dei fondamenti delle culture pedagogiche*. Turin: Il Segnalibro.
Foucault, M. (1977) *Microfisica del potere*. Turin: Einaudi.
Frabboni, F (2003) *Il domani dell'educazione*. Lecce: Pensa Multimedia.
Frauenfelder, E. (1994) *Pedagogia e biologia*. Naples: Liguori.
Freire, P. (2005) *Pedagogy of the Oppressed*. New York: The Continuum International Publishing Group.
Gennari, M. (2001) *Filosofia della formazione dell'uomo*. Milan: Bompiani.
Granese, A. (ed.) (1990) *La condizione teorica*. Milan: Unicopli.
Kincheloe, J. L. (2008) *Critical Pedagogy*. New York: Peter Lang.
Laeng, M. (1960) *Problemi di struttura della pedagogia*. Brescia: La Scuola.

Laporta, R. (1996) *L'assoluto pedagogico*. Florence: La Nuova Italia.

Manno, M. (1962) *L'esigenza critica come problema morale. E altri saggi*. Messina: Peloritana.

Mariani, A. (2003) *La pedagogia sotto analisi. Modelli di filosofia critica dell'educazione in Francia (1960–1980)*. Milan: Unicopli.

Mariani, A. (2006) *Elementi di filosofia dell'educazione*. Rome: Carocci.

Massa, R. (ed.) (1990) *Istituzioni di pedagogia e scienze dell'educazione*. Rome-Bari: Laterza.

McLaren, P. and Kincheloe, J. L. (eds.) (2007) *Critical Pedagogy: Where are we Now?* New York: Peter Lang.

Metelli di Lallo, C. (1966) *Analisi del discorso pedagogico*. Padua: Marsilio.

Muzi, M. (2009) *Pedagogia critica in Italia*. Rome: Carocci.

Nanni, C. (1984) *Educazione e scienze dell'educazione*. Rome: Las.

Porcheddu, A. (ed.) (1990) *Gli incontri mancati*. Milan: Unicopli.

Santelli Beccegato, L. (1998) *Interpretazioni pedagogiche e scelte educative*. Brescia: La Scuola.

Spadafora, G. (1992) *L'identità negativa della pedagogia*. Milan: Unicopli.

Scuola di Barbiana (1967) *Lettera a una professoressa*. Florence: Libreria Editrice Fiorentina.

Tolomelli, M. (2006) *Terrorismo e società*. Bologna: Il Mulino.

Visalberghi, A. (1965) *Problemi della ricerca pedagogica*. Florence: La Nuova Italia.

Xodo Cegolon, C. (ed.) (2004) *La persona prima evidenza pedagogica per una scienza dell'educazione*. Lecce: Pensa Multimedia.

5

Mass Schooling for Socialist Transformation in Cuba and Venezuela

Tom G. Griffiths and Jo Williams

At first glance, the experiences of both Cuba and Venezuela seem to simply align with the current global emphasis on *Education for All* (EFA) as promoted by UNESCO and other international institutions and Non Governmental Organisations. Indeed, Venezuela cites its progress toward this and other Millennium Development Goals as evidence of the government's social and economic achievements (Asamblea Nacional, 2008; República Bolivariana de Venezuela, 2004). The modest educational MDGs however, seeking universal access to primary schooling by 2015, highlight the apparent incapacity of such basic social outcomes to be achieved in sites exploited first by colonial rulers, then devastated by the new imperialism of global capitalism and the accompanying imposition of neoliberal policy by the World Bank, International Monetary Fund and World Trade Organisation, to reduce public expenditure and shift the cost of services like education away from the State and onto individuals (Brock-Utne, 2007; Jones, 2007; Robertson, 2005). The educational policies and enacted practices of Cuba and Venezuela, as critical components of society-wide struggles against the capitalist system, are accompanied by social and economic policies that provide the necessary material preconditions for students' access to and democratic participation in education, typically overlooked in other educational reform projects. What Cuba and Venezuela clearly demonstrate is that with a fundamental shift in the political economy towards socialism, universal access to education, with a high degree of equity in terms of opportunity and outcomes, is something that can be achieved quite quickly.

Prior to the Cuban Revolution the education system reflected the systemic social inequalities present under the Batista regime, with less than half of Cuban children in schools, more than 1 million illiterates, and an average educational level of less than Grade 3 (Gasperini, 2000). The new government launched an ambitious campaign to massively increase educational access, spearheaded by a nationwide literacy campaign (MacDonald, 1985). The campaign's success lay not only in its achievement of mass literacy, but in the politicisation of the hundreds of thousands of young volunteers who participated as teachers, and the new relationships they forged with predominantly peasant farmers who they taught.

This mass initiative involved hundreds of thousands of volunteers who, in addition to assuming teaching roles, helped to build large numbers of new schools and educational buildings, often in buildings left vacant by sections of the Cuban bourgeoisie who left the country to await the reversal of the Revolution. The popular literacy campaign was closely followed by the rapid but systematic expansion of child-care and schooling as children moved through the systems, alongside parallel programs of adult education to raise the education level of those who had been historically excluded from education. A contemporary example of this emphasis is *La Universidad*

Para Todos (The University for All), a government initiative involving a range of educational programs broadcast on Cuban television, accompanied by a range of broadsheets available at a nominal cost, covering specialised academic subjects like Physics, Linguistics, Chemistry, History etc, to more popular topics like healthy eating (see: http://www.medioambiente.cu/universidad_todos.asp).

In a very different context, Venezuela has emulated the Cuban focus on systematically overcoming illiteracy, extending adults' subsequent education, and rapidly expanding all levels of formal, public education. Since coming to power in 1999, the Chávez government has directed unprecedented levels of public resources to the reform of the public system of education, renamed the Bolivarian Education System (BES), and a system of parallel Adult education missions (see for example Asamblea Nacional, 2008; Ministerio del Poder Popular para la Planificación y Desarrollo, 2008). In particular, access has been extended to traditionally disadvantaged and/or excluded groups: the urban and rural poor, those of African descent, and indigenous communities. These achievements rest on the Constitutional reforms of the Bolivarian Republic of 2000, which affirmed for example that "Education is a fundamental human right and social obligation which is free, obligatory and democratic", and that "everyone has a right to comprehensive, quality, ongoing education, under equal conditions for equal opportunities, regardless of their abilities, aspirations or vocation" (see Article 103, Gaceta Oficial de la República Bolivariana de Venezuela, 2000, p. 103).

On this constitutional basis, immediate responses to these and other measures of exclusion from education, based on social class, indigenous status and ethnicity, included an increase in public expenditure on public education from 3.38% of GDP in 1998 when Chávez was first elected, to 5.43% in 2007 (Chávez, 2008). This figure increases to more than 7% if federal government expenditure on the educational missions is included, along with State and local government expenditure (p. 33). Between 1998 and 2006 participation rates have increased from 44.7% to 60.6% for pre-school (0–6) age children; from 89.7% to 99.5% for primary school age children; from 27.3% to 41% for secondary school age children; and from 21.8% to 30.2% for tertiary education (Chávez, 2008, pp. 47–57).

Cuba's literacy campaign highlighted to the government a range of other social issues, most notably in the area of health and childcare, requiring urgent attention as social policy objectives in and of themselves, and as actions to create the necessary conditions for equitable educational outcomes to be realised. Practical and immediate policies followed, providing material support to people to facilitate their full participation in the campaign and subsequent initiatives. These included serious attention to all areas of social infrastructure—for example housing, transport, utilities, health care—alongside employment, targeted education scholarships, the provision of meals, books and uniforms for students. Together these policies supported the rapid expansion of education in ways that simultaneously, directly confronted class-based disadvantage and exclusion. Carnoy et al. (2007) provide a recent, positive appraisal of the impact of such an approach, which they identify as "state generated social capital" (p. 144), on student performance.

In similar fashion, the Bolivarian project in Venezuela has explicitly identified and targeted the social and economic basis of educational disadvantage and social exclusion. In the Venezuelan context, the response has included a wide range of social programs (*misiones*) like the provision of free health care (*Misión Barrio Adentro* supported by Cuban doctors working in community health clinics), *Misión Mercal* providing subsidised food through a network of State run supermarkets and food kitchens to marginalised sectors, and improved public transport and general infrastructure (Germán Sánchez, 2005a; Germán Sánchez, 2005b). Education missions provide non-formal education for adults, coordinated through a national, state and municipal organisational structure. Each mission is distinct, but generally involves units addressing: teaching and pedagogy; the logistics of coordinating venues and equipment to facilitate classes; the administration of funding; and social units who work with local communities to ensure students have adequate housing, healthcare, recreation and cultural facilities. Furthermore, each mission involves a staff unit known as *Atención Laboral*, which monitors the work situation of students and their families, working with local communities to establish cooperatives in agriculture and other sectors.

Linked to programs like these are associated achievements like those cited by Chávez (2008), including the provision of meals in schools for over two million students (p. 58), reduced income inequality (p. 75), and high rates of popular satisfaction with Venezuelan democracy (p. 84), all underpinning efforts to extend participation in education toward universal access. A current focus is on incorporating all public schools into the BES, under a model of integral education that involves extended, single-session school days for students (with meals provided), subject specific classes in the mornings, and integrated projects linked to community needs in the afternoons. Weisbrot and Sandoval (2007) report that central government social spending in Venezuela increased from 8.2% of GDP in 1998 to 13.6% in 2006, this figure excluding social spending from the national oil company (PDVSA), which adds a further 7.3% of GDP (p. 2). These and other reforms amount to direct State investment in individuals' capacity to participate in education, aligning with Carnoy et al.'s (2007) conception of state generated social capital: an alternative take on the term "social capital", seen universally as a key factor for student participation and success in education, but increasingly left to individual families to provide according to their socio-economic status, thus reproducing class divisions through education.

The responses of the revolutionary governments of Cuba and Venezuela highlight perhaps the single most outstanding contrast with other systems, and hence a major element of difference impacting on educational outcomes: the role of social goals, including educational goals and policy, driving the political economy, rather than education being constructed by the demands of the political economy (López Hurtado, et al., 1996, pp. 14–25). Education in Cuba, and increasingly in Venezuela, is put forward then as a social good and a central factor shaping the system of production and general economic organisation.

Education for a democratic, protagonistic and participatory socialism

On the question of schooling for socialist transformation, significant gains have been made in Cuba since 1959, perhaps best evidenced by the capacity of the Cuban revolution to survive and reinvent itself in the post-Soviet period. In particular, we note Cuba's attempts to directly link mass education to other politicised social organisations, and its integration of manual labour as a core component of schooling. The overly instrumentalist application of Soviet orthodoxy to education, and other aspects of society post-1970, produced negative tendencies, which had a de-politicising effect. Some of these errors were officially acknowledged with the *rectification campaign* that began in 1986, well before the collapse of the Soviet Union, and which sought a return to Che Guevara's ideas and a renewed attention to the political and ideological formation of Cuba's youth. From here we move to the very different context of Venezuela's Bolivarian revolution in its initial stages of an attempted transformation of society towards a model of 21st century socialism, and identify radical possibilities to learn from the lessons of Cuba, and of socialist experiments more widely.

From the outset, education in Revolutionary Cuba was conceived in terms of its potential to contribute to and consolidate the revolution, and from the 1961 declaration of its socialist character, its potential to contribute to the socialist objectives of this political project. The development of Cuban students as conscious, critical participants in education and society emerged as an explicit political goal, positioning students as the future, youthful agents required for the transformation of society (see for example the then Minister for Education, Armando Hart, 1962). Education was considered as the arena in which the human subject could become conscious of their abilities to influence society and history, both by advancing in technological know-how and inventiveness and by developing their intellectual capacities as social interpreters and protagonists (López Hurtado, Hernández, Conte, Alfonso, & Rodríguez, 2000). Cole (2002) cites the well-known Cuban Marxist theoretician, Fernando Martínez Heredía (1993), who writes that the process of socialist development was "premised on the unleashing of the *power of the people*, who learn to change themselves along with their circumstances" (p. 44).

Although not normally associated with education, Che Guevara's writing played a significant role in the early development of a revolutionary approach to education. In the now famous text, *Man and Socialism in Cuba*, he referred to education as a fundamental aspect of liberation, and the key to unlocking all the creative and human potential of the human race (Guevara, 1964). He noted that alongside the structural changes made by the Cuban revolution, major and sustained efforts would be required to deepen the population's conscious participation, individual and collective, in all the structures of governance, management and production (Guevara, 1991, p. 216). For Guevara, such efforts demanded an approach to education that rejected formalistic or uncritical transmission of slogans and socialist values, and instead focused on more authentic and deep learning, debate, and the everyday practice of these values.

The political formation of students in Cuba was tied to the heightened levels of overt politicisation of society, and all aspects of social life, post-1959. Whereas in capitalist society the different social layers of young people's lives are frequently disconnected and contradictory, in Cuba the experiences of family, school and community were to be positively and explicitly connected in a learning environment that fostered both individual personal development, with an emphasis on its social value, and the development of collective values and outlooks (Cerda, Assaél, Ceballos, & Sepúlveda, 2000). Further, Robledo (1999) argues that Cuba's mass social organisations, its neighbourhood communities and councils, and its school and classroom structures of decision-making, were designed with a view to supporting and facilitating the empowerment of student, family, and community involvement in education systems.

One of the most distinctive aspects of Cuba's revolutionary education was the application of a model of work-study, as an integral part of students' civic and political formation. This policy involved students undertaking structured manual work via first *Schools to the countryside*, and then full boarding *School in the countryside* (see Figueroa, Prieto, & Guitérrez, 1974). This emphasis on manual labour, contributing directly to national economy and its model of socialist distribution of goods and services, was based in Marxist understandings of students' consciousness being shaped by these direct experiences and conditions, and hence was mirrored in programs of voluntary work for students in the cities, promoted by the Young Communist Union (UJC). While the outcomes of this approach were contradictory (see for example Griffiths, 2005), the work-study model complemented a curricular emphasis on social responsibility, whereby Cuban students actively take on a range of social tasks inside and outside the classroom. Examples of such activity include municipal inspections as part of the campaign to rid Havana of the Dengue carrying mosquito, preventative preparations for the cyclone season in July and the regular tasks of repairing books and cleaning the school and municipality. Cuban policy has set out to develop a methodology of learning through meaningful engagement in and reflection on the socio-historical process. This approach is quite distinct from many of the educational blueprints that various progressive educationalists have popularised, where the model takes on a certain independence from the socio-historical context, and where emphases on practical learning are connected to narrow industry driven objectives (e.g. workplace integrated learning) or to limited notions of experience that are non-global and ahistorical.

Rectification, Special Period, and Reassessment in Cuba

Economic and political difficulties in Cuba in the 1980s led to the formal *Rectification of errors and negative tendencies* campaign, launched by Castro in 1986. Presented in political and ideological terms, Petras and Morley (1992) argue that the campaign was the result of a "major internal policy debate over how best to confront Cuba's economic stagnation and its hard currency balance-of-payments problem" (p. 16), thus seeing the political and ideological character of the campaign as a way of enhancing public support for such measures. The result was a nation-wide collective reassessment of every aspect of economic and social organization in Cuba, including education. Having drawn earlier on some of the collectivist methods of Soviet education, the *rectification campaign* included a rejection of the Stalinisation of education that evolved through that tradition, which included for example a bureaucratic emphasis on promotion rates, leading to negative pedagogical practices in schools to maintain and improve such rates (see Castro, 1988). In education, the rectification campaign included a critique of the contradictions between the content of what students were receiving in school, and practices outside the school. For example, in a speech to close the Fifth Congress of the UJC in April 1987, Castro stressed the need for cadres and school teachers to model desired socialist and revolutionary behaviour, morals, attitudes, and the application of Marxism-Leninism, adding:

> We might have a teacher teaching Marxism, 400 hours in a semester if you like, and if they are a bad example to their students all the books and the 400 hours of Marxism-Leninism are worthless.
>
> (in Castro, 1988, p. 138)

It was here that the enduring influence of Che Guevara's ideas was critical, viewing Cuban collectivism in pedagogy not as the collectivism of control (Makarenko, 1955), but rather the collectivism of social action (Guevara, 2003, pp. 212–28). The attempts at reforming education were informed by Guevara's critical emphasis on the importance of individual consciousness and a revolutionary morality as distinct to the development of functional citizens in terms of economic growth. Some of the changes made in this period included criticism of authoritarian classrooms and the formalistic transmission of knowledge, with a renewed "…emphasis on active and participatory learning, to be facilitated with creative teaching methods" (Lutjens, 2000, p. 6); the decentralisation of educational administration, and greater autonomy for schools; and an emphasis on the ideological and political role of education, with more of a focus on Cuban history and civic education.

Following the collapse of the Soviet Union and the Eastern Bloc of 'real existing socialism', Cuba entered what was officially designated a "Special Period in Time of Peace" in which the country confronted the massive economic dislocation associated with the end of the Council of Mutual Economic Assistance (CMEA) and associated trade agreements with the socialist countries (Castro, 1991; Monreal, 2001; Pastor Jr & Zimbalist, 1995b). Between 1989 and 1993 the national economy experienced negative growth, with GNP contracting by some 45% and imports falling by around two-thirds (Carranza-Valdéz, Gutiérrez Urdaneta, & Monreal-González, 1995, pp. 18–19; Lage, 1995). The loss of sources for spare parts from the CMEA had significant effects on industry, while the end of the historic "sugar for oil" trade arrangements with the Soviet Union in particular brought major oil shortages that impacted transport and electricity generation (Pollitt & Hagelburg, 1994), causing frequent and extended blackouts for much of the population.

In this context education was again subject to critical reassessment as Cuba sought to save its socialist project in the post-Soviet world. The long-standing commitment to universal education was maintained, illustrated by the fact that, during the harshest moments of the Special Period, educational spending was maintained and then increased (Borotto López, 1999). Debate within Cuba in the mid-1990s highlighted major points of similarity between schooling on the island and in capitalist contexts (see for example Blanco, 1995a; Marí Lois, 1995), with a particular emphasis on its ongoing instrumental character of selecting and preparing students for work/the economy.

The preparation of labour for the national economy was qualitatively different in the context of socialist Cuba compared with, for example, capitalist Australia, most particularly given the relatively high level of socioeconomic equality. The critique by academics like Marí Lois, however, highlighted the persistence and strength of this instrumental aspect of education, and its capacity to work against students' political and ideological formation. Moreover, the critique of schooling was linked to a wider reassessment of the experience of "real existing socialism" and its influence, via the Soviet Union, on Cuba's revolutionary project (for some examples of this critique see Alonso-Tejada, 1995; Juan Antonio Blanco, 1995b; Martínez Heredia, 1995).

Education for 21st century socialism in Venezuela: some early signs

The Venezuelan approach, drawing on concepts of critical and popular education within the framework of a participatory model of endogenous socialist development, connects with the spirit of the Cuban education model, particularly as conceived by Che Guevara. At the forefront is the struggle to translate policy into practice in ways that are authentically democratic, that promote critical reflection and participation over formalistic and uncritical learning of the new hegemony that, as the Soviet experience demonstrates, can function to depoliticise in the name of political formation. Like the Cuban experience, formal school education in Venezuela's Bolivarian Education System is based on an explicit, politicized conception of education and its role in society.

Critical and popular education

The release in 2008 of a draft national curriculum framework for the Bolivarian system took the elaboration of the social and political role of public education for socialism a step further, building on the emphasis on critical and popular education, inspired by the work of Freire (1970), that followed Chávez's 2006 re-election. In a promising sign of further reforms, the framework foregrounds Che Guevara's fundamental approach to education in promoting the Bolivarian model of socialism (MPPCI, 2007), noting that the system is "oriented toward the consolidation of a humanistic, democratic, protagonistic, participatory, multi-ethnic, pluri- cultural, pluri-lingual and intercultural society..." (Ministerio del Poder Popular Para la Educación, 2007, p. 11), and critiquing the former system for reinforcing "the fundamental values of the capitalist system: individualism, egotism, intolerance, consumerism and ferocious competition ... [which also] promoted the privatisation of education" (p. 12). The framework was debated in parliament, and at the time of writing was the subject of an ongoing nation-wide consultation process with teachers, parents and communities, before its final draft is prepared.

While goals like those reported above may well be found in educational systems throughout the world, the Bolivarian system consistently refers these back to the underlying project to "promote the formation of new republicans, with creative and transformational autonomy, and with revolutionary ideas; with a positive attitude towards learning in order to put into practice new and original solutions for the endogenous transformation of the social-community context" (Ministerio del Poder Popular Para la Educación, 2007, p. 16). Moreover, Freirean influences are evident in references to schooling to "form girls and boys with a reflective, critical and independent attitude ... with a consciousness that allows them to understand, confront and verify their reality themselves; who learn from their surroundings, so that they are increasingly participating, protagonistic and co-responsible for their actions in the school, the family and the community" (Ministerio del Poder Popular Para la Educación 2007, p. 26).

According to the esteemed Venezuelan academic and political activist, Luis Bigott (2009), the expansion of education in Venezuela currently reflects two distinctive tendencies in popular education. The first comes out of 19th century Europe focused on the expansion of access to education, and the other based on 20th century South American critical/liberatory work of Freire and Fals Borda focused on the extension of education for the transformation of society. As documented above, the move toward universal access to State provided education, from childcare to primary and secondary schooling, technical and undergraduate tertiary education, and parallel adult education, has clearly been substantial (Chávez, 2008). In and of itself, in the global neoliberal context this reform program arguably takes on a revolutionary character.

A distinctly Venezuelan version of *Participatory Action Research* (PAR) is still being debated amongst academics and teachers, with some current examples of a working version being drawn upon offering glimpses of its potential. Founded in 2003 as a central feature of attempts to extend access to higher education, the Bolivarian University of Venezuela (UBV) offers free places to all students and seeks to fundamentally challenge the elitism of many of the traditional universities. Stating its commitment to social justice and equality at the core of all educational content and delivery, all courses undertaken at the UBV apply a PAR methodology, described as a multidisciplinary approach linking practice and theory.

In practice, the PAR methodology sees UBV students based in their local communities, working alongside a mentor on a community project, this being a core part of their formal studies. Examples include Community Health students working with doctors within the *Barrio Adentro* health mission, or Legal studies students establishing a community legal centre to advise and support families with civil law issues. Similarly, education students work with a teacher/mentor in schools in their local community. In the evenings all UBV students undertake classes in which they discuss theory linking back into and arising from their experiences in the project. The approach is designed to place day-to-day decision-making and problem solving in the hands of local communities, as part of the broader societal reconstruction underway, with all participants gaining skills through the process. The intent is that the PAR methodology places researchers in positions of political leadership, but with the projects being democratically controlled and driven by the communities themselves and their own leaders, and aimed at realising the objectives of the community based organisations.

The discussion is interesting but of greatest importance is *who* is taking part in this discussion. So much more than social and economic inclusion, this is political inclusion, with educational decision-making in the hands of staff, students, parents and the community.

Conclusion

Significant obstacles, tensions and contradictions remain in Cuba and Venezuela as they seek to define, debate and construct viable models of socialism for the contemporary times, and to develop systems of mass education that might contribute to the formation of citizens required for their respective political projects. In Cuba, for example, the training of new teachers, and retention of existing teachers for such a project remains a major challenge as teachers leave the profession for more highly remunerated work (see for example Espina Prieto 2001; Pérez Izquierdo 1998) in the post-Soviet context. In Venezuela, discussions with education academics and activists conducted by the authors during fieldwork in Caracas in 2007, 2008 and 2009 repeatedly raised the challenge of the political and pedagogical conservatism of existing teachers, who are often in opposition to the government's Bolivarian socialist project (e.g. Griffiths, 2008).

Historically, the expansion of public education has been a common feature of socialist revolutions, overtly presented as addressing legacies of educational inequity and exclusion. Impressive results frequently followed, including resources for new and/or refurbished schools, teachers and teacher training, and consequent increases in the participation rates of school-age children in schooling, as well as systems of parallel adult education for historically marginalised groups. The Cuban and Venezuelan cases reported here align with these general trends. These cases also highlight the many and complex difficulties associated with the overt political function of schooling in such societies: how to direct mass education to the formation of "new socialist citizens" committed to the transformation of society toward a model of socialism. We refer to "a" model of socialism, acknowledging the particular impact of the Soviet Union on the Cuban model, and in turn on its educational structures, curricula, and pedagogical practices; and the contrasting lack of clarity in Venezuela about the "twenty-first century socialism" and so the types of citizens, and associated educational practices, it requires.

One of the tensions at work in such processes, acknowledged in some of the Cuban research, is the potential for the political formation of students to be reduced to formalistic and uncritical responses to official ideologies that was antithetical to the official socialist objectives. Another, necessarily related, tension is the potential for socialist formation in schooling to be reduced to the functional identification and sorting of students for the requirements of the national economy, albeit with a more equitable allocation in a more equal socioeconomic structure/society. On both of these points, and others, the Venezuelan case holds particular interest given the historical context in which its Bolivarian socialist project is unfolding. The potential to benefit from lessons learned in Cuba, and in other former socialist States, alongside the consistent policy commitments to democratic, participatory socialism, is we think one of the most promising features of Venezuelan process. Progress on this political project, and the associated educational reforms, will therefore be crucial in our endeavours to contribute to more equal, just and democratic societies everywhere.

References

Alonso-Tejada, A. (1995). Marxismo y espacio de debate en la Revolución cubana. *Temas: Cultura Ideologia Sociedad* (3), 34–43.

Asamblea Nacional (2008). *Logros de la Revolución Bolivariana: No es poca cosa!* Caracas: Asamblea Nacional, Dirección General de Investigación y Desarrollo Legislativo.

Bigott, L. (2009). Popular Education in Venezuela and Latin America. In Presentation to a delegation of visiting education academics to Venezuela, coordinated by the authors, in January 2009. Caracas: National Assembly Building.

Blanco, J. A. (1995a). El compromiso con la etica del ser. *Acuario* (6), 25–29.

Blanco, J. A. (1995b). *Tercer Milenio: Una visión alternativa de la posmodernidad.* La Habana: Centro Felix Varela.

Borotto López, L. (1999). Education and development. Cuba, challenges for the second millenium. In J. Bell Lara (Ed.), *Cuba in the 1990s.* Havana: Editorial José Martí.

Brock-Utne, B. (2007). Worldbankification of Norwegian development assistance to education. *Comparative Education, 43* (3), 433–49.

Carnoy, M., Grove, A. K., & Marshall, J. H. (2007). *Cuba's Academic Advantage: Why Students in Cuba Do Better in School.* California: Stanford University Press.

Carranza-Valdéz, J., Gutiérrez Urdaneta, L., & Monreal-González, P. (1995). *Cuba: La restructuración de la economía, una propuesta para el debate.* La Habana: Editorial de Ciencias Sociales.

Castro, F. (1988). *Por el camino correcto: Compilación de textos.* La Habana: Editora Política.

Castro, F. (1991). The only situation in which we would have no future would be if we lost our homeland, the revolution and socialism. In G. Reed (Ed.), *Island in the Storm: The Cuban Communist Party's Fourth Congress* (pp. 25–79). Melbourne: Ocean Press.

Cerda, A. M., Assaél, J., Ceballos, F., & Sepúlveda, R. (2000). *Joven y Alumno: Conflicto de Identidad? Un Estudio etnográfico en los liceos de sectores populares.* Santiago: LOM Ediciones / PIIE.

Chávez, H. (2008). *Revolución Bolivariana: 9 Años de Logros.* Caracas: Ministerio del Poder Popular para la Comunicación y la Información.

Cole, K. (2002). Cuba: The process of socialist development. *Latin American Perpsectives, 29* (3), 40–56.

Espina Prieto, M. P. (2001). The Effects of the Reform on Cuba's Social Structure: An Overview. *Socialism and Democracy - Cuba in the 1990s: Economy, Politics, and Society, 15* (1), 23–39.

Figueroa, M., Prieto, A., & Guitérrez, R. (1974). *The basic secondary school in the country: an educational innovation in Cuba.* Paris: The Unesco Press.

Freire, P. (1970). *Pedagogy of the Oppressed.* Great Britain: Penguin Books.

Gaceta Oficial de la República Bolivariana de Venezuela (2000). Asamblea Nacional Constituyente. Retrieved March 20, 2006, from http://www.gobiernoenlinea.ve/docMgr/sharedfiles/059.pdf

Gasperini, L. (2000). The Cuban education system: Lessons and dilemmas. *Education Reform and Management Publications Series, 1* (5).

Griffiths, T. G. (2005). Learning 'To Be Somebody'. Cuban Youth in the Special Period. *International Journal of Learning, 11,* 1267–74.

Griffiths, T. G. (2008). *Preparing citizens for a 21st century socialism: Venezuela's Bolivarian Educational reforms.* Paper presented at the Social Educators Association of Australia National Biennial Conference, Newcastle, Australia.

Guevara, C. (1964). El Socialismo y el hombre en Cuba. *Nuestra Industria Económica* (5), 3–14.

Guevara, C. (1991). *Obras Escogidas 1957–1967.* Havana: Editorial de Ciencias Sociales.

Guevara, C. (2003). *Che Guevara Reader. Writings on politics and revolution* (2nd ed.). Melbourne: Ocean Press.

Hart, A. (1962). *Sobre organización y trabajo en el Ministerio de Educación.* La Habana: MINED Departamento de Publicaciones.

Jones, P. W. (2007). Global governance, social policy and multilateral education. *Comparative Education, 43* (3), 321–23.

Lage, C. (1995). Discurso del Vicepresidente Cubano, Carlos Lage Dávila, en el Foro Ecónomico Mundial de Davos, Suiza, 27 de enero, 1995. *Panorama Económico Latinoamericano February 1995, February* (484), 28–29.

López Hurtado, J., Chávez Rodriguez, J., Rosés Garcés, M. A., Esteva Boronat, M., Ruiz Aguilera, A., & Pita Céspedes, B. (1996). *El Carácter Científico de la Pedagogía en Cuba* Havana: Pueblo y Educación.

López Hurtado, J., Hernández, O., Conte, M., Alfonso, O., & Rodríguez, J. (2000). *Fundamentos de la Educación* Havana: Pueblo y Educación.

Lutjens, S. (2000). Educational Policy in Socialist Cuba: The lessons of Forty Years of Reform *Cuba: Construyendo el Future*: Spanish Foundation for Marxist Research.

MacDonald, T. (1985). *Making a New People —Education in Revolutionary Cuba.* Vancouver: New Star Books.

Makarenko, A. S. (1955). *Road to Life* (2nd ed.).

Marí Lois, J. (1995). Etica y Nación. *Acuario* (6), 6–11.

Martínez Heredia, F. (1995). Izquierda y marxismo en Cuba. *Temas: Cultura Ideologia Sociedad* .(3), 16–27.

Ministerio de Educación y Deportes (2006). *Escuelas Bolivarianas - Avance cualitativo del proyecto.* Caracas: Ministerio de Educación y Deportes.

Ministerio del Poder Popular Para la Educación (2007). *Currículo Nacional Bolivariano: Diseño Curricular del Sistema Educativa Bolivariano.* Retrieved October 30, 2007, from http://www.me.gov.ve/media.eventos/2007/dl_908_69.pdf.

Ministerio del Poder Popular para la Planificación y Desarrollo (2008). *Logros de a Revolución: En un país de 28 millones de habitantes* Retrieved 01/12/2008, 2008, from http://www.mpd.gob.ve/Logros-Revolucion/Nuevo-Encarte.pdf

Monreal, P. (2001). Cuba: the Challenges of Being global and Socialist … at the Same Time. *Socialism and Democracy - Cuba in the 1990s: Economy, Politics, and Society, 15* (1), 5–21.

MPPCI (2007). Tercer Motor Moral y Luces: Educación con valores socialistas. Retrieved May 8, 2007, from http://www.minci.gob.ve/motores/62/11852.

Pastor Jr, M., & Zimbalist, A. (1995b). Cuba's Economic Conundrum. *NACLA Report on the Americas (Special Issue), XXIX* (2), 7–12.

Pérez Izquierdo, V. (1998). Sector educación: reajuste en la situación actual. In Á. Ferriol Muruaga, A. González Gutiérrez, D. Quintana Mendoza & V. Pérez Izquierdo (Eds.), *Cuba: Crisis, Ajuste y Situación Social (1990–1996)* (pp. 115–44). La Habana: Editorial de Ciencias Sociales.

Petras, J. F., & Morley, M. H. (1992). Cuban Socialism: Rectification and the New Model of Accumulation. In S. Halebsky & J. M. Kirk (Eds.), *Cuba in Transition: Crisis and Transformation* (pp. 15–36). Boulder San Francisco Oxford: Westview Press.

Pollitt, B. H., & Hagelburg, G. B. (1994). The Cuban sugar economy in the Soviet era and after. *Cambridge Journal of Economics, 18* (6), 547–69.

República Bolivariana de Venezuela (2004). *Cumpliendo las Metas del Milenio.* Caracas: CD Publicaciones.

Robertson, S. L. (2005). WTO/GATS and the Global Education Services Industry. *Globalisation, Societies and Education, 1* (3), 259–66.

Robledo, L. (1999). *Cuba: Jóvenes en los 90.* Havana: Casa Editorial Abril.

Sánchez, G. (2005a). *The Cuban Revolution and Venezuela.* Melbourne: Ocean Press.

Sánchez, G. (2005b). *Barrio Adentro and Other Social Missions in the Bolivarian Revolution.* Melbourne: Ocean Press.

Weisbrot, M., & Sandoval, L. (2007). The Venezuelan Economy in the Chávez Years. Retrieved October 23, 2007, from http://www.cepr.net/documents/publications/venezuela_2007_07.pdf

Further Readings

Section 1: Critical Pedagogy and the Politics of Education

Abagi, O. (2005). 'The Role of the School in Africa in the Twenty-First Century: Coping with Forces of Change' in Abdi, A. A and Cleghorn, A (eds.), *Issues in African Education. Sociological Perspectives*, New York: Palgrave-Macmillan.

Andreotti, V. (2011). *Actionable Postcolonial Theory in Education*, New York and London: Palgrave-Macmillan.

Apple, M. & Novoa, A. (2002). *Paulo Freire, Politica e Pedagogia*. Porto: Porto Editora.

Araujo Freire, A.M. (2004). *La Pedagogia de la Liberación en Paulo Freire*. Spain: GRAO.

Baldacchino, J. (2012). *Art's Way Out: Exit Pedagogy and the Cultural Condition*, Rotterdam, Taipei and Boston, Sense Publishers.

Baral, K. C. (2006). 'Postcoloniality, Critical Pedagogy, and English Studies in India.' *Pedagogy*, 6(3), 475–91. doi 10.1215/15314200–2006–06

Batini, F., P. Mayo, and A. Surian. 2014. *Lorenzo Milani, the School of Barbiana and the Struggle for Social Justice*. New York: Peter Lang.

Berhard, A. (2011). *Pädagogisches Denken. Band 1: Einführung in allgemeine Grundlagen der Erziehungs- und Bildungswissenschaft* (Pedagogical Thinking. Volume 1: Introduction to general foundations of education and the education sciences), Baden Wuttemberg: Der *Schneider-Verlag Hohengehren*.

Betto, F and Freire, P (1985). *Essa Escola Chamada Vida* (The School called Life), São Paulo: Attica.

Bhattacharya, A. (2013).'Rabindranath Tagore and Mahatma Gandhi: Their Thoughts on Education from a Postcolonial Perspective', *Postcolonial Directions in Education*, Vol. 2 (1), pp. 100–44.

Bonal, X., Essomba, M.A. and Ferrer, F. (2005).'Política educativa e igualdad de oportunidades' (Educational Politics and Equality of Opportunity), in *Cuadernos de Pedagogía*, n. 344, pp. 82–87.

Bonal, X. (1998). *Sociología e la Educación. Una aproximación crítica a las corrientes contemporáneas*, Barcelona, Buenos Aires and Mexico: Paidós.

Borg, C. (2013). *L-Edukazzjoni hi Politika. Kitbiet Paulo Freire* (Education is Politics. Paulo Freire's Writings), Malta: Horizons.

Borg, C., and P. Mayo. 2007. *Public Intellectuals, Radical Democracy and Social Movements. A Book of Interviews*. New York: Peter Lang.

Borg, C. and Mayo, P. (2000). 'Reflections from a "Third Age" Marriage: Paulo Freire's Pedagogy of Reason, Hope and Passion.' In *McGill Journal of Education*, V. 35. N. 2, Spring (105–120).

Bourdieu, P., and J. C. Passeron. 1990. *Reproduction in Education, Society and Culture*. 2nd ed. London, Newbury Park and New Delhi: Sage.

de Morais, R. (1991). *Educação em tempos oscuros* (Education in dark times). São Paulo: Autores Asociados-Cortez Editores.

Epstein, I. (1989). 'Critical Pedagogy and Chinese Education.' *Journal of Curricular Theorizing*, 9(2), 69–98. Retrieved from http://works.bepress.com/irving_epstein/31

Freire, P. (1970). *Pedagogy of the Oppressed*. New York, Continuum.

Freire, P. (1970). *Cultural Action for Freedom*. Cambridge, MA: Harvard Educational Review.

Freire, P. (1983). *Education for Critical Consciousness*. New York, Seabury Press.

Freire, P. (1985). *The Politics of Education: Culture, Power, and Liberation*. South Hadley, MA: Bergin & Garvey

Freire, P. (2005). *Pedagogy of the Oppressed* (30th Anniversary Edition). New York: Continuum.

Freire, P. & A. Faundez, A. (1989). *Learning to Question: A Pedagogy of Liberation*. Trans. Tony Coates, New York: Continuum.

Freire, P. (2002). *Pedagogy of Hope: Reliving Pedagogy of the Oppressed*. New York: Continuum.

Freire, P. (1997). *Pedagogy of the Heart*. New York: Continuum.

Gentili, P. (2005). *La Falsificazione del Consenso: Simulacro e Imposizione nella Riforma Educativa del Neoliberalismo* (The Falsification of Consensus. Simulacra and Imposition in the Educational Reform of Neoliberalism), Pisa: Edizioni ETS.

Gezgin, U.B., Inal, K. and Hill, D. (Eds.) (2014). *The Gezi Revolt: People's Revolutionary Resistance against Neoliberal Capitalism in Turkey*, Brighton: Institute for Education Policy Studies.

Gounari, P. (2006).'Ακαδημαϊκοί, Διανοούμενοι και Κριτική Παιδαγωγική' (Academics, Intellectuals and Critical Pedagogy) in *Utopia: A Review of Theory and Culture* (Athens, Greece), Vol. 78 (January-February), pp. 61–75.

Gounari, P. and Grollios, G. (eds.) (2010). *Κριτική Παιδαγωγική*. (A Critical Pedagogy Reader), Athens, Greece: Gutenberg Publisher.

Gur-Ze'ev, I. (2003). *Critical Theory and Critical Pedagogy today. Toward a new critical language in education*. Haifa, Israel: Faculty of Education, University of Haifa.

Gur Ze'ev, I. (ed.) (2010). *The Possibility/Impossibility of a New Critical Language in Education*, Rotterdam, Boston and Taipei: Sense Publishers.

Kachur, J. L. (2012). 'The Liberal Virus in Critical Pedagogy: Beyond "Anti-this-and-that" Postmodernism and Three Problems in the Idea of Communism. Journal for Critical Education Policy Studies,' 10(1), 1–21.

Kupfer, A. (2011). *Bildungssoziologie: Theorien–Institutionen–Debatten* (Sociology of Bildung/Education: Theories, Institutions, Debates), Wiesbaden: VS Verlag für Sozialwissenschaften.

Kupfer, A (2015). *Educational Upward Mobility. Practices of Social Change*, London and New York: Palgrave-Macmillan.

Labidi, I. (2010). 'Arab Education Going Medieval: Sanitizing Western Representation in Arab Schools.' *Journal for Critical Education Policy Studies, 8*(2), 195–221. Retrieved from http://www.jceps.com/.

Larson, K. R. 'Critical Pedagogy(Ies) for ELT in Indonesia.' *TEFLIN Journal*, 25, 122–38. doi10.15639/teflin.v25i1.346t.

Leal Filho, W. (Ed.). (2006). *Innovation, Education and Communication for Sustainable Development*. Frankfurt: Peter Lang.

Mariátegui J.C. (2011). *José Carlos Mariátegui: An Anthology*. Vanden HE, Becker M (Eds. and Trans.). New York: Monthly Review Press.

Marti, J. (1979). *On Education*. New York: Monthly Review.

McKinney, C. (2005). 'A Balancing Act: Ethical Dilemmas of Democratic Teaching Within Critical Pedagogy.' *Educational Action Research, 13*(3), 375–91. Retrieved from http://www.tandfonline.com/doi/pdf/10.1080/09650790500200298.

Monasta, A (1993). '*L'educazione tradita*: criteri per una diversa valutazione complessiva dei Quaderni del carcere di Antonio Gramsci' (Education Betrayed. Criteria for a different comprehensive evaluation of Antonio Gramsci's Prison Notebooks), Florence: McColl.

Monasta, A (2003).'La Scuola di Tutti' *Testimonianze*,' No. 432–31–430, http://www.testimonianzeonline.com/pagina.asp?IDProdotto=295.

Neary, M. (2012). 'Teaching Politically: Policy, Pedagogy, and the New European University.' In *Journal for Critical Education Policy Studies*, V.10, N.2 (233–257).

Nyerere, J.K. (1968). *Freedom and Socialism*. Oxford: Oxford University Press.

Nyerere, J.K. (1979). 'Adult education and development' (H. Hinzen & V.J. Hundsdorfer, authors/ eds.), *The Tanzanian experience. Education for liberation and development*, 49–55, Hamburg, Germany: UNESCO Institute for Education; London: Evans Brothers.

Okçabol, R (2001). *Eğitim Hakkı [Gerçekleşmeyen Bir İlke]* (Right to Education [an inexistent policy]), Istanbul: Boğaziçi Üniversitesi Yayınevi / Araştırma – İnceleme Dizisi.

Pampanini, G. (2011). *La Complessità in educazione. Società cognitiva e sistema formativo integrato* (Complexity in Education. Cognitive Society and Integrated Educational System), Rome: Armando Editore.

Peters, M. (2003). 'Critical Pedagogy and the Futures of Critical Theory'. In I. Gur-Ze'ev (Ed.), *Critical Theory and Critical Pedagogy today. Toward a new critical language in education*, 35–48. Haifa, Israel: Faculty of Education, University of Haifa.

Polat, S. (2008). 'Neo-Liberal Education Policies in Turkey and Transformation in Education.' *Journal for Critical Education Policy Studies,* 159–78. Retrieved from http://www.jceps.com/wp-content/uploads/PDFs/11-4-08.pdf.

Reggio, P. (2014). *Lo schiaffo di don Milani. Il mito educativo di Barbiana* (don Milani's Slap. The Educational Myth of Barbiana), Trento: Il Margine.

Safari, P., & Pourhashemi, M. R. (2012). 'Toward an Empowering Pedagogy: Is There Room for Critical Pedagogy in Educational System of Iran?' *Theory and Practice in Language Studies* 2(12), 2548–55. doi:10.4304/tpls.2.12.2548–55.

Shakouri, N., & Abkenar, H. R. (2012). 'Critical Pedagogy: An ignis fatuus!' *Journal of Science, 1*(2), 21–25. Retrieved from www.worldsciencepublisher.org.

Silwadi, N., & Mayo, P. (2014). 'Pedagogy under Siege in Palestine: Insights from Paulo Freire.' *Holy Land Studies, 13,* 71–87. Retrieved from www.euppublishing.com/hls.

Takayama, K. (2011). 'A Comparativist's Predicaments of Writing about "Other" Education: a Self-Reflective, Critical Review of Studies of Japanese Education.' *Comparative Education,* 1–22. http://dx.doi.org/10.1080/03050068.2011.561542.

Telleri, F. (2003). *Educarsi per Educare. Teorie e Prassi* (Educate onself to Teach. Theory and Practice), Sassari: Carlo Delfino.

Teodoro, A., & Torres, C.A. (2007). 'Introduction. Critique and Utopia in the Sociology of Education.' In Torres, C. A. and Teodoro, A. (eds.), *Critique and Utopia: New Developments in the Sociology of Education.* Lanham, MD, and Boulder, CO: Rowman and Littlefield.

Teodoro, A. (2003). "Educational Policies and New Ways of Governance in a Transnationalization Period." In *The International Handbook on the Sociology of Education,* Torres, C.A and Antikainen, A (eds.), Lanham, MD: Rowman and Littlefield.

Viola, M. (2009). 'The Filipinization of Critical Pedagogy: Widening the Scope of Critical Educational Theory.' *Journal for Critical Education Policy Studies, 7,* 1–28. Retrieved from http://www.jceps.com/

Wardekker, W., & Miedema, S. (1997). 'Critical Pedagogy: an Evaluation and a Direction for Reformation.' *Curriculum Inquiry, 27,* (45–61).

Section 2
Globalization, Democracy, and Education

The more that social democracy develops, grows, and becomes stronger, the more the enlightened masses of workers will take their own destinies, the leadership of their movement, and the determination of its direction in to their own hands.

Rosa Luxemburg, *The Political Leader of the German Working Classes* (1905)

But democracy, by definition, cannot mean merely that an unskilled worker can become skilled. It must mean that every "citizen" can "govern" and that society places him [or her] in a general condition to achieve this.

Antonio Gramsci, *Selections from Prison Notebooks* (1971)

6

The Challenge of Inclusive Schooling in Africa

George J. Sefa Dei

Arguably, critical educational research on inclusive schooling in Africa has two challenges. First, critical studies must interrogate existing approaches and practices that alienate minorities and then suggest specific, creative ways for transforming conventional schooling so that it better serves the needs of diverse student bodies. Second, to ensure a sustained contribution to social development, educational studies must demonstrate how the knowledge obtained in individual schools, colleges and universities can be used effectively to contribute to the formulation of comprehensive strategies for genuine and fundamental structural change. This paper provides significant lessons on how discussions about 'inclusivity', 'minority' and 'difference' can inform debates about educational change and guide broad policy initiatives towards inclusive schooling in local, national and transnational settings. From the vantage points of diverse subjects (students and educators) this paper uncovers local Ghanaian conceptions of social difference in schooling practices and initiatives.

Instituting change in Ghanaian schooling is, first and foremost, a question of re-conceptualizing educational issues. This reconceptualization calls for an investigation of questions of process, content, objective and practice, as well as a critical interrogation of the structures established for educational delivery. Pursuing innovations in classroom instruction with the aim of pedagogic, communicative and curricular change grounded in a critical understanding of 'inclusivity' is the most promising alternative approach to educational change.

For the purpose of this study, the idea of 'inclusive education' is defined as education that responds to the concerns, aspirations and interests of a diverse body politic, and draws on the accumulated knowledge, creativity and resourcefulness of local peoples. A school is inclusive to the extent that every student is able to identify and connect with her/his social environment, culture, population and history. Discussions of difference are central to a redefinition of inclusive schooling. Inclusivity can be conceptualized as an approach to schooling that centres the lived experiences of students defined by the markers of difference: class, gender, ethnic, religious, linguistic and cultural differences, and the asymmetrical relations of power that such differences evoke.

In the Ghanaian context, like elsewhere, inclusive schooling is providing education that responds to and accounts for majority-minority relations and asymmetrical relations of power based on difference. This working definition of inclusivity contrasts with dominant definitions that view inclusive education simply as teaching students with a range of abilities and, specifically, integrating special education children into 'regular' classrooms. Schooling can be 'exclusive' by not responding adequately to difference and diversity among the student population. This paper extends the practice of inclusion to account for difference structured along lines of ethnicity, gender, class, religion, language, culture and ability.

Discussions contained in this paper examine how Ghanaian educators, learners and policy-makers link identity and knowledge production. More importantly this paper explores how the relational aspects of difference (e.g., ethnicity, culture, language, religion, socio-economic family background, gender) implicate the search for genuine educational options or alternatives for Ghana and the rest of Africa. These areas of investigation in the Ghanaian context have received sporadic attention in isolated academic enclaves, but never a comprehensive, coordinated examination or an examination specifically directed towards meeting the concrete needs of policy- makers, teachers, students and parents.

Historically, schooling and education in Ghana have been approached in terms of contributing fundamentally to national development. As Fanon (1963) observed, the process of decolonization within the colonial context necessitated the unification of the people on a national, sometimes racial basis, through the strategic radical decision to remove from them their heterogeneity. But in emphasizing the goal of national integration, post-independence, 'postcolonial' education in Ghana continues to deny heterogeneity in local populations, as if difference itself was a problem. With this orientation, education has undoubtedly helped create and maintain the glaring disparities and inequities, structured along lines of ethnicity, culture, language, religion, gender and class, which persist and grow. This pattern can, however, be disrupted. Education can meet the challenge of equitable minority education by acknowledging difference, while highlighting commonalities, even among peoples with conflicting interests. Since transformative change encompasses more than the reform of existing curricular and pedagogical practices, it must respond specifically to problems of discrimination, prejudice and alienation within schools. To promote the democratic participation of all citizens in a project of nation building and to provide lasting solutions to human problems, education in Ghana must acknowledge and affirm difference and diversity within the context of pursuing equity and social justice.

Context

As argued elsewhere the extensive literature on education in Africa focuses on specific themes such as curriculum, policy, language, teacher education, culture, science and development (Blakemore & Cooksey, 1983; Sifuna, 1992; Samoff, 1993; Obanya, 1995; Dei, 2004a). To varying degrees, other authors have sought to relate the discourse on educational reform to social development and change (Nyerere, 1979, 1985; Foster, 1965; Bray, 1986; Carnoy, 1986; Psacharopoulos, 1989, 1990; Carnoy & Samoff, 1990; Craig, 1990; Jones, 1992, 1997; Samoff, 1992; Banya & Elu, 1997). Existing works point to the problems in education that African countries face, including stagnating school enrolments, lack of textbooks and instructional materials, inadequacy of teacher training, diminishing educational finances and inefficiency in educational administration and management practices. While many of these problems are long-standing, others can be attributed to the 'postcolonial' state's dismal failure in altering the existing system to reflect changing times, circumstances and social realities (e.g., the problem of curriculum relevance and employment needs).

The adoption of western/colonial discourse of Ghanaian (racial) sameness has allowed educators to suppress difference. The goal of preserving unity as defined in 'peace and harmony' instead of discussing ethnic, class, religious, gender and other differences, detracts from key issues such as power differentials and social exclusions. The critical examination of the interplay of ethnicity, culture and politics in Ghana's history reveals that the culture and language of the Akans, the majority ethnic group, have dominated many sectors of society. Within the confines of schooling there is no direct historic evidence of the Akan forcing homogeneity upon other cultural groups (e.g., differentially excluding some students' learning based on unsaid difference). Nonetheless, dominant practices privilege certain ideas and social groups at school. For example, the concentration of schools in the south during colonial times has favoured the Akan of the south while other ethnic minorities in the north have struggled to 'catch up.' This imbalance in education is compounded by other sectoral and regional inequities in the distribution of social goods and resources. As postcolonial governments have sought to address this regional imbalance in education and to provide resources to assist students in/from the north, there has been resentment on the part of some southern students who view students from the north as receiving preferential treatment. Entrenched ideas about northerners and schooling only further the marginalization of minority ethnic groups in the north and other parts of the country.

Similarly, the colonizing discourses of 'sameness' have had the material and symbolic effect of 'hiding differences', in that Akan culture permeates much of the local Ghanaian setting as other differences are rendered unsaid or invisible.

In Ghanaian schooling today, (unequal) power relations exist, as seen in the differential allocation of, and access to resources among social groups and economic sectors, as well as regions of the country. Parental background and social composition of the students in 'high and low status secondary schools' appear to be widening over the last four decades. Foster's (1962, 1963) early works on ethnicity and education have been insightful and relevant to the discussion of difference and schooling. However such earlier works have not been followed up in order to understand the intricacies and implications of social difference for Ghanaian schooling. In fact, an interrogation of these 'external' influences suggests that they function to create and exacerbate inequities along lines of difference—particularly those of social class (Jones, 1988, 1992, 1997; and also Quist, 1994). Disturbingly, educational reforms in Ghana have failed to address critically questions of difference in relation to considerations of class, gender, ethnic, religious, linguistic and cultural differences (see also Foster, 1965; Bloch et al., 1998).

Gender is another area where difference is spoken about, as it also functions to demarcate life chances. The absence of female teachers and the male-centric presence in institutions of higher learning is disturbing, yet educational reforms in Ghana have failed to address this issue critically. The Ghanaian context illustrates that these issues are related to far more than differential hiring standards. At one level the disproportionate ratio of male to female students in universities works to ensure that there is not a sufficient pool of female candidates to apply for such positions. In reality, it is the patriarchal systems of schooling and the existence of entrenched traditional/ cultural values that work in conjunction with systemic barriers that continue to ensure low female representation in these institutions.

To redress some of the above-mentioned problems, educational researchers and theorists have endeavoured to interrogate the decline in formal education in post- independence Africa, and on the basis of their conclusions, have suggested a rethinking of the schooling process. Fafunwa (1974), Kinyanjui (1993), Banya (1991, 1993), Bledsoe (1992), Dei (1994a, b), Jegede (1994), Johnson (1995), Tedla (1995), Brock-Utne (1996) and Bloch et al. (1998), among others, have critiqued conventional African educational processes, suggesting ways of moving beyond the colonial and paternal discourse that has traditionally characterized interrogation of the field. In particular, these authors question the suitability of applying foreign ideas and institutions uncritically to Africa. They suggest an understanding of the continent on its own terms; that is, within the context of local culture, language, history and politics. Further, these authors locate their critiques in the lessons they have gleaned from countries that have attempted to implement educational reforms with the objective of maximizing social returns (Psacharopoulos, 1989, 1990; Achola, 1990; Craig, 1990; Eshiwani, 1990; Galabawa, 1990; Maravanyika, 1990).

It is clear from the above-mentioned works that, in identifying the important role education plays in national development, educational research must focus on ways of addressing social inequalities within the Ghanaian school system. This means under- standing how difference is perceived and acted upon by all educational stakeholders, and specifying the implications of this for formulating viable educational options. An increasing number of studies are examining class, gender, regional and sectoral imbalances in African education—see for example, Glick and Sahn (1999), Ansell (2002), Assie-Lumumba (2000), Harber (2002), and Vavrus (2002) on questions of gender, culture and class differences; as well as Adeyinka and Ndwapi (2002) and Hansen (2002) on religion, and Bunyi (1999) and Stroud (2003) on language and linguistic differences.

However, no attempts have been made thus far to explore majority-minority relations in schooling or to draw comparisons with approaches to minority education in other pluralistic contexts. In addition, little effort has been expended in examining the ways in which local teachers, students, parents and policy-makers understand difference, diversity and inclusion; specifically, how educators (in their classroom pedagogic, instructional, textual and discursive practices) respond to the needs of students from minority backgrounds.

Theorizing an anti-colonial approach to schooling and education

This paper utilizes a critical anti-colonial discursive framework to understand issues of, and questions about, culture, social difference, identity and representation in schooling. Discursively, 'colonial' is conceptualized here not simply as 'foreign' or 'alien', but rather as 'imposed' and 'dominating'. The anti-colonial framework is in fact comprised of a theorization of issues emerging from colonial relations; more specifically, an interrogation of the configurations of power embedded in knowledge production. The power of the anti-colonial prism is the recourse to local knowings and understandings as a starting base to frame key questions of domination, subordination and resistance. This approach sees marginalized groups as subjects of their own experiences (see Fanon, 1963; Memmi, 1969; and Foucault, 1980). In this framework, knowledge is understood to emanate from multiple sites, sources and conditions (e.g., gender, ethnicity, culture, religion and language). The strength of the anti-colonial theory is rooted in the experience of colonialism and the agency/ resistance of local peoples. Such experiential knowledge is critical to political projects of social and educational transformation.

The anti-colonial discursive framework acknowledges the role of the educational system in producing and reproducing racial, ethnic, religious, linguistic, gender, sexual and class-based inequalities in society. Further, anti-colonial discourse problematizes the marginalization of certain voices and ideas in the educational system, as well as the delegitimation, in the pedagogic and communicative practices of schools, of the knowledge and experience of subordinate groups. Fanon (1963), suggests paying attention to the voices of the colonized as having discursive power. Thus, the anti-colonial discursive approach means affirming the pedagogic need to confront the challenge of social diversity; and the urgency of creating an educational system that is both more inclusive and better able to respond to varied local concerns about formal schooling.

Anti-colonial as a conceptual framework for understanding difference is especially relevant to interrogating the concept of nation building. In African social thought, prominent anti-colonial thinkers such as Kwame Nkrumah, Amilcar Cabral, Sekou Toure, and Leopald Senghor (to mention a few) strategically evoked the goal of nation building for decolonizing the mind, the spirit and the state. Based on this strategic development of the nation, schooling in Ghana has proceeded to achieve the imperative of 'nation building', in contemporary times. Nation building in the post-colony, was meant to be a strategic temporal initiative to harness the strength and unity of the nation as part of an ongoing, critical process of decolonization, not as recolonization. However, in Ghana there continue to be underlying tensions between the imperative of nation building as a strategy for decolonization, and nation building as the production of discourses about difference on the ground (e.g., everyday schooling experiences of Ghanaian youth), which can be understood in colonial terms.

Anti-colonial prism theorizes the nature and extent of social domination and particularly the multiple places power, and the relations of power work to establish dominant-subordinate relations. Anti-colonial thought has roots in the decolonizing movements of colonial states that fought for independence from European countries at the end of the Second World War. The revolutionary ideas of Frantz Fanon, Mohandas Gandhi, Albert Memmi, Aime Cesaire, Kwame Nkrumah and Che Guevara, to name a few, were instrumental in fomenting anti-colonial struggles. Most of these scholars were avowed nationalists who sought political liberation for all colonized peoples and communities using the power of knowledge. In particular, Fanon's (1963) and Gandhi's (1967) writings on the violence of colonialism and the necessity for open resistance and Albert Memmi's (1969) discursive on the relations between the colonized and the colonizer, helped instil in the minds of colonized peoples the importance of engaging in acts of resistance to resist the violence of colonialism. In later years, particularly in African contexts, other scholars including Cabral (1969, 1970), Aime Cesaire (1972) and Leopold Senghor (1996) introduced questions of language, identity and national culture into anti-colonial debates for political and intellectual liberation.

After independence a new body of 'anti-colonial' discourse emerged. This discourse, appropriately located within the postcolonial discursive framework (see Said, 1978; Bhabha, 1990; Ashcroft *et al.*, 1995; Young, 1995; Gandhi, 1998) unde- niably shows powerful links to ideas of earlier anti-colonialists. The ideas of postcolonial theorists however, largely focused on the interconnections between imperial/ colonial cultures and the colonized cultural practices and the constructions of hybridity and alterity (see also Spivak, 1988; Bhabha, 1990; Suleri, 1992; Shohat, 1992; Slemon, 1995). The strength of postcolonial theory lies in pointing to the complexities and the disjunctures of the colonial experiences, and the aftermath of the colonial encounter. In fact, Bhabha (1990) has shown that the colonial encounter and discourse cannot be assumed to be unified or unidirectional. Spivak (1988) also emphasizes the possibility of counter knowledges that emerge or are constructed, from marginal spaces and the power of such voices for the pursuit of resistance. As Shahjahan (2003) has also argued, in a more general sense, postcolonial theorizing demonstrates the shift in anti-colonial thought from the focus on agency and nationalist/liberatory practice, towards a discursive analysis and approach, one that directs our attention to the intersection between 'western' knowledge production and the 'other', and western colonial power' (p. 5).

The anti-colonial discursive approach adopted in this paper reclaims the ideas of early anti-colonial theorizing. The adoption of an anti-colonial discursive gaze, while borrowing from the postmodern view of colonialism as espoused in the works of Young (1995, 2001), Said (1978, 1993), Bhabha (1990), and Loomba (1998), also has an important intellectual focus on local knowings and how colonizing practices can be unending and deeply embedded in everyday relations. In an anticolonial discursive approach, local/indigenous knowings become powerful sources of knowledge that allow for daily resistance and the pursuit of effective political practice to subvert all forms of dominance. This is not the case with postcolonial theorization.[1]

This paper takes the school system and the experiences of different bodies as an example to examine such colonial relations and experiences. It is maintained that within schools there is a material-structural, and socio-cultural-political dynamic whereby the social ecology of learning produces significant differential consequences for both dominant and minoritized bodies. For those who are asked to subsume their difference under the rubric of the 'common' the stakes are high. An anti-colonial approach raises new questions about schooling. It also exposes and challenges the hidden narratives surrounding discourse of nation building and nationhood. The normative claims of shared identity, inherent in nation building projects, can be interrogated to unravel how certain interests can be served when differences are erased. By sweeping social difference and identities under the carpet schooling is colonizing for some bodies.

By giving space to local subjects to articulate their understandings of the social relations of schooling, the voices of those who have been excluded and marginalized (along lines of ethnicity, gender, class, religion, culture and language) can be problematized. The production of certain dominant ethnic, gender, sexual, linguistic, religious and cultural identities, as well as colonial discourses and practices of schooling, are not innocent. If only some ethnic identities attain dominance, we need to understand how this occurs, how students, educators and communities interpret this occurrence and how the subject defines her or his relations to the dominant identity. As Fanon (1963) long ago noted, national cultures can be oppressive. Therefore there is a need for a new critical nationalist consciousness that reclaims diversity by connecting how the past histories, traditions and identities are themselves complicated by differences.

Notes

1. The argument is that the anti-colonial discursive framework must be viewed as a stand-alone framework that borrows from but objects to, some of what postcolonialism has to offer. This paper thus is a way to reclaim the anti-colonial as a political project of resistance.

References

Achola, P. W. (1990) *Implementing educational policies in Zambia* (Washington DC, The World Bank).

Adeyinka A. & Ndwapi, G. (2002) Education and morality in Africa, *Pastoral Care in Education* 20(2),17–23.

Ansell, N. (2002) Education reform in southern Africa and the needs of rural girls: pronouncements, policy and practice, *Comparative Education,* 38(1), 91–112.

Ashcroft, B., Griffiths, G. & Tiffin, H. (Eds) (1995) *The postcolonial reader* (New York, Routledge).

Assie-Lumumba, N. T. (2000) Educational and economic reforms, gender equity, and access to schooling in Africa, *Comparative Sociology,* 41(1), 89–120.

Banya, K. (1991) Economic decline and the education system: the case of Sierra Leone, *Compare,* 21(2), 127–42.

Banya, K. (1993) Illiteracy, colonial legacy and education: the case of modern Sierra Leone, *Comparative Education,* 29(2), 159–70.

Banya, K. & Elu, J. (1997) Implementing basic education: an African experience, *International Review of Education,* 43(5/6), 481–96.

Bhabha, H. (1990) *Nation and narration* (London, Routledge).

Blakemore, K. & Cooksey, B. (1983) *Education for Africa* (New York, St. Martin Press).

Bledsoe, C. (1992) The cultural transformation of western education in Sierra Leone, *Africa,*62(2), 182–201.

Bloch, M., Beoku-Betts, J. A. & Tabachnick, R. (Eds) (1998) *Women and education in sub-Saharan Africa: power, opportunities and constraints* (Boulder, CO, Lynne Rienner).

Bray, M. (1986) If UPE is the answer, what is the question? *International Journal of Educational Development,* 6(3), 147–58.

Brock-Utne, B. (1996) Reliability and validity in qualitative research within education in Africa,*International Review of Education,* 42(6), 605–21.

Bunyi, G. (1999) Rethinking the place of African indigenous languages in African education,*International Journal of Educational Development,* 19(4), 337–50.

Cabral, A. (1969) *Revolution in Guinea* (New York, Monthly Review Press).

Cabral, A. (1970) National liberation and culture. The 1970 Eduardo Mondlane Lecture, Programme of Eastern African Studies of the Maxwell School of Citizenship and Public Affairs, Syracuse University, 20 February.

Carnoy, M. (1986) Education for alternative development, in: P. Altbach & G. Kelly (Eds) *New approaches to comparative education* (Chicago, IL, University of Chicago Press), 73–90.

Carnoy, M. & Samoff, J. (1990) *Education and social transition in the third world* (Princeton NJ, Princeton University Press).

Cesaire, A. (1972) *Discourse on colonialism* (New York, Monthly Review Press).

Craig, J. (1990) *Comparative African experiences in implementing educational policies.* World Bank Discussion Papers, No. 83, Washington DC, The World Bank, 73–90.

Dei, G. J. S. (1994a) Afrocentricity: a cornerstone of pedagogy, *Anthropology and Education Quarterly,* 25(1), 3–28.

Dei, G. J. S. (1994b) The challenges of anti-racist education research in the African context,*African Development,* 19(3), 5–25.

Dei, G. J. S. (2004a) *Schooling and educational reforms in Africa: the case of Ghana* (Trenton, NJ, African World Press).

Dei, G. J. S. (2004b) Dealing with difference: ethnicity and gender in the context of schooling in Eshiwani, G. S. (1990) *Implementing educational policies in Kenya* (Washington DC, The World Bank).

Fafunwa, A. B. (1974) *History of education in Nigeria* (London, George Allen & Unwin).

Fanon, F. (1963) *The wretched of the earth* (New York, Grove Weidenfeld).

Foster, P. (1965) *Education and social change in Ghana* (London, Routledge & Kegan Paul).

Foster, P. J. (1962) Ethnicity and the schools in Ghana, *Comparative Education Review,* 6(2), 127–135.

Foster, P. J. (1963) Secondary school and social mobility in a West African nation, *Sociology of Education,* 37(2), 150–71.

Foucault, M. (1980) *Power/knowledge: selected interviews, 1972–77* (C. Gordon, Ed.) (Brighton, Harvester Press).

Galabawa, C. J. (1990) *Implementing education policies in Tanzania* (Washington DC, The World Bank).

Gandhi, L. (1998) *Postcolonial theory: a critical introduction* (New York, Columbia University Press).

Glick P. & Sahn, D. E. (1999) Schooling of girls and boys in a West African country: the effects of parental education, income, and household structure, *Economics of Education Review,* 19(1), 63–87.

Hansen, D. T. (2002) The moral environment in an inner-city boys' high school, *Teaching and Teacher Education,* 18(2), 183–204.

Harber, C. (2002) Education, democracy and poverty reduction in Africa, *Comparative Education,* 38(3), 267–76.

Jegede, O. J. (1994) African cultural perspectives and the teaching of science, in: J. Solomon & G. Aikenhead (Eds) *Science, technology and society education for the future citizens* (New York, Teachers' College Press), 120–30.

Johnson, D. (1995) Introduction: the challenges of educational reconstruction and transformation in South Africa, *Comparative Education,* 31(2), 131–40.

Jones, P. W. (1988) *International policies of third world education* (London, Hutchinson).

Jones, P. W. (1992) *World Bank financing of education* (New York, Routledge).

Jones, P. W. (1997) Review article: 'Policies and strategies for education: a World Bank review' *Comparative Education,* 33(1), 117–30.

Kinyanjui, K. (1993) Enhancing women's participation in the science-based curriculum: the case of Kenya, in: J. Ker Conway & S.C. Bourque (Eds) *The politics of women's education* (Ann Arbor, MI, University of Michigan Press), 133–48.

Loomba, A. (1998) *Colonialism/postcolonialism* (London, Routledge).

Maravanyika, O. E. (1990) *Implementing educational policies in Zimbabwe* (Washington DC, The World Bank).

Memmi, A. (1969) *The colonizer and the colonized* (Boston, MA, Beacon Press).

Nyerere, J. (1979) Adult education and development, in: M. Hinzel & C. V. H. Hundsdorfer (Eds) *Education for liberation and development: the Tanzanian experience* (Paris, UNESCO).

Nyerere, J. (1985) Education in Tanzania, *Harvard Educational Review,* 55(1), 45–52.

Obanya, P. (1995) Case studies of curriculum innovation, *International Review of Education,* 41(5), 315–36.

Psacharopoulos, G. (1989) Why educational reforms fail: a comparative analysis, *International Review of Education,* 35(2), 179–95.

Psacharopoulos, G. (1990) *Why educational policies can fail: an overview of selected African experiences* (Washington DC, The World Bank).

Quist, H. O. (1994) The missionary element in the development of education in the Volta Region of Ghana, 1920–1950, *Journal of the Institute of Education, University of Cape Coast Ghana,* 3(1), 119–33.

Said, E. (1978/1985) *Orientalism: western representations of the orient* (Harmondsworth, Penguin).

Said, E. (1993) Intellectual exile: expatriates and marginals, *Grand Street,* 12(3), 112–24. Samoff, J. (1990) Educational reform in Tanzania: schools, skills and social transformation, in: B. Nasson & J. Samuels (Eds) *Education: from poverty to liberty* (South Africa, David Phillip Publishers Ltd.), 132–40.

Samoff, J. (1992) The intellectual/financial complex of foreign aid, *Review of African Political Economy,* 53, 60–75.

Samoff, J. (1993) The reconstruction of schooling in Africa, *Comparative Education Review,* 37(2), 181–222.

Senghor, L. S. (1996) African socialism, in: M. K. Asante & A. S. Abarry (Eds) *African intellectual heritage* (Philadelphia, PA, Temple University Press), 342–54.

Shahjahan, R. (2003) Mapping the field of anti-colonial discourse to understand issues of indigenous knowledges, paper presented at the congress meeting of the *Canadian Sociology and Anthropology Association,* Dalhousie University, Halifax, 28–30 May.

Shohat, E. (1992) Notes on the 'Postcolonial', *Social Text,* 31/32, 99–113.

Sifuna, D. N. (1992) Diversifying the secondary school curriculum: the African experience, *International Review of Education,* 38(1), 5–20.

Slemon, S. (1995) The scramble for postcolonialism, in: B. Ashcroft, G. Griffiths & H. Tiffin (Eds) *The postcolonial studies reader* (New York, Routledge), 45–52.

Spivak, G. C. (1988) Can the subaltern speak?, in: C. Nelson & L. Grossberg (Eds) *Marxism and the interpretation of culture* (Basingstoke, Macmillan), 271–313.

Stroud, C. (2003) Postmodernist perspectives on local languages: African mother-tongue education in times of globalisation, *International Journal of Bilingual Education and Bilingualism,* 6(1), 17–36.

Suleri, S. (1992) *The rhetoric of English India* (Chicago, IL, Chicago University Press).

Tedla, E. (1995) *Sankofa: African thought and education* (New York, Peter Lang).

Vavrus, F. (2002) Uncoupling the articulation between girls education and tradition in Tanzania, *Gender and Education,* 14(4), 367–89.

Young, R. (1995) *Colonial desire: hybridity in theory, culture and race* (New York, Routledge).

Young, R. (2001) *Postcolonialism: an historical introduction* (Oxford, Blackwell Publishers).

7

Neoliberalism and Its Impacts

Dave Hill and Ravi Kumar

Inequalities both between states and within states have increased dramatically during the era of global neoliberalism. Global capital, in its current neoliberal form in particular, leads to human degradation and inhumanity and increased social class inequalities within states and globally. These effects are increasing (racialized and gendered) social class inequality within states, increasing (racialized and gendered) social class inequality between states. The inequality within societies has acquired new forms. While one finds an increasing class-based polarization at ground level, there is an effort by the ruling classes to substitute for class, as the fundamental defining characteristic of social identity, different social identities such as race and caste. The efforts at rejecting the primacy of class as the primary constituent of social relations are being put forth also by some "celebrated" progressive educationists (such as Apple, e.g. 2006). Sadly enough, progressive working-class movements across the globe also fall prey to such discourses. And ultimately, they facilitate the unhindered march of neoliberal capital and the degradation and capitalization of humanity, including the environmental degradation impact primarily in a social-class-related manner.

Markets in Education

Markets have exacerbated existing inequalities. There is considerable data on how poor schools have, by and large, become poorer (in terms of relative education results and in terms of total income) and how rich schools (in the same terms) have become richer. Whitty, Power, and Halpin (1998) examined the effects of the introduction of quasi-markets into education systems in the United States, Sweden, England and Wales, Australia, and New Zealand. Their book is a review of the research evidence. Their conclusion is that one of the results of marketizing education is that increasing "parental choice" of schools, and/or setting up new types of schools, in effect increases school choice of parents and their children and thereby sets up or exacerbates racialized school hierarchies.

In the United Kingdom, for example, while in government between 1979 and 1997, the Conservatives established a competitive market for 'consumers' (children and their parents) by setting up new types of schools in addition to the local (state, i.e., public) primary school or the local secondary comprehensive school. Thus they introduced new types of school such as City Technology Colleges and Grant Maintained schools, schools that removed themselves from the control of Local (democratically elected) Authorities. And to confirm this creation of a "quasi-" market in school choice, they extended the "parental choice" of schools—letting parents, in effect, apply for any school anywhere in the country.

77

Not only that, but the Conservative governments also stopped redistributive, positive discrimination funding for schools. Decisions about funding were substantially taken out of the hands of the democratically elected local education authorities (LEAs) by the imposition of per capita funding for pupils/school students. So students in poor/disadvantaged areas in an LEA would receive the same per capita funding as "rich kids." Furthermore, this funding rose or fell according to intake numbers of pupils/students, itself affected by henceforth compulsorily publicized "league table" performance according to pupil/student performance at various ages on SATs (Student Assessment Tasks) and 16+ examination results. (This "equality of treatment" contrasts dramatically with the attempts, prior to the 1988 Education Reform Act, of many LEAs to secure more "equality of opportunity" by spending more on those with greatest needs—a power partially restored in one of its social democratic polices by the New Labour government following its election in 1997).

The result of this "school choice" is that inequalities between schools have increased because in many cases the "parental choice" of schools has become the "schools' choice" of the most desirable parents and children—and rejection of others. "Sink schools" have become more "sinklike" as more favored schools have picked the children they think are likely to be "the cream of the crop." Where selection exists the sink schools just sink further and the privileged schools just become more privileged. Teachers in sink schools are publicly pilloried, and, under "New Labour" the schools are "named and shamed" as "Failing Schools," and, in some cases either reopened with a new "superhead" as a "Fresh Start School" (with dismissals of "failing" teachers), or shut down (see, for example, Whitty, Power, and Halpin, 1998).

These Conservative government policies are classic manifestations of neo-liberal, free-market ideology, including the transference of a substantial percentage of funding and of powers away from LEAs to "consumers" (in this case, schools). "Ostensibly, at least, these represent a "rolling back" of central and local government's influence on what goes on in schools" (Troyna, 1995, p.141).

Conservative government/ Party policy in England and Wales remained and remains a mixture of neoliberalism and neoconservatism. An aspect of its neoconservatism is its "equiphobia"—fear of equality (Myers in Troyna, 1995; cf. Hill, 1997a), its hostility to agencies or apparatuses thought to be involved in promoting equality and equal opportunities—such as (democratically elected) LEAs (Gamble, 1988; Hill, 1997a, 1999, 2001b).

New Labour's education policy modifies and extends Radical Right principles and anti-egalitarianism (Hill, 1999, 2001b). Its policy for more *com- petitiveness* (between schools, between parents, between pupils/students, and between teachers) and *selection* (by schools and by universities) are a continuation, indeed, an extension, of most of the structural aspects of the 1988 Conservative Education Reform Act, in terms of the macrostructure and organization of schooling. The Radical Right principle of competition between schools (which results in an increasing inequality between schools) and the principle of devolving more and more financial control to schools through local management of schools are all in keeping with preceding Conservative opposition to comprehensive education and to the powers of LEAs, as are the ever-increasing provision of new types of school and attacks on "mixed-ability teaching" and the increased emphasis on the role/rule of capital in education.

Governments in countries such as Britain, the United States, Australia, and New Zealand have marketized their school systems. Racialized social class patterns of inequality have increased. And at the level of university entry, the (racialized) class-based hierarchicalization of universities is exacerbated by "top-up fees" for entry to elite universities, pricing the poor out of the system, or at least into the lower divisions of higher education. And, to control the state apparatuses of education, such marketization is controlled by heavy systems of surveillance and accountability (Hill and Rosskam, 2009).

On an international level, diktats by the World Bank, the International Monetary Fund, and other agencies of international capital have actually resulted in the actual disappearance of formerly free nationally funded schooling and other education (and welfare, public utility) services (Hill, 2006a, c). One of the "fast growing economies" in the world, India has principally been doing away with the agenda of equality in education. While the discourse of "choice" has legitimized private education at all levels, those sections which lack purchasing power are being systematically deprived of equal access to good quality education (Kumar, 2006a, Kumar and Paul, 2006). Government schools are the only option left for them.

The Growth of Undemocratic (Un)Accountability

Within education and other public services business values and interests are increasingly substituted for democratic accountability and the collective voice. This applies at the local level, where, in Britain for example, private companies—national or transnational—variously build, own, run, and govern state schools and other sections of local government educational services (Hatcher and Hirtt, 1999; Hatcher, 2001, 2002; Hirtt, 2008). As Wilson (2002) asked,

> There is an important democratic question here: is it right to allow private providers of educational services based outside Britain (and, I would add, inside Britain, too, indeed, wherever they are based). In the event of abuse or corruption, where and how would those guilty be held to account? …Who is the guarantor of "the last resort"?
>
> (p. 12)

This antidemocratization applies at national levels, too. As Barry Coates (2001) has pointed out, "GATS locks countries into a system of rules that means it is effectively impossible for governments to change policy, or for voters to elect a new government that has different policies." (p. 28).

In connection with the principle of democratic control, quite interestingly, the discourse on "community participation" and decentralization has been consistently put forth by the World Bank (Kumar, 2006b, pp. 308–13) and by United Nations agencies. However, far from being democratic they ultimately become a top-down approach of governance. Under pressure from such global developmental discourses many states in the so-called third world have factored in what they claim as "democratic accountability" in their state-run educational programs. But it has remained a failure because (a) it runs as a program and not as a permanent concern of the state towards its citizens,[1] and (b) it does not take into consideration the societal politics or economic context of the masses which determine their participation.

The Loss of Critical Thought

The increasing subordination of education, including university education, and its commodification, have been well documented (e.g., Levidow, 2002, Hill, 2001a, 2002, 2004a, b, 2007; Giroux and Myrsiades, 2001; Giroux and Searls Giroux, 2004; Ross and Gibson, 2007; Rikowski, 2007; CFHE, 2003).[2] One aspect is that other than at elite institutions, where the student intake is the wealthiest and most upper-class, there is little scope for critical thought. Scholars have examined, for instance, how the British government has, in effect, expelled most potentially critical aspects of education from the national curriculum, such as sociological and political examination of schooling and education, and questions of social class, "race" and gender for what is now termed *teacher training,* which was formerly called *teacher education.* Across the globe and more so in the newly liberalized economies such as India there is a trend towards looking down upon social sciences on the grounds that they do not produce an employable population.

The mantra is of job-oriented courses, which is reflected when many universities and colleges transform their history courses into travel and tourism courses (*The Hindu,* 2004). The change in nomenclature is important both symbolically and in terms of actual accurate descriptiveness of the new, "safe," sanitized and detheorized education and training of new teachers (e.g., Hill, 2001a; 2004a; 2007). Even in those parts of the world where the neoliberal processes were set in motion by the 1990s we find not only that teacher education is transformed into teacher training, but that even the training period has been progressively declining (Sadgopal, 2006; Kumar, 2006c). What can be more disastrous than the systematic degeneration of the role of a teacher to a member of the informalized workforce, which lacks job security and works with a meager salary of as little as twenty-five dollars per month in some of the provinces in India (Leclercq, 2003).

McMurtry (2001) describes the philosophical incompatibility between the demands of capital and the demands of education, inter alia, with respect to critical thought. Governments throughout the world are resolving this incompatibility more and more on terms favorable to capital. One example in England and Wales is the swathe of redundancies/dismissals of teacher educators specializing in the sociology, politics, and contexts of education following the conforming of teacher education and the imposition of a skills-based rigidly monitored national curriculum for teacher training in 1992–1993. One dismissal was, for instance, of one of the authors (Dave Hill) himself. At a stroke, numerous critical teacher educators were removed or displaced. So too were their materials/resources—no longer wanted by the government. Thus, at the College from which I was dismissed, the Centre for Racial Equality, was closed down—its resources no longer required by the new technicist, detheorised, anticritical "teacher training" curriculum (Hill, 1997b, c, 2003). At a more general level, Mathison and Ross (2002) note that

> [the] university's role as an independent institution is increasingly threatened by the interests of corporations in both subtle and obvious ways. "Globalization,"—which Bertell Ollman (2001) defines as "another name for capitalism, but it's capitalism with the gloves off and on a world scale. It is capitalism at a time when all the old restrictions and inhibitions have been or are in the process of being put aside, a supremely self-confident capitalism, one without apparent rivals and therefore without a need to compromise or apologize"— has transformed internal and external relations of university from teaching and research to student aid policies and pouring rights for soft drink manufacturers. Decreased funding for higher education has made universities increasingly susceptible to the influence of big money and threatens the academic freedom and direction of research.

Education, Class, and Capital

Glenn Rikowski's work, such as *The Battle in Seattle* (2000, 2001, 2007), develops a Marxist analysis based on an analysis of labor power. With respect to education, he suggests that teachers are the most dangerous of workers because they have a special role in shaping, developing and forcing the single commodity on which the whole capitalist system rests: labor power. In the capitalist labor process, labor power is transformed into value-creating labor, and, at a certain point, surplus value—value over and above that represented in the worker's wage—is created. Surplus value is the first form of the existence of capital. It is the lifeblood of capital. Without it, capital could not be transformed into money, on sale of the commodities that incorporate value, and hence the capitalist could not purchase the necessary raw materials, means of production and labor power to set the whole cycle in motion once more. But most importantly for the capitalist is that part of the surplus value that forms his or her profit—and it is this that drives the capitalist on a personal basis. It is this that defines the personal agency of the capitalist!

Teachers are dangerous because they are intimately connected with the social production of labor power, equipping students with skills, competences, abilities, knowledge, and the attitudes and personal qualities that can be expressed and expended in the capitalist labor process. Teachers are guardians of the quality of labor power! This potential, latent power of teachers explains why representatives of the state might have sleepless nights worrying about the role of teachers in ensuring that the laborers of the future delivered to workplaces throughout the national capital *are* of the highest possible quality.[3]

Rikowski suggests that the state needs to control the process for two reasons: first, to try to ensure that this occurs, and second, to try to ensure that modes of pedagogy that are antithetical to labor power production do not and cannot exist. In particular, it becomes clear on this analysis that the capitalist state will seek to destroy any forms of pedagogy that attempt to educate students regarding their real predicament—to create an awareness of themselves as future labor powers and to underpin this awareness with critical insight that seeks to undermine the smooth running of the social production of labor power. This fear entails strict control of teacher education and training, of the curriculum, and of educational research.

Capitalism's Education Agendas

How, in more detail, do education markets fit into the grand plan for schooling and education? What is capitalism's "business plan for education"?

In pursuit of these agendas, new public managerialism—the importation into the old public services of the language and management style of private capital—has replaced the ethic and language and style of public service and duty. Education as a social institution has been subordinated to international market goals, including the language and self-conceptualization of educators themselves (see Mulderrig, 2002; Levidow, 2002). Mulderrig shows how

> education is theoretically positioned in terms of its relationship with the economy and broader state policy (where) an instrumental rationality underlies education policy discourse, manifested in the pervasive rhetoric and values of the market in the representation of educational participants and practices.

She theorizes this

> as an indicator of a general shift towards the commodification of education and the concomitant consumerisation of social actors [within which] discourse plays a significant role in constructing and legitimizing post-welfare learning policy as a key aspect of the ongoing project of globalization.

And the Campaign for the Future of Higher Education slams the commodification of higher education by pointing out that

> students are neither customers nor clients; academics neither facilitators nor a pizza delivery service. Universities are not businesses; producing consumer goods. Knowledge and thought are not commodities, to be purchased as items of consumption, whether conspicuous or not, or consumed and therefore finished with, whether on the hoof as take-away snacks or in more leisurely fashion. Education is not something which can be "delivered," consumed and crossed off the list. Rather, it is a continuing and reflective process, an essential component of any worthwhile life—the very antithesis of a commodity.
> (Campaign for the Future of Higher Education, 2003)

Within universities and vocational further education the language of education has been very widely replaced by the language of the market, where lecturers "deliver the product," "operationalize delivery," and "facilitate clients' learning," within a regime of "quality management and enhancement," where students have become "customers" selecting "modules" on a pick 'n' mix basis, where "skill development" at universities has surged in importance to the derogation of the development of critical thought.

Richard Hatcher (2001, 2002, 2006a, 2006b) shows how capital/business has two major aims for schools. The first aim is to ensure that schooling and education engage in ideological and economic reproduction. National education and training policies in the business agenda *for* education are of increasing importance for national capital. In an era of global capital, this is one of the few remaining areas for national state intervention—it is *the* site, suggests Hatcher, where a state can make a difference.

The second aim—the business agenda *in* schools—is for private enterprise, private capitalists, to make money out of it, to make private profit out of it, to control it.

The Capitalist Agenda for Schools

Business wants education fit for business—to make schooling and higher education subordinate to the personality, ideological, and economic requirements of capital, and to make sure schools produce compliant, ideologically indoctrinated, procapitalist, effective workers.

This first agenda constitutes a broad transnational consensus about the set of reforms needed for schools to meet employers' needs in terms of the efficiency with which they produce the future workforce. The business agenda *for* schools is increasingly transnational, generated and disseminated through key organizations of the international economic and political elite such as the Organisation for Economic Co-operation and Development (OECD). In that global context there is a project for education at the European level, which rep- resents the specific agenda of the dominant European economic and political interests. It is expressed in, for example, the various reports of the European Round Table (ERT) of industrialists, a pressure group of forty-five leaders of major European companies from sixteen countries, and it has become the motive force of the education policies of the European Commission and its subsidiary bodies. Monbiot quotes the ERT as saying "the provision of education is a market opportunity and should be treated as such" (ERT, 1998, cited in Monbiot, 2001, p. 331; see also Hatcher and Hirtt, 1999; Hirtt, 2008).

The Capitalist Agenda in Schools

Second, business wants to make profits from education and other privatized public services such as water supply and health care. The work of Molnar (2001, 2005), Monbiot (2000, 2001, 2002), Robertson (Robertson, Bonal, and Dale, 2001) in the United States and in Britain by Rikowski (2001, 2002a, 2002b, 2002c, 2002d, 2003) and Hill (1999, 2006b) highlight another aspect of what national and multinational capital wants from schooling and education—it wants profits through owning and controlling them. Thus privatization of schools and educational services is becoming "big business" (so, too, are libraries—see Ruth Rikowski, 2002). As the weekly radical newsletter *Schnews* exclaims, in an April 2000 article entitled "The Coca-Cola Kids,"

> Education in the West is fast becoming indistinguishable from any other industry. Privatization of education was this week put in the spotlight with the National Union of Teachers threatening strike action not just over performance related pay, but also over big business moving in on the classroom. But what the hell is "Best Value," "Out-sourcing," "Action Zones," and the "Private Finance Initiative"? Shall we peer into the New Labour Dictionary of Gobbledee Gook to find out just what it all means?
>
> How about "Privatization, privatization, privatization." Yes, New Labour is busy selling off everything—they just dress it up in fancy jargon to try and pull the wool over our eyes. Still, why would private companies want to move into education? McDonalds' "operations manual" gives us a clue: "Schools offer excellent opportunities. Not only are they a high

traffic (sales) generator, but students are some of the best customers you could have." And with £38 billion spent on education a year, there's a lot to play for.

Of course, ultimate responsibility within private-company-owned schools and colleges and libraries is not to children, students or the community—it is to the owners and the shareholders.

Notes

1. One needs to differentiate between a program of education and the educational edifice as such. While programs are temporary arrangements to allow spaces for private capital to be created in contemporary times, the educational edifice in the form of government schools is permanent in character, which the neoliberal seeks to destroy.
2. In capitalist society, "well-being" is now equated with "well-having"—we are what we consume. In educational terms our worth is how many years and credits we have accumulated. Indeed, being a student is now a serious game, to build up credits to get a better job. In the United States and in England and Wales today, as in other advanced capitalist states, economic goals of education have sidelined social/societal/community goals, the traditional social democratic goals of education, and have also replaced education/learning for its own sake, the traditional liberal and liberal-progressive goals of education.
3. Perhaps the easiest way of understanding the concept of "national capital" is with respect to Rikowski's definition in terms of *national labour markets:* "the labour-power needs of national capitals refer to those labour-power capacities required for labouring in any labour process throughout the national capital... [There] is the drive [to increase] the quality (of labour-power) vis-a-vis other national capitals for gaining a competitive edge" (Rikowski, 2001b, p. 42). This particular definition points towards the national capital (when being viewed in relation to labor power) as the national labor market.

References

Althusser, L. 1971. Ideology and ideological state apparatuses: Notes toward an investigation. In *Lenin and philosophy and other essays,* ed. L. Althusser. New York and London: Monthly Review Press. http://www.marx2mao.com/Other/ LPOE70ii.html#s5.

Apple, M. 2006. Rhetoric and reality in critical educational studies in the United States. *British Journal of Sociology of Education* 27, no. 5: 679–87.

Bircham, E., and J. Charlton. 2001. *Anti-capitalism: A guide to the movement.* London: Bookmarks.

Campaign for the Future of Higher Education. 2003. http://www.cfhe.org.uk.

Coates, B. 2001. GATS. In *Anti-capitalism: A guide to the movement,* ed. E. Bircham and J. Charlton, 27–42. London: Bookmarks.

The Coca Cola Kids. 2000. *Schnews 257.* http://www.schnews.org.uk/archive/ news257.htm#Top.

Gamble, A. 1988. *The free economy and the strong state.* London: Macmillan.

George, S. 2004. *Another world is possible if ...* London: Verso.

Giroux, H. and S. Searls Giroux. 2004. *Take back higher education.* London: Palgrave MacMillan.

Giroux, H. and K. Myrsiades. 2001. *Beyond the corporate university.* Lanham, MD: Rowman and Littlefield.

Hatcher, R. 2001. Getting down to the business: Schooling in the globalised economy. *Education and Social Justice* 3, no. 2: 45–59.

——2002. *The Business of education: How business agendas drive labour policies for schools.* London: Socialist Education Association. *http://www.socialist- education.org.uk.*

——2006a. Business sponsorship of schools: For-profit takeover or agents of neoliberal change? *Volumizer,* November 5, 2005. http://journals.aol.co.uk/ rikowskigr/Volumizer/entries/651.

——2006b. Privatisation and sponsorship: The re-agenting of the school system in England. *Journal of Education Policy* 21, no. 5: 599–619.

Hatcher, R., and N. Hirtt. 1999. The business agenda behind labour's education policy. In *Business, business, business: New Labour's education policy,* eds. M. Allen, C. Benn, C. Chitty, M. Cole, R. Hatcher, N. Hirrt, and G. Rikowski. London: Tufnell Press.

Hill, D. 1997a. Equality and primary schooling: The policy context intentions and effects of the conservative "reforms." In *Equality and the national curriculum in primary schools,* ed. M. Cole, D. Hill and S. Shan, 15–47. London: Cassell.

——1997b. Critical research and the dismissal of dissent, *Research Intelligence* 59, 25–26.

——1997c. Reflection in initial teacher education. In *Teacher education and training,* Vol. 1 of *Educational dilemmas: Debate and diversity,* ed. K. Watson, S. Modgil, and C. Modgil, 193–208. London: Cassell.

——1999. *New Labour and education: Policy, ideology and the third way.* London: Tufnell Press.

——2001a. Equality, ideology and education policy. In *Schooling and equality: Fact, concept and policy,* ed. D. Hill and M. Cole, 7–34. London: Kogan Page.

——2001b. *The Third Way in Britain: New Labour's neoliberal education policy.* Paper presented at the Conference Marx 111, Universite de Sorbonne/Nanterre, Paris. http://www.ieps.org.uk.

——2001c. Education, struggle and the left today: An interview with three UK Marxist educational theorists: Mike Cole, Dave Hill and Glenn Rikowski by Peter McLaren, *International Journal of Education Reform* 10, no. 2: 145–62.

——2002. The radical left and education policy: Education for economic and social justice. *Education and Social Justice* 4, no. 3: 41–51.

Hill, D. 2003. second edition. *Brief autobiography of a Bolshie dismissed.* Brighton: Institute for Education Policy Studies. http://www.ieps.org.uk.cwc.net/ bolsharticle.pdf.

——2004a. Books, banks and bullets: Controlling our minds: The global project of imperialistic and militaristic neoliberalism and its effect on education policy. *Policy Futures* 2, nos. 3–4. http://www.wwwords.co.uk/pfie/content/pdfs/2/issue2_3.asp.

——2004b. Educational perversion and global neo-liberalism: a Marxist critique. *Cultural Logic: An Electronic Journal of Marxist Theory and Practice.* http:// eserver.org/clogic/2004/2004.html.

——2006a. Education services liberalisation. In *Winners or losers? Liberalising public services,* ed. E. Rosskam, 3–54. Geneva: International Labour Organisation.

——2006b. Six theses on class, global capital and resistance by education and other cultural workers. In *Introductory reflections: From re-action to action in contemporary social* thought, ed. O.-P. Moisio and J. Suoranta, 191–218. Jvaskyla, Fin- land: SoPhi. http://www.sensepublishers.com/catalog/files/90–77874–17–8.pdf.

——2006c. Class, capital and education in this neoliberal/ neoconservative period. *Information for Social Change* 23. http://libr.org/isc/issues/ISC23/B1%20 Dave%20Hill.pdf.

——2007. Critical teacher education, New Labour in Britain and the global project of neoliberal capital. *Policy Futures* 5, no.2.

Hill, D., and E. Rosskam, eds. 2009. *The developing world and state education: Neoliberal depredation and egalitarian alternatives.* New York: Routledge.

The Hindu. 2004. Choice-based credit system helpful in meeting demand for jobs. http://www.thehindu.com/2004/02/03/stories/2004020309770400.htm.

Hirrt, N. 2008. Markets and education in the era of globalized capitalism. In *Global neoliberalism and education and its consequences,* ed. D. Hill and R. Kumar, 206–24. New York: Routledge.

International Marxist Tendency. 2008. *In defence of Marxism: World perspectives, Part One,* 6 Feb. International Marxist Tendency. http://www.marxist. com/world-perspectives-2008-draft-one.htm.

Kumar, R. 2006a. ed. *The crisis of elementary education in India.* New Delhi: Sage Publications.

——2006b. Educational deprivation of the marginalized: A village study of Mushar community in Bihar. In *The crisis of elementary education in India,* ed. R. Kumar, 301–42. New Delhi: Sage Publications.

——2006c. State, class and critical framework of praxis: The missing link in Indian educational debates. *Journal of Critical Education Policy Studies* 4, no.2. http://www.jceps.com/index.php?pageID=article&articleID=68.

Kumar, R., and Rama P. 2006. Institutionalising discrimination: Challenges of educating urban poor in neo-liberal era. In *Managing urban poverty,* ed. A. Sabir, 253–89. New Delhi: Council for Social Development and Uppal Publishing House.

Leclercq, F. 2003. *Education policy reforms and the quality of the school system: A field study of primary schools in Madhya Pradesh, India.* Developpement et Insertion Internationale, Document de Travail DT/2003/12. http:// www.dial. prd.fr/dial_publications/PDF/Doc_travail/2003–12.pdf.

Levidow, L. 2002. Marketizing higher education: Neoliberal strategies and counter-strategies. *The Commoner* 3, January. http://www.commoner.org. uk/03levidow.pdf.

Mathison, S., and E. W. Ross. 2002. The hegemony of accountability in schools and universities. *Workplace: A Journal for Academic Labor* 5, no. 1. http://www.lou- isville.edu/journal/workplace/issue5p1/mathison.html.

McMurtry, J. 2001. "Why is there a war in Afghanistan?" Speech, University of Toronto, Science for Peace Forum and Teach-In, "How Should Canada Respond to Terrorism and War? http://scienceforpeace.sa.utoronto.ca/Special_Activities/ McMurtry_Page.html.

Molnar, A. 2001. *Giving kids the business: The commercialization of America's schools.* 2nd ed. Boulder, CO: Westview.

——2005. *School Commercialism: From Democratic Ideal to Market Commodity.* New York: Routledge.

Monbiot, G. 2000. *Captive state: The corporate takeover of Britain.* London: Pan.

——2001. How to rule the world: Rich nations should stop running the planet and give way to global democracy. *The Guardian,* July 17, 2001. http://www.guardian. co.uk/globalisation/story/0,7369, 522903,00.html.

——2002. Public fraud initiative. *The Guardian,* June 19, 2002. http://society. guardian.co.uk// futureforpublicservices/comment/0,8146,739525,00.html.

Mulderrig, J. 2002. *Learning to labour: The discursive construction of social actors in New Labour's education policy.* http://www.jceps.com/index.php?pageID=art icle&articleID=2.

Ollman, B. 2001. *How to take an exam ... and remake the world.* Montreal: Black Rose.

Rikowski, G. 2000. *That Other Great Class of Commodities: Repositioning Marxist Educational Theory,* BERA Conference Paper, Cardiff University, 7–10 September. http://www.leeds.ac.uk/educol/documents/ 00001624.htm.

——2001. *The battle in Seattle.* London: Tufnell Press.

——2002a. *Globalisation and education.* A paper prepared for the House of Lords Select Committee on Economic Affairs, Inquiry into the Global Economy. http://www.ieps.org.uk%20or%20rikowski@ tiscali.co.uk.

——2002b. *Schools: Building for business.* http://www.ieps.org.uk.

——2002c. *Schools: The great GATS buy.* http://www.ieps.org.uk.

——2003. *The suppression and compression of critical space in education today.*

Paper presented at University College Northampton.

——2007. *Marxist educational theory unplugged.* A paper prepared for the Fourth Historical Materialism Annual Conference, November 9–11th, School of Oriental & African Studies, University of London. http://www.flowideas. co.uk/?page=articles&sub=Marxist%20Educational%20Theory%20Unplugged.

Rikowski, R. 2002. *The WTO/GATS agenda for libraries.* http://www.ieps.org. uk.cwc.net/rikowski2002a. pdf.

Robertson, S., X. Bonal, and R. Dale. 2001. GATS and the education service industry: The politics of scale and global re-territorialization. *Comparative Education Review* 46, no. 2: 472–96.

Ross, E. W. and R.Gibson. 2007. *Neoliberalism and education reform.* Cresskill, NJ: Hampton Press.

Sadgopal, A. 2006. Dilution, distortion and diversion: A post-Jomtien reflection on education policy. In *The crisis of elementary education in India,* ed. R. Kumar, 92–136. New Delhi: Sage Publications.

Whitty, G., S. Power, and D. Halpin. 1998. *Devolution and choice in education: The school, the state and the market.* Buckingham: Open University Press.

Wilson, C. 2002. Assault on our rights. *Morning Star,* September 12.

8

Pedagogy and Democracy
Cultivating the Democratic Ethos

Maria Nikolakaki

Neoliberalism has transformed our lives since society is transformed in the image of the market and the state itself is now "marketized." Citizens are regarded as consumers. It follows that neoliberals privilege the market mechanisms, as the most "efficient" and "rational" tool to construct human agency, by promoting individualism, and by assuming social and political determination. As Polanyi (1957, pp. 14–15) has persuasively shown, the establishment of the market economy implied sweeping aside traditional cultures and values and replacing the values of solidarity, altruism, sharing and cooperation (which usually marked community life) with the values of individualism and competition as the dominant values. New modes of subjectivity and citizenship are forged through a social mandate to provide for one's survival solely through individual "choice," leading to, according to Habermas (1986), an "instrumentalism of existence". As a result, people are brought together in competition rather than in cooperation in finding a living. The prevailing motto derived from neoliberal global capitalism is consume, compete, and win at any cost.

All the major communication institutions of a modern society—including the media and education, facilitate the replacement of democratic values by market values. As Beder (2008) writes, "the market values of competition, salesmanship and deception have replaced the democratic ideals of truth and justice," and

> The conflict between democratic values and corporate values is even more evident at a personal level, given that in the new global culture—where people are rewarded for their greed—increasingly there is little room for the expression of higher human values and qualities such as generosity, compassion, selflessness, willingness to seek out and expose the truth, courage to fight for justice.

A new inclusive education will intend to shape new citizens in a democratic society. As Zinn and Macedo support (2011), a miseducation has been always a device for conformity. "Those who are the victims of the educational system are considered to be disposable bodies, which were never supposed to be educated in the first place." This has to be stopped. There are no simple solutions. Hence it becomes crucial for educators at all levels of schooling to provide alternative democratic conceptions of the meaning and purpose of both politics and education.

Polis versus individualism as social re-location

The dominant social paradigm promoted by mass media and other cultural institutions expresses only the values and beliefs of the ruling elites, which have a vested interest in the reproduction of the existing institutions of capitalism that secures also the reproduction of their own political, economic and social power. As Cliff DuRand (1997, pp. 1–3) asserts, the core of the historical idea of democracy is "the possibility of collective decision-making about collective action for a common good." He says this is the opposite of the concept found in popular consciousness today which defines democracy as the freedom of individuals to decide on their own on actions to pursue their own purposes.

Unlike what took place in the classical polis, the individual and the state are polarized entities, in conflict, and adversaries rather than partners in a common pursuit. As John Anton (1995: p.17) describes, "hidden forces of oppression continue to show up just as unexpected acts of violence against the tyranny of the state become unavoidable. The polis is absent from the operation of the state. The state is not a polis, cannot be. At best, it is a benevolent despot, and has found a place in all of us, who in vain believe ourselves to be citizens. If we are citizens, we relate to the state in radically different ways from what the citizens of the polis thought their function to be". Ancient Greeks sought justice to secure eudaimonia, whereas nowadays, in neoliberal global capitalism there is strife for "justice" to deliver rights to satisfy the cravings of the individualized will. In this on-going struggle for freedom of this will, the pursuit of power has become the centrepiece of political conduct. This individualized will according to the Greeks was a peculiar and unfathomable entity, if any entity at all. According to Aristotle (Politics, H3, 1325B14–32), the greed that goes with human needs and desires motivates the citizen to interpret justice and equality according to their own good and not the common good. He believes that justice and friendship are elements of a political community, where friendship is to be seen as a community for the sake of self-interest and the participation in common values. Aristotle did not believe this to be an easy task and "differences that arise to contentions that fuel strife concerning the individual and common good lead to revolutions, which bring about political changes".

The real issue in contingencies, as Aristotle would say, is the formulation of the principle of the Architechtonic: how to conceive of the art and science of politics as the overarching source of value and conduct, for without it human dignity is compromised and peace becomes short-lived. According to Aristotle (Pol.1278b 29 1253a 7–8), man is by nature a political animal in that he is by nature inclined to associate; he is a being that partakes of language and has a sense of what is right or wrong, of what is beneficial or harmful. He believes that the city-state (polis) as a community came about on accounts of the needs of life, but exists for the sake of good life, on the basis of "homonoia" (political friendship), which is linked to a cooperative endeavour to bring to fruition the associative conditions, the "common good", within which endelecheia may be fulfilled (p. 92). According to Konstantinos Kalimtzis (1995, p. 95), "if we interpret Aristotle's comments on the defining characteristics of homonoia, from the standpoint of the relationship of homonoia to human fulfilment, we find a number of objective conditions must be met for political friendship to be actual:

— As polis friendship, it must sustain the common good and produce reciprocated benefits in all things that contribute to shared polis life.
— At the same time homonoia can never become a collective "oneness"; it must preserve and enrich the autonomy of the individual, for friendship is only possible among citizens who are free and equal and empowered to act for the good of another;
— It must promote stable values according to which each citizen becomes truly worthy of mutual regard and cooperative affection."

This means that in order to become humanized again, what is needed is a renegotiation of human values. According to Castoriadis, "the existing state of affairs is self–destructive politically. It produces a growing glacier of privatization and apathy; it dislocates the social imaginary significations that hold institutions together. An apathetic and cynical society cannot maintain for long even the few institutions existing today. And a society of social institutions based upon the relentless pursuit of individual self-interest is sheer nonsense". Instead, Castoriadis claims (2003, p. 48), "one who wants to institute a people has to change the mores of the people." Through individualism and competition people in a society are marginalized, disempowered and manipulated. Instead, communitarian values, solidarity and responsibility, for individual and community autonomy, need to be fostered.

Solidarity can become an enriching experience. It makes sense when its definition takes into account the needs of *all* the exploited and oppressed. It must be based not only on unity in struggle but also on learning from other people about the forms of oppression and exploitation that they face. One need to take action whether it is to support Third World's struggles, refugees resisting deportation, anti-poverty actions, assertions of women's rights, struggles for the needs of the disabled, or a strike. Capitalism has destroyed previous forms of community and solidarity. Castoriadis (2003, p.78) says on this: "The only value in liberal- capitalist societies is money, media notoriety, or power in the most vulgar, most derisory sense of the term. Here, community is destroyed. Solidarity is reduced to a few administrative measures." A politics of solidarity is not simply a politics of defense against attack; it also needs to be developed more offensively as a politics of social transformation. The struggle against oppression is not simply a fight for representation. It also needs to get to the social roots of the forms of oppression people face and the transformation of social relations producing oppression. This is what an anti-racist, feminist, class politics needs to be all about. This approach is about developing a broader sense of class struggle and anti-capitalism that is centrally defined by struggles against oppression. Facing capitalism and exploitation requires an approach to solidarity that views it as taking up and learning from all our struggles.

Personal freedom in society is inextricably and dialectically linked with personal responsibility. The existence of either is dependent on the existence of the other. However, responsibility needs to be seen in a context of community feeling, since it is essential not only for the defense against neoliberal global capitalism, but mainly for humanization, according to Paulo Freire. Feeling responsible for social exclusions is an inextricable feature of human dignity. "Responsibilization" in this form becomes an essential component of social prosperity and it is a prerequisite for unity and mutual support.

Neoliberalism promotes a kind of individualized responsibility, which is not ours to take:[1] we (not multinational corporations that overuse resources) are held responsible for global warming, we (not the system with its segregating politics) are responsible for our social exclusion, we are responsible if our politicians fail or are corrupted (as if we have a say to what "representative" politicians do once elected or even who gets into politics—these decisions are made for us by default). A new "responsibilization" should be built on hope, on the faith that something can be done and on the determination that we are not passive receptors of the will of others but agents of our destiny in the recreation of our common future. In essence, this means feeling responsible for the present state of society. As Henry Giroux (2004, p.124) maintains, "politics demands more than understanding, it demands that understanding be coupled with responsibility to others".

Political disobedience, dissidence and resistance seem to be a way out of this havoc. It is the only way to protect democracy from extinction. Resistance must be more than a protest against elite policies or disruption of the institutions through which they rule. It can only affect their actions marginally, perhaps restricting their choices in time and place, but cannot alter their course. Popular forces may succeed in driving elites to seek more secure locations in which to meet (G8 and G20) and 15 million people may protest worldwide against their wars, but the ruling elite still has the power to make decisions and impose them. According to Takis Fotopoulos

(2008b), "The inevitable conclusion is that only the struggle for the building of a massive movement aiming at the creation of a new institutional framework of equal distribution of power, and the parallel development of the corresponding culture and social paradigm, might have any chance to lead to the emergence of a new world society, which would reintegrate the economy and polity as well as Nature with society, and transcend the present huge and continually deteriorating multi-dimensional crisis."

The fact is that there is a growing discontent amongst peoples. The global economic crisis has made things obvious: either the banks will take over society or society will survive by taking back its power. In a real economy of 57 trillion dollars the financial system that the ruling elite has fostered is more than 1000 trillion dollars. About 950 trillion dollars is nothing more than thin air… but on the excuse of debt made in order to serve this thin air states are attacking their nations serving the ruling elite and not the people who they pressumingly represent. Even in USA, there is a percentage of about 50% who can now see that there are class divisions to their dismay. This discontent needs to be transformed into widespread mobilization for social change. The strengthening of the struggle against neoliberalism requires unity of mass struggles and recognition that the ruling elite's interests patronize politics. Attempts to organize popular dissatisfaction and despair in an effective manner have not produced satisfactory results. Although there is clearly a highly organized and extremely effective trans-national capitalist class, the global organization of the 'popular', as opposed to the 'capitalist' classes, has been far less effective. Therefore there is ample ground for the ruling elite to play the game, the only rules being determined by profit, which translates into the 'computation of lives'. Under such a set of morals, you can, for example, justify the dumping of nuclear wastes on Indian reservations in the U.S., (what's the use of a few million lives, when balanced with such huge profits?) You can also justify the elimination of millions of peasants and indigenous communities in Mexico, so that land which was once cultivated collectively, can now pass to the hands of multi-national companies which will use it to cultivate crops for exportation, a much more profitable activity.

Neoliberalism is a predatory system. The neoliberal bias in favor of financial interests has had devastating effects on growth, employment and the environment. It is not only humankind, who is in danger; nature and the environment are also threatened. The basic concept of Bacon that man can conquer nature in order for development to be achieved (Adorno and Horkheimer, 1996) was detrimental to the environment. Neoliberalism promotes a "blind" development, as rapid as possible, whatever the cost may be. Over the past decades, the planet has been suffocating in a "non-sustainable" development, because neoliberal capitalists' greed for short-term profit making led to consuming resources and wasting common goods which are in danger of extinction. The conception of "sustainable" development is a farce, because what causes environmental problems is the neoliberal conception of "development."[2] Sustainable development was a "sugaring the pill" practice, an excuse for keeping on doing the same things under different names. It is striking that those who harm the environment present themselves as its saviors. For example, World Council for Corporate Governance, pretending to protect the environment, consists of those who pollute and exploit it, mainly firms like 3M, Monsanto, Unilever, Novartis, Nestle, Coca Cola, Total, Fina etc. Capitalism is in fact profitably wasting the capital that Nature has been producing for three billion years, a waste that is accelerating each day. To say that the environment must be saved is to say nothing less than that society has to change its frantic consumer race. As Castoriadis maintains, this potentially constitutes the fiercest political, psychological, anthropological and philosophical quest of humanity today. And it takes the whole of society to overcome it.

Education under the Neoliberal Regime

Under neoliberalism education faces a dual trauma. On the one hand, there is a continuation and intensification of teaching as indoctrination, in order for future citizens to have no critical conscious and to passively accept the neoliberal dogma. The teaching of indifferent, useless and out-of-context knowledge has been used as a means to this end. On the other hand, education in neoliberalism has been given over to marketization, with devastating consequences.

As Castoriadis (1998, p.19) describes, the student is considered a passive vessel to which the teacher pours in a certain amount of knowledge. The student is considered a simple executor in a process whose aim is the student him/herself as a fixed product of a certain type and quality of education. In all this procedure s/he has no initiative—s/he just has to learn what /he is told and that is that. This training or miseducation will continue to exist if teachers, as John Dewey (1954) had already described, continue to teach (and preach) certain collections of fixed, immutable subject matter that they were taught which they in turn transmit to students under them. The educational regime thus consists of authorities at the upper end handing down to the receivers at the lower end what they must accept. This is not education but indoctrination, propaganda. It is a type of "education" fit for the foundations of a totalitarian society and, for the same reasons, fit to subvert, pervert and destroy the foundations of a democratic society.

Paulo Freire (1970) described this as the "banking concept," and according to that, "it is the people themselves who are filed away through the lack of creativity, transformation and knowledge in this (at best) misguided system. For, if disassociated from inquiry, from the praxis, individuals cannot be truly human" (p. 53). Freire (1970) insightfully describes that "implicit in the banking concept is the assumption of a dichotomy between human beings and the world: a person is merely *in* the world, not *with* the world or with others; the individual is a spectator, not re-creator" (p. 56).

Castoriadis (1988) remarks that:

> If someone really thinks about it, away from his superstitions, school is a monstrous institution. The child goes into an artificial world for X hours, immobilized on a desk, amongst four walls, forced to learn things which are, for the most part, strange, useless, and indifferent. S/he is forced to be passive against someone who stuffs him/her with knowledge. S/he suffers a complete separation of his/her physical and mental development, a fragmentation in which the curriculum inserts some ridiculous beautifying aspects, like 1 hour of gymnastics or 1 hour of art, etc. The result is that when s/he leaves school s/he is a disabled person, who shouldn't—if the educational system had had its way—have either body or mind. If s/he has still a body or mind it is because of his/her resistance to the system.
>
> (own translation) (p. 35)

The values of education have been eroded during the last 30 years. Under this neoliberal dominance, schooling takes the form of miseducation, an apaideia; it becomes a domain for the promotion of ignorance. The student in this school has to be filled with useless knowledge and must be mentally and psychologically amputated. S/he must be rendered unable for critical analysis and for linking knowledge with his/her own reality, personal or political. In a world of blurred and shifting boundaries under the neoliberal regime, the purpose of education has certainly shifted from that of a public good to a commodity, while meanings of education have become reconstituted, as have the roles of educators and students. As Castoriadis (2003) explains and is worth quoting at length:

> Not so very long ago, school was, for parents, a venerated place, for children an almost complete universe, for teachers more or less a vocation. At present, it is for teachers and pupils an instrumental form of forced labor, a site for present or future bread-winning (or an incomprehensible and rejected form of coercion), and, for parents, a source of anxiety: "Will my child get into the right schools [*l'enfant, sera-t-il ou non admis à la filière menant au Bac*

C]" . . . It is only apparently a paradox. Economic value, having become the only value, educational overconsumption and anxiety on the part of the parents of all social categories concerning the scholarly success of their children is uniquely related to the piece of paper their children will or will not obtain. This factor has become ever weightier these past few years. For, with the rise in unemployment, this piece of paper no longer automatically opens up the possibility of a job; the anxiety is redoubled, for now the child must obtain a good piece of paper. School is the place where one obtains (or does not obtain) this piece of paper; it is simply instrumental—it no longer is the place that is supposed to make the child a human being. Thirty years ago, in Greece, the traditional expression was: "I am sending you to school so that you may become a human being—*anthropos.*"

(p. 34)

On the other hand, educational institutions have become a principal target of marketization agendas that have sought to discursively reconstitute and redefine the nature of education by transforming it from a collective public good into an individualistic commodity that can be bought and sold in the marketplace. Education, as an ideological state apparatus, insidiously works to ensure the perpetuation of the dominant ideology by immersing students in ideologically determined practices like measuring student learning and the quality of teaching by percentage improvement of test scores and standardized tests. Then funding of education is based on this measurement. This fact ignores a basic thesis of sociology of education: that the social background of students reflects competence. As Macedo so repetitively argues, when a student goes hungry to school, it is impossible to learn. So instead of working on the source of their underperformance, schools under the neoliberal regime are to be punished. One thing is sure: This will contribute even more to increasing inequalities of education, leading the poor to become poorer and more ignorant and the rich richer.

Markets have gradually taken over education as a commodity. Many governments, under pressure from the International Monetary Fund (IMF) and the World Bank to cut government funding, have imposed fees for public schooling—a de facto privatization. In the U.S., neoliberalism has taken a variety of forms in education; perhaps the most important of these being the running of formally public school systems by private, for-profit companies. In order for schools to be taken over by the market, standardized testing has been used:

While ensuring accountability through standardized testing may seem somewhat paradoxical—since education is meant to extend far beyond standardized test scores and graduation rates—this craze with standardized testing not only promotes teaching to the test, but has also become a vehicle to restrict educational opportunities from those who need those opportunities the most.

(Makris, 2009, p. 2).

Contrary to these recent changes, societies have long designed school systems to meet a broad set of social needs—including the creation of social equality, social cohesion, common values and language. When schooling is privatized and education becomes a commodity, these broader social needs take second place before the need of the private- school operators to make a profit and the decisions of individuals who are buying an education to meet their particular needs. As education becomes a commodity, the nature of this "product" gets transformed. As Kincheloe (2007)writes, "In this milieu, students are transformed from citizens into consumers, capable of being bought and sold." Democratic control over what goes on in the schools is harshly curtailed, if not eliminated entirely.

Schools increasingly resemble prisons, and policing is the only pedagogy the system is able to apply. Since there is no more intention of creating jobs, security, or a viable future of any kind, as

Giroux (2004) supports, the system insidiously promotes the limitation of personal creativity and freedom, while it attempts to create a culture of fear to ensure that the Youth will not resist the dominant ideology in its various manifestations. The system's ultimate goal is to subordinate the Youth, which, left to their own devices, will perform actions, the implications of which the system definitely wants to avoid. In other words, they want to kill the soul of the Youth before it becomes expressive or offensive. At the same time, since the Youth is no longer a social "investment" and it has lost its established cultural position, schooling is restricted to utilizing mainly policing facilities, which is hard for society to swallow. Giroux (2004) notes this: "As despairing as these conditions appear at the present moment, they increasingly have become a basis for a surge of political resistance on the part of many Youth, intellectuals, labor unions, educators and social movements" (p. 103).

Marcuse (1989), a major figure in the Frankfurt school, so insightfully points out, "No qualitative social change, no socialism, is possible without the emergence of a new rationality and sensibility in the individuals themselves: no radical social change without a radical change of the individual agents of change." As for the radicalization of individual agents, education is a site for struggle. According to Freire (2004), "If education alone cannot transform society, without it society cannot change either" (p. 47). The final crucial issue refers to what Castoriadis called "the riddle of politics," i.e., how within a heteronomous society and a heteronomous education we may create autonomous institutions and the infrastructure of *paideia*.

This is where critical pedagogy seems to be a necessary component of awareness, resistance, and social struggle. Critical pedagogy is about how to be in the world with the world, and as Macedo (2007) so correctly remarks, it is a "never-ending process that involves struggle and pain, but also hope and joy maintained by a humanizing pedagogy". Critical pedagogy, according to Giroux (1994), signals how questions of audience, voice, power, and evaluation actively work to construct particular relations between teachers and students, institutions and society, and classrooms and communities. Pedagogy in the critical sense illuminates the relationship between knowledge, authority, and power (Giroux, 1994, p. 30). It is at this place where critical pedagogy becomes an important vehicle for social resistance and social transformation.

Critical Pedagogy as Democratic Practice

Since education is the ideological apparatus of the state, according to Althusser (1994), the aim of education is explicit: It is the construction of the desired citizen. Under neoliberalism, this person has become a passive citizen who accepts the neoliberal agenda. It is for teachers to change that. Critical pedagogy as a social theory necessitates that the teacher has taken a stand and has recognized his/her ideological basis. It means that whatever and however they teach, they connect knowledge to the social and political agenda and install democratic values to their students in an effort to make them agents of social change.

According to Castoriadis (2003), the goal of emancipation is individual and social autonomy. In order to achieve an autonomous society, an autonomous activity of collectivities is required. At the individual level, a democratic ethos needs to be cultivated. Commenting on the crisis of democracy, Castoriadis (2003) says:

> Democracy is possible only where there is a democratic *ethos*: responsibility, shame, frankness (*parrhssia*), checking up on one another, and an acute awareness of the fact that the public stakes are also personal stakes for each one of us. And without such an ethos, there can no longer be a "Republic of Letters," but only pseudotruths *administered* by the State, by the clergy (whether monotheistic or not), or by the media.
>
> (p. 6)

What is needed then is a critical pedagogy in the classroom cultivating the democratic ethos of the student and creating the conditions for a citizen, through conscientization, to struggle for a just world. In such an emancipating pedagogy, egocentrism, narcissist certainties, and the constant accumulation of experiences are put into question. Instead, communitarian values are to be developed. According to Aristotle in *Nicomachean Ethics* (1.2.1094b7–10), a life guided by moral virtue is a political life. He maintains that the good person and the good citizen are one, at least in the ideal state. To be a good person is simply to use one's faculties well, and political activity constitutes a way in which one can exercise one's faculties well.

Hence, to perform one's tasks as a citizen is to exercise one's faculties for the sake of the community that one shares in (Harper, 1995, p. 81). Aristotle claims that the good of the community is nobler and more divine than the good of any individual; to secure and preserve the former is greater and more complete than the latter. Since the good person is someone who leads a good life, and since one who works with other citizens improves his own life too, the good person should be a good citizen. On the other hand, not only is the good citizen a good person, but it is through acts incumbent upon citizens that they can realize their human potential. In an ideal state, personal and civic interest, private and public interest converge. In other words, the individual cannot be happy alone, but only within a community, and the community cannot prosper without its citizens' contribution.

Educating the active, critical citizen to participate in the *polis* is considered by critical pedagogy as an essential means for the emancipation of society. In Castoriadis's words:

> Only the education (paideia) of the citizens as citizens can give valuable, substantive content to the "public space." This paideia is not primarily a matter of books and academic credits. First and foremost, it involves becoming conscious that the polis is also oneself and that its fate also depends upon one's mind, behaviour, and decisions; in other words, it is participation in political life.
>
> (quoted by Fotopoulos 2008)

According to Freire (2004), "Dealing with the city—the polis—is not simply a technical matter; it is above all a political one" (p. 17). The polis is an area for political action. Also, as an expression of individual autonomy, it secures more than human survival. Politics makes possible man's development as a creature capable of genuine autonomy, freedom, and excellence, according to ancient Greek practice. Education as a means of cultivating the democratic ethos for a genuine democracy to be realized needs to open up pedagogical spaces, where interaction between the educators and the students promotes this self- realization and self-institution of society.

Critical pedagogy contributes to a democratic ethos for the benefit of both the individual and the collective. Critical pedagogy is about acquiring both knowledge and the ability to maximize individual *and* social autonomy, as a means of individual *and* social liberation. This democratic ethos is cultivated in a sense of freedom. Freedom cannot be taken for granted; it is something that needs to be taught. Aristotle claims that freedom is not a means; it is a coordinated end. According to Freire (2004):

> Freedom is not a gift given, but is rather earned by those who enrich themselves through the struggle for it. That is true to the extent that there can be no life without at least a minimal presence of freedom. Even though life in itself implies freedom, it does not mean in any way that we can give it gratuitously.
>
> (p. 120)

Giroux (2004) argues, "Democracy necessitates forms of education that provide a new ethic of freedom and a reassertion of collective identity as central preoccupations of a vibrant democratic culture and society" (p. 53). This necessitates commitment to the democratic project with passion. Democracy is impossible without a democratic passion, a passion for the freedom of each and of all, a passion for common affairs, which become, as a matter of fact, the personal affairs of each individual. Freedom facilitates the understanding of human conditionality and the potential of humankind to shake off any kind of oppression and exploitation. Freedom, personal initiatives, and resistance to any form of compliance and to any form of power should be an integral part of the educational process.

However, using Reason to teach freedom is a paradox, as "Reason itself presupposes freedom—autonomy. Reason is not a mechanical device or a system of ready-made truths; it is the movement of a thought that doesn't recognize any authority other than its own activity" (Castoriadis, 2003, p. 292). The sense of freedom necessitates Reason because excessive freedom can lead to selfishness, hedonism, and egoism, that is, people who love and strive for their own freedom but ignore the freedom of others. This neoliberal egoistic notion of freedom that equates freedom with personal interests has been successfully cultivated by capitalism through competition and individualism.

In a state of freedom, autonomy is cultivated. Autonomy according to Castoriadis is not hedonic fulfillment of desires: doing whatever one wants, whenever one wants. The word is a combination of Greek words *auto* (self) and *nomos* (law). So there is a law, but the question is who lays down the law (2003, p.158). Critical pedagogy aids the subject in becoming as autonomous as possible in a collective autonomy. As Freire (2004) commented, "It is necessary for the child to learn that his/her own autonomy can only attain legitimacy if it respects the autonomy of others" (p. 38).

Freedom and autonomy have to be based on the cultivation of *nous* and embedded in a communitarian context—to use Castoriadis's (2003) words, "in a collective identity—of a whole with which one might, in key respects, identify, in which one participates and about which one might bear some concern, and for whose fate one feels oneself responsible" (p. 98).

According to Castoriadis (1988), for the self-institution of society, *nous* as critical thinking and praxis as critical outcome, are required. This distinction resembles Freire's concept of conscientization. As Freire (1970) stressed, conscientization focuses on achieving an in-depth understanding of the world, allowing for the perception and exposure of social and political contradictions. This conscientization, as *nous,* is an inner-self-procedure and cannot be indoctrinated. Conscientization leads to praxis, taking action against the oppressive elements in one's life that are illuminated by that understanding. So we see that both Castoriadis and Freire supported similarly: conscientization as *nous,* has to do with the realization of suppressive circumstances and leads to praxis, which has to do with forms of resistance.

This freedom and autonomy (through the creation of a democratic ethos) is essential for conscientization as *nous.* Conscientization within a democratic ethos is about an agent who wants to belong to a community based on equality (regardless of race, age, sex, culture, class, disability, sex orientation), feeling responsibility for the injustices of this world. This responsibility feeling is not a state; it is a procedure. This "responsibilization" grows with conscientization and makes us feel that we are an organic part of what is going on around us, that we are equally liable for the injustices being done in this world as they evolve, unless we speak up and strive for their elimination. It is clear that "responsibilization" based on autonomy does not mean imposing one's value system upon others, but implementing dialogue and maintaining empathy, an attitude of openness in order to understand others, while always respecting them. It dictates justice as each individual contributes to the community, according to each one's capabilities and needs. Personal freedom as discussed earlier is inextricably tied to the question of personal responsibility. About this, Freire states, "If I lack responsibility, I cannot speak of ethics or of hope" (Freire, 2004, p. 99). Responsibility, however, is not to be founded on guilt. Guilt immobilizes the individual, neutralizes every tendency for freedom, and overshadows and numbs human feelings.

Conscientization as praxis means acting with solidarity, where the collectivity by no means consists of homogenized and identical masses. Responsibilization, as a procedure of conscientization, concludes to solidarity, to a communal feeling, connecting to society and working towards a common goal, which is defined by society and not the markets. This is where responsibilization connects conscientization as *nous* with praxis. Conscientization leads to praxis as a revolutionary action. When Castoriadis was asked if he was a revolutionary, he replied, "Revolution does not mean torrents of blood, the taking of the Winter Palace, and so on. Revolution means a radical transformation of society's institutions. In this sense, I certainly am a revolutionary(1988)." This is where critical pedagogy comes along as an essential emancipatory device for social self-institution (auto-thesmisis, to use Castoriadis's term). Challenging neoliberal hegemony as a form of domination is crucial to reclaiming an alternative notion of the political and rearticulating the relationship between political agency and substantive democracy (Giroux, 2004, p. 53).

Notes

1. Barack Obama said that: "Solving this crisis will require more than resources—it will require all of us to step back and take responsibility". "Government must take responsibility for setting rules of the road that are fair and fairly enforced. Banks and lenders must be held accountable for ending the practices that got us into this crisis in the first place. And each of us as individuals must take responsibility for their own actions. That means all of us must learn to live within our means again." In this way he equates the victims and the victimizers, through a generalized responsibility.
2. From 2002 Latouche promotes a discourse for the need of de-development, which signals the need to escape from the imperialism of economy, and the colonization of our imaginary of the economy. (Latouche Serge (2008). *The challenge of de-development*. Polis. In Greek)

References

Adorno T. and M. Horkheimer. (1947–1996). *Dialektik der Aufklarung, Querido*, Amsterdam, in Greek translation. Athens: Nisos Publications.

Althusser, L. (1994). *Ideology and ideological mechanisms. Σύγχρονη Σκέψη*, 5, 69–95.

Anton, J. (1995). Timely observations on Aristotle's Architectonic of Politike Techne. In *Aristotelian Political Philosophy*. Athens: International Center for Greek Philosphy and Culture &KB.

Apostolopoulos, A. (2008). Poverty, charity and NGOs. *Diaplous, August-September,* p. 49.

Apple, M. (2009). Some ideas on interrupting the right: On doing critical educational work in conservative times. *Education, Citizenship and Social Justice*, 4, 87.

Aristotle. (1964). *Politics* (W. D. Ross, Trans.). Oxford, England: Clarendon Press.

Beder, S. (2008). The corporate assault on democracy. *The International Journal of Inclusive Democracy,* 4(1).

Bourdieu, P. (1998). The essence of neoliberalism. *Le Monde.* Retrieved from http://www.analitica.com/Bitblio/bourdieu/neoliberalism.asp

Castoriadis, C. (1988). *The revolutionary problem today.* Athens, Greece: Ypsilon.

Castoriadis, C. (2003). *The rising tide of insignificancy.* Retrieved from http://www.notbored.org/RTI.pdf

Castoriadis, C. (2005). *Figures of the thinkable.* Retrieved from http://www.costis.org/x/castoriadis/Castoriadis-Figures_of_the_Thinkable.pdf

Castoriadis, C. (2007). *The rationality of capitalism.* Retrieved from http://indy.gr/library/kornlios-kastoriadis-i-orthologikotita-toy-kapitalismoy/kastoriadis-i-orthologikotita-toy-kapitalismoy.

Darder, A., & Mirón, L. F. (2006). Critical pedagogy in a time of uncertainty: A call to action. *Cultural Studies- Critical Methodologies,* 6(1), PP: 5–20.

Dewey, J. (1954). *The public and its problems.* Chicago, IL: The Swallow Press Inc.

DuRand C. "The Idea of Democracy." (University of Havana Conference: *Socialism Toward the 21st Century.* October 21, 1997)p: 1–3

Fotopoulos, T. (2008a). The globalization of poverty. *Diaplous,* August–September .Also retrieved from: http://www.inclusivedemocracy.org/fotopoulos/greek/grvarious/diaplous_aug_08.htm

Fotopoulos, T. (2008b). Values, the dominant social paradigm and neoliberal globalisation. *The International Journal of Inclusive Democracy*, 4(1). Retrieved from http://www.inclusivedemocracy.org/journal/vol4/vol4_no1_takis_values.htm

Freire, P. (1970). *Pedagogy of the oppressed.* London, England: Penguin.

Freire, P. (1985). *Politics of education: Culture, power and liberation.* Westport, CT: Bergin & Garvey Publishers.

Freire, P. (1995). *Letters to Christina: Reflections on my life and work.* New York, NY: Routledge.

Freire, P. (2001). *Pedagogy of freedom.* Lanham, MD: Rowman and Littlefield Publishers.

Freire, P. (2004). *Pedagogy of indignation.* Boulder, CO: Paradigm.

Freire, P., & Macedo, D. (in press). *Ideology matters.* Lanham, MD: Rowman & Littlefield Publishers.

Giroux, H. (1994) *Disturbing pleasures: Learning popular culture.* New York, NY: Routledge.

Giroux, H. (2004). *The terror of neoliberalism-authoritarianism and the eclipse of democracy.*Boulder, CO: Paradigm.

Giroux, H., & Giroux, S. (2008). Beyond bailouts: On the politics of education after neoliberalism. Retreived from http://www.truthout.org/123108A.

Giroux, H., & McLaren, P. (1994). *Between borders: Pedagogy and the politics of cultural studies.*New York, NY: Routledge.

Habermas, J. (1986). *Autonomy and solidarity.* Athens, Greece: Ypsilon.

Harper, E. C. (1995). Virtue and the state. In K. I. Boudouris (Ed.), *Aristotelian political philosophy* (pp. 79–90). Athens, Greece: Boudouris.

Harvey, D. (2003). *The new imperialism.* Oxford University Press.

Kalimtzis K. (1995). *Aristotle's Theory of Homonoia and the Democratic Institutions in Aristotelian Political Philosophy.* Athens.

Macedo, D., & Gounari, P. (Eds.). (2006). *Globalization of racism.* Boulder, CO: Paradigm.

Macedo, D. (2006). *Literacies of power: What Americans are not allowed to know.* Boulder, CO: Westview Press.

Macedo, D. (2007). In P. McLaren & J. Kincheloe (Eds.), *Critical pedagogy: Where are we now?* (pp.TK). New York, NY: Peter Lang.

MacEwan, A. (2005). Neoliberalism and democracy: Market power versus democratic power. In A. Saad-Filho & D. Johnston (Eds.), *Neoliberalism: A critical reader* (pp. TK). London, England: Pluto Press.

Makris, V. (2009). The dominance of neoliberal ideology in public schooling and possibilities for reconstructing the common good in education. Unpublished Master's thesis. University of Alberta, Edmonton, Canada.

Marcuse, H. (1989). *Counterrevolution and revolt.* Boston, MA: Beacon Press.

McLaren, P., & Kincheloe, J. (Eds.). (2007). *Critical pedagogy: Where are we now?* New York, NY: Peter Lang.

Nikolakaki, M. (ed.). (2011). *Critical Pedagogy In The New Dark Ages: Challenges And Possiblities.* NY: Peter Lang

Oikonomou, Y. (2005). Plato and Castoriadis: The concealment and the unravelling of democracy.*The International Journal of Inclusive Democracy, 2*(1), pagesTK.

Orwell, G. (1949). *Nineteen eighty-four.* New York, NY: Harcourt, Brace and Company.

Polanyi, K. (1957). *The great transformation.* Boston, MA: Beacon Press.

Pykett, J. (2009). Pedagogical power: Lessons from school spaces. *Education, Citizenship and Social Justice, 4*(2), 102–16.

Ronaldi, R. (2008). The movements against poverty. *Diaplous,* August–September. Rousseau, J. (1762). *The social contract.* Amsterdam, TNT: Chez M. M. Rey.

Stavrianos, L. (1976). *The promise of the coming dark age.* San Francisco, CA: Freeman.

Steinberg, S. (2007). In P. McLaren & J. Kincheloe (Eds.), *Critical pedagogy: Where are we now?*(pp. TK). New York, NY: Peter Lang.

Trifonas, P., & Balomenos, E. (2003). *Good taste: How what you choose defines who you are.* Cambridge, England: Icon.

The World Bank Group. (2001). *Administrative and civil service reform.* Retrieved from http://www1.worldbank.org/publicsector/civilservice/center.htm

Wood, E. M. (1995). *Democracy against capitalism.* Cambridge University Press.

9

Critical Pedagogy and the Idea of Communism

Jerrold L. Kachur

All those who abandon [the communist] hypothesis immediately resign themselves to the market economy, to parliamentary democracy–the form of state best suited to capitalism–and to the inevitable and "natural" character of the most monstrous inequalities.

Alain Badiou, 2010a, *The Communist Hypothesis*

Developing critical pedagogy requires conjoining committed adherents in a discourse dedicated to the Idea of communism, formulating and debating ideas about communism and pedagogy, and asserting an intellectual line of argument (inside and outside communist fora) that pragmatically accounts for the problems of *power, authority* and *social change*. This debate assumes an immanent logic in the development of communist ideals and practices and relates to the production of communist theology, world-views, philosophies, historical materialisms and social theories; the identification of political ideologies, identities, and interests; and the formulation of insights on appropriate strategies and tactics. However, there are three key problems in the development of critical pedagogy within a pragmatic communist paradigm related to questions of power, authority and social change. For power there is a tension between personal enlightenment versus social enlightenment; for authority there is the contradiction between enlightenment which presupposes unequal authority) versus egalitarianism which presupposes equal ignorance); and, for the relationship between the theory and practice of communism, there is the transition from a liberal democratic society to a communist society.

According to Jacques Rancière (2010: 166–78), the communist hypothesis is the hypothesis of emancipation intrinsic to the very practices of emancipation and, fundamentally, a pedagogical problem that must be solved before anything worthwhile is worth doing. For him there are two fundamental tensions tearing at the relationship between enlightenment and equality: one between the idea of individual emancipation versus the idea of social emancipation through education; and, two, between the idea of emancipation and the idea of egalitarianism in education.

First, on individual emancipation and social emancipation, Rancière suggests that the key difficulty in answering the question of power is NOT about the inequality of authority but that the communism of intelligence is different than the forms of social implementation of this communism. Rancière (2010: 169) asks:

How far can the communist affirmation of the intelligence of anybody coincide with the communist organization of a society? Emancipation is a form of action transmitted from individuals to individuals and is opposed to the logic of social bodies. Anybody can be emancipated; a society can never be emancipated. How can the collectivization of the capacity of anybody coincide with the global organization of a society?

The communist society will not arise accidently or spontaneously; therefore, it will either not arise at all from a pre-communist society (such as liberal democracy that reproduces itself through the generation of new inequalities) or it will rise in the name of enlightenment but use repressive or oppressive practices that impose themselves on the ignorant with a future promise of an egalitarianism which never comes.

What, then, would the discipline of emancipation look like *as an Idea of communism*? According to Rancière (2010: ibid.), a tension exists between individual communists and the community. The settlement of a social order either (1) erases heterogeneity through the logic of emancipation with respect to the logic of development and erases what is the core of emancipation, that is, heterogenetic forms of individual freedom or (2) undermines the capacity for gaining and transmitting intelligence about the possibility of communism. Disillusion rests on a presupposition: individuals are impotent in gaining the very competence that is required to change the social order without breaking with their egalitarian principle.

Understanding this point in a more concrete way requires the identification of the primary axis of political power is between authoritarianism and anarchism. Neo-communist politics, for example, must address the relationship between a neo-Leninist Left versus neo-anarchist Left that goes back to the Marx-Bakunin split in the 19th century or the split between Red and Green politics in the Germany in the 1970s. In pedagogical debates this tension is represented in debates about the emancipatory possibilities for state-based schooling or institutionalized education. The anti-statist orientation of anarchist in the free-school movement (e.g., Summerhill) and deschooling movement (e.g., Ivan Illich, Walter Mignolo) identifies that individuals or communities should be left to spontaneously localized practices of personal enlightenment.

However, Lenin's critique in *The State and Revolution* identified anarchists as unrealistic and naïve and inherently bourgeois. They cannot accept the necessity of institutions or the cruelty of everyday reality. They fail to understand or condone the progressive necessity of physical and symbolic violence as inherently linked to freedom or the fact that individual persons or local communities (however altruistic with each other) will be unable to defend themselves against more powerful foreign enemies and more institutionally organized territorial aggressors. In authoritarian politics for liberation, the state must be seized, not ignored or evaded. State-based education is transformed for imperatives defined for the communist revolution. Generalized enlightenment as symbolic violence is imposed on a population in need of re-education. Because I have articulated the existence of such a harsh posture on the relationship between politics, violence, emancipation and education today will strike those who were socialized through liberal education as strangely anachronistic or positively evil (i.e. forgetting, of course, that the English Revolution, the American Revolution, and the American Civil War laid the basis for Anglo-American liberal education today).

On a broader scale, in the interests of revolutionary education, the Russian Revolution needs revisiting as an historical record and not as an artefact of Cold War myth. The logic of authoritarianism versus anarchism was reproduced even within communist circles in USSR in the 1920 debates between the Traditional Pavlovians and the Nietzschean Communists over how to remake the new education system. Lenin created The Commissariat of Enlightenment, and through his People's Commissar of Education, Anatoly Lunacharsky, and Deputy Commissar of (Adult) Education, Nadezhda Krupskaya, he initiated a truly revolutionary mass curriculum for the whole population. State-based education broke with elitist Russian traditionalism and

Orthodox mystification and the new system also produced two generations of upward mobility for women, ethnic minorities, and the working class (Fitzpatrick 1970, 1979, 1992). Lenin, thus, pragmatically mediated a middle way through the core paradoxes of institutionalizing enlightenment in renovating Russian schools. Today, important thinkers on education are highly praised for their pedagogical insights, such as Lev Vygotsky and Mikhail Bakhtin; yet, these thinkers are rarely acknowledged as significant *communist* pedagogues in the USSR before Stalinization set in. While the Bolshevik revolution also led to the tragic elevation of the state, Russian chauvinism and many human disasters, the good and bad lessons of communist pedagogy and state reformation should be recovered and re-evaluated.

If analysis moves from the axis of power, another problematic exists for communist pedagogy: the axis of authority relations whereby the relationship between the unequal authority of the enlightened conflicts with the equalizing authority of the ignorant. According to Rancière (2010: ibid.), not only is there a conflict between the idea of individual emancipation versus the idea of social emancipation in education, there is a conflict between the idea of individual enlightenment and individual equality. The emancipation of one's own self-knowledge via self-critique to a higher education as a matter of self-creation (emancipation as enlightenment) can only happen for individuals without the conditions of authority. However, the free conditioning in the development of a community of equals is not a problem for liberals because liberalism justifies a community that reproduces the inequality of property ownership while at the same time supposedly freeing morally equal individuals to compete for a position in the hierarchy they are creating. Because liberalism assumes that the starting and end point is a hierarchy of enlightened authority, there is no paradox in leading the minority culture of the subordinate group (e.g., children) into the majority culture of the community (e.g., adults) so individuals cannot be left to their own means because they may go astray.

Built into the assumption of an individual's emancipation and the logic of Enlightenment is the schoolmaster who starts from the situation of ignorance which belongs to the student and who works to replace ignorance with knowledge, leading the student to science and republican progress. The cultivated elites guide the ignorant and the superstitious onto the path of progress. The promise of equality infinitely reproduces the inequality. The gap separating the intelligence of the master from the intelligence of the ignorant is the knowledge of ignorance. The master's knowledge of ignorance presupposes an in egalitarian principle built into the division of labour, that is, the pedagogical act is necessarily marked by an inequality in knowledge. Here, equality is not the goal; it is a starting point for verification of the potential equality of intelligence between student and master whereby the student's new knowledge is the knowledge of one's own ignorance. Since liberals have only equality of opportunity as a goal, the paradox is not a problem for them in the same way and is built into the very Idea of liberalism as a fact and value in life; however, the Idea of communism demands not merely equality of opportunity to learn but presumes also the precondition of the equality of the learners. The communist pedagogue must claim both (1) the authority to enlighten and presuppose a precondition of unequal authority or (2) claim equality as an ignorant "schoolmaster" and presuppose a precondition with no authority.

As a concrete case today, pedagogues can witness the liberating and detrimental aspects of a liberal education that promotes a child-driven and anti-teacher model based on mobilizing consumer desire for commodities; however, traditional authoritarian models of teacher-directed discipline have fallen out of favour. For students on the margins of power, without an intensive socialization contrary to liberal modes of control, they never develop the discipline to challenge the capitalist system in an organized and systematic way. On the other hand, too much and the wrong kind of authoritarianism can create a weak ego and subordination to capitalist power. On the broader political level, this mirrors the debates between those calling for an enlightened "vanguard" to lead and teach others the hard lessons of history and those calling for all of us to just wait for the "spontaneous" revolution to unfold through the natural intelligence of the population–or, what might be called, the Forrest Gump philosophy of anti-intellectualism popularized by Tom Hanks in the 1994 Hollywood film. Paulo Freire clarifies his position about the tension and falls in line with Marx, Lenin, and Gramsci's critique of authoritarianism and anarchism: "The mythification of popular knowledge, its superexaltation, is as open to challenge as is its rejection. As the latter is elitist, so the former is 'basist'. Still, both elitism and basism, so sectarian in themselves, when taken *in* and *at* their truth become capable of transcending themselves" (Freire and Freire 2004: 71).

The liberal defence of child-driven education infantilizes children and extends infantilization into adulthood in the name of "positive thinking," self-expression, and the self-esteem agenda. The resulting demotion of critique, science, intellect and social resilience increasingly focuses the processes of learning on sustaining mandatory happiness and no longer understands education as the *making* of a substantively informed and intelligently creative and critical person. In this way, the market plays an increasingly important role in defining an "educated" person as one who buys and sells commodities and *is* a commodity (Barber 2007; Ehrenreich 2009). On the other hand, a communist pedagogy that ignores the emotional fulfilment and happiness of children and adults will create a cold-hearted future and terror for the soul.

Rancière (2010: 171–73) captures the problematic. If intelligence is treated as One and does not belong differentially to any single student, legislator, or artisan, emancipation (freedom and equality in community) will mean the appropriation of one intelligence that belongs to all participants as communal property. Emancipation in the communal sense means a communism of intelligence that must be enacted in the demonstration of the capacity of the "incapable": the capacity of the ignorant to learn by herself on her own. In, an extended quotation, he writes:

> The communist hypothesis is the hypothesis of emancipation… [but] we must not forget the historical tension between the two hypotheses. The communist hypothesis is possible on the basis of the hypothesis of emancipation, meaning the collectivization of the power of anyone. It is possible on the basis of the egalitarian presupposition. At the same time, the communist movement -meaning the creation of the communist society as its goal—has been permeated from its inception by the opposite presupposition: the in egalitarian presupposition with its various aspects: the pedagogical /progressive hypothesis about the division of intelligence{…}. The hypothesis of emancipation is a hypothesis of competence. But the development of Marxist science and communist parties mixed it up with its contrary, a culture of distrust on the presupposition of incompetence…[It is illusory to return to the debates of spontaneous freedom versus disciplined organization]. If something has to be reconstructed under the name of communism, it is the form of temporality singularizing the connection of those moments [and of collectivizing the power of the equality of anyone with everyone].

However, the Idea of communist pedagogy has to address Rancière's two contradictions (i.e. a fourfold problematic) regarding (1) enlightened authority versus egalitarian ignorance and (2) personal versus social power in the enlightenment process. In addition, Alessandro Russo (2010: 179–94) identifies a third major contradiction. This third contradiction relates to the *transition* from communist theory within a liberal democratic capitalist society to communist practice for a communist society: that is, there is the conflict between a pedagogy that intends to transition from a non-communist society to a communist society versus developing a pedagogy that lives out the kind of teaching and learning that should exist in a communist society.[1] The third logic evokes the interesting problematic about means and ends, that is, between acting as a communist in the present versus acting in non-communist or liberal ways to bring about the communism in the future. What is the best way to teach communist democracy in a liberal democratic capitalist society?

For example, Paulo Freire has written extensively about the praxis of liberation and could be given a neo-communist turn by emphasizing his quasi-Marxist Left Hegelian Liberation Theology. However, Ronald Glass (2001: 15–25) gives us some indication of the pervasiveness and power of liberal modernity, the Idea of liberalism and how anarchist tendencies in critical pedagogy reproduce bourgeois habits of mind. Glass takes up a liberal line in addressing the problematic of theory and practice with a historical humanist argument for the liberating power of modernism and its critique of dehumanization. He (2001: 15) sees Freire as someone who "recognizes the malleability and contradictions of identity, embraces epistemic uncertainties and the varieties of reason in knowledge, and respects the plural conceptions of the good which can shape moral and political life." Exhibiting anarchist tendencies he naively concludes that liberation education be based on an ethics grounded in militant nonviolence–clearly showing affinity with a kind of weak-kneed liberalism that I have already addressed. Glass simplistically assimilates the anarchist praxis of liberation into radical liberal education for a liberal society without moral standing or commitment to anything beyond liberalism. Such *radicalization* does not lead to socialism or communism because it lacks commitment to any Idea other than liberalism. So where does radical democratic *liberal* education lead us? Peter Berkowitz (2007: 25), a leading *liberal* theorist, makes Lenin's point about the bourgeois connection between liberalism and radicalized liberalism (i.e. anarchism, postmodernism):

> The greatest source of instability in the liberal spirit is the momentum that freedom develops in a free society. ... It dissolves toleration into indifference or neutrality; it dissipates generosity into busy bodiness or bossiness; it unravels reason and leaves in its place creativity and self-assertion; and it collapses enlightened self-interest into petty selfishness. By placing the individual at the center, freedom also creates fertile ground for the growth of age-old vices, particularly narcissism, vanity, and sanctimoniousness. At every turn, the spread of freedom emboldens the liberal spirit's inclination to expose and overthrow claims of arbitrary authority. However, as the claims of freedom themselves acquire authority in a free society, the liberal spirit has difficulty limiting its campaign against authority to that which is arbitrary. With each new success, the liberal spirit comes closer to viewing all authority as arbitrary. Eventually, the liberal spirit turns upon the authority of freedom itself, attacking the very source of its moral standing. Thus does postmodernism arise out of the sources of liberalism.

So, even if the Idea of communism can be resurrected and transmuted from a variety of conservative and liberal conversations from around the world and a variety of different persons and communities, translating the Idea of communism into a theory of critical pedagogy as communist practice has its own specific social logical contradictions which have yet to be worked out.

The error, delusion, fiction or lie in liberal and communitarian (republican) commitments to pedagogical liberation is that working for the equalization of individual or group opportunity is neither necessary nor sufficient in itself to challenge the stratified systems of property ownership, whether it be the capitalist economy, bureaucratic state, patriarchal family or white-supremacist ethnoculture. In fact, in believing that equalizing opportunity is also reducing hierarchical stratification of properties, well-intentioned liberals and communitarians unintentionally work to increase structural inequalities that act through the practical logics of modernity: the logics of capital, violence, sexuality and distinction.[2] However, critical pedagogy must explore the "gap" within and between the suturing of liberal and communitarian commitments to the Idea of education as enlightenment and equality in community to specify an idea of communism and an idea of a "socialist" transition or what Marx called "the lower stage of communism" that can address distributional issues that also challenge the privileges of property, hierarchy and authority.

Furthermore this pedagogy must articulate the emergence of the many past and present moments of singularity as they connect with the communist hypothesis.

However, I pose the eightfold problematic in the Idea of communist pedagogy to suggest that Rancière and Russo seem to assume that the most relevant insights are those that can be garnered from the axis of communist politics that has emerged outside the Anglo-Saxon-Nordic. The potential for an Idea of pragmatic communism that addresses the contradictions specified by Rancière and Russo finds some purchase in attempts to address these struggles within North American liberalism rather than French republicanism (e.g., Cohen 1995; Cunningham 1987; Macpherson 1964, 1973; Sayer 1987). Also, this struggle has been played out in critical pedagogy's failure to inoculate itself against the worst elements of radicalized liberal education.

Due to its unique history and socio-spatial expansion, the US has emerged as a unipolar Empire on the global stage. American liberalism has increasingly dominated thinking about education in Anglo-American countries (e.g., USA, UK, Canada, Australia, NZ, Northern Ireland) as well as having significant influence on global practices through the rule-oriented International Organizations (e.g., WTO, WB, OECD), relationship-oriented bilateralism (e.g., NAFTA, APEC) and various states of exception (e.g., The Velvet and Colour Revolutions, Arab Spring etc.) which it dominates in directing and developing. Responses to critical pedagogy in defence of "democracy" have mirrored the general tendencies of liberal education when asserting it in more radicalized forms instead of developing post-liberal modes, strategies, and tactics of education (e.g., labour, socialist, communist).

The influences of globalization and empire in the semi-core, semi-periphery and periphery provide new opportunities for rethinking critical pedagogy and teaching the core new lessons as long as it recognizes that critical pedagogy has become 1) too micro-politically oriented (i.e. too anti-systemic); 2) too ultra-egalitarian (i.e. anti-elitist and anti-enlightenment); and 3) too anti-authoritarian and anti-authoritative (i.e. too easily genuflecting to "democracy" as a cure all for social ills). In short, it suffers from ultra-leftism, the post-modernized condition of Lenin's infantile disorder.

I recommend four analytical projects for the emerging global intelligentsia of the Left. First, more social theory and historical materialist contextualization and the development of a practical-critical revolutionary consciousness which modifies the critical traditions of Franco-Germanic Republicanism (e.g., Poststructuralism [e.g., Foucault, Deleuze, etc.], Post-marxism [Balibar, Badiou, Rancière, etc.] with an infusion of Anglo-American Marxism oriented toward a revolutionary pragmatic and democratic communism [e.g., Derek Sayer, E. P. Thompson, C. B. Macpherson, G. A. Cohen, etc.]). Second, draw less on liberal postmodernism and beware of its anarchist tendencies, compliance with neocapitalism, and the emergent ideology of imperialist neoliberal cosmopolitanism. Third, draw more on the intellectual resources and cultural understandings of non-liberal and illiberal states and identify their *revolutionary* democratic responses to American domination and hegemony and the expansion of "liberal democracy" in both its domestic, international and geo-regional dimensions (e.g., "Arab Spring"). That is, consider the hegemonic power of Roosevelt's ground rules which organize the post-Cold War global security system along with how inter-civilizational dynamics play themselves out in the struggle between the Anglo-Saxon centre and the Euro, Slavic, Sinic, Indic, Turkic, Arabic, Hispanic, Afro and Indigenous variations of capitalism. And, fourth, develop intellectual institutions for making pragmatic judgements from the core and periphery about the world system with an eye on the selective integration of marginal and minority points of view.

Notes

1. This dilemma raises critical sub-issues about communist means and communist ends as well as about the role of the State and the relationship between political knowledge and philosophical knowledge in the modern political épistème along the three primary dimensions of contemporary political culture: "(i) the

party-state, as the sole seat for politics; (ii) the class-based vision of politics and the state; and (iii) the most decisive figure of the worker into the state" (Russo 2010: 183).
2. These logics and their categorization are debatable. For example, Agnes Heller (1999) argues for three logics of modernity: (1) technology-science; (2) division of social positions, functions, and wealth; (2) political power (domination). Feminist urgings no doubt require considering the logical primacy of sexuality in modernity and patriarchal contradictions in social development: see for example, Pierre Bourdieu (2001) *Masculine Domination*.

References

Badiou, Alain. 2008. *The Meaning of Sarkozy*. English translation by David Fernbach. London and New York: Verso Press.
Barber, Benjamin. 2007. *Consumed: How Capitalism Corrupts Children, Infantilized Adults, and Swallow Citizens Whole*. New York: W. W. Norton.
Berkowitz, Peter. 2007. "The Liberal Spirit in America and Its Paradoxes." *Liberalism for a New Century*. Edited by Neil Jumonville and Kevin Mattson. Berkeley: University of California Press.
Bourdieu, Pierre (2001) *Masculine Domination*. Palo Alto, CA: Stanford University Press.
Cohen, G. A. 1995. *Self-Ownership, Freedom and Equality*. Cambridge: Cambridge University Press.
Cunningham, Frank. 1987. *Democratic Theory and Socialism*. Cambridge: Cambridge University Press.
Ehrenreich, Barbara. 2009. *Bright-sided: How the Relentless Promotion of Positive Thinking Has Undermined America*. New York: Macmillan.
Fitzpatrick, Sheila. 1970. *The Commissariat of Enlightenment: Soviet Organization of Education and the Arts under Lunacharsky, 1917–1921*. Oxford: Oxford University Press.
Fitzpatrick, Sheila. 1979. *Education and Social Mobility in the Soviet Union, 1921–1932*. Cambridge, UK: Cambridge University Press.
Fitzpatrick, Sheila. 1992. *The Cultural Front: Power and Culture in Revolutionary* Russia. Itaca, NY: Cornell University Press.
Freire, Paulo, and Ana Maria Araújo Freire. 2004. *Pedagogy of Hope: Reliving Pedagogy of the Oppressed*. New York: Continuum.
Glass, Ronald. 2001. "On Paulo Freire's Philosophy of Praxis and the Foundations of Liberation Education." *Educational Researcher*, *30*(2), 15–25.
Heller, Agnes. 1999. *A Theory of Modernity*. Oxford, Blackwell.
Losurdo, Domenico. 2011. *Liberalism: A Counter-history*. London: Verso Press.
Macpherson, C. B. 1964. *The Political Theory of Possessive Individualism: Hobbes to Locke*. Oxford: Oxford University Press.
Macpherson, C. B. 1973. *Democratic Theory: Essays in Retrieval*. Oxford: Clarendon Press.
Rancière, Jacques. 2010. "Communists without Communism?" *The Idea of Communism*. Edited by Costas Douzinas and Slavoj Žižek. London: Verso Press.
Russo, Alessandro. 2010. "Did the Cultural Revolution End Communism?" *The Idea of Communism*. Edited by Costas Douzinas and Slavoj Žižek. London: Verso Press.
Sayer, Derek. 1987. *The Violence of Abstraction: The Analytical Foundations of Historical Materialism*. Oxford: Basil Blackwell.

Further Readings

Section 2: Globalization, Democracy, and Education

Allman, P. (2010). *Critical education against global capitalism: Karl Marx and revolutionary critical education.* Rotterdam: Sense Publishers.

Apitzsch, U (ed.) (1993). *Neurath, Gramsci, Williams. Theorien der Arbeiterkultur und ihre Wirkung* (Neurath, Gramsci, Williams. Theories of Workers' Culture and its Effects). Hamburg: Argument Verlag.

Borg, C. and Mayo, P. (2005). Challenges for critical pedagogy: A southern European perspective. *Cultural Studies-Critical Methodologies, 6,* 143–154. doi: 10.1177/1532708605282809

Canaan, J. (2013). Resisting the Neoliberal University: What Critical Pedagogy Can Offer. In *Journal for Critical Education Policy Studies,* v11 n2 p16–56 Mar 2013

Darder, A (2015). *Freire and Education.* New York: Routledge.

Freire, P. (1993). *Pedagogy of the City.* New York: Continuum.

Freire, P. (1998a). *Pedagogy of Freedom: Ethics, Democracy and Civic Courage.* Lanham, MD: Rowman & Littlefield Publishers.

Gatimu, M. W. (2009). Rationale for critical pedagogy of decolonization: Kenya as a unit of analysis. *Journal for Critical Education Policy Studies, 7*(2), 67–97. Retrieved from http://www.jceps.com/

Gezgin, U. B, Inal, K and Hill, D (2014) *The Gezi Revolt: People's Revolutionary Resistance against Neoliberal Capitalism in Turkey,* Brighton: The Institute for Education Policy Studies (www.ieps.org.uk)

Gomez, A. (2004). *La cultura escolar en la sociedad neoliberal.* Madrid: Morata.

Gor, H. (2005). *Critical pedagogy, pedagogy for human rights education.* Paper presented at the International Symposium on Human Rights Education and Textbook Research. Kibbutzim college of Education.

Griffith, T. and R. Imre (2013). *Mass Education, Global Capital and the World.* New York: Palgrave Macmillan.

Guha, R (2009). 'Omaggio a un Maestro' (Homage to a Master). In *Gramsci, le Culture e il Mondo* (Gramsci, Cultures and the World). Schirru G (ed.) Rome: Viella.

Kemal, I. and Akkaymak, G. (eds.) (2012). *Neoliberal Transformation of Education in Turkey Political and Ideological Analysis of Educational Reforms in the Age of the AKP,* New York and London: Palgrave-Macmillan.

Kumar, R. (2012). *Education and the Reproduction of Capital.* New York: Palgrave Macmillan.

Landri, P. (2009). 'Temporary Eclipse of Bureaucracy. The Circulation of School Autonomy in Italy', *Italian Journal of Sociology of Education,* 3, pp. 76–93.

Ledwith, M. (2010). Community work as critical pedagogy: re-envisioning Freire and Gramsci. *Oxford University Press and Community Development Journal, 36*(3), 171–182.

Mancini, F. (1973). 'Worker Democracy and Political Party in Gramsci's Thinking, 'occasional paper, Bologna, School of Advanced International Studies, The Johns Hopkins University.

Magendzo, A. (2005). Pedagogy of human rights education: A Latin American perspective. *Intercultural Education, 16*(2), 137–143. doi: 10.1080/14675980500133549

Mayo, P. (2013). Italian signposts for a sociologically and critically engaged pedagogy. Don Lorenzo Milani (1923-1967) and the schools of San Donato and Barbiana revisited. *British Journal of Sociology of Education*, 1–18. doi: 10.1080/01425692.2013.848781

Milani, L. (1988a). "Letter of Don Lorenzo Milani to the Military Chaplains of Tuscany Who Signed the Communiqué` of 11 February 1965." In *A Just War no Longer Exists. The Teaching and Trial of Don Lorenzo Milani*, edited by J. T. Burtchaell, 18–28. Indiana: University of Notre Dame Press.

Milani, L. (1988b). "Milani's Letter to the Judges." In *A Just War no Longer Exists. The Teaching and Trial of Don Lorenzo Milan*, edited by J. T. Burtchaell, 52–77. Indiana: University of Notre Dame Press.

Nikolakaki, M. (2011). Critical pedagogy and democracy: cultivating the democratic ethos. *Journal for Critical Education Policy Studies, 9*, 48–70. Retrieved from http://www.jceps.com/wp-content/uploads/PDFs/09-1-03.pdf

Nikolakaki, M. (2012). 'Building a Society of Solidarity Through Critical Pedagogy: Group Teaching as a Social and Democratic Tool', *Journal for Critical Education Policy Studies*, Vol. 10 (2) pp. 392–417.

Nikolakaki, M. (2012). 'Critical Pedagogy in the New Dark Ages: Challenges and Possibilities: An Introduction.' In Nikolakaki, M (ed.), *Critical pedagogy in the New Dark Ages. Challenges and Possibilities*, New York-NY, Berne, Vienna, Brussels, Oxford and Frankfurt a M: Peter Lang.

Nuryatno, M. A. (2005). In search of Paulo Freire's reception in Indonesia. *Convergence, 38*, 50–68. Retrieved from http://connection.ebscohost.com/c/articles/27761030/search-paulo freires-reception-indonesia

Nyerere, J.K. (1968). *Freedom and socialism*. Oxford: Oxford University Press.

O'Cadiz, M.., Wong, P. L., and Torres, C.A. (1997). *Education and Democracy. Paulo Freire, Social Movements and Educational Reform in São Paulo*, Boulder CO: Westview.

Papastephanou, M. (2009). *Educated Fear and Educated Hope: Utopia, Dystopia and the Plasticity of Humanity*. Rotterdam, Taipei and Boston: Sense Publishers.

Papastephanou, M. Christou, M and Gregoriou, Z (2013). 'Globalisation, the Challenge of Educational Synchronisation and Teacher Education', *Globalization, Societies and Education* 11 (1), pp. 61–8

Pannu, R.S. (1996). 'Neoliberal project of Globalization: Prospects for Democratisation of Education' in *Alberta Journal of Educational Research*, Vol. XL11, No. 2, pp. 87–101.

Puigvert, L. and Santacruz I. (2006). 'La transformación de centros educativos en comunidades de aprendizaje: calidad para todas y todos.' (the transformation of education centres into communities of learning: quality for all, women and men) *Revista de Educación*. 339, 169–176. [ISI-JCR, Q4]

Rodney, W. (1973). *How Europe Underdeveloped Africa*, London and Dar Es Salaam: Bogle-L'Ouverture Publications.

Rosa, R. and Rosa, J. (2015). *Capitalism's Educational Catastrophe*. New York: Peter Lang.

Schugurensky, D. (2002). 'Transformative Learning and Transformative Politics. The Pedagogical Dimension of Participatory Democracy and Social Action' in, *Expanding the Boundaries of Transformative Learning*, O'Sullivan, E., Morrell, A. and O'Connor, M. (Eds.), New York, Palgrave.

Sousa Santos, B. (2014). *Epistemologies of the South. Justice against Epistemicide*. Boulder/London: Paradigm Publishers.

Sousa Santos, B. (2006). *The Rise of the Global Left. The World Social Forum and Beyond*. London: Zed Books.

Sousa Santos, B. (2002). *Toward a New Legal Common Sense. Law, globalization, and emancipation*. London: Butterworths.

Sousa Santos, B. (1995). *Toward a New Common Sense: Law, Science and Politics in the Paradigmatic Transition*. Nova Iorque: Routledge.

Sousa Santos, B. (2013). *Se Deus fosse um ativista dos direitos humanos*. São Paulo: Cortez Editora.

Sousa Santos, B (1999). "Porque é tão difícil construir uma teoria crítica?", *Revista Crítica de Ciências Sociais*, 54, 197–215.

Shiva, V. (2003). The living democracy movement: Alternatives to the bankruptcy of globalization. In W. Fisher & T. Ponniah (Eds.), *Another world is possible. Popular alternatives to globalization at the World Social Forum* (pp. 115–124). London: Zed Books Books; Nova Scotia: Fernwood Publishers; Malaysia: SIRD; South Africa: David Philip.

Silwadi, N. and Mayo, P. (2014). 'Education Under Siege in Palestine. Insights from Freire', *Holy Land Studies*, Vol. 13 (1), 71–87.

Sotiris, P. (2014). 'The New 'Age of Insurrections' and the Challenges for the Left (Thoughts on the aftermath of the Turkish revolt) in *The Gezi Revolt: People's Revolutionary Resistance against Neoliberal Capitalism in Turkey*, Gezgin, U.B, Inal, K and Hill, D (Eds.), Brighton: Institute for Education Policy Studies.

Sotiris, P. (2013). Reading revolt as deviance: Greek intellectuals and the December 2008 revolt of Greek youth. *Interface, 5*(2), 47–77.

Stoer, S. R. (2008). 'Construindo a escola democrática através do "campo de recontextualização pedagógica'. (Constructing a democratic School through @the field of pedagogical reconstruction) *Educação, Sociedade & Culturas, 26*, 133–147.

Stoer, S. R. (2008). 'A Revolução de Abril e o sindicalismo dos professores em Portugal.' (The April Revolution and the Teachers' Union in Portugal), *Educação, Sociedade & Culturas, 26*, 49–70.

Strech, D (2010). *A New Social Contract in a Latin American Context*, London and New York: Palgrave-Macmillan.

Sunker, H. (2006). Globalization, democratic education (Bildung), educating for democracy. *Journal of International Association for the Advancement of Curriculum Studies, 3*(2), 16–30. Retrieved from http://ojs.library.ubc.ca/index.php/tci/article/viewFile/26/47

Sünker, H. (1997). *Education and Fascism: Political Formation and Social Education in German National Socialism*, London and New York: Routledge.

Sünker, H. (2003). *Politik, Bildung und Soziale Gerechtigkeit. Perspektiven für eine Demokratische Gesellschaft* (Politics, education and social justice. Perspectives for a democratic society), Frankfurt a M.

Sünker, H. (2005). 'How much does Education need the State' in Fischman, G, McLaren, P. Sünker, H and Lankshear C (eds.), *Critical Theories, Radical Pedagogies and Social Conflicts,* Lanham, MD: Rowman & Littlefield.

Suoranta, J., and Vadén, T. (2010). *Wikiworld*. (Revised Edition). London: Pluto Press.

Surian, A (2013) 'Mr. Palomar and Youth 2.0: Beyond the Faustian bargain' in *Italian Journal of Sociology of Education, 5*(1), pp. 82–100

Torres, C.A. (2006). *Pedagogia de la Lucha* (Pedagogy of Struggle). Valencia: Denes Editorial-Edicions del CReC

Torres, C.A. (2010). 'Introdução. La Educación Superior en Tiempos de la Globalización Neoliberal' (Introduction. Higher Education in a time of Neoliberal Globalization' . In Teodoro, A (ed.) *A Educação Superior No Espaço Iberoamericano. Do Elitismo á Trasnacionalização*. Lisbon: Edições Universitarias Lusófona

Torres Santome, J. (2007). *Educación en tiempos de Neoliberalismo*. Madrid: Morata.

Torres Santome, J. (2012). *La justicia curricular: el caballo de Troya de la cultura escolar*. Madrid: Morata.

Ty, R. (2011). Social injustice, human rights-based education and citizens' direct action to promote social transformation in the Philippines. *Education, Citizenship and Social Justice, 6*(3), 205–221. doi: 10.1177/1746197911417413

Ünlü, D (2014). 'Resistance is the Cure' in *The Gezi Revolt: People's Revolutionary Resistance against Neoliberal Capitalism in Turkey*, Gezgin, U.B, Inal, K and Hill, D (Eds.), Brighton: Institute for Education Policy Studies.

Vigilante, A and Vittoria, P (2011). *Pedagogie della Liberazione. Freire, Boal, Capitini, Dolci* (Pedagogies of Liberation. Freire, Boal, Capitini, Dolci), Foggia: Edizioni del Rosone.

Willhauck, S. (2009). Crossing pedagogical borders in the Yucatan Peninsula. *Teaching Theology and Religion, 12*(3), 222-232. Retrieved from http://onlinelibrary.wiley.com/doi/10.1111/j.1467-9647. 2009.00524.x/abstract

Section 3
History, Knowledge, and Power

Colonial education induced attitudes of human inequality, and in practice underpinned the domination of the weak by the strong, especially in the economic field. Colonial education in this country was therefore not transmitting the values and knowledge of Tanzanian society from one generation to the next; it was a deliberate attempt to change those values and to replace traditional knowledge by the knowledge from a different society.

Julius Nyerere, *Education for Self-Reliance* (1967)

[Those in power] mean to try and destroy living tradition in the colonial framework. They believe it lies in their power to give the initial impulse to the nation, whereas in reality the chains forged by the colonial system still weigh it down heavily. They do not go out to find the mass of the people. They do not put their theoretical knowledge to the service of the people.

Frantz Fanon, *The Wretched of the Earth* (1967)

10
Education in Liquid Modernity
(or late modernity)

Zygmunt Bauman

Liquid/late modernity is marked by the global capitalist economies with their increasing privatisation of services and by the information revolution. Bauman, Beck + Giddens maintain (against postmodernists) that modernization continues into the contemp. era change is occurring more + more rapidly) 'modern' world.

Let me start by discussing a few seminal and interconnected departures from the old social order which are currently happening (at least in the 'developed' part of the planet) and which are creating a new and indeed unprecedented setting for the educational process, thereby raising a series of never-before-encountered challenges for the educators.

First of all, society is being transformed by the passage from the 'solid' to 'liquid' phase of modernity, in which all social forms melt faster than new ones can be cast. They are not given enough time to solidify, and cannot serve as the frame of reference for human actions and long-term life-strategies because their allegedly short life-expectation undermines efforts to develop a strategy that would require the consistent fulfilment of a 'life-project.'

The second departure from the past involves the divorce between power and politics, until recently a married couple cohabiting 'till death do us part' the shared household of the nation-state. Power now circulates within the politically uncontrolled global (and in many ways extraterritorial) space. By contrast, politics, that historically-shaped way of linking individual and public interests and of engendering purposeful collective action, remains as before local; as such, it is unable to effectively operate at the planetary level. The absence of political control makes power into a source of pro found and in principle untameable uncertainty; while the dearth of power makes the extant political institutions, their initiatives and undertakings, increasingly irrelevant to citizens' most haunting life-problems and, for that reason, less likely to draw citizens' attention. This situation also prods the state organs to drop, transfer away, or 'subsidiarize' an increasing number of previously performed functions. Having been abandoned by the state and left to the private initiative and care of individuals, those unregulated functions now become a playground for notoriously capricious and inherently unpredictable market forces.

Third, the withdrawal of communal insurance against individual mishaps and ill fortune devalues collective action and indeed the social foundations of solidarity, exacerbating the frailty and impermanence of interhuman bonds. Such an undermined security net hardly seems worthy of a large and continuous investment of time and effort and of the sacrifice of immediate individual interests (or whatever is seen as being in individual interest). Individual exposure to the vagaries of commodities and labour markets inspires and promotes divisions, not unity; it puts a premium on competitive attitudes and degrades collaboration and teamwork to the rank of temporary stratagems that need to be suspended or terminated the moment their benefits have been exploited in full and used up. 'Society' is increasingly viewed and treated as a 'network' rather than 'structure' (let alone a solid 'totality'): it is perceived and treated as a matrix of random connections and disconnections, and of essentially infinite volume of possible permutations.

Fourth, the collapse of long-term thinking, planning and acting—and the disappearance or weakening of social structures in which thinking, planning, and acting could be inscribed for a long time to come—leads to the splicing of both political history and individual lives into series of short-term projects and episodes that do not combine into the logically consistent and cohesive sequences to which concepts like 'development,' 'maturation,' 'career,' or 'progress' (all suggesting a preordained order of succession) could be meaningfully applied. Such fragmentation of human lives stimulates 'lateral' rather than 'vertical' orientations. Any next step needs to be a response to a different set of opportunities and distribution of odds, and so it calls for a different set of skills and arrangement of assets. Past successes do not necessarily increase the probability of future victories, let alone guarantee them; in fact, the methods successfully tested in the past need to be constantly inspected and revised since they may prove useless or downright counterproductive in changed circumstances. Swift and thorough *forgetting* of outdated information and aged habits can be as much or more important for success than the memorizing of past moves and building one's strategies on the hardened and lasting sediment of previous *learning*.

Fifth, the future, now largely out of control and unpredictable, is increasingly turning from a land of hope into a major source of apprehension. Lives of even the happiest people among us (or, by common opinion, the luckiest) are far from trouble-free. Not everything works in life as one would like it to work. Unpleasant and uncomfortable events abound: things and people keep causing worries we would not expect and certainly not wish them to cause. But what makes such discomforts particularly irksome is that they tend to come unannounced. They hit us, as we say, 'as bolts out of the blue'; no one expects a thunderbolt from a cloudless sky, and no one can take precautions against and avert a catastrophe from that which is unexpected. The blows come suddenly, with irregularity; and their nasty ability to appear from anywhere and at any moment makes them unpredictable, and renders us defenseless. Insofar as the dangers are eminently free-floating, freakish, and frivolous, we are their sitting targets—we can do little, if anything at all, to prevent their arrival. Such hopelessness of ours is frightening. Uncertainty breeds fear.

Sixth, the responsibility for resolving the quandaries generated by these volatile and constantly changing circumstances is shifted onto the shoulders of individuals, who are now expected to be 'free choosers' and to bear the consequences of their choices. Every choice involves risks that may be produced by forces transcending the comprehension and active capacity of the individual; nevertheless, it is the individual's lot and duty to take on these risks, as there are no authoritatively endorsed recipes which, if properly learned and dutifully followed, would enable one to avoid error or to transfer blame in case of failure. The virtue proclaimed best to serve individual interests is not *conformity* to rules (which at any rate are few and far between, and often mutually contradictory) but *flexibility*: readiness to change tactics and style at short notice, to abandon commitments and loyalties without regret, and to pursue opportunities according to their current availability rather than following one's own established preferences.

It is time to ask how this set of departures modifies the range of challenges men and women face in their life-pursuits and how it obliquely influences the way people tend to live their lives.

We can say that if the common, indeed 'normal,' premodern posture towards the world was akin to that of a *gamekeeper*, then it is the *gardener* 's attitude that best serves as a metaphor for modern world-view and practice.

The main task of a gamekeeper is to defend the land assigned to his wardenship from (mainly human) interference, in order to defend and preserve its 'natural,' so to speak, balance or equilibrium. The gamekeeper must promptly discover and disable the snares set by poachers and keep alien, illegitimate hunters from trespassing. A gamekeeper's vocation rests on the belief that things are at their best when not interfered with; that the world is a divine chain of being in which every creature has its rightful and useful place, even if human mental abilities are too limited to comprehend the wisdom, harmony, and orderliness of God's design.

Not so the gardener. He assumes that there would be no order at all in the part of the world in his charge were it not for his constant attention and effort; until that effort is undertaken, blind accident will prevail, bringing by chance some felicitous results, but also many numerous regrettable errors. The gardener knows better what kind of plants *should*, and what sort of plants *should not* grow on the plot entrusted to his care. He works out the desirable arrangement first in his head, and then tries, persistently and assiduously, to engrave the image on the plot: to re-make the plot in the likeness of that image. He implants his preconceived vision by the twin efforts of encouraging the growth of the right type of plants and of uprooting and destroying all the others (now renamed 'weeds'), whose uninvited and unwanted presence disagrees with the overall harmony of the design and challenges the very idea of preconceived, planned, and supervised order.

Both postures of the gamekeeper and the gardener are now, in the liquid-modern world, increasingly rare and at best half-hearted, giving ground to that of the *hunter*. Unlike the preceding types, sport hunters could not care less about the overall 'balance of things,' whether 'natural' or contrived. The sole task they pursue is another 'kill,' large enough to fill their game-bags to capacity. Most certainly, they would not consider it their task to make sure that the supply of game roaming in the forest is replenished after being decimated in the course of the hunt. If the woods have been emptied of game due to a particularly successful hunting escapade, sport hunters would rather move swiftly to another relatively unspoiled wilderness, still teeming with prospective hunting trophies. They may be aware that in some distant and still undefined future the planet may run out of virgin forests and undepleted game-havens. This is not, however, an *immediate* worry; and since it won't bear on the results of the current hunts it is surely not *their* worry, and therefore not a prospect about which a single hunter or a single hunting association would see the need to concern themselves and do something.

We are all like game hunters now, or told to be hunters and compelled to act like hunters, on the penalty of eviction from the hunting world; and in case we don't repent and correct our ways, the penalty may mean relegation to the ranks of the game itself. No wonder then that looking around we see mostly other lonely hunters like us, or hunters gathering in packs for the occasion, which we also sometimes try to do. What we practice ourselves, and see other people practicing, is called 'individualization.' We would need to try really hard to spot a gardener who aims at predesigned harmony stretching beyond the fence of his private garden. We certainly won't find a gamekeeper with such vast ambitions (this being the prime reason for people with 'ecological conscience' to feel alarmed and try their best to alert the rest of us). That increasingly salient absence of gamekeepers and gardeners with a wider vision is called 'deregulation.'

As Jacques Attali (2004) recently observed in *La Voie Humaine*, "nations lost influence on the course of affairs and have abandoned to the forces of globalization all means of orientation in the world's destination and of the defence against all varieties of fear.... Individualism is triumphant. No one, or almost no one, believes any longer that changing lives of others has importance for him or her. No one, or almost no one, believes that voting may change significantly his or her condition, and so the condition of the world."

On the rare occasion when the word 'progress' appears these days in the public discourse (or for that matter on the homepages of commercial websites), it no longer refers to a forward drive. Rather than implying a joyful chase after a spinning-along utopia, it inspires fear of an imminent danger and instils the urge of salvation, or rather of lucky escape; it arouses fearful vigilance and cultivates the desire to run away from an impending disaster. Progress seems no longer to be about *improvement*, but about *survival*. Progress is no longer about rushing ahead and winning the race, but about staying on the track. It's not about the rise in stature, but about staving off the fall. It's not about a promotion, elevation, or any other advancement, but about the *avoidance of being excluded*.

We learn, for instance, from the widely read and diligently obeyed glossy magazines, that this coming year Brazil is 'the only winter-sun destination this winter' and so you must avoid being seen where people of aspirations similar to yours were obliged to be seen the winter before. Or that you must 'lose the ponchos' which were so much en vogue last year, since if you wear a poncho now, 'you look like a camel.' Donning pinstripe jackets and T-shirts is over, simply because 'nobody' wears them. And so it goes, if you don't wish to sink, keep surfing; and that means changing your wardrobe, your furnishings, your wallpapers, your look, your habits—in short, yourself—quickly, and as often as you can manage.

I don't need to add, since this should be obvious, that the new emphasis on the *disposal of things*, rather than on their *appropriation*, suits well the logic of a consumer-oriented economy. People sticking to yesterday's clothes, computers, mobiles, cosmetics, and habits would spell disaster for an economy whose main concern and the condition sine qua non of survival is a rapid and accelerating acquisition of purchased products and their subsequent consignment to waste, and for which swift waste disposal is a cutting-edge industry. Increasingly, timely *escape* is now the name of the most popular game in town.

Semantically, escape is the very opposite of early modern utopias, but psychologically it is their sole available substitute: one could say it is their new rendition, refashioned to the measure of a deregulated, individualized society of consumers. You can no longer seriously hope to make the *world* a better place to live; you can't even make really trustworthy and secure that 'relatively better' *place* in the world which you might have managed to cut out for yourself. You are left concentrating your concerns and efforts on the fight against *losing*. The most you can do is to try to stay among the hunters, since the only alternative is to find yourself among the hunted. And the fight against losing is a task that requires your full, undivided attention—vigilance twenty-four hours a day, seven days a week—and keeps you moving as fast as possible.

Joseph Brodsky (1997), the Russian-American philosopher-poet, vividly described the kind of life set in motion and prompted by the compulsion to escape. The lot of the *losers* (that is, of the poor) is sometimes a violent rebellion, but more commonly drug addicion: "In general, a man shooting heroin into his vein does so largely for the same reason you buy a video," Brodsky told the students of Dartmouth College in July 1989. As to the potential winners (or the 'haves'), which the Dartmouth College students aspire to be, you'll be bored with your work, your spouses, your lovers, the view from your window, the furniture or wallpaper in your room, your thoughts yourselves. Accordingly, you'll try to devise ways of escape. Apart from the self-gratifying gadgets mentioned before, you may take up changing jobs, residence, company, country, climate, you may take up promiscuity, alcohol, travel, cooking lessons, drugs, psychoanalysis....

In fact, you may lump all these together, and for a while that may work. Until the day, of course, when you wake up in your bedroom amid a new family and a different wallpaper, in a different state and climate, with a heap of bills from your travel agent and your shrink, yet with the same stale feeling toward the light of day pouring through your window.

Andrzej Stasiuk (2002), a remarkable Polish novelist and perceptive analyst of the contemporary human condition, suggests that 'the possibility of becoming someone else' is the present-day substitute for a now largely discarded and dismissed salvation or redemption. "Applying various techniques, we may change our bodies and re-shape them according to different patterns.... When browsing through glossy magazines, one gets the impression that they tell mostly one story—about the ways in which one can remake one's personality, starting from diets, surroundings, homes, and up to rebuilding of psychical structure, often code-named a proposition to 'be yourself.' " Stawomir Mrożek (2003), Polish satirist of a worldwide fame, seems to endorse and complement Stasiuk's hypothesis: "In old times, when feeling unhappy, we accused God, the then world's manager; we assumed that He did not run the business properly. So we fired Him and appointed ourselves the new directors." But, Mrożek suggests, the change of management has not improved the business. Once the dream and hope of a better life had been re-focused on our own egos and reduced to tinkering with our own bodies or souls, "there is no limit to our ambition and temptation to make that ego grow ever bigger.... I was told: 'invent yourself, invent your own life and manage it as you wish, in every single moment and from beginning to end.' But am I able to rise to such a task? With no help, trials, fittings, errors and overhauls, and above all without doubts?" The strife produced by unduly limited choice of one painful option or another is caused by the obligation to choose while having no trust in the choices made, and no confidence that further choices will bring the target any closer. Mrożek compares the world we inhabit to a "market-stall filled with fancy dresses and surrounded by crowds seeking their 'selves.' ... One can change dresses without end, so what a wondrous liberty the seekers enjoy.... Let's go on searching for our real selves, it's smashing fun—on condition that the real self will be never found. Because if it were, the fun would end."

The dream of making uncertainty less daunting and happiness more permanent by changing one's ego, and of changing one's ego by changing one's dress and other wrappings, has become the current 'utopia' of hunters: the 'deregulated,' 'privatized,' and 'individualized' version of the old-style vision of a good society understood as a society hospitable to the humanity of its members.

Hunting is a fulltime task: it consumes a lot of attention and energy; it leaves time for little else; and so it averts attention from the infinite task and postpones *ad calendas graecas* the moment of reflection in which the sheer impossibility of the task at hand needs to be faced point blank. As Blaise Pascal (1966) centuries ago prophetically noted, what people want is "being diverted from thinking of what they are ... by some novel and agreeable passion which keeps them busy, like gambling, hunting, some absorbing show. We want to escape the need to think of "our unhappy condition," and so "we prefer the hunt to the capture." "The hare itself would not save us from thinking" about the formidable but intractable flaws in our shared condition, "but hunting it does so."

The snag is that once tried, the pursuit of prey turns into compulsion. Catching a hare is an anticlimax; it only makes the prospect of hunting more seductive even as the desire to hunt becomes an obsession. The hopes that accompanied the pursuit seem in retrospect to have been the most delightful (the only really satisfactory) gain of the affair. Catching the hare presages the end to those hopes, that is, unless another hunt is immediately planned and undertaken.

If early modern utopias envisaged a point in which time will come to a stop (indeed, the end of time as history), there is no such point in the hunter's life, no moment where one would say in clear conscience that the job has been completed, the mission accomplished. In a society of hunters, a prospect of an end to hunting is frightening—since it may arrive only as a personal defeat. The horns will go on announcing the start of another hunting escapade; the greyhounds will go on barking and resurrecting the sweet memory of past chases; everyone around will go on hunting; there will be no end to universal excitement. Only *I* will be left standing or pushed aside, excluded and no longer wanted, barred from other people's joys: just a passive spectator on the other side of fence, watching the party but forbidden or unable to join the revellers, enjoying the sights and sounds of revelry at best from a distance and by proxy.

If a life of continuing and continuous hunting is another utopia, it is—contrary to the utopias of the past—a utopia of *no* end. A bizarre utopia indeed, if measured by orthodox standards. The original utopias promised the end to the toil; but the hunters' utopia encapsulates the dream of a toil never ending. Strange, unorthodox utopia it is—but utopia all the same, as it promises the same unattainable prize all utopias brandished, namely the ultimate and radical solution to human problems past, present, and future, and the ultimate and radical cure for the sorrows and pains of the human condition. It is unorthodox mainly for having moved the land of solutions and cures from the 'far away' into 'here and now.' Instead of living *towards* the utopia, hunters are offered a living *inside* the utopia.

For the gardeners, utopia was the *end of the road*; for hunters, however, it is *the road itself.* Gardeners visualized the end of the road as the vindication and the ultimate triumph of utopia. For the hunters, the end of the road would be the utopia's final, ignominious defeat. Adding insult to the injury, it would also be a thoroughly personal defeat and proof of personal failure. Other hunters won't stop hunting; and non-participation in the hunt can only feel like personal exclusion, and so (presumably) personal inadequacy. Utopia brought from the misty 'far away' into the tangible 'here and now,' utopia *lived* rather than being *lived towards*, is immune to tests (there can be always another trial, and another trial after that .. .). For all practical intents and purposes, this utopia seems to be immortal. But its immortality has been achieved at the price of frailty and vulnerability of each one who has been enchanted and seduced to live in it.

Unlike the utopias of yore, the hunters' utopia does not offer a meaning to life—whether genuine or fraudulent. It only helps to chase the question of life's meaning away from the mind of living. Having reshaped the course of life into an unending series of self-focused and self-referential pursuits, each episode lived through as an overture to the next, it offers no occasion for reflection about the direction and the sense of it all. When (if) finally such an occasion comes, at the moment of falling out or being banned from the hunting life, it is usually too late for the reflection to bear on the way life is shaped, and so too late to oppose its present shape and effectively dispute its propriety.

So where does this leave education and its practitioners? I suggest that the sole imaginable answer to such a question has been put into Marco Polo's lips by the great Italo Calvino (1974) in *Le Citt`a Invisibile*:

> The inferno of the living is not something that will be: if there is one, it is what is already here, the inferno where we live every day, that we form by being together. There are two ways to escape suffering it. The first is easy for many: accept the inferno and become such a part of it that you can no longer see it. The second is risky and demands constant vigilance and apprehension: seek and learn to recognize who and what, in the midst of the inferno, are not inferno, then make them endure, give them space.
>
> (my translation)

> L'inferno dei viventi non e` qualcosa che sara`; se ce n'e` uno e` quello que e` gia` qui, l'inferno che abitiamo tutti i giorni, che formiamo stando insieme. Due modi ci sono per non soffrirne. Il primo riesce facile a molti: accettare l'inferno e diventarne parte fino al punto di non vederlo piu` . Il secondo e` rischioso ed esige attenzione e apprendimento continui: cercare e saper riconoscere chi e cosa, in mezzo all' inferno, non e` inferno, e farlo durare, e dargli spazio.
>
> (p. 164)

It is a contentious matter whether living in a society of hunters is or is not like living in hell (most hunters will tell you that being a hunter among hunters has its blissful moments). It is hardly contentious, however, that 'many' will go for the 'easy' strategy and so become 'part of it,' no longer puzzled by its bizarre logic nor irritated by its ubiquitous and mostly fanciful demands. Also beyond doubt is the prospect that the educators who seek for 'what and who is not hell' would face a daunting task when wishing to gain the attention and arouse the vigilance of their pupils, and would find themselves under all sorts of pressure to accept the 'inferno' and, moreover, help their pupils to make the application of the 'easy for many' life-strategy still easier yet.

Let us recall that, according to Gregory Bateson (1987), 'tertiary learning' (which trained the skills of dismantling the previously learned cognitive frames) would make learners akin to plankton, carried by random waves and unable to adhere to anything to resist the tide. In this way, tertiary learning is at cross-purposes with the 'deutero-learning,' which in Bateson's view could make the learners able to 'build upon a firm foundation,' adding new knowledge to the already acquired volume and thereby enabling the pursuit of the selected trajectory under any, even the most volatile, circumstances. If deutero-learning could make the learners creative and their conduct autonomous, tertiary learning was bound to make them confused and their behaviour heteronomous. Tertiary learning left no lasting sediment, no firm foundation on which to build, and no knowledge fit for accumulation and growth over the course of study. The process of tertiary learning (if one can speak at all of a 'process' in such a case) was an unending succession of new beginnings, moved more by a swift forgetting of the previously acquired knowledge than by an acquisition of new knowledge; it militated against retention and memorizing. Tertiary knowledge was, one could say, an 'anti-memory' contraption. It is for such reasons that Gregory Bateson saw 'tertiary learning' as a pathology, a cancerous growth bound to eat into the body of education and—if not excised—leading to its demise.

However, the assumption on which Bateson's verdict was resting holds true no more; under the liquid-modern condition it has, so to speak, become 'counterfactual.' Tertiary learning might have looked pathological, hovering on the brink of madness and appearing potentially suicidal, if we had first accepted the assumption that the notoriously volatile and relatively brief individual life is inscribed in a stable and long-lasting world. In liquid-modern surroundings, however, the relation between life and the world has been reversed. It is now the opposite assumption which feels more acceptable: that of a longish individual life dedicated to its survival in frail and volatile settings through a series of successive 'new beginnings.' In the light of such new experiential evidence, Bateson's verdict is no longer safe, and seems ready to be quashed—if not yet by the educators sitting in judgment, called to the bench with the instruction to observe that the law is done, than by the jury, meant (and presumed) to represent the current mood and common sense of the public.

The practitioners of a life sliced into episodes, each with its new beginning and abrupt ending, have little use for an education that aims to equip its objects for an unchanging world (or at least for a world moving at a slower pace than the knowledge required to grasp and reveal its momentum). Hunters live from one hunting escapade to another, moving from one forest to another; we all live, as Luc Boltanski and Eve Chiapello (1999) convincingly demonstrated, through projects and by projects, moving from one project to another, to the projects-yet-to-come, undetermined by the projects already passed through. Don't mind the breath-taking speed with which knowledge is changing tack, old knowledge is aging, and new knowledge is born only to start aging right away; the volatility of the disjointed, poorly integrated, and multi-centred liquid- modern world makes it certain that each successive episode of a life-through-projects will call for another set of skills and information, invalidating the skills already acquired and the information already memorized (as it will surely be shown to no avail). Loading oneself with information, absorbing and retaining information, struggling for a completeness and cohesion of the information stored—it all looks suspiciously like offering oneself as a dumping site for prospective waste, and thus like an outrageous waste of time.

Images of the world in general, and of human consciousness in particular, tend to be *praxeomorphic*: it is *what we can do* thanks to the technology we use, and particularly to the newest, 'state-of-the art,' 'cutting edge' technology; this most recently acquired technology works surreptitiously as a metaphorical frame for the understanding of human mind. It is when (and because) the freshly invented, adopted, and mastered technology is applied to the description of the mind's working that we experience the gratifying revelation of 'eureka!'—'now we understand!' Since the beginning of modern science (that is, the beginning of the technology-run era), the progress of philosophical and scientific models of human consciousness ran parallel with the progress of technology, following closely the successive breakthroughs in technologically framed praxis. In the position of 'the last words of science,' mechanical models were succeeded by chemical, electric, cybernetic, and electronic models.

It is no wonder therefore that the latest model offered today for scientific acceptance and quickly gaining wide recognition is Daniel C. Dennett's idea that the 'mind's unloading' (first elaborated in *Kinds of Minds Towards an Understanding of Consciousness*, 1997) is the prime moving force in the historical development of the human mind and its capacity. As could be expected in the era of computers, Dennett's version downplays the role of the 'hardware' (that is, of the human brain, already fully formed well before the mind's explosion started) while assigning the principal role to the 'soft- ware' (that is, to the socio-cultural uses to which humans have managed to put their brains). The most symptomatic innovation in Dennett's story is, however, the role imputed to the ways and means of storing information *outside* the brain (let us note that this is precisely the function for which the advent of computers brought a genuinely revolutionary advance). In Dennett's version of the rise of human intelligence and mental capacity, it is not the production, assimilation, and retention of knowledge by 'biological humans' that has marked the progress of human mental powers, but the *un-burdening of brains* through the expedient of storing information in technological artifices, from the most primitive stone tools up to the most capacious servers and worldwide web of computers.

Dennett's model implies that human intelligence is improved, and the human brain's potential is better used, for the vacation of the brain's contents and the squeezing-out of information away from the 'natural' warehouse made of brain cells. Having dislodged knowledge that otherwise would clog it and severely constrain its processing powers (the volume of knowledge which the brain can absorb, just like the volume which a single PC can accommodate, is at any rate irrevocably limited by the capacity, respectively, of the brain's tissues or hard drive), the human brain needs to retain only a relatively small set of 'indices' and 'clues'; this would be enough to allow humans access to the virtually unlimited amounts of information lodged away from the brain in the artifices scattered all over the human-made world. With the help of indices and clues, small and manageable samples of information, appropriate to the current problem which the mind is aiming to tackle, can be time and again retrieved—only to be returned to the external storage devices once the problem in question has been solved, thereby freeing the brain's capacity again for another batch of information required by the next problem or task.

One cannot vouch for Dennett's scheme to be the final, incontrovertible, and incontestable version of the history of human mind (prudence would advise to suspend the verdict until another technological revolution in human praxis takes shape, as it most probably will, sooner or later). What is however highly credible is the guess that Dennett's scheme faithfully reflects contemporary knowledge handling-and-deploying practices, and for that same reason its suggestions seem at the moment to most of us quite convincing, perhaps even self-evident.

A number of other credible implications follow. Instead of an image of an edifice erected floor by floor, from the foundations up to the roof, signalling the completion of building, it is better to think of knowledge as offered and consumed in small bites, each one separately cooked and quickly chewed and digested, and then just as quickly vacated from the digestive track, clearing the space for further portions. It is better as well not to think of the whole intake as ordered in any specific menu-like sequence (for instance, the main course preceded by hors d'oeuvres and followed by dessert), but of the successive morsels consumed in a random succession, each time improvised anew according to the needs of the moment. Further, it is better to think of knowledge production and consumption after the pattern of fast food, prepared rapidly and eaten fresh, hot, and on the spot, rather than in terms of haute cuisine's meticulous composition and laborious cooking of dishes that need a long time of rest and settle before being fit for consumption. Finally, it is currently better to think of every food on offer as a product with an admittedly short shelf-life and a clearly printed 'use-by' date. Expeditious removal from shop shelves of the pieces that have 'expired' is equally important as, perhaps even more important than, their timely inclusion in the assortment of foods on offer.

All this militates against the very essence of school-centred education, known for its predilection for a stiff curriculum and predetermined succession of learning. In a liquid-modern setting, centres of teaching and learning are subjected to a 'de-institutionalizing' pressure and prompted to surrender their loyalty to 'canons of knowledge' (whose very existence, not to mention utility, is increasingly cast in doubt), thus putting the value of flexibility above the surmised inner logic of scholarly disciplines. Pressures come from above (from the governments eager to catch up with the volatile and capricious shifts in 'business needs') as much as from below (from prospective students exposed to the equally capricious demands of labour markets and bewildered by their apparently haphazard and unpredictable nature). Another factor, the loss by teaching establishments of their past monopoly on the office of gatekeepers of knowledge and the subsequent sharing of that office (or competing for it) with market suppliers of computer software, adds force to the above mentioned pressures.

A most prominent effect of the above pressures on the theorists and practitioners of education is the marked shift of emphasis from 'teaching' to 'learning'. Transferring to individual students the responsibility for the composition of the teaching=learning trajectory (and, obliquely, for its pragmatic consequences) reflects the growing unwillingness of learners to make long-term commitments that constrain the range of future options and limit the field of manoeuver. Among the conspicuous effects of de-institutionalizing pressures are the 'privatization' and 'individualization' of the teaching-learning settings and situations, as well as a gradual yet relentless replacement of the orthodox teacher-student relationship with the supplier-client, or shopping-mall-shopper pattern.

This is the social setting in which today's educators find themselves bound to operate. Their responses, and the effectiveness of the strategies deployed to promote them, are likely to remain a paramount concern of pedagogical science for a long time to come.

References

Attali, J. (2004). *La voie humaine* (pp. 9–10). Paris: Fayard.

Bateson, G. (1987). *Steps to an Ecology of Mind: Collected Essays in Anthropology, Psychiatry, Evolution, and Epistemology*. Jason Aronson Inc.

Boltanski, L. and Chiapello, E. (1999). *Le nouvel e`sprit du capitalisme* (pp. 143).

Brodsky, J. (1997). *On Grief and Reason: Essays* (pp. 107–8). Farrar, Strauss, and Giroux.

Calvino, I. (1974). *Le citta` invisibile*. Giulio Enaudi Editore.

Dennett, D. C. (1997). *Kinds of Minds: Towards an Understanding of Consciousness*. Basic Books.

Mrożek, S. (2003). *Male listy (Little Letters)* (p. 184, 273). Noir sur Blanc.

Pascal, B. (1966). *Pensees* (pp. 67–68). A. J. Kreilsheimer (transl.), Penguin.

Stasiuk, A. (2002). *Tekturowy samolot (Cardboard Aircraft)* (pp. 59–60). Wydawnictwo Czarne.

11
Images Outside the Mirror?
Mozambique and Portugal in World History

Maria Paula Meneses

Não vamos esquecer o tempo que passou,
Quem pode esquecer o que passou?

We will not forget the time that passed.
Who can forget what passed?

Popular revolutionary song of Mozambique

One cannot only listen to the tale of the hunter;
The lion has its version too.

African proverb

The history of Africa has been marked by the devaluing of memories—in the plural—where the past acquires similar forms to the future, full of problems and populated with dense silences. The crises of time—when it seems that one does not have time for memories—do not occur only because of the increasingly dominant presence of neoliberal globalization; they also derive from a present replete with amnesias. Further, they are connected to the crises of singular explanations of the world, the crisis of the meta-narrative in history, specifically regimes of totalitarian power that sought to control the regimes of memory in a centralized manner.

Strategies of colonial interpretation of post-colonial situations operate by essentially trying to conserve an explanation that justifies and does not challenge the underlying colonial presence in the knowledge produced. Even today, years after achievements of political independence, the countries of the African continent are often identified as Lusophone, Francophone or Anglophone. The exceptionality of these countries draws from their 'belonging' to an old colonial project, relentlessly present in their foundation, erasing other histories or exceeding them—the ubiquitous link to Portugal.[1]

But colonialism is a confrontation of different societies, each with its own memory. The Portuguese colonial ideology, seemingly monolithic and supported by expansionist practices, regarded the mass of African social formations—each having different and often particular memories, competing with each other—as a single entity, binding them together. This pitiful picture persists and is reproduced in many ways (Meneses 2010a). What has actually changed, if anything?

One can no longer speak of a single macro-narrative, of only one interpretation of history. In other words, the problem operates inside of a 'single analytical field' and is seen only at the discursive level. The issues, the scale, and the location of these places remain unresolved. And this brings back the question of decolonization.[2] This thorny concept claims for a broader reconceptualization of the ruptures associated with the end of political colonization. Did the representations of the colonial world change the same way both in the former colonies and in the metropoles?

Europe planted its memory in the very core of Africa. This phenomenon is not particularly European; rather, is in the nature of all colonial conquests and systems of foreign occupation. Attempting to (re)create the land and its people, to reconfigure the territory, the Portuguese, like other colonizers, asserted their right to name the land and its subjects, demanding that the subjects accept the names, references, culture and history of the conqueror (Thiong'o 2009:9). Thus, one must question why there is such a resistance to opening up the canon of macro-history, the macro- narrative of world history. As several people interviewed in Mozambique would state, it does not make sense to exist with- out remembering the past and without imagining the future; questioning from where we came and to where we will go. Walter Benjamin writes that memory "*is not an instrument for exploring the past, but rather a medium*" to do so (1999:576). Memory is essential to constructing an identity, that of an individual as much as that of a collective. To starve or destroy memories results in liquidating the past, the history that binds people together, that makes them what they are.

To impose a single history is to impose the weight of experiences it carries and its conceptions of self and otherness—indeed, the weight of its memory, which includes several factors, such as religion and education.[3] The signs of this project can be traced everywhere, especially in claiming the memory or memories of collective pasts which, being unique, are distinct from a single and vague general past. The quality of being unique is not allowing them/others to identify with us. While the persistent routes of nationalisms are not always healthy in their principles and intentions, they at least signify that the situation of amnesia generates much conflict when imposed on a global scale, as Aquino de Bragança and Jacques Depelchin once anticipated (1986) when analyzing the construction of Mozambican history after the country's independence.

This, in part, signifies that we remain involved in the search for other parts of history/histories, of other people/peoples, facts, and other institutions that are silenced and almost erased. This is a sign of the continuation of the struggle for liberation, against amnesia, against attempts at silencing. Again, one needs to cautiously approach the relationship between forgetting, these intentional memory lapses and the work of the ethnographic collection undertaken by Africanist researchers, by ethnographers that fill the infinite shelves of the colonial library. The practices of producing knowledge about the African continent were, in actuality, guided by objectives designed to operate and legitimize one determined project: the colonial mission (Meneses 2008). Possibly one central problem of this work has not been failing to develop some conceptual aspects such as rituals, magic, fetishism, paternalism, and the traditional local authorities, but the reaffirmation of tradition, of a primal space and the continent's inescapable mark of delay. This is not to argue that the colonial archives cannot be used, quite the contrary. They should be used with necessary precautions that analytically take their potential biases into consideration. Accentuating tradition impedes us from seeing and questioning the problems of a Mozambican working class that has been present for more than a century,[4] and the dilemmas it confronts with the current economic crisis. Emphasizing the study of rural tradition prevents us from analyzing and conceptualizing the urban complexity of many African countries. Or rather, we risk making them immune to the modernization that also happens within these spaces and within the present. We risk making them immune to discussing the implication of authoritarian regimes in situations of multiparty, of the implication of cultural 'uprootings,' etc. The present, which constructs narratives about the past, is also worth celebrating.

Mozambique: The Struggle Continues

The nationalist struggle in Mozambique, as in other contexts, brought about the need to reconstruct the history, confronting the dominant colonial narrative. In short, independence called for a reanalysis of the histories, now in the plural.

The end of authoritarian narratives does not necessarily mean that delayed realities remain incompatible with time forever, or even worse, suspended outside of it. It is not a synonym for the end of history because whatever existing society is, it is part of time. On June 25, 1975, Mozambique woke up independent, with a sense of urgency regarding the reconstruction of its history. As we sang at the time, "*we will not forget the time that passed*." A current challenge is the recuperation and the production of memories. Identities were created and political alliances forged, to give a meaning to life and to help explain the importance of fighting Portugal's colonial-fascist presence in Mozambique.

Colonial relations came in many forms, such as conquest, rebellions, religious missions, scientific exploration, education, medical services, commerce and economic exploitation, voyages, art, etc. In addition to the absolute denial of the colonized, colonial relations, often marked by domination and violence, are also characterized by multifaceted processes of appropriation. There were numerous forms of appropriation, such as religions, economics, demographic, political, linguistic, artistic, intellectual, etc. With different intensities in space and time, these appropriations and (re)creations generated contradictions and conflicts throughout this process. Although asymmetrical, any process of appropriation encompassed a double relationship. This aspect is extraordinarily important because it reveals how colonization describes situations of political control over a given territory by a foreign force with objectives to incorporate and exploit it. Colonization hence goes much further than the restricted meanings we sometimes use to discuss the subject. Secondly, questioning these colonial relations in our time opens the subject to perceiving the ruptures and continuities of the colonial relation. If decolonization is a political relationship, as a political process it impacts upon the multiple parts involved in the colonial relation, now confronted with a dramatic change of power relations. Analyzing the Mozambican reality, Aquino de Bragança would dare to affirm that the power transfer occurred without any impositions from Portugal. Thus, the Mozambican case could mean the possibility of a political transition without the weight of the neocolonial relationships usually attached to it (Bragança 1986).

In this context, to speak of colonial legacies is to recognize, firstly, that colonial relationships contributed to formatting any history, suggesting that this relationship persists in how the world is perceived today—even though this legacy is not always recognized in a legal or cognitive sense by its potential heirs. This means that what remains in the past is more than a memory. To question the place of memories implies questioning the place where we inquire into the memories about ourselves. Portugal's colonization of the African continent can be analyzed in terms of how the situation impacted the regions[5] and where the process took place and by examining how the very meaning of being European was objectively [6] and subjectively constructed by the colonial experience. Within colonial juridical thought, the concept of Portuguese citizenship does not refer to an abstract category—quite the contrary.

Portuguese citizenship identified a specific, socially concrete, and moral standard: it applied only to white men and women born in Portugal, well-educated and wealthy, the "*genteel soul of colonization*." In such a manner, to be European became a category that defined a status and deter- mined these relationships. To be European came to mean being part of a certain geopolitical strategy of power, a space dominated by a modern rationality which wore the color white.

Part of this reflection reflects my place of questioning. As a Mozambican researcher working in Portugal, my perspective on contemporary Portuguese society begins its interrogation from spaces that are most familiar and from my places of belonging, Mozambique. These reflections also reflect my path, my commitment to research in the field of social sciences. The political turbulence of the 1970s and the 1980s in Mozambique was informed by scholarship, including empirical analysis, debates about agency and intervention, philosophy and history. It also included scholarly and activist publications (Borges Coelho, 2007). A peculiar aspect of this knowledge production was the fact that many of the persons involved in its production were not professionally trained academics. Still, it became possible to bring other voices, other problematics to the process of decolonizing Mozambique and freeing the country from the weight of colonial history.

Portugal and Mozambique shared places with each other but they hardly share memories. It might be more adequate to say that they have shared silences and a lack of contact. In the more than three decades since its independence, Mozambique has come to grasp the difficulties that recognizing this aspect of sharing entails. This awareness raises very complex questions inherent to the memory of the relationship between the colonized and the colonizer. Beyond historiography of a common period, it would be more precise to speak of two historical macro-narratives developed upon a common denominator within the same territory and the same conflict: a macro-narrative about a colonial war in the final era of the Portuguese imperial colonization,[7] and another one, seen from the Mozambican side, about the process that led to the national independence of Mozambique.

These two histories have distinct paths that were influenced by the social memory of what 'happened' and by how it was politically generated. Working now as a researcher in Portugal, it has been a curious transition from forgetting the 'omitted' to a growing presence of this relationship and sharing. Yet even here, no one speaks of the reasons behind this war. Very few seek to understand why the war has two names that reflect different paths and different interpretations. After all, when did the colonial war begin? What was the colonial war? Why is it said to have started only in 1960 when all who ponder over this theme have 'other' colonial wars in mind? The 'other' colonial wars date back to the very end of the 19th century and the early 20th century and were at the time called "*campaigns of occupation.*"[8]

In the south of Mozambique, where the military campaign was against the state of Gaza, the struggle ended at the very end of the 19th century (Albuquerque 1935; Ennes 2002). When the Portuguese finally imprisoned the head of Gaza state, Ngungunyane, they condemned him—together with his closest political advisors—a life of exile in the Azores, that is, in Portugal. Ngungunyane died there, in semi-captivity, without ever being submitted to trial. A thread of violence connects these violent campaigns with the final stage of the colonial presence of Portugal in Mozambique, in the 1960s. There are shared moments united by distinct memories; they rest upon the thin lines that link the military vehicles, the 'Chaimites,'[9] which occupied parts of Lisbon, on the dawn of the coup d'etat of April 25th—and which came to symbolize the liberation from the colonial dictatorship in Portugal—to the war against the state of Gaza.

The fate of Ngungunyane—simultaneously acts of triumph and humiliation—embodies the colonial relationship between Portugal and Mozambique (Meneses 2010b). This colonial act was both a practice of power, intended to pacify a populace, and a performance of power intended to produce docile minds. The fate of Gaza state also symbolized the dismemberment of the colonial subjects from the individual and collective body. The colonial fracture, represented in the exile of Ngungunyane, was characterized by dismemberment and omission of former political structures, by the attempt to bury all the memories these subjects carried.

On the other side, in Mozambique, the quest for memory has followed a different path. Or rather, from a strong remembrance of Portugal as a symbol of the colonial relation aimed at creating a sense of national unity,[10] people have been sliding toward forgetting.

Throughout most of its short history, the Mozambican state has pursued a nation-building policy that includes the political adoption of an official history grounded in a set of public (and intensely publicized) memories about its colonial past, both recent and distant (Meneses 2007a).

The Mozambican state has thereby sought to eliminate, silence or make invisible the diversity of memories generated by the complex social interactions between the colonizers and colonized over the long period of Portuguese colonialism. Soon after independence, FRELIMO,[11] the leading political force in the country, carried out a complex political strategy that sought to deal with the ambivalent and hybrid identities that constitute the intricate colonial legacy. To put an end to all forms of possible continuities with the colonial past, the target of this policy became those caught in 'transition,' i.e., the *'collaborators'*—a rather diverse group that is rarely spoken of, if not virtually omitted (the estimated size of the group is 100,000 people).[12] The *'collaborators'* were accused of having collaborated with the colonial system, up to the independence of Mozambique; FRELIMO's politics of memory was founded upon the idea of "*not forgetting the time that passed.*" This strategy aimed "*to transform the collaborators based on presumption of guilt, repentance, punishment and re-education*" (Coelho 2003:191). In the aftermath of this political process, in the early 1980s, most of the 'collaborators' were recognized as politically re-educated and accepted as full citizens. Their subsequent rehabilitation was obtained at the cost of erasing their past from the public sphere and treating it as a past that was to be kept a private, silenced memory.

The guerrilla nationalist was projected as the icon of the truly Mozambican citizen, the model of the 'new man.' The myth of the guerrilla nationalist was created as an attempt to generate new political identities during the first years of independence. Mozambique was cast as being made up of two main groups: those who had fought for independence and the others who made up the mass majority of Mozambican society. These moments of hierarchization after independence derived from the necessity to "*limit the electoral capacity of the citizens who were committed to fascist colonialism.*"[13]

The category of second-class citizens included many of those whom FRELIMO identified as having been allies or supporters of the Portuguese colonial presence (Meneses 2007b). Shortly after independence, FRELIMO sought to overcome the separation thus created between those deemed to be 'collaborators' and the 'Mozambican population.' In 1977–78, the first signs of a political strategy seeking to deal with the memory of these colonial connections emerged. Samora Machel, then the president of Mozambique, had not opted to form a Truth and Reconciliation Commission. He addressed this issue in several speeches, culminating in an important public meeting in 1982. The multiple meetings and the integration processes for the 'collaborators' can be seen as an unofficial Truth and Reconciliation Commission, which sought to elucidate, clarify, and offer knowledge about the coplexity of these Mozambicans' history.

The 'collaborators' were a significant and extremely heterogeneous group, lumping together all who did not ' fit' into the epic story that fabricated the 'new man': the project of the new Mozambican citizen.[14] They were those who had given in to temptation, having committed themselves to the colonial system. Among them were former members of the Portuguese political colonial police, the PIDE-DGS; members of ANP,[15] soldiers in the Portuguese army; the godmothers of war, traditional authorities, politicians, members of the lower echelons of the administrative apparatus, or those who "*were not with us* [with FRELIMO]." Seen as the traces of the colonial presence, re-routing and re-educating memory through forgetting was an important task that Mozambique sought to fulfill.

However, if the question of political content and ideology confronted within the liberation movement in Mozambique is present in political analyses of these struggles, it is directed towards comprehending the distinct geopolitical contexts of these countries. In Portugal, I have learned about the peculiarities of this situation. My work is not on Portugal and it is my objective to debate the course of historiography or the collective Portuguese memory from this period. What is surprising when analyzing the situation from Mozambique, nevertheless, is the rediscovery of African issues by academia in Portugal, which still largely declines to recognize other memories of this war, the reasons behind it, and the political projects involved in it.

In Mozambique, the heart of national history is located in the memory of the struggle for national liberation. The heroes are those produced by this struggle, with which Mozambique began. The construction of this history rests upon a politicization that was exacerbated by the process of constructing the national political memory. The construction of membership was founded upon a political analysis that accentuated the dichotomization of spaces between *"liberated areas"* where *"the new man was being produced"* and the colonial territory perceived as a negative space of past legacies. Even if the territory was inhabited by a great majority of Mozambicans up to that point in time, it was, as I previously mentioned, necessary to extirpate it. These too are colonial legacies (Mbembe 2002).

A Map of Conflicts: the National History

The tension between the national project, or the modern territorial base that was mapped, legislated and historicized by the hand of colonialism, and the successive (re)constructions of various identities that were present in the geocultural territory identifiable as the Mozambique of our times, has translated into a co-habitation that was never peaceful (even when interpreted as such by those in power) and involved very little dialogue. This reality manifests itself in the successive recon figurations of conflicting identities (ideological, ethnic, racial, and religious) that have generated other presuppositions and concepts that have helped to de fi ne other geo-cultural places that came to be named as Mozambique, but in which other peoples, other cultural, linguistic, and religious archives were also present. The long duration of the history requires some analytical breath when focusing on the specificity that Mozambique is today.

In modern times, the most visible expression of opposite narratives to those of the colonizers is the grand narrative generated by the anti-colonial struggle, centered upon denouncing colonialism and its vices (discrimination, subalternization, concealing of knowledges, etc.) and the elaboration of a national project for the future. From this narrative, promising more of a new future than of a possible review of the past—and nationalist although quite Eurocentric in its core, but organically local—emerged the idea of a Mozambique for Mozambicans, and what came to be designated as Mozambican- ness. The country's call for equality caused the dramatic erasure of the differences that made its social fabric, generating profound contradictions, synonymous with the continuities of imperial mechanisms that remain active (Meneses & Ribeiro 2008). For example, how does one situate the idea of the nation driven by the anti-colonial struggle with other grand narratives, such as ethnicity, race, religions, and gender? Where is it situated in relation to the 'new' discursive hegemony that is linked to the national project? Before independence, but mainly after independence, the political project of Mozambique and the political project of FRELIMO seemed to coincide.

The 'literature of combat'[16] was one of armored weapons; it promoted the nation's struggle for 'recovery' and was imbued with the mission of inventing a single past that could create 'Mozambicans,' who, without fracture and without difference, were united against a common enemy, colonization. In short, proposals that rejected, amended and, finally, posed a challenge to the hegemony of the national project created in the midst of an exogenous proposal,[17] questioning its value as representing the Mozambican nation, while simultaneously debating its discontinuity with the Mozambican state.[18] Such narratives question the single sense of historiography, with its heroes and national myths, which are more elaborated than organic.[19] In fact, in the literature of combat, found upon the figure of revolutionary 'combatant,' it became possible to integrate only very partially and in a very subaltern way the urban intellectual. The project of constructing the 'new man' did not captivate the memories of the past or the diversity of the present. Nevertheless, diversity insisted upon its presence, finding other forms of protests and affirmation: art, music, literature, etc.

The construction of proposed political alternatives to the colonial situation both denounced the empire and sought, simultaneously, to make a *"new revolutionary subject"* visible—the revolutionary Mozambican who identified with the people and whose purity was filtered by the modern nationalism distinguished by FRELIMO. This political context explains the trial of various nationalist ex-political prisoners (including such renowned poets as José Caveirinha and Rui Nogar, and the painter Malangatana Valente[20]), in 1977, for contradicting the monopolizing vision of FRELIMO over the meaning of national- ism.[21]

If we allow decolonization to question the impact of violent and exploitative relationships, we will find that our legacies and memories are far short of decolonization. Recognizing this problem brings us to the urgency of a critical engagement with current political consequences, both intellectual and social, of centuries of Western 'expansion' in the colonized world to dispute the naturalization and depoliticization of the world. In one sense, postcolonialism is greater than the meeting of various perspectives and concepts of power, for it is a language which seeks to reflect upon processes of 'decolonization' as they take place in the spaces of the metropole and those in colonized spaces.

In the latter, historical reinterpretations were necessary to rescue Mozambique from the silence of interpretations imposed by colonial history. From the outset, this reinterpretation was imbued with revolutionary purity and was indisputable because it was constructed from the testimonies of FRELIMO's leaders, the living heroes that fought for national liberation. This process did not need a mediating historiography; rather, what was needed was to avoid inquiring about sources and about alternative interpretations that were likely to cause disputes.

Thus, the time and space of liberation came to be 'made history,' which was more likely to be disseminated than questioned or interpreted. For academic consolation, the colonial situation emerged into an excellent space for research and inquiry into a new history from silenced memories. For Aquino de Bragança and Jacques Depelchin (1986), history, as an academic discipline, had to play a key role in constructing national political memory. However, the opening to democracy and to a multiparty system that Mozambique witnessed in the 90s allowed the surfacing of other moments of questioning and other hidden spaces of violence. (Re)constructing 'Mozambican-ness' was necessary, yet this new political project now had to integrate these other, less politically instrumental memories. These memories, however, did not meet great challenges through new interpretations and new versions. A political reading of the complex situation in Mozambique reveals a peculiar characteristic of its political process: the multipartidarism of a single party (Meneses & Santos 2008). The armed struggle for national liberation could not be claimed as the only foundation of Mozambican unity since there were other conflicts and other political processes. As the elders frequently say, "*because our dead still speak very loud,*" in Mozambique it was not worth speaking of the past because that brings back the shadows of memories we do not want to remember. Contrary to Portugal, the emphasis in Mozambique was on the need to struggle for liberation, the roots of the struggle and not the struggle itself. Nevertheless, the evolution of the nationalist movement can only be understood within its broader context, taking into account, not just influential internal factors, but all the factors resulting from the confrontation with colonial power. In this sense, the conjoining of memories was due to a convocation of all memories—nationalist and colonial—to comprehend this moment of rupture. Mozambican history needs colonial sources, and Portuguese history also needs to analyze the sources of the liberation movements involved in the war. These are two sides of many remaining histories to be studied.

Let us return to the factor of time in our analysis. Always speeding ahead, time constructs the past. An immaterial shadow of what happened, the past is a narrative created in the present. Its discourse approaches the past, but it is not the past. Such constructions occur in many forms: music, art pieces, oral history, etc.; all are forms of conjugating the past into the present. All are forms of organizing time beyond formally written narratives.

Public narratives, explanations, constructions of official memories are always complex due to the number of players and the number of intentions that produce them. Yet again, these plural memories reflect power relations by being one of many versions produced by players that predominate over others. There are many actors that participate in the production of memories: individual actors, collective actors, institutional, private, etc. A historical memory that is produced by historians is only one of many strands.

There are in fact others that we cannot forget if we seek to make the analysis of our societies more complex. It is not possible to construct official narratives by ignoring the collective memories of groups that are silenced for some reason. Political memory or official history already seeks to construct a unifying narrative within the national space to create social cohesion and legitimize political options. The *History of Mozambique* is the history found and taught through textbooks, but it collides with other, parallel memories.

Therefore, one needs to address these various 'locations' of memories, the epistemic 'discovery' of an otherness, the presence of multiple memories. This is the first moment that announces changes in relation to the official memory, with history as a macro-narrative of our societies. The second is recognizing the process of constructing history from this otherness and from its recuperation.

Conclusion: Weaving Narratives, Constructing History

The debate about investigation and presentation of the African continent exposes a problematic reality, a *"theoretical extroversion"* characterized by the importation of uncritical paradigms, problems and perspectives, by politicians and African intellectuals alike (Hountondji 2002, 2009). Today, contemporary Africa needs to confront two major inquiries: analysis of the implications of the colonial legacy for itself, and the quest to recover that which came before colonization and has remained present in its social structures, its political structures and its identities. The objective is not to create a conceptual space for the other, but recognizing that otherness is a constant in processes of social development.

During the colonial period, the denial of this condition resulted in keeping otherness outside the time of civilization and its transformation into the time of culture, the time outside the space of Western (read: colonial) modernity.

Today the problem is more complex. On one hand, we often continue to make our interpretations from a center that still has not been 'decolonized.' It is hence through the eyes of Imperial Europe that these African spaces are still perceived through epistemically colonial lenses. On the other hand, while we want to (re)construct other histories and (re)introduce ourselves to the debate of other memories, the situation we observe reflects the difficulty of constructing another analytical grid which would escape from dominant interpretations and allow us to introduce the memories of other actors.

Imperial projects have hardly been reformulated, maintaining themselves in the essentially hegemonic conception of the Global North over the Global South despite the independence of African countries and the end of the so-called Cold War.[22] The questions raised by debt, migration, weak or "problem" states, world poverty, and institutional and epistemic racism are among the moments that bring to our attention the persistence of colonization. Many academic relations in the fields of anthropology and history express and treat this colonial expression as the persistent memory of colonization and as a power relation. In this sense, constructing contemporary histories in our times is perhaps one of the principal elements necessary for the (re)emergence of another subject as well as an active political actor. We become aware of ourselves and others, recognizing that the presence of an 'other' implies that we must know the past and the paths of other(s).

To think of memories in the plural, placing them as diverse narratives of histories about locations, involves an obligation to think of identity processes, or the social and political metamorphoses known to societies. If we agree that recognizing signifies remembering the other, the relation- ships between 'I' and the 'other' become spaces of struggle for recognition, spaces of democratizing memory and of the knowledges that they convey.

Even the collective memory that we call 'our memory' and which seems to overlap with others, is not anything real or concrete. On the contrary, 'our memory' is also a narration, a story of 'arrival' and the resulting construction of memories (history, community, etc.) articulated within present power relations. The integration of memories into a whole occurs through a political filter managed by political memory; or rather, by the 'officially' established bodies of power.

Historians tend to use the notion of memory to incorporate unauthorized or unofficial versions of the past while groups whose identities rest upon a specific history challenge legitimate versions of the past and the monopoly of experts, as a *"duty to memory"* (Bensoussan 1998; Ferenczi & Boltanski 200; Ruscio 2005).

As a result, new silencing occurs, and, as previously mentioned, since there are many variables at work in constructing these memories, there will always be segments of memory that feel excluded or insufficiently integrated. What to remember, and for whom? Who are we and where are we going?

The way to address the questions of memory is therefore to recognize two essential questions. On the one hand, collective memories have various producers originating from a plural origin, whether it be the point of view of the distinct locations of distinct narrators or perspective of that which is being narrated and the forms the material assumes. On the other hand, if we are to accept the plural origin of collective memory, it is fundamental to manage these diverse producers in an inclusive and democratic manner (Borges Coelho 2007). We often speak of democratizing our societies, yet the histories, memories, knowledges and experiences of these groups escape from the space of this democratization. In this sense, and borrowing from Boaventura de Sousa Santos (2007), the 'silences' that other memories have been subjected to and their absence from imperial academic circuits strongly indicates the presence of alternative discourses that question insistently the centrality of a single, universal history.

Questioning the colonial raises infinite questions in both imperial metropolitan and colonized spaces. The struggle for Mozambique's independence was linked not only to other political processes via aid from the African continent, but also to other outside processes including the struggle against fascism in Portugal. This involved rejecting racial discrimination and the boundaries of difference in a call to join forces to resist colonial and fascist oppression, transforming them into a unified cause against a common oppressor.

To reclaim the past, as Frantz Fanon insisted, *"triggers a chance of fundamental importance"* (Fanon 1963: 210) for the subaltern other. Instead of shame, the past should be branded with *"dignity, glory and solemnity"* (Ibid.). From this perspective, the silences of the Otherness are not a synonym for the victimization of alterity, but of an increasingly active, and even radical presence of these 'other' historical actors—a condition for transforming the memories and narratives they produce.

This kind of knowledge, or better yet, inter-knowledge, rests upon recognizing the mutuality of differences and similarities, which allows relationships between societies to be reconstructed. The legacies distilled in the memories would not simply be transmitted: they would be repudiated, selectively accepted, falsified and modified through numerous demands and negotiations. They would involve sentiments, nostalgia and envy, remembering and forgetting, fighting for recognition and suspicions of illegitimacy. Like the colonial question, historical legacies create relations (many times quite conflictive) between the potential heirs, simultaneously dividing and connecting the parts together.

Historical scholarship entails distancing the self from the objects of knowledge, which in the case of the activist involvement with a 'new subject'—the history of Mozambique—is the unfair world present 'out there', which the researcher only tackles minimally. On the other side, and as Radha d'Souza reminds us, *"activism involves transcending the subject-object divide, crossing the boundaries between the self as the knower and the knowledge of the world, about a state of being when the knower identifies with the knowledge so completely, where the distinction between the knower and the knowledge is so blurred that the knower is able to make a qualitative leap into the unknown"* (2009:35). The production of this 'new' historical knowledge requires the acknowledgment of and distinguishing between the subject *and* the object. Speaking about others will therefore always have to be sustained by knowledge produced with others in a complex and symbiotic relationship.

Notes

1. What made Mozambique unique in 'Portuguese colonial Africa,' along with Angola, was the settlement of white colonists who were expected to form the economic and political leading backbone of the colony.
2. To explore the concept of decolonization from a postcolonial perspective, in African contexts, see, for example, Bragança 1986 and Sheppard 2006.
3. Cheikh Hamidou Kane, in his novel Am*biguous Adventure,* insightfully remarks the power of colonial schools in the subjugation of the colonized. He credits the schools as having even more power than the cannons for they made conquest permanent, as *"the cannon compels the body and the school bewitches the soul"* (1963:49).
4. In this sense, the role of migrants from Mozambique in the mines of South Africa since the nineteen century must also be taken into consideration to broaden studies on how the revolutionary consciousness was developed in this region of the continent.
5. "Amor e vinho (idílio pagão)" article published in the newspaper, O Africano, 11 June 1913.
6. An attentive reading of the legal codes reveals an abyssal frontier between nationality and citizenship. The 'blacks' were nationals of Mozambique and were deprived of rights to citizenship and submitted to a specific and extremely repressive disciplinary regime, the "Regime of Indigenato," abolished only in 1961. Under this regime, legal citizens (legal being the Portuguese)—acknowledged themselves as invested with the right to govern the subjects that were declared to be further behind on the road to progress and civilization. The legitimacy of their political power rested on the colonial mission to assimilate the 'less developed' into a model of life that was defined superior by the 'citizens' (Meneses 2007a).
7. The Portuguese colonial war, fought simultaneously in Angola, Guinea Bissau and Mozambique.
8. On this subject see Albuquerque 1935; Caetano 1947; Ennes 1971, 2002.
9. Chaimites were armored military vehicles, produced in Portugal to fight the guerrilla nationalist movements. They were named after 'Chaimite,' the sacred capital of Gaza state (now in Mozambique), defeated by the Portuguese in 1895. Chaimite became the symbol of the submission of the 'colonial other.'
10. Contained in the attribution, for years, of the political conflicts and errors of Portuguese colonialism.
11. FRELIMO is the nationalist movement that led the fight for the independence of Mozambique from Portuguese colonization. Afterwards, it turned into a political party and has been in power since independence, both during the single-party and multi-party periods.
12. A process of 'Portuguese indoctrination' started in Mozambique during the 1960s (Borges Coelho 2003; Souto, 2007) when colonial enlargement policy sought to extend Portuguese identity to the overseas populations overseas in Africa. When the pressure of the liberation movement increased, especially in the military, such actions were taken to convey the idea that Mozambique was an integral part of the Portuguese nation and that all the former colonial subjects were Portuguese.
13. In this manner, the introduction to the first electoral law in 1977 distinguished between those that were involved *"in the colonial structures of the oppresso*r" and the *"Mozambican people,"* the former being prohibited from political participation.
14. See, on this subject, Meneses 2007b.
15. *PIDE-DGS*: the repressive police during the dictatorship. *Acção Nacional Popular*: the single political party that ruled Portugal throughout the period of the dictatorship
16. Literature produced during the nationalist army struggle.
17. As a geopolitical project, Mozambique is the result of the division of Africa carried out in the Berlin Conference in the late 19th century.
18. The 2004 national constitution, for example, recognizes the multicultural character of the country (art. 4).
19. For example, see Ncomo 2003.
20. See Laban, 1998.
21. As Craveirinha later explained, these former political prisoners, who were accused of treason and then submitted to re-education processes, underwent a difficult period of political marginalization after independence (Laban 1998).

22. Indeed, the cold war, as a concept, applies to very restricted areas of the globe; specifically, in the case of the African continent, wars and severe conflict situations were experienced throughout the entire 20th century, thus questioning the validity of the use of 'cold war.'

References

Albuquerque, Joaquim Mouzinho de (1935). *Livro das Campanhas*. Lisboa: Agência Geral das Colónias.

Benjamin, Walter (1999). *Selected Writings. Vol. 2 (1929–1934)*. Cambridge, MA: Belnap Press.

Bensoussan, Georges (1998). *Auschwitz en héritage? D'un bon usage de la mémoire*, Paris: Mille et une nuits.

Bragança, Aquino (1986). "Independência sem Descolonização: a transferência de poder em Moçambique, 1974–1975." *Estudos Moçambicanos*, 5 / 6: 7–28.

Bragança, Aquino; Depelchin, Jacques (1986). "Da idealização da Frelimo à compreen-são da história de Moçambique," *Estudos Moçambicanos*, 5 / 6: 29–52.

Borges Coelho, João Paulo (2003). "Da Violência Colonial Ordenada à Ordem Pós-colonial Violenta: sobre um Legado das Guerras Coloniais nas Ex-Colónias Portuguesas," *Lustopie 2003: 175–93*.

Borges Coelho, João Paulo (2007). *Memória dos Dias Moçambicanos de Ruth First*. Paper presented at the Colóquio Moçambique no Contexto da África Austral e os Desa fi os do Presente: Repensando as Ciências Sociais. Maputo (mimeo).

Caetano, Marcello (1947). *As campanhas de Moçambique em 1895 segundo os contem- porâneos. Prefácio e notas do Prof. Dr. Mar- cello Caetano*. Lisboa: Agência Geral das Colónias.

D'Souza, Radha (2009). "The Prison Houses of Knowledge: activist scholarship and rev- olution in the era of 'Globalization,'" *Mcgill Journal of Education*, 44 (1): 19–38.

Ennes, António (1971 [1893]). *Moçambique: Relatório apresentado ao governo*. Lisboa: Agência Geral do Ultramar.

Ennes, António (2002). *A Guerra de África*. Lis- boa: Prefácio.

Fanon, Frantz (1963). *The Wretched of the Earth*. New York, Grove Press.

Ferenczi, Thomas; Boltanski, Christian (eds.) (2002). *Devoir de Mémoire, Droit à l'oubli?* Paris: Complexe.

Hountondji, Paulin J. (2002). *The Struggle for Meaning: reflections on philosophy, culture, and democracy in Africa*. Athens: Ohio University Center for International Studies.

Hountondji, Paulin J. (2009). "Conhecimento de África, Conhecimento de Africanos: duas perspectivas sobre os estudos africanos," *in* Santos, B. S.; Meneses, M. P. (eds.) *Epistemologias do Sul*. Coimbra: Almedina.

Kane, Cheikh Hamidou (1963). *Ambiguous Adventure*. New York: Walker and Co.

Laban, Michel (1998). *Moçambique - Encontro com Escritores*. Porto: Fundação Eng. António Almeida, 3 Volumes.

Mbembe, Achille (2002). "African Modes of Self-writing," *Public Culture*, 14 (1): 239–73.

Meneses, Maria Paula (2007a). "Os Espaços Criados pelas Palavras - Racismos, Etnicidades e o Encontro Colonial," in N. Gomes (ed.) *Formação de Professores e a Questão Racial: uma visão além das fronteiras*. Belo Horizonte: Autêntica Editora.

Meneses, Maria Paula (2007b). "Pluralism, Law and Citizenship in Mozambique: mapping the complexity," O fi cina do CES, 291.

Meneses, Maria Paula (2010a). "O 'indígena' africano e o colono 'europeu': a con- strução da diferença por processos legais," E-cadernos CES, 68–93, available at http://www.ces.uc.pt/e-cadernos/media/ecadernos7/04%20-%20Paula%20Meneses%2023_06.pdf.

Meneses, Maria Paula (2010b). Legal Pluralism and Plural Memories: a view from Mozambique. Paper presented to the 2010 Conference of the Law and Society Association, Chicago, May 2010.

Meneses, Maria Paula; Ribeiro, Margarida Calafate. (2008). "Cartogra fi as Literárias Incertas," in M. C. Ribeiro; M. P. Meneses (eds.). *Moçambique: das palavras escritas*. Porto: Afrontamento.

Meneses, Maria Paula; Santos, Boaventura de Sousa (2008). *The Rise of a Micro Dual State: the case of Angoche (Mozambique)*. Paper presented at the CODESRIA Yaounde Conference, December 2008.

Ncomo, Barnabé Lucas (2003). *Uria Simango: um Homem, uma Causa*. Maputo: Edições Novafrica.

Ruscio, Alain (2005). *1931: L'Apogée de la Bonne Conscience Morale*. Paris: La Dispute editi- ons.

Santos, Boaventura de Sousa (2007). "Beyond Abyssal Thinking: from Global Lines to Ecology of Knowledges," *Review Fernand Braudel Center*, XXX (1): 45–89.

Souto, Amélia Neves (2007). *Caetano e o Ocaso do 'Império': Administração e Guerra Colonial em Moçambique durante o Marcelismo (1968–1974)*. Porto: Afrontamento.

Thiong'o, Ngugi wa (2009). *Something Thorn and New: an African Renaissance*. New York: Basic Civitas Books.

12
Theorizing from the Borders

Walter D. Mignolo and Madina V. Tlostanova

Border thinking or theorizing emerged from and as a response to the violence (frontiers) of imperial/territorial epistemology and the rhetoric of modernity (and globalization) of salvation that continues to be implemented on the assumption of the inferiority or devilish intentions of the Other and, therefore, continues to justify oppression and exploitation as well as eradication of the difference. Border thinking is the epistemology of the exteriority; that is, of the outside created from the inside; and as such, it is always a decolonial project. Recent immigration to the imperial sites of Europe and the USA—crossing the imperial and colonial differences—contributes to maintaining the conditions for border thinking that emerged from the very inception of modern imperial expansion. In this regard, critical border thinking displaces and subsumes Max Horkheimer's 'critical theory' which was and still is grounded in the experience of European internal history (Horkheimer, 1937). 'Critical border thinking' instead is grounded in the experiences of the colonies and subaltern empires. Consequently, it provides the epistemology that was denied by imperial expansion. 'Critical border thinking' also denies the epistemic privilege of the humanities and the social sciences—the privilege of an observer that makes the rest of the world an object of observation (from Orientalism to Area Studies). It also moves away from the post-colonial toward the de-colonial, shifting to the geo- and body-politics of knowledge.

Epistemology is also woven into language and, above all, into alphabetically written languages. And languages are not something human beings have but they are part of what human beings are. As such, languages are embedded in the body and in the memories (geo-historically located) of each person. A person formed in Aymara, Hindi or Russian who has to learn the rules and principles of knowledge mainly inscribed in the three imperial languages of the second modernity (French, English and German), would of necessity have to deal with a 'gap'; while a person formed in German or English who learns the rules and principles of knowledge inscribed in German or English is not subject to such a gap. But there is more, since the situation is not one that can be accounted for in terms of the universal history of human beings and society. Knowledge and subjectivities have been and continue to be shaped by the colonial and imperial differences that structured the modern/colonial world.

Thus, any languages beyond the six imperial European ones, and their grounding in Greek and Latin, have been disqualified as languages with world-wide epistemic import. And of course, this impinges on subject formation: people who are not trusted in their thinking, are doubted in their rationality and wounded in their dignity. Border thinking then emerges from the colonial and the imperial wound. If we consider, instead, Hindi or Aymara, the epistemic difference with modern European languages and epistemology will be colonial. In both cases, the coloniality of knowledge and of being goes hand in hand with modernity's rhetoric of salvation. The rhetoric of modernity and the logic of coloniality are mutually constituted and are the two sides of the same coin. Today the shaping of subjectivity, the coloniality of being/knowledge is often described within the so-called globalization of culture, a phrase, which in the rhetoric of modernity reproduces the logic of coloniality of knowledge and of being.[1]

Borders Not Only Geographic, but Epistemic

'Borders' are not only geographic but also political, subjective (e.g. cultural) and epistemic and, contrary to frontiers, the very concept of 'border' implies the existence of people, languages, religions and knowledge on both sides linked through relations established by the coloniality of power (e.g. structured by the imperial and colonial differences). Borders in this precise sense, are not a natural outcome of a natural or divine historical processes in human history, but were created in the very constitution of the modern/colonial world (i.e. in the imaginary of Western and Atlantic capitalist empires formed in the past five hundred years). If we limit our observations to the geographic, epistemic and subjective types of borders in the modern/colonial world (from the European Renaissance till today), we will see that they all have been created from the perspective of European imperial/ colonial expansion: massive appropriation of land accompanied by the constitution of international law that justified the massive appropriation of land (Grovogui, 1996; Schmitt, 1952); control of knowledge (the epistemology of the zero point as representation of the real) by disqualifying non-European languages and epistemologies and control of subjectivities (by conversation, civilization, democratization) or, in today's language– by the globalization of culture.

Our second thesis is the following. 'Border thinking' (or border epistemology) emerges primarily from the people's anti-imperial epistemic responses to the colonial difference—the difference that hegemonic discourse endowed to 'other' people, classifying them as inferior and at the same time asserting its geo- historical and body-social configurations as superior and the models to be followed. These people refuse to be geographically caged, subjectively humiliated and denigrated and epistemically disregarded. For this reason, the de-colonial epistemic shift proposes to change the rule of the game–and not just the content–and the reason why knowledge is produced: de-colonization, instead of working toward the accumulation of knowledge and imperial management, works toward the empowerment and liberation of different layers (racial, sexual, gender, class, linguistic, epistemic, religious, etc.) from oppression, and toward the undermining of the assumption upon which imperial power is naturalized, enacted and corrupted. Second, border thinking could emerge also from the imperial difference, i.e. the same mechanism of the colonial difference but applied to people in similar socio-economic conditions as the ones who are in a dominant position. Western (Christian and secular) discourses about Indians and Blacks (that is, Africans transported to the Americas) founded the colonial difference and the modern matrix of racism. During the same period, the sixteenth and seventeenth centuries, Western Christian and secular discourse founded the imperial difference with the Ottoman and the Russian Empires. Turks and Russian, in other words, were obviously not Indians and Blacks in the Western hegemonic geo- and body-classification of the world. However, it was clear to everybody in the West that Turks and Russians might not be Blacks or Indians, but they were not European either. However, 'second-class' empires in the history of Western capitalist ones also had to deal with colonies. Empires like the Russian/Soviet (and also Japan, 1895–1945) and the Ottoman, before its demise, are all Janus-faced empires: one eye is pointing toward Western capitalist and dominant empires, while the other looks toward their own colonies (Tlostanova, 2003).

Zero point epistemology configured by the theo- and ego-politics of knowledge has shaped Western imperial expansion throughout five centuries. Border thinking is configured by the geo- and body-politics of knowledge. What are the relations between geo-historical locations and epistemology, on the one hand, and between identity and epistemology, on the other? These questions have not been asked by theological and egological epistemologies.[2] The array of possibilities for border thinking is indeed vast but they all have one thing in common: how do people in the world deal with Western economic, political and epistemic expansion if they do not want to assimilate but choose to imagine a future that is their own invention and not the invention of the empires, hegemonic or subaltern? Someone born and raised in British India does not have much in common with someone born and raised in Latin America; the languages and religions are different, the histories are incommensurable. However, they have a common history: the imperial/colonial history of Western capitalist and Christian empires—Spain and England. From the imperial perspective—either of the dominant empires (England, America) or the subaltern empires (Russia, China, the Ottoman Empire of the past), border thinking is almost an impossibility (one would have to give up the epistemic privilege of Western modernity and admit that knowledge and understanding are generated beyond institutional norms and control) and, from the colonial perspective, border thinking is straightforwardly a necessity. The next question is whether border thinking could emerge from the perspective of subaltern empires or its chances for emergence are better in the colonies and what kind of colonies at that—the (ex-)colonies of a subaltern empire (e.g., Uzbekistan, Ukraine) or a hegemonic empire (e.g., India during the British rule; Iraq under US imperial moves; Bolivia and Ecuador in the history of the Spanish empire and the present of US domination in Latin America; or South Africa in its past and present)?[3] Border thinking and the de-colonial shift cannot be reduced to an abstract universal (e.g. critical theory, semiotics of culture, or nomadology for everyone on the planet) that will account for all universality, is the major claim made by border thinking and the justification for the de-colonial shift. Once again, there is no pluriversality from the perspective of theo- and ego-politics of knowledge. Pluriversality is only possible from border thinking, that is, from shifting the geography of reason to geo- and body-politics of knowledge.

While imperial epistemology is based on theological and egological principles, the shift to geo- and body- political principles is indeed a de-colonial move. Geo- and body-politics are the 'displaced inversion' of theo- and ego-politics of knowledge. It is an 'inversion' because it is assumed that John Locke's 'secondary qualities' cannot be bracketed in the process of knowing and understanding. And in a world order in which the imperial and colonial differences establish all hierarchies, from economy to knowledge, 'secondary qualities' that matter are colonial local histories (geo-politics) subordinated to imperial local histories, on the one hand, and colonial subjectivities (e.g. what Frantz Fanon described as 'the wretched of the earth'), on the other. Colonial subjectivities are the consequences of racialized bodies, the inferiority that imperial classification assigned to everybody that does not comply with the criteria of knowledge established by white, European, Christian and secular men. Thus, 'displaced inversion' means that it is not just a change in the content but fundamentally in the terms of the conversation: the geo- and body-political perspectives de-link from the imperial and totalitarian bent of theo- and ego-logical principles. It is hardly enough to question the secularity of the social sciences from the perspective of theology, as John Milbank does. It is of the essence to move away from inversions internal to imperial epistemology and to shift the geography and the biography of reason.

These positions are hard to reconcile, which is clearly seen in any juxtaposition of Western and radical non-Western theorizing of borders. From the perspective of the imperial difference, the conditions and possibilities of border thinking and de-colonization are not only different but also more difficult. If in the history of borders marked by colonial differences the opposition to the empire is clear and loud; in the history of borders marked by imperial differences, the assimilation (e.g. Peter and Catherine in Russia) and desire to become the West, or competition (the Soviet Union confronting Western capitalist empires) takes precedence over decolonization (which would be a sort of de-imperialization), as we see in case of Russia today. China offers still another example of border thinking through the imperial difference: adaptation without assimilation. Overall, the conditions for de-colonization seem to be more promising in the colonies and ex-colonies; or in empires that had been reduced to colonies (e.g. the Islamic empire, which by the nineteenth century, was already subdivided and found itself at the mercy of the new imperialism of England and France). The ex-second world, or better yet, the world marked by the imperial more than colonial differences, lives on/in the border, and yet instead of border thinking we find there blurred, smudged, in-between models (the Ottoman Empire, Russia/USSR, Central and South-Eastern Europe).[4] Their differences with the West are also of a blurred and unstable nature and this makes it difficult to conceptualize such locales and epistemic and existential configurations from the viewpoints of both West and radical non-West, as well as from the viewpoint of these very people who were colonized by Western thinking, infected with secondary Euro-centrism and not able to analyse their own split subjectivity (their double consciousness, the necessary condition for border thinking), because it is always easier to analyze binary polar structures than soft and blurred difference–same but not quite, different, but too similar. Geo- and body-politics of knowledge as well as border thinking implies the awareness of the double consciousness.

Double consciousness, as conceptualized by the African-American sociologist W.E.B. Dubois (see note 2) lies at the very foundation of border thinking. Double consciousness is border thinking and border thinking is double consciousness. There cannot be border thinking without double consciousness. Imperial consciousness is always territorial and monotopic; border thinking is always pluri-topic and engendered by the violence of the colonial and imperial differences. Internal imperial critique (be that of Bartolomé de las Casas or Karl Marx) is territorial and monotopic and assumes the 'truth' of abstract universals (peaceful Christianization by conversion, free market, international revolution of the proletarians, etc.). Double consciousness emerges from the experiences of being someone (black, inscribed in the memory and histories of the slave trade in the Atlantic economy) who was classified by the imperial-national gaze (the European imperial frame of mind, the emerging US imperial nationalism at the turn of the twentieth century). Thus, the problem of identity and of identity politics is a direct consequence of imperial knowledges making all the inhabitants of the New World Indians and Blacks and all of Asia the Yellow Race. If border thinking is the unavoidable condition of imperial/colonial domination, critical border thinking is the imperial/condition transformed into epistemic and political projects of de-colonization. For that reason, de-colonial thinking is always already critical, it is border thinking and it is double consciousness border thinking and double consciousness. Hegel, Kant and Marx--to name just three European luminaries—denied internal others, be they Slavic people or Turks, a place in the universal history, in the march of modernity, in the unfolding of global proletarian revolution, etc. Their dis-incorporated epistemology and their belief in universal parameters blinded them to the subjectivity of otherness and more so to internal others. It was beyond their scope to understand why a Russian feels himself to be a cockroach in Europe (Yerofeyev, 2000), while a Turk buying a coat from a French store is in fact buying a European dream (Pamuk, 2000).[5]

The reaction of the internal others to this rejection has been that of an unconscious border, divided between the first and third worlds, wanting to see itself as part of a center. The border's painful division is being masked and at once reinforced when in Istanbul they change the alphabet to Latin or make slightly crooked, but recognizably Parisian boulevards; when in Moscow they speak only French or destroy their own economy in order to please the IMF. Today the split configuration of internal others is expressed in the continuing hierarchy of othering: the ex-second world, on the one hand, plays the role of unwanted and threatening immigrant in the West; on the other hand, the West guards its own borders (including epistemic borders) against the unwanted immigration from the ex-Soviet republics and ex-third world. However, when border thinking does not emerge, the alternatives are competition, assimilation, or resistance without a vision of the future.

For instance, when the European imperial/colonial model was replicated and transformed in subaltern empires or empires-colonies, such as Russia or the Ottoman Empire (which became mirror reflections of each other, one a quasi- Western and the other a quasi-Islamic empire), it led to ideological and intellectual dependency on the West and the epistemic colonization by the West which resulted in the phenomenon of two cultures–the culture of a European-oriented imperial/national elite with secondary Eurocentric inferiority complexes, and the impenetrable culture of people, that the elite is either ashamed of or attracted to, in the importing of the Western discourses of nationalism, cosmopolitanism, liberalism, socialism, modernization, progress, etc. (Tlostanova, 2004).

The imperial and colonial epistemic differences create the condition for border thinking, but do not determine it. In the hierarchical structure of the modern/colonial world, four main types of dependency relations can be identified: (1) the oppositional attitude consisting of total rejection of Western epistemology and subjectivity based on fundamentalist defense of languages, religions, knowledges, etc.; (2) the assimilating attitude, consisting in wanting to become like the superior other and, therefore, yielding to the imperial language, knowledge and subjectivity at the high price of alienating oneself into the imperial Other (this is the case of the trickster empire Turkey, making its own subaltern status work for its benefit–through transcultural and trans-religious mediation of Western ideologies and establishing of new alliances based not on abstract principles of democracy and freedom, but on religious, linguistic, indigenously economic and cultural expansionism and soft penetration, which today turns out to be more effective than many European and American strategies (Griffiths and Özdemir, 2004; Özbudun and Keyman, 2002); (3) competition within the capitalist rules of the game or adaptation without assimilation (e.g. China or modern defeated Russia, to some extent, which is still grounding itself in the doomed imperial myths of grandeur and dominance, finding solace in understanding the border as an aggressive expansionistic 'third way' and reviving the dusty ideology of Eurasianism); and (4) border thinking and critical border thinking, consisting in the incorporation of Western contributions in different domains of life and knowledge into an epistemic and political project that affirms the difference, colonial and/ or imperial to which most of the population of the world has been subjected throughout the five hundred years of economic, religious, epistemic imperial expansion and its consequences in the formation of split subjectivities.

Dependency relations are established, through the imperial and colonial differences, with the exteriority of Europe. But these dependency relations with the colonies revert back to its internal others like the Jews, the immigrants and the states, the ex-Soviet colonies, now joining the European Union. Aimé Césaire clearly saw, in the 1950s, that the colonial matrix of power set up and implemented through 450 years of colonization had been implemented by the Nazi regime in Germany and by the communist regime in the Soviet Union (Césaire, 1955). These are all different historical conditions from which border positions could be developed as active de-colonizing projects, both epistemic and political from the lived experiences (e.g. subjectivity) of diverse communities. Geo- and body-politics of knowledge would be of the essence to disengage from the epistemology of the zero point in which the geo- and the body-politics has been repressed. The epistemology of the zero point that privileges political economy and political theory continues to repress the geo-historical and body-graphic politic of knowledge in which critical border thinking is founded. The interconnections between geo-historical locations (in the modern/colonial order of things) and epistemology, on the one hand, and body-racial and gender epistemic configurations on the other, sustain 'the inverted displacement' we describe here as geo-politics and body-politics of knowledge. If, say, René Descartes or Immanuel Kant suppressed (in their theo- and ego-political epistemic foundations) the geo- and body-political component of their thinking, Frantz Fanon (1952) and Gloria Anzaldúa (1987) (Saldívar-Hull, 2000) brought both (geo- and body-politics) wide and loud into the open.

Border thinking needs its own genealogy and its own history; a history and a genealogy that emerge in the very act of performing border thinking. Without it, border thinking will remain either an appendix of modern Western imperial epistemology and the variants of canonical history of Western civilization told from the imperial perspective (from the Renaissance, to Hegel, to Marx); or an object of study for the social sciences (like the savage mind for earlier anthropologists). If border thinking is to emerge and prosper in the ex-second world today, it would have to happen in the colonial and ex-colonial locales of the subaltern empires, among the people who were multi-marginalized and denied their voice by Western modernity–directly and through subaltern imperial mediation. It is the Caucasus and Central Asia (with regard to Russia), the Kurds, the Greeks and the Armenians (with regard to the Ottoman Empire), the Yugoslavian bundle of contradictions in the Balkans, etc. But these voices are never heard and will hardly be heard soon. These mutes colonized by the subaltern empires are split between the original of Western culture (now also accessible to them) and its bad subaltern empire copies, the ex-mediators of civilization, plus their own native ethnic traditions continue to play their part in the process of the already split selves being shattered into even smaller pieces.

Notes

1. The logic of coloniality is one side (the hidden and darker side) of imperial governance. Imperial governance was and continues to be predicated on the rhetoric of modernity (reluctant imperialism, light imperialism, e.g. justification for the invasion of Iraq). The rhetoric of modernity is a rhetoric of salvation (conversion, civilization, development, market democracy) while the logic of coloniality is the logic of land appropriation, exploitation of labour, control of gender and sexuality, of knowledge and subjectivity.
2. For example, John Milbank's (1993) theological critique of the social sciences reverses the order of the secular and the sacred in epistemology, but the geo-historical location of his thought as well as the unspoken male, white and Christian identity of his discourse are grounded in Greek and Latin categories of thought and articulated in English language. On the other hand, when Harvard Black sociologist W.E.B. Dubois asks 'how can one be American and Black at the same time', he established the foundation of a 'double consciousness' as an epistemic foundation grounded on the racial colonial difference (Dubois 1904).
3. 'Third World nationalism' (e.g. India or Algeria) reproduced in the ex-colonies the model of 'Imperial nationalism' (e.g. England or France), and all ended up in the impasse we all know about. 'Internal colonialism' was the end result, since the first post-colonial nation-states, in the modern/colonial word, that emerged in the Americas at the end of the eighteenth and first decades of he nineteenth centuries. Bolivia is going now through an interesting process of border thinking and constitutional de-colonization. And we may see a similar experience in Iraq. 'Third World nationalism' furthermore remained within the monotopic and exclusionary imperial logic, just in the hands of the 'locals or natives'. Frantz Fanon, instead, opened up the possibility and the need for a double consciousness and border thinking of and from the experience of *Les damnés de la terre*. His thoughts were far removed from national fundamentalisms.
4. In Eurasian space, there also existed instances of border thinking, created by people who experienced double and multiple marginalization and discrimination by several empires and powers at once, but these histories remained undocumented; the views of these people (if ever they were put on paper) were erased by the empires and by Western modernity (e.g. a nineteenth-century Caucasus anti-colonial movement activist and Cherkess Prince called Saferbi Zan, a late nineteenth-century Muslim intellectual, and a Tartar enlightener and journalist, Ismail Bey Gasprinksii, etc.), or had to make a compromise with the dominant power by choosing the assimilative position of Ariels (Suleimenov, 1974).
5. See, for instance, Kant's description of Russian and Turkish national characters in his *Anthropology From a Pragmatic Point of View* (1798).

References

Anzaldúa, G. (1987) *Borderlands/La Frontera: The New Mestiza*. San Francisco: Aunt Lute.

Bataillon, Marcel and O'Gorman, Edmundo (1955) *Dos Concepciones de la Tarea Histórica, con Motivo de la idea del Descubrimiento de America*. Mexico: D.F. [Bataillon's essay was originally published under the title 'L'idée de la découverte de l'Amérique chez les Espagnols du XVI siècle', *Bulletin Hispanique* 55(1): 23–55.

Bogues, Anthony (2003) 'C.L.R. James and W.E.B. Du Bois: Heresy, Double Consciousness and Revisionist Histories', in *Black Heretics, Black Prophets. Radical Political Intellectuals*, pp. 69–94. Oxford: Blackwell.

Castro-Gómez, Santiago (2000) 'Traditional and Critical Theories of Culture', *Nepantla*, 1(3): 503–18.

——(2002) 'La hybris del punto cero: Biopolíticas imperiales y colonialidad del poder en la Nueva Granada (1750–1810)', unpublished manuscript.

Césaire, Aimé ([1955] 2000) *Discours sur le colonialism*, trans., J. Pinkham. *Discourse on Colonialism*. New York: Monthly Review Press.

Dubois, W.E.B. ([1904] 1995) *The Soul of the Black Folks*. New York: Penguin.

Fanon, Frantz (1952) *Peau noire, masque blanche*. Paris: Maspero.

——(1961) *Les damnés de la terre*. Paris: Masperó.

Griffiths, Richard T. and Özdemir, Durmus (2004) *Turkey and the EU Enlargement: Processes of Incorporation*. Istanbul: Bilgi University Press.

Grovogui, Siba N'Zatioula (1996) *Sovereigns, Quasi Sovereigns, and Africans*. Minneapolis: University of Minnesota Press.

Habermas, Jürgen (1998) *The Inclusion of the Other: Studies in Political Theory*, ed. C. Cronin and P. de Greiff. Boston: MIT Press.

Horkheimer, Max ([1937] 1999) 'Traditional and Critical Theory', in *Critical Theory: Selected Essays*, pp. 188–243. New York: Continuum.

Kant, Immanuel ([1798] 1978) *Anthropology From a Pragmatic Point of View*, trans. Victor Lyle Dowedel, Book II, Section II. Carbondale: Southern Illinois University Press.

Las Casas, Bartolomé de ([1552] 1967) *Apologética Historia Summaria*, ed. E. O'Gorman. Mexico: Universidad Autónoma de México, vol. II, 'Epílogue'.

Milbank, John (1993) *Theology and Social Theory: Beyond Secular Reason*. Oxford: Blackwell.

Mignolo, W. (1995) Ann Arbor: The University of Michigan Press.

—— (2000) *Local Histories/Global Designs: Coloniality, Subaltern Knowledges and Border Thinking*. Princeton, NJ: Princeton University Press.

——(2002) 'Geopolitics of Knowledge and the Colonial Difference', *South Atlantic Quarterly* 101(1): 57–96.

Özbudun E. and Keyman, E.F. (2002) 'Cultural Globalization in Turkey. Actors, Discourses, Strategies', in Peter L. Berger and Samuel P. Huntington (eds) *Many Globalizations: Cultural Diversity in the Contemporary World*, pp. 296–320. New York: Oxford University Press.

Pamuk, O. (2000) Chernaja Kniga. Sankt-Peterburg: Amfora.

Paranjape, Makarand (2002) 'The Third Eyes and Two Ways of (Un)Knowing: Gnosis, Alternative Modernities and Postcolonial Futures'; http://www.infinityfoundation.com/indic_colloq/papers/paper_paranjape2.pdf.

Quijano, Anibal (1992) 'Colonialidad y modernidad-racionalidad', in Los conquistados: 1492 y la población indígena de las Américas., ed. H. Bonilla, pp. 437–47. Quito: Tercer Mundo Editores/FLACSO/Libri Mundi.

Quijano, Anibal (2000) 'Coloniality of Power, Eurocentrism and Latin America', Nepantla 1(3): 533–80.

Saldívar-Hull, Sonia (2000) *Feminism on the Border: Chicana Gender Politics and Literature*. Berkeley: The University of California Press.

Schmitt, Carl ([1952] 2003) *The Nomos of the Earth in the International Law of* JusPublicum Europeaum, trans. G.L. Ulmen. New York: Telos Press.

Suleimenov, O. (1975) Az i Ja. Kniga Blagonamerennogo Chitatelja. Alma-Ata.

Tlostanova, M. (2003) *A Janus-Faced Empire*. Moscow: Blok.

——(2004) *Postsovetskaja Literatura i Estetika Transkulturatsii*. Moscow: Editorial URSS.

Yerofeyev V. (2000) *Pjat Rek Zhizni*. Moscow: Podkova.

13
Palestinian History and Memory from-Below and from-Within

Nur Masalha

The methodologies of history-from-below (Thompson 1966: 279–80) (often referred to as people's history) seek to challenge hegemonic top-down approaches to history. They focused on the narrativisation of the past from the perspectives of ordinary people or social movements rather than political, social, economic or religious elites or statement. Their primary focus is the oppressed, silenced and forgotten people. History-from-below narratives of resistance would produce an alternative to Palestinian elites. In order to understand and appreciate the complexities and richness of Palestinian individual, social and cultural memories, rather than imposing a top-down, elite or single narrative, a range of voices and multiple narratives of competing memories, the archaeology of a people crisscrossed with individual experiences–including narratives of suffering and *sumud* (steadfastness), of courage and resistance born out of anger and revolt against oppression–must be allowed to flourish and be nurtured further. The history-from-below approach, with its emphasis on multiplicity of popular memories and people's voices rather than high politics, political elites, decision makers or top-down approaches, can, potentially, challenge elite discourses or dominant methodologies based on Israeli or Western-dominated archival sources.

Oral history and oral traditions are not Western imports to the Middle East. The deeds and sayings of the Prophet Muhammad, famously known as the Hadith, were oral traditions which originated in and evolved from the earliest years of Islam. The storyteller/narrator, *Al-Hakawati* is part of a long popular oral tradition in Palestinian and Arab societies and cultures. In modern times the memoirs of Jerusalemite Wasif Jawhariyyeh (1897–1973), *Storyteller of Jerusalem: The Life and Times of Wasif Jawhariyyeh, 1904–1948* (2013), written on the basis of notebooks he had kept from the Ottoman until the Nakba, highlights oral testimony, story-telling, memoir, folk tradition, poetry, music and dance as a rich source for different forms of representation of the Palestinian past and for writing the social history of Palestine.

While both Israeli official and revisionist historiographies have long emphasised Israeli state papers, official documents, high politics and elite narratives rather than the people's voices behind the documents, Palestinian social history and people's voices and narratives are often richer and go much deeper than the official records. Furthermore, in recent decades, Palestinian oral history–which is partly inspired by the popular *Al-Hakawati* tradition and partly by the oral and cultural traditions of Islam–has attempted to redress the imbalance of modern historiography and the hegemonic Zionist narrative, by developing methodologies for understanding the contexts, objects and meanings of documents, facts and evidence and generally for exploring the history and voices of the people.

Palestinian oral history and memory are evolving methodologies. Not until the 1970s did published Palestinian oral history begin to offer a picture of traumatic events through the eyes of the disenfranchised and forgotten refugees who had experienced dispossession and dispersal. It should be pointed out, however, that this new oral history perspective based extensively on interviews with and testimonies of the refugees began in the early 1970s–before the opening of the Israeli governmental and institutional archives in the late 1970s and, at least a decade before the emergence of the Israeli 'new historiography' in the mid-late 1980s and two decades before the appearance of Israeli post-Zionist methodologies in the 1990s.

The 1960s were a turning point in the post-Nakba Palestinian resistance literature. From the early 1960s onwards Ghassan Kanafani and other Palestinian novelists began producing important fictional accounts of the Nakba. Combining facts and fiction, these imaginative social memory accounts of the refugees are important works of representation of the Palestinian past. Also during the 1960s and early 1970s the Palestinian collective nationalist resistance discourse about history, as articulated by the PLO, was homogenising, and dominant, effectively marginalising personal narratives of individual refugees. Typically this 'heroic' nationalist discourse was designed to paint an ideal type of history and suppress the darker sides of Palestinian history, including accounts of internal infighting and stories about many Palestinian collaborators with Zionism. From the early 1970s onwards, however, *Journal for Palestine Studies*, *Shuun Filastiniyah*, the Centre for Palestine Studies, Palestinian Research Centre and *Arab Studies Quarterly* began publishing pioneering articles and books based on individual oral evidence, personal narratives and interviews with ordinary refugees to tell the history of Palestine before and during the Nakba. This included works by Elias Shoufani (1972: 108–21), Nafiz Nazzal (1974: 58–76), Fawzi Qawuqji (1975), Rega-e Busailah (1981: 123–51), Elias Sanbar (1984), Walid Khalid (1984), 'Ajaj Nuwayhid (1993). In 1978 the Institute for Palestine Studies in Beirut published Nafiz Nazzal's *The Palestinian Exodus from Galilee 1948*, based on his doctoral dissertation (1974a), which brought important oral accounts of Galilee dispossession as recalled by refugees exiled in Lebanon to academic attention.

Ironically Israeli historian Benny Morris, who claims to distrust Palestinian oral evidence on 1948 (Morris 1988: 2), cited Nafiz Nazzal's work on oral history of the refugees repeatedly and extensively in *The Birth of the Palestinian Refugee Problem, 1947–1949* (1987). Despite his anti-Palestinian polemics Morris found Nazzal's oral history research to construct several of the Israeli massacres of Palestinians in 1948 extremely useful.

In recent decades, Palestinian oral history and individual memory accounts have attempted to redress the imbalance of modern historiography by developing methodologies for understanding the contexts, objects and meanings of documents, facts and evidence and generally for exploring the history and voices of the people behind state papers and official documents. Oral history revolutionised historical methodologies by bringing to light hidden, suppressed or marginalised narratives. Oral history has, in fact, brought together academics, archivists and librarians, oral historians, museum professionals and community-based arts practitioners. As a producer of meaning, oral history has become a major catalyst for creative practices and interpretations in history-related fields and for the construction of alternative histories and memories of lost practices.

Archival documents, like oral histories, are constructs; they are never the 'reality itself' or the 'past itself'. Oral history, like written documentation, is never free from factual error or bias and has to be treated critically. Oral history and written documentation have also to be explored in connection with socially-framed and socially-acceptable memory. Benny Morris argues that written documents (and Israeli archives) distort far less than interviews with Palestinian refugees (2004: 4). But archival documentations are often based on memory; they can distort, misinform, omit or even fabricate evidence (Humphries 2009 79–80). Memory is an evolving process shaped by processes of identity construction and creative imagining; its evolution overtime ought to be explored both synchronically and diachronically. As Louis Starr notes, memory is selective and 'fallible, ego distorts and contradictions sometimes go unresolved', nevertheless

> Problems of evaluation are not markedly different from those inherent in the use of letters, diaries, and other primary sources ... the scholar must test the evidence in an oral history memoir for internal consistency and, whenever possible, by corroboration from other sources, often including the oral history memoirs of others on the same topic.
>
> (Starr 1984: 4–5)

From the 1970s onwards, oral history began to be considered in a more positive light by the academy following work by scholars such as Luisa Passerini who studied the history of the Turin working class under Italian Fascism (Humphries 2009: 78; Passerini 1998: 53–62). Since then there has been a proliferation of memory projects throughout the world, promoting the collection, preservation and use of recorded memories of the past and people's voices. In the UK the BBC has developed an 'Archive of World War Two Memories', based on oral history and written by the public and ordinary people,[1] and 'BBC Memoryshare' which is described as 'a living archive of memory from 1900 to the present day... the majority of content on memoryshare is created by Memoryshare contributors, who are members of the public'.[2] Ordinary people can contribute memories, research events and link to context material relating to any date back to 1 January 1900. As for the 'WW2 People's War Archive', the BBC asked the public to contribute their memories of World War Two to a website between June 2003 and January 2006. This 'people's memory archive' has got 47,000 stories and 15,000 images–stories not just of air raids, military operations and the armed forces, but also of the concentration camps in Europe, on the roles of women, on resistance and occupation, on civilian interment and conscientious objectors.

Palestinian oral history is a significant methodology not only for the construction of an alternative, counter-hegemonic, history of the Nakba and memories of the lost historic Palestine but also for an ongoing indigenous life, living Palestinian practices and a sustained human ecology and liberation. In contrast with the hegemonic Israeli heritage-style industry of an exclusively biblical archaeology, with its obsession with assembling archaeological fragments–scattered remnants of masonry, tablets, bones, tombs–and officially approved historical and archaeological theme parks of dead monuments and artefacts destined for museums, in recent decades Palestinians have devoted much attention to the 'enormously rich sedimentations of village history and oral traditions' as a reminder of the continuity of native life and living practices (Said 2004: 49; Masalha 2008: 123–56; 2012; 2012a).

Drawing on research from other colonial and post-colonial contexts, new approaches to liberating Palestinian history and historiography can combine a wide range of historical sources with the study of knowledge and power, historiography and popular memory accounts, oral, subaltern and resistance narratives, indigenous, counter-hegemonic, post-colonial and decolonising methodologies (Foucault 1972; 1980; Young 2003; Prakash 1994: 1475–1490, 1476; Guha 1997; Guha and Spivak 1988; Hooks 1990: 241–43; Abu-Sa'ad 2005: 113–41; 2008: 17–43; Smith1999). In the context of rural and peasant Palestinian society, Palestinian oral history is a particularly useful decolonising methodology; throughout much of the twentieth century the majority of the Palestinians lived in villages and were fellahin (peasants); in 1944 sixty-six percent of the Palestinian population was agrarian with a literacy rate, when last officially estimated, of only fifteen percent (Esber 2003: 22). Their experiences in the fields, in their villages and in exile are largely absent from history- writing and much recent historiography ('Issa 2005: 179–86). Moreover the Nakba itself, and the political instability and repression faced by the dispersed Palestinian communities since 1948, have also impeded Palestinian research and studies (Khalidi, R. 1997: 89). In *Palestinian Identity*, Rashid Khalidi argues that modern Palestinian historiography has suffered from 'inherent historical biases' and that "The views and exploits of those able to read and write are perhaps naturally more frequently recorded by historians, with their tendency to favour written records, than those of the illiterate." (Khalidi 1997: 98)

As is the case with other subaltern groups, Palestinian oral testimony is a vital tool for recovering the voice of the subaltern: peasants, the urban poor, gypsies (often described as *Nawar* people in Palestine and the Middle East), women, refugee camp dwellers, and bedouin communities. An important feature of the Palestinian oral history effort from its inception has been its popular basis with the direct participation of the displaced community (Gluck 2008: 69). Since the mid-1980s this grassroots effort has shown an awareness of the importance of recording the events of the Nakba from the perspective of those previously marginalised in Palestinian elite and male-centred narratives. Although gender (both female and male) imagery and symbols have always been prevalent in Palestinian nationalist discourses (Khalili 2007: 22–23)–the Palestinian National Charter of 1964 (revised in 1968) and the Palestinian Declaration of Independence of 1988 had both imagined the Palestinian nation as a male body and masculinised political agency (Massad 1995: 467–83; also 2008).

In 1949 Constantine Zurayk published *The Meaning of the Nakba* (1956) which was translated into English. This was followed by Palestinian historian and native of Jerusalem 'Arif Al-'Arif, who published six volumes in Arabic in the period 1958–1960, entitled: *Al-Nakba: The Catastrophe of Jerusalem and the Lost Paradise*. Also in the late 1950s and early 1960s Palestinian historian Walid Khalidi published three pioneering articles on the circumstances surrounding the Nakba (Khalidi, W. 1959: 21–24; 1959a: 22–32; 1961: 22–28). However, with the exception of these three articles, based on written documentation, and an important article by Irish journalist Erskine Childers in 1961,[3] in fact little was published in English about the Nakba during the first two decades following 1948. In 1972 Palestinian author Mustafa Dabbagh began publishing in Arabic his eleven volume, encyclopaedic work, entitled *Our Country: Palestine*, describing all villages of Palestine during the British Mandate (Dabbagh 1972–1986). However, with their emphasis on the loss of property in 1948, with the exception of a few sympathetic books in English on the Palestinian elite voices but never brought people's voices.[4] This almost total silencing of the Palestinian Nakba, which was associated with defeat and shame, went largely unchallenged until the 1970s.

Walid Khalidi's own publications have contributed to the monumen-talisation of the collective memory of the Nakba. Khalidi himself in December 1963 co-founded (and since then has served as Secretary General) of the Institute for Palestine Studies (IPS), established in Beirut as an independent research and publishing centre focusing on the Palestinian refugee problem and the Arab-Palestine conflict. Under his guidance the IPS produced a long list of publications in both Arabic and English and several important translations of Hebrew documents, texts and books into Arabic. In 1984, the IPS published Walid Khalidi's *Before Their Diaspora: A Photographic History of the Palestinians, 1876–1948*. However Khalidi will always be known for his encyclopaedic knowledge on the Palestinian villages occupied and depopulated by Israel in 1948, *All That Remains* (1992). This work of monumental and commemorative collective memory includes several hundred photographs and has clearly benefited from the contribution of Palestinian oral historians. According to the blurb

> This authoritative reference work describes in detail the more than 400 Palestinian villages that were destroyed or depopulated in 1948. Little of these once-thriving communities remained; not only they have been erased from the Palestinian landscape, their very names have been removed from contemporary Israeli maps.
>
> No experience has shaped Palestinian attitudes since 1948 more than this loss of hearth and home … Well-wishers of Israel, as well as diplomats seeking peacefully to resolve the Palestinian-Israeli conflict, need to know this informative component of Palestinian collective memory and history. Such knowledge could be useful in formulating reasonable

parameters for a just redress of the terrible suffering inflicted upon the Palestinian people in the process of the establishment of the State of Israel.

The culmination of nearly six years of research by more than thirty participants, *All That Remains* goes beyond the scope of previously published accounts of depopulated and destroyed Palestinian villages. Unlike earlier studies, it has relied extensively on field research to pinpoint the exact location of village sites through former residents and local guides. The body of the text is devoted to the villages themselves … Each village entry comprises statistical data … and several narrative sections. These include a section on the village before 1948 summarizing its history from a wide variety of Arab and Western sources (works of ancient and medieval historians, geographers, travellers, etc.), and synthesizing information about the village's topography, architecture, institutions, and economic activity.

In recent decades two distinct historiographical approaches concerning the history and memories surrounding the birth of the Palestinian refugee problem have evolved. Recent debates about 1948 tell us something about the historian's method and the meaning of the 'historical document' (Pappe 2004a: 137). Methodologically, many historians have displayed a bias towards archival sources; Israeli revisionist historians, in particular, believe they are both ideologically dispassionate and empirically impartial (Masalha 2011: 1–53), and that the only reliable sources for the reconstruction of the 1948 war are in the IDF archives and official documents. This bias towards high politics and 'archives' has contributed to silencing the Palestinian past. The silencing of the Nakba by Israeli historians follows the pattern given by Michel-Rolph Trouillot in *Silencing the Past: Power and the Production of History*:

> Silences enter the process of historical production at four crucial moments: the moment of fact creation (the making of sources); the moment of fact assembly (the making of archives); the moment of fact retrieval (the making of narratives); and the moment of retrospective significance (the making of history in the final instance).
>
> (1995: 26)

I myself, like other historians, could not resist the opportunity presented by the availability of mountains of Israeli and Hebrew archival sources on 1948 and the Mandatory period. However as in the case of other decolonising methodologies, subaltern groups, Palestinian oral testimony is an important tool for researchers to recover the voices of the victims of the Nakba: the Palestinian refugees (Pappe 2004b: 188). Furthermore in recent years, more and more historians have been paying attention to the idea of social history-from-below–or 'from the ground up' and thus giving more space to the voices and perspective of the refugees, rather than that of 'policy-makers'; and also incorporating extensive oral testimony and interviews with the refugees. In that sense, the oral history of the Nakba is not only an intellectual project dictated by certain ideological commitments; it can provide an understanding of the social history of the refugees 'from below' that Palestinian elite narratives and political history often ignore or obscure.

Of course the two sets of methodologies can complement each other. But, also crucially, in recent years Palestinian authors have been producing memories of the Nakba, compiling and recording oral testimony and studying annual commemorations. While many authors in the West continue to rely on Morris and his publications as a key source for recovering and reconstructing the past, at least some authors, influenced by the emergence of decolonising methodologies, post-colonial theory and post-modern studies in recent decades, are beginning to raise question marks concerning the reliability and 'objectivity' of the IDF archives.

Moreover it is important to point out that a report by an Israeli officer from 1948 is as much an interpretation of the reality as any other human recollection of the same event; archival documents are never the reality itself (Masalha 2011: 1–53); the reality of 1948 Palestine can only be reconstructed using a range of sources. Even historians who rely extensively on written documents often resort to guesswork and imagination when reconstructing the past from official documents (Pappe 2004b: 189). Therefore the vitality and significance of Palestinian 'oral history' methodologies in the reconstruction of the past is central to understanding the Nakba. The most horrific aspects of the Nakba—the dozens of massacres that accompanied the ethnic cleansing of the Nakba, as well as a detailed description of what ethnic cleansing was from the point of view of the one 'ethnically cleansed'—can only be recovered when such an historiographical approach is applied (Pappe 2004a: 137).

Notes

1. http://www.bbc.co.uk/ww2peopleswar/timeline/
2. http://www.bbc.co.uk/dna/memoryshare/lincolnshire/about
3. Erskine Childers, 'The Other Exodus', *Spectator* (London), 12 May 1961.
4. Rosemary Sayigh, interview by Toine van Teeffelen, in *The Jerusalem Times,* 10 October 1997, at: http://www.palestine-family.net/index.php?nav=3–83&cid=90& did=671.

References

Abu-Sa'ad, Isma'el (2005) 'Forced Sedentarisation, Land Rights and Indigenous Resistance: The Palestinian Bedouin in the Negev', in Nur Masalha (2005) (ed.), *Catastrophe Remembered: Palestine, Israel and the Internal Refugees* (Zed Books: London): 113–41.

Al-'Arif, Arif (1958–1960) *Al-Nakba: Nakbat Bayt al-Maqdis Wal-Firdaws al-Mafqud, 1947–1952* [*The Catastrophe: The Catastrophe of Jerusalem and the Lost Paradise- 1947–52*], 6 Volumes (Beirut and Sidon, Lebanon: Al-Maktaba al-'Asriyya [Arabic]).

Busailah, Reja-e (1981) 'The Fall of Lydda, 1948: Impressions and Reminiscences', *Arab Studies Quarterly* vol. 3 no. 2 (Spring): 123–51.

Dabbagh, Mustafa Murad (1972–1986) *Biladuna Filastin* [Our Country, Palestine] (Beirut and al-Khalil: The Research Centre and Matbu'at Rabitat al-Jami'yyin fi-Muhafazat al-Khalil [Arabic]).

Esber, Rosemarie (2003) *War and Displacement in Mandate Palestine, 29 November 1947 to 15 May 1948.* Thesis submitted for the Degree of PhD, in History, SOAS, University of London).

Foucault, Michel (1972) *The Archaeology of Knowledge* (New York: Harper and Row).

——(1980) *Power/Knowledge: Selected Interviews and Other Writings, 1972–1977* (New York: Pantheon).

Gluck, Sherna Berger (2008) 'Oral History and *al-Nakbah*', *Oral History Review* 35, No.1 (Winter/Spring): 68–80.

Guha, Ranajit (1997) (ed.), *A Subaltern Studies Reader, 1986–1995* (Minneapolis: University of Minnesota Press).

Guha, Ranajit and Gayatri Chakravorty Spivak (1988) (ed.), *Selected Subaltern Studies* (New York: Oxford University Press).

Hooks, Bell (1990) 'Marginality as a site of resistance', in Russell Ferguson *et al.* 1990 (eds.), *Out There: Marginalisation and contemporary Cultures* (Cambridge, MA: MIT): 241–43.

Humphries, Isabelle (2009), 'Displaced Voices: The Politics of Memory amongst Palestinian Internal Refugees in the Galilee (1991–2009)'. Doctoral Dissertation, St Mary's University College and University of Surrey, England.

Issa, Mahmoud (2005) 'The Nakba, Oral History and the Palestinian Peasantry: The case of Lubya', in Nur Masalha (2005) (ed.), *Catastrophe Remembered* (London: Zed Books): 179–86.

Jawhariyyeh, Wasif (2013) *Storyteller of Jerusalem: The Life and Times of Wasif Jawhariyyeh, 1904–1948* (New York: Olive Branch Press).

Khalidi, Walid (1959) 'Why Did the Palestinians Leave?' *Middle East Forum*, 24 (July): 21–24. Reprinted as 'Why Did the Palestinians Leave Revisited', *Journal of Palestine Studies* 34, No. 2 (2005): 42–54.

——(1959a) 'The Fall of Haifa', *Middle East Forum*, 35: 22–32.

——(1961) 'Plan Dalet: The Zionist Master Plan for the Conquest of Palestine', *Middle East Forum*, 37(9) (November): 22–28.

——(1984) *Before Their Diaspora: A Photographic History of the Palestinians, 1876–1948* (Beirut: Institute for Palestine Studies).

——(1992) *All That Remains: The Palestinian Villages Occupied and Depopulated by Israel in 1948* (Washington DC: Institute for Palestine Studies).

Khalidi, Rashid (1997) *Palestinian Identity: The Construction of Modern National Consciousness* (New York: Columbia University Press).

——(2007) *Heroes and Martyrs of Palestine: The Politics of National Commemoration* (Cambridge: Cambridge University Press).

Masalha, Nur (1991) 'Debate on the 1948 Exodus: A Critique of Benny Morris', *Journal of Palestine Studies* 21, No.1 (Autumn): 90–97.

——(2008) 'Remembering the Palestinian Nakba: Commemoration, Oral History and Narratives of Memory', *Holy Land Studies: A Multidisciplinary Journal* 7, No.2 (November): 123–56.

——(2011) 'New History, Post-Zionism and Neo-Colonialism: A Critique of the Israeli "New Historians"', *Holy Land Studies: A Multidisciplinary Journal*, Vol. 10, No.1 (May): 1–53.

——(2012) *The Palestine Nakba: Decolonising History, Narrating the Subaltern, Reclaiming Memory* (London: Zed Books, 2012).

——(2012a) Naji Al-Ali, Edward Said and Civil Liberation Theology in Palestine: Contextual, Indigenous and Decolonising Methodologies', *Holy Land Studies: A Multidisciplinary Journal*, Vol.1. No.2 (November): 109–34.

Massad, Joseph (1995) 'Conceiving the Masculine: Gender and Palestinian Nationalism', *Middle East Journal* 49, No.3 (Summer): 467–83.

——(2008) 'Resisting the Nakba', *Al-Ahram Weekly On-line* (15–21 May), Issue No. 897, at: http://weekly.ahram.org.eg/2008/897/op8.htm.

Nazzal, Nafiz (1974) 'The Zionist occupation of Western Galilee, 1948', *Journal of Palestine Studies* 3, No.3: 58–76.

——(1974a) 'The Flight of the Palestinian Arabs from the Galilee: A Historical Analysis', (Doctoral dissertation, Georgetown University, Washington DC).

——(1978) *The Palestinian Exodus from Galilee* (Beirut: Institute of Palestine Studies). Nimni, Ephraim (2003) (ed.), *The Challenge of Post-Zionism: Alternative to Israeli Fundamentalist Politics* (London: Zed Book).

Nuwayhid, 'Ajaj (1993) *Mudhakkirat 'Ajaj Nuwayhid: Sittuna 'Aman ma' al-Qafila al- 'Arabiyya* [The Memoirs of 'Ajaj Nuwayhid: Sixty Years with the Arab Caravan], edited by Bayan Nuwayhid al-Hout (Beirut: Dar al-Istiqlal lil-Dirasat wal-Nashr [Arabic]).

Pappe, Ilan (2004a) 'Palestine and Truth, Culture and Imperialism: The Legacy of Edward W. Said', *Holy Land Studies: A Multidisciplinary Journal* 2, No.2 (March): 135–39.

——(2004b) 'Historical Truth, Modern Historiography and Ethical Obligations: The Challenge of the Tantura Case', *Holy Land Studies: A Multidisciplinary Journal* 3, No.2 (November): 171–94.

Passerini, Luisa (1998) 'Work ideology and consensus under Italian Fascism', in Robert Perks and Alistair Thomsen (1998) (eds.), *The Oral History Reader* (London: Routledge): 53–62.

Prakash, Gyan (1994) 'Subaltern Studies as Postcolonial Criticism', *The American Historical Review* 99, No.5 (December): 1475–1490, 1476.

Qawuqji, Fawzi (1975) *Filastin fi mudhakirrat al-Qawuqji, 1936–1948* [Palestine in the Qawuqji Memoirs, 1936–1948], edited by Khayriyya Qasmiyya (Beirut: Markiz al-Abhath [Arabic]).

Said, Edward W. (2004) *Freud and the Non-European* (London: Verso, in association with the Freud Museum).

Sanbar, Elias (1984) *Palestine 1948: L'Expulsion* (Paris: Revue d'études palestiniennes).

Shoufani, Elias (1972) 'The Fall of a Village', *Journal of Palestine Studies* 1, No.4 (Summer): 108–21

Smith, Linda Tuhiwai (1999) *Decolonizing Methodologies: Research and Indigenous Peoples* (London: Zed Books).

Starr, Louis (1984) 'Oral History', in David K. Dunaway and Willa K. Baum (1984) (eds.), *Oral History: An Interdisciplinary Anthology* (Tennessee: American Association for State and Local History).

Thompson, E. P. (1966), 'History from Below', *Times Literary Supplement* (April) 279–80.

Trouillot, Michel-Rolph (1995) *Silencing the Past: Power and the Production of History* (Boston, MA: Beacon Press).

Young, Robert J. C. (2003) *Postcolonialism: A Very Short Introduction* (New York: Oxford University Press).

Zurayk, Constantine (1949, 1956) *Ma'na al-Nakba* [The Meaning of the Catastrophe] (Beirut: Khayat [Arabic]),

14
Predicaments of 'Particularity' and 'Universality' in Studies of Japanese Education

Keita Takayama

Two dominant discourses—the 'discourse of particularity' and the 'discourse of universality'—condition the articulation of Japanese education (and by implication 'other' education in general) in education scholarship. The discourse of particularity is produced and circulated by the writings whose primary aim is to introduce Japanese education to non-Japanese readers. In this discourse, disseminating knowledge about Japanese education to the international scholarly community is the end in and of itself. While the writings in this camp draw on either Japanese-language scholarship, English-language scholarship on Japanese education, or both, they are commonly disarticulated from the theoretical debates in English-language comparative education and other disciplines in education (e.g. sociology of education). Hence, these writings tend to circulate rather exclusively within the closed circle of Japanese education 'specialists' in English-language scholarship.

The 'discourse of universality' is produced and circulated when authors closely articulate their discussion of Japanese education to the larger theoretical themes and debates in English-language comparative education or other disciplinary studies in education. The writings in this camp either situate their analysis of Japanese education in the themes and conceptual tools developed in larger education research communities beyond Japanese education specialists, or use their findings of Japanese education to participate in the 'universal' knowledge production in respective fields of educational research. The participation in the universal knowledge work, however, is partial and indirect, because it is always through an analysis of the 'particular' case of Japanese education. This partial participation needs to be differentiated from a theoretical exposition often undertaken by Anglo-American 'theorists' who are not expected to explicitly situate their theoretical discussion in an analysis of a particular national case.

While drawing on either or both of these discourses, all the existing studies on Japanese education indicate a particular inclination towards one or the other discourse.

Discourse of particularity

Both Japanese and Anglo-American scholars participate in the production and circulation of the discourse of particularity. In Japanese scholars' writings, it manifests itself in the form of general introduction books and journal articles on Japanese education wherein the authors provide descriptive accounts of particular topics on Japanese education (e.g. Aso and Amano 1982; Horio 1986; Kobayashi 1986, 1993; Takeuchi 1991; Shimizu 1992; Fujita 2000, 2009; Otsu 2000; Imai and Saito 2004; Tsuneyoshi 2004; Motani 2005; Nabeshima 2009; Takayama 2009a)[1] or Japanese education in general (e.g. Okano and Tsuchiya 1999; Yamashita and Williams 2002). They tend to have a general topic in the titles such as *The internationalisation of Japanese education* (Kobayashi 1986), *Civics education in Japan* (Otsu 2000), *Education reform and education politics in Japan* (Fujita 2000), and *Progressive struggle and critical education scholarship in Japan* (Takayama 2009a). As is clear from the list of authors here, some of the leading education scholars from Japan undertake such introductory writings—often in response to an invitation to edited 'international' books and journal special issues—as the 'representatives' of Japanese education scholarship. English-language translations of Japanese writings are another example of this kind (e.g. Horio 1986). These writings draw primarily on Japanese-language studies with a limited number of references to the English-language literature.

Many Anglo-American scholars also produce and circulate the discourse of particularity on Japanese education (e.g. Singleton 1989; Shimahara 1997; S.D. Hoffman 1999; Green 2000; Cave 2001, 2003; Hood 2001, 2003; Duke 2009; Howe 2009). While they commonly draw on existing English-language writings of Japanese education and the Japanese government's policy documents, the extent to which they reference Japanese-language studies differs considerably. For instance, while Cave's (2001) discussion of Japanese education reform is substantively informed by some of the key figures in the domestic discussion of education reform at the time, Howe (2009) cites only a handful of Japanese authors in his discussion of Japanese pre-service teacher training, and S.D. Hoffman (1999) cites no Japanese studies in his historical study. In contrast, Benjamin Duke's (2009) latest work on early modern Japanese education distinguishes itself from other English-language studies of Japanese education; the book draws almost exclusively on studies by Japanese historians (see also Duke 1989). Whether drawing on Japanese- or English-language literature on Japanese education, these writings are similar in that they are disconnected from theoretical discussions in wider scholarly communities. They constitute a rather closed, 'thick' discursive community within which mutual referencing is extensive due to its lack of articulation to wider scholarly communities and the limited amount of English-language scholarship on Japanese education.

The primary scholarly contribution of this discursive community is the introduction of Japanese-language studies and discussions to non-Japanese education researchers who do not necessarily have access to them, or who lack the required linguistic competency to read them. Occasionally, these writings are taken up by English-speaking, Anglo-American scholars who pursue 'theoretical' work in comparative education.[2] They use these writings as the 'raw materials' (Connell 2007, 140) against which their supposedly 'context-free' theoretical work is tested for wider global applicability. Furthermore, some of the aforementioned Japanese scholars write in English in a structure and style that reflects the Japanese scholarly writing styles and conventions (see Horio 1986, 1988; Shimizu 1992; Yamashita and Williams 2002; Fujita 2009; Nabeshima 2009), although many are compelled to conform to the English writing conventions to avoid having their work 'dismissed as incomprehensible or as inferior products' (Miyoshi in Kuwayama 2004, 29). The diversification of what counts as quality scholarly writings should be recognised as an important contribution of these writings, especially those written by Japanese scholars who consciously or unconsciously do not conform to the dominant English-language academic conventions. The inclusion of such writings can challenge the Eurocentricity of academic discourses in English-language publications (see Canagarajah 2002; Kuwayama 2004; Singh and Han 2010). Furthermore, these writings could reflect particular epistemological and theoretical traditions of Japanese educational research and thus can be celebrated as addressing the issue of 'epistemological diffidence' (Appadurai 2001) in English-language educational scholarship.

Despite these scholarly contributions, the writings drawing on the discourse of particularity can set discursive limitations on the way Japanese education can be articulated in English-language publications. As discussed earlier, these writings are disarticulated from current themes and debates in English-language education research communities. Duke's (2009) aforementioned historical study, for instance, documents the early development of Japanese modern schooling at the time of state formation in the late nineteenth century. Though his study does an exceptional job of piecing together Japanese historians' works, it does not engage with any wider scholarly discussions on the relevant topics. As I point out elsewhere, his study could have made a significant contribution to the sociological literature on the role of education in state formation (see Takayama 2010b). Likewise, Tsuneyoshi's (2004) discussion of the recent scholastic 'crisis' in Japanese education, though providing a comprehensive summary of the key debate participants, is hardly articulated with the theoretical discussion of 'crisis' and its politics in comparative education and sociology of education (see Takayama 2007, 2010a).

Because of this lack of articulation to the wider discussions, the scholarly legitimacy of these studies centres largely on the use value of their discussion, either to those who specialise in Japanese education or those who engage in theoretical work, most likely Anglo-American comparative education 'theorists'. Hence, by uncritically accepting the discursive position as 'area specialists' offered by the Anglo-American-centric, international division of academic labour (Ben-Ari and van Bremen 2005, 17), these authors tacitly endorse the very world system of education scholarship that defines 'other' scholars' knowledge as partial and localised and thus excludes them from the process of theoretical knowledge production (Kuwayama 2004, 55; Connell 2007, 44).

More problematically, these studies are tacitly premised upon, and thus reinforce, the problematic belief that 'it is possible to make sense of Japanese education in terms of Japan alone'.[3] Hence, the publication of these studies naturalises methodological nationalism—'the epistemological assumptions about the primacy of the nation state as the fundamental unit of social analysis' (Sugimoto 2003, 17). Lastly, not being situated in the English-language scholarly debates can be justified by and thus reinforce the prevailing thesis of Japanese 'exceptionalism' (Mouer and Sugimoto 1986; Befu 2001a; Sugimoto 2003, ch. 1): Japanese education can only be understood through the terms of references that are specific to it, because it is so 'unique'.

In fact, the lack of articulation to the larger theoretical debates could also reflect Japanese scholars' tacit belief about the 'uniqueness' of their education system and associated phenomena (Takayama 2009b). Accepting the Eurocentric view of non-Western knowledges as 'partial', Japanese scholars take for granted the limited applicability of their discussions beyond Japan. Drawing on the discourse of Japanese cultural nationalism (*nihonjinron*) (see Befu 2001a; Sugimoto 2003, ch. 1), they tend to accentuate the 'unique' characteristics of Japanese education often defined in clear opposition to what they construct as 'Western education' (Befu 2001a, 6; Takayama 2008a; Nozaki 2009). As I will discuss in the next section, this self-Orientalising preoccupation about Japanese 'special characteristics' (Kobayashi 1993, 4) echoes with many Anglo-American studies of Japanese education that draw on the discourse of universality in identifying the 'uniqueness' of Japanese schooling.

Discourse of universality

Just like the discourse of particularity, both Japanese and Anglo-American scholars participate in the production and circulation of the discourse of universality. This discursive community consists of not only English-language, predominantly Anglo-American, researchers specialising in Japanese education but also Japanese scholars who were trained in English-language academic institutions (myself included). These researchers discuss Japanese education by closely relating it to the theoretical themes and debates in English-language academic discourses. They draw on theoretical constructs and frameworks developed primarily in Anglo-American scholarly communities to analyse things about Japanese education (see Shimahara 1984; Schoppa 1991; Parmenter 1999; Aspinall 2001; Sato 2004; Okano 2006; Cave 2007; Rappleye 2007, 2009, 2011; Takayama 2007, 2008b, 2008c, 2010a; Nitta 2008; Ohkura 2008; Bjork 2009). In these writings, the data on Japanese education are framed by the concepts, debates and research strategies that have evolved out of discussions in Anglo-American scholarly communities with little participation of Japanese researchers. For instance, my recent publications on the politics of discourse borrowing in Japanese education reform (Takayama 2007, 2008c, 2010a; Takayama and Apple 2008) subscribe to this orientation, because they draw heavily on the theoretical discussions of educational transfer and critical sociology of education, both of which centre in Anglo-American scholarly communities. Rappleye (2011) does the same, when utilising the discussion of postwar Japanese education reforms to achieve a conceptual coherence in the ongoing debate on educational transfer engaged in predominantly by Anglo-American comparativists. These studies treat Japanese education as a site where Anglo-American theoretical constructs and frameworks are tested and refined to gain 'universal' reach (Connell 2007). While the extent to which these writings refer to Japanese-language literature considerably differs, even those that extensively reference many Japanese-language studies tend to use them not as a source of theoretical insights but more as 'raw data' with which to refine their conceptual arguments relevant to Anglo-American scholarly debates (e.g. Parmenter 1999; Aspinall 2001; Cave 2007; Takayama 2007, 2010a; Rappleye 2007, 2009, 2011; Bjork 2009). These researchers therefore help maintain the existing unequal global production, distribution, and consumption of educational knowledge and reinforce the hegemony of 'Western' theoretical knowledge.

While similarly using Japanese education as a 'testing ground', others use Japanese cases more consciously as an 'anomaly' to expose the particular situatedness of existing theoretical constructs and frameworks that are developed in Anglo-American scholarly communities (e.g. Cummings 1980; Tobin 2000; Takayama 2009b). Many comparative studies of Japanese schooling for instance discuss Japanese pedagogical assumptions, such as the Japanese notion of self, to highlight the 'particularity' (non-universality) of the Western conceptualisation (e.g. White 1987; Lewis 1995; D.M. Hoffman 1999, 2000; Sato 2004; Cave 2007). I have also used the case of the Japanese textbook controversy over 'comfort women' to denaturalise what is taken for granted in the Anglo-American critical education scholarship, exposing what I call 'conceptual nationalism' which reflects the particular geopolitical location of Anglo-American critical scholars of education (see Takayama 2009b). These works use the Japanese 'anomaly' to identify the shortcomings of the existing theoretical tools and frameworks and thus attract wider readership than the first kind of writings—drawing on discourse of particularity—which are disconnected from the discussions outside the circle of Japanese education specialists.

These 'universal' studies also pose serious dilemmas, however. First, they are more likely written in a style and structure that closely conform to the conventional English-language academic discourse, thus hardly making a dent in the hegemony of English-language academic discourse. Second, they tend to define Japanese 'particularities' within the framework of 'universality' that the English-language scholarly discourse unreflectively assumes. Hence, they tacitly reinforce the normative status of Western scholarship and the associated Orientalist epistemology upon which Japanese 'particularities' and 'differences' are constructed. These studies inherit the long tradition of Western scholarship of Japanese society wherein Japanese 'uniqueness' is defined in contrast to what is deemed 'Western' (or 'American') (Befu 2001a; Nozaki 2009). They construct the 'unique' features of Japanese schooling through an implicit contrasting with 'Western' schooling; the elements of Japanese schooling that are rendered the 'essence' of Japanese schooling (Befu 2001a, 5; Sugimoto 2003, 17; Takayama 2008a, 2011).

This particular construction of Japanese 'uniqueness' is so uncritically accepted that few English-language studies dare to relativise it by comparing Japanese schooling to non-Western national counterparts [Tobin, Wu and Davidson (1991) is one of very few exceptions]. In fact, some of the supposedly 'uniquely Japanese' pedagogical beliefs and practices—such as the use of small groups (*han*) in classrooms (Tsuney-oshi 1994)—are not distinctively Japanese at all when compared with those in non-Western nations, especially in Asian nations. While these studies certainly 'make Japanese schooling more understandable to Anglo-American readers, whether they help Koreans and Pakistanis to understand Japanese schooling is totally a different question' (modified from Befu in Kuwayama 2004, 39). By failing to recognise the 'partiality of the truth' that the binary contrasting between Japan and the West generates, these studies marginalise alternative representations of Japanese education attainable when it is examined in different, non-Western academic reference communities (Befu 2001a, 6, 66). Third, treating Japanese education as a testing ground for Eurocentric theoretical constructs and frameworks, these studies often ignore the 'indigenous' discourse of Japanese educational research and debates as a valuable source of theoretical insights.

Fourth, studies that use the Japanese 'anomaly' to expose the Eurocentricity of the existing theoretical constructs often draw on the essentialist discussion of Japanese culture as manifested in Japanese cultural nationalism. This trend is particularly seen in the large volume of literature on Japanese schooling (e.g. White 1987; Lewis 1995; Shimahara and Sakai 1995; D.M. Hoffman 1999, 2000; Tsuneyoshi 2001; Sato 2004; Cave 2007). For instance, D.M. Hoffman's (2000) use of the Japanese 'anomaly' to expose the culturally situated (thus not universal) nature of the 'Western' theory of self and learning is premised upon the binary construction between Japanese and Western cultural theories of self and learning. She draws extensively on the so-called 'Japanist' studies,[4] the English-language, anthropological and socio-psychological studies of Japanese culture and society (e.g. Nakane 1972; Doi 1973; Lebra 1976) and comparative studies of Japanese schooling (e.g. White 1987; Lewis 1995) that were published in the 1980s and the early 1990s and are heavily informed by the Japanist studies, or what I have called elsewhere 'foundational studies' of Japanese schooling (Takayama 2010c). The Japanist studies tend to 'abstract(s) "cultural average" or "dominant value orientations" in an effort to define national character as the major independent variable' (Mouer and Sugimoto 1986, 13; Sugimoto 2003, 13). This classic anthropologists' holistic view of culture (Tai 2003, 5) leaves unaddressed issues of power, social conflict, and internal diversity in terms of gender, class, ethnicity, age, location, and other factors (McConaghy 2000; Nozaki 2009). 'Foundational studies' uncritically accept the Japanist notion of 'national culture' and view schooling primarily as a cultural institution where children are socialised into *the* Japanese way of being. They use the notion of 'Japanese cultural patterns' as drawn from the Japanist studies in explaining the 'unique' Japanese pedagogical practice and theory. By uncritically accepting the same essentialist discourse of 'contrasting cultural difference' between Japan and the West (White 1987, 5; Tsuneyoshi 2001, 2), these 'deconstructive' studies take the 'fundamental difference' as a given. In so doing, they fail to recognise that 'difference' is always produced within given power relations (Said 1978; Gupta and Ferguson 1992). The effort to deconstruct the hegemonic, Eurocentric discourse of teaching and learning in the West through the use of the Japanese 'anomaly', therefore, ironically naturalises another hegemonic discourse in the discussion of Japanese education [see Takayama (2010c, 2011) for an extended discussion on this].[5]

Lastly, imbedded in these 'deconstructive', comparative studies is a problematic notion of 'American (Australian, British, or Canadian etc. for that matter) culture' and 'American schooling' which serves as the implicit reference point of comparison. As much as the Japanese model of schooling that these studies construct ignores the internal ethnic, gender, and socio-economic diversities within Japan, the 'American model of schooling' also excludes these social variables from the discussion of American cultural practices and schooling. Smuggled in the essentialist construction of Japanese schooling therefore is the implicit presumption that the 'distinctiveness' of Japanese schooling means its difference from the unmarked, white, middle-class self (Gupta and Ferguson 1992, 14). Just as the construction of 'Japanese schooling' is racist in that it ignores the existence of ethnic diversity within Japan, its dialectic counterpart, the construction of 'American schooling', is equally racist in that it normalises a particular segment of the population as 'true Americans' and their schooling experience as 'true American schooling'.[6]

To sum up, many existing English-language writings on Japanese education, including my own, unreflexively subscribe to and reinforce the discourses of particularity and universality that situate writing about Japanese education deeply in what Kuwayama (2004, 139) calls a 'conspiracy'—the problematic collaboration between Western Orientalist discourse and Japanese self-Orientalising cultural nationalism (Tai 2003; Takayama 2007, 2008a). The discursive condition has been established in English-language educational scholarship wherein those who write about Japanese education could either participate in the conspiracy or become complicit with the global hegemony of Western academic discourses. The more education scholars uncritically accept the discursive position that the field offers them as the 'Japanese education specialist', the more entrenched the discursive constraints become, making it extremely difficult to articulate Japanese 'differences' and 'particularities' in a manner that dissociates them from either of these dominant discourses.

Notes

1. See also many chapters written by leading Japanese education scholars in Shields' (1993) edited volume on Japanese schooling.
2. For instance, see how Cowen (1996, 164) uses the English-language translation of Horio's (1988) work among others to advance his 'theoretical' argument.
3. This quote is inspired by Dale and Robertson's (1997, 209) assertion that 'it is not possible to make sense of New Zealand education policy in terms of New Zealand alone'.
4. 'Japanism' is a term that Brian Moeran created after Said's *Orientalism* (see Nozaki 2009, 485).
5. This issue of 'essentialism through comparison' is not specific to the comparative studies of Japanese education. As many leading comparativists claim, 'only by seeing the *uniqueness* in the way others carry on education can one genuinely appreciate the *distinctiveness* of education at home' (Mallinson in Epstein 1988, 9, my emphasis added; see also Rohlen and LeTendre 1998, 3; Crossley 2001, 45; Bray 2003a, 7). None of these scholars discuss the problematic inclination of cultural relativism towards cultural essentialism (see McConaghy 2000).
6. More recent studies (e.g. Tsuneyoshi 2001; Sato 2004; Cave 2007) attempt to diversify the rather monolithic representation of the earlier 'foundational studies' with their explicit focus on gender (Cave), class (Sato), and ethnicity (Tsuneyoshi) in their discussion of Japanese schooling. However, as I have discussed elsewhere (Takayama 2011), their treatment of domestic diversities is often localised in particular sections of their books

References

Appadurai, A. 2001 Grassroots globalization and the research imagination. In *Globalization,* ed. A. Appadurai, 1–21. Durham, NC: Duke University Press.
Aso, M., and I. Amano. 1982. *Education and Japan's modernization.* Tokyo: The Japan Times Ltd.
Aspinall, R.W. 2001. *Teachers' unions and the politics of education in Japan.* Albany, NY: State University of New York Press.
Befu, H. 2001a. *Hegemony of homogeneity.* Melbourne: Trans Pacific Press. Ben-Ari, E., and J. van Bremen. 2005. Asian anthropologies and anthropologies in Asia. In *Asian anthropology,* ed. J. van Bremen, E. Ben-Ari, and S.F. Alatas, 3–39. London:RoutledgeCurzon.
Bjork, C. 2009. Local implementation of Japan's integrated studies reform. *Comparative Education* 45, no. 1: 23–44.
Canagarajah, S.A. 2002. *A geopolitics of academic writing.* Pittsburgh, PA: University of Pittsburgh Press.
Cave, P. 2001. Education reform in Japan in the 1990s. *Comparative Education* 37, no. 2:173–191.
Cave, P. 2003. Japanese educational reform. In *Can the Japanese change their education system?,* ed. R. Goodman and D. Phillips, 87–102. Oxford: Symposium Books.
Cave, P. 2007. *Primary school in Japan.* London: Routledge.
Connell, R. 2007. *Southern theory.* Crows Nest, NSW: Allen & Unwin
Cummings, W.K. 1980. *Education and equality in Japan.* Princeton, NJ: Princeton University Press.
Doi, T. 1973. *The anatomy of dependence.* Tokyo: Kodansha International.
Duke, B.C., ed. 1989. *Ten great educators of modern Japan: A Japanese perspective.* Tokyo: Tokyo University Press.
Duke, B.C. 2009. *The history of modern Japanese education.* Piscataway, NJ: Rutgers University Press.

Fujita, H. 2000. Education reform and education politics in Japan. *American Sociologist* 31, no. 3: 42–57.

Fujita, H. 2009. Whither Japanese schooling? In *Challenges to Japanese education,* ed. J.A. Gordon, H. Fujita, T. Kariya, and G. LeTendre, 17–53. New York: Teachers College Press.

Green, A. 2000. Converging paths or ships passing in the night? An 'English' critique of Japanese school reform. *Comparative Education* 36, no. 4: 417–35.

Gupta, A., and J. Ferguson. 1992. Beyond 'culture': Space, identity, and the politics of difference. *Cultural Anthropology* 7, no. 1: 6–23.

Hoffman, D.M. 1999. Culture and comparative education: Toward decentering and recentering the discourse. *Comparative Education Review* 43, no. 4: 464–88.

Hoffman, D.M. 2000. Pedagogies of self in American and Japanese early childhood education. *The Elementary School Journal* 101, no. 2: 193–208.

Hoffman, S.D. 1999. School texts, the written word, and political indoctrination: A review of moral education curricula in modern Japan (1886–1997). *History of Education* 28, no. 1:87–96.

Hood, C.P. 2001. *Japanese education reform: Nakasone's legacy.* London: Routledge

Hood, C.P. 2003. The third great reform of the Japanese education system. In *Can the Japanese change their education system?,* ed. R. Goodman and D. Phillips, 73–85. Oxford: Symposium Books.

Horio, T. 1986. Towards reform in Japanese education. *Comparative Education* 22, no. 1: 31–36.

Horio, T. 1988. *Educational thought and ideology in modern Japan.* Tokyo: University of Tokyo Press.

Howe, E.R. 2009. Teacher induction across the Pacific: A comparative study of Canada and Japan. *Journal of Education for Teaching: International Research and Pedagogy* 34, no. 4: 333–46.

Kobayashi, T. 1986. The internationalisation of Japanese education. *Comparative Education* 22, no. 1: 65–71.

Kobayashi, T. 1993. Japan's teacher education in comparative perspectives. *Peabody Journal of Education* 68, no. 3: 4–15.

Kuwayama, T. 2004. *Native anthropology.* Melbourne: Trans Pacific Press.

Lebra, T.S. 1976. *Japanese patterns of behavior.* Honolulu: University of Hawaii Press.

Lewis, C.C. 1995. *Educating hearts and minds: Reflections on Japanese preschool and elementary education.* Cambridge: Cambridge University Press.

McConaghy, C. 2000. *Rethinking Indigenous education.* Flaxton Qld: Post Pressed.

Motani, R. 2005. Hopes and challenges for progressive educators in Japan. *Comparative Education* 41, no. 3: 309–27.

Mouer, R., and Y. Sugimoto. 1986. *Images of Japanese society.* New York: Kegan Paul International.

Nabeshima, Y. 2009. Invisible racism in Japan: Impact on academic achievement of minority children. In *Challenges to Japanese education,* ed. J.A. Gordon, H. Fujita, T. Kariya, and G. LeTendre, 109–30. New York: Teachers College Press.

Nakane, C. 1972. *Japanese society.* Berkeley, CA: University of California Press.

Nitta, K.A. 2008. *The politics of structural education reform.* New York: Routledge.

Nozaki, Y. 2009. Orientalism, the West and non-West binary, and postcolonial perspectives in cross-cultural research and education. In *International handbook for critical education,*ed. M.W. Apple, W. Au, and L. Gandin, 482–90. New York: Routledge.

Ohkura, K. 2008. Dewey and ambivalent modern Japan. In *Inventing the modern self and John Dewey,* ed. T. Popkewitz, 279–99. New York: Palgrave.

Okano, K.H. 2006. The global–local interface in multicultural education policies in Japan. *Comparative Education* 42, no. 4: 473–91.

Okano, K., and M. Tsuchiya. 1999. *Education in contemporary Japan.* Cambridge: Cambridge University Press.

Otsu, K. 2000. Civics education in Japan: Values promoted in the school curriculum. *Asia Pacific Journal of Education* 20, no. 1: 53–62.

Parmenter, L. 1999. Constructing national identity in a changing world: Perspectives in Japanese education. *British Journal of Sociology of Education* 20, no. 4: 453–63.

Rappleye, J. 2007. *Exploring cross-national attraction in education.* Oxford: Symposium Books.

Rappleye, J. 2009. Re-contextualizing foreign influence in Japan's educational history. *Encounter* 10. http://library.queensu.ca/ojs/index.php/encounters/article/viewArticle/1951.

Rappleye, J. 2011. *Educational policy transfer in an era of globalization.* Frankfurt: Peter Lang.

Said, E.W. 1978. *Orientalism.* New York: Pantheon Books.

Saito, N., and Y. Imai. 2004. In search of the public and the private: Philosophy of education in post-war Japan. *Comparative Education* 40, no. 4: 583–94.

Sato, N.E. 2004. *Inside Japanese classrooms: The heart of education.* New York: Routledge.

Schoppa, L.J. 1991. *Education reform in Japan: A case of immobilist politics.* London: Routledge.

Shimahara, N.K. 1984. Toward the equality of a Japanese minority: The case of Burakumin. *Comparative Education* 20, no. 3: 339–53.

Shimahara, N.K. 1997. Restructuring Japanese high school. In *The challenge of East Asian education,* ed. W.K. Cummings and P.K. Altbach, 87–100. Albany, NY: State University of New York Press.

Shimahara, N.K., and A. Sakai. 1995. *Learning to teach in two cultures: Japan and the United States.* New York: Garland.

Shimizu, K. 1992. Shido: Education selection in a Japanese middle school. *Comparative Education* 28, no. 2: 109–29.

Singh, M., and J. Han. 2010. Peer review, Bourdieu and honour: Connecting Chinese and Australian intellectual projects. *British Journal of Sociology of Education* 31, no. 2: 185–98.

Singleton, J. 1989. Gambaru: A Japanese cultural theory of learning. In *Culture theory: Essays on mind, self, and emotion,* ed. J. Shields, 8–15. University Park, PA: Pennsylvania State University Press.

Sugimoto, Y. 2003. *An introduction to Japanese society.* 2nd ed. Cambridge: Cambridge University Press.

Tai, E. 2003. Rethinking culture, national culture, and Japanese culture. *Japanese Language and Literature* 37: 1–26.

Takayama, K. 2007. A nation at risk crosses the Pacific: Transnational borrowing of the U.S. crisis discourse in the debate on education reform in Japan. *Comparative Education Review* 51, no. 4: 423–46.

Takayama, K. 2008a. Beyond Orientalism in comparative education: Challenging the binary opposition between Japanese and American education. *Asia Pacific Journal of Education* 28, no. 1: 19–34.

Takayama, K. 2008b. The politics of international league tables: PISA in Japanese crisis debate. *Comparative Education* 44, no. 4: 387–407.

Takayama, K. 2008c. Japan's Ministry of Education 'becoming the right': Neoliberal restructuring and the Ministry's struggles for political legitimacy. *Globalisation, Societies, and Education* 6, no. 2: 131–14.

Takayama, K. 2009a. Progressive struggle and critical education scholarship in Japan. In *International handbook for critical education,* ed. M.W. Apple, W. Au, and L. Gandin, 354–67. New York: Routledge.

Takayama, K. 2009b. Globalizing critical studies of 'official' knowledge: Lessons from the Japanese history textbook controversy over 'comfort women'. *British Journal of Sociology of Education* 30, no. 5: 577–89.

Takayama, K. 2010a. Politics of externalization in reflexive times: Reinventing Japanese education reform discourses through 'Finnish success'. *Comparative Education Review* 54, no. 1: 51–75.

Takayama, K. 2010b. Book review: The history of modern Japanese education: Constructing the national school system, 1872–1890. *Asia Pacific Journal of Education* 30, no. 2: 243–45.

Takayama, K. 2010c. Rethinking 'culture', 'difference', and 'comparison': A genealogical review of the comparative studies of Japanese education. Paper presented at the World Congress of Comparative Education Society XIV World Congress, Istanbul, Turkey.

Takayama, K. 2011. Other Japanese educations and Japanese education otherwise. *Asia Pacific Journal of Education.*

Takayama, K., and M.W. Apple. 2008. The cultural politics of borrowing: Japan, Britain, and the narrative of educational crisis. *British Journal of Sociology of Education* 29, no. 3: 289–301.

Takeuchi, Y. 1991. Myth and reality in the Japanese educational selection system. *Comparative Education* 27, no. 1: 101–12

Tobin, J. 2000. Using 'the Japanese problem' as a corrective to the ethnocentricity of Western theory. *Child Development* 71, no. 5: 1155–58.

Tobin, J., D. Wu, and D. Davidson. 1991. *Preschool in three cultures.* New Haven, CT: Yale University Press.

Tsuneyoshi, R. 1994. Small groups in Japanese elementary classrooms. *Comparative Education* 30, no. 2: 115–29.

Tsuneyoshi, R. 2001. *The Japanese model of schooling: Comparison with the United States.* New York: RoutlegeFalmer.

Tsuneyoshi, R. 2004. The new Japanese educational reforms and the achievement: 'Crisis 'debate. *Educational Policy* 18, no. 2: 364–94.

White, M. 1987. *The Japanese educational challenge.* New York: Collier Macmillan.

Yamashita, H., and C. Williams. 2002. A vote for consensus: Democracy and difference in Japan. *Comparative Education* 38, no. 3: 277–89.

Further Readings

Section 3: History, Knowledge, and Power

Abdo, N. (2002). *Women and the Politics of Military Confrontation. Palestinian and Israeli Gendered Narratives of Dislocation*, New York and Oxford: Berghahn.

Bekerman, Z and Zembylas, M (2012). *Teaching Contested Narratives Identity, Memory and Reconciliation in Peace Education and Beyond*, Cambridge, New York, Melbourne, Madrid, Cape Town, Singapore, São Paulo, Delhi, Tokyo, Mexico City: Cambridge University Press.

Castiglione, A. (ed.) (2004). *Danilo Dolci. Memory and Utopia*, Partinico: Centro per lo Sviluppo Creativo 'Danilo Dolci' (www.danilodolci.net).

Christou, M and Puigvert, L. (2011). 'The Role of "Other Women" in Current Educational Transformations.' *International Studies in Sociology of Education*, 21(1), 77–90.

Darder, A. (2011). *A Dissident Voice: Essays in Culture, Pedagogy & Power.* New York: Peter Lang.

Darmanin, M. (2011). 'On a Hard Rock: Trying to Be Radical in a Conservative Context.' in *Educators of the Mediterranean….Up Close and Personal. Critical Voices from South Europe and the MENA Region.*, Sultana, R. G. (ed.), Rotterdam, Taipei and Boston: Sense Publishers.

Elsheikh M. S (1999). 'Le Omissioni della Cultura Italiana' (The Omissions of Italian Culture) in *L'Islam nella Scuola* (Islam in the School), Siggillino, I (Ed.), Milan: Editore Franco Angeli.

Fagan, G. H. (1991). 'Local Struggles: Women in the Home and Critical Feminist Pedagogy in Ireland.' *Journal of Education, 173*, 65–75. Retrieved from http://eprints.nuim.ie/494/1/local_struggles.pdf.

Foucault, M. (1980). *Power/Knowledge: Selected Interviews and Other Writings 1972–1977.* New York: Pantheon.

Foucault, M.(1988). 'Technologies of the Self.' In L.H. Martin, H. Gutman, & P.H. Hutton (Eds.), *Technologies of the self* (pp. 16–49). Amherst: University of Massachusetts Press.

Galeano, E. (2009). *Open Veins of Latin America.* London: Serpent's Tail.

Gregoriou, Z (1991). *The Encounter with the Other in Its Alterity and Corporeality*, Urbana Champaign: University of Illinois at Urbana-Champaign.

Gregoriou, Z. (1998). *Learning Performances of Dislocation, Receptivity and Hybridity in Women's Utopian Writing*, Urbana Champaign: University of Illinois at Urbana-Champaign.

Kashope Wright, H. (2012). 'Is This an African I See Before Me? Black African Identity and the Politics of (Western, Academic) Knowledge' in *The Dialectic of African Education and Western Discourses*, Kashope Wright, H and Abdi, A. A (Eds), New York City: Peter Lang.

Liasidou, A. (2012). 'Inclusive Education and Critical Pedagogy at the Intersections of Disability, Race, Gender and Class.' *Journal for Critical Education Policy Studies, 10*, 168–84. Retrieved from http://www.jceps.com/.

Lynch, K, Grummel, B. and Devine, D. (2012). *New Managerialism in Education Commercialization, Carelessness and Gender*, New York and London: Palgrave-Macmillan.

Macías, F and Redondo, G. (2012). 'Pueblo gitano, género y educación: investigar para excluir o investigar para transformar' (Gypsy People, Gender and Education. Research to Exclude or Research to Transform), *International Journal of Sociology of Education*, Vol. 1 (1), 71–92.

Marx, K. and Engels, F. (1970). *The German Ideology*, ed. C.J. Arthur, London: Lawrence and Wishart.

Meneseses, M. P. (2011).'Images Outside the Mirror? Mozambique and Portugal in World History.' *Human Architecture: Journal of the Sociology of Self-Knowledge*, 121–36.

Mignolo, W. D. & Tlostanova, M. V. (2006).'Theorizing from the Borders: Shifting to Geo- and Body-Politics of Knowledge.' *European Journal of Social Theory*, 9(2), 205–21. doi: 10.1177/1368431006063333.

Paredes-Canilao, N. (2007). Engendering Asian Critical Pedagogies. Proceedings of the Redesigning Pedagogy: Culture, Knowledge and Understanding Conference. http://conference.nie.edu.sg/2007/paper/papers/PanelA3.pdf.

Pisani M (2012). 'Addressing the "Citizenship Assumption" in Critical Pedagogy: Exploring the Case of Rejected Female Sub-Saharan African Asylum Seekers in Malta,' *Power and Education*, Vol. 4 (2), 185–95.

Schulz, S. (2007). 'Inside the Contract Zone:White Teachers in the Anangu Pitjantjatjara Yankunytjatjara Landa.' *International Education Journal*, 8(2), 270–83. Retrieved from http://iej.com.au.

Smith, G. H. (1999). 'Reform of the New Zealand Education System and Responses by the Indigenous Maori of New Zealand.' *Journal of Educational Studies*, 21, 60–72. Retrieved fromhttp://www.directions.usp.ac.fj/collect/direct/index/assoc/D770159.dir/doc.pdf.

Smith, L. T. (2005). 'On Tricky Ground Researching the Native in the Age of Uncertainty.' In N. K. Denzin & Y. S.

Sousa Santos, B. (2007). *Another Knowledge is Possible*. London: Verso.

Sousa Santos, B. (2014). *Epistemologies from South*. Boulder: Paradigm.

Lincoln (Eds.). *The Sage Handbook of Qualitative Research* (3rd ed., 85–108). Thousand Oaks, CA: Sage Publications.

Smith, L. T. (2012). *Decolonizing Methodologies*. London: Zed Books.

Thomas, M., & Rugambwa, A. (2011). 'Equity, Power, and Capabilities: Constructions of Gender in a Tanzanian Secondary School.' *The John Hopkins University Press*, 23(3), 153–75. doi: 10.1353/ff.2011.0030.

Ventura, M. (2012). 'Between Intercultural and Critical Pedagogy: The Subtle Exclusion of Immigrant Students.' *Intercultural Education*, 23(6), 555–65. http://dx.doi.org/10.1080/14675986.2012.731206.

Zoletto, D. (2012). *Pedagogia e studi culturali. La formazione tra critica postcoloniale e flussi culturali transnazionali* (Pedagogy and Cultural Studies. Education between Postcolonial Critique and Transnational Cultural Influences), Pisa: ETS.

Zygmantas, J. (2009). 'Understanding Critical Pedagogy and Its Impact on the Construction of Knowledge.' *Acta Paedagogica Vilnensia*, 23, 63–78.

Section 4
Society, Politics, and Curriculum

The highest education is that which does not merely give us information but makes our life in harmony with all existence. But we find that this education of sympathy is not only systematically ignored in schools, but it is severely repressed. From our very childhood habits are formed and knowledge is imparted in such a manner that our life is weaned away from nature, and our mind and the world are set in opposition from the beginning of our days. Thus the greatest of educations for which we came prepared is neglected, and we are made to lose our world to find a bagful of information instead.

Rabindranath Tagore, *My School* (1933)

The individual consciousness of the overwhelming majority of children reflects social and cultural relations which are different from and antagonistic to those which are represented in the school curricula: thus the 'certain' of an advanced culture becomes 'true' in the framework of a fossilized and anachronistic culture. There is no unity between school and life, and so there is no automatic unity between instruction and education.

Antonio Gramsci, *Selections from Prison Notebooks* (1971)

15

Curriculum and Society
Rethinking the Link

Alicia de Alba

There are different modes of integration, transformation, combination, distortion and appropriation, which make it difficult to delimit movements into classifiable identities. This multiplicity cannot be reduced to a tabular order – fixed and stable – because of differences, on the one hand, between diverse cultural traditions and states, and the opening of spaces among disciplines, on the other.
Michael Peters, *Nietzsche, Poststructuralism and Education : After the Subject?*

In contrast to the situation in the 1960s and 70s, and even parts of the 80s when the school was accorded a particular social role, the link today between curriculum and society has become profoundly uncertain. In the complex and crisis-ridden times we live in, it has become almost impossible to define a role for the curriculum in debates about the shape of the world we wish to inhabit. The making of this link between curriculum and society is rendered all the more difficult because of the absence of what we might call utopian visions.[1] In the past we had access to utopian visions which spawned important social projects, such as socialism, which in turn inspired particular under standings of the role of the school in promoting social change.

The rapid changes that have occurred around the globe after the collapse of the Berlin Wall in 1989, combined with the erosion of the epistemological foundations of Western thought, have placed the educational field and, within it, the curriculum, in an extremely complex situation. This condition can be looked at in a number of ways. Among these, it might be said that:

1. academics have not been able to constitute themselves as subjects *(as agents)* in the context of the process of curricular overdetermination (de Alba 1995a);
2. the complex surface of inscription of education and the curriculum (i.e. the space in which discourse might be inserted), is marked by the presence of split subjects (i.e. subjects who are the products of processes of hybridisation, contestation and negotiation) and is overlaid by the social contours of a multiplicity of movements, social trends and emergent practices;
3. there is an absence of adequate theoretical tools (until recently these tools were sufficient for helping us understand educational problems);
4. there has been an increase in cultural contact and this has had a large impact on both the social and educational spheres.

This article seeks to develop these ways of understanding the relationship between curriculum and society and begins with the premise that there is a need to rethink this relationship to enable us to recapture a purposeful, critical and analytical view of our work in education. In seeking to recapture such a purposeful, critical and analytic view, it is important to understand the nature of the crisis in which the field of curriculum finds itself. The field is characterised by a generalised crisis exemplified by the retreat of grand narratives and the emergence of a multiplicity of competing social trends and movements. Contemporaneous with this crisis, has been an intensification of cultural contact in a multiform and multidirectional way which has not only contributed to processes of decentring amongst individuals (hence the notion of split subjects), but has also served to decentre the centre itself.

Surface of inscription:[2] social traits and contours

I have argued elsewhere (de Alba 1991) that the curriculum is a political educational project constituted by a synthesis or an articulation of cultural elements derived from fights, impositions and negotiations amongst different social subjects. These conflicts and negotiations embrace a range of social political projects and portend how society is to be educated.

As mentioned above, one of the most serious developments confronting us in the area of the curriculum is the retreat of sociopolitical projects which involve particular narrations of the curriculum-society relationship and which help to constitute and sustain the subjects (agents) of the processes of curricular overdetermination. Such subjects play formative roles and sustain educational projects in relation to these socio-political projects. With the weakening of the grand narrative in education and curriculum, the question that arises is twofold:

How do we understand and reconstitute the curriculum-society link within societies that are in crisis and that lack wide and ambitious socio-political projects? And what is the position of the social and curricular subject in these societies, given the absence of utopian horizons and projects?

Towards understanding this crisis and the role of subjects within it, it could be put that through the processes of crisis, what can be observed is the emergence of social traits and contours which prefigure the articulation of incipient hegemonic practices. Traits, in this explanation, refer to new or residual elements from current and precarious or [previous] social configurations, which show themselves in a significant way, in a social space and accomplish two functions. In the first instance, they contribute to the dis location of the order of things within the crisis situation. In the second, they emerge as traces in the contours of new discursive social configurations. Traits are thus elements which do not have the ability to articulate the past, present and the future, and their importance resides in their ability to erupt (unexpectedly) and to disrupt the textured overlays of meaning which permeate the society. They are, therefore, elements that linger on dangerously in new discursive[3] configurations; but at the same time, because of their very residualness, they might wither altogether (de Alba 1995a). They emerge and are present during the early stages of a social crisis.

Contours are shaped by a set of emerging elements in society in the process of generalised structural crisis. Contours are traits which coalesce and can be identified by their eruptive tendencies. Contours have a greater capacity for articulation than traits and can be observed in advanced moments of the crisis. They are constituted and are present as the articulation of initial and incipient meanings in the making (and genealogy) of a social configuration. They can have, thus, the ability to articulate and constitute themselves as master signifiers.[4] Like traits they can also go in the opposite direction. As new social configurations unfold, they can disappear and be excluded from the social and curricular terrain (de Alba 1995a.)

Seen in this way, social traits and contours are constituted elements on the surface of the inscriptive field of the curriculum. They, in turn, provide the contextual space for the constitution of specific social and curricular subjects. Social traits and contours thus interpellate[5] and provide for the constitution of subjects and, critically, the possibility for the creation of the curriculum society link. I wish to argue, therefore, that in the contemporary world, it is social traits and contours, as opposed to grand projects, which constitute the surface of inscription of the curriculum. They are inextricably linked with the broad social changes that have impacted on the different spaces and levels of reality which make up our social reality. Amongst the most important, these changes are: environmental crisis, the meteoric advances in science and technology (particularly in information technology), the intensification of cultural contact, geopolitical recomposition, poverty, famine, globalisation[6] and the increasing emphasis of difference.

Subjects of curriculum. After the death of the subject?

The conceptual tools in the field of education and, within that, the field of the curriculum, which were dominant until the 1970s and 80s, have shown themselves to be inadequate in explaining some of the most urgent problems we are facing today. One such problem relates to the withering of a coherent notion of the subject, that is to say the individual self as a conscious source of thought and action.

The notion of a coherent subject – a corner stone of Western thought – has been seriously eroded. The work of Nietzsche, Heidegger and Wittgenstein, amongst others, has produced new discursive frameworks in which autonomous subjects have all but disappeared in the face of the totalising discourses of science and progress which have prefigured "the death of the subject". This work has been significantly advanced in post-structuralist thought, with authors like Lacan, Foucault and Derrida. Peters (1997), reflecting on the power of this new theory, suggests that we now cannot continue thinking about the subject in the same way.[7]

The modern subject has been characterised as centred, rational and avant garde. He/she is a subject centred in a strong, primary identification with rationality as his/her main *motif*. This rationality is embodied in the ideal of a subject able to contribute to the acceleration of structural change and able to shape history. The modern subject is thus the subject of social change operating through and with strong socio-political projects. He/she is the subject of the modern curriculum and has been interpellated for and constituted by the great historical, social and political projects, by the great meta-narratives (Lyotard 1979). However, the modern subject has immense difficulty in realising his or her subjecthood or subjectivity in post-modern societies which are governed by suspicion, uncertainty and scepticism.

Foucault (1972, 1980 and 1982), Lacan (1956–57, 1964, 1987a and 1987b), Derrida (1966 and 1968), Laclau (1990 and 1996), Hall (1996), and Zizek (1990), among others, have reformulated [resettled] the concept of the subject in different ways since its "subject death". They have represented the position of the subject in terms of the subject as lack, the subject as a moment of decision, the subject as reiterative power of discourse (effect of power), and as a subject split by the multiciplicity of discourses surrounding him or her. We thus have a subject that is not pre-determined but rather can be constructed in successive and persistent processes of identification and reidentification.

In the field of education, authors from around the world have concerned themselves with the question of the subject for the last decade: Peters and Marshall (1997) in Australasia, Giroux (1992) and McLaren (1989, 1995 and 1997) in the United States, Puiggros (1990, 1992 and 1995), Buenfil (1991 and 1994), Gomez Sollano (1992) and de Alba (1991, 1995a, 1996a and 1997) in Argentina and Mexico, amongst others.

The split subject, the subject that is constituted in the moment of decision, is post-foundational, anti-essentialist, and post-modern. He/she is the subject of the crisis and of the uncertainty of today's world. He/she is the current subject in the process of curricular overdetermination. This subject is interpellated by the social traits and contours emerging from the crisis and is defined by his/her ability to respond to such interpellations.

The question may be asked why it is important to (re)incorporate this split subject into the field of the curriculum (after its supposed 'death') and how it can be done. Reincorporating the split subject is of profound importance because split subjects, in comparison with their singular and 'coherent' antecedents operating in the discursive ether of the grand-narrative, are constituted as subjects with a number of different positions and postures to the world. They do not seek to resolve problems once and for all, and assume their historical and generational responsibility with the awareness that the world they inhabit is one of infinite complexity.

In these new conditions of intelligibility and with these new surfaces of inscription, it is possible to face the crisis, either from a very pessimistic point of view, or to regard it as a terrain of new possibilities. With reference to this discussion, Laclau and Mouffe say:

> There is no room here for disappointment …Hopelessness in this matter is only proper to those who, to borrow a phrase from J. B. Priestley, have lived for years in a fool's paradise and then abruptly move on to invent a fool's hell for themselves. We are living, on the contrary, in one of the most exhilarating moments of the twentieth century: a moment in which new generations, without the prejudices of the past, without theories presenting themselves as 'absolute truths' of history, are constructing new emancipatory discourses, more human, diversified and democratic. The eschatological and epistemological ambitions are more modest, but the liberating aspirations are wider and deeper.
>
> (Laclau and Mouffe 1990: 98)

In seeking to pursue this possibility, it is important that the notion of the subject's positionality is examined as a way of understanding how we might proceed conceptually and politically in the field of the curriculum. Positionality is crucial in the context of the crisis in which we find ourselves. Faced with social traits and contours – instead of grand social projects – what we have in the field are split subjects who live in a world of intense cultural contact which serves as a constant challenge. I want to argue that it is impor tant to confront the issue of positionality and to locate and specify our own positionality in order to construct new modalities of communication with others in a world where cultural contact is increasing each day.

Positionality must be understood as the psychic, cultural, social, geopolitical, economic, etc. space, from which the world is enunciated and through which it is constructed. Discourse positionality is defined by the specificity of the social fabric in which the enunciator belongs. It might, therefore, be understood as an enunciative space (de Alba 1996a: 10).

Curricular overdetermination, cultural contact and traits and contours

We have now seen that the contemporary subject, after the "death of the subject", is constituted and inscribed on the surface of inscription of education by social traits and contours emerging from the dislocated society and is profoundly affected, as a generational subject, by cultural contact.

Even though, in different times in history, there have been moments of intense cultural contact which have given rise to new cultures and nations, it is true to say that the frequency, depth and diversity of cultural interaction is more intense than it has been before. Cultural contact[8] refers to the exchanges of cultural goods and interrelationships among groups, sectors and/or individuals of different cultures. It refers to the transaction of different semiotic codes and the different use of signs (signifiers and signified). As a space in which different discourses interact, its outcomes are new semiotic fields which produce changes in the different subjects inhabiting it. It occurs in several social spaces in a multiplicity of ways interpellated by complex power relationships. Cultural contact is thus relational, unequal, conflictive and productive. It is produced through complex identification processes.[9]

Cultural contact is relational because it is generated, produced and defined in the context of open and precarious relationships. It is constituted and produced within and amongst several articulated meaning systems. That is, it occurs among diverse cultures that have different symbolic economies where symbolic goods and different ways of symbolisation are transacted. The entry of one culture into another and the complex and conflictive encounter which results produce a cultural dislocation that affects the relationality of the meaning systems or cultural systems.

Cultural contact is also conflictive because the subjects involved in it experience structural difficulties in establishing modalities of communication. They are, thus, compelled to construct new arenas of meaning that work as bridges among and between their distinct semiotic codes. While building these arenas, however, they are under pressure to honour and reproduce the constitutive traits of their identity. This struggle is constituted as a relational tension between culture as metonomy and culture as metaphor. One can say it is the expression of different signifiers in their fight to hegemonize the symbolic and cultural space, by trying to reconstitute some signifiers as empty and master signifiers.

From a historical point of view, cultural contact is often unequal because when two or more cultures come into contact they have to negotiate the tension between the desire to dominate and the longing to develop mechanisms which preserve the constitutive traits of their identities. Domination produces its own conditions of possibility in so far as the very conditions of the cultural contact bring with them access to new technology, ideas and practices. A certain productivity emanates from this situation because the relationality, the conflictive characteristics and the unequal relationships which develop during cultural contact permit and accelerate the dislocation of the subjects identities. Multiple interpellations are produced among the subjects, floating signifiers proliferate and through mechanisms of identification new traits and new condensations of meanings are generated. New semiotic and semantic elements permit not only communication among cultures and their subjects but also their transformation and, with long and intense periods of contact, the emergence of new cultures.

The productive character of the process thus refers to its capacity to over determine and articulate several discontinuous and uneven moments. It refers to its metaphorical or paradigmatic capacity to take one or several empty signifiers and to make them nodal in so far as they condense and articulate new meanings.

Cultural contact also plays the role of dislocating old certainties as well as producing new and incipient understandings. It changes the language games [10] in which the split subject is constituted and performs. In doing this, it also changes the language games' rules and goes further than any kind of multiculturalism.

In the current context of crisis, cultural contact is constitutive of new social spaces characterised by traits and contours. Within those spaces are to be found arenas for public discourse from which emanates the curricula. Public spaces are characterised by a) visibility of speech and action (information); b) the possibility of the exchange of ideas, opinions and arguments about information; and c) the possibility of reaching agreements and taking action based on this information and as a result, discussion about this information (see Arditi 1996, and Arendt 1958).

These characteristics – flow and visibility of messages, discussions, agreements and actions – are found in traditional public spaces, what we might call intermittent public spaces, and also virtual public spaces. Traditional public spaces are usually located around issues which are located in specific and known space and time. Intermittent public spaces are located in specific moments and places which appear and disappear and change. And virtual public spaces take place in cyberspace, internet and e-mail, amongst others. This last kind of public space is particularly marked by cultural contact as a result of the necessity of new communicative language forms and the unlimited possibilities of communication and contact.

In the field of the curriculum, the cultural contact serves to disrupt the surface of inscription of the field and presents itself as a challenge to rethink the curriculum and to formulate new proposals. It reveals itself as an experience which is constitutive of the new public spaces in which the curriculum is overdetermined and developed.

Conclusion

In our current crisis-ridden societies it is important to rethink how work in the field of the curriculum might be conducted. While the trajectory of the crisis has been leading towards the disempowerment of the active subject, subjectivity remains possible and might even be pursued. As I have tried to argue in this article, this possibility might be pursued along the following lines:

a) The retrieval and the incorporation of the concept of the subject "after the death of the subject" and the introduction of the notion of positionality;

b) The recognition of new forms of the curriculum-society link, located in the social traits and contours that emerge from the current processes of crisis; and,

c) the incorporation of cultural contact as a challenge and as a constitutive force within new social spaces.

What an approach such as this makes possible is the recovery of the notion of a social project. Cast in this light, the social project, however, is fundamentally less imperialistic and is underscored by a deep sense of its partiality. It is through this the possibility of establishing the curriculum-society link, from social traits and contours, is enhanced. What this permits is a broad conceptual framework which recognises the possibilities for the emergence of new articulations and the emergence, through cultural contact, of a new and vibrant public sphere, in which many divergent subjects can participate and a new democracy might be forged.

Notes

1. I agree with Laclau (1998) that Neo-Liberalism is in crisis too. In that sense, one cannot consider it a hegemonic social project.
2. I use "surface of inscription" in the Derridean sense. See Derrida 1966 and 1968.
3. Discourse is "a meaningful totality which transcends the distinction between the linguistic and the extra-linguistic. ... the impossibility of a closed totality unties the connection between signifier and signified. In that sense there is a prolifera tion of 'floating signifiers' in society, and political competition can be seen as attempts by rival political forces to partially fix those signifiers to particular signifying configurations" (Laclau 1993: 435).
4. See Zizek 1990 and Lacan 1987.
5. I am using the notion of interpellation in a Lacanian and Laclaunian way.
6. Globalisation, however, is used mainly in an economic sense. It is used here in the sense of a social contour in the sense that what happens in one part of the world impacts in a multiplicity of ways in other parts of the world too.
7. "I am inclined to paraphrase Ferry and Renault thus: it is impossible to return innocently to the Hegelian or phenomenological subject after Foucault, Derrida, Deleuze and Lyotard (and here these proper names stand as emblems) Peters 1997: 12.
8. About cultural contact, see de Alba and Gutierrez 1986, Gonzalez Gaudiano and de Alba 1994 and de Alba 1995.
9. The notion of identification is used mainly from a psychoanalytic view and also from a discourse analaysis view.
10. The notion of language games derives from Wittgenstein, 1953.

References

Arditi, B. 1995. *An Archipelago of Public Spaces.* Department of Government, University of Essex, England. 25 pp.

Arendt, Hannah. 1958. *The Human Condition.* Chicago: The University Chicago Press.

Buenfil Burgos, Rosa Nidia. 1991. *El debate sobre el sujeto en el discurso marxista: notas criticas sobre el reduccionismo de clase y educaci6n.* Mexico: DIE (Tesis DIE 12).

Buenfil Burgos, Rosa Nidia. 1994. *Cardenismo. Argumentaci6n y antagonismo en educaci6n.* Mexico: DIE-CINVESTAV-IPN/CONACYT.

de Alba, Alicia and Gutierrez, M. 1986. La pluriculturalidad en la escuela primaria mexicana: un reto hacia la consolidaci6n de la identidad nacional. In: *Educaci6n primaria* (1–101). Mexico: SEP.

de Alba, Alicia. 1991. *Curriculum: crisis, mito y perspectivas.* Mexico: CESU-UNAM.

de Alba, Alicia. 1995a. *Expectativas docentes ante la problematica y los desaffos del curriculum universitario en Mexico.* Madrid: UNED.

de Alba, Alicia. 1995b. Posmodernidad y educaci6n. Implicaciones epistemicas y conceptuales en los discursos educativos. In: *Posmodernidad y educaci6n Mexico* (129–175). Pomia: CESU-UNAM.

de Alba, Alicia. 1996a. *Sujetos educativos: la tarea de reescribirlos conceptualmente.* Paper presented at International Congress of Education "Education, Crises and Utopias". Buenos Aires, Argentina. 12 pp.

de Alba, Alicia. 1996b. *Crisis y curriculum universitario: Horizontes postmodernos y ut6picos.* International Congress of Education "Education, Crises and Utopias". Buenos Aires, Argentina. 19 pp.

de Alba, Alicia. 1997. *Curriculum: crisis y sujetos.* Mexico: CESU-UNAM, 19 pp.

Derrida, Jacques. 1966. Freud y la escena de la escritura. In: *La escritura y la difer encia* (271–317). Barcelona: Anthropos, 1989.

Derrida, Jacques. 1968. La Difference. In: *Margenes de la Filosoffa. Catedra.*

Foucault, Michel. 1972. *The Archaeolog y of Knowledge.* London: Tavistock Publications.

Foucault, Michel. 1980. *The History of Sexuality,* Vol. 1. New York: Vintage.

Foucault, Michel. 1982. Afterword: The Subject and Power. In: H. Dreyfus and P. Rabinow (eds) *Michel Foucault: Beyond Structuralism and Hermeneutics.* Chicago: The Harvester Press Ltd.

Giroux, H. 1992. *Border Crossings: Cultural Workers and the Politics of Education.* New York: Routledge.

Gonzalez Gaudiano, E. and de Alba, Alicia. 1994. Freire - Present and Future Possibilities. In: Peter McLaren and Colin Lankshear (eds) *Politics of Liberation. Paths from Freire* 023–141). London and New York: Routledge.

Hall, S. 1996. Who Needs 'Identity'? In: *Questions of Cultural Identity* (1–36). London: Thousand Oaks/New Delhi: SAGE Publications.

Lacan, Jacques. 1956–1957. *"La relacion de objeto" Seminarios de Lacan 4.* Barcelona: Paidos, 1994.

Lacan, Jacques. 1964. *"Los cuatro principios fundamentales del psicoanalisis" Seminarios de Lacan 11.* Barcelona: Paid6s, 1987.

Lacan, Jacques. 1987a. "El estadio del espejo como formador de la funci6n del yo (je) tal y como se nos revela a la experiencia psicoanalftica", "Del sujeto por fin cuestionado" in Escritos 1. Mexico: Siglo XXL

Lacan, Jacques. 1987b. Psicoanalisis y estructura de la personalidad: subversion del sujeto y dialectica del deseo en el inconsciente freudiano. In *Escritos 2.* Mexico: Ed. Siglo XXL

Laclau, E. and Mouffe, C. 1990. Post-Marxism without Apologies. In: E. Laclau (ed) *New Reflections on the Revolution of our Time* (97–132). London and New York: Verso.

Laclau, E. 1993. Discourse. In: R. Goodin and P. Pettit (eds) *A Companion to Contemporary Political Philosophy* (431–437). Oxford: Blackwell.

Laclau, E. 1996. *Emancipation(s).* London and New York, Verso.

Laclau, E. 1998. La ideologfa neoliberal esta perdiendo su capacidad integradora. In: *Excelsior.* Mexico: DF: Sunday 19 April (El Mho).

Lyotard, J-F. 1979. *The Postmodern Condition: A Report on Knowledge.* Trans by G. Bennington and B. Massumi. Manchester: Manchester University Press.

McLaren, P. 1989. *Life in Schools,* 3rd edition. New York: Longmans, 1997.

McLaren, P. 1995. *Critical Pedagogy and Predatory Culture.* London and New York, Routledge.

McLaren, P. 1997. *Revolutionary Multiculturalism.* Boulder, CO: Westview Press.

Peters, M. 1997 Nietzsche, Poststructuralism and Education: After the Subject? In: *Educational Philosophy and Theory,* Vol. 29 No. 1, 1997, pp. 1–19.

Puiggros, A. 1990. *Sujetos, Disciplina y Curriculum,* Second edition. Buenos Aires: Editorial Galerna, 1994.

Puiggros, A. 1992. Las alternativas pedag6gicas y los sujetos. Reflexion critica sobre el marco teorico de APPEAL. In Puiggr6s, Adriana and Marcela Gomez Sollano (coord.) Alternativas Pedagogicas: Sujetos y Prospectiva de la Educacion Latinoamericana. Mexico: Facultad de Filosoffa y Letras, DGAPA-UNAM. Pp. 68–85.

Puiggros, A. 1995. *Volver a educar. El desaj(o de la enseiianza argentina a finales del siglo XX*. Buenos Aires: Ariel.

Puiggros, A. and Sollano. M. (coord.) (N.D.) *Alternativas Pedag6gicas: Sujetos y Prospectiva de la Educaci6n Latinoamericana*. Mexico, Facultad de Filosofia y Letras, DGAPA-UNAM.

Wittgenstein, Ludwig. 1953. Investigaciones Filosoficas. Translation by Alfonso Garcia Suarez and Ulises Moulines. Mexico: Ed. Crftica/lnstituto de Investigaciones Filosoficas UNAM, 1988.

Zizek, S. 1990. *The Sublime Object of Ideology*. London: Verso.

16

The Constructivist Curriculum Reform in Turkey in 2004

In Fact What Is Constructed?

Kemal İnal, Güliz Akkaymak and Deniz Yıldırım

The Justice and Development Party (AKP), which came to power as a single party in Turkey, has signed very important changes in education until the year 2014. These educational changes have fundamentally shifted the philosophy of education in Turkey (Inal, 2005). One of the main effective and extensive amendments in the educational system has been done with the primary school curriculum reform. The curriculum change was put into implementation in 2004 and reorganized teaching methods, teacher training, textbooks, and so on. The AKP declared that renewed curriculum would replace the former old-fashioned behaviorist approach, which had been criticized for being supportive of rote learning and teacher-centered education, with a constructivist approach (Ministry of National Education [MoNE], 2004a, pp. 227–28). The constructivist approach has introduced a number of new concepts into the educational system, such as student-centered education, guidance teacher, multiple intelligence approach, and educational duties on efficiency and performance.

Neoliberalism and Transformation of Education

Neoliberalism has been the dominant economic model for almost all Western countries as well as for some Eastern countries since the early 1980s. To define neoliberalism, the words of Teeple (1995) are very illuminating:

> Neo-liberal free market economics—the purpose of which is to avoid states and keep businesses in healthy flux-functions as type of binding arbitration, legitimizing a host of questionable practices and outcomes: deregulation, unrestricted access to consumer markets, downsizing, outsourcing, flexible arrangements of labor, intensification of competition among transnational corporations, increasing centralization of economic and political power, and finally, widening class polarization. Neo-liberalism is currently embarking on ways of "re-imagining" democracy through the importation of the market discourse of parasitic financial oligarchies into increasingly domesticated democratic practices and through the valorization of capital and the unrestrained economic power of private poverty.
>
> (cited in McLaren and Farahmandpur, 2001, p. 137)

In line with the principles of neoliberalism, education has been increasingly transformed to meet the competitive needs of corporations within globalizing markets. In other words, education has been reorganized to support the dominant neoliberal economic policies promoted by governments and corporations (Hursh, 2000). Moreover, neoliberalism and globalization go hand in hand and a neoliberal agenda in education heavily stresses "*global competitiveness, the reduction of the (publicly financed) costs of education, and of social reproduction in general, the necessity for greater market choice and accountability and the imperative to create hierarchically conditioned, globally oriented state subjects*" (Mitchell, 2003, p. 388).

In the recent years, a high number of educational systems over the world have stressed the "importance" of multi-skilled flexible workforce that will constantly be in the process of trying to fit the needs of the business community. To support the demands of the business community, governments in various countries have called for educational subjects such as schools, teachers, and students to meet the changing challenges of international competition and the changing workplace (ibid.). Therefore, educational reform efforts have been put into practice to develop students' knowledge, skills, and attitudes that will eventually make them productive workers. These efforts have further aimed at centering learners (i.e., students) in the teaching process and promoting the idea of individuality. A number of countries, such as China and those in sub-Saharan Africa readjusted their societies to the demands of the market economy (Carney, 2008) through educational reforms. Discourse of these reforms concentrates on the rhetoric of curriculum change and modernization (Bonal, 2003), and they are based on the constructivist education approach (Kosar-Altinyelken, 2010). Constructivist curriculum and/or pedagogy has been instantly appealed since governments and the business community assume that it will carry *the promise of intellectual liberation from 'oppressive' traditional approaches*" (Nykiel-Herbert, 2004, p. 249). Not surprisingly, then, the focus of the constructivist approach is on individual and it stresses that an individual needs to construct knowledge himself/herself.

The AKP and the Education System

It has been well-acknowledged by various circles that the AKP is a neoliberal political party (Yavuz, 2010; Inal, 2009; Uzgel, 2009; Bedirhanoglu, 2009). Indeed, Yavuz (2010) declared clearly the fact that the AKP has a tendency to promote market forces and to support the neoliberal project in Turkey. In addition, the hegemonic project of the AKP can be called "neoliberal populist" due to the fact that the Party has also tried to create a historical bloc by subordinating the poor segments of the society to the hegemonic project of the ruling classes. This hegemonic project of neoliberal populism does not contradict with the general rules of capital accumulation. In a way it deepens the neoliberalization process through the implementation of a populist agenda which is in conformity with the agenda of international institutions of the financial capital such as World Bank and the IMF (Yildirim, 2009).

Although the AKP comes from an Islamic fundamentalism, namely National View (Milli *Görüş*) tradition of Necmettin Erbakan and is governed by a Muslim staff, it is a political party which accepts the globalizing capitalist system based on the logic of the free market relations and economic competition. Indeed, the party chairman and Prime Minister, Recep Tayyip Erdoğan, has repeatedly declared that the AKP is a liberal party on the basis of "conservative democracy." The language and discourse used by the prime minister and party staff manifest the political space on which the party stands. For example, the AKP described education in the 60th government's educational program as an activity to be continued lifelong to create human capital needed to compete in the world (Memurlar.net, 2008). Due to the passion and the goal to be an important actor on the world stage by adapting to the globalization and neoliberalism, the party's educational view has been established through a language of neoliberal education. Some other concepts such as competition, quality, responsiveness to the needs of globalization, adaptation to the business world's needs, which all reflect neoliberal understanding at the party program, indicate the educational framework of the Party. Several statements and articles by the former

Minister of National Education, Hüseyin Çelik, and the architect of the new primary school curriculum reform, Ziya Selçuk, suggest that the two main planes of AKP are neoliberalism and globalization (Inal, 2009, p. 690). For instance, the AKP defines students and their parent as "customers" under the concept of "Total Quality School" (EARGED, 2003, p. 27). At this point words by Ziya Selçuk are very meaningful:

> a] kind of education which was not integrated with the world, unable to make a connection between education and production, insensitive to national and global sensitivities, unable to perform functions has emerged. The pressure of globalization which was experienced today thoroughly exposed the failure of the system. Globalization today has become a threat against the national and local things. After 50 years, continuation of strong presence of national cultures and local wealth depends on balanced configuration of local and globalization.
>
> (Inal, 2009, p. 691)

As shown in the expression above, AKP's official experts prefer, on the one hand, to bustle the globalization train, while on the other hand demand this process not to have a negative impact on the local culture. When the applications were examined, it has been observed that since 2002 many of the AKP's educational applications are realized within a huge educational market: e.g. publishing millions of textbooks at the private printing houses instead of the state printing houses, requesting the sale of state schools in central areas of the cities due to the their high price, promoting privatization in education through facilitating the establishment of private educational institutions, collaborating with the private sector for vocational and technical training schools, and forcing the School-Parent Associations (*Okul Aile Birliği*) to work as a commercial enterprise (Inal, 2009, pp. 691–92; Yildirim, 2006). AKP's supports to neoliberal ideology and globalization have been explicitly reflected in the primary school curriculum reform.

Curricula: A Comparative Outlook

The new curriculum is prepared in line with a thematic approach and different than the 1968 curriculum: there are learning spheres, competencies and skills which will be discussed later. It is divided into four main parts: Introduction, social studies sample activities for the fourth grade, social studies sample activities for the fifth grade, and sample forms for assessment. The 1968 curriculum is organized under four major purposes of the social studies course: duties and responsibilities of citizenship, relationship among human beings living in a society, informing students about their environment, country and the world, and teaching students to acquire a decent life.

Compared to the new curriculum, the 1968 curriculum has more emphasis on being a member of the society. Several parts of the 1968 curriculum stress that the primary school education has to teach students the idea that interests of the society come before their own interests. Additionally, the curriculum states that students learn in the primary school that "in order to attain an individual well-being, first of all the society has to be developed" (MoNE, 1968, p. 8). The 2005 curriculum, on the contrary, does not underline the importance of society's interest. The curriculum first underlines the importance of individual development and then stresses that "education teaches students to live in collaboration" (MoNE, 2004b, p. 7). The new curriculum signals the importance of knowledge production and knowledge usage stating that knowledge has become the main factor determining everything in the world. In this respect, the people who produce and use knowledge are superior to everyone else. The new curriculum also focuses on the developments in science and technology.

The emphasis on science and technology in the new curriculum indicates the impact of a shift from an industrial economy to a knowledge economy. Especially in the last decade, knowledge began to be considered as a capital which signals the necessity of making rearrangements in the educational system accordingly with the knowledge economy (Olssen and Peters, 2005, p. 330). Furthermore, as a result of the shift to knowledge economy the role of education in the creation of human capital becomes more significant (ibid. 332). Considering Turkey as a knowledge economy, the MoNE reorganized primary school social studies course with the idea of knowledge production and knowledge usage.

Another difference between the old and new curriculum is the assessment methods. The new curriculum combines classical and alternative methods. In the old curriculum, the main assessment methods were tests and essay questions. However, assessment methods and tools in the new curriculum are: Observation, performance homework, interviews, self-evaluation forms, student folders (portfolio), projects, posters, tests, matching, filling the blanks and essay questions. By increasing the number of assessment methods and tools, the social studies curriculum committee aimed to make the assessment process sensitive to differences among students. However, addition of alternative assessments is a clear implication of neoliberal ideology on education. Some of these methods address the individual's adaptation abilities to the market rather than his/her multi-faceted development. The most prominent of these alternative methods is "performance homework," since performance has become one of the main reference points of thinking in the neoliberal ideology (Harris, 2007, p. 135). In this context, "a further consequence of marketization of education has been the increased emphasis on performance and accountability assessment, with the accompanying use of performance indicators and personal appraisal systems" (Olssen and Peters, 2005, p. 327).

The new curriculum defines learning sphere (*öğrenme alnani*) as a structure which defines a relationship among skills, concepts and values, and thus organizes the education process (MoNE, 2004b, p. 96). In the curriculum, there are eight learning spheres in each grade. These include individual and identity; cultural and heritage; human beings: places and environment; production, delivery, and consumption; science, technology and society; groups, foundations, and organizations; power, management, and society; and global linkages. Learning spheres indicate specific emphasis of each unit. From 12 to 15 class hours are devoted to each learning sphere. There are no great differences between the spheres or units in terms of their percentage within the curriculum or class hour. In addition to the skills, there are seven intermediate/minor competencies in the curriculum as components of the skills: Disaster education competencies, entrepreneurial competencies, human rights and citizenship competencies, development of career awareness competencies, individual education competencies, psychological counseling and guidance competencies, and health culture competencies.

As explained previously, there is no section in the 1968 curriculum on competencies or skills, which mean that the skills and competencies listed above were added to the social studies curriculum with the 2004 reform. Instead of those skills and competencies, there is an emphasis on the 1968 curriculum on being a good citizen, which is described as a person who lives for his/her country. Among the skills and competencies listed in the new curriculum, entrepreneurship, entrepreneurial competencies, and development of career awareness competencies are especially important in terms of signaling the impact of the neoliberal discourse on education. Many scholars note the entrepreneurial nature of the neoliberal world (Apple, 2001; Harris, 2007; Hursh, 2005; Read, 2009). They argue that the creation of entrepreneurs and entrepreneurial culture is one of the most significant and perceived signals of neoliberal policies.

Furthermore, educational systems serve neoliberalism through leading students to skills and competencies necessary to be a part of the marketplace. For the new curriculum, student is more than a social individual; he/she is also an "enterprising individual." It aims to familiarize students with the entrepreneurial culture. To illustrate, the entrepreneurship skill set consists of seven targets: Recognizing occupations and workplaces around them, recognizing well-known and successful entrepreneurs around them, exploring the roles of individuals in the economy as a worker and consumer, realizing the importance of education for their future, acquiring essential economic terms, understanding the difficulties that entrepreneurship faces, presenting innovative ideas and designing new products (MoNE, 2004b, p. 48).

Therefore, the neoliberal discourse is heavily integrated into the renewed curriculum and students have become to be regarded as human capitals that will be defined according to market rules and work for the continuity of the market. In other words, 2004 reform made the capitalist messages in the curriculum explicit.

Conclusion

Educational policies have been in the process of transformation during the neoliberal years of the last three decades. In the first part of the neoliberal reform agenda, marketization of educational services was at the top. With the introduction of the new wave of neoliberal reforms in the 1990s, the emphasis of reforms have been enlarged towards the inclusion of "reforms" in all aspects of the education sphere including the curriculum, teaching and governance. In this sense, the global agenda of the neoliberal strategy aimed at transforming both the financing and the teaching aspects of education in order to create a standardized educational sphere all over the world. The curriculum reforms implemented in the different corners of the world were not an exception. In the last decade, from Bolivia to Romania, a new standardized, market-friendly curriculum has been introduced and the agenda of the capitalist classes to harmonize the content of education with the "necessities" of the market gained strength.

Turkey has not been an exception in this transformation process. The aim of this article hence has been to illuminate the curriculum aspect of the neoliberal "harmonization" process. Following the general picture of the transformation in education and focusing on the different factors affecting the neoliberalization process in Turkey, this article has put an emphasis on which concepts and practices specific to the neoliberal ideology were constructed in which ways in the 2004 curriculum reform which provided a new but controversial basis for Turkish educational system in terms of the constructivist educational approach. Drawing on analysis of the previous and renewed curricula, and the in-depth interview data, the article has manifested that the 2004 curriculum reform in Turkey in fact was part of a pedagogical reform wave which has been simultaneously implemented in many developing countries throughout the world. The discourse in education, however, should not be a tool solidifying neoliberal ideology (Robertson, 2005), and critical educators should take up the struggle against "neoliberalization" of all aspects of education.

References

Apple, M. (2001). Comparing neo-liberal projects and inequality in education. *Comparative Education* 37 (4): 409–423.

Bedirhanoglu, P. (2009). Türkiye'de neoliberal otoriter devletin AKP'li yüzü. In Uzgel İ. & Duru, B. (Eds.) *AKP kitabı: Bir dönüşümün bilançosu* (pp.40–65). Ankara: Phoenix.

Bikmaz, F.H. (2006). New elementary curricula and teachers. *Ankara University, Journal of Faculty of Educational Sciences* 39(1): 97–116.

Bonal, X. (2003). The neoliberal educational agenda and the legitimation crisis: old and new state strategies. *British Journal of Sociology of Education* 24(2): 159–175.

Carney, S. (2008). Learner-centered pedagogy in Tibet: International education reform in a local context. *Comparative Education* 44(1): 39–55.

Egitimi Arastirma ve Gelistirme Dairesi Baskanligi [EARGED]. (2003). *Öğrenci Merkezli Eğitim Uygulama Modeli*, Milli Eğitim Basımevi, Ankara.

Harris, S. (2007). *The governance of education: how neo-liberalism is transforming policy and practice.* London: Continuum International Publishing Group.

Hursh, D. (2005). Neo-liberalism, markets and accountability: transforming education and undermining democracy in the United States and England. *Policy Futures in Education* 3(1): 3–15.

Hursh, D. (2000). Neo-liberalism and the control of teachers, students, and learning: the rise of standards, standardization, and accountability. *Cultural Logic* 4(1): 1–9.

Inal, K. (2005) Yeni ilköğretim müfredatının felsefesi. *Muhafazakar Düşünce* 6: 75–92.

Inal, K. (2009). AKP'nin neoliberal ve muhafazakar eğitim anlayışı. In Uzgel İ. & Duru, B. (Eds.) *AKP kitabı: Bir dönüşümün bilançosu* (pp.689–719). Ankara: Phoenix.

Justice and Development Party [AKP]. (2001). Party program. [Online] Available from: http://www.belgenet.com/parti/Programmes/ak_1.html [Accessed: 12th March 2010].

Kosar-Altinyelken, H. (2010). *Changing Pedagogy: A Comparative Analysis of Reform Efforts in Uganda*. PhD diss., University of Amsterdam.

McLaren, P. & Farahmandpur, R. (2001). Teaching against globalization and the new imperialism: toward a revolutionary pedagogy. *Journal of Teacher Education* 52(2): 136–150.

Ministry of National Education [MoNE]. (2012). *12 yıl zorunlu eğitim, sorular-cevaplar* [Online] Available from: http://www.meb.gov.tr/duyurular/duyurular2012/12Yil_Soru_Cevaplar.pdf [Accessed: 22nd March 2013].

Ministry of National Education [MoNE]. (2005a). *Eğitim Bülteni* [Education Bulletin]. Ankara: MEB Yayınları.

Ministry of National Education [MoNE]. (2005b). *Eğitimde Değişim Yılları 2003–2005* [Transition Period in Education 2003–2005]. Ankara, MEB Yayınları.

Ministry of National Education [MoNE]. (2004a) Programların geliştirilmesini gerekli kılan nedenler. [Online] Available from: http://programlar.meb.gov.tr/prog_giris/prog_giris11.html [Accessed: 2nd October 2004].

Ministry of National Education [MoNE]. (2004b). *İlköğretim sosyal bilgiler dersi (4–5. sınıflar) öğretim program*. Ankara: Devlet Kitapları Müdürlüğü Basım Evi.

Ministry of National Education [MoNE]. (1968). *1968 Programı*, Ankara: MEB Yayınları.

Memurlar.net (2008). *İşte 60. hükümet programı eylem planı*. [Online] Available from: http://www.memurlar.net/haber/98630/ [Accessed: 20th May 2010].

Mitchell, K. (2003). Educating the national citizen in neoliberal times: from the multicultural self to the strategic cosmopolitan. *Transaction of the Institute of British Geographers* 28(4): 387–403.

Nykiel-Herbert, B. (2004). Mis-constructing knowledge: the case of learner-centred pedagogy in South Africa. *Prospects* 34(3): 249–265.

Olssen, M. & Peters, M. (2005). Neo-liberalism, higher education and the knowledge economy: from the free market to knowledge capitalism. *Journal of Education Policy* 20(3): 313–345.

Read, J. (2009). A genealogy of homo-economicus: neoliberalism and the production of subjectivity. *Foucault Studies* 6: 25–36.

Robertson, T. (2005). Class issues: a critical ethnography of corporate domination within the classroom. *Journal for Critical Education Policy Studies* 3(2): 184–212.

Uzgel, I. (2009). AKP: neoliberal dönüşümün yeni aktörü. In Uzgel İ. & Duru, B. (Eds.) *AKP kitabı: Bir dönüşümün bilançosu* (pp.11–39). Ankara: Phoenix.

Windschitl, M. (2002). Framing constructivism in practice as the negotiation of dilemmas: an analysis of the conceptual, pedagogical, cultural, and political challenges facing teachers. *Review Educational Research* 72(2): 131–175.

Yavuz, M. H. (2010). Giriş: Türkiye'de islami hareketin dönüşümünde yeni burjuvazinin rolü. In Yavuz M. H. (Ed.) *Ak Parti: toplumsal değişimin yeni aktörleri* pp. 7–28, İstanbul: Kitap Yayınevi.

Yildirim, D. (2009). AKP ve neoliberal populizm. In Uzgel İ. & Duru, B. (Eds.) *AKP kitabı: Bir dönüşümün bilançosu* (pp.66–107). Ankara: Phoenix.

Yildirim, D. (2006). Okul aile şirketlerinin katılımcılık vurgusu neyi gizliyor? *Evrensel Kültür*, 178, pp. 77–80.

World Bank. (2002). Education reform. [Online] Available from: http://web.worldbank.org/WBSITE/EXTERNAL/TOPICS/EXTEDUCATION/0,,contentMDK:20283533~isCURL:Y~menuPK:624454~pagePK:148956~piPK:216618~theSitePK:282386,00.html [Accessed: 6th September 2006].

17
Justice Curriculum and Teacher Formation

Jurjo Torres Santomé

The concern with understanding how education systems function and more importantly, with understanding the reasons why a large percentage of children are labeled as school dropouts and expelled from educational institutions, is one of the most pressing issues of today's societies. We cannot overlook the importance of education and knowledge, as they exist within the new social models in which we live. We are dealing with a subject with a history that requires we question what type of society we consider to be ideal and, therefore, the society towards which we should direct our intentional efforts and actions. This always turns out to be a most controversial topic. Adopting an educational system model also involves expecting certain functions to exist within it, in order to bring into being the socio-political project considered most appropriate and logical in terms of theories, information, ideals, values and skills possessed by those who really have a chance to participate democratically in this debate, or in the event that this is restricted or forbidden, then by those within the structures of political power and government.

Awareness concerning the political, philosophical and socio-educational concepts underlying the legislative frameworks is a matter of utmost importance when trying to analyze real possibilities and more appropriate courses of action that should be taken in classrooms and schools. Not to consider these worldviews that frame and guide the educational systems of each society, can lead teachers and even families and students to assume the role of facilitators resulting in a sort of perverse and unfair Pygmalion Effect: perceiving as logical either school success or failure of the students based on their social and economic status, ethnicity or place of birth. This is something that usually happens in corrupt education systems primarily designed to facilitate academic success for the most advantaged social groups, and therefore, when students from disadvantaged socio-cultural environments fail or dropout, many teachers and less politicized families end up seeing it as something "natural", a nearly impossible to break out curse, which renders all of our sincere efforts to turn the tide of the situation useless and ineffective.

In what ways, and through what kind of practical school experiences do the students belonging to the most disadvantaged social groups usually experience the stigma of school failure in schools? Through what unjust and wicked means do this type of pupils and students come to see themselves as solely responsible and guilty? These are some of the questions that cannot be deferred by the entire educational and social community, otherwise it would be to tantamount to assuming as logical that tomorrow these students should accept their destinies without protest, considering them to be fair and reasonable. Questions such as these should always become a compass and an invigorating element in the work of the teaching staff, as these are truly urgent social issues within the knowledge societies of the present moment.

If we analyze the hidden curriculum in many of the routines that govern life in the classroom, subject content, homework, assessment models and interactions of students and with faculty, we can see that even the education system, as in other social spheres (the workplace, the field of justice, government, law enforcement, social services, …) do not pay due attention and will often even treat those groups and people living in poverty with indifference or what is even worse, with contempt. Hegemonic psychological and pedagogical thinking, as well as dominant praxis in the classroom, reduces too many children to silence, turning them into passive and resigned beings– even if neither the education system, let alone the teaching staff, intend to encourage this.

Classrooms are still privileged spaces in which to build our interpretations of reality, in which to open our imagination to other worlds and, in particular, to envision other possibilities and alternatives. The explicit curriculum and the hidden curriculum stimulate, promote and make obvious and natural certain explanations, knowledge, realities and aspirations as neutral and fair, while simultaneously stigmatizing, repressing and condemning others.

Even today, in our analyses of the hidden curriculum for example, we end up selecting the culture an educational institution works with, in a way that continues to reveal a chronic, almost pathological silence regarding numerous present realities as well as the most significant realities of the past, which have a greater potential for explaining and understanding what is happening in the world of today. The continued silencing or distortion and manipulation of the explanations about racism, sexism, homophobia, the existence of social classes, neocolonialism, poverty and marginalization, injustice in the workplace, the daily reality for people with intellectual and/or physical disabilities, diseases and consequences of all kinds etc., is too outrageous. This type of information censorship is helping to build a sense in which these realities of our time that are so unfair, are not perceived, except by the people who are most affected by them directly and explicitly. In this way it is easier and more "natural" to perpetuate situations of oppression and the injustice that many human beings are suffering.

That this should happen within the framework of the school system is something we should regard very seriously because it means we are depriving students of developing cognitive and socio-emotional capabilities as well access to knowledge and procedures that will inform them, help them make judgements, develop collaborative strategies, and organize and take actions to resolve the most urgent and vital community and personal problems. A policy guided by social justice principles, moreover, requires relying on redistribution and recognition policies; by redistributing resources and opportunities, since today's societies have even fewer equal opportunities.

Even in a minimal follow-up of educational policy in most countries, it is very striking to see the enormous attention and obsession that exists among ideologically conservative groups to monitor the content legislated by the state. It is almost always these conservative and fundamentalist sectors who, when the State does not submit to their will, accuse it of meddling and even raise complaints of all kinds to impede the normal functioning of the education system, by claiming it is an attack on the freedom of families. These complaints tend to emphasize the interference of the state, because it legislates and imposes certain cultural contents that should be dealt with in educational institutions that impact on freedom and democracy. This phenomenon draws much attention, since truthfully and in fact, there is nobody like these conservative and neo-liberal groups who have been imposing their own cultural and political interests, and therefore benefitting themselves from the cultural world views used and that will continue to be used by educational systems and educational institutions to shape the concept of common sense of most of the population.

Constructed sociohistorically, *"common sense"* is used to explain and justify the school system's preferred cultural content. It makes clear what *can* and *could* be done, as well as what *should* be done. Simultaneously, it makes other possible and real alternatives seem *illogical, irrational* or *impossible.* It is the weight of this common sense, built on the silence of many voices, generated and maintained regardless of what can be questioned and debated, that allows us to understand the many forms of resistance to the change and innovation in the education system. Likewise, on occasion, this hegemonic common sense conflicts with the most progressive educational innovation proposals that are promoted by the most innovative sectors of the school system, and this can generate some personal and group crisis.

The success of neoliberal, conservative and neoconservative organizations is not because they have better or fairer objectives than the left, and that therefore this is why they even get the most votes in the electoral process. What explains their success has more to do with the greater possibilities available to them through their media networks to shape the mentality and common sense of the majority of the population. The media blitz serves to facilitate consent and implements the selfish interests and goals of those same and most powerful sectors of society.

This explains the existence of significant segments of the population who think it is rationally logical, and therefore considered common sense to accept, that *someone must fail*. For many years schools have traditionally been classifying and labeling the students through all manner of routines, even using more or less sophisticated instruments such as intelligence tests, objective performance testing, etc. These instruments masquerade as being objective and neutral, but they end up blaming each of these students, convincing them that they are solely responsible for their failure. These types of labeling strategies ignore the contexts and social conditions in which the life of each student and their families develops.

Years ago, this type of labeling was performed assuming that the fate of each person was decided by divinities. Later, this pseudo explanation grew to include other equally exculpatory statements of innocence regarding the responsibilities of humans, for instance by referring to the structure of the vault of heaven at the time of birth of each human being. Subsequently, the foundations for success and failure are thought to be rooted in the genes with which we were born. At the same time we continue to blame the student's environment, and we especially blame the lazy or uninspiring role performed by fathers and mothers from ethnic and disadvantaged social groups, etc.

Conservative and fundamentalist binary logic tells us that if we have "winners" we must have "losers", and becomes a key mechanism for the operation of the capitalist market and also of our educational system. This logic always serves to excuse the model of society that we have given to ourselves, and is and must be changeable to the extent that we do not like it. Darwinian logic has seized more areas than it should have.

"Scientific" deficit models reinforce this logic or selective determinism in the school system. We implicitly assume that we live in societies where equality of opportunity reigns, and therefore it is assumed that we all have the same opportunities. At the start line, we all started out with equal opportunities in which like in an Olympic race or Oca game, there can only be one winner and many losers. This explains why a commercial orientation is so easily seizing our education system every day.

One of the many obstacles to saving any educational reform and innovation designed to address these shortcomings seen in our schools and classrooms, is the revision and reconstruction of conceptual and theoretical frameworks. Frameworks should enable us to become aware of how our own common sense is not the most relevant thing in order to understand what happens in schools, and consequently, for the design and evaluation of the most relevant and meaningful educational intervention proposals for the students; in short, to accommodate the aims of the education system in light of current social aspirations and demands for greater social justice and curriculum. In any educational policy it is urgent to direct much more attention to the curriculum, to the everyday life that takes place in schools; ie, to force us to take on the question of a justice curriculum.

Curriculum justice is the result of analyzing the curriculum that has been designed. It triggers, evaluates and investigates. It takes into account the degree to which everything that is decided and done in the classroom is respectful and caters to the needs and emergencies of all social groups; helps them to see, analyze, understand and judge themselves, as ethical, supportive, collaborative people and as stewards of a larger sociopolitical intervention destined to build a more humane, just and democratic world (Torres, 2011) people.

Teacher Formation and Inclusive Education

Educating someone involves teaching them to become critical, reflective, and creative, not mechanical beings who reproduce and enunciate the truths according to the authority. This is the optimal way to train people facing indoctrination and dogmatic thinking. To become a critical and reflective person leads one to question opinions, truths, traditions in a thoughtful way, providing arguments and looking for ethical coherence. To be a creative human being requires knowing that the problems, dilemmas, doubts and situations in which we find ourselves have multiple solutions. To educate creatively, requires the encouragement of divergent thinking, dreaming, imagining and putting into action other ways to solve problems that are different than the ones that result from routines.

This educational philosophy requires that we consider to what extent this critical and reflective concept excludes or does not exclude cultures and realities that hegemonic systems mute and/or deform in a scandalous way, as is this case: the reality and culture of the gypsy people. That is why we consider it to be of great urgency that both the educational authorities as well as teacher training institutions rely with greater emphasis on education models that are truly more just and inclusive. Inclusive education, by necessity, must consider a political project destined to overcome the obstacles that prevent or hinder people from accessing schools and from participating democratically in the classroom and succeeding. It is a way to dismantle the architecture of exclusion and inequality and simultaneously to dismantle the self-blaming and/or self-hatred of excluded people.

There are far too many scandalous examples regarding this lack of recognition of Gypsy culture and of the cultural reality of an entire group of students with whom it is compulsory to co-exist in the classroom. Some of these are genuinely crimes, but everyone knows that too many schools practice selective and clearly racist student admissions, to the extent that they tolerate ghetto groups. We must not forget that we are talking about a Spanish community, the Gypsies, who have lived here for centuries and with whom, obviously, we co-exist both inside and outside of the classroom.

A truly inclusive conception requires paying close attention to the selection of the culture we present to the students in order to enable learning, to contribute to their individual development, socialization and integration as citizens in society.Teachers must become very aware that inside of the classroom we work within the framework of cultural "selection". Hence the importance that the process of cultural critical analysis should have during the initial training and continuing education of this professional group. In this area, teacher formation, from an inclusive philosophical point of view still suffers from significant deficits, although there have been decisive breakthroughs.

The concern for Gypsy students started at the beginning of the restoration of democracy, where small groups of teachers were more politicized and therefore more sensitive and concerned for the students belonging to such a marginalized group as the Gypsies. Students who were coming to ordinary classrooms for the first time (where they previously had not attended school or remained enrolled in the famous *"bridge schools"*) were without preparation, resources or an adequate environment with which to meet this new challenge.

This is how the Association of Teachers with Gypsies arose in the late seventies. Groups of teachers from different autonomous regions who work with these students come into contact and generate dynamics that allow the sharing of problems, and experiences, and allows them to form a team to improve the retention of these students in the educational system, offering them a more relevant and higher quality education. Due to pressure by the most progressive educational groups, education administrators slowly began to include this line of action in their programs; but it almost exclusively affected educational psychology programs, in order to facilitate the integration of these students into regular classrooms by offering training and refresher courses for teachers in the newly created Teacher Centers.

But really in order to speak of a truly inclusive school a key element was always lacking: a review of the cultural contents with which they worked in classrooms, of the content in various subjects areas in order to confirm the image being offered in terms of the achievements and realities of the Gypsy people. At most what was done, was to draw on the experience of the analysis of sexism in curriculum materials, mainly from textbooks, attempting to apply a similar model in order to verify the presence or absence of people from this ethnic group in the textbooks; to check what was said about them, and to notice the very rare ocassions when they were named in textbooks and in which subject matter areas this mentioning ocurred, and that was pretty much it.

Regarding the teachers most committed to the Gypsy community, along with some members of this community, they were also developing the first curriculum materials in which the history and characteristics of Gypsy culture is described. However, in most cases these were teaching units greatly intended to incorporate the mandatory learning content legislated by the Ministry of Education and the Boards of Education of the various Autonomous Communities, which ended up being almost exclusively for consumption by Gypsy children who were in the classrooms where this minority of teachers with more political and social sensitivity worked.

Educational Psychology Reductionism in Teacher Training

For years, the results of research being carried out on this topic have denounced a remarkable disregard for the cultural training of teachers, most especially at the Pre-School and Primary educational levels. In the curricula of their university training, priority is given in a very striking way to an emphasis on pedagogical and psychological training, dimensions that are essential and which logically should not suffer any cuts; but it is essential to expand and complete these with greater sociological and cultural training. If teachers must also be motivators in order to allow students to become enthusiastic for culture, through the cultural content that is taught in various subjects, logically, there must also be a relevant and meaningful training in these same areas of knowledge. Traditionally, there was a belief that a person who knows more about something is the one who creates the conditions to start, disseminate and encourage people who are newer to this area of knowledge, that they master. But for decades we know that in order to educate, it is not enough to know the subject being taught. Rather, it is necessary to know many other things that will facilitate learning for girls and boys and adolescents. For example, how is knowledge constructed in the minds of students; how do their cognitive structures and types of intelligence condition the use of methodologies and resources; with what strategies can we motivate and keep their interest; which tasks facilitate learning, and result in ethical education, etc. It is based on these training needs that we find sense and usefulness for training in pedagogy, psychology, didactics, philosophy and sociology; aside from having expertise in the disciplines that each teacher will be in charge of.

Reductionism assumes relying exclusively on psychoeducational interventions, disregarding a thorough review of what is said, what is omitted, what is distorted, what is exaggerated, what is assumed about the history, the reality and culture of the Gypsy people, contributes to blaming the Gypsy students for their own problems in the schools. An education policy with this outlook only serves to pretend to culturally assimilate Gypsy men and women; to force them to renounce their identities and even worse, to "self-convince" them that their culture is inferior, that in fact theirs does not even deserve to be labeled as a culture.

Neither the importance nor the reality of cultural mixing that has occurred as a result of many years of sharing territory is made visible in training programs and educational update. A question related to this last point is the ongoing absence of historical language, of Caló or Romani in the education system. It is a language that should be offered to all students, as Caló is a cultural heritage language of the Spanish State and of all humanity. Coming to terms with this historical injustice should serve to make us aware of the very limited availability of teachers with sufficient command of the language, as well as a huge vacuum in terms of its existence in school curriculum, information and materials in this language. Although there are now materials in this language at present, their availability in most school libraries is still completely inadequate. A policy based on fighting injustice forces us to take decisive action in order to remedy this injustice towards the Gypsy people.

Another issue that education administrators have neglected is the incentives given to Gypsy people to study university courses that encourage them to become teachers and professors. The existence of Gypsy teachers in mainstream schools is a measure of enormous educational power which can provide benchmarks for Gypsy students, as well as in terms of visibility for the non-Gypsy students and other ethnic immigrants making them fully aware that all human beings are equal.

Regarding the New Education Policies

The urgency of the realities we have been mentioning here also requires that we pay attention to the Educational Reforms currently pending, as these will determine everything from the conception itself and aims of the education system, to the type of model society and person to be considered as logical, obvious, natural. We are moving from a capitalism "softened" by a certain Welfare State, -concerned with the existing inequality of opportunities and therefore committed to a certain policy of redistribution of wealth, profits and resources, of recognition and of participation - towards a neoliberalism that carries a more frontal attack on the current Welfare State. This explains the orientation of the legislative measures that are being taken by different government ministries and departments.

The current education reform project is a clear example of how conservative and neoliberal policies promoted by the Popular Party government presided by Mariano Rajoy, are ceasing to be a strategy in the fight against social, cultural and economic inequalities in order to transform the schools and classrooms into a valuable resource to meet the needs of a staff gifted with the professional expertise and the cultural capital needed by companies operating in the new globalized markets; in other words, to facilitate and accommodate the consolidation of a neoliberal neo-colonialist capitalism. A radical change is being sought: going from educating citizens in order to further consolidate the existing Welfare State, to completely and decisively reorient the education system in order to build the new neoliberal personalities destined to live in neoliberal societies; In other words, relying on instrumentalizing the school apparatus in order to shape personalities that are *"rulers of themselves"*, something that would be like the conservative solution to the class struggle. If we are all rulers of ourselves, there is no longer a valid distinction between workers and employers, between exploiters and exploited.

If to educate citizens it is necessary to ensure a more comprehensive, humanistic, scientific and artistic education, then in order to shape the world of work and consumption we must seek to primarily influence the knowledge and skills that are needed by and of interest to the market. What the LOMCE seeks is to educate students with an eye on the profitability of everything it does, and therefore it is obsessed with technical, instrumental and marketable knowledge for the job market; humans who are dominated by economic concerns in their analysis when making decisions about what to study and choose in the educational system; people, therefore, who are fascinated by consumer goods, one of the main engines of their efforts and their reasoning.

Hence, to carry out this change they intend to cutback the subjects that make up the social sciences, humanities and the arts, as well as the time assigned to them. This educational policy is the reason for the disappearance of subjects such as *Education for Citizenry and Human Rights* and why *Cultural Values* was placed in the same category as *Religion* to choose from. In the same way, compulsory curriculum is augmented by financial education content. But we must not forget that historically and even in the present, what has served to mobilize the educational community and society in general is to realize that education is part of a project to build a better future that will try to maintain the achievements and the memory of its failures, in order to avoid repeating past mistakes and to overcome the ruins of history.

In this sense, the humanities, social sciences and arts are precisely the great critical witness to history, the constant renewal of ideals, interventions, the achievements and construction of human beings. The humanities, social sciences and the arts, as a product of culture, are always a political task, since they are the result of a selective gaze at what is visible and it is what those in control who have more decision-making power try to ignore; these are fields of knowledge in which there is always the option of giving priority to some voices over others.

These areas of knowledge study the world as a lived as experience, as a result of human will and socio-historical conditions; not in an impersonal manner, as is frequently the case in the experimental sciences and technologies. The social sciences, humanities and the arts contribute decisively in order to make sense of and to explain human ideals and frustrations. It is this form of reflexivity that allows us to understand concepts, knowledge, values, techniques, procedures, which give meaning to our existence, that illuminate our technical, scientific, political, artistic and social productions.

If we curtail these dimensions in the content of the compulsory curriculum in the education system, we will be facing the type of training that will educate people to assume that the injustices present in today's world and therefore also in the future can hardly be remedied. They will consider social inequalities to be the obvious result of genetic or religious determinism, or to be due to random causes, but they will have too many limitations to understand how policies and legislations preferably favor certain social groups and individuals, and harm others.

It is with this type of educational policies and amplification as well as, normally, through media manipulation used to explain to the citizenry and get their consent that they will learn to see economics as the only engine and rationale for decisions and measures that need to be implemented. Politics, philosophy, ethics and, in general, social and human sciences are shown as spheres of knowledge of minor importance. All questions, expressed or unexpressed, regarding why things happen in our societies are too conditioned by the structure of the cultural content that the education system presents to new generations, as being more relevant and pertinent. This is seen in the procedures and skills they develop as they pass through each classroom, and the moral dilemmas that will arise and be put to them, as well as the ways of thinking about them and facing them.

It is obvious that with this kind of economist and positivist emphasis in the curriculum that is now being proposed, the students will be hard put to be able to question and deal with any situation of injustice and privilege. We have an instrumental and economic vision of all that is studied in the classroom; an education that prevents other problematizations and the development of more comprehensive and interdisciplinary insights about the true meaning, value and functions of knowledge in general education in order to build more democratic, just and caring societies.

Hand in hand with the educational reforms promoted in recent decades, we have been enabling education to be placed at the service of an intense de-politicization, an education which is clearly individualist and tries to isolate each student-citizen, to incapacitate them from seeing themselves as part of a community, and this is jointly responsible for the present and future of their community. There is an attempt to disguise this mercantil emphasis by using words which during an actual financial crisis have a certain appeal and turn out to be quite convenient, but, more importantly, they are attempting to interpret the situation in a very biased way. In other words, these words are instruments put to the service of the most powerful economic sectors.

It is important to highlight how we are being bombarded with business terms among the slogans and concepts of the Ministry of Education, and of large corporations and philanthropic capitalist foundations that try to seek our consent towards a neoliberal and conservative reorientation of education systems. This is the case with today's buzzwords in educational discourse with which these agencies try to force an acceptance of the new neoliberal educational reforms, with word such as: *employability* and the *culture of entrepreneurship*. Both the discourse of *employability* and the *culture of entrepreneurship*, in the context in which they are articulated, never question the current capitalist production system and therefore neither do they question the current labor market. This philosophy, therefore, will decisively condition the education that educational systems offer, their cultural content, instruction, and evaluation methods.

Betting on Optimism in the Curriculum

We must assume pedagogical perspectives that go beyond the speeches and models that put the main emphasis on the deficit. Obviously, there are students that the schools find harder to understand and motivate, and for whom they must propose a curriculum that is appropriate to their current capabilities, interests and prior knowledge. But this means that we are in situations that require a teaching staff and the collaboration of relevant experts to try to more precisely identify the characteristics and strengths and weaknesses of each student in particular, always assuming that it must be possible to overcome those barriers that at this particular time hinder certain learning. We need to try different strategies other than the ones we were using, until we find the most effective ones.

What we cannot consent to are negative expectations about the possibility that every person can overcome their difficulties, something that contradicts the goals of scientific knowledge. Science has always progressed on the basis of optimism. It is possible to solve any problem, any challenge. It is only a matter of research and testing until you find the right method. Otherwise, what we are doing is adopting models of predestination for individual lives or the existence of a determining genetic code for the success and social failure of individuals. It also involves relying on blame-based models, on an exaggerated sense of individualism in which everyone's future is always in their hands. In other words, we are reinforcing the unjust and immoral logic of "every man for himself", by blaming their situation on the people from the most disadvantaged groups with higher deficits. Is each of these people to be blamed for their situation of neediness, and therefore for the fact that their education has all kinds of deficits?

We cannot ignore that an important segment of problem students with antisocial behavior in the schools, belong to economically and socially oppressed families, or families who are going through difficult circumstances of interpersonal, social, medical or labor issues. It is often a common reality for girls and boys living in many cases, on the frontlines of those huge tensions; who feel rejected or undervalued in their own neighborhood environment and even within the family, then also feel unwelcome at the schools they attend. These negative experiences do nothing but accumulate in their lives, leading them quickly to see themselves as failed beings and therefore they look for alternative solutions, no matter if they are violent solutions and/or a wide range of disruptive behaviors.

Let us keep in mind that by studying the curriculum content as it is integrated and treated in the vast majority of textbooks with which we work in our schools, Gypsy children, though not intentionally, will be subjected to the various experiences that manifest and reproduce inequalities: a lack of presence and recognition. We must be very aware, and therefore immediately remedy the lack of information and educational resources in schools, so that their outstanding cultural contributions are apparent and where their history is treated with rigor and respect. Due to the fact that many of these students also live in situations of poverty and their families have a low cultural capital, their manners and appearance cause them not to receive enough affection, care, support and solidarity from other students and too often from teachers as well. (Lynch, Baker, & Lyons, 2009). They don't tend to be the kind of students who receive more attention and for a longer time, on the contrary, they are frequently targeted by glances directed at surveillance and suspicion. However, we must never forget that whenever the teaching staff becomes aware of these situations, problems begin to be solved much faster. We need to short-circuit the perversely reproductive effects of the classist racist, sexist and homophobic concept of *common sense* that we built on our own journey as students who went through the education system.

An educational institution committed to a justice curriculum requires that the professional practice of teachers be governed actively and reflectively with ethical principles such as fairness and intellectual integrity, moral courage, respect, humility, tolerance, trust, responsibility, fairness, openness and solidarity (Torres Santomé, 2009, pp. 74–75). To be optimistic about the possibilities of education requires good professionals who can diagnose and understand the causes and social, cultural, political, labor and health conditions that are becoming more difficult and problematic in the everyday life of children from families who are going through major difficulties. Teachers should not avoid problems, but should help girls and boys to articulate their own answers. Different options for addressing such problems will be more effective through a political understanding of the difficulties and opportunities. It is also important that students growing up in poverty can appreciate the hard work and effort that is needed to get out of that situation; but they must also be able to engage institutions, social organizations and many people, including the teaching staff, who work alongside them, their families and neighbors to help address these unfair situations.

We live in a world where the exercise of the rights and obligations of citizenship requires people with information, knowledge, sufficient and relevant procedures to understand and intervene at local, national and global levels; active human beings, critics, aware of their responsibilities. And in achieving this goal, the education system must and should play a key role. If we really work with an optimistic curriculum in our classrooms through which we learn to see the strategies used by other countries and social groups that in other historical moments were themselves objects of discrimination very similar to those that came to pass and continue to affect the Gypsy people, future generations will also learn that their problems are solvable and, therefore, that they can articulate really effective actions in that direction.

To ensure and enhance democratic life is a permanently open process and requires an informed, educated and alert citizenry with faith in the future, because starting today we are working to guarantee this.

References

Lunch, K., J. Baker, & M. Lyons (eds.) (2009). *Affective Equality. Love, Care and Injustice.* New York. Palgrave, 2009.

Torres Santomé, J. (2009). *The Demotivation of Teachers.* Madrid. Morata, 2nd ed.

Torres Santomé, Jurjo (2011). *Justice Curriculum. The Trojan Horse of School Culture.* Madrid. Morata.

18

Indigenising Curriculum
Questions Posed by Baiga *Vidya*

Padma M. Sarangapani

In India, one of the policy responses to the perceived gap in the case of children of tribal or socially underprivileged communities[1], is derived from the concept of 'educability'. It interprets difference as disadvantage, and the 'gap' is to be bridged by minimising the influence of the home through structures such as residential schools for these children. In several states, the tribal welfare department runs residential schools called *ashram shalas*. The converse approach, of making the school closer to the child's world, has also been explored in some initiatives, particularly by non-government organisations (NGOs). The suggestion to include 'traditional games, jokes, riddles, tales, songs and dances in the curriculum of the school to make the child feel at home' (Nanda, 1989, p. 11) arises from this second way of 'bridging the gap'. But in either case, this group of words, 'gap', 'polarity', etc., is metaphorical. Apart from communicating a value judgement, they do not indicate what constitutes the difference. For this we need conceptual tools that will enable us to understand the composition of the curriculum in terms of whose knowledge is selected for inclusion and how it is represented, or its consequences for learners using concepts such as Bernstein's 'linguistic codes' and 'framing' (Bernstein, 1977), or Bourdieu's habitus (1977) (see for example, Kumar, 1989; Kundu, 1994; Singh, 1995).

The second contemporary concern that forms a backdrop to this paper is the growing official interest in incorporating 'indigenous knowledge' into curriculum at the school level as is evident in the National Curriculum Framework (NCERT, 2000). In India there is a variety of indigenous knowledges, from theological and philosophical studies to the performing arts and crafts. Astrology has already been accepted as a subject of study at university level. Sundar (2002) argues that gaining legitimacy and patronage for some kinds of indigenous knowledge is a reflection of the status and power of the group involved. Astrology has the backing of the Hindu right which is closely associated with the political party currently in power at the national level, and has gained official recognition, but the indigenous knowledge of tribal groups without political clout is unlikely to be included in the formal education system. The dimension which I wish to add to this debate, through the issues raised in this paper, is to do with the epistemological compatibility of indigenous knowledges, especially oral knowledges, with the practices and structures of the modern formal school which derives from the literate tradition.

The Baiga of Northern Kawardha

The Baiga are a small tribe living in and near the forested regions of Central India, in the Maikal hills around up-stream Narmada. Other tribes such as the Gond, Agaria and Pardhan and other castes such as the Ahir (Yadav) and Panka also live in the area, but the Baiga are believed to be the autochthons of the area. They speak a language which may be called '*Baiga-boli*' which is recognised to be a form of Chhatisgarhi, the common language spoken in the region.

The earliest systematic anthropological account of the Baiga is to be found in Russell and Hiralal's *Tribes and Castes of Central India* (Russell & Hiralal, 1916/1975), but the most important anthropological work describing in detail their nomadic lifestyle, the practice of shifting cultivation, magic and medicine is by Verrier Elwin (Elwin, 1938/1986). British colonial forest policies forced the Baiga to settle and begin cultivation with the plough (Rangarajan, 1996). Their current land holdings are small and typically not irrigated; agriculture is at a subsistence level. They are dependent on the forests for a number of their needs: fuel and bamboo for construction and basket weaving, minor forest produce which they sell, tubers, fruits and prey with which they supplement their diet, for medicinal plants and for recreation (Nag, 1958; Bose *et al.*, 1987). The Baiga are categorised by the government of India as a 'primitive tribe' (living in very remote areas and with very low levels of literacy, in this case about 5%). They are targeted by the State with many special development and welfare programmes.[2]

The villages of Baghmara and Kasaikunda, with a total of about 52 families, are located in the northernmost part of the district, in the valley of a small river, about one kilometre away from each other. The Kanha reserved forest is nearby. Daldali, the largest village on the plateau, is about seven kilometres from Baghmara. It has a residential school, a small weekly market, and an outlet of the Public Distribution System. The school—actually two schools: a girls' school and a boys' school in the same building—is an *ashram shala* run by the Tribal Welfare Department, and it was recently upgraded to a middle school (up to grade eight).

The castes and tribes of the region typically live in mixed villages. Baghmara and Kasaikunda, being more remote villages, are both predominantly Baiga, with a few Gond and Yadav (Ahir) families. In contrast to areas that have more access to roads and government-sponsored development programmes, the Baiga of this region have retained their traditional appearance and attire. Women have distinctive tattoos on their forehead and bodies, and their distinctive red and white checked *saree* is worn knee-length. Men usually grow their hair which they knot into a bun on the side of their head. Older men still wear only a loin cloth. All men always carry an axe, when they move away from their homes toward the forests. Women carry a sickle when they go into the forest.

The social and economic conditions of the various tribe and caste groups living in this area are similar in many respects. There are traditional occupational interdependencies, e.g. the Ahir family is given responsibility for looking after cattle, for a payment in kind, or a skilled Baiga may be requested to make a bamboo winnow, or a Baiga *gunia* called in to treat an illness. All people in this region depend on the forest, but the Baigas claim to have a special relationship with, and fearlessness of, the forest. They have the reputation of having extensive knowledge of the forests, herbal medicines and magical treatment of illness and disease. Both Baghmara and Kasaikunda had several medicine men, both '*vaidi*' (herbalist) and '*gunia*' (diviner), who have learnt this craft-knowledge from teachers and now practise it. Families are also networked, through relationships, or friendships (they may be formal 'ritual' friendships or the more loose and inclusive notion of the *sanghvari*, or peer group). The reasons are both social and labour/economic.

Culturally, there are aspects that are distinctive to each of these groups, but there are also aspects that are shared. The Baiga dance and songs differ from those of other groups in the area, and they pride themselves on their superiority in this matter. In every new generation, the creation myth of the Baiga is learnt by some men, and it is recounted at the important yearly rituals of '*bidri*', making of seed, and '*devli*', to ensure a good harvest. The myth continues to be an important source of their understanding of themselves in relation to the other communities inhabiting the area, their relationship with the world and their sense of destiny. On one of my visits, as the time for the annual *bidri* making drew near, several older Baiga spoke of the importance of this ritual and the role of Baiga people in performing it. All communities in the area collect mahua flowers in April and brew alcohol from it. The liquor is considered sacred, and is offered and drunk at the time of all worship. Baiga men and women remember the original Baiga man and woman every time they drink by sprinkling a few drops on the earth. Occasions such as *bidri* and *bida*, the biannual prophylactic rite, and festivals, such as *cherta*, for children, involve families of all castes and tribes living in the village.

Formal School

The village of Daldali has two residential *ashram* schools, one for boys and one for girls, set up by the Tribal Welfare Department. Although such *ashram shalas* were supposed to be based on different curricula more suited to the language and ethos of tribal children (National Policy on Education, 1986), most run like mainstream government schools (Ananda, 1994). The *ashram* schools at Daldali are no exception. The medium of instruction is Hindi, which is quite different from both Chhatisgarhi and *Baiga-Boli*, and which is unfamiliar to the children. The teachers, all of whom come from the plains, are not only unaware of, but also do not think very highly of, the culture of tribal peoples in this interior area. Many of them feel that the primary lessons that the children need to be taught are regarding cleanliness and proper ways of eating and dressing. The school runs quite irregularly and when it does, the teaching-learning approach is based on endless repetition of texts. There is no attempt made either by teachers or by children to seek meaning in what they are memorising. A Baiga, Hare Singh, preferred to send his children to *ashram* schools that were located further away. In these places the classes are more regular, but the pedagogy is identical.

In the last five years, more government schools have come into the area. Kasaikunda has a school which runs in the front porch of the village headman, and has two teachers, at least one of whom spends a fair proportion of his time in the village and conducts his classes every day. The school in Baghmara is an 'Education Guarantee Scheme' (EGS) school of the government. The teacher is around for only about two to three weeks of the month. Very few Baiga children come to either school. Parents are distinctly uninterested and do not compel their children to go. For their part, children often run away, preferring to roam the jungle or hunt for crabs in the river rather than endure the monotony and the harsh comments of teachers that marks schooling. Several children at Baghmara admitted that this was the reason they did not like to come to school. The EGS schools are supposed to have a more 'child-friendly' curriculum. But the books, which are in Hindi, are still inaccessible. Both the mainstream books and the EGS use a language and present objects, scenarios and values that are completely alien to the Baiga and their children. The headman of the Daldali area was of the opinion that the new techniques of singing songs and reciting poems were 'backward' and would not help children who were already 'backward'.

A Knowledge Repository

Saraswathi's 1972 paper 'Traditional modes of learning' is an important study of traditional knowledge systems in India. Based on a spectrum of indigenous knowledge traditions, which includes theology, logic, grammar, architecture, medicine and crafts such as pottery and weaving, he proposed that a conceptual distinction be made between *sastric* knowledge and *laukic* knowledge. The former includes theoretical study and applied areas such as architecture and medicine for which there are treatises and recognised instructional procedures and courses of study—they are well systematised and form a part of the literate traditions. The crafts, including pottery and weaving, are classified as *laukic*; they are learnt experientially and through practice, trial and error, and are of a non-literate character. Following the distinction made by anthropologists, the former also belong to the 'great tradition' while the latter belong to the 'little tradition' (Sinha, 1957). However, in this scheme there is no provision for including the kind of knowledge the Baigas have and use, of medicinal plants, diagnosis and healing, which is transmitted, learnt and remembered in an oral, non-literate tradition, and which is also 'local' in the sense of being culturally and ecologically integrated. The diversity, complexity and specialisation of the information involved, and its application makes this knowledge comparable to other indigenous *sastric* systems such as *ayurveda* (a holistic system of medicine) or architechture. Yet, like the crafts, it is oral and is a product of the non-literate world of the 'little traditions'. The sociocultural and particularly the ecological context in which it is learnt and practised are important features of the knowledge. Furthermore, this knowledge system is realised, practised and transmitted in a 'habitus' constituted by the subsistence economy lifestyle.[3]

Baiga villages can be regarded as epistemic communities (Holzner, 1968) engaged with the application and the transmission of medicinal knowledge. There is a distribution of this knowledge among various members of the community. In Baghmara village, for instance, virtually all the adults have a fairly extensive knowledge of the trees and plants in the forest, and varying degrees of knowledge about the medicinal properties of various plants. Children, both boys and girls, from the age of about five or six years can identify several of the more common medicinal plants around the village. On a few occasions they mentioned what it was used to treat; typically stomach ailments. By the age of about eight or nine years, the scope of the child's environment and knowledge both widen quite dramatically. On some of our visits together to the forest, they named over 60 plants with medicinal properties, and many more that bore fruits that could be eaten or were useful. They stopped their list out of consideration for me because I could no longer keep track. The Baigas themselves appear to take their knowledge of the plant life of the forests for granted, although they do recognise that there are a few men in every village whose knowledge is far more extensive and specialised.

Regarding medicinal knowledge, they are of the opinion that this is more specialised and has to be learnt from a *guru*, a teacher. They refer to this knowledge as *vidya* and believe that it is of divine origin: the first Baiga, Nanga Baiga, was also the first medicine man and received his knowledge from god *mahadev*. Many of the incantations include mention of a series of gurus through whom *vidya* has been transmitted and whose names are now also powerful. (The present incumbents regard themselves a part of this lineage although they rarely know who their *guru's guru* was.) Included in the knowledge is a wide range of herbal and root preparations, and also divine beings, both godlike and evil, that cause illness and who need to be propitiated. Some of the healers are more knowledgeable about medicinal preparations and are called *vaidi*. Others are more knowledgeable in magic and the ways of the divine and are called *gunia*. In addition to divination, both *gunia* and *vaidi* also read the pulse and use physical examination and enquiries about bowel and urinary movements to arrive at a diagnosis. *Vidya* is considered a male preserve. Women who know *vidya* are regarded as witches. The specialised knowledge about pregnancy and childbirth which is known by women who perform the function of a *suni mai* or midwife, is not regarded as *vidya*.

This description of the specialised knowledge of the Baigas conforms well with references to 'indigenous knowledges' in international discourse. Most of these are references to non-western, oral knowledge about biodiversity and medicinal plants and ecology, of autoch-tonous groups who have become marginalised and dispossessed typically as a consequence of colonisation (Burger, in Aikman, 1999). Anthropologists such as Beteille (1986, 1998) have argued persuasively against the use of this term in the Indian context as not only is the segregation it proposes invalid, but it is also dangerous. On account of the moral force inherent in the term, it lends itself to chauvinistic and communal identity politics.

My own use of the term as a generic description of Baiga *vidya* is not to stake any claim to a privileged status. It is to emphasise its non-western origin and also to ensure that it is included in current discussion on indigenous knowledge systems. As Saraswathi (1972) reminds us, 'Indigenous Knowledge Systems' in India includes a variety of epistemologies and epistemic practices: from text-based to oral systematised knowledge, to performing arts and crafts, from both the great and the little traditions.

Learning *Vidya*

The ethical code of *gunias* and *vaidis* does not permit the Baiga to charge or accept any payment for their services. By virtue of possessing *vidya*, they are obliged to use it when requested. The belief is that refusal is dangerous. The motivation to learn therefore does not seem to come from the prospect of monetary gain. When asked, many of the children said they had learnt the uses of various plants and trees from their fathers, mothers or older siblings. They recalled occasions when a particular plant had been pointed out to them, or they had been present when it was collected for use. But this knowledge did not include details on how the medicine is to be made or when and to whom it is to be administered. The *mantra* (sacred chants) and ritual aspects of diagnosis or treatment too were not a part of common and informal knowledge, but known only to those who had formally learnt it. Some of the men seem to have decided to learn a little *vidya* formally when they were married and had children—they spoke of it as useful knowledge, akin to 'first aid', to handle the frequent ailments and illnesses of childhood. 'After a boy is married and he has children, then he feels he too needs to know and he begins to learn' (Hare Singh). For this they had either gone to a guru for a short period of time, or had acquired it by what they called '*susangati*' which literally means 'good company', i.e. by spending time in the company of a knowledgeable person.

The pursuit of more specialised knowledge was restricted to a few. Baghmara had only three people, out of which only two were recognised in other villages also as healers. Hare Singh was very highly reputed but said he had given up his practice after he took a job in the *ashram* school at Daldali village nearby. Kasaikunda had three who had more formidable reputations. All these men had learnt their *vidya* from gurus. Only in two cases was the guru a close relative—in one case his father and in another case his grandfather. Most of them were young men when they began learning. They had to take the initiative to seek out their guru. The *mukkaddams* (village chief) of Kasaikunda and of Baghmara and Hare Singh, all of whom knew *vidya*, said that *vidya* is a hard taskmaster. It requires sacrifices and hard work.

Learning *vidya* is also an expensive matter for the student as it involves providing *daru*, alchohol made from mahua flowers, to the guru. It also calls for a great deal of perseverance. Most of the teachers did not teach willingly or readily but had to be cajoled over several bottles of *daru* and several visits. From the descriptions given, it seems that the process of instruction required a lot of patience and waiting. It was also fairly leisurely. Typically, it was to be had at the end of the day, when the day's labour was over. Sitting around, drinking *daru* brought by one or more of his *chelas*, the guru would teach incantations, repeating until they were learnt by heart. A few mantras I heard seemed to be in the local dialect and not some unknown, specialised language. Some were very long and there were sections that were in a dialogic form.[4] It seemed important that the incantations should be remembered well—heard and spoken without break. The men I spoke with were firm that their *vidya* is not to be written. Knowledge that required to be mediated by the eye was believed to be less direct and therefore not as pure as that which is remembered and spoken—'*sumiran*'. When asked about it they also mentioned that their guru had taken them on one trip to the forest where the names of plants and their uses were shared.

The period between the festivals of *hareli* and *dewali* (roughly July to October) was believed to be particularly auspicious for learning. A *chela* would 'enter' on *hareli* and if his guru so decreed, would 'emerge' on *dewali*. The whole process of apprenticeship seemed to be cloaked with secrecy. Who is learning from whom was always referred to as being rumoured. There was a notion of being tested by your guru at different times during the apprenticeship—two of them claimed they had been given tests in divining. They also referred to being 'tested' at the end of the course, before being declared 'pass', when their guru patted them on the back and gave them some *daru* to drink. There did not seem to be any period of practising with the guru. But it seemed that both during and after the period of this formal learning, there were occasions to witness, and participate in the diagnosis and treatment.

A *chela* could learn from several gurus—it was recognised that different gurus could have different specialties to offer. For example, curing snake-bite was a recognised specialisation. But excessive *vidya* was regarded as being dangerous. There was a strong belief that if you possessed *vidya* but did not use it, it could harm you. So also, if it was not properly respected every year during the festival of *dewali*, it could make the knower go mad. Although *vaidis* and *gunias* did not receive any payments, they were known by their reputation and were important people. Miraculous cures wrought by these specialists using plant and root extracts, were often related and savoured. But the men themselves were required to be modest and self-effacing about their knowledge. Indeed, with the exception of Hare Singh, they never directly admitted to me that they knew anything above the ordinary. They were quite secretive but they seemed to take a little pleasure in my curiosity regarding their learning.

Many of the features of 'learning *vidya*' are anticipated in childhood socialisation. Perhaps the most important feature is the learner's autonomy and initiative-taking. This aspect of initiative-taking by the learner is a common feature throughout childhood where the child is almost never coerced into doing anything, but is given ample opportunity to take initiative and participate in ongoing activity. Equally important is the fact that the pace of learning is set by the learner, depending on his own judgement regarding his readiness. In most situations, children could opt out of an ongoing activity at any point when they wished, without fear of any stigma or teasing. The same level of proficiency or interest was not expected of everyone. It was also acceptable that different people would learn to different degrees, and accordingly practice differently. Most learning took place in the course of, or alongside, productive work. Thus the boundaries between work and play, leisure and labour are quite fluid. In the learning environments, whether in the family or among the peer group, there were niches for several levels of proficiency and learning by participating and direct engagement with the task.

In two cases, *vaidis* had learnt *vidya* when they were still boys, from their relatives for whom they had been working at that time. In these cases it seems that their older relatives had wanted to teach them. There had been mutual respect; i.e. not only of the child for the older relative, but also vice versa. On the whole, Baiga society is marked by non-hierarchical relationships between children and adults, and amongst adults themselves. The volition of children was respected from the time they were young, and their abilities were noticed and appreciated. Age was respected; *siyaan* and *siyaanin*, i.e. older men and women, were all given a special place in meetings, functions and rituals in the community. But neither deferential nor authoritarian attitudes marked these relationships. Many courses of action and decisions were arrived at by the process of consultation, *salahi*; the opinions of older men were sought, but younger people also spoke. Everyone spoke equally sparingly and with as much thought, hesitation and gentle humour.

The students visited the forest in the company of their guru perhaps only once or twice. This brief visit to the forest seemed to presume a level of familiarity with the plant world around, which perhaps was not unreasonable. From a very young age children exhibited an awareness of the forest landscape in its details. It was first and foremost a landscape of edible things and full of objects of human interest—useful plants and trees, plant roots and fruit and animals to eat, plants, insects and animal activity to be noticed and perhaps to be careful and wary of. Names of many plants and insects were known to a high degree of specificity; e.g. *koilad* and *kachnar* were names for two kinds of trees which were identical in every respect save that the former had leaves that were edible and the other did not, and while most Baiga could distinguish between two types of bamboo, some could distinguish between five types.

Out of School and School

Many of the features I have described are similar to descriptions of knowledge-related activities in oral cultures as described by Ong (1982) and Goody (1968), and from an educationalist's perspective by Teasdale (1990) and Aikman (1999). This includes features such as context embeddedness of thought and activity, aggregative and cumulative organisation of thought rather than analytical categorisation, and learning through performance of real tasks rather than abstract learning tasks. It is significant that the Baiga recognise a period of learning for more formalised knowledge, that is for learning *mantras*. (Studies such as Aikman (1999) or Rogoff (1990) are about informal learning.) In marked contrast to the observation of 'conservativeness' of oral communities, there is a conscious flexibility regarding the actual content and form of the orally transmitted and remembered sacred knowledge. More than one *gunia* observed that the '*charcha*' (i.e. sacred knowledge and *mantras*) known by different people is essentially the same, but there may be differences because after all it is '*bath-kaha*', that which is told and said, and therefore apt to change. This is a contrast to the conservatism found in other Indian traditions of oral transmission of literate forms of knowledge, *sastric* knowledge, where elaborate devices are imposed to ensure that there is no distortion (see Mookerji, 1988 and Narasimhan, 1992 for details relating to Vedic learning traditions). The ease with silence, either being on one's own or of companionable silence even between two *gunia* who have come together to treat a patient, is an essential feature of the Baiga attitude of being at ease with not having or needing to speak.

Along with this, one must also recognise features that are linked to the subsistence economy. One is that childhood (after infancy) is not clearly differentiated from adulthood, so that while children are integrated into productive work at an early age, adults retain a childish playfulness. Another is the non-hierarchical structure of society and non-authoritarian structure of the family. The acceptance of children's volition and initiative is linked to a production process where children's labour is valuable and valued.

The institution of the modern school is based on different premises regarding the nature of knowledge, learning and childhood. The literate tradition which is foundational to the modern school necessarily presents knowledge 'out of context', not directly experienced. Schools teach how to act on a modelled world—not the real world. This necessitates explicit characterisation of details and interconnections. All aspects of things, even the obvious, must be talked about in order to render them comprehensible, to analyse and reflect on them. Narasimhan (1987) suggests that this is also the primary strength of knowledge obtained from school, that it is articulated and has a wide scope of applicability as it is analytical, precise and abstract. Cole and Scribner (1981), in their study of forms of literacy in Liberia noted that the most visible and indisputable consequence of schooling was that it fostered abilities in expository talk in contrived situations. Syllogistic reasoning was also followed by those who were schooled rather than non-schooled.

Sting (1998) points out that literacy also alters the relationship of the subject and society and generates a shift in subjectivity. Although the framework of literacy is contingent on social rules and cultural traditions, these do not completely determine the individual who preserves a critical detachment and autonomy. '[H]is social and cultural integration [is] dependent on processing and mediation of his own' (Sting, 1998, p. 49). Although writing permits the social repertoire of knowledge to be permanently fixed, distanced from particular situations and individuals, abstract, systematised and in principle generally accessible, it also opens up a gap between the individual subject/knower and the written cumulative knowledge. The social and cultural horizon of the literate world, constituted by overlapping subjectivities, is thus fragmentary and pluralistic.

In his study of the Bondo Highlander tribals, Bikram Nanda observed that the school presumes not only a material surplus, but also a symbolic surplus: 'the school curriculum willy nilly presupposes a certain concept of childhood for those who have to consume it. But childhood as a distinct phase in a biography may be unknown in a society based on a subsistence production system' (Nanda, 1989, p. 4). Furthermore there is also an authority inherent in the pedagogic device of the formal school. Learning is also privatised and competitive.

The purpose of presenting these two contrasting pictures is not to mount an attack on formal education. The 'decontextualised' nature of learning or of pedagogic authority are features to be noted along with the realisation that this is not a 'problem' of the institution of formal school, but this is both a part of its foundational character and what makes it an institution of modernisation and suited to the modern world, both in terms of the conception of knowledge from which it draws, its perceived relationship to the world of production, and to the nature of childhood which it presumes and upon which it is conditional. Both Bernstein's (1977) observations regarding the linguistic requirement of elaborated code and the weak framing in promoting 'active' learning in which the learner is cognitively situated, are to do with this modern institution. We are obliged to recognise the deep disjunction in the habitus of children in the oral subsistence Baiga community vis-à-vis the school.

My purpose in presenting this contrast is to suggest that the Baiga knowledge tradition, at least in its present form, cannot survive in the modern school institutional structure. It is not to identify the contour points of a rapprochement. One could consider generating from Baiga knowledge learning tasks that could be carried out in the school; for example, taxonomic and herbarium-like tasks. But turning each plant into an object to be observed and talked about may amount to simplifying or trivialising the way in which the plant is known in a living dynamic culture, or accord it with properties and dimensions that are of no interest and perhaps even distracting in the Baiga system. Chants and *mantras* rendered into writing may not be able to survive and retain their sanctity when subject to the decontextualised scrutiny which the technology of writing makes possible. The consequences of being turned into an object of study could be even more disastrous. Consider, for example, having to answer comprehension types of question based on text whose content is derived from magic.

It is far from obvious that the flexibility, initiative-taking, and peer group interaction that the knowledge of *vidya* is built upon and which is in the Baiga child's habitus, can be rediscovered in an institution in which pedagogic authority is central. On the other hand, the discipline which learning *vidya* requires places a far greater responsibility on the learner as a practitioner, which formal schools do not engender. Clearly reinventing this indigenous knowledge to suit the literate culture of the school would require that a lot more be known about its content, form and practice.[5]

I say this not only of the indigenous knowledge possessed by tribal communities, but also of the more literate *sastric* knowledge systems. Including astrology as a university course may be a disaster for astrological knowledge as it now lays itself open to a new level of awareness of the knowledge itself, made possible by the epistemic practices of modern institutions. This includes new types of objectification of knowledge in the form of texts, comprehension and questions to answers, and also examinations.[6] The survival of indigenous knowledge systems is probably better assured by being kept out of the purview of the formal modern educational system.

Notes

1. The Constitution of India recognises some communities as requiring special provisions and privileges to counteract the extreme forms of deprivation they suffered through traditional social organisation. These specific castes and tribes that are beneficiaries are listed in a Schedule of the Constitution.
2. Savyasachi (1991) feels that as a consequence of this constitutional provision, the identity of 'tribal' has acquired a definiteness it lacked in the past. The borderline between 'tribal' and 'non tribal' is no longer permeable. Beteille also points out that '[u]ntil recently tribe was a part of a regional system, and tribes

from different regions had little to do with each other. Now there is not only a definite tribal identity enjoying legal sanction, but a political interest in maintaining and strengthening that identity' (Beteille, 1986, p. 318).

3. Nanda (1989) notes the importance of the economic basis of life and productive activities in understanding the ethos of tribal communities. Reducing subsistence economy uni-dimensionally to poverty desensitises one to this dimension. See Antweiler (1998) for an analysis of characteristics of 'local' knowledge and a review of the various senses of the term.

4. The dialogic form has been noted and commented upon as a feature of oral thought and compositions of oral cultures. The chanting also had a rhythmic quality and a 'somatic component' i.e. hand activity to manipulate rice on a winnow or short sticks held in the hand. Other features such as 'ritual language use' and 'copiousness' seemed to be absent (Ong, 1982).

5. The perception of the requirements of formal learning, also leads to indigenous cultures inventing new products that they feel are more suitable or worthy of the 'modern' contexts. Krishna Kumar (1991) argues that the form of the 'essay' came into existence in the Hindi literary tradition in response to the need created by including Hindi as a subject of school study, in the British colonial educational system. A friend involved with the literacy movement in Tamil Nadu noted that when they had organised a competition for neo-literate women to demonstrate their traditional 'kolam' drawing skills, the women made drawings of motifs associated with the literacy slogans rather than their own traditional patterns.

6. Krishna Kumar recently observed to me that the recent heated debates on the inclusion of astrology as a subject of study in Indian Universities has not included this epistemological dimension.

References

AIKMAN, S. (1999) *Intercultural Education and Literacy: an ethnographic study of indigenous knowledge and learning in the Peruvian Amazon* (Amsterdam, John Benjamins Publishing Company).

ANANDA, G. (1994) *Ashram Schools in Andhra Pradesh* (New Delhi, Commonwealth Publishers).

ANTWEILER, C. (1998) Local knowledge and local knowing: an anthropological analysis of contested 'cultural products' in the context of development, *Anthropos*, 93, pp. 469–94.

BERNSTEIN, B. (1977) *Class Codes and Control Volume 3: towards a theory of educational transmission*, 2nd edn (London, Routledge & Kegan Paul).

BETEILLE, A. (1986) Concept of tribe with special reference to India, *Archive European de Sociologie*, 27, pp. 297–318.

BETEILLE, A. (1998) The idea of indigenous people, *Current Anthropology*, 39 (2), pp. 187–91.

BOSE, S., SINGH, A. K., DUTTA, A.& GANGOPADHYAY, S. (1987) *Changing Patterns of Land Use Among the Baigas of Madhya Pradesh* (Calcutta, Anthropological Survey of India).

BOURDIEU, P. (1977) *Outline of a Theory of Practice* (Cambridge, Cambridge University Press).

COLE, M.& SCRIBNER, S. (1981) *The Psychology of Literacy* (Cambridge, MA, Harvard University Press).

ELWIN, V. (1938/1986) *The Baiga* (New Delhi, Gyan Publishing Company).

GOODY, J. (1968) *Literacy in Traditional Societies* (Cambridge, Cambridge University Press).

HEREDIA, R. C. (1996) Tribal education for development: the need for liberative pedagogy for social transformation *Journal of Education and Social Change*, 10 (1&2), pp. 51–68.

HOLZNER, B. (1968) *Reality Construction in Society* (Cambridge, MA, Schenkman).

KUMAR, K. (1989) *The Social Character of Learning* (New Delhi, Sage).

KUMAR, K. (1991) *Political Agenda of Education* (New Delhi, Sage).

KUNDU, M. (1994) *Tribal Education, New Perspectives* (New Delhi, Gyan Publishing House).

MOOKERJI, R. K. (1988) *Ancient Indian Education: Brahminical and Buddhis* (Delhi, Motial Banarsidass).

NAG, D. S. (1958) *Tribal Economy* (Delhi, Bharatiya Admijati Seva Sangh).

NANDA, B. N. (1989) Pedagogy and prescription in Highland Orissa: the role of teachers and doctors in tribal development. Unpublished paper presented at the Comparative Education Conference, New Delhi, December 26–28, 1989.

NARASIMHAN R. (1987) Literacy: its characterization and implications. Unpublished paper presented at the International Conference on Orality and Literacy, Toronto, 19–21 June.

NARASIMHAN R. (1992) The oral-literate dimension in Indian culture, in: M. LOCKWOOD (Ed.) *Indological Essays: commemorative volume no. 2 for Gift Siromoney* (Chennai, Department of Statistics, Madras Christian College). *National Policy on Education* (1986) (New Delhi, Ministry of Human Resource and Development, Government of India).

NCERT (2000) *National Curriculum Framework for School Education* (New Delhi, NCERT Publications Division). ONG, W. J. (1982) *Orality and Literacy* (London, Routledge).

RANGARAJAN, M. (1996) *Fencing the Forest Conservation and Ecological Change in India's Central Provinces 1860–1914* (Delhi, Oxford University Press).

ROGOFF, B. (1990) *Apprenticeship in Thinking: cognitive development in social context* (New York, Oxford University Press).

RUSSELL, R. V.& HIRALAL, L. (1916/1975 reprint) The Baiga, in: R. V. RUSSELL & L. HIRALAL *Tribes and Castes of the Central Provinces of India Vol II* (Delhi, Rajdhani Book Centre).

SARASWATHI, B. (1972) Traditional modes of learning in Indian civilization, in: S. SINHA (Ed.) *Aspects of Indian Culture and Society* (Calcutta, the Indian Anthropological Society).

SAVYASACHI (1991) Modernisation and tribal identity, *Seminar*, 389, pp. 24–29.

SINGH, A. K. (1995) The cultural construction of home and school knowledge in tribal India, *Prospects*, 25 (4), pp. 735–47.

SINHA, S. (1957) Tribal cultures of Peninsular India as a dimension of little tradition in the study of India civilization. A preliminary statement, *Man in India*, 37 (2), pp. 93–118.

STING, S. (1998) Literacy and Education, *Education*, 57, pp. 49–59.

SUNDAR, N. (2002) Indigenise, nationalise and spiritualise—an agenda for education, *International Social Science Journal*, 173, pp. 373–83.

TEASDALE, G. R. (1990) Interactions between 'traditional' and 'western' systems of learning: the Australian experience, in: A. LITTLE (Ed.) *Understanding Culture: a precondition for effective learning* (mimeo) (Paris, UNESCO).

TOPPO, S. (1985) *Dynamics of Educational Development in Tribal India* (New Delhi, Classical Publishing Company).

WALSH, J. E. (1983) *Growing Up in British India* (New York, Holmes and Mercer).

YOUNG, M. F. D. (Ed.) (1971) *Knowledge and Control: new directions for the sociology of education* (London, Collier Macmillan

Further Readings

Section 4: Society, Politics, and Curriculum

Anttila, E. (2003). *A Dream Journey to the Unknown: Searching for Dialogue in Dance Education.* (Doctoral dissertation). Theatre Academy Helsinki, Finland: Acta Scenica 14.

Baldacchino, J. and Vella, R (eds.) (2013). *Mediterranean Art and Education. Navigating Local, Regional ad Global Imagnaries Through the Lens of the Arts and Learning*, Rotterdam, Taipei and Boston, Sense Publishers.

Bauman, Z. (2013). 'Learning to Walk on Quicksand. Lifelong Learning in Liquid Modernity' in Mayo, P. (ed.), *Learning with Adults. A Reader*, Rotterdam, Boston and Taipei: Sense Publishers.

Borg, C., and P. Mayo. 2006. *Learning and Social Difference. Challenges for Public Education and Critical Pedagogy.* Boulder: Paradigm.

Buhler, S., Settee, P., & Styvendale, N. V. (2014). 'Teaching and Learning About Justice through Wahkohtowin.' *Annual Review of Interdisciplinary Justice*, 4, 182–210.

De Alba, A. (1999). 'Curriculum and Society: Rethinking the Link.' *International Review of Education*, 45(5/6), 479–90. Retrieved from http://www.jstor.org/stable/3445098.

Ditchburn, G. M. (2012). 'the Australian Curriculum: Finding the Hidden Narrative?' *Critical Studies in Education, 53*(3), 347–60. http://dx.doi.org/10.1080/17508487.2012.703137.

Gadotti, M, Freire, P and Guimaraes, S (1995), *Pedagogia, Dialogo e Conflitto* (Pedagogy, Dialect and Conflict), Bellanova, B and Telleri, F (eds.), Turin: Società Editrice Internazonale.

Gadotti, M. (2000). *Pedagogia da terra.* (Pedagogy of the Earth). Rio de Janeiro: Editorial Peirópolis.

Gregorcic, M. (2009). 'Cultural Capital and Innovative Pedagogy: a Case Study among Indigenous Communities in Mexico and Honduras.' *Innovations in Education and Teaching International, 46*(4), 357–66. doi:10.1080/14703290903301750.

Gutierrez, F and Prado, C. (1999). *Ecopedagogia e Cidadania Planetaria* (Ecopedagogy and Planetary Citizenship). São Paulo, Brazil: Cortez.

Henry, P. (2000) *Caliban's Reason.* New York: Routledge.

Lazar, S. (2010). Schooling and critical citizenship: Pedagogies of political agency in El Alto, Bolivia. *Anthropology and Education Quarterly, 41*(2), 181–205. doi:10.1111/j.1548–1492.2010.01077.x.

Manacorda, M. A. (1970) *Il Principio Educativo in Gramsci* (The Educational Principle in Gramsci), Rome: Armando Editore.

Martinelli, E. (2007) *Don Lorenzo Milani. Dall' motivo occasionale al motivo profondo* (Don Lorenzo Milani. From the Occasional Motive to the Profound Motive). Florence: Società Editrice Fiorentina.

Nelles, W. (2008). 'Towards a Critical Pedagogy of Comparative Public Diplomacy: Pseudo-Education, Fear-Mongering and Insecurities in Canadian-American Foreign Policy.' *Comparative Education, 44*(3), 333–44. http://dx.doi.org/10.1080/03050060802264876.

Nugi, W.T'O. (1981). *Decolonizing the mind. The politics of language in African literature.* Oxford: James Currey & Heinemann.

Paraskeva, Joao, M. (2007). *As Dinamicas Ideologicas e Culturais na Fundamentacao do Curriculo.* Porto: Didactica Editora.

Paraskeva, Joao, M. (2007). *Educao e Poder. Abordagens Criticas e Pos-estruturais.* Lisboa: Edicoes Pedago.

Paraskeva, Joao, M. *et al* (2006). *Marxismo e Educacao.* Porto: Profedicoes

Paraskeva, Joao, M. (2011). *Conflicts in Curriculum Theory. Challenging Hegemonic Epistemicides.* New York: Palgrave.

Paraskeva, J., E. W. Ross, & D. Hursh (2006). *Marxismo & Educacao.* Porto: Profedicoes.

Paraskeva, J. M., Gandin, L. A., & Hypolito, A. M. (2004). A imperiosa necessidade de umateoria e pratica pedagogica radical critica: Diálogo com Jurjo Torres Santomé. *Currículo sem Fronteiras, 4*(2), 5–32. Retrieved from www.curriculosemfronteiras.org

Paraskeva, J. Hypolito, A. & Gandin, L. (2001). 'Manifesto.' *Journal Curriculo sem Fronteiras.* www.curriculosemfronteiras.org.

Paraskeva, Joao, M. et el (2005). *Reinventar a Pedagogia Critica.* Lisbon: Edicoes Pedago

Portelli, J. P (1993). 'Exposing the Hidden Curriculum,' *The Journal of Curriculum Studies,* Vol. 25 N.4 (343–358).

Sacristan, J. G. (1988). *Currículum: una reflexión sobre la práctica.* Madrid: Morata.

Sultana, R. G (1995). 'A Uniting Europe, a Dividing Education? Eurocentrism and the Curriculum,' *International Studies in Sociology of Education,* 5(2), pp. 115–44.

Sultana, R. G (ed.) (1997). *Inside/Outside Schools: towards a Critical Sociology of Education in Malta,* Malta: PEG Publications.

Tagore, R. (1993). 'My school'. *Personality.* London: MacMillan.

Veuglers, W. (2007). 'Creating Critical-Democratic Citizenship Education: Empowering Humanity and Democracy in Dutch Education.' *Compare, 37,* 105–19.

Section 5
Critical Praxis and Literacy

The philosophers have only interpreted the world, in various ways; the point, however, is to change it.

Karl Marx, *These on Feuerbach* (1845)

Before going back to college, i knew i didn't want to be an intellectual, spending my life in books and libraries without knowing what the hell is going on in the streets. Theory without practice is just as incomplete as practice without theory. The two have to go together.

Assata Shakur, *Assata: An Autobiography* (1987)

19
Critical Literacy
Theories and Practices

Vanessa de Oliveira

Introduction

This essay explores the idea of critical literacy in development education, used in this article also with reference to global and global citizenship education recognizing multiple orientations, theories and practices of critical engagement within these related fields. Critical literacy, as defined in this text, emphasizes the need for a careful examination of different 'root' narratives as a practice of responsible intellectual engagement across all sectors. In the first part of this chapter, I review the idea of critical literacy in the context of development education offering examples of my own academic and pedagogical practice in this area. In the second part I expand on the idea of soft and critical approaches to global citizenship and development education by presenting a new heuristic with four different 'root' narratives as a critical literacy stimulus for dialogue and analyses that may open new possibilities of signification.

Critical literacy in global citizenship and development education

Critical Literacy: Theories and Practices is the title of an academic open access journal I founded with Lynn Mario de Souza in 2006. When we first started the journal we were aware that different groups in education used the term in different ways, which is evident in the wide variety of articles we have received and published so far. Therefore, as an editor, I have used a very open and general definition of the term as 'an educational practice that emphasizes the connections between language, knowledge, power and subjectivities'. Authors have traced the origins of the term to different sources and associated critical literacy with different traditions, including critical pedagogy (e.g. Paulo Freire), the New/Multi-Literacies groups (e.g. Brian Street), discourse analysis (e.g. Norman Fairclough), and poststructuralism and postcolonial studies (e.g. Michel Foucault and Edward Said). The way I use critical literacy in my own work has been informed by the latter. In this chapter, I intend to outline some of the ways I have used this concept in research and teacher education related to global citizenship and development education as a strategy of examining the politics of knowledge production and the limits and possibilities of different knowledge systems.

In the article 'Soft versus Critical Global Citizenship Education' (2006), drawing on the works of Dobson (2006) and Spivak (2004; see also Andreotti 2007; Andreotti 2011), I stated that there were at least two common trends in educational initiatives that promoted concern for others (especially distant others). The first was based on the idea of a common humanity. I represented it as a 'soft' approach to global citizenship and development education. The second was based on the idea of justice and complicity in harm. I represented it as a critical approach to global citizenship and development education. I argued that 'soft' approaches based on a modernist understanding of linear time, progress and development, although productive in certain contexts, tended to close down the possibility of more critical approaches, particularly of approaches that offered alternative ways to conceptualize development, knowledge and solutions from the perspective of historically subjugated peoples (see also Bryam and Bracken 2011; Martin 2011; Bourn 2011). I asserted that 'critical literacy' as an educational practice that critically examines origins and implications of assumptions as well as other possibilities for signification, could be a viable way to address this problem.

The conceptualization of critical literacy I used in that article combines questions within two orientations. The first orientation challenges imbalances in power and representation. This can be illustrated in questions such as: who decides (something is true or ideal), in whose name and for whose benefit? The second orientation challenges the notion that meaning is objective and self-evident. It emphasizes the social, cultural and historical 'construction' of realities and highlights the limits and blind edges of any system of signification, promoting openness to suppressed knowledges and subjectivities and to what is unknown. This orientation is illustrated in questions such as: where is this understanding coming from (in terms of collective 'root' narratives), where is it leading to (in terms of social, cultural, political and environmental implications), and how can this be thought 'otherwise' (what possibilities of signification have been 'forgotten' in this context)?

Within the multiplicity of critical literacy traditions, this approach differs slightly from critical engagements based on other orientations. Cervetti, Pardales and Damico (2001), for example, establish a distinction between traditional reading, critical reading and critical literacy, emphasizing that each orientation of 'reading critically' will result in different questions being asked. Using their framework, I illustrate these differences through the scenario of a teacher and a student in a classroom, where the teacher is telling the student he needs schooling in order to 'be somebody in life.' Within their framework, a traditional form of reading would enable 'decoding' questions such as: what did the teacher say, how did she substantiate her arguments, is what she said true or false? A critical form of reading would look further into the context and political framework of the scenario: where was this school, when did it happen, what was the socio-economic situation of the teacher and student, what was the motivation and political orientation of the teacher, what power relations are reproduced in the teacher's statement, how did the teacher's views affect the student and his/her family? A critical literacy approach would focus on the production of knowledge/power and enable questions like: who decides what 'being somebody' means, in whose name for whose benefit then and now, how do we come to think about the ways we do, who makes choices about understandings of reality, whose interests are represented in these choices, who benefits or loses with them, what choices are forgotten, how do people in different contexts understand the idea of 'being somebody'?

When introducing critical literacy in development education, I choose scenarios that make evident dominant taken for granted perspectives and assumptions about the benevolence of progress, charity and schooling in international engagements. One of the scenarios I use is a poster with pictures of children in need with the title 'education for all can solve all problems.' I use the idea of 'critical reading' to explore the context of production of that poster: what is the purpose of the poster, who created it and with what motives, where was it placed and why, how and why were pictures and words chosen, how is the reader manipulated through the language? I use the idea of 'critical literacy' to start to open up questions related to complicity in harm at a very basic level, such as: who decides what problems and solutions are (in the poster, historically and in 'our' context), what assumptions inform these decisions, how are unequal relationships between donors and recipients reproduced through these significations, what other conceptualizations of problems and solutions could be designed by communities that have been historically subjugated in these relationships, and so on.

I also usually emphasize a strategic distinction between reflexivity and reflection in the practice of critical literacy in teacher education. 'Reflection on practice' in teacher education has been mainstreamed as a form of thinking that looks at individual processes of meaning and decision making in order to improve educational practice amongst teachers. I suggest the term self-reflexivity to contrast the practice of reflection (thinking about individual journeys and assumptions), to the practice of tracing individual assumptions to collective socially, culturally and historically situated 'stories' with specific ontological and epistemological assumptions that define what is real, ideal and knowable (i.e. 'root' narratives). This highlights that possibilities for thinking available to individuals, and individual 'choices' are never completely 'free,' 'neutral' or only 'individual,' as the things we say, think and do are conditioned (but not necessarily determined) by our contexts (see Andreotti 2010a; 2010b). Self-reflexivity also challenges the assumption of the self-evident subject – the idea that there is a direct correlation between what we say, what we think and what we do. It draws attention to the complex constitution of subjectivities, to the interdependence of knowledge and power, and to what is sub- or unconscious in our relationships with the world.

I have used the metaphor of a three-layered cake (see figure 19.1) to illustrate these differences. At the top layer there is what we say, what we think and what we do, which are generally perceived to be directly related. A 'Cartesian' understanding of subjects states that we say exactly what we think and that we can describe objectively exactly what we do. However, our capacity to describe what we think is limited by what can be said: what is appropriate and intelligible to both ourselves and to others (e.g. we can think things that are not appropriate to say in specific contexts, or that we cannot articulate, acknowledge, or make sense of). Our capacity to describe what we do is limited by what we can notice and by what we want to present to others (e.g. we can say we are open and flexible, but fail to notice that we act in a contradictory way). This recognition of the limits of language is part of critical literacy practices.

The second layer of the cake is that of individual experiences. It acknowledges that what we say, think and do are based on our individual journeys in multiple contexts. They are rooted in our unique 'baggage' of concepts and traumatic, inspiring and ordinary learning experiences and dependent upon what we have been exposed to. The third layer of the cake recognizes that our experiencing and interpretation of these experiences are conditioned by collective referents grounded in the languages we have inherited to 'make sense' of reality and communicate with others. These languages have specific criteria for what counts as real (ontology), what can be known and how (epistemology), what is ideal and how to get there (methodology). These collective criteria are socially, culturally and historically 'situated' – it depends on a group's social, cultural and historical background and therefore it changes (slowly) over time, as contexts change and criteria of different groups intersect and contradict each other. Therefore, there is always

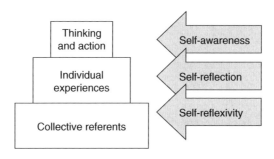

Fig. 19.1. Awareness, reflection, and reflexivity

diversity within a group of same criteria, as things are never static, but there is also always a dominant set of criteria that represents the 'common sense' of a group or groups. I suggest that an analysis of the first layer could be named 'self-awareness,' an analysis of the second layer 'self-reflection' and an analysis of the third, 'self-reflexivity.' All three are important for development education.

In order to address some of the pedagogical challenges of introducing this conceptualization of critical literacy in the classroom context in my work as a teacher educator, I created a matrix of the relationship between knowledge, power, the construction of realities in the classroom, and ideas about the control of pedagogical outcomes (see Andreotti 2008). I illustrate this matrix with examples from development education, as the practice of critical literacy is sometimes accused of either 'indoctrinating' or 'paralysing' learners (see Vare and Scott 2007 for a similar discussion on Education for Sustainable Development). Critical literacy is perceived to indoctrinate learners when a specific critical analysis of injustice and position on justice are presented as the only morally justifiable path. Critical literacy is perceived as paralyzing learners in questioning everything, when it emphasizes a multiplicity of perspectives, the limits of knowledge and the complexity and context dependency of positions on justice. Thus, the matrix helps think through these issues and present these perceived problems as part of a more general discussion on the role of education. This matrix combines two ways of thinking about education (i.e. 'think as I do and do as I say' and 'think for yourself and choose responsibly what to do') and two ways of thinking about knowledge (i.e. 'there is one right answer independent of context' and 'answers are socially constructed and context dependent').

Therefore, there are (at least) four different possibilities for thinking and action. The first possibility is 'think as I do, do as I say, there is only one right answer.' The example from development education I use is a quote from a teacher: 'I teach my students that people in poorer countries lack technology, education and proper work habits. I make sure my students understand that we have a moral obligation to help them by providing assistance through charity and expertise.' The second possibility is 'think for yourself and choose responsibly what to do, but there is only one right answer,' which is illustrated in the quote: 'I teach my students that they need to be critical thinkers –to separate facts from opinions and to search for impartial, objective information to construct their arguments. I believe rational and scientific thought is the only way to achieve a just and prosperous society.' The third possibility is 'answers are context dependent, but in my class, you should think as I do and do as I say,' illustrated in: ' I teach my students that textbook history is always told from the point of view of the winners and that the perspective of the oppressed peoples is seldom promoted. So, I teach my students the perspective of the oppressed. I want them to be willing to fight for social justice.' Last, the fourth possibility is 'answers are context dependent, you should learn to think for yourself and choose responsibly what to do,' exemplified in: 'I teach my students that there are always different perspectives on any issue, that these are grounded in social, cultural and historical processes, and that whatever choice they make there will be systemic implications. My job is to create spaces for them to engage with the ethics of global challenges, processes, and dilemmas in ways that create a sense of interdependence and responsibility for themselves and towards the world.' I emphasize that decisions about possibilities are also context dependent (a teacher may legitimately choose the first under certain circumstances), but that the fourth possibility has not been very common in formal Western schooling where the first and second possibilities have been dominant and also imposed or exported all over the world.

In terms of engagements with historically subjugated communities who may offer alternative perspectives on international development issues, in the Through Other Eyes Initiative (TOE), Lynn Mario de Souza and I developed a resource and framework of a critical literacy practice based on Spivak's ideas of learning to unlearn, learning to learn, learning to listen and learning to reach out (see Andreotti and Souza 2008; Souza and Andreotti 2009; Andreotti 2011). I also framed this kind of practice of critical literacy as a response to increasing complexity, uncertainty, diversity and inequality in contemporary societies related to two different conceptualizations of the 'post-' in postmodernism (i.e. post- as 'after,' and post- as questioning) that could prompt an educational process that would enable students to move from the desire for absolute certainties, fixed identities/communities, and predictable and consensual futures towards being comfortable with contingent and provisional certainties, complex and hybrid identities/communities and open co-created futures in the context of global education (Andreotti 2010b).

More recently, I have been framing my own work on critical literacy in global citizenship and development education around the task of addressing recurrent patterns of relationships, flows and representations between over-exploited and over-exploiting communities. I have created the acronym 'HEADS UP' to represent these patterns, which refer to common practices of engagements and education that are:

1. Hegemonic (justifying superiority and supporting domination);
2. Ethnocentric (projecting one view, one 'forward,' as universal);
3. Ahistorical (forgetting historical legacies and complicities);
4. Depoliticized (disregarding power inequalities and ideological roots of analyses and proposals);
5. Salvationist (framing help as the burden of the fittest);
6. Un-complicated (offering easy solutions that do not require systemic change);
7. Paternalistic (seeking affirmation of superiority through the provision of help).

(Andreotti 2012a, 2)

I have put together a checklist of questions to help to identify each pattern in education (see Andreotti 2012a) and also a list of questions that complicate further common/easy solutions for each of the patterns (see Andreotti 2012b). At the heart of this work is the idea that education is about preparing myself and those I work with to enlarge possibilities for thinking and living together in a finite planet that sustains complex, plural, uncertain, inter-dependent and, unfortunately, deeply unequal societies. In order to do this, perhaps what is needed is an attitude of skeptical optimism or hopeful skepticism (rather than naïve hope or dismissive skepticism) in order to expand our inherited frameworks in terms of four educational priorities. First, it is necessary to understand and learn from repeated historical patterns of mistakes, in order to open the possibilities for new mistakes to be made. Second, we need to recognize how we are implicated or complicit in the problems we are trying to address. Third, we need to learn to enlarge our referents for reality and knowledge, acknowledging the gifts and limitations of every knowledge system and moving beyond polarized antagonisms towards agonistic solidarities (Andreotti 2011). Fourth, we must engage with more complex social analyses acknowledging that if we understand the problems and the reasons behind them in simplistic ways, we may do more harm than good.

In relation to the latter, it is also important for the field that these analyses are accessible and available to different discursive communities (e.g. academics, non-governmental organisation (NGO) practitioners, teachers and students). Therefore, work that translates and synthetizes discussions in different fields (e.g. politics, development, sociology, social movements) can be very useful and important in moving the debate in the field forward in a more organic way (see for example Andreotti 2011b). The downside of translations and syntheses is that they simplify complex discussions and can create seemly fixed distinctions that are more fluid than their representations. Nevertheless, if used as a starting point for discussion (that is also open to critique), they are necessary tools in the creation of a tradition of responsible, non-exclusive, critical intellectual engagement in the field (see also Richardson 2008; Evans, Ingram, McDonald and Weber 2009; Khoo 2011; Marshall 2011). It is in this spirit that, in the second part of this chapter, I offer a new heuristic which represents a revision of the popular distinction between soft and critical approaches to global citizenship education (Andreotti 2006).

Mapping narratives as a key critical literacy exercise

Tracing narratives to collective 'root' narratives (or meta-narratives) is a central exercise of the kind of critical literacy I advocate in this chapter. As an intellectual exercise, mapping discourses helps people clarify their own positions by making evident the ambivalence of signification (the fact that words mean different things in different contexts), and by promoting the productive identification of inherent assumptions, patterns, trends, differences, similarities, paradoxes, and contradictions between and within different worldviews. Mapping exercises can also help people to explore the problem spaces that generated the questions they are seeking answers for in order to check if they are still relevant or if questions have already changed (Scott 1999). However, each mapping exercise is not neutral or transparent: as all interpretations are socially, culturally and historically situated, so is the 'picture' presented by a map. Therefore, it is important to remember that maps are useful as long as they are not taken to be the territory that they represent and are used critically as a starting point of discussion.

The mapping exercise I present below establishes distinctions between a) technicist instrumentalist, b) liberal humanist, c) critical and postcritical, and d) 'Other' narratives of society, education, development and diversity. I characterize the first three orientations as framed by, or in response to, modernist tenets. These narratives reproduce similar characteristics of privileging: anthropocentrism (putting 'mankind' at the centre); teleology (aiming for a predefined outcome in terms of progress); dialectics (expecting a linear progression towards a synthesis); universal reason (the idea of one rationality); and the Cartesian subject (who believes that he can know himself and everything else objectively). I propose that these basic characteristics should not be seen as all good or all bad, but as historically situated, and potentially restrictive if *universalised as a single story* through social, political or educational projects, as they prevent the imagination of other possibilities.

The technicist instrumentalist root-narrative frames *social engineering as economic rationalization decided by experts*. This narrative can be seen at work in educational and development initiatives concerned with the creation of human capital for national economic growth in knowledge societies. From this perspective education is perceived as a way to maximise the performance of individuals in global markets driven by services and innovation, in order to improve their employability or entrepreneurial capacity with a view to contribute to their country's competitiveness in global economies. Economic growth is associated with the acquisition and accumulation of universal knowledge (in contrast, for example, to the explanation that economic growth is based on hegemonic control of means of production) and poverty is defined as an individual or a country's deficit of knowledge, competencies and skills to participate in the global economy. The rationale for education is presented as a business case, as an individual responsibility of lifelong learning and adaptation to ever-changing economic contexts. From this perspective, global/development education, often associated with ideas of 'social responsibility' involves the export of expertise from those heading the way in terms of economic development to those lagging behind. Engagements with other cultures are defined in relation to national interests, such as the protection of national labor markets, the expansion of consumer markets, and the perceived threat of unwanted immigration, creating a need for controlled and market oriented internationalization based on nationally defined objectives.

The root-narrative of liberal humanism frames social engineering as *human progress decided by national representatives*. From this perspective, education serves as enculturation into a national culture defined by its political or intellectual representatives, as well as an international culture perceived as an encounter between nationally defined groups of individuals primarily concerned with a combination of individual, national and humanitarian interests. What human progress looks like is decided by national representatives in supranational governance institutions like the United Nations, through a process of international consensus on key universal aims to be delivered by nation states, generally focusing on human rights, substantial freedoms or human capabilities. From this perspective, education should disseminate the international consensus on universal human progress defined in terms of access to education, healthcare, democracy and economic development. In this sense, obstacles to human progress become the focus of government agreed targets (such as the Millennium Development Goals), campaigns (like Education for All), and other charitable and humanitarian interventions which generally define help as the moral responsibility of those who are ahead in terms of international development.

Poverty is explained as a deficit in terms of human progress, thus education becomes a vehicle for poverty eradication through partnerships between donors/dispensers and receivers of aid, knowledge, education, resources (e.g. books, computers, etc.), technical assistance, human rights, or volunteer labour. From this perspective, education is a means to prepare world leaders to bring order and progress for all (generally through education itself). Engagements with difference are also defined in national or ethnic terms: global learners are encouraged to acquire knowledge about different cultures/nationalities, including different perspectives, in order to be able to work with diverse populations towards common/consensual goals (predefined by national or supranational governance institutions). Therefore, different perspectives and critical engagement are welcome within pre-defined frameworks (i.e. as long as there is acceptance of human rights, specific ideas of development, progress, governance, etc.).

Critical and postcritical root-narratives frame *social engineering as fair distribution done by ordinary people* (rather than experts or representatives). These perspectives are based on a critique of both technicist instrumentalist and liberal humanist root-narratives highlighting injustices and inequalities created or maintained by their ideals and means of implementation. In terms of state governance, critical and postcritical narratives emphasize the complicity of initiatives based on economic or humanist ideals in the creation and maintenance of poverty and marginalization in order to sustain exponential compound economic growth and improvements in quality of life that benefit only small sections of the world population. A critical narrative (still drawing on humanism) focuses its critique on the primacy of economic growth imperatives in nation state agendas, as well as the erosion of autonomy and accountability of governments to their own populations due to lobbying and increasingly closer relationships with corporations. This type of critical humanism attempts to expand the notion of consensual human progress to include the rights of those who have historically been marginalized working against patriarchy, sexism, class divisions, racism and hetero-normativity (e.g. approaches grounded on critical pedagogy).

Post critical narratives claim that the consensus on human progress, based on modern development, is manufactured by elites and imposed around the world as a form of imperialism that eliminates other conceptualizations and possibilities of progress and development, therefore, they challenge the idea of social engineering. Post critical narratives will tend to focus on relationality, complex subjectivities, difficulties of representation (of hybrid and fluid communities/identities), intersectional violence, and agonism (rather than antagonism) in politics. Education, from critical and postcritical perspectives, is concerned with the transformation of society and the creation of a new social order more inclusive of or led by those who have been silenced or exploited by the current dominant system – it involves an emphasis on critical social analyses of unequal power relations, distributions of labour and wealth (emphasized in critical narratives) and the politics of representation and knowledge production (emphasized in post critical narratives).

Education, therefore, is about the creation of a critical mass of people who could see and imagine beyond the limitations and oppression of the current system in order to bring a different reality into being. Engagement with difference involves listening to and empowering those who have been marginalised and insisting on the need for spaces of dissent where other alternatives can emerge. The World Social Forum, the Occupy Wall Street Movement, the Idle No More Movement in Canada, and the occupation of the Syntagma square in Athens are examples of initiatives based on critical humanist narratives in civil society. Several educational initiatives inspired by anti-colonial, feminist and anti-oppressive movements since the 1960s also enact critical humanist ideals.

Through education in contemporary metropolitan and industrialised societies people are exposed to different degrees to the three configurations of thinking described so far. The common theme of social change as social engineering in the three configurations is also not a coincidence. All these narratives can be traced to common roots in the Renaissance, the Industrial Revolution, the Reformation, European colonialism and resistance to colonialism, and, particularly, the European Enlightenment. However, since these cultural, social and economic transitions have framed our ideas of what is good, ideal and normal, it is important to acknowledge our constitutive blindness to other forms of seeing, knowing and being in the world that do not fit what we can recognize through the frames of references we have become used to.

For this reason, I presented the fourth option 'Other(s)' as a question mark: non-anthropocentric, non-teleological, non-dialectical, non-universal and non-Cartesian possibilities. For people over-socialized in the first three options (i.e. most of us who have been schooled), these possibilities would be extremely difficult to even begin to identify or to experience. Thus, it may be more useful to present them as absences rather than categories. The closest and most intelligible example that I have of an 'Other' narrative is that of a global education centre in Pincheq, a tiny village between Pisac and Cuzco in Peru (see below). Even though their principles for global education may seem self-evident and understandable, a deeper cognitive-relational engagement with the metaphoric ontology of the puma, the serpent and the condor in their Incan cosmology would be necessary to unlock possible contingent meanings that are not obvious in what we can represent in writing. I use this here to illustrate the limited nature of our interpretations (that always rely on inherited concepts) and the complexity and difficulty of translating and representing these worldviews outside of their contexts; both of these preoccupations are key to critical literacy.

The Apu Chupaqpata Global Education Centre's Global Education Principles are:

1. The entire planet Earth (i.e. Pachamama) is my home and country, my country is my mother and my mother knows no borders.
2. We are all brothers and sisters: humans, rocks, plants, animals and all others.
3. Pachamama is a mother pregnant of another generation of non-predatory children who can cultivate, nurse, and balance forces and flows, and who know that any harm done to the planet is harm done to oneself.
4. The answers are in each one of us, but it is difficult to listen when we are not in balance, we hear too many different voices, especially in the cities.
5. The priority for life and education is balance: to act with wisdom, to balance material consumption, to learn to focus on sacred spiritual relationships, to work together with the different gifts of each one of us, with a sense of oneness. Our purpose is to learn, learn and learn again (in many lives) to become better beings.
6. There is no complete knowledge, we all teach, learn and keep changing: it is a path without an end. There is knowledge that can be known and described, there is knowledge that can be known, but not described and there is knowledge that cannot be known or described.
7. Our teachers are the Apus (the mountains-ancestors), Pachamama, the plants, what we live day by day and what has been lived before, the animals, our children, our parents, the spirits, our history, our ancestors, the fire, the water, the wind, all the different elements around us.

8. The serpent, the puma and the condor are symbols of material and non-material dimensions, of that which can be known, of that which cannot be known or determined, and of the connections between all things.

9. The traditional teachings of generosity, of gratitude, and of living in balance that are being lost are very important for our children – it is necessary to recover them.

10. The world is changed through love, patience, enthusiasm, respect, courage, humility and living life in balance. The world cannot be changed through wars, conflicts, racism, anger, arrogance, divisions and borders. The world cannot be changed without sacred spiritual connections.

(Apu Chupaqpata Global Education Centre, 27/07/2012)

Conclusion

I started this essay with an overview of the ways I have used critical literacy in global citizenship and development education, particularly in the context of teacher education. I offered examples of how critical literacy may trigger new questions and directions in relation to global and development education in terms of how we can move beyond repeated problematic patterns of thinking and engagements and how we can start to approach increasing complexity, uncertainty, plurality and inequality in contemporary societies. I emphasized the importance of intellectual depth, of multiple and complex social analyses and of making these analyses accessible to different communities in order to build a strong foundation for the field. In the second part of the chapter, I presented a new heuristic that traces assumptions in three common sets of narratives in education and that frames a fourth set of narratives as a question mark, something that the related fields of global and development education should further engage with to pluralize knowledge in the present in order to pluralize the future.

References

Andreotti, V. (2006). 'Soft Vs. Critical Global Citizenship Education.' *Policy and Practice: A Development Education Review*, 3, 40–51.

Andreotti, V. (2007). 'An Ethical Engagement with the Other: Gayatri Spivak on Education.' *Critical Literacy: Theories and Practices*, 1(1): 69–79.

Andreotti, V., Souza, L. (2008). 'Global Learning in the Knowledge Society: Four Tools for Discussion.' *Journal of Development Education Research and Global Education*, 31:7–12.

Andreotti, V. (2010a). 'Global Education in the 21st Century: Two Different Perspectives on the 'Post-' of Postmodernism.' *International Journal of Development Education and Global Learning*, 2(2), 5–22.

Andreotti, V. (2010b). 'Glimpses of a Postcolonial and Postcritical Global Citizenship Education.' In G. Elliott, C. Fourali and S. Issler (Eds.) *Education for Social Change* (238–50). London: Continuum.

Andreotti, V. (2011a). *Actionable Postcolonial Theory in Education*. New York, NY: Palgrave Macmillan.

Andreotti, V. (2011b). 'Engaging the (Geo)Political Economy of Knowledge Construction: Towards Decoloniality and Diversality in Global Citizenship Education.' *Globalization, Society and Education Journal*, 9(3–4):381–97.

Andreotti, V. (2012a).' HEADS UP: Editor's Preface.' *Critical Literacy: Theories and Practices*, 6(1):3–5.

Andreotti, V. (2012b). 'Education, Knowledge and the Righting of Wrongs.' *Other Education: The Journal of Educational Alternatives*, 1(1): 19–31.

Bourn, D (2011) 'Discourses and Practices around Development Education: From Learning about Development to Critical Global Pedagogy.' *Policy & Practice: A Development Education Review*, Vol. 13, Autumn 2011, 11–29, available: http://www.developmenteducationreview.com/issue13-focus1

Bryam, A. and Bracken, M. (2011). *Learning to Read the World? Teaching and Learning About Global Citizenship and International Development in Post-Primary Schools*. Dublin: Irish Aid.

Cervetti, G., Pardales, M., & Damico, J. (2001). 'A Tale of Differences: Comparing the Traditions, Perspectives, and Educational Goals of Critical Reading and Critical Literacy.' *Reading Online*, 4(9). Available: http://www.readingonline.org/articles/art_index.asp?HREF=/articles/cervetti/index. html

Dobson, A. (2006). 'Thick Cosmopolitanism.' *Political Studies*, 54, 165–84.

Evans, M., Ingram, L. A., Macdonald, A., & Weber, N. (2009). Mapping the 'Global Dimension' of Citizenship Education in Canada: the Complex Interplay of Theory, Practice and Context. *Citizenship Teaching and Learning, 5*(2), 17–34.

Khoo, S. (2011). Exploring Global Citizenship and Internationalisation in Irish and Canadian Universities.' *Globalisation, Societies and Education*, 9 (3 Apr):337–353.

Marshall, H. (2011). 'Instrumentalism, Ideals and Imaginaries: Theorising the Contested Space of Global Citizenship Education in Schools.' *Globalisation, Societies and Education, 9*(3–4), 411–26.

Martin, F. (2011).' Global Ethics, Sustainability and Partnership.' In Butt, G. (Ed.) *Geography, Education and the Future* (206–22), London: continuum Books.

Richardson, G. (2008). 'Conflicting Imaginaries: Global Citizenship Education in Canada as a Site of Contestation.' In M. O'Sullivan & K. Pashby (Eds.), *Citizenship Education in the Era of Globalization: Canadian Perspectives* (53–70). Rotterdam, The Netherlands: Sense.

Scott, D. (1999). *Refashioning Futures: Criticism after Postcoloniality*. Princeton, NJ: Princeton University Press.

Souza, L., Andreotti, V. (2009). 'Culturalism, Difference and Pedagogy: Lessons from Indigenous Education In Brazil.' In Jennifer Lavia and Michelle Moore (eds.) *Cross- Cultural Perspectives on Policy and Practice: Decolonizing Community Contexts* (72–85). London: Routledge.

Spivak, G. (2004). 'Righting Wrongs.' *The South Atlantic Quarterly*,Vol.103, 523–81.

Vare, P. and Scott, W.(2007). 'Learning for a Change: Exploring the Relationship between Education and Sustainable Development.' *Journal of Education for Sustainable Development*, 1 (2), 191–98.

20

Postcoloniality, Critical Pedagogy, and English Studies in India

Kailash C. Baral

We in India have a complex relationship with the legacy of English both as a language and as a literary discipline. This legacy, a product of both colonialism and postcoloniality, is also entwined with the global status of English today in the wake of technological revolution, especially in the form of the World Wide Web, Internet networks, and e-mail.[1] Although only 4 percent of the Indian population uses English on a regular basis, India has the third largest English-speaking population in the world. The Ethnologue database puts this figure at around 50 million who use English as a second language. Not tied to a specific ethnic group or region, English plays an important role as the lingua franca in the country. A wide variety of English is used in India with local and regional flavor starting with "the pukka enunciations of Oxbridge-educated Maharajahs … to the near-incomprehensible patois of the slums and streets. But it all remains English, varied and wonderful, as Anthony Burgess puts it, 'A whole language, complete with the colloquialisms of Calcutta and London, Shakespearian archaisms, bazaar whinings, references to the Hindu pantheon, the jargon of Indian litigation and shrill Babu irritability all together'" (Green 1998: 111).[2]

Even so, English has been overtly politicized in postcolonial India in spite of its constitutional status as an Indian language and as the second official language along with Hindi. The tirade against English in a state like West Bengal, ruled by the Left front, is symbolic in that it is a fight against imperialism. In the northern states of Uttar Pradesh and Bihar, the slogan "Angreji Hatao" (remove English) has more to it than simply a fight against a colonial legacy. At one level the movement seeks to ensure the superiority of the Hindi language, and at another, it participates in the politics of caste. English is identified with the educated upper caste, politically categorized as the dominant class. They are pitted against the *dalits* and other marginalized castes that constitute the vote bank of some of the political parties. Nonetheless, globalization has brought in its wake a radical change in the attitudes of people toward English in all walks of life, including those who were earlier opposed to it. Instead of being a symbol of imperialism and identified with a certain class or caste of people, English is now considered as the language of opportunity, thanks to multinational corporations, free trade, and outsourcing of software services. It is one of the most sought after curricular subjects as each state in the country, in spite of the ideological inclinations of the ruling class, has started acknowledging its functional primacy. Mastery of the English language now equates with economic success. This impetus is catalyzed in different ways: for example, English is now a required subject from the first grade in West Bengal and from the third grade in states such as Bihar and Uttar Pradesh.

Caste, class, and ideological imperatives apart, the primacy of English in India is marked by three parallel and often overlapping developments: (1) as a language of trade, commerce, and economic opportunity; (2) as a language of communication and creative expression; and (3) as a disciplinary study. The expediency of English as a language for trade, commerce, and economic empowerment in a climate of economic liberalization is caught up with the political class across the ideological divide. Even the Bharatiya Janata Party (BJP), a right-wing political party, has recognized the primacy of the English language and has toned down its anti-English rhetoric, moving away from its advocacy of cultural nationalism borne out by the slogan "Hindi, Hindu, and Swadeshi." English has been commodified to such an extent today that one comes across shops for Spoken English, Business English, and so on in every city in India small or big, training people for the bourgeoning services sector. In spite of occasional political hiccups, English has moved from being the subject of politics to an object of economic empowerment having significant impact on the political economy of the state. From its initial role in independent India as a "library language" and the "window to the world,"[3] English has steadily gained importance, and today it has become a symbol of people's aspiration for quality education, economic opportunities and a fuller participation in national and international life.

Further, the authenticity of English in the Indian sociocultural matrix, manifested in the modes of living and cultural practices of the people, is creatively expressed in the English language by authors from the last quarter of the nineteenth century to contemporary times; India is inscribed in English in multiple ways. Writers such as Salman Rushdie, Arundhati Roy, Vikram Seth, Upamanyu Chatterjee, and Amitav Ghosh not only have demonstrated their mastery over the language but also have earned global recognition. In their works, they have clearly marked the narrative address of the nation projecting a pan-Indian consciousness.

Beyond the historical and political contexts of its development, English studies as an academic discipline has drawn critical attention to critics and theorists of diverse ideological persuasions across disciplines. Initially implicated in the political agenda of colonialism for producing a set of people by birth and blood Indian but by attitude and manners British, the location of English studies within a postcolonial curricular structure today has intensified the debate on its sociohistorical and cultural implications. In recent years issues such as caste, class, gender, nationalism, secularism, democracy, and pedagogy have marched into and exploded the English studies discipline. Issues concerning syllabus design and pedagogical practice have further deepened the problematic. My endeavor in this essay is to examine the curricular politics and the pedagogical issues of English in India in the context of English studies as a discipline.

The Colonial Legacy and Plural Debates

The discipline of English studies in India has come a long way, with a tradition of more than 170 years, dating from Macauley's notorious Minute of 1835. Its discursive history intersects the colonial/postcolonial trajectory while the debate concerning the shifting terrain of English as a discipline continues.[4] Either as a language or as a disciplinary study, English in India has been always a site for and of conflicts, alliances, and resistances.

In "The Caste of English," Raja Rao (1978: 421) writes, "As long as we are Indians—that is, not nationalists, but truly Indians of the Indian psyche—we shall have the English language with us and amongst us, and not as guest or friend, but as one of our own, of our caste, our creed, our sect and of our tradition." By qualifying English with the sociological term of "caste," Rao has naturalized English in our cultural context.[5] Probing a little further, Braj Kachru (1983), an eminent linguist, observes that English is not a homogenous product in India as it is subdivided into its regional as well as local varieties. He examines those processes which have been used in India to nativize the "guest and friend" as one of our own, of our caste and tradition. Contrary to Kachru's sociolinguistic thesis of the Indianization of English, P. Lal, an Indo-English poet and critic of repute, and Meenakshi Mukherjee, an important postcolonial critic, argue in favor of its literary naturalism (Dasgupta 1993: 116–17). This debate serves only an academic interest, for whatever critical position is favored or status is accorded to English, it has been naturalized linguistically as a variety called "Indian English" and through literary production, as a body of literature called "Indian Writing in English" (IWE). Probal Dasgupta is amused to see in the debate a lack of concern for vernacular languages and for linguistic and cultural pluralism vis-à-vis English in India. Taking into account the pluralistic paradigm, which serves as the basis of his thesis, Dasgupta (1993: 30) argues that "while a Western scholar faced with massive linguistic heterogeneity and pluriculturalism would start with a 'why' question, the Eastern scholar (or call him the noble man from the 'South' following the Brandt Report of 1980) being accustomed to living within a pluralistic situation would start with an explanation as to 'how' the communication pattern was organized in such a nation." In trying to explain the "how" of linguistic pluralism and multiculturalism, Dasgupta posits that the study of English in India should not be considered independent of a serious study of the cultures and languages of the country.

Besides the linguistic implications of English in India, its curricular context as a literary discipline is interrogated from diverse critical positions. If a few decades back English studies was at the center of debates over colonial administration and its impact upon Indian nationalism and historical consciousness, the scenario is different now under postcolonial conditions marked by the regime of critical theory. The penetration of critical theory into Indian academia has disquieted English studies previously secured within an almost static inherited colonial institutional and instructional structure. The debate on the complex destiny of English studies in India in the wake of critical theory has deepened as some express their anxiety about the stability of the discipline while others cry for change. Such a disjuncture calls for some elaboration. Placing English studies in the larger cultural context, Kapil Kapoor (2002: 81) argues that if the "knowledge and appreciation of English literature" is considered to be "synonymous with being cultured," its interpretation should be opened to Indian theories as well. He adds, "Using our own theories makes sense because 'habits' of mind differ from one community to another" (83). Kapoor believes that if we were grounded in our own thought it would enhance "our understanding of even the live issues of Western debate. For example, the Buddhist *apohavad* and its critique by Mimamasaka Kumarila Bhatta and Bhartrihari's elaborately argued theory of linguistic conservatism—all these provide an explanatory perspective for recent Western history of ideas about language and interpretation" (83). Drawing a parallel to Plato's discussion in the *Sophist* with the *Advaita* critique of difference, Kapoor suggests that one can even evaluate Derrida's use of this concept in his theory of meaning. Kapoor not only underlines the critical and theoretical parallels between Indian and Western theories but also seeks a possible synergy between the two that may result in collapsing the divide while opening up hitherto unmarked perspectives in English studies.

Contrary to Kapoor's position, among others who are suspicious of theory, A. V. Ashok (2002) argues against Western theories, claiming that the discipline of English, under the influence of theory, has become indisciplined and disturbed. For him deconstruction, one of the major theoretical-critical strategies, relishes "breaking disciplines" and champions a brave new post-disciplinary order. To him, English studies has moved away from its primary objective of studying literature on "aesthetic merit"; therefore English studies in India should be reconstituted under another name to rescue it from the "cult of irrationalist perceptions" created by "post-absolute relativism, post-disciplinary revolt and subaltern politics" (106). Judged as genuine or dismissed as downright sentimentality out of sync with the times, Ashok's fears raise some significant questions about theory in a postcolonial country like India.

A paradigm shift has taken place. English studies not only has taken a critical and theoretical turn but also has been overtly politicized because of the rising empowerment of the marginalized groups exerting tremendous pressure on academic institutions. Such a situation demands a serious look at the discipline of English studies in the context of its content, institutional politics, and, most importantly, its pedagogical practices.

Institutional Politics and Fixing the English Curriculum

English studies in India today is struggling to unfetter itself from the past in order to reinvent itself as a postcolonial discipline. Its curricular formation is undergoing dramatic changes as new courses in women's studies, *dalit* studies, environmental studies, and so on are being added to the existing syllabus. The imperatives of such syllabi, in the larger context of English studies in India, need to be explored, and the historical and the political have to be considered along with the cultural and the canonical.

In India, fixing the curriculum is tricky, as it is impelled by the question of relevance. Relevance is both a validation of utilitarian expectation and a subjectivist formulation. However, in India relevance has been an uncontested notion and is often glossed as what is good for the nation or for its unity, and not necessarily for the individual or the community of learners in multicultural locations. Thus diversity becomes a cliché and freedom is advocated in its negation. The curriculum war is fought with the suggestion that the canon should on the one hand be liberated and on the other be regulated or standardized across the country. During the 1970s the emphasis was on developing language skills with a linguistic orientation to the teaching of English, but by the 1990s most universities in the country had opened up the curriculum to include several new and emerging areas.

Although the universities are supposed to be autonomous, funding agencies exert a measure of control. Unlike in the United States where the curriculum is largely free from any external control, in India the University Grants Commission (UGC), a statutory body under the federal government, plays a role in fixing the syllabus.[6] This agency is mandated by the federal government to promote and coordinate university education in maintaining a uniform standard in teaching, examination, and research across the country. Questions are raised regarding the competence of the UGC in these matters even as universities perforce follow its guidelines. The UGC guidelines do not normally originate from academic debates and discussions but on most occasions from the political decisions of the federal government.

The UGC normally convenes a committee of academics chaired by a subject expert for preparing a syllabus. This committee decides what should be taught across the country without any debate on the status of the discipline, the learners' requirements, or pedagogy. The committee meets a few times in Delhi or in some other convenient location and prepares a syllabus, a model curriculum. A recent curriculum committee on English observed that to serve the expectations of the academia, employers and society at large, programmes simply designated as "English" should primarily ensure training in the language and/or its literature. Programmes of newer design may still incorporate a modicum of literature in the English language, and use English as the medium of study; but they should adopt titles properly indicating their scope. Ultimately they may break quite free of traditional "Eng. Lit." and move into totally new areas with appropriate new titles eschewing the word "English." (University Grants Commission 2003: 16–17)

As a teacher of English for over two decades now, I find this account confusing and ambiguous. The committee has not examined the so-called expectations of different groups in concrete terms. More significantly, it does not say anything about the learners' expectations. The committee has suggested two curricular models: one is titled "English Language and Literature," dividing the syllabus into periods in the traditional way, and the second is called "English and Literary Studies," with a generic classification having a maximum of ten courses. Although the document advocates flexibility, the choice before the English departments is limited, for they have to adopt one of the two models and select texts from the recommended list. The committee has done mostly a cut-and-paste job of adding some things and removing some others in fixing the curriculum. What is the usefulness of the recommendations of such a committee that proposes, on the one hand, to introduce new courses in the curriculum with a "modicum of literature in English language," and, on the other, *also* recommends that such courses "may break quite free"? If such courses are thought to be suitable for inclusion in the "Eng. Lit." curriculum and are also allowed to break free, why should such courses be part of an "Eng. Lit." syllabus in the first place?

The ambiguity deepens in drawing the boundary between courses considered worthy and unworthy and the contexts of their content. This confusion arises simply because no one is sure of the cohesiveness of and the demands on the discipline. This document proposes a syllabus having the scope "for new items and areas that may be opened up by the future development of the discipline" (7), while circumscribing the syllabus by its own recommendations. Likewise, the committee does not throw any light on a recent move by many universities to bring English under the rubric of cultural studies. As a core component of cultural studies, English may contribute to the production of new knowledge; however, the shifting emphasis points not only to the instability but also at the internal crises of English studies as a discipline today. The committee would have done well had it provided a thematic model instead of dividing the syllabus by period or making a selection of canonical texts to suit a particular course. The two models recommended by the committee are not different in content and character from the traditional syllabus that was in operation in many universities until the 1990s, whereas the English studies syllabus should provide an inter/multidisciplinary perspective. For example, a course on romanticism should include selections from the works of English Romantics, key European and Indian thinkers, critics, and creative writers so that such a course would initiate a learner into reading these texts in a perspective that is self-reflexive to his or her postcolonial location. Such a perspective underlines Ernesto Laclau's understanding that "one must construct one's discourse as difference in relation to that tradition and this implies at the same time continuities and discontinuities" (qtd. in Giroux 1992: 16). Continuities and discontinuities become contingent factors in planning a syllabus for a postcolonial country like India. If discontinuity implies a rupture with the colonial past, continuity means reinventing precolonial practices and validating those practices in a postcolonial context.

If the UGC committee obliquely promotes standardization or some sort of regimentation in the name of flexibility and freedom, interestingly, it does not offer any pedagogical guideline for the implementation of the so- called model curriculum. If one were to assume that a teacher is free to adopt any teaching strategy, why is he or she not free to prescribe texts to be taught? If we have to reinvent English studies and delink it from a colonial and elitist frame, it has to be placed at the intersection of contingency and history. The key to any curricular planning or pedagogical practice is freedom. Although unbridled freedom of any kind is not favored, freedom remains a necessary condition for allowing autonomy to stakeholders within a system. India has a tradition of valorizing academic freedom, but this tradition has not been critiqued and recontextualized because of colonial intervention and other factors.

Sharma's Alternative Pedagogy

Such an imperative is implicated in the very objective of education to give voice to the voiceless, enfranchise the marginalized, and enable learners to set themselves free from the discursive struggle. In service to that ideal, I would like to elaborate here on a precolonial pedagogical model developed by Vishnu Sharma in the form of the text *Panchatantra*.[7] If *Panchatantra* is characterized by the selection of material for a specific objective, Sharma's pedagogical strategy is notable for its consideration of dialogue as a necessary condition of learning in a world of multiple conversations.

Acknowledged primarily as a collection of stories for moral and philosophical instruction, *Panchatantra* (a treatise in five parts) is considered the first Indian text on pedagogy. Told in a simple and elegant style, these stories lead a reader through constant displacement of locations and characters, engaging in dialogue birds, beasts, and humans on philosophy, psychology, astronomy, politics, music, human relationship, and so on. Sharma understands the first principle of teaching: that nothing can be taught in the absence of favorable conditions for teaching. He nonetheless proceeds successfully to teach the unruly and almost unteachable princes the wide expanse of different discourses. In response to the king's desperate (and coercive) request, after having tried all other methods and many teachers, to the eighty-year-old Sharma to take charge of his wards, the confident Sharma replies, "If I do not teach your sons in such a manner that in six months time they have complete mastery over all the wide expanse of political and practical wisdom, then let my name be thrown away and forgotten. And your majesty may show me His Bare Royal Bottom" (Sarman 1949: 5).

Vishnu Sharma recognizes that the freedom to pursue one's own method of teaching depends on the type of material one uses for effective instruction. To him, any kind of learning has to maintain the vital link with the life stream out of which its very subject matter springs. A pedagogical strategy for Sharma is efficient if it enriches one's understanding of the human predicament. As such, his pedagogical philosophy embraces the universe of discourse that makes inter/multidisciplinarity the very norm of efficient instruction. It encourages dialogue to proliferate where learning becomes a self-propelling process.

Through this example I am not advocating for an alternative *gurukul* or suggesting dismantling of the existing institutional structure.[8] Freedom, however, remains the key for the self-actualization of a teacher and also of a learner. If we consider pedagogy as a cultural practice, then Vishnu Sharma's method of teaching has relevance even today. Why cannot our teachers frame the syllabus and also devise a method of teaching it with the goal of empowering the learners? Why prescribe, direct, and dictate? In our context, any kind of freedom is denied; we as teachers are perpetually threatened with being shown the bare bottoms of politicians and royals.

Postcoloniality and Critical Pedagogy

In a postcolonial context, the study of English literature can no longer be underpinned by its twin traditional functions of pleasure and prophecy: pleasure as a product of the colonial bourgeois' leisure that celebrates the reading of English literature as a means of acquiring the correct cultural taste underscored by colonial standards, and prophecy that privileges the Western/Christian cultural worldview over an Indian learner's own on the premise that the West is the repository of civilizational values. All these have changed. The study of English is now far less symbolic of elitism than of economic empowerment and entrepreneurship. Operating under the props of necessity and power, English studies has to recognize the intellectual forces that have shaped our present, and these forces in turn will provide a critical context for an appropriate pedagogy for its study.

Any pedagogical strategy today needs to address the process of decolonization while examining the political dynamics, economic imperatives, and social concerns of a postcolonial state. Exploring the postcolonial pedagogical problematic, Kostas Myrsiades and Jerry McGuire offer an interesting context in their work *Order and Partialities: Theory, Pedagogy and the Postcolonial* (1995). Introducing the theme, Lalita Pandit and Jerry McGuire (1995: 7) argue that there is a need for reexamining the postcolonial pedagogy that will assist redefining our objectives, reorienting learning vis-à-vis existing models. They take note of "the failure of global models, global aspirations, global assumptions, of the necessity to recognize distinctions and the subversion of distinctions, of a new regime of inquiry marked both by passionate intensities and the peculiar demands of multicultural selectivity. What emerges is a postmodern multidiscipline whose analysis of postcolonial pedagogy repeatedly reflects back on its own enmeshed participation in the global exercise of postcolonial power." The critical turn in the postcolonial pedagogical structure has challenged the older paradigm; it undermines the authority of the author, democratizes the canon, and considers the cover- age model dead. Each one of the skills— such as reading, writing, listening, and thinking—that stimulates the learning process under the earlier model becomes problematic: "Reading, what? Thinking, how? Writing, why? The first question brings up issues of the canon and the archeology of ideas; the second raises issues of construction of knowledge, and the hierarchy of cultural anthropology; and the third presents issues of production of texts as cultural artifacts" (Kar, Baral, and Rath 2003: 13). Besides these critical issues, the larger concern is how education can provide individuals with the tools to better themselves and strengthen democracy by creating a more egalitarian and just society—in other words, how to deploy education for social change.

To ensure desired social change, critical pedagogy is relevant in both its liberating and strategic dimensions. In the words of Antonia Darder (1991: 77), "Unlike traditional perspectives of education that claim to be neutral and apolitical, critical pedagogy views all education theory as intimately linked to ideologies shaped by power, politics, history and culture." The strategic goal of liberation is problematic in a multilingual, multicultural country like India, where identity and history are crucial issues. Politically sensitive and contested issues such as secularism, marginalization, and minority rights assume significance in what we teach and learn. Issues of representation, ethnicity, and nationalism further problematize the context of English studies in India. To make English studies sensitive to the multifaceted predicament of a postcolonial country we need both a critical and an engaged pedagogy: critical because in contrast to the unitary and homogenized colonial model we need a model that can negotiate between and among a plurality of language, culture, and ethnicity, and engaged because those who teach need to commit and transgress to guide the learners through ways of learning differently.[9]

Derived from the ideological underpinnings of the Frankfurt school, the concept of critical pedagogy developed by Paulo Freire presents a good starting point for a discussion on some of the core issues here. At the heart of Freire's articulation is a revolutionary concept of education for liberation, which underlines the fact that "man's ontological vocation is to be a subject who acts upon and transforms his world, and in so doing moves towards ever new possibilities of fuller and richer life individually and collectively" (1986 [1972]: 12). Freirean critical pedagogy is not simply a method but a process that would ensure "conscientization," or the coming to critical consciousness of the learning subject. It is possible only when the "banking education" system— which perceives knowledge as a gift bestowed by those "who consider themselves knowledgeable upon those whom they consider to know nothing" (46)—is replaced with "problem-posing education," which ensures liberation. Postmodernist educators question Freire's thesis on the grounds that his critical pedagogy deploys static definitions and categories, assumes reality as a given, and relies upon a dialectical Marxist metanarrative of liberation. In spite of the fact that some of Freire's positions are problematic and essentialist, his concept of critical pedagogy can be productively deployed alongside the postmodernist thesis of plurality and relativized concepts of truth and reality. It would be unfair to address Freire as dogmatic, for in *Pedagogy of Hope* (2005 [1992]), he defends "progressive postmodernism" while rejecting "conservative" and "neoliberal postmodernity." A postcolonial pedagogy cannot ignore Freire, but neither should it bury postmodernist insights; it has to work in tandem with both.

Critical Pedagogy and Post-disciplinary English

In *Language and Silence*, George Steiner (1969: 89) maintains that the current relevance of humanistic studies/teaching depends on "our interest between that which is primarily of historical or local significance and that … which has in it the pressure of sustained life." If English studies, as a core area of humanities, hopes to sustain itself, then, as Steiner observes, it should be able to strengthen the continuity of life and culture. Hence the curriculum that we prescribe for our learners needs to be simultaneously pragmatic and open to global aesthetics within a humanistic perspective. From Steiner to John Guillory (1993), the debate about formalizing the canon and fixing the curriculum has been wide open.[10] Guillory makes a useful distinction between a canon and a syllabus, arguing that the canon itself is never the object of classroom study: "Where does it appear, then? It would be better to say that the canon is an *imaginary* totality of works. No one has access to the canon as a totality" (30). At the level of curriculum, then, we must work to infuse critical post- modern principles of openness and multivalent social action into our syllabus design, something the UGC has not successfully undertaken.

As a postdiscipline, English studies is on trial today. Teaching of English within marked boundaries and a contained pedagogical situation is no longer operative or even desirable. Instead, it is necessary to liberate the learner from "disciplinary ghettos." As Gayatri Spivak (1992: 281) remarks, in these most definitely postcolonial times, a teacher needs to consider how the object of study is to be constructed or gets constructed in the classroom to make it meaningful. *What* one reads is immaterial, *how* one reads is pre- eminent. We should therefore continue to engage ourselves in an unending dialogue with the texts, the teachers, and the institutions, for we know that finding meaning, making our learning relevant, and knowing our private worlds is too complex a process to be dictated by curricular mandate from afar.

In the absence of any pedagogical strategy laid down or proposed by the UGC model curriculum, a learner is mostly subjected to the banking system of education. Within the traditional method of teaching, a teacher is invested with the moral authority for guiding his or her pedagogical subjects. In contrast, a critical pedagogy asserts that what is important is not what texts a student reads, or what theories a student applies in interpreting those texts, but the student's location, identity, history, and cultural self-possession. What is at stake is not the extension of the study into new areas, but a reconstruction of teaching-learning practice in which the learner is exposed to the provisionality and the contradictions of national, ethical, cultural, racial, gender, and other discourses while engaging with the West and its other.

In the foreword to *Pedagogy of the Oppressed*, Richard Shaull (1986 [1972]: 14), reiterating Paulo Freire's position, maintains that education is never a neutral process; it either "functions as an instrument which is used to facilitate the integration of the younger generation into the logic of the present system," thereby encouraging them to internalize its values, or "it becomes a 'practice of freedom', the means by which men and women deal critically and creatively with reality and discover how to participate in the transformation of their world." People become agents of change only when they understand the forces of change and act upon them as human subjects, regardless of their intent. Freire distinguishes between transitive and critical consciousness. Transitive consciousness emerges as people begin to perceive and respond to the themes and myths that characterize their world. He argues that at the initial stage transitive consciousness is marked by gross simplifications and generalizations of problems lacking in critical investigation. Such a stage is marked by polemics rather than dialogue. On the other hand, critical consciousness is characterized by depth in the interpretation of the problems by substitution of causal principles for magical explanations in testing one's findings with openness and avoiding distortions through the practice of dialogue (14).

We know that the process of knowledge production undergoes transformation not only because of historical necessity but also due to changes in our situation and consciousness. The study of English literature, therefore, should be organized not only around authors and texts and the specific contexts of their interpretations but also through an interrogative process that should lead the learner, as Freire says, toward a "practice of freedom." Further, following Robert Scholes (1985: 39), we must note "the ways in which teachers can help students recognize the power texts have over them and assist the same students in obtaining a measure of control over textual processes, a share of textual power for themselves." Critical pedagogy in the present context provides a way out and allows us articulation and self-reflexivity. Armed with its radical possibility, we can inquire into and respond to the diversity of our engagement with English studies as a discipline. Such a pedagogical strategy would signal "how questions of audience, voice, power, and evaluation actively work to construct particular relations between teachers and students, institutions and society, and classrooms and communities ... [for it] illuminates the relationship among knowledge, authority, and power" (Giroux 1994: 30).

As pedagogies are always institutionalized, we should begin with institutional reforms that allow more freedom and flexibility to teachers and learners, so that the larger goal of education is served in uniting the private and the public spheres. This proposition validates the argument that knowledge is culture, a claim that can draw together disparate theories, methods, and pursuits in creating and transmitting cultural dispositions, meanings, and categories. Plurality of reading strategies, whether theory driven or otherwise, should work to the advantage of the learners, simultaneously relating the world of the book, a public world, to students' own private worlds while developing an attitude for open enquiry, looking at the cultural and intellectual roots of our diverse world in exciting and challenging ways. For this to happen, the study of English has to follow a strategy of collective engagement that not only would encourage dialogue between the taught and the teacher but also would set different courses in the curriculum, authorities, and agencies into dialogue with each other with the objective of making a learner an agent in the production of knowledge.

If that is the Holy Grail, the final aspiration, then we need a critical pedagogy that will enable a learner to ask questions beyond and alongside the aesthetic, stylistic, or thematic organization of a text. For example, Kar, Baral, and Rath (2003: 13–14) delineate the following list:

Race: are texts written by dead white European males more valuable than those writers elsewhere, living or otherwise? Gender: are texts by men about their life experiences more valuable than those by women? Are heterosexual experiences more normative than homosexual ones? Culture: are texts produced in the West more significant than those produced elsewhere? Politics: does the colonial text qualitatively excel the subaltern discourse? Textuality: is the written text to be privileged over the oral? Are printed books more worthy of preservation than hand-written palm-leaf manuscripts? Code: is one language a more reliable vehicle for communication than another? Value: is New Historicism a more efficient interpretive approach than deconstruction? Ideology: are some political institutions (constitution or rule of law) or systems (democracy or dictatorship) inherently better or worse than their counterparts? Epistemology: is intuitive, experiential insight more reliable than scientific, acquired knowledge?

Starting from the ancient Greek model of *skol* to the medieval model of learning and revelation, followed by modernism's foundational and edificational model of enlightenment and the postmodern model of displacement and dispersal, the search for an appropriate pedagogy is always on. However, at the heart of all these the learner is somewhere marginalized, rendered voiceless, or is coercively integrated into the dominant discourse and ideology. Particularly in the unique postcolonial context of India, there is a need for a pedagogy that initiates learners into "critical consciousness" and sets them free to explore the relationship between theory and praxis, self and other, and history and ideology in understanding and transforming their own lives and worlds.

Notes

1. In his work *English as a Global Language*, David Crystal (1998) makes a couple of significant assertions besides making the claim that English deserves to be and is the global language. Although his position regarding bilingualism and multiculturalism in a comparison between the Welsh and English cultures and languages may not be tenable in the Indian situation, the English language certainly facilitates multilingual communication in India.
2. Jonathon Green (1998: 107) is not surprised that even a prime minister of the country chooses to address the nation in the English language on its independence day. According to him, the continuance of the English language in India serves a vital purpose: "English, no matter how many sectors of society may complain, and no matter how little it impinges on the hundreds of millions of peasants who form the backbone of society, has been the language of administration and of business for well over a century and a half. It is a convenient alternative to the mutual incomprehensibilities of, say, Urdu and Tamil, and used as such."
3. The successive National Education Commissions from 1948 to 1966 have emphasized English as the medium of instruction at the collegiate and university level on the ground that it serves as a window to

the world. A mythology has been built around the metaphor of a window, in that the English language is privileged as the language of knowledge, reason, and liberal, modern thinking, with a general relevance in the fields of education, economy, and communication. See Kapoor 1992.

4. The history and politics of the teaching of English in India have been extensively dealt with in works such as *The Lie of the Land: English Literary Studies in India* ([1992] 1993), ed. Rajeswari Sunder Rajan; *Provocations: The Teaching of English Literature in India* (1993), ed. Sudhakar Marathe et al.; Svati Joshi's edited volume *Rethinking English in India: Essays in Literature, Language, History* (1994); and Gauri Viswanathan's *Masks of Conquest: Literary Study and British Rule in India* ([1990] 1998).

5. In the foreword to *Kanthapura*, Rao (1974: v) argues, "One has to convey in a language that is not one's own, the spirit that is one's own. One has to convey the various shades and omissions of a certain thought-movement that looks maltreated in an alien language. I used the word 'alien,' yet English is not an alien language to us. It is the language of our intellectual make-up — like Sanskrit or Persian was before — but not of our emotional make-up."

6. The present University Grants Commission has its genesis in the Inter-University Board established in 1925 by the colonial government. The present body was formally established by an act of Parliament in 1956. The UGC has the unique distinction of being the only grant-giving agency in the country that has been vested with two responsibilities: that of providing funds and that of coordination, determination, and maintenance of standards in institutions of higher education. The different education commissions constituted under its aegis have contributed through their recommendations to the continuation of the English language as the medium of instruction and as a discipline of study.

7. In A. Ryder's 1949 translation, Vishnu Sarman is given as the name of the author of *Panchatantra*. Although examples and a citation are taken from Ryder's translation, I have retained the popular title of Sharma in place of Sarman.

8. The *gurukul* is the ancient form of the Indian institution of learning. Etymologically, *gurukul* means "teacher's domain." This is a place where students live with or in close proximity to the teacher. In such a school the teacher ensures full development of a *shishya*, or student, teaching him or her the wide expanse of all knowledge along with training in practical aspects of life. In its contemporary sense, a *gurukul* is an institutional and instructional learning domain that ensures the teacher's freedom in pedagogical practices.

9. Following Freire, bell hooks (1994) develops her method of "engaged pedagogy." The central concern of her thesis is that teaching is a process of transgression. Teachers who have the courage to transgress the boundaries should approach students with the will and desire in response to their unique beings. Such an approach works within the Freirean concept of the practice of freedom.

10. Guillory's elaboration of the imaginary nature of the literary canon as opposed to the concrete character of a pedagogical canon highlights the ways in which conservative arguments concerning the canon often fail to acknowledge that canon formation is an imprecise process. Although the biblical canon was intentionally formed in a series of church councils, it is a deceptive namesake for the literary canon, which never was systematically identified by any formal deliberation of white males dead or alive. Rather, as numerous historical studies have demonstrated, the literary canon is a loose, baggy monster, a fluid movement of ebbs and flows, ins and outs — therefore, abstract instead of concrete.

References

Ashok, A. Venkabarao. 2002. "English in India Today: Discipline, Postdiscipline, and Indiscipline." In *Humanities and Pedagogy: Teaching of Humanities Today*, ed. Kailash C. Baral, 97–106. Delhi: Pencraft International.

Crystal, David. 1998. *English as a Global Language*. Cambridge: Cambridge University Press.

Darder, Antonia. 1991. *Culture and Power in the Classroom*. New York: Bergin and Garvey.

Dasgupta, Probal. 1993. *The Otherness of English: India's Auntie Tongue Syndrome*. New Delhi: Sage.

Freire, Paulo. 1986 [1972]. *Pedagogy of the Oppressed*, trans. Myra Bergman Ramos. Harmondsworth, UK: Penguin.

——. 2005 [1992]. *Pedagogy of Hope*, trans. Robert R. Barr. New York: Continuum.

Giroux, Henry A. 1992. "Paulo Freire and the Politics of Postcolonialism." *JAC* 12: 15–26.

——. 1994. *Disturbing Pleasures: Learning Popular Cultures*. New York: Routledge.

Green, Jonathon. 1998. "English in India: The Grandmother Tongue." *Critical Quarterly* 40: 107–11.

Guillory, John. 1993. *Cultural Capital: The Problem of Literary Canon Formation*. Chicago: University of Chicago Press.

hooks, bell. 1994. *Teaching to Transgress: Education as the Practice of Freedom*. New York: Routledge.

Joshi, Svati, ed. 1994. *Rethinking English in India: Essays in Literature, Language, History*. New Delhi: Oxford University Press.

Kachru, Braj B. 1983. *The Indianization of English: The English Language in India*. New Delhi: Oxford University Press.

Kapoor, Kapil. 1992. "Teaching English as Second Language in India." In *English in India: Theoretical and Applied Issues*, ed. Omkar Kaul, 69–81. New Delhi: Creative.

——. 2002. "Teaching English Literature: Cultural Determination." In *Humanities and Pedagogy: Teaching of Humanities Today*, ed. Kailash C. Baral, 81–89. Delhi: Pencraft International.

Kar, Prafulla C., Kailash C. Baral, and Sura P. Rath. 2003. "Introduction." In *Theory and Praxis: Curriculum, Culture, and English Studies*, ed. Prafulla C. Kar, Kailash C. Baral, and Sura P. Rath, 11–22. Delhi: Pencraft International.

Marathe, Sudhakar, Mohan Ramanan, and Robert Bellarmine, eds. 1993. *Provocations: The Teaching of English Literature in India*. Hyderabad: Orient Longman.

Myrsiades, Kostas, and Jerry McGuire, eds. 1995. *Order and Partialities: Theory, Pedagogy, and the Postcolonial*. Albany: State University of New York Press.

Pandit, Lalita, and Jerry McGuire. 1995. "Introduction." In Myrsiades and McGuire 1995: 1–12.

Rao, Raja. *Kanthapura*. 1974. New Delhi: Oxford University Press.

——. 1978. "The Caste of English." In *Awakened Conscience*, ed. C. D. Narasimhaiah, 420–22. New Delhi: Sterling.

Sarman, Vishnu. 1949. *Panchatantra*, trans. (with commentary) A. Ryder. Bombay: Jaico. Scholes, Robert. 1985. *Textual Power: Literary Theory and the Teaching of English*. New Haven, CT: Yale University Press.

Shaull, Richard. 1986 [1972]. Foreword to *Pedagogy of the Oppressed*, trans. Myra Bergman Ramos. Harmondsworth, UK: Penguin.

Spivak, Gayatri Chakravarty. 1992. "The Burden of English Studies." In Sunder Rajan 1993: 275–99.

Steiner, George. 1969. *Language and Silence*. Harmondsworth, UK: Penguin.

Sunder Rajan, Rajeswari, ed. [1992] 1993. *The Lie of the Land: English Literary Studies in India*. New Delhi: Oxford University Press.

Viswanathan, Gauri. [1990] 1998. *Masks of Conquest: Literary Study and British Rule in India*. New Delhi: Oxford University Press.

University Grants Commission. 2003. *UGC Model Curriculum*. New Delhi: UGC.

21

Critical Pedagogy in a Conflicted Society
Israel as a Case Study

Moshe Levy and Yair Galily

Israeli anthropology and sociology have changed dramatically since the 1970s. This change included the abandonment of "conservative" theories and an overwhelming adoption of "critical" perspectives. Those perspectives introduce themselves as a vehicle that can promote social change and provide justice and equality to disadvantaged minorities in Israel. This paper aims to examine how the different critical perspectives are being accepted by Israeli students from different groups and minorities (Jewish, Muslim, women, men, Ashkenazi, Mizrahi, middle class, and lower class) who attended sociology classes that took place in four different Israeli academic institutions. The social heterogeneity of the students in these geographically scattered institutions, together with the turbulent political and social times experienced by Israeli society during the process of data collection, enabled different comparisons that shed a new light on the role of the critical knowledge reproduced in the educational systems of conflicted societies.

Knowledge and the Reproduction of Structure

Different structural approaches view educational systems such as schools, colleges, and universities as tools that reproduce culture and knowledge and, by doing so, conserve social structures and hierarchies (Anderson, 1991; Billing, 1995; Bourdieu, 1977; Bowles and Gintis, 1977; Gellner, 1983; Walkerdine, 1986). These approaches have analyzed the reproduction of domination by looking, on the one hand, at the ways that educational institutions provide differential knowledge and cultural capital to different social groups. This differentiation leads to inequalities and stratification between those different social groups (ethnic, national, gender, class) (Bernstein, 1977; Bourdieu & Passeron, 1977). On the other hand, the knowledge reproduced in these institutions promotes a "hidden curriculum" (Apple, 1990) whereby students are socialized and behaviorally conditioned to accept hierarchical structures of power. The "authoritarian classrooms" (Shor, 1992) in these institutions, where students are conditioned to become passive, conformist, and obedient members of society, legitimize social order, state ideology, and power, and delegitimize any intention to promote social or cultural change (Apple, 1985; Braa & Callero, 2006; Poulantzas, 1978).

Whether in its Marxist or poststructuralist form, these reproduction approaches focus on the hegemonic system itself and the ways it works to reproduce social structures and bodies of knowledge. While doing so, they fail to understand the important rule of social agents in opposing, manipulating, and interpreting the knowledge being provided to them (Giroux, 1983).

This study would like to adopt the phenomenological resistance approach in order to explore the way social agents react to knowledge provided to them. For Giroux (1983), such an approach, that takes human agency seriously, leads to possibilities of oppositional pedagogy and meaningful interventions in schools. The main question presented in this paper is what happens when the knowledge being reproduced and provided is critical of the social order, hegemonic ideology, and inequalities in the distribution of power and other resources among social groups. How do students from different groups and minorities react to this knowledge being reproduced institutionally? These questions will be examined by analyzing the way different "critical" sociological theories were accepted by students from different Israeli groups and minorities that attended sociology classes that took place in four different Israeli academic institutions.

The Rise of "Critical" Sociology in Israel

Israeli sociology has changed dramatically since the 1970s. This change, which parallels similar changes in other fields of Israeli humanities and social sciences, includes an abandonment of "conservative" theories and an overwhelming adoption of "critical" perspectives. While the first are accused of providing academic legitimization of Zionist institutions and ideology, "critical" perspectives introduce themselves as a vehicle that can promote social change, and provide justice and equality to disadvantaged minorities in Israel (Ram, 1995).

The paradigmatic change in Israeli sociology led to the rise of five major "critical" approaches: Elite theory (Shapiro, 1975, 1977, 1984, 1996), feminism (Azmon & Izraeli, 1993; Bernstein, 1992; Swirski & Safir, 1991, Sasson-Levy, 2006), Marxism (Swirski, 1995, 1999; Swirski & Bernstein, 1980), Pluralism (Sasson-Levy, 2008; Smooha, 1978, 1992; Yiftachel, 2010), and Colonialism (Azoulay & Ophir, 2008; Kimmerling, 1983, 2004; Sa'di, 2008; Shafir, 1989; Shenhav, 2010).

As noted above, the aim of this research was to examine how the different "critical" sociological perspectives were accepted by students from different Israeli groups and minorities. The data analyzed was gathered from students who participated in classes on the sociology of Israeli society that took place in four Israeli academic institutions between 2000 and 2008: Bar Ilan University, Ariel University Center of Samaria, Achva College, and Dina Nursing School. The social heterogeneity of the students in these geographically scattered institutions, together with the turbulent political and social times experienced by Israeli society during the process of data collection, enabled different comparisons between the students' reactions. Although these reactions were not analyzed statistically and might not represent accurately all the students' views and sentiments, we believe they shed a new light on the role of critical thought in conflicted societies and of social agents in opposing, manipulating, and interpreting the knowledge provided to them. The following sections will present some of the students' typical reactions to each of the "critical" theories presented above. Since students were not informed their responses might be used outside the classroom, this paper will not provide the names of the students nor their academic affiliation.

Findings

Feminism

It seems that in each class introducing feminist ideas, this always leads to chauvinist remarks, usually by male students (who in many cases are in the minority): "What do you call the kitchen window? A woman's point of view" (2001). Despite these remarks, the overall reactions of students to feminist theories and research about Israeli society imply these ideas are accepted by the vast majority of students in all four institutions, leading to reactions such as: "Even without this table [data about gender stratification presented in the classroom–ML & YG], it is quite clear that women are discriminated against, and this is very sad" (female student, 2005). It must be noted that all students are familiar with some feminist thought from mandatory introduction courses, which might make it easier to understand and accept these concepts when presented again in courses on the sociology of Israeli society.

Despite this wide consensus, one group undermines some of the basic arguments of the feminist critique of Israeli society. This group consists mainly of female students from the national-religious sector. Their disapproval focuses on the feminist notion of women's roles in the Israeli Army (IDF) and in the Jewish family. According to these students, Israeli women should not seek equality in the IDF because such equality is not possible: "Do you want women to be raped in captivity?" (female student, 2006); "Can I perform the same tasks as male soldiers?" (female student, 2008); "I just can't lift the heavy load that a male solider can" (female student, 2010). These remarks show such students see the gendered inequality in the IDF as something deterministic based on gender differences, and not on gendered socialization and discrimination by men and state institutions.

While these claims are based on women's "nature" and "biology," when demonstrating their disapproval of the feminist quest for equality within the Jewish family, female students tend to base their arguments on free choice:

> Who says we want the same things as men? Who are you to decide that we [women–ML & YG] all want money and power? These are male standards and women should not be measured by them…I would rather be with my kids at home and take care of their education. No one is forcing me. This is my prerogative, and that is why I choose to stay at home.
>
> (female student, 2003)

Despite and aside from the objections cited (which confront the core of feminist critique), these national-religious female students join the vast majority of their classmates in a demand for gender equality in Israeli society, projecting an overall impression that accepting feminist ideas is the right thing to do.

The Elite Theory

As with the feminist critique of Israeli society, Elite Theory too was found to be the most accepted and approved by students in all four academic institutions examined. However, while the first approach leads students to ask for social action and political solutions to the problem raised, in the case of the Elite Theory, students' conclusions are quite the opposite. Despite students' awareness of the flaws of Israeli democracy and of the destructive effect of some elites and interest groups, most students perceive the situation as incorrigible: "Nothing can be done. The state has always been and will always be corrupted" (2006). "I have voted Likud, I have voted Labor, I have voted NRP, each time I vote differently and nothing changes. So why bother?" (2006).

These and similar reactions do not encounter any counter remarks from the other students and imply most of the students take Israeli democracy and its flaws for granted. These flaws are perceived as a constant and inseparable part of the democratic system.

Marxism

The Marxist critique of Israeli society frequently is greeted with antagonism by students from various groups. Most students attend the classes after having been introduced to Marxist thought in previous courses but without an understanding of the Marxist interpretation of the social and economical processes that affect Israeli society. When the theoretical framework is presented, some students do not hesitate to remark: "We saw what happened in the Soviet Union" and "Communism failed."

The main objection is aimed at the Marxist theory of surplus value, which perceives employer profits as a product of worker exploitation: "The factory owner risks his money, so why shouldn't he be the one to profit? When he loses money no one will help him" (2005).

Students' fierce rejection of this theory fades when presented with the Israeli context. Marxist analysis of various economical processes such as privatization brings most students to the realization that the capitalist system they have embraced has its disadvantages, affecting the quality and quantity of health, education, and welfare services provided or not provided in Israel. Despite their slow and gradual acceptance of this critique, most students (usually in their 20s) react in a manner that implies they don't think this critique, whether right or wrong, has anything to do with their lives: "If I make enough of an effort I will succeed" (2003); "You can't stop the progress. If people don't work, it is their problem; if there are sick or old people, we should help them individually" (2005).

These remarks indicate many of these students, who lack significant experience in the workforce and are not dependent on state welfare services, partially accept the Marxist analysis of Israeli society and regard it as suitable for some weak sectors of society but definitely not for them.

The students who are most persistent in their rejection of the Marxist paradigm in general, despite the data presented in the classroom, are those who immigrated to Israel from the former Soviet Union. Their familial and personal experience and socialization seem to lead them to the concept of the evils of socialism and the promise embodied by the Israeli capitalist system. In contrast, many students who show a relative acceptance of socialist ideas come from the Arab sector. It may be easier for this sector, from its place at the bottom of the Israeli economical hierarchy, to break free from the grasp of capitalist ideology. In addition, it seems some of the Arab students think that by endorsing these ideas they can bridge the ethnic, religious, and national gaps separating them from their Jewish classmates.

Pluralism

The main debate in this part of the course deals with the inequality of Ashkenazi Jews (of European origin) and Mizrahi Jews (whose families originated from the Muslim or Arab world). One of the theories presented in the classroom claims that Mizrahi Jews underwent a process of assimilation in which they were forced to erase their Arab culture and identity. During this debate, Mizrahi Jews are labeled "Arab Jews." This presentation encounters fierce opposition of the radical terminology by two groups within the classroom.

The first group rejecting the label of "Arab Jews" is comprised of orthodox religious Ashkenazi Jews: "How dare you compare Mizrahi Jews to Arabs? Arabs are a different people who 'happen to' want to destroy us" (2008). The recurring theme in students' arguments is the defense of Jewish solidarity by rejecting the concept of "Arab Jews," as it undermines their dichotomous perspective of all Jews as a unified group opposed to all Arabs.

Surprisingly, the second group rejecting claims of pluralism consists of middle-class Mizrahi Jews who insist that ethnic inequality among Jews in Israel has no racial roots: "Enough of this 'ethnic demon.' When I want to export my farm's merchandise, no one asks me what my ethnic origin is. When I invest in the stock market, my ethnic origin makes no difference" (2006). While these arguments try to portray Israeli stratification mechanisms as indifferent to ethnicity, other Mizrahi Jews blame their fellow Mizrahis for not succeeding to elevate themselves from the bottom of the socioeconomic hierarchy: "The truth should be proclaimed. You ["unsuccessful" Mizrahi Jews–ML & YG] are to blame for your situation. Nothing will be changed by more crying. Instead of having eight children you should begin thinking about caring for them and for their education like Ashkenazim" (2006).

However, Mizrahi Jews who have encountered racism or didn't enjoy substantial social mobility embrace the pluralist critique while providing examples of its validity from their own experience:

This subject is very important. I thought that it was relevant in my mother's generation but I see it again and again. My daughter, an excellent student, was accepted to a prestigious course in the Air Force. She told me about the [racist–ML & YG] attitude she encountered from the other girls.

(2008)

These students are mainly disturbed that their fellow Mizrahi students do not see the same picture and that, instead of blaming the racist system, they tend to blame the victims of this system: "Even Ashkenazim don't think like you do! You think like a Nazi!" (2006).

Colonialism

Of all "critical" perspectives presented in the classroom during the academic year, the colonialism perspective seems to encounter the most antagonism. Most of the Jewish students protest against the presentation of Israel as aiming to disinherit the Palestinians from their lands. The main concept of "occupation" presented in the classrooms meets with the objection of most students who do not perceive the sovereign territories of Israel as occupied land. Some of the students even make such claims regarding Judea, Samaria, and the Gaza strip, which in their opinion should be described as liberated and not occupied.

It was interesting to follow students' reactions to the colonialist critique over time, particularly during the period of the second Palestinian intifada in the early 2000s. Thus, for example, it was interesting to see the change in some students' attitudes toward the claim that Israel suffers from militarism. Traditionally, students with right wing views and those who live in the West Bank and Gaza would reject the criticism and present arguments supporting the IDF and its important role in Israeli society and culture. An e-mail one of us received after he gave an assignment to write a paper about Israeli militarism exemplifies the support of militaristic culture among some of the students:

I read your instructions for the second assignment and I would like to change them so it will be possible for me to explain through my analysis why Israeli society is not militaristic.… This way I will be more "comfortable" writing about something I believe in. As far as I understand, a militaristic society is a society which adopts and sometimes sees as holy, values such as organization, order, discipline, power and so on. I don't think this is the case in Israel, where everyone speaks about peace and no one dares to speak out in support of war. There is no order, culture and entertainment are flourishing, and no one is afraid of the military or the police.

(2008)

While these kinds of statements, which mourn the decline of militaristic values in Israel, were voiced during the entire period of the research, the last two years have seen new criticism expressed by groups formerly supportive of the IDF. Students who live in Jewish settlements that experienced the disengagement from Gaza either directly or indirectly began to show some acceptance of the anti-militaristic critique of the colonialist perspective. Thus, some of them objected to using the army against civilian groups. Students from these same groups had previously supported such action when it was practiced exclusively against non-Jewish civilians, but their traumatic experience caused them to accept the same criticism rejected by their social sector several years earlier.

While this example proves the ability of the colonialist perspective to convince students, it does not succeed in its attempt to present the Israeli society as holding racists attitudes toward Israeli Arabs and Palestinians. It would be accurate to say an overwhelming majority of Israeli students reject this criticism and do not accept the demand for civil, political, and economical equality between Jews and Arabs in Israel: "All the data presented [concerning inequality between Jews and Arabs–ML & YG] is not worth much. The Arabs do not pay taxes but are eligible for unemployment benefits. Believe me, no one should feel sorry for them" (2005). Similar arguments were voiced during the entire period examined, but as time went by and the second intifada began, these arguments became more stringent and even led to racist remarks that almost ended in physical altercations between Jews and Arabs in the classroom.

Conclusions

This research found that while the feminist and elite perspectives incurred overall positive reactions from most students, the remaining three perspectives (Post Colonialism, Marxism, and Pluralist Theory) provoked the students and frequently encountered antagonism. These reactions indicated most students adopted a critical theory only when it promised to provide them with an advantage over competing groups. Accordingly, "critical" perspectives were rejected by students when they were perceived as endangering the interests and position of the groups to which they belonged. Thus, the findings of this research show that studying "critical" theories toward Israeli society does not develop universalistic points of view that perceive equality and freedom as rights to which all human beings are eligible. Critical ideas are accepted in a manner conditioned by the students' social background as well as by immediate sociopolitical events.

If these theories merely serve as tools in conflicts between different social groups, one must ask what is the use of teaching critical thought in conflicted societies. The findings of this study seem to indicate that critical ideas have a very limited effect and that reproduction and resistance overlap, rather than oppose each other. While other researchers of Israeli society see a potential for change in this overlap (Erdrich et al., 2005), the present study implies that teaching "critical" theories might even further means of domination and preserve the power relations and animosity between social groups in conflicted societies. Other studies of marginal groups in educational systems have shown that when social agents resist knowledge presented to them institutionally, this often serves to reproduce power relations and social hierarchies (Erdrich et al., 2005; Fine 1982; McRobbie 1978; Willis 1978). The finding presented in this article suggests that even when the knowledge presented in the classroom is critical to the social order, it paradoxically might be interpreted, used, and accepted as a mean for the reproduction of dominance.

References

Apple, M. (1985). *Education and power.* Boston: ArPaperbacks.

Apple, M. (1990). *Ideology and curriculum.* New York: Routledge.

Azmon, Y., & Izraeli, D. N. (Eds.) (1993). *Women in Israel: Studies of Israeli society.* New Brunswick, NJ: Transaction Books.

Azoulay, A., & Ofir, A. (2008). *The Regime which is not one: Occupation and democracy between the sea and the river (1967-).* Tel Aviv: Resling.

Bernstein, D. (1992). *Pioneers and homemakers: Jewish women in pre-state Israel.* New York: State University of New York Press.

Braa, D., & Callero, P. (2006). Critical pedagogy and classrom praxis. *Teaching Sociology, 34,* 357-59.

Erdreich L., Lerner, J., & Rapoport T. (2005). Reproducing nation, redesigning positioning: Russian and Palestinian students interpret university knowledge. *Identities: Global Studies in Culture and Power 12*(4), 539–62.

Fine, M. (1982). Examining inequity: View from urban schools. Unpublished dissertation, University of Pennsylvania, Philadelphia.

Giroux, H. (1983). *Theory and resistance in education. A pedagogy for the opposition.* South Hadley: Bergin and Garvin Publishers.

Kimmerling, B. (1983). *Zionism and economy.* Cambridge: Schenkman.

Kimmerling, B. (2004). *Immigrants, settlers, natives.* Tel Aviv: Am Oved.

McRobbie, A. (1978). Working class girls and the culture of femininity. In Centre for Contemporary Cultural Studies (Ed.), *Women take issue* (pp. 96–108). London: Hutchinson.

Ram, U. (1995). *Changing agenda of Israeli sociology: Theory, ideology and identity.* New York: State University of New York Press.

Sàdi, A. (2008). Remembering Al-Nakba in a time of amnesia: On silence, dislocation and time. *Interventions, 10*(3), 381–99.

Sasson-Levy, O. (2006). *Identities in uniform: Masculinities and femininities in the Israeli military.* Jerusalem: Eshkolot series, Magnes Press.

Sasson-Levy, O. (2008). I don't want an ethnic identity: The marking and erasing of boundaries in contemporary discourses of Ashkenaziyut. *Theory and Criticism, 33,* 101–29.

Shafir, G. (1989). *Land, labor and the origins of the Israeli-Palestinian conflict 1882–1914.* Cambridge: Cambridge University Press.

Shapiro, Y. (1975). *The historical Achdut HaAvoda: The power of a political organization.* Tel Aviv: Am Oved.

Shapiro, Y. (1984). *Elite without followers.* Tel Aviv: Sifriat Hapoalim.

Shapiro, Y. (1996). *Politicians as a homorganic class: The case of Israel.* Tel Aviv: Sifriat Hapoalim. Shapiro, Y. (1997). *Democracy in Israel.* Ramat Gan: Masada.

Shenhav, Y. (2010). *The time of the green line: Towards a Jewish political thought.* Tel Aviv: Am- Oved.

Shor, I. (1992). *Empowering education: Critical teaching for social change.* Chicago: University of Chicago Press.

Smooha, S. (1978). *Israel: Pluralism and conflict.* Berkeley, CA: University of California Press.

Smooha, S. (1992). *Arabs and Jews in Israel.* Boulder, CO: Westview Press.

Swirski, B., & Safir, M. (Eds.) (1991). *Calling the equality bluff.* New York: Pergamon Press.

Swirski, S. (1995). *Seeds of inequality.* Tel Aviv: Breirot.

Swirski, S. (1999). *Politics and education in Israel.* New York: Palmer Press.

Swirski, S. & Bernstein, D. (1980). Who worked, in what, for whom and for what? *Notebooks for Research and Criticism, 5,* 5–66.

Willis, P. (1978). *Learning to labor.* Westmead, England: Saxon House.

Yiftachel, O. (2010). The Palestinians in Israel: Majority-minority relations and the colonial momentum. *Society and State (Hevra u-Medina), 7*(1), 101–18.

22

Toward an Empowering Pedagogy
Is There Room for Critical Pedagogy in the Educational System of Iran?

Parvin Safari and Mohammad R. Pourhashemi

Over the last two decades, language teaching profession experienced an unequivocally critical shift. In Kumaravadivelu's (2006) terms, it can probably be considered as one of the last academic principles in the field of humanities and social sciences to go critic. In his words, this critical turn is simply concerned with connecting word to the world and the recognition of language as an ideology, not just as a system. It is also concerned with extending the educational space to the social, cultural, and political dynamics of language use and the realization that language learning and teaching are more than learning and teaching language. It is also about creating the cultural forms and knowledge that give meaning to teachers' and learners' lived experiences.

Within a decade or so, the trend moved so fast that critical pedagogy along its themes emerged on the scene. The themes include discourse analysis (Fairclough, 1995), language and identity (Norton, 1997), critical approaches to TESOL (Pennycook, 1999), teaching for academic purposes (Benesch, 2001), language in development (Markee, 2002), and also gender and language education (Davis & Skilton-Sylvester, 2004). In fact, critical pedagogy as a postmethod approach which is the offspring of this pedagogical revolution according to Kincheloe (2005) suggests novel ways of looking at classroom practices, aiming at humanizing and empowering learners to be emancipated through transforming relations of power which are oppressive. As Benesch (2001) puts it, critical pedagogy is used as a means of linking the linguistic texts, sociopolitical context, and the academic content with the larger community for the purpose of changing classroom input and interaction into effective instruments of transformation.

Regarding the significance of social change, Noroozisiam and Soozandehfar (2012) state that when we focus on social transformation, education proves to be considered as a political issue in the need of being politically dealt with. This kind of education influences everything including curriculum, materials, teachers, and learners. In deed, critical pedagogy creates a healthy non-alienating classroom-social relationship with no dominant policy overhanging in the minds of individuals. Therefore, due to the fact that language learning classrooms are far removed from historical and political conditions (Okazaki, 2005), many researchers advocate the inclusion of CP at the heart of language classrooms with the purpose of examining the sociohistorical and political aspects of language learning (Benesch, 2001; Canagarajah, 1999, 2002; Morgan, 1998; Norton, 1997; Norton & Toohey, 2004; Pennycook, 1999, 2001; Ramanthan, 2002).

In addition to what was mentioned above, failures and successes of an educational system depend on the people's linguistic and socio-cultural interaction which are under the influence of dominant ideology, institutional practice and social relations (Heras, 1999). Critical pedagogy thus endeavors to enhance the students' critical consciousness to challenge the domination and subjugation that may distort and constraint their modes of thinking and acting (Sadeghi & Ketabi, 2009). Critical pedagogy deals in fact with considering the socioeconomic and political inequities and injustices in the society which are oppressive and undemocratic. Its main occupation is to critically prepare students to interrogate and act upon social inequalities through challenging the status quo, deep-seated knowledge and taken-for-granted assumptions transferred by means of schools to students. This aim cannot be achieved if language learning is taken as a mere acquisition of language skills and communicative competence without any consideration of the cultural and sociopolitical context in which it occurs.

In order to be satisfactorily implemented in ELT classrooms, any innovative approach encounters ups and downs in the process of development to reach to its burgeoning phase. Critical pedagogy as a new approach to language teaching has not long been introduced, studied, and researched in the educational settings of Iran. It is no exaggeration to say it is like a new born infant in the educational system of Iran, in need of maturity and development. Hence, lots of researches and studies are required to theoretically and practically indicate a vivid picture of its application in such an EFL context. Reviewing the literature of CP, we can obviously see a wide range of researches across the globe attempting to theoretically and conceptually appreciate the different aspects of CP. However, much less has been reported to explore the practical considerations and problems of CP in EFL contexts like Iran.

Akbari (2008b), in this regard, asserts that despite its potential implications, however, the practical implications of CP have not been well appreciated and most of the references to the term have been restricted to its conceptual dimensions. Davari among others (2012) also points out that although the concept of CP has been around for some time in education, it has been recently explored in the practice of English Language Teaching. Thus, as Zacharias (2003) argues, in any study in the field of ELT, teachers and their beliefs play a central role in the delivery of language instruction. Accordingly, it seems to be necessary for the language teachers, professionals, practitioners, and planners of ELT to be aware of beliefs and attitudes they are operating from. This study, in fact, attempts to illuminate teachers' beliefs and attitudes concerning the problems, limitations, and hardships associated with the application of such a postmethod approach in educational system of Iran.

Key Findings

In the pursuing parts, the different derived themes based on the analysis of the data illustrate and address the respective issue:

Lack of Familiarity with the Approach

How do we expect our teachers to be fully cognizant of such an innovative approach while there are a few Iranian universities in which CP as a subject is taught and researched? In deed, Iranian teachers seem to be in need of a breath of knowledge on CP, good schemes of work, appropriate content and critical skills to enable them to teach according to the principles of CP (Aliakbari & Allahmoradi, 2012). The best means through which Iranian teachers can gain awareness concerning the theoretical tenets and practical aspects of CP can be universities, institutes, pre-service and in-service classes. After all, the number of professors and lecturers whose academic syllabuses are based on this issue is relatively few.

The books and internet-based materials on the respective issue can also be of great assistance. But the availability of the materials can be another demand which needs to be carefully taken into account. This concern is rightly stated by a teacher as:

To tell you the truth, I have heard about critical pedagogy so I am not familiar with it. I've read some books on methodology and learned a lot of techniques to apply in my language classes. Just recently a friend of mine introduced critical pedagogy to me very briefly. I liked to know more about it. Unfortunately not many teachers have enough information of it let alone applying it in their own language classes.

Shortage of Fluent and Competent Teachers

Critical approach demands highly fluent and competent teachers to naturally and spontaneously handle the challenging issues. Undoubtedly, not only CP, but any other approach dealing with speaking, communication, dialogue, and interaction is also in urgent need of fluent and competent teachers. In Richard's (2011) terms, to teach effectively, a language teacher needs to possess language-specific competencies of which the ability to maintain fluent use of the target language is of great importance. Medgyes (2001) also asserts that a threshold proficiency level a teacher needs to have reached in the target language so as to be able to teach effectively in English. A teacher who has not reached this level of proficiency will be less likely to engage in improvisational teaching.

The most prevalent methods which are yet in vogue in educational system of Iran are GTM, ALM, and CLL. The first of these is widely used in state schools while the other two are the most favorites used in institutional settings. Unfortunately, due to the use of GTM in English classes of state schools and shadowing the banking education over Iranian educational contexts, teachers' fluency and competency have become infertile after so many years. Therefore, teachers are necessarily required to equip themselves with fluency and enhance their professional qualifications in English language so as to overcome the possible hardships and problems demanded by this approach. A teacher in his personal journal described this problem as:

> The most important skills that our students must have are reading comprehension, vocabulary, and grammar. The school textbooks are generally working on these skills. I do not need to speak English in my class all the time or discuss different issues at all. We have to translate all sentences to Persian and explain grammatical points in our students' mother tongue. This process has blocked our fluency. We, teachers, have mostly been fluent in English as university students. But after some years, we are not as we used to be regarding our fluency in English. I assume it is just due to lack of using language in class by us as teachers.

Inaccessibility to the Critical Textbooks and Published Instructional Materials for both Teachers and Learners

In fact, course book selection largely has an impact not only on the topics to be covered but also on the tasks and activities to be implemented in EFL classrooms. While suffering from poor ELT materials, critical pedagogy discourages the use of commercially produced textbooks and instructional materials (Rashidi & Safari, 2011), since such materials alienate learners from realities of life, and eliminate creativity and responsibility from learners. However, one of the major criticisms that is directed toward CP is its practicality which can be enhanced through the provision and accessibility to the fully worked-out sample materials. With the aid of these materials, teachers can gain more insights and get familiar with the theories playing out in CP (Crooks, 2009). During the interview that I had with one of the teachers, she opined that:

> I have heard about critical pedagogy when participating in an EFL conference held in Yazd. One of the papers presented at this conference was on the issue of critical pedagogy. I tried

to understand it but I didn't get it well. But I got interested in it. So I went to the bookstore to get some materials on it. Unfortunately even the bookseller did not have any idea about that issue. I could not find any book on this topic at all.

In Iranian educational settings, both teachers and learners face with the paucity of respective materials which should be resolved in some way. In this regard, Aliakbari and Allahmoradi (2012) also state that due to the absence of standard textbooks on CP, Iranian teachers have no time and instructional resources to integrate CP into their daily instruction. In educational system of Iran, not all teachers and learners have access to other resources like Internet, rich libraries, magazines and newspapers to pay off the dearth of such materials. Accessibility to the instructional materials and course books including provocative topics is a major concern for English teachers. As one of them referred to this reality:

As an English teacher who is going to implement critical pedagogy in my classes, I think our textbooks are devoid of any topics concerning the respective issue. So the best thing we can do is to choose some topics from magazines, newspapers and Internet based on our students' interests and needs. But I think it's also so time consuming that with a low salary we receive monthly, no teacher is likely to do so.

In Akbari's (2008a) words, many of the available textbooks are sanitized and neutralized in order not to lose their market potential and in this process most of the topics for critical pedagogy are removed. In his terms, most of the topics one faces in commercially prepared textbooks deal with harmless issues which leave no room for social transformation and political awareness rising.

Actually, it is noteworthy to mention that both English textbooks used in ministry of education of Iran and most of the commercially prepared instructional course books available on the market include politically and socially neutral topics which bear no relationship with learners' social lives and immediate community. Also, most of the instructional materials and textbooks used in Iranian state schools are replete with the compilation of information and taken-for-granted knowledge which do not reflect any social issues related to learners' lives and experiences. In other words, they are on the basis of traditional banking education not aiming at developing learners' skills and awareness of the socio- economic, political, and cultural issues existing in the contemporary society.

With respect to the importance of using challenging issues and activities which exploit learners' fruitful experiences related to the cultural and sociopolitical contexts, Akbari (2008b) nicely suggests that CP should "connect word to world", so in order this connection to take place, marginalized learners must tackle world problems. It means they must learn to "read world" before they "read word" (Freire & Macedo, 1999). In this regard, Noroozisiam and Soozandehfar (2011) also state that individuals are required to connect the class to their community, and as a result to activate their minds so as to solve problems, and work for transformation; this is simply what "going beyond words" means.

In sum, it is suggested that textbooks should include topics which cultivate learners' understanding and awareness of the sociopolitical injustices and inequalities existing in the community and the ones which exploit learners' lived experiences related to the society and outside world. Therefore, instructional materials designers, curriculum developers and policy makers of education are expected to keep in mind that the materials should include provocative issues, hot topics and activities aiming at improving learners' abilities to come to an understanding of social, political, and cultural practices reflecting the wider community.

Resistance of School Principals against any Innovative Approach

According to Kanpol (1998), the authoritarian nature of schools is guided by control mechanisms, standardized curriculum, rigid rule structures, and top-down hierarchy. Within this authoritarian structure of education, obviously defined structural leaders and their subordinates constitute the ladder of control. This kind of school structure in deed deskills the teacher and robs her/him of the enthusiasm to proceed with their job creatively. Based on this argument, in this kind of system, for instance, division between principals and teachers, authority of principals over teachers, and that of teachers over learners in addition to the division of tasks and roles can clearly be examined.

It can be said that the educational system in Iran pursues a rigid rule structure with clearly pre-defined roles for principals, teachers and learners. Even when an innovative approach comes into play and all the private institutional settings are seriously armed to use their forces to adequately apply it, there would be severe and negative reactions on the part of state school principals. In fact, this can be related to the same authoritarian nature of educational system in which principals exert their authority over teachers and other members. As an state school English teacher, I myself remember those unpleasant days that I wished to apply CLL in my own classes but I was so badly behaved that I preferred to leave it midway and continue the orthodox GTM as the favorite which fulfilled the immediate needs of principal and learners. This unfavorable reality has also been witnessed by other teachers, as one of them stated:

> Last year, I decided to avoid speaking Persian in my class. It was about less than a week that the school principal called me into her office. She asked me about the reason I spoke English in class. She said that a lot of students and even some parents had told her that many students did not understand anything in my class. At the end, the principal made me change my teaching method and avoid using English in my English class.

Fossilized Unequal Power Relationship between Teacher and Students

What makes Freire's (1970) pedagogical approach absolutely distinctive can be the assigned roles for both teacher and learners that are totally different from the traditional banking education. Based on the so-called "banking model", the passive student is considered to be an empty account which needs to be filled with the knowledge that the teacher with the epistemological authority imparts to his or her discretion. In this process, the unequal distance and asymmetrical relations between teacher and learners lead to the perpetuation of the assumed roles for both learners and teacher that according to Freire (1970) are in deed the reflections of the colonialist and oppressive nature of the society. Moreover, teacher confuses the authority of knowledge with the authority of his or her professional authority which is in contrast with learners' freedom.

Critical pedagogy or liberatory education, on the other hand, revolves around an anti-authoritarian and interactive approach which assumes an equal relation between learners and teacher. The teacher is no longer merely the one who teaches, but the one who is himself/herself taught in dialogue with the students, who in turn while being taught also, teaches (Freire, 1993). Based on this approach, teachers and learners' dialogical relations can shape and reshape the roles. They are jointly in charge of a process in which all grow. The ways in which teachers perform their roles and the ways in which the whole environment of the class contributes to the transformational process that learners bear in order to be emancipated from society's negative labels and empowered to take control of their academic, social, political and economical destinies. In this process, authority no longer functions against freedom but must be on the side of freedom.

It seems to be really unlikely that Iranian English teachers who have long been accustomed to possessing the absolute authority of traditional classes as the main source of knowledge and information can modestly quit their presumed roles at the cost of applying an anonymous innovative approach. Actually, these roles and unequal relations have been so profoundly ingrained in the texture of Iranian educational system that any violation from these taken-for-granted roles sounds weird and unusual. Hence, all the learners unquestioningly and submissively accept their roles as something true and unchangeable. Thus, this trend incessantly strengthens and legitimates the atmosphere of silencing, oppression and the maintenance of the status quo that in turn are in lieu of the existing banking system of education. The following statements reveal the respective theme:

> Teachers are in charge of their classes. They should be able to efficiently manage and control the classes. They have to decide what or how to do the job. So students should listen to them carefully, and do their assignment as they are instructed. Teachers are the source of information who can guarantee learners' success. Students just depend on teachers as the main source of information because there is not enough explanation for some vocabulary and grammatical items in the book.

Absence of Culture of Critical Thinking in Education

According to Burbules and Burk (1999), over the past two decades, critical thinking and CP are considered to be two literatures which have shaped much of the writing in the educational foundations. In deed, critical thinking shares some common concerns with CP in that they both invoke the term "critical" as a valued educational goal. Critical thinking advocates believe that all the people need to be better critical thinkers and that critical thinking could have a general humanizing effect across all social groups and classes. The authors of both literatures would argue that by helping people become more critical in thought and action, minded educators can progressively assist the process of liberating learners to see the world as it is and to act up on social injustices. Furthermore, education in this sense can increase freedom and enlarge the scope of human possibilities.

Teachers are, thus, assumed to provide students with skills and knowledge necessary for them to expand their capacities both to question deep-seated assumptions and myths that legislate the most archaic and disempowering social practices and to take responsibility for intervening the world they inhibit (Mclaren & Kincheloe, 2007). Through CP and critical thinking, educators can also make learners react toward institutionalized functions and educational institutions to raise questions about inequalities of power and about the belief systems, which have been so internalized that the individuals abandon any questioning regarding their legitimacy.

In sum, as Burbules and Burk (1999) claim, in the language of critical pedagogy, a critical person is the one who is empowered to seek justice, to seek emancipation. So not only is the critical person adroit at recognizing injustice but, for critical pedagogy, that person is also moved to change it. In this sense, critical thinking lets people be more discerning in recognizing faulty arguments, hasty generalizations, and assertions lacking evidence, truth claims based on unreliable authority, ambiguous or obscure concepts, and so forth. It means that the people are required to learn how to express and criticize the logic of arguments that underpin their every day activities.

With respect to what was mentioned, it seems to be a futile and unwise effort to apply CP without any consideration of the necessity of creating the culture of critique and critical thinking among learners and teachers. In Iranian educational settings, criticizing has not yet appropriately evolved and is necessarily avoided since the culture of silencing is so commonplace that any critique in education counts as an unruly and unmanageable behavior which should be reprimanded. So this issue also deserves serious attention from language teachers in advance of taking any action. A teacher expressed his concern as below:

I don't see any necessity to teach my students critically or make them think or study critically. In our educational system or even in our community and culture there is no room for critiques. The students are not culturally rich enough to criticize the text or material they are learning in class.

Inefficiency of Pre-service and In-service Classes for English Teachers

The most efficient means of cultivating teachers' academic awareness is through pre-service and in-service teacher training courses, which should be organized to enhance teachers' professional abilities (Hui, 1994). Throughout the world, teacher training programs are efficiently targeted at the service of teachers to update their professional knowledge of ELT and to provide them with the fruitful pedagogical practices, contemporary language learning theories and practical considerations of language learning classrooms.

However, what really matters in the in-service classes of ministry of education in Iran, is nothing but the provision of linguistic and grammatical knowledge aiming at the improvement of teachers' professional knowledge. I myself spent more than 300 hours of participating in the so-called "in-service classes" through which the instructors mentioned some grammatical points and structures leading to the subsequent discussion over formality or informality and their usage in American or British English and etc. While the educational system in Iran centers irrationally on the development of language knowledge and is even incapable of proceeding toward learner-centered approaches, life long professional development and teacher autonomy, thinking about an anonymous approach like critical pedagogy is beyond our expectations. As one of the teachers wisely referred to this fact:

> To be frank, we have participated hundreds of hours in in-service classes, but no new material or innovative issues have been introduced to us. The same instructors are in charge of these classes and they work on the same material they did before. This bitter fact has discouraged many of us and we have such a negative feedback toward these useless classes. If we were not obliged to take part in those in-service classes, the majority of us would never ever did. When you see nothing valuable, or useful to our career it does not seem logical to waste time on it.

Culturally and Politically Inappropriate for our Education

One teacher participating in the project mentioned another problem which is worth quoting here:

> We live in a traditional community dominated by rituals. The texts books are generally prepared based on these rules and principles. So not only the students but the teachers also have no right to criticize those rules or principles to cross the red line; otherwise they may lose their jobs. So teachers do their best to avoid speaking about or discussing the issues that might be politically or religiously misinterpreted.

Have those who theoretically developed the corner stones and principles of CP realized the limitations of moving from theory to practice in other societies with different traditions and cultures? Is it worth for teachers taking risks to be agents of social change at the cost of losing jobs or professional positions?

According to Sadeghi and Ketabi (2009), most teachers show no interest in politics and politically controversial issues. It is, indeed, considered to be something taboo, which might endanger their job positions, personal and professional, lives. It does not mean teachers be politically negligent and retrieve themselves from political projects. Rather, we should take into account the stakes for teachers in such an effort. In this regard, a note of caution seems appropriate in that according to Aliakbari and Allahmoradi (2012), critical pedagogy and its principles can be infused into the Iranian educational context provided that it does not contradict its culture and tradition. Thus, every teacher should behave vigilantly towards politically and challenging issues so as not to be underprivileged in such a risk.

Conclusion

Critical approach as a new approach which has a particular focus on teaching English as a sociopolitical enterprise connected to learners' lived experiences in the wider community has immensely influenced the field of ELT in various educational contexts throughout the world. In fact, it has also particularly contributed to the process of transforming both teacher and students to become social agents to act upon inequalities in the society. Moreover, education can better evolve through dialogical exchanges among teacher and students concentrating on the issues related to their sociopolitical contexts. However, in order to appropriately and feasibly move from theory to practice in an EFL context, I do suggest that taking necessarily its associated problems and constraints into account be significant for the intellectuals in advance of attempting to bring about any social transformation. This study was in deed an attempt to throw more light on the appropriacy of CP and the probable problems, concerns and limitations of its applicability in educational system of Iran. Through the use of a multi-method approach including observation, semi-structured interview and dialogic conversation, a crystal clear picture of the themes was derived. The respective themes which are culturally and socially bound to the educational context of Iran precisely reflect what teachers as intellectuals might face in such an EFL context. Thus, it is recommended that teachers should cautiously behave in this regard and meticulously consider all the possible impediments. Surely, if they evaluate the pros and cons of such an approach before application, undoubtedly, they can feasibly cope with any probable problems at the time of its use.

References

Akbari, R. (2008a). Postmethod discourses and practice. *TESOL Quarterly 42.2*, 641–52.
Akbari, R. (2008b). Transforming lives: Introducing critical pedagogy into ELT classrooms. *ELT Journal 62.3*, 276–83.
Aliakbari, M. & N. Allahmoradi (2012). On Iranian school teachers' perceptions on the principle of critical pedagogy. *International Journal of Critical Pedagogy 4.1*, 154–71.
Benesch, S. (2001). Critical English for academic purposes: Theory, politics and practice. Mahwah, NJ: Lawrence Erlbaum Associates.
Burbules, N.C. & R. Burk (1999). Critical thinking and critical pedagogy: Relations, differences and limits. In T. S. Popkwitz, & L. Fendler (eds.), *Critical theories in education: Changing terrains of knowledge and politics*. NY: Routledge, 45–66.
Canagarajah, A. S. (1999). Revisiting linguistic imperialism in English teaching. Oxford, England: Oxford University Press.
Canagarajah, S. (2002). Reconstructing local knowledge. *Journal of Language, Identity and Education 1*, 234–59.
Crookes, G. (2009). Values, philosophies, and beliefs in TESOL: Making a Statement. Cambridge: Cambridge University Press.
Davari, H., A. Iranmehr & S. M. Erfani (2012). A survey on the Iranians' ELT community's attitudes to critical pedagogy. *English Language Teaching 5.2*, 101–11.
Davis, K.A. & E. Skilton-Sylvester (2004). Looking back, taking stock, moving forward: Investigating gender in TESOL. *TESOL Quarterly 38.3*, 381–404.
Eisner, E. W. (2002). The arts of the creation of mind. New Haven: Yale University.
Fairclough, N. (1995). Discourse analysis: The critical study of language. London: Longman. 13.
Freire, P. (1970). Pedagogy of the oppressed. New York: Continuum.

Freire, P. (1993). Pedagogy of the oppressed. New York: Continuum.

Freire, P. & D. Macedo (1987). Literacy: Reading the word and world. Westport, CT: Bergin & Gravery Publishing.

Giroux, H. A. (1992). Border crossings: Cultural workers and the politics of education. New York: Routledge.

Gur-ze'ev, I. (1998). Toward a nonrepressive critical pedagogy. *Educational theory 48*.4, 463-86.

Heras, A. I. (1999). Taking action with family and community members: Critical pedagogy as a framework for educational change. In Z. Cline & J. Necochea (eds.), *Advances in confluent education.* Stanford, CT: JAI Press.

Hui, L. (1997). New bottles, old wine: Communicative language teaching in China. *English Teaching Forum 35*.4, 34–41.

Kanpol, B. (1998). Critical pedagogy for beginning teachers: The movement from despair to hope. Retrieved from http://www.wmc.edu/academics /library/pub/jcp/issuell-1/kanpol.html (accessed 4/8/2008).

Kincheloe, J. L. (1998). Critical research in science education. In B. Fraser & K. Tobin (eds.) *International Handbook of Science Education* (part 2). Boston: Kluwer.

Kincheloe, J. L. (2004). Critical pedagogy. New York: Peter Lang.

Kincheloe, J. L. (2005). Critical constructivism. New York: Peter Lang.

Kincheloe, J. L. (2007). Critical pedagogy in the twenty-first century: Evolution for survival. In P. Mclaren & J.L. Kincheloe (eds.), *Critical pedagogy: Where are we now?* New York: Peter Lang.

Kumaravadivelu, B. (2006). TESOL methods: Changing tracks, challenging trends. *TESOL Quarterly, 40 .1*, 59–61.

Lather, P. (1998). Critical pedagogy and its complicities: A praxis of stuck places. *Educational Theory, 48*.4, 487–97.

Luke, A. (1988). Literacy, textbooks, and ideology. London, England: Falmer.

Markee, N. (2002). Language in development: Questions of theory, questions of practice. *TESOL Quarterly 36*.3, 265–74.

Mclaren, P. (1989). Life in schools: An introduction to critical pedagogy in the foundations of education. White Plains, NY: Longman.

Mclaren, P. (2000). Paulo Freire's pedagogy of possibility. In S. Steiner, H. Frank, P. Mclaren & R. Bahruth (eds.), *Freirean pedagogy, praxis and possibilities: Projects for the new millennium.* New York: Falmer Press, 1–21.

Mclaren, P. (2003). Life in schools: An introduction to critical pedagogy in the social foundations of education (4th edn.). New York: Falmer Press.

Mclaren, P. (2007). Life in schools: An introduction to critical pedagogy in the foundations of education (5th edn.). Boston, MA: Pearson.

Medgyes, P. (2001). When the teacher is in a non-native speaker. In M. Celcie-Murcia (ed.), *Teaching English as a second or foreign language* (3rd edn.). Boston: Heinle & Heinle, 415–27.

Morgan, B. (1998). The ESL classroom: Teaching, critical practice, and community. Toronto, Ontario, Canada: Toronto University Press.

Noroozisiam, E. & S. M. A. Soozandehfar (2011). Teaching through critical pedagogy: Problems and attitudes. *Theory and Practice in Language Studies 1*.9, 1240–1244.

Norton, B. (1997). Language and identity, and the ownership of English. *TESOL Quarterly 31*.3, 409–29.

Norton, B., & K. Toohey (eds.) (2004). Critical pedagogies and language learning. Cambridge, England: Cambridge University Press.

Palmer, J. & K. Emmons (2004). Critical pedagogy: An overview. Retrieved from http://www.case.edu/artsci/engl/emmons/writing/pedagogy/critical.pdf (accessed 21/5/2012).

Okazaki, T. (2005). Critical consciousness and critical language. *Second Language studies 23*.2, 174–202.

Pennycook, A. (1999). Introduction: Critical approaches to TESOL. *TESOL Quarterly 33*.3, 329–48.

Pennycook, A. (2001). Critical applied linguistics: A critical introduction. Mahwah, NJ: Lawrence Erlbaum.

Ramanathan, V. (2002). The Politics of TESOL Education: Writing, knowledge, critical pedagogy. New York: Routledge Falmer.

Rashidi, R. & F. Safari (2011). A model for EFL materials development within the framework of critical pedagogy. *English Language Teaching 4*.2, 250–59.

Richards, Jack C. (2011). Competence and performance in language teaching. New York: Cambridge University Press.

Sadeghi, S. & S. Ketabi (2009). From liberal ostrichism to transformative intellectuals: An alternative role for Iranian critical pedagogues. *Journal of English Language Teacher Education and Development12*, 52–60.

Simon, R. (1992). Teaching against the grain: Texts for pedagogy of possibility. New York: Bergin and Garvey.

Zacharias, N.T. (2003). A survey of tertiary teachers' beliefs about English language teaching in Indonesia with regard to the role of English as a global language. Unpublished M.A. thesis, Thailand University.

23

Critical Pedagogy and a Rural Social Work Practicum in China

Hok Bun Ku, Angelina W. K. Yuan-Tsang,
and Hsiao Chun Liu

In the midst of the financial and social transformations of the past 20 years, China has made significant economic progress in terms of its gross domestic product (GDP) and its GDP growth rate. However, its impressive economic performance has been accompanied by an increase in the magnitude of social problems. The introduction of a market economy has led to greater rural poverty, unemployment, family breakdowns, youth delinquency, street children, HIV/AIDS, prostitution, disabilities, mental illness, corruption, ethnic tensions, environmental pollution, and other deleterious effects. These problems have received attention from government ministries and recently established nongovernmental organizations (NGOs); however, the magnitude of the problems is so overwhelming that many issues have been left unattended and unresolved.

In an effort to promote the education of professionals who can address these acute social problems, the Chinese government reintroduced social work education programs in its universities in 1986, after a lapse of more than 30 years. The number of social work training programs expanded rapidly in the 1990s and the number of higher education institutions offering social work programs reached 172 in 2006.[1] However, there is still a severe shortage of professionally trained social work teachers to staff these programs, and the quality of social work education is an issue of grave concern.

In response to this situation, The Hong Kong Polytechnic University (PolyU), with the support of Peking University, launched a Master of Social Work (MSW; China) Program[2] for social work educators in 2000, with the aim of training a critical mass of social work educators to take up future leadership roles in developing indigenized social work and social work education. The program also aims to train a group of social work educators and practitioners to lead social development and social change in China. Social work is a Western-oriented discipline, which was invented in a Western urban context: its curriculum focuses on individualized practice and a clinical approach. We feel that, given the geographical vastness of China and the magnitude and complexity of its problems, individualized practice is not the best response in the Chinese context. We agree with Wang Sibin, the chair of the China Association of Social Work Education, who maintains that "social development and poverty alleviation should be the primary focus of social work education in China and that individualized practice should only constitute a supplementary and secondary role in the social work curriculum" (Wang, 1995). Given this orientation, we are committed to establishing programs in rural social work, which is an essential component of the indigenization of Chinese social work. Thus, when we designed our program, our main concern was to promote an effective rural social work theory and practice model.

Our Rural Practicum

The practicum allows students to put their theories of social work into practice and adapt Western concepts to the Chinese context. The students in our MSW program must complete three practicums in different settings and contexts. In the first practicum, each student selects one agency or governmental unit for their placement and each is matched with one teacher as their supervisor. Intensive skills training workshops are held before, during, and at the end of the practicum. The third practicum is conducted in Hong Kong; students are grouped into pairs and are placed in Hong Kong's social work organizations. It is hoped that by offering practicums in different cultural settings, the students will not only learn new skills but also acquire sensitivity to various workplace cultures.

The second practicum is the most critical and the longest: students are required to spend 400 hr (around 8 weeks) in one of the practicum bases, with the support of supervisor and teaching assistants. To expose students to various community services and approaches to learning, we are careful in choosing our practicum sites. For example, in Beijing, we have developed a community-based networking project to aid in the development of social support for laid-off female workers and urban families undergoing social and economic transitions. In Shanghai, we have initiated a home/school/community delinquency prevention project in collaboration with the legal department. In Wuhan, students participate in a community inclusion project for the elderly and families with special needs, including poor families that suffer from violence and abuse. In Kunming of Yunnan province, we also established a practicum in a hospital that offers a community-based mental health clinic. In Yunnan's another rural practicum site, the students engage in integrated community development. In Hunnan's rural site, they are involved in a community health project to help people with disabilities. As noted, we make it compulsory for some students to undertake at least one of their placements in a rural setting. In this article, we will focus on the teaching activities in one rural practicum site.

This practicum lasted for 8 weeks, from 24 June to 28 August 2001. We let students choose their practicum site, and five students picked Pingzhai village as their first choice. All of our students are from social work teaching faculties at universities in Mainland China. All have, at minimum, the rank of associate professors. One of the students from Beijing had already earned a PhD in sociology. The field supervisors were social work educators from Hong Kong and Taiwan, with extensive experience in rural development in China and Taiwan. More importantly, they have a passionate commitment to the development of social work in China.

The aims of the practicum were to explore the social needs of the villagers, make a preliminary determination of what the scope of community development should be, and propose a model for community development. The team of seven—two field-work supervisors and five students—stayed in Pingzhai village, an administrative village populated by Han Chinese with some Zhuang residents, located in one of the poorer counties in Yunnan province. The county where we resided was among the first designated as poor by the Leading Group for Economic Development of Poor Areas.

The population of the village in 2001 was about 26,122, with Han Chinese making up 68.61% of the population and the Zhuang minority accounting for 23.14%. The income of the local villagers depended mainly on rice production. Due to the difficulty of farming the hilly area and the scarcity of arable land, the average income of the township was about 376 yuan, much lower than the national average income. Because it is the poorest township in the county, the county government has gone to great lengths to implement poverty-reduction programs in areas such as education, road-building, tourism, and the cultivation of cash crops (including high-quality rice, sugar cane, and potatoes). The institutional features of the poverty-reduction programs implemented in Pingzhai village were similar to those of other poor townships. The purpose of our program was to apply a TCB approach that uses ethnographic methods and participatory action research to promote knowledge that would both enhance the effectiveness of social work practitioners and lead to positive social transformation.

Dialectical Dialogue and The Learner-Based Approach in The Teaching/Learning Process

Before entering the village, the fieldwork supervisors and students held an orientation workshop on rural development where they discussed China's development and its poverty. The workshop was important because it was an opportunity for the instructors and the students to engage in a dialogue and achieve a better understanding of each other's views on rural development and the conditions of Chinese peasants. We also used the occasion to introduce the learner-based approach to the students, stressing that the student should be at the centre of the learning process. At the outset of the workshop, we outlined the principles of the practicum as follows:

> We are not in a position to criticize whether or not your work is well done. All we can do is share this working experience with you. All of us should not be preoccupied with results (marks), theories, or the goals that we have set out for ourselves; instead, we should remember that we are not here to fulfill the requirements of this course only. Rather, you should come with the purpose of satisfying your own learning needs.

The students were given the freedom to choose their work placements. We pointed out that the learning process itself should be a pleasant one and that the members of the team should cooperate with each other. They should learn how to deal with the inevitable conflicts that ensue when different methods, values, and ideologies are brought together. Both the field supervisors and the students were partners in this course, and the teachers were by no means manipulators of the learning process.

The learner-based model is very different from the nonreflective conventional teaching/learning method used in Mainland China. According to Freire, as a result of such oppressive pedagogy, students are unable or unwilling to think critically about the world. Freire proposes 'conscientization' as a means of reviving people's reflexivity toward themselves, their community, and their society (Freire, 1972). The rural practicum was intended to emancipate the students' cultural self and revive their reflexivity. To encourage students to see themselves as the subjects of learning, dialectical dialogue is an important teaching strategy.

Conventionally, a social work educator is treated as an expert and a student is seen as a novice. This expert–novice duality in educational institutions is intertwined with a culturally instituted divisive relationship between the educated and uneducated; these attitudes determine the relationship between educator and student in rural development practice and teaching. To avoid this, we substituted a learner-based method and dialectical dialogue for the traditional method of supervision. To promote dialectical dialogue and emancipate instructors and students from long-standing educational and cultural assumptions, we recognized that, as educators, we needed to adopt a nonexpert attitude toward students and to encourage them, in turn, to adopt a nonexpert attitude toward the villagers. We wished to challenge the students' ambition to become an expert in rural development practices, an attitude that tends to diminish the power of the local people and discourage them from taking charge of their lives.

We modified all the individual and group supervision sections accordingly. Dialectical dialogues were initiated by fieldwork supervisors in all team meetings to encourage students to become creative subjects, participating both in the rural development practice and the learning process. It was anticipated that, through the dialectical dialogue process, both students and instructors would learn to think critically about their selves, surroundings, and society. Through this mutual inquiry, the participants could work cooperatively to acquire knowledge of rural developmental practices in China. As teachers, we hoped that this learning process—dialectical dialogue between educated and uneducated—would be adopted by the students and characterize their interactions with the villagers. We also hoped that mutual learning instead of individual learning flows would be established through dialectical dialogue among all participants, including field supervisors, students, and villagers. In the end, all participants would have a greater sensitivity to the inequity and oppression within themselves, their community, and society, and could act as a reflexive agent of transformation. We addressed the students as follows:

> What is more, you should not have come for the purpose of alleviating poverty but to participate on an equal footing with the local inhabitants and to conduct dialogues based on a culture of diversity. The locals are not objects on which we practice our theories. Instead, they are equal subjects in their relation with us. We should therefore see them as the starting point for our practice, so as to face up to ourselves, face up to power, and face up to social relations. Education is a tool; the process of education is a process of emancipation.

To put the learner-based approach into practice, we asked the students to develop their own study plan and their proposals for its actualization. At first, the students felt very much at a loss and ambivalent about the process: they had never considered that learning could be negotiated through dialogue. For the first 3 weeks, the students struggled with the meaning of "learner-based." They were not used to developing their own study plans and searching for their own methods of learning. As one student observed,

> As far as I was concerned, it was the first time that I had to actualize the notion personally. From the moment of my birth until now, as a teacher myself, I always felt it to be a process of interaction between the object and the subject, a process of interaction between the educator and the learners. All of a sudden, I became the subject of education, and it was somewhat awkward. As one of my classmates said, we had become children without a mother.

Not only were the students nervous, they also felt powerless. They did not know what they could do in the village. At the beginning of the practicum, the students, who were senior academics and experts from Mainland China, had a fixed conception of rural development. Some students even boasted, "Rural China, we know it well. We came from villages. We know the problems of rural development in China better than you teachers." Some students thought that the peasants were poor, backward, uncivilized, and desperately in need of outside experts. During the dialogues in team meetings, the instructors continually challenged the students' mistaken assumptions and led them to realize that their own ideals might, if not presented carefully, do harm to the local community. For example, the students were accustomed to thinking that the best way to eradicate poverty was to provide training in modern agricultural technology. However, they had not considered the destructive impact of modern technology on the rural community in terms of environmental degradation. The dialogue made them aware of the ecological issues in rural development and widened their perspective on the best courses of action.

Oral History as a Bridge between Students and Villagers

According to Weissner (2001), narratives of human experience are one of the key influences on what we learn and how we approach learning. These narratives are so rich and diverse, whether they are told to us by elders or shared with our peers, that they expand and deepen our understanding. To help our students accept their position as learners, we suggested that they gather the oral histories of the villagers. By establishing a means of dialogue between the MSW students and the villagers, we hoped to transform the existing power relationship. However, when the instructors first encouraged the students to seek out the oral histories of the villagers, the students were not keen: they could not see how oral history, as a method of participatory rural appraisal, could be a significant way of mobilizing community participation and exploring the needs of the local community. The students thought that they would be able to mobilize the community by using the conventional needs-assessment methods. However, due to language barriers[3] and to their status as outsiders, the students had not become integrated into village life and were, therefore, unable to understand the deeper needs of the community. How did the villagers respond to birth, aging, illness, and death? What were their needs during work and rest? How did they deal with the various pressures resulting from social changes? To answer these questions, the students began collecting oral histories: they hoped that through this process, they would create closer bonds with the villagers and thus gain a better understanding of the villagers' lives and needs.

The process of collecting oral histories was divided into several phases. First, we recruited the local people from various natural villages[4] as our research partners. The response was positive and a total of 42 people agreed to participate in our oral history collection. These local participants were young adults: some were married and some were junior secondary school graduates. Seven teams were formed to carry out the oral history interviews in seven villages, with a team leader for each village. The team members selected their leader by means such as drawing lots, so everyone had an equal chance of becoming leader. We organized several workshops on oral history for the students and for the local villagers. With the villagers, we used drawing, drama, and games to convey the meaning of oral history and to encourage them to share their own narratives and those of other villagers. We also worked alongside the students to formulate the interview questions and drew a life-course map to generate interview topics.

During the process, we lent the villagers tape recorders, which they mastered very quickly. After training workshops led by their team leader, each team collected oral histories. When we were finished, we had oral histories of the elderly, young schoolgirls, middle-aged women, husbands, and wives. At every stage in the project, we reminded ourselves to play a secondary role and allow the villagers to become the owners and leaders of the project.

We emphasized the participation of local people in the process of collecting life stories. Because our students were handicapped by the language barrier, they had to rely on the villagers' aid throughout the entire process. The villagers collected the stories in their native language and became our interviewers, translators, and teachers. In the course of collecting stories, the villagers became the experts: they told their own stories and, of course, they had more knowledge of their own affairs than outsiders did. During this process, the outside "experts" became the students: they learned to respect the experience and knowledge of the local people. In this sense, we exchanged roles with the locals and reversed the power relationship. The right to speak was returned to the villagers. The oral histories became a means of empowerment for the locals and an important means of education for our students (Campbell, 2001; Perks & Thompson, 1998; Slim & Thompson, 1995).

Collecting oral histories also transformed the relationship between our students and the villagers. After collecting oral histories, the students were totally accepted by the villagers and they felt themselves to be members of the community. As one of them observed,

> At the beginning, I was an observer and outsider, but then the village became part of my life …. It is so amazing that in this practicum we choose the 'oral history' as a method. It is really a participatory method.

The students participated in many affairs of the village: they helped with the harvest, joined in games, and attended village funerals, among other activities. One student commented,

I was very pleased with all these opportunities, because they enabled me to discover new things about myself and to adjust myself accordingly. My relationship with the villagers was greatly transformed after I relaxed. In return, the villagers began to identify with us and tried to get close to us. Three weeks later [after collecting oral histories together with the villagers], the relationship was transformed, paving the way for a very smooth start to our work.

Gathering oral histories also facilitated dialogues between people of different ages, genders, and backgrounds. It established communal relationships among the local people, strengthened their social cohesion, led them to choose community spokespeople, and, overall, was a catalyst for community organization. For example, when working with us, the young villagers had an opportunity to listen to the stories of their fellow villagers and to learn the histories of "marginalized" individuals. In the process of collecting oral histories, the young and the old were able to find common topics of conversation and to narrow the generation gap. Moreover, the elderly villagers gained confidence and rediscovered their strengths through narrating the history of their life and finally participating in the community once again. It was a process of education and empowerment for them as well (Grele, 1991; Perks & Thompson, 1998; Portelli, 1998; Slim & Thompson, 1995; Yow, 1994).

More than a simple method for collecting data, oral history gives us an opportunity to hear voices outside the mainstream discourse, and uncovers personal details and aspects of life that are buried or hidden in the public realm. It is an important tool of needs assessment because it enables us to acquire greater understanding of the local community. Still, collecting oral histories was only the first step of the rural social work practicum. The students needed to learn how to plan and actualize a rural community development project.

Students' Reflections on Their Learning Experience

During the 8-week practicum, the students came to realize that their relationship with the villagers was akin to that between their teachers and themselves. In the learner-based practicum, the teachers assumed a nonexpert role in relating to the students and the students became the subject of their own learning. The teachers, who came from urban Hong Kong, clearly knew that they were at the same level as the students: neither group was familiar with rural conditions. Their only course was to dispense with hierarchical relationships and work together with the students and the villagers to discover the best paths to rural development. This process helped the students discover their own value and develop a strong sense of confidence and competence. As one student commented,

> In the process, I felt myself to be like a teacher …. What are we to do? How shall we do it? We had to make decisions all by ourselves. Now the villagers had also become the subject of their own learning process; they had to make decisions about what to do and what not to do in community development.

The students realized that their interactions with the villagers should resemble their instructors' interactions with them. They found the villagers to be highly motivated and very capable. Once the power of decision making was passed into the villagers' hands, they made full use of it and did their utmost to succeed. One student remarked,

> Peasants are not as stupid as we had thought. Actually, they're full of wisdom. They have their local knowledge. They don't need our supervision and imposition; instead, they need encouragement and support.

The villagers also grew to appreciate their own value. Although they did not know what group work meant in the context of social work, they did understand the motto "unity is strength," and they were willing to work with us and to search for their own methods of development. The villagers learned how to organize themselves and realize their goals. They became both the agents and the beneficiaries of community development, which is the goal of people-centered development.

The transformation of the villagers was very encouraging. At the end of the practicum, one student wrote in his journal,

> Suddenly, I had a sense of satisfaction [from seeing the villagers make their own decisions] because I could observe the changes in the villagers in only seven weeks: their potential was realized. In the beginning, they thought we were playing, and observed us from afar. Later, they began to get close to us, to chat and to sing with us. And finally, they started working with us [collecting oral histories] and organized themselves to plan their own future. How encouraging! There were a few girls in particular who were so shy at first that they would not even lift their heads. After working with their own groups, they became bold enough to sing some ditties at evening gatherings and participate in group discussions. What an amazing change!

As teachers, we noticed that the students, too, had developed their own capabilities. This was a learning process that served two purposes. In the early days of the practicum, the students remained remote from the villagers, but after working together with the local residents, the students became more relaxed and confident, and happy to engage in conversation on an equal footing. They abandoned their role as expert and listened attentively to the villagers' concerns, which they seriously considered. They shared more personal emotions. No longer objective observers, they were involved and concerned participants.

The teaching and learning process not only enhanced students' competence and confidence but also developed their capacity to rethink issues of power and domination in China's rural development. They had, in Paulo Freire's words, developed the "ability to reread the world." They began to ask: What is development? Whom does development serve? Who benefits? Who pays the greatest cost? What are the forces driving development?

Encouraged to reflect on their own roles, the students realized the perils of abusing their position. As one of them said,

> Our ideals, if not handled with care, could possibly represent an invasion to others. It is indeed noble to fight for our ideals, but we should also pay more attention to realities and experience them more.

They often reminded themselves that it did not matter what position they were in. The key issue was whether or not they were receptive enough to reexamine and reconsider the nature of social work in China, so as to make their practice culturally sensitive. One student remarked,

> Now I realize what we believe in and the position we are in is irrelevant, for the most important thing is whether or not we have re-examined ourselves enough, understood our limitations and advantages, and become adequately alert. It is important to acknowledge the coexistence of different values and to approach issues from all sides.

The students gained a new outlook on development work in rural China. The learning process forced them to reconsider the simplistic "plan—intervention—conclusion" model; usually, the reality is more complex. Learning should be a process of self-emancipation and continuous reexamination, in the course of which students construct, deconstruct, and then reconstruct their professional knowledge. The students found such knowledge lies in everyday life experiences: it is a process of discovering meanings together with others. They also experienced diversity and inclusiveness, which enabled them to appreciate the richness of life and realize their own limitations.

> The fifty days of fieldwork in the village were a time I will not forget for the rest of my life, for they gave me inspiration and have had a great impact on me. I have made new discoveries with regard to myself, others, and villages in China, as well as the peasants. I have been made to rethink and reflect on the idea of social work as a profession, the conventional theories of rural development, and, in particular, my character as well as that of others.... .

These are the heartfelt words of a student; they convey the significant impact of the teaching/learning experience. Other student feedback also confirmed that the students gained the ability to reflect on conventional social work teaching and its application in the context of Mainland China. It has also enhanced the ability of the students to see the relationship between their studies and the process of social work.

Notes

1. Figures were provided by the China Association of Social Work Education (CASWE), which is an umbrella organization consisting of almost all the social work training institutions in China.
2. The English term "conscientization" is a translation of the Portuguese term *conscientização* that is also translated as "consciousness raising" or "critical consciousness," which was coined by Paulo Freire. It is a process in which educator endeavors to help student achieve an in-depth understanding of the world, allowing for the perception and exposure of social and political contradictions. It also includes the process of taking action against the oppressive elements in one's life that are illuminated by that understanding.
3. The local people speak the Zhuang dialect. Only few of the young villagers or educated adults can speak official Chinese—Mandarin. Therefore, it was difficult for the students to communicate directly with the local villagers. On one hand, it was a handicap, but, on the other hand, it became an advantage because the students had to humble themselves and work closely with the educated villagers, who often became our translators.
4. In China, villages are classified according to two categories—administrative villages and natural villages. An administrative village is so classified by the government and it normally will include several natural villages.

References

Freire, P. (1972). *Pedagogy of the oppressed.* New York: Continuum.

Grele, Ronald J. (1991). *Envelopes of Sound: The Art of Oral History,* Praeger, New York.

Perks, R., & Thompson, A. (1998). *The oral history reader.* New York: Routledge.

Portelli, A. (1998). *Narrative and genre.* London: Routledge.

Wang, S. B. (1995). The experience and development of social work in China. *Social Science in China, 2,*97–106.

Weissner, C. (2001). *Stories of change: Narrative in emancipatory adult learning.* Digital Dissertations. New York: Teachers College, Columbia University.

Yow, V. R. (1994). *Recording oral history.* London: SAGE.

Further Readings

Section 5: Critical Praxis and Literacy

Abdi, A. (ed.) (2012). *Decolonizing Philosophies of Education*, Rotterdam, Boston and Taipi: Sense Publishers.

Araujo Freire, A.M. (1997). 'A Bit of My Life with Paulo Freire' in *Taboo. The Journal of Culture and Education*, 2, Fall: 3–11.

Araujo, Freire, A.M. (1995). Literacy in Brazil: The Contribution of Paulo Freire. In de Figueiredo-Cowen & D. Gastaldo (eds.). *Paulo Freire at the Institute* (25–37). London: Institute of Education.

Araujo Perreira, A and Vittoria, P. (2012). 'A luta pela descolonização e as experiências de alfabetização na Guiné-Bissau: Amilcar Cabral e Paulo Freire' (The liberation struggle and the experiences of literacy in Guinea-Bissau: Amilcar Cabral and Paulo Freire), *Estudos Históricos (Rio de Janeiro)*, Vol. 25 (n. 50) http://www.scielo.br/scielo.php?pid=S0103–21862012000200002&script=sci_arttext.

Biko, S. (2002). *I Write What I Like*. Chicago: University of Chicago Press.

Bloch, E. (1986). *The Principle of Hope*. Cambridge, MA: MIT Press.

Borg, C. & Mayo, P. (2000). 'Reflections from a "Third Age" Marriage: Paulo Freire's Pedagogy of Reason, Hope and Passion.' *McGill Journal of Education*, *35*(2), 105–20.

Cortesao, L. (2011). 'Paulo Freire and Amilcar Cabral: Convergences.' *Journal for Critical Education Policy Studies*, *9*(2), 260–96. Retrieved from http://www.jceps.com/wp-content/uploads/PDFs/09-2-15.pdf.

Cortesão, L. (2012). 'Paulo Freire ve Amilcar Cabral' (Paulo Freire and Amilcar Cabral). *Elestirel pedagoji– Critical Pedagogy* Vol. 4 (19), 23–26. (In Turkish).

Da Silva, A. B. (2010). 'Amilcar Cabral's Pedagogy of Liberation Struggle and His Influence on FRETILIN 197501978,' in M. Leach, N. C. Mendes, A. B. Da Silva, A. D. C. Ximenes and B. Boughton (eds), *Hatene kona ba/ Compreender/ Understanding/ Mengerti Timor-Leste. Proceedings of the Timor-Leste Studies Association Conference, Dili, 2–3 July 2009*. Hawthorn: Swinburne Press, 266–71.

Derince, Z. M. (2011). 'Language Learning through Critical Pedagogy in a "Brave New World."' *International Review of Education*, *57*, 377–95. doi:10.1007/s11159-11-9218-8.

De Robbio Anziano, I., (1987). *Antonio Gramsci e la Pedagogia del Impegno* (Antonio Gramsci and the Pedagogy of Engagement), Naples, Ferraro.

De Vita, A (2009). *La Creazione Sociale. Relazioni e Contesti per Educare* (Social Creation. Relations and Contests to Educate), Rome: Carocci.

Ferrer I Guardia, F. (2002). *La Escuela Moderna. Póstuma explicación y alcance de la enseñanza racionalista* (The Modern School. Posthumous Explanation and Scope of Rationalist Teaching). Barcelona: Tusquets.

Freire, P. and D. Macedo (1987). *Literacy: Reading the Word & the World*. South Hadley, MA: Bergin & Garvey Publishers.

Freire, P. and D. Macedo (1995). 'A Dialogue: Culture, Language, and Race' in *Harvard Educational Review*, vol. 65, no. 3, fall, (p. 377-402).

Gadotti, M (1996). *Pedagogy of Praxis. A Dialectical Philosophy of Education*, Albany: SUNY Press.

Hirschfeld, U (2006), '...und Brecht'(...and Brecht) in Mayo, P, *Politische Bildung bei Antonio Gramsci und Paulo Freire/ Perspektiven einar verändernden Praxis* (Political Bildung/Education in Antonio Gramsci and Paulo Freire. Perspectives regarding a Changing Praxis), Hamburg: Argument Verlag.

Inal, Kemal. (2010). 'A Modern Emancipatory Approach to and in Education.' *Journal of Alternative Education*, 1–10. Retreived from http://dergi.alternatifegitimdernegi.org.tr/eng//content/view/20/29/.

Jules, D. (1993). 'The Challenge of Popular Education in the Grenada Revolution.' In C. Lankshear and P. McLaren (Eds.), *Critical Literacy, Politics, Praxis and the Postmodern*, Albany: State University of New York Press.

Macedo D (1994). *Literacies of Power: What Americans Are Not Allowed to Know*. Expanded edition. Boulder, CO and Oxford: Westview Press.

Martin, G. (2005). 'You Can't Be Neutral on a Moving Bus: Critical Pedagogy as Community Praxis.' *Journal for Critical Education Policy Studies, 3*(2), 1–29. Retrieved from http://www.jceps.com/.

Mayo, P. 2007. "Critical Approaches to Education in the work of Lorenzo Milani and Paulo Freire." *Studies in Philosophy and Education* 26 (6): 525–44.

Mayo, P (2013). 'Museums as Sites of Critical Pedagogical Practice,' *Review of Education, Pedagogy, and Cultural Studies*, 35:2, 144–53, DOI: 10.1080/10714413.2013.778661.

McInerney, P. (2009). 'Toward a Critical Pedagogy of Engagement for Alienated Youth: Insights from Freire and School-Based Research.' *Critical Studies in Education, 50*, 23–35. http://dx.doi.org/10.1080/17508480802526637.

Puiggrós, A. (2005). *De Simón Rodríguez a Paulo Freire, Educación para la integración Iberoamericana* (From Simon Rodriguez to Paulo Freire: Education for Iberoamerican integration). Bogotá, Colombia: La Organización Internacional Convenio Andrés Bello.

Relys Díaz, L. I. (2013). *De América Soy Hijo… Crónica de una Década de Alfabetización Audiovisual* (I am Son [*sic*] of America…History of an Audiovisual Literacy Decade), Girona: La Guerilla Comunicacional.

Shin, H., & Cookes, G. (2009). 'Exploring the Possibilities for EFL Critical Pedagogy in Korea: a Two-Part Case Study.' *Critical Inquiry in Language Studies, 2*(2), 113–36. http://dx.doi.org/10.1207/s15427595cils0202_3.

Tagore, R. 'The Parrot's Training.' In V. Bhatia (Ed.) 1994. *Rabindranath Tagore: Pioneer in Education*. New Delhi: Sahitya Chayan.

Vittoria, P. (2008) *Narrando Paulo Freire. Per una Pedagogia del Dialogo* (Narrating Paulo Freire. For a Pedagogy of Dialogue), Sassari: Carlo Delfino Editore.

Wu, Y-J. (2011).' Comparing the Cultural Contents of Mandarin Reading Textbooks in China, Hong Kong, Singapore and Taiwan.' *Journal of International Cooperation in Education, 14*, 2 (67–81).

Section 6
Critical Pedagogy and the Classroom

No man can be a good teacher unless he has feelings of warm affection toward his pupils and a genuine desire to impart to them what he believes to be of value.

Bertrand Russell, *On Education* (1926)

Teacher preparation should go beyond the technical preparation of teachers and be rooted in the ethical formation both of selves and of history.

Paulo Freire, *Pedagogy of Freedom* (1998)

24

Critical Theories and
Teacher Education in Portugal

New Possibilities for Teacher Education
to Make the Difference

Fátima Pereira

Teacher education is currently facing major challenges in Portugal. Indeed, it needs to assert its fundamental role in building professional identities and in producing a teaching profession able to provide educational alternatives to the education crisis that has been affecting, over the past decades, not only Portugal but all Western countries in general. In the new millennium, educational and training policies for a more democratic and equitable School are still to be devised. In the second half of the twentieth century, critical theory/critical pedagogy became a particularly relevant approach to all questions concerning the social and the educational world and the world of scientific research. In Portugal, little is known about the extent of its influence in the educational field.

In this text, I reflect on the incidence of critical theory and critical pedagogy in teacher education in Portugal, based on partial results gathered through research projects that I developed in the last few years and in my own experience as a researcher and a teacher working in the field of teacher education. This reflection not only takes into consideration the changes suffered by teacher education in Portugal in the broader context of late modernity; but it also clarifies the different conceptions of critical theory that underlie this analysis. The results examined lead to the identification of narratives about School, the Teaching Profession and Teacher Education that may, in the current context of crisis, be conducive to a reconfiguration of the incidence and type of critical approaches to teacher education, and favour new epistemologies and rationalities regarding professionalization and the teaching profession.

Social Changes and Teacher Education in Portugal

Nowadays, the social relations and conventions that founded modern institutions face a great instability. Defined as a late modernity (Giddens 1997) shaken by the decline of former key institutions (Dubet 2002), the present is an intense, complex, uncertain and permanently transient time. School has been deeply affected in its matrix and has, accordingly, been facing a deep crisis over the past decades. Teacher education is intrinsically bound up with this crisis. In tune with the educational system, it has suffered successive changes and reforms in order to adjust to social and scientific demands of transformation in professionalization, professionalism and in the teaching profession (cf. 2013a).

The transformations that occurred after April 25, 1974, are particularly relevant, when the "Carnation Revolution," as it is commonly known, toppled a totalitarian political regime that had, for 40 years, sentenced education and the teaching profession back to obscurantism and scientific poverty. The restoration of democracy in Portugal, in 1974, led to profound changes in initial and continuing teacher education. These changes focused on the democratisation of education – by increasing compulsory schooling and implementing measures to combat school failure and dropout –on the reformulation of curricula and of the conditions of their development, and also on the forms of school administration and management. In the domain of initial teacher education, the changes focused on an increase of years of training (particularly visible in the qualification of teachers of the 1st cycle of basic education),[1] on professionalization, a component of teacher qualification that became a mandatory requirement in all courses of initial teacher education,[2] and on the reconfiguration of the disciplinary areas of training, depending on the curriculum reforms operated in the educational system and on the cognitive and epistemic changes in scientific knowledge.

In the domain of continuing teacher education, a national system overseen by the state was institutionalised in 1992. It sought to "improve the quality of teaching and of the teachers' professional and pedagogical competence, encourage self-training, practical research and educational innovation, and promote the feasibility of retraining" (Santos 2009: 15, my translation). At the core of this national system are the Training Centres of Schools Association (Centros de Formação de Associação de Escolas–CFAE) which foster the development of projects and actions for continuous education of teachers, in close coordination with School dynamics.

On the other hand, today, Portuguese education, teaching and teacher education do not escape the globalised neoliberal drift that has been going on for decades and with particular intensity in this new millennium. The neoliberal drift in educational policies integrates a broader and more intricate socio-cultural and ontological chain of changes brought by the so-called late modernity. Indeed, with states grappling with the crisis of modernity and its institutional development model, neoliberalism insinuates itself as a potential solution, offering management practices that deviate the social, political and economic risks from the state to the individuals, by mechanisms of self-regulation that make the latter responsible for their own care (cf. Webb, Gulson, and Pitton 2012).

Critical Theory and Critical Pedagogy: Main Topics for Analysis

In order to understand the impact of critical theory on teacher education in Portugal, a theoretical clarification of the concepts that guide this analysis is required. Critical theory has been object of numerous conceptual debates within different scientific communities. Today, critical theory is particularly relevant in the field of social and political philosophy and in education sciences, but it emerged in the field of economics, sociology and psychoanalysis and it is intrinsically bound up with the thought and work of authors of the Frankfurt School, especially Horkheimer, Adorno and Marcuse, theorists of the School's first generation, and Habermas, member of the School's second generation. Starting from a revision of Marxist theory–but keeping as essential to social analysis the concepts of alienation and domination–and a critique of "traditional theory," in the 1930s, the first generation of authors of the Frankfurt School, devised a "critical theory of society." This theory would establish an epistemological break with positivist science, presenting itself as a "project of rationalisation of society" founded on the intentionality of promoting "an emancipatory/rationalising practice" epistemologically sustained in the relationship between theory and *praxis* (Ruz 1984: 10). This approach is particularly influenced by the American pragmatism of Dewey and his conceptions of democracy and reflexivity, later developed by Habermas when reflecting on universal pragmatics in his theory of communication. Despite taking into consideration the Marxist concepts of domination and capitalist exploitation, Habermas's "critical social theory" intends, above all, to "apprehend the subjective and communicative elements of the interpersonal power relations as well as the possibilities of their transformation" (Morrow and Torres 1998: 127, my translation).

It is not surprising, therefore, that Habermas is one of the theorists of the Frankfurt School more frequently evoked in critical analysis of education, and, predominantly, in critical pedagogy. Since its main premise is the assumption that the educational relationship is in keeping with a structure of domination, "critical pedagogy is particularly focused on the constantly changing role of the subjectivity in power relations, on the transformation of these relations and on discourse as a transformer" (*ibid.*: 141, my translation). This approach is particularly developed by Paulo Freire and Henry Giroux whose work became an obvious reference towards a pedagogy for liberation, in Freire's case, and radical pedagogy, in Giroux's. Critical pedagogy aims not only at transforming the educational relationship in the micro-context of the classroom, but also at transforming the forms of knowledge production in education and in all relations of domination of micro, meso and macro-type involved in education that might be potential factors of alienation, oppression and social injustice.

One can also agree with Santos (1999) and endorse a broader theoretical and epistemological perspective on critical theory that deems critical all theory that does not reduce reality to the things that currently exist, but see it, instead, as a field of possibilities and alternatives boosted by theoretical knowledge: "The critical analysis of all that exists is based on the assumption that existence does not exhaust its possibilities and, therefore, there are alternatives that can overcome what is inappropriate in existence. Discomfort, discontent or disgust regarding existence are driving forces to theorise how to overcome them" (Santos 1999: 197, my translation).

In this rather comprehensive perspective, there is room for some hybridity and flexibility in defining boundaries with the so-called post-critical theories. These theories are particularly relevant in the field of post-structuralist and post-Marxist studies and, in the last two decades, they have gained importance in education sciences. All these studies break with the intention of formulating scientific metanarratives and essentialist axioms and put emphasis on interpretive approaches focusing on issues of identity, culture and difference, with strong mobilisation of conceptions within the field of language and speech (cf. Lopes 2013).

The Incidence of Critical Theory and Critical Pedagogy in Teacher Education in Portugal

My analysis is based on partial results of research projects developed by myself in recent years. These results lead to the identification of concepts and authors pertaining to critical theory and critical pedagogy studied both in research and analysis in the field of teacher education and in the programmes of teacher education offered in Portugal.

Analysis of Masters and PhD Dissertations

A literature search was performed in the national repository of theses and dissertations, using search terms such as the name of authors working within the framework of critical theory and critical pedagogy and also keywords such as "emancipation" "transformation," "reflection," "critical," etc. This search was restricted to theses and dissertations concerning teacher education, published from 2000 to the present day. 208 reports were collected;[3] 48 of them (that is, 22.3%) contained words connected with critical theory/critical pedagogy; 27 were Masters' dissertations; and 21 were PhD thesis.

The search results here presented are organised in terms of referenced authors, themes/problematics and research methodologies. The different formatting styles are meant to provide information on the items more frequently mentioned in the reports studied. Although there is a great diversity of national and international authors whose work is inscribed in the field of critical theory/critical pedagogy or in a broader theoretical and epistemological critical perspective, this study only focuses on authors that have been referenced in more than two reports. International authors include Paulo Freire; Henry Giroux; Jürgen Habermas; Donald Schön; Moacir Gadotti; Kenneth Zeichner; Stephen Kemmis; Wilfred Carr; Edgar Morin; Frankfurt School, without reference to specific authors; Michael Apple; Robert Ennis; Philippe Perrenoud; Tomás Tadeu da Silva. While national authors include: José Alberto Correia; Boaventura de Sousa Santos; Isabel Alarcão; António Nóvoa; Carlinda Leite; Idália Sá-Chaves; Rui Canário; Stephen Stoer.

Themes/Problematics

The main themes/problematics were: the teacher as a reflective professional; professional development; *the autonomy of teaching; pedagogical supervision; emancipation; constructing identity; the production of professional knowledge; and technologies of information and communication.* Less frequent themes/problematics included: pedagogical innovation; the school-family relationship; professional communication; cultural diversity; pedagogical praxis; the training curriculum; contextualising school knowledge; and childhood governance.

Professional development was the main concern in this category, followed in terms of occurrence by educational transformation and education and information technologies. *The construction of professional identity, collaborative work, training models and e-learning* were themes focused in more than one report. The themes mentioned in only one report included: management training; educational innovation; cultural diversity; the curriculum; emancipation; sex education; inclusion; school libraries; the educational project; learning communities; civics; research-training; the development of critical thinking; socio-educational mediation; the teacher as a professional researcher and reflective practitioner; training supervision; and the theory-practice relationship.

Methodologies

The most relevant fact concerning methodologies is that only 1 report (in a total of 48) adopted a quantitative methodology. Three reports adopted a hybrid method and the great majority of studies adopted a qualitative methodology that favoured an interpretive/comprehensive approach, namely through action-research, case study and narrative approaches.

Initial Teacher Education: Curriculum Analysis

The sample used in this study includes the curricula and programmes of 11 courses of initial teacher education currently offered by 5 Portuguese higher education institutions. A search was conducted in a total of 309 subject programmes, using as key-words critical theory, critical pedagogy and critical, and also the names of authors associated with critical theory/critical pedagogy. Relevant references for analysis were found in 58 (19%) subjects, 4 being explicit references to critical theory/critical pedagogy and 54 being references to critical reflection, attitude and/or analysis. The programmes identified were studied according to items such as Institution, Course, Year, Subject, Concepts, Authors and/or Works pertaining to critical theory/critical pedagogy, Aims and Critical skills developed. In this paper they are divided in three items: Authors, Key concepts and Professional profile of the future teacher.

Subjects that deal with critical theory/critical pedagogy explicitly include Critical pedagogies; Educational Communication and Technology II; Human Resources Training and Management; and Curriculum Theory and Development. Authors referenced in these subjects: Henry Giroux, Paulo Freire; *Max Horkheimer; Tomaz Tadeu da Silva;* and Theodor Adorno. Key concepts discussed included culture; critical pedagogy, ethics and aesthetics; politics; awareness; social justice; collaborative work; globalisation; the information society; critical deconstruction of discourse; critical reflection; ideology; and power. Also discussed were the professional profile of the future teacher, including reflective; critical; transformer; proficient in ICT; and curriculum manager.

Subjects that don't deal with critical theory/critical pedagogy explicitly included are: Education Sciences: Education and School Organisation; Sociology of Education and of the School; History of Education; Elements of Sociology of Education; Educational Organisation and Management; Citizenship and Educational Intervention; Educational Intervention Projects; Mediation in Childhood Educational Contexts; Educational Management and Leadership; Trends in Contemporary Pedagogy; Playful Pedagogy; Curriculum Theory and Development I; Educational Policies; Training and Mediation Devices and Methodologies I; Training and Mediation Devices and Methodologies II; Human Resources Training and Management II; Child Pedagogy; Educational and Professional Practice Contexts; and Fundamentals of Educational Thought. Speciality Sciences included Concepts of Mathematics I; Integrated Natural Sciences I; Motor Expression and Education; Integrated Natural Sciences II; Elements of Geometry; Literature and Reading Training; Literature for Children and Youth; Physical and Human Geography of Portugal; Mathematics and Education; Theory of Text; Study of the Physical and Natural World; Portuguese IV; Supervision of Education and Training; History of Portugal; and Society and Culture.

Other important topics included 1) Didactics, including didactics of Natural and Social Sciences; Didactics of Social Sciences; Didactics of Integrated Sciences; Didactics of Physical and Social Environment; Didactics of Mother Tongue; Didactics of Portuguese; Experimental Science Education; Didactics of Elementary Mathematics; and Didactics of History and Geography of Portugal. 2) Pedagogical practice, including Supervised Pedagogical Practice A1; Supervised Pedagogical Practice A2; Supervised Pedagogical Practice B1; Supervised Teaching Practice; Supervised Teaching Practice in the 1st Cycle of Basic Education; Introduction to Professional Practice I; Introduction to Professional Practice IV; and Supervised Teaching Practice in Early Childhood and Basic Education I. And, 3) Methodology, including Educational Research Seminar B2; Research Methodology in Education; and Quantitative Methods of Analysis.

Authors who develop a critical analysis referenced in these subjects[4] at the international level included Andy Hargreaves; Philippe Perrenoud; Anthony Giddens; Donald Schön; Edgar Morin; Jean Claude Passeron; Marguerite Altet; Maria Carme Torremorel; Michael Apple; Paulo Freire; Pierre Bourdieu; Basil Bernstein; Bernard Charlot; Célestin Freinet; Christian Baudelot; Gimeno Sacristán; John Elliot; Kenneth Zeichner; Louis Althusser; Philippe Corcuff; Roger Establet; and Tomaz Tadeu da Silva. National authors included Isabel Alarcão; Almerindo Janela Afonso; António Nóvoa; Idália Sá-Chaves; Flávia Vieira; Boaventura de Sousa Santos; José Alberto Correia; Luíza Cortesão; Licinio Lima; Rui Canário; Stephen Stoer; Fátima Antunes; Fátima Pereira; José Augusto Pacheco; Raul Iturra; Sérgio Grácio; Abílio Amiguinho; Amélia Lopes; Ana Benavente; António Teodoro; Carlinda Leite; Filomena Mónica; João Paraskeva; and Pedro Silva.

The key concepts discussed within a critical perspective were found to be: critical reflection; critical analysis; critical thinking; (social and personal) change; emancipation; critical attitude; autonomy; collaborative work; divergent thinking; discussion; active citizenship; critical awareness; democracy; equal opportunities; complexity; praxis; communication; social exclusion; school autonomy; shared responsibility; and action-research. Also discussed was the professional profile of the future teacher within a critical perspective, including professional critical; reflective; researcher; creative; transformer; ethically-driven; research-driven; autonomous; cooperative; self-critical; and politically conscious.

Continuing Teacher Education Analysis[5]

Within the framework of a project that assessed the Portuguese System of Continuing Teacher Education[6] (cf. Lopes et al. 2011), and with the purpose of learning more about the theoretical conceptions of reference and the results of studies and reports produced in the field, I analysed a set of documents published between 1992 and 2008 (cf. Pereira 2013a). This analysis resulted in the identification of concepts, policies and training practices and this paper presents a systematising interpretation of the conceptual frameworks that have been mobilised in the assessment studies and analysis of continuing teacher education and in regulatory system documents, with a particular focus on the activity of the Training Centres of Schools Association.

Table 24.1 presents a meta-analysis of conceptions identified in the studies and documents that examined or regulated the continuing teacher education provided by the Training Centres between 1992 and 2008. It shows, succinctly, that all conceptual references mobilised in the analysis of continuing teacher education, since its institutionalisation in 1992, follow a constructivist approach that, according to Nóvoa (1991), presents reflection and research focused on professional practices and their contexts as the basis for building continuing teacher education devices.

Figure 24.1 provides a mapping of the conceptual reference points analysed, according to a chronological perspective that aims at enlightening associated problematics. This chronological arrangement may induce the conclusion that each problem relates to a given period exclusively, but that is not the case. They may be felt in the remaining periods, but they are simply given less importance in the approaches analysed.

Table 24.1. Reference display of the analysis of in-service teacher education

Rationalities	Disciplines/Subject areas	Training instruments	Training models
Cognitive-instrumental Communicational-transformative Socio-critical Composite	Pedagogy Psychology School administration Sociology Curriculum development Evaluation	Reflection Research Project work Teamwork Ability to work with colleagues Context of practical teaching	Directed towards research and reflection Centred on analysis

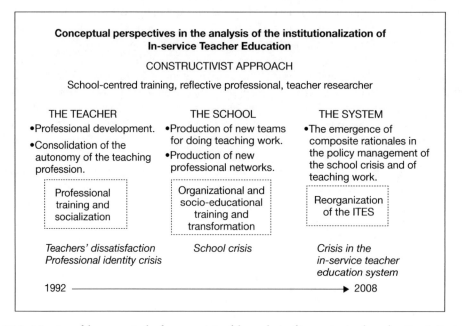

Fig. 24.1. Mapping of the conceptual reference points of the analysis of in-service teacher education in Portugal

Critical Perspective and Narrativity of Teacher Education: Research, Reflection and Emancipated/Emancipatory Identities

Although resulting from different projects, the data gathered in this paper and their articulation leads to relevant considerations regarding teacher education. Generally speaking, in the field of teacher education, critical theory linked to the Frankfurt School has a more significant impact on scientific research and especially through the work of Habermas. In the remaining corpus analysed its presence is insignificant. Critical pedagogy also emerges more strongly in scientific research and through the works of Paulo Freire and Henry Giroux. However, when a broader theoretical and epistemological perspective is taken into account, other references are found along with evidence of a very significant critical perspective with impact on conceptions of professional development of teachers, with emphasis on the analysis of continuing teacher education, but also with relevance for initial teacher education curricula.

Another important point is the association between critical theory/critical pedagogy and the option for a qualitative methodology in education, namely through action research, case study and narrative approaches. Postulating an interpretative paradigm and understanding of reality, this methodology introduces a rupture with the nomological and monolithic perspective of modern positivist science. The specificity of a qualitative research is on the shared and instrumented search for the meaning of human action, oriented towards the apprehension of heterogeneous systems of meaning attribution and discursive interpretation. In this context, action-research techniques enhance the intentionality of transformation and change, scientifically grounded. Conceptions pertaining to critical theory/critical pedagogy converge into the epistemological, theoretical, and ethical frame of reference of a qualitative approach to education, which explains, thus, the association established and elucidated in this paper. It is also in the field of education research that the hybridity of critical and post-critical theories is most felt and there are a substantial number of authors who, although working within the grounds of theoretical critical analysis, differ significantly from the perspective of the Frankfurt School.

Perceived through its hybridity, a critical approach to teacher education leads to the identification of narratives about School, the teaching profession and teacher education in itself that may have some influence on processes, actions and the construction of identities. Narratives are public or private stories with which we can relate and which we integrate in our perception and cognition of the world, affecting our interpretation of events and social relations and guiding our actions and attitudes. In this paper, I have identified conceptions revealing narratives about a communicative, multicultural, emancipatory, democratic and just School, and about a reflective, analytical, critical, intellectual, transformer, ethically-driven, communicative and in permanent development teacher. Initial teacher education and continuing teacher education are fundamental in building professional identities and fostering professional development, but they have their own specificities. The conceptions identified in the curriculum of initial teacher education reveal narratives of an investigative paradigm of training (cf. Zeichner 1993). Indeed, the structure of the curriculum promotes inquiry on social institutional contexts and focuses politico-social awareness and on research, reflection and critical analysis as a professional epistemology, giving a prominent place to the theory-practice relationship.

In continuing teacher education, the conceptions related to a critical theoretical perspective suggest narratives of a transformational paradigm centred in the world of school life and in a new epistemology of professional practice. This new epistemology draws on collaborative research and critical reflection as shared forms of educational innovation and cognitive construction of individual and collective professional action, according to a praxiological and communicative perspective (in Habermasian terms 1987).

Final Considerations or How Can Teacher Education Make a Difference?

Without wishing to disregard the importance of specific disciplinary and didactic knowledge pertaining to different types of professional teaching, levels of education and educational disciplines, it is important to emphasise that the cognitive-instrumental rationalities and techniques employed in teacher education as a whole have not been able to promote a construction of professional identities adjusted to the current times of crisis and decline of School. Indeed, the School crisis is associated with the crisis of Western models of development and the collapse of the European social model that underlie the construction of the Democratic School, intensifying the difficulty in finding ethical references to emancipatory and solidarity-driven educational action. In Portugal, the effects of this crisis disturb the teachers' work and the education of children and young people, triggering the promotion of an exaggerated individualism and the establishment, in education and in the teaching profession, of a competitive socio-economic rationality and logic; and worsening social inequalities and social exclusion intrinsically compromised in School's action.

It is in this context of disruption of the School's ethical and social missions that critical theories can rediscover their primary aim in teacher education, both through the construction of scientific objects oriented towards an epistemology of listening and meaning (Berger 1992) and through their communicative, praxiological and socio-critical nature.

Multiple conflicting and competing principles legitimising school justice and educational forms of organisation cohabitate in School today (Derouet 1992), each claiming for itself the legitimacy of their educational ethics and social practical reason. On the other hand, the globalisation of neoliberal ideology has imposed an educational rhetoric that should be deconstructed.

Currently, the conceptual narratives on a communicative, multicultural, emancipatory and just School identified in critical theory approaches are fundamental to the School's social legitimation, but also, and above all, to its social (re)construction according to a communicative rationality and ethical and political awareness of the subjective and social effects of schooling (cf. Pereira 2011). Teacher education plays an irreplaceable role in this social (re)construction and so does critical theory (or theories), in its hybridity with post-critical (or neo-critical) theories.

Initial teacher education is responsible for primary professional socialisation and for the construction of basic professional identities (cf. Dubar 1996). The educational research paradigm studied in this paper seems to offer the possibility of creating a reflective and critical theory-practice relationship in favour of the construction of basic professional identities, cognitively informed about school reality and ethically sensitive to the implication of this reality in the lives of children, young people and their families. Informed by a critical, communicative and hermeneutical rationality, research may provide the necessary cognitive mediation to overcome reality shock in the beginning of a teaching career (cf. Korthagen 2010), and provide support to a professional development actively involved in the social (re)construction of a School more committed to social justice. Nevertheless, the promotion of social justice in School is not limited to a greater awareness of the causes of its devaluation in school life and in the school's institutional project. Indeed, it requires professional skills to contextualise school knowledge and build pedagogical devices as well as social and institutional conditions adapted to each particular milieu in order to guarantee that all children and young people have access to the cultural assets offered by School, regardless of their social, cultural, and ethnic origin or any other characteristic that makes them different and potentially subject to discrimination (cf. Pereira 2013b). Continuing teacher education is vital in this process.

The transformational paradigm centred in the world of school life and in a new epistemology of professional practice that has been identified as the conceptual narrative of critical theories can create the necessary conditions to devise new educational and professional systems and to bring change to organisational contexts and work situations. Reflective and research-driven practice may provide teachers with knowledge about the school's community (including other teachers, students, their families, and themselves) as well as knowledge about the numerous (ethical, social and political) implications of education, encouraging, therefore, a prudent professional attitude regarding their everyday decision-making process. Understood in a complex and plural, subjective and intersubjective intelligibility, educational action is, together with communicative action, a web of times and places that enables the "talk where meaning is built" (Hameline 1991: 56, my translation) and where action and Institution are simultaneously reconstructed.

Furthermore, School cannot overlook more general principles that provide its social legitimacy. The agreements reached within the dynamics of School's social reconstruction demand a broader discussion on the local common good and its relationship with universal principles for the creation of a fairer society. As Derouet observes, the failure of the equal opportunities model turned School into the basic unit of "work in the reconstruction of the social place in education" (1992: 239, my translation). To carry out this work, School must be seen as a "political small town" where "conflicting demands" are arbitrated according to the adequacy of educational principles to real situations, that is, "a school, in many records, justified" (*ibid.*: 281, my translation) by local needs, but without losing sight of global concerns. It requires a theoretical effort to produce, amidst a diversity of possibilities, a broader framework to identify the principles that are at stake and locate them in relation to each other, understanding "that each offers a fulcrum to move from the particular to the general, from everyday life to History and from local to national" (*ibid.*, my translation). This paper and the analysis here presented aimed at illustrating the essential role of critical theories applied to teaching education in this complex process of School (re)construction.

Notes

1. In 40 years of democracy, the academic qualification of the teachers of the 1st cycle of basic education passed from mid-level (that is, 11 years of schooling) to higher level, Masters (that is, 17 years of schooling).
2. Until 1974, only the courses for teachers of the 1st cycle of basic education and physical education integrated a component of professionalization.
3. This number does not correspond, however, to the total of dissertations and theses held in the country for not all of them are available in the repository.
4. Mentioned in more than one subject.
5. Table 1 and Figure 1 can be found in Pereira (2013a).
6. 'Evaluation of the effects of continuing teacher education in Portugal,' developed by a research team from the Faculty of Psychology and Education Sciences of the University of Porto, funded by the Portuguese Ministry of Education.

References

Berger, G. (1992). A investigação em educação: modelos sócio-epistemológicos e inserção institucional. *Revista de Psicologia e de Ciências da Educação*, 3/4, 23–6.
Derouet, J.-L. (1992). *École et justice*. Paris: Métailié.
Dubar, C. (1996). *La Socialisation: Construction des identités sociales & professionnelles*. Paris: Armand Colin.
Dubet, F. (2002). *Le déclin de l'institution*. Paris: Seuil.
Giddens, A. (1997). *Modernidade e identidade pessoal*. Oeiras: Celta.
Habermas, J. (1987). *Théorie de l'agir communicationnel (I et II)*. Paris: Fayard.
Hameline, Daniel (1991). O educador e a acção sensata. In A. Nóvoa, A. (Org.). *Profissão Professor* (33–60). Porto: Porto Editora.
Korthagen, F. (2010). 'Situated Learning Theory and the Pedagogy of Teacher Education: Towards an Integrative View of Teacher Behavior and Teacher Learning.' *Teaching and Teacher Education* 26: 98–106.
Lopes, A. C. (2013). Teorias Pós-críticas, Política e Currículo. *Educação, Sociedade e Culturas, no 39*, 7–23.

Lopes, M. A. et al. (2011). *Formação Contínua de Professores 1992–2007. Contributos de investigação para uma apreciação retrospectiva.* Porto: Livpsic/Conselho Científico Pedagógico da Formação Contínua.

Morrow, R., e Torres, C. A. (1998). Jürgen Habermas, Paulo Freire e a Pedagogia Crítica: novas orientações para a educação comparada. *Educação Sociedade e Culturas, 10, 123–55.*

Nóvoa, A. (Org.) (1991). *Formação Contínua de Professores: realidades e perspetivas.* Aveiro: Universidade de Aveiro.

Pereira, F. (2011). 'In-Service Teacher Education and Scholar Innovation: The Semantics of Action and Reflection on Action as a Mediation Device.' *Australian Journal of Teacher Education, 36*(11), article 3, 33–50.

Pereira, F. (2013a). 'Concepts, Policies and Practices of Teacher Education: An Analysis of Studies on Teacher Education in Portugal.' *Journal of Education for Teaching: International Research and Pedagogy, 39*(5), 474–91.

Pereira, F. (2013b). 'Initial Teacher Education for Social Justice and Teaching Work in Urban Schools: An (Im)Pertinent Reflection.' *Alberta Journal of Educational Research, 59*(2), summer, 162–80.

Ruz, J. (1984). Teoria Crítica e Educação. *Perspectiva,* Florianópolis, 1(3), 9–50, jul/dec.

Santos, B. de S. (1999). Porque é tão difícil construir uma teoria crítica? *Revista Crítica de Ciências Sociais, no 54 197–215.*

Santos, S. M. (2009). *Percurso da formação contínua de professores: Um olhar analítico e prospectivo.* Braga: Conselho Científico-Pedagógico da Formação Contínua.

Webb, T. Gulson, K., e Pitton, V. (2014). 'The Neo-Liberal Education Policies of Epimeleia Heautou: Caring for the Self in School Markets.' *Discourse: Studies in the Cultural Politics of Education, 35:1,* 31–44.

25
Striving for a Better World
Lessons from Freire in Grenada, Jamaica and Australia

Anne Hickling-Hudson

GRENADA: Dialogic Education for Teachers

In 1980, Paulo Freire was invited to run a two-week teacher education workshop with 50 teachers on the Caribbean island of Grenada. It was a unique setting in that it was not a workshop to train adult literacy facilitators, which was usually Freire's main sphere of interest. Instead, it was a professional development workshop for teachers and a few community workers. For me, it provided "insider" light not only on the critical praxis core of Freire's pedagogy, but also on its social implications. The political context of the workshop was the end of the first year of the popular revolutionary regime led by Maurice Bishop and his colleagues in the New Jewel Movement (NJM).[1] It was a time of new possibilities. A corrupt former regime had been overthrown and the new, youthful and idealistic leaders of the revolution set out a vision that would decolonise Grenada, not only in the sense of modernisation, but also in the sense of a radical, socialist-oriented rethinking and restructuring of relationships. Grenada, a small society of just over 100,000 people, had obtained independence from Britain in 1976, a decade or more after independence had been won by some of the other, larger societies of the Caribbean. The socio-economic structure was still colonial, characterised by poverty for the majority, social division and a dependent economy. In the four and a half years of the revolution, the People's Revolutionary Government (PRG) laid foundations for social transformation. Moving towards decolonising and postcolonial goals included improving the economic structure, in this case with an expanded role for the public sector, enhanced opportunities for the dominant private sector, and a small new sector comprising economic cooperatives. The country was galvanised into becoming involved in planning and implementing many new projects in agriculture, small business and education (see Hickling-Hudson 1995, 2012).

Grenadians saw the education and upgrading of teachers as an important method of urging along change. Many of the teachers were an enthusiastic part of the revolution. In the 18 months before Freire arrived, they had met in workshops to discuss their role as change agents, and it was in these workshops that they had emphasised the necessity of adopting a work-study concept[2] in education. The work-study approach was to counter the dysfunctional educational system left by British colonialism. As in other British colonies, high-status learning in elite schools was theoretical, divorced from practical matters and Anglocentric, while education for the masses was vocational in emphasis, minimalist, and divorced from theory.[3] How would teachers re-frame education for the new society in a manner that would see practical work informing study and vice versa? The Freire seminar was intended to give them a forum to sort out their many questions and work out a strategy for changing education.

The seminar group consisted of 51 participants (47 Grenadian teachers and 4 agricultural officers), together with Paulo Freire and his team of 4 facilitators. As a Caribbean teacher-educator who had also had some experience in non-formal adult education, I was invited by the Grenadian PRG to be one of these facilitators. I was the only woman and the only Caribbean native English-speaker in Freire's team.[4] Our task was to help participants consider how to develop a model or models of "work-study" that would pursue the vision of the Revolution to develop the society by forging strong and mutually enriching links between school and community. Together with the officers of Grenada's Ministry of Education, I expected that the seminar would be structured around a timetable which included lectures, discussion groups and prepared readings. However, this did not accord with the dialogic style of Freirean pedagogy. Neither timetable nor readings were provided, because Freire wanted the group to draw on their own mental and cultural knowledge in discussing the problems of education and working out solutions and alternatives.

Freire organised the 51 participants into five study circles which engaged in collaborative learning. Each circle had a member of the teaching team as a facilitator. The study circles, including the facilitators, discussed topics during the mornings. Each afternoon the whole group met for plenary discussion and sharing, when the facilitators added more comments and questions. Extensive notes were made of the discussions, both by the learners and by the facilitators. Contrary to my misgivings, this dialogic structure did not imply lack of preparation on the part of the facilitators. Before the seminar started we spent a few days preparing for it by visiting workplaces and institutions, talking with personnel, and studying the nature of the educational and social changes that were taking place in Grenada. Each day after the seminar, we met and prepared for the next day by discussing topics which had been raised and which were likely to be discussed on the following day (see Hickling-Hudson 1988, pp. 15–16). We were building up a picture of the local circumstances, contextualising this with knowledge from our rich and varied experience as educators in different settings, and expanding our knowledge and understanding by the daily discussions and debates with the Grenadian teachers.

As facilitators, we utilised guiding questions to orient the thoughts of participants towards the goal of analysing the changes needed in the education system. Our guiding questions were along the lines Freire remembers in his book *Pedagogy of Hope* (1995), asking the study circle members to describe the schools in which they taught, the best and worst aspects of the relationships between teachers and students, and what they thought was good or bad "about a rural school in whose programmatic content there is nothing, or almost nothing, about rural life?" (Freire 1995, pp. 173–74.) Once the groups started to talk, our responses helped to deepen the dialogue. At first they saw work-study as the timetabling of practical subjects into the curriculum – agriculture, handicraft, school games, festivals. The facilitators asked them to diagnose the deeper meanings of concepts of work, study, community, programme and approach. After intense discussion both in small groups and plenary sessions, they decided to abandon the concept of a work-study programme, and replace it with that of a more holistic work-study *approach*. An approach did not consist of discrete subjects. An approach was a philosophy that would pervade the whole learning experience of school and community. The production goals and projects of the revolution would be the basis of the work-study approach.

In Freirean terms, the learners were naming their world and interrogating their reality. In the cycle of communications praxis they sought solutions to the problems they raised, discussed how the solutions would be tested, shared ideas in the plenary group, modified their ideas and deepened them through further dialogue each day. In the culminating activity of the workshop, the teachers co-wrote and produced a manuscript[5] of their deliberations, describing how their thinking had developed in setting out a concept of work-study for Grenada's schools and communities.

Freire's belief, shared with us at several points of the workshop, was that "The thinking subject cannot think alone [...] it is the 'We think' that establishes the 'I think' and not vice versa."

Evaluation of the discussion is jointly pursued, as the learners deepen the historical context of their knowledge, and as they think about their thinking. The process leads people towards conscientisation, or a state of being able to engage in an informed critique of their world, which raises political literacy. This can enhance the confidence that is a step towards collectively challenging the status quo to bring about transformative action "to change the present to create the future" (Hickling-Hudson 1988, pp. 14–15).

Another important principle that Freire shared with the workshop participants is that a group needs a theory of transformative action, in order to move from critically analysing a situation to envisaging how to change it. The discussion groups reorganised themselves into workshops, and each of these produced a booklet on the goals, practice and methods of the work-study approach, based on their deliberations so far. This work took them two days. Then a committee was elected to combine the five booklets into one. The final manuscript included: a report on the deliberations of the seminar, a theoretical explanation of work-study and its objectives, illustrations of procedure and techniques for facilitators assisting development projects in local communities. It ended with a hypothetical illustration of a facilitator's work in a rural community. The group had an anxious discussion about where the school and its students would fit into the change process. Then someone made the point that "The children live in the same reality as their parents. We deal with each at their particular stage." Children in school and parents in the community would be constantly interacting, at their own levels, in the adventure of practising social change as well as learning about it.

The entire group – participants and facilitators – had experienced a process of conscientisation (Hickling-Hudson 1988, p. 23). This meant that we had moved slowly towards an informed, analytical articulation of the challenges for a decolonising Grenada, and of the possibilities of change. The workshop's production of the booklet represented the first stage of transformative action. The next stage should have been for the group to organise its members to carry the new approach into their communities and implement it there – to take it into the public sphere.

But this was not exactly what happened. The seminar group did not stay together as a collective, since many of them moved on to other careers or study programmes. Therefore, they could not work together to implement and monitor the changes they had envisioned in the workshop (see Hickling-Hudson 1988). Yet, although most of the participants were not in a position to carry out, as an activist collective, the process of school-community educational change in the manner envisaged in the workshop, they undoubtedly helped to contribute to change in education. The Freirean learning process influenced the thinking and orientation of the participants and all the facilitators, many of whom devoted their careers to working for radical reform in educational as well as other social settings.

The educational programmes of the four and a half years of the revolution (both before and after the Freire workshop) had a firmly postcolonial ethos that resonated with the philosophy and teaching of Freire and the broader tradition of socialist- oriented popular democracy. The revolutionary leaders followed policies which freed people's voices to articulate social concerns, draw on their cultural roots and collectively design local problem-solving strategies (see Hickling-Hudson 2013a). In the education system, the reforms introduced included the upgrading of the most neglected schools, the training of teachers, and preparation for taking school-leaving examinations set by the Caribbean Examinations Council rather than British examination syndicates (see Hickling-Hudson 2012). The pedagogy of the adult literacy programme in the new Centre for Popular Education (CPE) was based on pre-designed textbooks or reading primers, which is not a method advocated by Freire (Walker 1980). However, a pedagogy based on primers was what was possible at the time, as few of the volunteer literacy teachers could have carried out a fully dialogical teaching programme along Freirean lines.[6] The Grenadian adult literacy primers were part of the broader programme of the CPE, which was an ambitious and innovative structure designed to suit the circumstances of the society (see Hickling-Hudson 1988, 2013a).

The Freire workshop, in my view, made a unique contribution to Grenada's struggles for a better society. It was an example of an interactive and affirming pedagogical model that was hitherto little known, or perhaps even completely unknown, to educators from the English-speaking Caribbean. The approach demonstrated to more than fifty Caribbean participants the effectiveness of dialogic and interactive pedagogy in the search for informed practical strategies that would move marginalised communities forward.

The Grenada revolution achieved four and a half successful years of important, positive change in many key areas of the economy, society and education system. But because of the inadequacies of its model of political organisation, the NJM, the party of the revolution, was unable to manage internal conflict and degenerated into fighting amongst party members in what Joseph Ewart Layne (2014, p. 186) describes as a "lose–lose situation". This led to events that culminated in horrific violence and killings of leaders and members. It exposed the society to the U.S. invasion in October 1983, the killing by invading forces of a number of Grenadians, the imprisonment for two decades of many of the political leaders, and the reversal of many of the social changes put in place by the revolution (see Ambursley and Dunkerley 1984; Payne et al. 1984; Lewis 1987, chapter 7; Thorndike 1991; Henry 1991; Bigelow 2013). Yet, some of the educational changes endured, and have provided the basis for people to continue striving for a better society (Hickling-Hudson 2012).

JAMAICA: Theatre Arts Pedagogy

A few years after the U.S. invasion of Grenada, my trajectory as an educator took me to Australia, where I continued my career in teacher education and where, in 1995, I completed a doctoral dissertation on Grenada's adult education programme. Continuing my research focus on adult education, I became interested in the work of the Area Youth Foundation (AYF) in Jamaica.[7] The AYF works with young adults from marginalised communities of Kingston, providing young people from some of the most neglected and disadvantaged sections of Kingston with new opportunities, and putting them on a path that in many cases leads to skilled and creative careers. Across seventeen years, the programme has involved over 1,000 young people. What particularly interested me was not only the Freirean pedagogy consciously used in this project, but also the way in which the effectiveness of this pedagogical approach was deepened by combining it with the transformative power of the creative arts. This is expressed in an interactive dramatic mode drawing on the work of Augusto Boal among other drama educators. As I have argued in an article providing a detailed analysis of the AYF (Hickling-Hudson 2013b), this pedagogical model has achieved significant success in strengthening the participants in their struggles to improve their own and their society's circumstances.

The genesis of the AYF project was the decision of "The Company", an innovative amateur theatre group led by dramatist and cultural activist Sheila Graham, to experiment with using drama-in-education methods to help challenge the damaging effects of political conflict on the lives of young people (see Graham 2007). In interviews that I carried out with Graham over a ten-year period (2003–2013), and in observations, with her permission, of AYF workshops on occasional visits to Jamaica, I learnt how the group developed and operated. Graham explained its genesis: "Our overall goal was to give youths in rival zones of the city an opportunity to work together—to create understanding across chasms of misunderstanding that were literally deadly: cross the street and you could be dead" (interview with S. Graham, 2003). This refers to the situation of warring two-party politics that was blighting the lives of many people in Jamaica, particularly those from areas of the society which are socially and economically disadvantaged (Levy 2009). The young people in the AYF project come from the section of the society affected by problems such as a 20.1 per cent illiteracy rate (JFLL 2008), a high unemployment rate of 14.2 per cent in 2012, a high poverty rate, a high rate of crime, and a high rate of homicide, particularly in poorer communities. Many of these problems are exacerbated by a low rate of educational success for the majority of students in the island's socially stratified school system (see Hickling-Hudson 2013b, pp. 16, 30).

Educated Jamaicans from professional backgrounds and a socially influential section of the society crossed the social class divide to work in this project with youths from disadvantaged Jamaican communities in a sustained and systematic way. The founders and leaders of the AYF, Sheila Graham and her colleagues Winston Bell and Owen Ellis, combine learner-centred pedagogy with the creative arts.

The bedrock of all of the arts-based work in the AYF is the pedagogical process that helps the young people to develop their life skills and their educational competence. The interaction between learners and teachers in AYF workshops vividly illustrates topics from Paulo Freire's *Pedagogy of the Oppressed* (1972). It is based on a view of knowledge as a process of critical praxis, made and remade after reflection of themes critical to the lives of learners. The AYF participants are organised into Freirean-style "culture circles" engaging in intense dialogue and discussion about the issues that matter to them. This is followed by extended learning that builds on the discussion. The young people move on from their dialogic learning to take on the intense learning journey of expressing their newly developed insights in the form of drama, music, film, visual art and print text. Their dramatic expression is influenced by the approach taken by the Brazilian dramatist, Augusto Boal, who shaped a method that gave creative voice to Freire's dialogical pedagogy and political philosophy. In this technique, expressed in his book *Theatre of the Oppressed* (Boal 1993), actors, during the course of the play, invite audiences to engage directly with them in representing or finding solutions to the problems being acted out on stage. Boal's methods in turn influenced the technique of process-drama, an interactive, improvisational, problem-posing drama teaching method now utilised by many drama educators (see O'Neill 1995, Neelands and Goode 2000). It is the process-drama method of exploring a situation or theme through unscripted drama and reflection-in-action that is utilised in AYF pedagogy. The AYF teaching team helps the young people to articulate their own experiences and turn these into creative works. In the process, the youths encounter many aspects of the education that they have missed. In spite of the non-formal setting of the AYF, there is a carefully structured curriculum, taught by the AYF leader plus at least two additional tutors and regular guest speakers who extend knowledge of particular topics. Working through the curriculum takes approxi- mately nine months, but some members stay on indefinitely as AYF associates, who help when needed as facilitators or assistants in artistic productions. The topics centre around issues such as sexuality, parenting and family life, gender and group relations, conflict resolution, psychology and the development of Jamaica and its social structure and tensions.

AYF leader Sheila Graham expresses the teaching/learning significance of the process in this way:

> The discussions with the participants give us the basis for teaching and working with them. We now know who they are, what they are thinking, what is important to them. Everything flows from that. Our building blocks are who they are and what they already know. Everything they create comes out of this– they write a poem, create a dance, or a song, or do a small skit.[8] Then we can further develop the storyline from that material. It can even become a musical stage show that develops as we rehearse it. The group talks about the story expressed in the skit, poem or song they created. Who is the hero? The protagonist and antagonist? What are some of the ways in which it could end? We, the facilitators, become directors who will make it work as a work of art. We might say: that piece doesn't work there, let's try it somewhere else.
>
> (2012 interview with S. Graham)

The four outcomes briefly described below particularly illustrate the effectiveness of the work of the AYF teaching team in developing the education, social understanding, practical skills and career-orientation of the young AYF members.

The design and staging of musical theatre shows

The first musical theatre show created by the group was *Border Connection*. This musical revue became so popular that it was performed for several years in communities around Jamaica, attracting large audiences as well as requests for it to be performed again and again. The theme of *Border Connection* addressed the violence and social decay of neglected communities, asking, in the first half: "How we come to this?" The second half of the revue projected positive solutions: "Yes, there is better way".

Family, another musical theatre production written and staged by the group, emerged from workshop sessions in which the young people explored the intimate side of what happens at home. This opened social sores, such as lack of love and care, and social as well as sexual abuse. The AYF youths became so recognised for staging challenging and thought-provoking performances that they received several invitations to travel and perform overseas. They developed *Border Connection* into another version of a musical revue that they called *Link Up*, maintaining and extending the theme of healing the divisions between hostile local communities. The AYF performed *Link Up* to popular acclaim and sold-out houses in several locations in England and Italy.

The design and production of a series of photo-novella booklets

In the *All in Pictures* project, group members produce stories in a series of "photo- novella" booklets in comic-book style about issues that deeply concern young people (HIV awareness, unemployment, violence, drug abuse and child abuse). The AYF members are taught the skills of constructing and writing stories – learning about plot, protagonist, antagonist, problem, resolution, conclusion. They enact dramatic improvisations on the topics that they select, design costumes and sets, act out and photograph each scene for the booklets, select photos and up-link them into a computer graphics programme, write conversation "bubbles" in a combination of Jamaican Creole and Standard English, edit the booklets for final production, publish and finally market them. The teaching/learning process involved in producing these photo-novellas is as intense as that involved in developing musical theatre shows. The comic books were self-published by AYF in Kingston in 2005. They were entitled: *Di Crack and Di Whip, Di Test of Love, Dun Di War* and *No Vacancy*.

The involvement of AYF members as apprentices and assistants in theatre and media work

Some AYF members have worked as apprentices and assistants on film sets such as with the film *Third World Cop*.[9] Some of them made video productions of local docu-dramas and documentaries. Their music videos, made in-house with songs of their own creation, have been played on TV and cinema screens, and two of them have been used in national peace-building public education campaigns. This led the young people to develop skills and competence as film and media production assistants in the entertainment industry. Several of them have progressed to obtaining jobs in these fields.

The contribution of AYF members to working with troubled communities in peace-building efforts

An important part of the work of the AYF has been to contribute to peace-building in troubled communities. It organised "Peace Boat",[10] an unprecedented community sports and cultural celebration which brought hostile communities together after violent local elections in 2003, and initiated collective mural creations in some of these communities. The lives of the AYF learners are stabilised through the facilitators' skilful use of Freirean-style pedagogy in the culture circle, which enables them to interrogate their reality. Their lives are also transformed – not only individually through the new career-oriented skills and attitudes that are nurtured by their work in the AYF, but also collectively through their work in the public sphere. These young people have helped to create new community cultures in a variety of ways. Their music-theatre performances have raised awareness of their deep-seated longing for peace and equity, their photo-novellas have sparked debate of pressing social issues among adolescent groups, and their artistic mural projects and social "Peace Boat" activities have contributed to healing, peace and friendships within warring communities. Some of them are motivated to pursue their formal school and post- school education, and many are now working in skilled, influential and satisfying careers (see Graham 2007, Hickling-Hudson 2013b).

The success of the work of AYF members contrasts with the marginalisation they suffered while growing up in divided and troubled inner city communities. The topic "transforming lives" (Yard Edge blog 2008) relates aptly to the lives of many of them. For young adults who have been disadvantaged by substandard schooling, the powerful learning experiences provided by the AYF help them to have a chance of becoming successful and effective, not only in their careers and social relationships, but also in their ability to challenge and change entrenched public injustices, as is suggested by their success in reducing antagonism and violence among different community groups.

AUSTRALIA: Curriculum Development in an Indigenous Community

My work as a teacher-educator in Australia brought me into contact with a sphere of knowledge that I had never before encountered, that of issues in the education of Indigenous "First Peoples". From the perspective of my experience in radical, de-colonising education in the Caribbean, it seemed to me that one of the most intractable problems in the education provided for Indigenous people in Australia was the imposition by the dominant Anglo-Australian majority of neo-colonial norms and expectations. What I have seen and read of the education provided by Anglo-Australia for Aboriginal and Torres Strait Island students confirms my view that it is usually Anglocentric in content, and assimilatory rather than cross-cultural in ethos (see Hickling-Hudson and Ahlquist 2003 and 2004). Despite much rhetoric about the need for change, it appears to be extremely difficult for meaningful change to take place.

In this example of educational work with radical potential for changing the public sphere, my particular interest lies in the cultural significance of the creation of an innovative programme of early literacy materials, the *Honey Ant Readers*, within an Indigenous school-community partnership at the Yipirinya School in Alice Springs, a town in Australia's Northern Territory. I have selected it as an example of curriculum development which exemplifies Freirean principles, since it utilises a method of conscientisation, co-learning, co-development of the materials, and praxis in terms of how they are tried out and improved. The potentially powerful impact of this project is that it is an example of one means of achieving culturally authentic Indigenous educational progress in Australian society.

The Yipirinya School is independent, not in the sense that parents pay fees, but in that it is controlled by an independent board of Elders. The school was founded in 1979 on the initiative of the Indigenous Elders of the camps on the margins of Alice Springs, a site in which Indigenous people and families live in a situation of socio-economic disadvantage. The school's website explains that Elders struggled to establish it, in the face of resistance, as "a school where Indigenous Languages and Culture were prominent, where there was a strong Aboriginal presence and where their children felt comfortable". Eventually the school was given government support, including buildings, teachers and resources.[11]

Margaret James, a lecturer in Education, with a background in linguistics, at an Indigenous tertiary institution in Australia, works with Aboriginal Elders as well as with Aboriginal teachers and teacher aides to develop the *Honey Ant Readers* to promote literacy. This project is implemented both inside and outside of the Yipirinya school. The school curriculum is a nurturing setting that promotes bi- lingual and bi-cultural education, and provides tuition in English as well as in four Aboriginal languages. The *Honey Ant Readers* literacy team, coordinated by Margaret James, develops texts – reading primers – which utilise a vocabulary based on the everyday life experiences and cultural context of the school and its community. The language style is Aboriginal English. The children relate well to this material, as they learn through the concepts surrounding them and the stories that are familiar.

In this project, James' work with Aboriginal Elders is central in her co- development of material for the *Honey Ant Readers*. In discussion circles, she describes to the Elders how the reading primers utilise stories to develop early literacy, and asks them to decide what stories they would like to tell and what concepts they would like to be emphasised in the readers. Then the Elders lead the discussion. She stresses that she never takes control of their decisions. In her words: "I don't argue with their decisions. If they want a story used in the readers, I use it. You'll notice *Honey Ant Reader*[12] isn't what a mainstream teacher would normally use, but they want me to, and the children and adults love it" (interview with M. James, 17 June 2013).

Honey Ant Reader No. 14 is indeed a surprise to an educator used to safer stories in early-reading primers. It is called "A Big Man Grabs Sister", and words and pictures recount the tale of how a man stalked two young sisters as they went hunting for goanna and honey ants, some distance from their family camp. When night came and both sisters slept under a mulga tree, the man grabbed Big Sister and carried her away. When Little Sister woke up, she realised what had happened from looking at the tracks in the desert sands, and ran back to the family to raise the alarm. The family went searching for Big Sister, and eventually rescued her from the man's camp while he was out hunting. They walked for a whole day to set up their camp at a new spot, far away from the man who had taken Big Sister, and warned the sisters never to get separated from each other while they were hunting. Several of the *Honey Ant Readers* portray equally dramatic tales, for example: No. 12 "Drowned Him, Drowned Him", and No. 13 "Gotta Get the Baby". The very earliest readers use familiar words and pictures in stories such as "Stop the Bus", "Wet Baby", "Nana Dig in Red Sand", and "Honey Ants Yum".

After recording the stories told by the Elders, Margaret James designs the readers so that they present these stories in a way that gradually develops ten levels of reading competence suitable for the first two or three years of school. The bright illustrations of the stories add to the Indigenous contextualisation and attractiveness of the text.[13] The words of the stories relate to a specific word list for each reading level. Different and new sounds and concepts, as well as mathematics and music activities are systematically introduced. Numbers and counting games are incor- porated in some of the stories. For example, in the tale of "A Big Man Grabs Sister", the sisters find honey ants after they have walked a long way, and dig up 14 honey ants to put on the sand in their *coolamons* [bowls carved out of wood], "7 for big sister and 7 for little sister (7 ? 7 = 14)" (page 7). Singing, too, is incorporated into this reader, in that when the sisters continue next morning to look for honey ants, they sing a tune of "Dig for honey ants" to music written in staves, clefs and notes in the text (page 8). Notated songs and rhymes are included in all of the books, as they can be effectively used to teach Standard English and reinforce the four macro skills of language learning: reading, writing, speaking and listening. The songs are part of a series of learning activities that include word and number games and puzzles relating to the particular reader.

In 2013, this literacy method was evaluated as being very successful by a team of independent university evaluators. Citing comments from their impact evaluation report (Broughton and Gahan 2013), I will skip the technical points about literacy method (phonics, phonemes, decoding, encoding etc.), focusing instead on their cultural points. These relate to my observation that the project resonates with Freirean-style pedagogy in its method of drawing on and enhancing the cultural consciousness and articulateness of all the project participants. The evaluators assessed the *Honey Ant Readers* as having a high level of cultural relevance. They observed the children responding with excitement and enthusiasm to the stories, relating to their cultural and family significance. They noted the examples of children's progress in literacy learning. Particularly important are the points made by the evaluators about the language of the readers, and the connections that the reading project facilitates between school and community.

The evaluators state that "The *Honey Ant Readers* create a symbolic bridge between […] home and school languages" (ibid., p. 13). The vital importance of this language strategy must be understood in a context of a fierce debate on language teaching methods for Australian Indigenous children in communities where English is not the first language. The old view is that children should be immersed in Standard English from their earliest years, even those who do not speak it at home. Bilingual learning is either not catered for, or given a subordinate role. The *Honey Ant Readers* take a different approach. They aim to meet the needs of "Aboriginal children who speak multiple languages and Aboriginal English, but [who] may not be adept in Standard Australian English" (ibid., p. 15). Thus, they make distinctive use of:

1. "Aboriginal English that matches children's oral language, thus validating their home culture and language and facilitating the earliest stages of reading";
2. "Gradual progressions from Aboriginal English to Standard Australian English [SAE], providing a learning pathway towards reading a wider range of texts in SAE, essential for ongoing learning at school"; and
3. "Culturally relevant illustrations reflecting the environments of children's lives; inviting engagement; encouraging prediction of the written text; supporting comprehension and providing motivation for reading."

(ibid., p. 3)

An important feature is that Readers are being translated into Aboriginal languages to meet the desire of Indigenous people to have children learn to read their own languages. In the 3rd edition, Books 1 to 3 have been translated into 6 Aboriginal languages: Luritja, Western Arrente, Central Arrente, Warlpiri, Pitjantjatjara and Yakunytjatjara.[13] The use of Aboriginal English and the translation into Aboriginal languages in these books is of special significance in Australia, where the majority of basal texts available in schools fail to recognise and represent the culture of Indigenous learners. When texts devalue, distort or render invisible the Indigenous world, this can generate the impression that reading is "a ritual practice of the school that has no pleasurable or communicative function" (Rose et al., 1999, p.29). In the bi-dialectical approach of the *Honey Ant Readers*, learning in the home language makes learning to read more accessible, values home culture, and also offers a bridge to reading in the official language, Standard Australian English. When learners master reading in one dialect or language, they can transfer their reading skills to reading in other dialects and languages (see Bialystok 1991, Baker 1993). By the 20th *Honey Ant Reader*, learners are expected to be able to navigate the textual conventions of Standard Australian English. Margaret James points out that

The books build in vocabulary and complexity of words, pictures (from simple, to complex multi-actor events) and grammar as they scaffold learners from AE (Australian English) to SAE (Standard Australian English). Over 650 words are progressively introduced into the series, repeated frequently. [...]These words are listed at the back of each reader for review [...] In the *HARs* scaffolding takes the form of supporting learners along a spectrum of language structures from AE structures towards SAE academic discourse required for, and rewarded by, schooling.

(James 2014, p. 84)

The second area of cultural significance is that the *Honey Ants* project is fostering significant interaction between the school and its community.

The *Honey Ant Readers* create a symbolic bridge between school and community [...] supporting a genuine two-way exchange of ideas and information [...] Significantly, elders and community members have been central to the development of the *Honey Ant Readers* [HAR] from the beginning, and the HAR project remains a catalyst for connecting the school and community in many ways. Community members who have a formal, acknowledged role in the development and production of the *Honey Ant Readers* are involved in telling traditional stories, providing evaluative comments on drafts of books, and translating and recording books in language.

(Broughton and Gahan, p. 13)

The *Honey Ants* project is indeed a bridge between school and community, but it is more than that. The books are a means of preserving stories and languages that face steep decline. Of 250 known Aboriginal languages, only 20 are still in daily use (Gamble 2011).[14] This is of vital importance in a context in which only 11 per cent of Indigenous children are involved in Indigenous language programmes in Australian schools (see Obata and Lee 2012). Not only are the *Honey Ant Readers* for the children being translated into several Indigenous languages, as pointed out above, but additional material is also being produced that prints the stories as stories, not as a series of reading texts. As Margaret James explains: "I am also putting out an edition which is exactly the way the stories were told to me, in the language of the speaker, in most cases Aboriginal English" (interview with M. James, 17 June 2013). "The book printed from these is a direct transcript. This delights the adults. It is print literacy in their words, unedited by anyone" (written communication from M. James, 3 November 2013).

The process of translating the stories from Aboriginal English into Aboriginal languages is significant. Different language groups deal with translating in their individual ways. In James' account:

The Warlpiri people, for example, translated page 1, book 1, "nana" as "*Jajangka karrimi karlangu kurlu*" (literally: "Nana is running with the digging stick"). The Luritja just wrote "*kami*" (literally: "Nana") [...] Some of the translators translated the songs and rhymes, and others chose not to [...] In this way these books in traditional languages are no longer a progressive reading series, but a set of books. The translations have been a huge success in terms of communities wanting them. Many communities have asked us to print more books in their languages. We printed 660 in each language. Bearing in mind the small numbers of speakers, that is a significant show of hands.

(James, written communication, 3 November 2013)

This aspect of the project shows potential for improving literacy levels among the adults who use the books – literacy in English as well as in Indigenous languages. "Many adults in the community are not print literate, but they read the environment and pictures. While their children learn to read via the *Honey Ant Readers*, many of the parents learn to read too, also the cre`che carers and the Aboriginal classroom assistants" (M. James, written communication, 19 June 2013). The project also contributes to making a record of oral language pronunciation. "We made an audio CD for each book, with Elders reading the books. That has been a great addition as it means that adults and children alike can enjoy the books, whether they can read or not. Also this way the pronunciation is preserved, as we know that it changes once a language is written and read, rather than just oral" (M. James, written communication, 3 November 2013).

The project of the *Honey Ant Readers* allows us to reflect on the postcolonial significance of working with adults to transform education for children in their communities. Indigenous education has been held back under the regime of internal colonialism imposed by Anglo-Australia, and the consequences of that regime still linger. Although the levels of school success, school completion and tertiary education of Indigenous Australians have recently started to improve, they are still extremely low compared to those of non-Indigenous Australians (Mellor and Corrigan 2004). Levels of Indigenous adult literacy and school literacy are still relatively low. Projects such as the *Honey Ant Readers*, which develop modern skills based on the authentic cultures of Indigenous communities, are vital to help turn around this situation.

Margaret James notes the powerful impact

of giving minority people from ancient, living cultures written, modern material in their language and about their world. There's no doubt it draws them towards the books. They feel part of the story, even saying things like "That's my nana; that's me in the green shirt!" They feel proud and also of course as they know the stories so well they feel comfortable and I guess "in control" (they can predict what's next) in an otherwise rather "out of control" world. They seem to "grow", especially when recognised for the work. I notice this at conferences and other places I visit with Elders. They start off shy, then gradually realise they are supported and people are interested in what they have to say [...] and they really do seem to grow in stature & confidence.

(James, written communication, 19 June 2013)

Conclusion

The three case studies in this paper exemplify the process of encouraging the creation of knowledge rather than teaching preconceived knowledge. The central aim of all projects that exemplify the pedagogy of Paulo Freire is that they will strengthen the confidence, courage and skill of people to push for transformative developments in their societies. The most powerful impact of my three case study projects is in their strengthening of the culture and societal knowledge of the participants in a manner that leads to praxis – reflective activism. However, in the dialectics of real life, pockets of praxis are not enough to bring about the social change that is necessary to halt and turn around the conditions that continue to oppress and marginalise large numbers of people. Material, political and educational changes need to be combined to achieve transformation towards equity.

Notes

1. The New Jewel Movement (NJM) was the acronym for the New Joint Endeavour for Welfare, Education and Liberation, a coalition of socialist-oriented groups emerging in the 1970s in Grenada. The NJM dedicated itself to replacing the existing government, which was seen as corrupt, dictatorial, and perpetuating some of the most negative patterns of colonialism. In 1979, the NJM overthrew the government and formed the People's Revolutionary Government (PRG), which launched revolutionary change in the economy, social services, education, cultural expression, and governance of the island. The

PRG was in power for four and a half years until October 1983, when the revolutionary coalition imploded politically with fratricidal killings culminating in the execution of Prime Minister Maurice Bishop and others by some of their colleagues. Combined forces led by the United States supported by some Caribbean governments then invaded Grenada, and eventually the pre-revolutionary Grenadian constitution was re-established. 2 A work-study concept of education combines formal theoretical elements with practical vocational elements.

3. Problems and possibilities of Caribbean education within a development context are discussed in Hickling-Hudson (2004).

4. Freire's colleagues, three educators from Argentina, Bolivia and Colombia, were Spanish speakers who were fluent in English. Freire's English was not strong enough to convey complex ideas, so he usually spoke in Spanish, which his colleagues translated into English.

5. After the collapse of the revolution and the U.S. invasion of Grenada in 1983, many of the educational materials developed and produced during the 1979 to 1983 period were destroyed. It is not known whether any copies of the manuscripts from the Freire workshop still exist in Grenada.

6. The Grenada Centre for Popular Education (CPE) was set up in 1980 to combat adult illiteracy. Its adult literacy programme was based on a Cuban-style model of "Each one teach one". Volunteers were given basic training through the CPE, and went into the homes of people who requested classes. Their main pedagogical tool was the set of reading primers, which were designed by Grenadian adult educators and printed with the assistance of the Cuban government.

7. According to its homepage, "AYF is a charitable, non-governmental organization which, since 1997, has been working with young people in the inner cities to assist them in developing additional life skills and business training. AYF often uses an arts-based approach and focuses on building bridges of friendship between the divided, marginalized communities of Kingston" (http://www.areayouthfoundation.com/ [accessed 2 May 2014]).

8. A skit is a short theatrical sketch, usually comic, dramatising a situation, concept or character.

9. Third World Cop is a 1999 action-crime film set in Kingston, Jamaica, produced by Chris Blackwell's company "Palm Pictures".

10. The name is derived from Jamaican popular culture in which people in some collaborative situations "run-a-boat", that is, pool their resources to make a meal.

11. "In the 1970's the town camp Elders wanted a school of their own. They felt that the Government Schools did not properly cater for their children because traditional Languages and Culture were ignored, and because their children felt that they were outsiders and were frequently teased." The Elders wanted a school where Indigenous languages, culture and people were respected. "In 1978 the Yipirinya School Council was formed and in 1979 the first classes were started in the town camps. In 1981 the Council applied for registration of the School but this was originally rejected. After an appeal to the Supreme Court the School was finally registered in September 1983" (Yipirinya School n. d.; History section).

12. Illustrated information on the Honey Ant Reader project is available both on the Yipirina school website at http://www.yipirinya.com.au/education/honey_ant_readers.phtml and on the project's own website at http://honeyant.com.au/. Margaret James (2014) describes the project and analyses its theoretical context.

13. For pictures see: http://www.facebook.com/pages/Honey-Ant-Readers/201066696622268.

14. "Indigenous language endangerment in Australia is clearly illustrated by the decline of Indigenous language speakers among all age groups of the Indigenous population aged 5 years and over. At the 1996 Census, 12.1% of the Indigenous population were Indigenous language speakers, declining to 11.1% at 2001 and 9.2% at 2006" (Obata and Lee 2012).

References

Ambursley, F., & Dunkerley, J. (1984). *Grenada: Whose freedom?*. London: Latin America Bureau.

Baker, C. (1993). *Foundations of bilingual education and bilingualism*. New York: Multilingual Matters Ltd.

Bialystok, E. (1991). *Language processing in bilingual children*. New York, NY: Cambridge University Press.

Bigelow, B. (2013). Grenada: A lovely little war. In *If we knew our history series*: Zinn Education Project. Accessed 8 January 2014, from http://zinnedproject.org/2013/10/grenada-a-lovely-little-war/.

Boal, A. (1993). *Theater of the oppressed*. New York: Theatre Communications Group.

Broughton, B., & Gahan, D. (2013). *An impact evaluation of the Honey Ant Readers resource and its implementation at Yipirinya School*. Alice Springs: Unpublished Report.

Caribbean Journal. (2012). Jamaica's murder rate falls to seven year low, but still Caribbean's highest (8 February). Accessed 8 January 2014, from http://www.caribjournal.com/2012/02/08/jamaicas-murder-rate-falls-to-seven-year-low-but-still-caribbeans-highest/.

Freire, P. (1972). *Pedagogy of the oppressed*. Harmondsworth: Penguin.

Freire, P. (1995). *Pedagogy of hope. Reliving pedagogy of the oppressed*. New York: Continuum.

Gamble, B. (2011). A mission to save indigenous languages. *Australian Geographic*, 19 August. Accessed 2 May 2014, from http://www.australiangeographic.com.au/news/2011/08/a-mission-to-save-indigenous-languages/.

Graham, S. (2007). The arts in violence prevention: The case of the Area Youth Foundation. In F. W. Hickling (Ed.), *Dream a world. Carimensa and the development of cultural therapy in Jamaica* (pp. 44–50). Kingston: CARIMENSA (Caribbean Institute of Mental Health and Substance Abuse).

Henry, P. (1991). Socialism and cultural transformation in Grenada. In J. Heine (Ed.), *A revolution aborted: The lessons of Grenada*. Pittsburgh: University of Pittsburgh Press.

Hickling-Hudson, A. (1997). Caribbean experiments in education for social justice: The Case of Grenada. In T. Scrase (Ed.), *Social justice and third world education* (pp. 133–62). New York: Garland.

Hickling-Hudson, A. (1988). Towards communication praxis: Reflections on the pedagogy of Paulo Freire and educational change in Grenada. *Journal of Education, 170*(2), 9–38.

Hickling-Hudson, A. (1995). *Literacy and literacies in Grenada: A study of adult education in the revolution and afterwards (Unpublished doctoral dissertation)*. Australia: University of Queensland. Hickling-Hudson, A. (2004). Caribbean "knowledge societies": Dismantling Neo-colonial Barriers in the Age of Globalisation. *Compare, 34*(3), 293–300.

Hickling-Hudson, A. (2012). Grenada, education, revolution. In R. Lewis (Ed.), *Caribbean reasonings: Caribbean political activism – essays in honour of Richard Hart*. Kingston: Ian Randle Publishers. Hickling-Hudson, A. (2013a). A theory of literacies for considering the role of adult and community education in postcolonial change. In R. Arnove & C. Torres (Eds.), *Comparative education: The dialectic of the global and the local* (4th ed.). Lanham, MD: Rowman & Littlefield.

Hickling-Hudson, A. (2013b). Theatre-arts pedagogy for social justice: Case study of the Area Youth Foundation in Jamaica. *Current Issues in Comparative Education, 15*(2), 15–34.

Hickling-Hudson, A., & Ahlquist, R. (2003). Contesting the curriculum in the schooling of indigenous children in Australia and the USA: From Eurocentrism to culturally powerful pedagogies. *Comparative Education Review, 47*(1), 64–89.

Hickling-Hudson, A., & Ahlquist, R. (2004). The challenge to deculturalisation: Discourses of ethnicity in the schooling of indigenous children in Australia and the USA. In A. Hickling-Hudson, J. Matthews, & A. Woods (Eds.), *Disrupting preconceptions: Postcolonialism and education* (pp. 39–56). Brisbane: Post Pressed Publisher.

James, M. (2014). The Honey Ant Readers: An innovative and bold approach to engaging rural indigenous students in print literacy through accessible, culturally and linguistically appropriate resources. *Australian and International Journal of Rural Education, 24*(1), 79–89.

JFLL (Jamaican Foundation for Lifelong Learning). (2008). *The development and state of the art of adult learning and education*. Jamaica: Ministry of Education. Accessed 8 January 2014, from http://www.unesco.org/ fi eadmin/MULTIMEDIA/INSTITUTES/UIL/confi ea/pdf/National_Reports/Latin%20 America%20-% 20Caribbean/Jamaica.pdf.

Jules, D. (1993). The challenge of popular education in the Grenada revolution. In C. Lankshear & P. McLaren (Eds.), *Critical literacy: Policy, praxis and the postmodern*. Albany, NY: State University of New York Press.

Layne, J. E. (2014). *We move tonight. The making of the Grenada revolution*. Grenada: The Grenada Revolution Memorial Foundation.

Levy, H. (2009). *Killing streets and community revival*. Kingston: Arawak Publishers.

Lewis, G. K. (1987). *Grenada: The jewel despoiled*. Baltimore, MD: Johns Hopkins University Press. Mellor, S., & Corrigan, M. (2004). The policy and research position: Synthesis and proposal. In S. Mellor & M. Corrigan (Eds.), *Australian education review: The case for change. A review of contemporary research on indigenous education outcomes* (pp. 42–50). Melbourne: Australian Council for Educational Research (ACER) Press.

Neelands, J., & Goode, T. (2000). *Structuring drama work: A handbook of available forms in theatre and drama*. Cambridge: Cambridge University Press.

Obata, K., & Lee, J. (2012). Languages of aboriginal and Torres Strait islander Peoples: A uniquely Australian heritage. In Australian Bureau of Statistics *Year Book Australia, 2009–10*, updated 2012. Accessed 2 May 2014, from http://www.abs.gov.au/ausstats/abs@.nsf/Previousproducts/1301. 0Feature%20 Article42009%E2%80%9310?opendocument&tabname=Summary&prodno=1301. 0&issue=2009%9610&num=&view.

O'Neill, C. (1995). *Drama worlds: A framework for process drama (The dimensions of drama)*.Portsmouth, NH: Heinemann.

Payne, A., Sutton, C., & Thorndike, T. (1984). *Grenada: Revolution and Invasion*. London: Croom Helm.

Rose, D., Gray, B., & Cowey, W. (1999). Scaffolding reading and writing for indigenous children in school. In P. Wignell (Ed.), *Double power: English literacy and indigenous education*. Language Australia: Melbourne.

Searle, C. (1984). *Words unchained: Language and revolution in Grenada*. London: Zed.

Thorndike, T. (1991). People's power in theory and practice. In J. Heine (Ed.), *A revolution aborted: The lessons of Grenada*. Pittsburgh, PA: University of Pittsburgh Press.

Torres, C. (2013). *Fifty years after Angicos: Paulo Freire, popular education and the struggle for a better world that is possible*. Paper presented at the XV Comparative Education World Congress (WCCES) held in Buenos Aires, 24–28 June 2013.

Walker, J. (1980). The end of dialogue. Paulo Freire on politics and education. In R. Mackie (Ed.), *Literacy and revolution. The pedagogy of Paulo Freire* (pp. 120–50). London: Pluto Press.

Yard Edge blog. (2008). Area Youth Foundation—Transforming lives. Accessed 20 August 2013, from http://www.yardedge. net/interviews/the-area-youth-foundation-transforming-lives.

Yipirinya School. (n. d.). School website. Accessed 2 May 2014, from http://www.yipirinya.com.au/our_community/history.phtml.

26

'Queer Goings-on'

An Autoethnographic Account of the Experiences and Practice of Performing a Queer Pedagogy

Mark Vicars

If you want to know me, then you must know my story, for my story defines who I am. And if I want to know myself, to gain insight into the meaning of my own life, then I, too, must come to know my own story. I must come to see in all its particulars the narrative of the self and the personal myth that I have tacitly, even unconsciously composed over the course of my years. It is a story I continue to revise, and to tell myself (and sometimes to others) as I go on living.

(McAdams, 1993: 11)

Is It All About Me? How Queer!

What am I trying to do with this writing? I have never found writing easy, never quite sure out of which voice I should speak, Hallet (1999). I feel nervous in experimenting with a methodological approach that 'denaturalises conceptions of "appropriate" forms of educational theorizing, practice and research', Miller (1998: 371) to tell of my experience as a 'queer' teacher. Brandt et al. (2001) thinks that my feeling is a predictable state but suggests that it is useful in that 'such states give us direct access to the ways in which what is felt internally as "personal experience" is intimately connected to the institutions outside the self that foster and promote such feelings',

(Brandt et al., 2001: 21).

I would like to engage the active reader, for them to produce their own pleasures of this text, Barthes (1976). However, I am mindful of the personal and professional risks involved in such an endeavour, of laying myself open to 'the trivializing charge of self-indulgence that is so readily levelled by mainstream academics', Sparkes (2003: 73). I am attempting to create impressions of places and people that led me to question the ways that I belong, act, speak and represent myself as a Gay/Queer man and as a teacher. I am finding it impossible to reproduce a neutral account veiled in an objective representation. An attempt to do so would be mechanistic, technical and methodologically invalidate a critical reflexivity weaved within the process of identifying and reconstructing the contexts which formed my reality of the events, McNamee (1993: 5).

The claim has been made that reflexive authors are paradigmatically circumscribed, Pollner (1991). In gazing once again at past events, I find myself doing this autoethnography from a Queer perspective that uses what Hill (1996) has called 'fugitive knowledge'. Fugitive knowledges are forms of knowing that are used to disrupt heterosexualizing pedagogies. Queer, as a term, a theory and a way of being, is increasingly being contested and usefully problematized. The potential of Queer as a conceptual tool is that it can productively fuse the divisions between practice, politics and theory. Within the academy, it has shot out disruptive rhizomes that have challenged orthodoxies of knowing and generated discursive activity that has focused critical attention on the ways in which the regime of the normative habitually constructs and naturalizes within everyday practices of life. To adopt a Queer stance is to resist essentialist notions of sexual identity. It is a position that abruptly reconsiders the politics of identity by reconstructing allegiances across disparate communities that are framed, found out and made visible by their differences. Queer embraces the provisional in its refusal to be pinioned by any one single definition. It can be rooted in embodied experiences that inform, propel and fashion meaning around its use. In this context, it has been employed politically to agitate, the most notable illustrations being the direct action taken by the protest groups Queer Nation, and Act-Up. Theoretically, it has been utilized to analyse the effects of communities of practice (Lave and Wenger, 1991), on dissident subjectivities and as the anonymous author of Queers read this, a leaflet distributed at a New York Pride march in June 1990, states: 'Being Queer means leading a different sort of life. It's about defining ourselves. Using "queer" is a way of reminding how we are perceived. Queer can be a rough word but it is also a sly and ironic weapon' (Anon, 1990: 1). I offer my understanding of it as positionality that focuses on actions not actors (Britzman, 1995) and epistemologically as a way of knowing, rather than something to be known (Kopelson, 2002).

A Queer reflexivity raises the significance of employing ontology for unsettling thinking about reality, agency and ways of being and relating. Leonard (1997) has pointed out that a 'Queer theory urges the discovery of subjugated knowledge, and the positing and exploration of sites of resistance within the pressured "subject" who knows' (1997: 4). Ways of being, traditionally categorized as perverse, are able to be explored without pathology. Queer is a process of constant becoming and movement and Morris (1998) suggests that 'A queer identity is a chameleon-like refusal to be caged into any prescribed category or role' (1998: 279). Honeychurch (1996) has commented that:

A queering standpoint in social science research is a vigorous challenge to that which has constrained what may be known, who may be the knower, and how knowledge has come to be generated and circulated ... [and] queers participate in positioning themselves through both authoring and authorising experience. (Honeychurch, 1996: 342)

If, as Chia (1996) suggests, reflexivity can assist in understanding the process of becoming, the recovering of emerging experiences, and the making strange of what is familiar, then it finds a home within this text that attempts to complexify as opposed to simplify and question instead of answer the contradictions and dissonances between the social roles I have come to inhabit. A Queer reflexivity would resist the appeal of constructing an authorial identity to unify narratives told of a sovereign self, Crawley (2002). I am conscious that in placing myself within this text as a speaking subject I have been constituted and reconstituted by discourse, embedded in an intricate network of social relations (Foucault, 1972) and am spoken by language (Lacan, 1977). My voice has become a necessary fiction from which I am able to speak back and about the multiple subjectivities of self that have been discursively constituted and reiteratively performed. Talburt (1999) has commented that:

For ethnography to engage queer theories can be a difficult task, particularly when voice, visibility, the self and experience have inherently mediated forms and when knowledge and ignorance do not readily offer evidence of their workings. A difficulty is to discover how epistemologies that rely on seeing and hearing can be brought into dialogue with epistemologies that question what is seen and heard.

(Talburt, 1999: 529)

In trying to overcome the difficulties, I am attracted by Heidegger's (1966) appeal to employ 'meditative thinking' as a way of opening up possibilities and to query the orthodox rules that discipline what questions are asked and how we seek the answers. Meditative thinking offers a space in which truth and knowledge are constructed as a dialectical social practice (Cunliffe, 2001). It requires me to think about my own practices of self as a process of continual negotiations (Butler, 1997; Probyn, 1996) in relation to the knowledge derived from performing rigid, dichotomous identities' produced out of social categories (Evans, 2002). Talburt (1999) suggests,

> Queer theory pushes the limits of ethnography ... that seeks to understand the formation of subjectivities and practices in relations of power, in that it explicitly draws presences from discursive silences as it questions the constitution and effects of social and institutional norms.
>
> (Talburt, 1999: 537)

What, then, are the potential sites in which a Queer identity can find expression within everyday experiences of teaching and learning and within schools? It is perhaps in the refusal to be pinioned by the weight of professional role, one that rigidly delineates student from teacher, private from public, that I can come to articulate what I mean by a Queer pedagogy. Thomas (1993) has commented that: 'It is difficult to separate convincingly and reliably, self from professional persona. It seems ... to be in the nature of teaching, that the mask of the role player is likely to slip' (Thomas, 1993: 239).

It would seem to me that a Queer presence in pedagogy would trouble 'the very relationships of the day to day lived experience of school life' (Morris, 1998: 285) and 'offer an alternative to move beyond the limiting homo/hetero binary' (Quinlivan and Town, 1999: 253). In doing so, making possible a critique of what is constituted as normal behaviours, roles and expectations.

In critiquing my professional practice as a teacher and of the social and cultural contexts in which my sexual identity had been constituted, I have come to realize that schools and classrooms are places where I become invisible or am made to become invisible. It seems to me that I have always felt pressured to legitimize and explain what it is that I am and what I do, especially to myself. Tierney (1997) suggests this feeling could be a product of a heterosexualizing culture and discourse, one in which: 'The widespread notion that heterosexuality is normal and that everything that is not heterosexual is somehow aberrant and has placed queers in a constant existential state of questioning ourselves, our identity, and how we should act' (Tierney, 1997: 39).

My unaccomplished performances of normative gender and sexuality in educational settings have subsequently continued to shape and provide a pattern to how I have come to have an experience of what it means to be a teacher who is gay. My feelings of being an outlaw in the educational process have a genealogy. Constantly being positioned in relation to the force of dominant institutional discourses and agendas is how I have come to understand and interpret the intersections of the personal on professional practices (Vicars, 2003; 2005).

In this text I have chosen to reconstruct and critically reflect on a key moment from my past. The slippage of the private into the public disrupted the social and cultural roles I was expected to perform and problematised my cultural identities as teacher and Gay/Queer man. Said (1989: 225) suggests that '... the crossing of boundaries are experiences that can therefore provide us with new narrative forms'.

Telling Tales: Revisiting the Past in the Present and Towards the Future

> Conscious and unconscious are asymmetrically co-present: the inner structure maps the outer conceptualisings. This mapping is above all governed by linguistic experience.
>
> *(Wright, 1984: 107)*

I reorganize the space at my desk in order to begin writing. Does the coffee pot need refilling? Do I have another packet of cigarettes? Have I remembered to switch on the answer phone? I start to tap away at my keyboard scouring experience, aware that it already exists as an 'interpretation and is in need of interpretation' (Scott, 1992). As I settle down in front of the computer screen, the taste of bitter coffee is blended with cigarette smoke and I reach for the mediating forces of memory and language and wait for them to assert authority on my unconscious.

I am getting lost in past imaginings and struggle to find the language to share and interpret my world. How do I start to give a form to a narrative that will hopefully reveal how my identity as a teacher and my educational practice has been constituted through 'material, cultural and interpsychic relations' Smith and Watson (2001: 25). Grasping at images from the past, I selectively revise scenes and reorder fragments in an attempt to make sense of those critical, defining transitional moments located in a multiple embodied life. What order can I impose on the illusions of myself and of others that claim to be truthful expressions? I am becoming aware how the events I select are constantly up for negotiation. With each churned and filtered motion, they recoil from immediate analysis. Hesitantly, they emerge into words, phrases, sentences and paragraphs that require structure and 'emplotment' (Bruner, 1990; Polkinghorne, 1988; Ricoeur, 1984). It is in the writing that I find the interpretation is being formed. It is through this developing narrative that I hope to be able to find the threads of my story. I light another cigarette and draw deeply, pulling the nicotine-laced smoke deep into kippered lungs. I observe the yellowed surface of the monitor tarnished by numerous nocturnal sessions spent reading and thinking in this room that I converted to a study on my return to England. I recall the comments of a friend, an ex-smoker, who on quitting claimed that smokers are people who suppress unresolved emotional conflicts. I light another cigarette and think about my father who lay dying from emphysema in a flock-wallpapered room for 13 months. I returned to his house having spent 10 years overseas teaching. On my return, I obstinately clung to the remnants of a life I had known, a life I had created. Artefacts from that life (hand-crafted Japanese fans, earthenware sake sets and stone-carved Theravada Buddhas) clutter this new space that I have consciously created in my father's house. Garishly announcing their origins, they reside in stark contrast to my father's collections of porcelain figurines and are a visual reminder of the distance and differences that existed between us and that neither of us managed to breach.

I never wanted to be a teacher. I based my perceptions of the profession on the grey suited, pallid-faced disciplinarians of my youth. They embodied the substance of control that was my secondary educational experience. Even today, the dictums of the maths teacher, 'silence is golden', and taunts of the PE teacher ring in my ears and sound the death knell for any endeavour vaguely mathematical or activity in which I have to compete physically.

Five years ago I had arrived at a strange airport with no job, nowhere to live and I created a life for myself. I carved out a home amidst the chaos of that uncanny city. Beguiled by the charms and anarchy of the metropolis, I quickly adapted to the myriad ways of knowing this exotic geography and its difference imprinted indelible patterns on my psyche. The pungent aroma of spices blended with eye-watering carbon monoxide fumes that infused skin, bone and connective tissue, worming a way through my outer defences. I embraced its toxicity. It was a place that I thought at the time I would never want to leave.

Three months after arriving, I had applied for a job teaching English and drama at an international school and I could not believe my good fortune when I got it.

Welcome to the smokers balcony!

Sue, a formidable Geordie who taught special needs took me immediately under her wing.

We're not really allowed to smoke but the head turns a blind eye if we are discreet.

Dipping in and out of conversations, she maintained a constant dialogue and was the lynch pin that kept everything and everyone together.

> You canne have any secrets on the balcony pet. I love it here, been here for three years now. The head is a good un and we're like one big family. Great place to work, kids are wonderful, staff is best I've ever worked with. Now tell me 'bout you.

Four years later and my leaving day approached. In the interim, there had been a change of leadership and the incoming Head had established a regime that reminded me of those tortuous times I had spent under the disciplining gaze of former PE masters. Increasingly, I felt I had nowhere to turn and just as I had aimlessly floundered on the football pitch I had for the past 12 months questioned whether I could sustain the humiliations that resulted from not being one of the lads. There had been a plethora of new appointments, all men and the emphatic performances of masculinity that I had believed secured them jobs in the first place had a dramatic impact across the school. Steve, the newly appointed Head of English, in a department of two, had recently allotted himself the role of captain for the newly formed staff football team and set about establishing his order on and off the pitch.

> Now then tiger, I've decided to start an English Speaking Club. The little bastards keep talking their own language and I've got to do Something to stamp it out. Here is how it works, every time one of the little fuckers uses ***** put their name on the board. At the end of each week the names will be collected and if a name appears more than once it will be published in the school magazine that is sent home to the parents. Naming and shaming tiger, that is what it's all about.

And so it continued, aggression seemed to characterize his every act. I had grown accustomed to his commentary on my sexuality in terms of 'was I able to sit down after the weekend' and 'had I had it up the arse?' My resistance to what Steve represented, personally and professionally, was making my position within the school increasingly vulnerable. I worked hard to maintain my approach to teaching in the classroom and a way of being with the students that encouraged openness, challenged prejudices, and attempted to restore equity to the teaching/learning interface. This stance had attracted attention from the senior management team who had on more than one occasion commented that my pedagogic style would be better suited to the 'progressive' philosophy of education advocated by Alexander Neill's Summerhill School. I knew that in their comparison of my classroom, and by implication my practice that I was being told I did not fit in with his concept of how a school should operate. I had a feeling that my days were increasingly numbered because I persistently remained sceptical of the changes that were being introduced. I disrupted the view held by senior management and Steve that in the classroom an effective teacher should only: '… deal with the part of the child that is above the neck; and … the emotional, vital part of the child is foreign territory' (Summerhill School).

The differences were to become more pronounced. That Steve tolerated me was apparent. Using the status of Head of Department, he asserted authority and I was informed of departmental decisions as opposed to being involved in creating policy. He increasingly started to question my choice of texts from the IGCSE (International General Certificate in Secondary Education) syllabus and began to regulate how it should be taught. With each confrontation, it became clear that his need to win was driving the encounter. Agreeing to disagree was not an option. Metaphors of football, of playing on the same team, were drawn upon and it was made abundantly clear to me that in 'playing offside' I was disrupting 'his game'. The time of year approached when timetables are suspended and there is a sense of the daily life of school shuddering to a stop. It was exam time. It had been decided by the Headmaster that subject teachers would invigilate their own exams. Steve and I were thrust together for a week in the claustrophobic assembly hall.

Look at em, a couple of shittas. Eh?

Returning from giving out extra sheets of paper, I did not have a clue to what he was referring.

Them, a couple of shittas! What are you on about now? Them!

He gestured to where two Year 11 lads were sitting industriously working through the question paper.

For crying out loud, stop it, they're kids. They're a couple of pussies. You know what they said 'bout me?

I knew that he was 'pissed off'. These students had asked to be transferred to my class two terms previous. Having to produce a valid reason for their wanting to move from what was the top set down to the bottom set, the Headmaster had demanded to know the reason. A meeting had been organized where their parents had explained that the two lads were uncomfortable and fed up with being made fun of. Both had long hair and wore hair bands to keep it out of their face.
It was at the annual sports day that the situation finally came to a head.

You're on shot-putt with Steve.

I inwardly groaned and made my way over to where a bunch of the less able and less physically streamlined kids were lining up.

Duuur, are you stupid or what, I told you to line up over there.
I was not quite sure if he was talking to me or the kids. I looked around to check and spied Pete, the music teacher, lurking in the shade eating an ice cream and resplendent in a specially purchased, and it has to be said, rather camp red ensemble. Pete was not in the least sporty but felt that he should at least look the part. The lucky so-and-so had been given crowd control and, as there was not that much of a crowd to control, had found a quiet spot to observe the proceedings.
That fat queer cunt! Oh leave it out, what has he ever done to you? He makes me want to spew. You know what I want to do? I wanna tie that fat queer fucker down to a chair and stuff my fist down his throat till he gags. I want to ram it down so hard that his teeth break and he starts to choke. How very sexual! What phallic imagery! It sounds like you want to fuck him? Maybe that's it, you secretly fancy a bit of cock? Fuck off, that's disgusting! Uurgh, is that all you think about?

I had had enough and walked away to join Pete and have a lick of his ice cream. As it was the time of year when contracts were up for renewal, I had decided enough was enough. My decision had just been made. In between mouthfuls of vanilla whip, I told Pete.

You're doing what? I'm leaving. Why?

Pete could not understand.

Look, I've had two years working with Steve and let's face it this is not the place it used to be. It is virtually unrecognisable from the school we started at four years ago. I don't look forward to coming in any more, yeah the kids are still great but it's the rest of it that is a nightmare. Steve has re-signed for another two years and I have had enough.

The last day of term arrived and I was running late for the ritual line up for the school photograph. Making my way along the bleachers, I shouted out my apologies to the sweating bodies bunched together in a forced pose of institutional togetherness. We were anything but one big happy family.

Sorry I'm late, sooorrry.!
Watch yer back boys, Vicars is coming through!

I had made the right decision. I felt such a sense of relief knowing that I would no longer have to put up with any more of it. I returned to my classroom to finish off packing up my things.

Dahhhhling!

Karla the art teacher announced herself, bounded into my room and gave me a hug. I was bustled out of my classroom to an awaiting taxi. I demanded to know what was going on. I had come to hate surprises considering the amount I had had to accommodate during the previous couple of years.

Now, close your eyes.

Clutching onto Karla I made my way up the narrow winding stairs.

Surprise!

Opening my eyes I found myself in a small restaurant packed with year 10 and 11 students. A buffet was laid out and ominously a karaoke machine was buzzing on a raised platform stage.

Isn't it fabulous! They organised it all. Happy leaving!

The next couple of hours were spent eating, drinking, saying goodbye and swapping email addresses. I was surprised to see Bank there, for the last two years he had been visibly reluctant to have anything at all to do with me. I had taught him at the beginning of year 10, he was in my English IGCSE set and we had always got on well. Steve had decided that those students who did not stand a chance of passing the exam would not be entered as it would look bad on the department's pass rate. They would be taken out of mainstream English classes and would have to do extra EFL. I had argued against the decision but, as it was supported by the senior management, I had to tell Bank that he would be leaving the class.

But I don't want to Mr. Vicars, I will try harder, I really will.
I'm sorry, Bank, it has already been decided.
What if I got my parents to pay?
I'm sorry, Bank, there is nothing I can do.

I knew as well as he did that his departure from my class would be read by his peers that he was not that bright as only the less able kids were being creamed off and separated into the sink category.

Hello Bank, how are you?

    I wasn't going to come. I hated you, you know! Why did you throw me out of your class? I was trying hard. …

As I explained to him what had happened and that it had not been my decision, he started to cry.

    I'm sorry, Mr. Vicars, I didn't know …

How could I explain?

Why didn't you tell me at the time?

Visibly upset and crying harder, he went to put his arms around me.

    Mr. Vicars, Karaoke time.

Saved by a song, I felt uncomfortable about being physical with Bank. I knew it was not appropriate behaviour for a teacher. I understood what he was trying to tell me and regretted not being totally honest with him at the time. Amid cheers and shouts of my name I was dragged to the microphone just in time to launch into Gloria Gaynor's Gay disco anthem

    I will survive.

The whole room erupted with the refrain, Karla was being encouraged to join me on the stage and the amassed throng were on their feet dancing and singing at the top of their voices. Suddenly, Bank jumped on to the stage and started to take off his tie, then his shirt. Dancing around me to the cheers of onlookers, he flung his arms around my waist and planted a kiss on my cheek. What on earth was happening now? What did he think he was doing? What did I think I was doing?

Picking Up the Pieces

Clough (2002) asks the question of function and purpose of stories in educational research and proposes that narrative can disturb ways of knowing, it can be used to reframe the enquiring gaze. Contexts of the familiar are rendered strange and the strange can become familiar. He comments:

> … in setting out to write a story, the primary work is in the interaction of ideas; in the act of thinking, tuning in, decision making and focusing on the primary intent of the work … writing a story … is not carried out outside of a need, a community, a context.
>
> (Clough, 2002: 8)

By challenging conventional assumptions of what constitutes legitimate pedagogical knowledge within educational research (Bridges, 1998, 1999; Husu, 2002; Whitehead, 1997), I wanted to create an authentic voice (Errante, 2000, 2001; MacDaniels, 2000) embedded in an embodied form of knowing. I have wanted to create an accessible and 'writerly' text that is immediate and captures the attention and interest of whoever is turning the page (Barthes, 1988). Sparkes (2003) has spoken of the effects of using voice in this way to situate a specific response in the reader: 'I don't want readers to sit back as spectators. I want to engage them and evoke a response. I want readers whatever their positioning in relation to me, to feel care and desire when they read my stories' (Sparkes, 2003: 67).

In questioning the ethical and moral implications of performing pedagogy that enunciates a 'vulnerable self' (Ellis, 1999; Ellington, 1998), I have tried to draw together the fragments of lived experience to construct a narrative where lifeless data is transformed into a lived landscape (Oates, 1999). Smith and Watson (2001) suggest that:" Embodied subjects are located in their bodies and through their bodies in culturally specific ways–that is, the narrating body is situated at the nexus of language, gender, class sexuality and other specificities, and autobiographical narratives mine this embodied locatedness". (Smith and Watson, 2001: 38)

I am aware that in using autobiographical incidents the story I have written of myself will become a 'story-telling performance shot through with conflicting cultural meanings' Chapman, (1997: 7). Each memory that has been triggered, its interpretation and analysis is already imbued with a situated morality and ethics. I have been careful to obscure factual traces and have used fictitious names, other than my own, to fashion what I hope could be considered as a substantial representation of experience.

In actively disrupting allegiances of belonging, in crossing over and becoming part of the stories that are told, I am inhabiting the borderlands that Rosaldo (1989: 207–8) considers as 'sites of creative cultural production' and I have been mindful of Laurel Richardson's (1990: 12) remark that: 'No textual staging is ever innocent, we are always inscribing values in our writing, it is unavoidable.' I have tried to be a good informant (Sikes, 2001) by creating scenes that draw on literary and poetic devices to illuminate for the reader my perceptions and experience of the events (Ellis, 1995; Richardson, 1990). In using dialogue in different forms to show and produce verisimilitude, I have hopefully extended an invitation to the reader to engage with my reconstructed account of experience, one in which language ceases to be objective and the self becomes simultaneously object and subject. I have tried to illustrate how a Queer reflexivity can be used to frame autobiographical writing and I have challenged the notion of a unified subject with agency, in doing so problematizing lived experience as a site of self-hood and writing. Denzin (1997: 140) has noted that 'Stories are not waiting to be told; they are constructed by the writer who attempts to impose order on perceived events' and Winterson has commented that:

> Everyone, at sometime in their life, must choose whether to stay with a ready-made world that may be safe but which is also limiting, or to push forward, often past the frontiers of common-sense, into a personal place, unknown and untried.
>
> (Winterson, 1991: xiv)

Reconceptualizing the act of writing as a performative act, I am attempting to make available representations of experience that are informed by and emerge out of an understanding of how writing operates as an enactment of freedoms and a way of resisting systems of domination. I have experimented with different modes of composition to address the problem of trying to make queer voices visible within the largely heteronormative framework of hegemonic educational discourse. Disrupting the doxa (Bourdieu, 1984) of normative representational method has enabled me to explore and represent aspects of pedagogy previously unthinkable. Challenging the legitimacy of the symbolic capital of the academic field has meant thinking about the ways texts position readers in relation to claims of truth and authority. I have found that by utilizing creative and dramatic modes that is it possible to attend to the social/cultural habits of being/ doing that are performatively constituted through language and that shape and influence the textual practice of representing identities.

The reality in the story is mine and is filtered through my lexis and phrasings. That is not to say the representations are inaccurate or untrue, they are a synthesis of the days, months and years spent working alongside and with these people. They are my understandings of them through time, they are how I have interpreted motives and actions and they have been staged with the goal of recognition, communication and hopefully connection (Tierney, 1993). Experimentation in this way seems to fulfil my readings and interpretations of events and travel in some way to realizing Tierney's (1993) suggestion that there are occasions when there is a 'need to create texts that enable the reader to reflect on his or her own life and see if the text resembles any sense of reality' (Tierney, 1993: 313).

The reconstruction of my journey in education resists teleological statements. Miller (1998) has suggested that:

> … addressing 'self' as a site of permanent openness and resignifiability opens up possibilities for queering autobiography, for speaking and writing into existence denaturalised ways of being that are obscured or simply unthinkable when one centred self-knowing story is substituted for another.
>
> Miller (1998: 368)

Bank's performance on that stage and our performance together caused/causes me to reconsider what happened to my identification as a teacher up to and on that day. I had never made a verbal declaration of my sexuality and I had not really thought about whether the students I taught knew if I was gay. I knew that they interacted with me differently from the other teachers, but I had put that down to the fact that I had made an effort to interact with them differently. After reeling from the initial shock of what was unfolding my immediate (professional) thoughts were that this should not be happening. I have come to realize this rupture of personal and professional was a critical incident in my development as a teacher.

The rigid, dichotomous identities of teacher/student, gay/straight had been breached and our performance on that day re-inscribed how we performed our given identities of student and teacher. Transgressing what could be read as appropriate or 'normal' behaviour, a heteronormative reading might present Bank as being 'at risk'. As the teacher, should not I have been acting to determine closure to the event? To what extent can I determine which of us unruly subjects were in a position of power and therefore agency? To be quite honest, I am still flummoxed by what happened on that day and I do not think that I will ever fully understand. It seems to me that we were both vulnerable. I had much to lose and so did Bank. I could have stopped him; I could have walked off the stage and reasserted my authority by stepping back in to the role of teacher. Bank could, if he had wanted to, have got revenge, by placing me in an awkward situation. It seems to me, with the advantage of hindsight, that we were both inscribing ourselves against hegemonic social discourses. Our performative refusal to be pinioned within and defined by a heteronormative matrix made it possible for us to eschew a normative regime of identity and identification by challenging personal and pedagogic boundaries.

However, I am loathe to provide a definitive interpretation, to close off and shut down the past. I leave it to live with me and maybe at some point in the future I will come to an understanding that might make more sense.

References

Anon. 1990: Queers read this!/I hate straights! New York.

Barthes, R. 1976: The pleasure of the text, trans. R. Miller. London: Jonathan Cape.

——1988: The death of the author. In Lodge, D., editor, Modern criticism and theory: a reader, London: Longman, 167–72.

Bourdieu, P. 1984: Distinction: a social critique of taste. London: Routledge & Kegan Paul. Brandt, D., Cushman, E., Gere, A. et al. 2001: The politics of the personal: storying our lives against the grain. College English 64: 41–62.

Bridges, D. 1998: Educational research: pursuit of truth or flight into fancy. Paper presented at BERA Annual Conference 27–30 August 1998. <http://www.leeds.ac.uk.educol/documents000000774.htm> (accessed 25 June 2003).

——1999: Faction and friction: educational narrative research and 'the magic of the real'. Paper presented at the BERA Annual Conference, 2–5 September 1999,University of Sussex at Brighton, UK. <http://www.leeds.ac.uk.educol/documents/ 00001218.htm>

Britzman, D. 1995: Is there a queer pedagogy? Or, stop reading straight. EducationalTheory 45, 151–65.

Bruner, J. 1990: Acts of meaning. Cambridge, MA: Harvard University Press.

Butler, J. 1997: The psychic life of power. Stanford, CA: Stanford University Press.

Chapman, V. 1997: A woman's life remembered: autoethnographic reflections of an adult educator. Paper Presented at SCUTREA 29th Annual Conference 5–7 July1999, University of Warwick, UK. <http://www.leeds.ac.uk.educol/documents. 000000980.htm>

Chia, R. 1996: The problem of reflexivity in organizational research: towards a postmodern science of organization. Organization 3: 31–59.

Clough, P. 2002: Narratives and fictions in educational research. Buckingham, UK:Open University Press.

Crawley, S. 2002: They still don't understand why I hate wearing dresses! An autoethnographic rant on dresses, boats and butchness. Critical Methodologies 2: 69–92.

Cunliffe, A.L. 2001: Managers as practical authors: reconstructing our understanding of management practice. Journal of Management Studies 38: 351–71.

Denzin, N. 1997: Interpretative ethnographic practices for the twenty first century. London: Sage.

Ellis, C. 1995: Final negotiations. Philadelphia: Temple University Press.

——1999: Heartfelt autoethnography. Qualitative Health Research 9: 669–83. Ellington, L. 1998: Then you know how I feel: empathy, identification and reflexivityin fieldwork. Qualitative Inquiry 4: 492–512.

Errante, A. 2000: But sometimes you're not part of the story: oral histories and ways of remembering and telling. Educational Researcher 29: 16–27.

Evans, K. 2002: Negotiating the self: identity, sexuality, and emotion in learning to teach. London: Routledge Falmer.

Foucault, M. 1972: The archaeology of knowledge and the discourse on language, trans. A. Sheridan. New York: Pantheon Books.

Hallet, N. 1999: Lesbian lives–identity and autobiography in the twentieth century. London: Pluto Press.

Heidegger, M. 1966: Discourse on thinking, trans. of Gelassenheit by J.M. Anderson and E. Hans Freund. New York: Harper and Row.

Hill, R. 1996: Learning to transgress: a socio-historical conspectus of the American gay life world as a site of struggle and resistance. Studies in the Education of Adults 28: 253–79.

Honeychurch, K. 1996: Researching dissident subjectivities: queering the grounds of theory and practice. Harvard Educational Review 66: 339–55.

Husu, J. 2002: Learning to live with a lesser form of knowledge–coming to terms with the characteristics of teacher's pedagogical knowing. Paper presented at the European Conference on Educational Research, University of Lisbon, 11–14September 2002. <http://www.leeds.ac.uk.educol/documents00002368.htm>

Iser, W. 1971: The reading process: a phenomenological approach. New LiteraryHistory 3, 279–99.

Kopelson, K. 2002: Dis/integrating the gay/queer binary 'Reconstructed identitypolitics' for a performative pedagogy. College English 65, 17–35.

Lave, J. and Wenger, E. 1991: Situated learning: legitimate peripheral participation.Cambridge: Cambridge University Press.

Lacan, J. 1977: Ecrits: a selection. London: Tavistock.

Leonard, G. 1997: Introduction. Pedagogy 24, 152.

McAdams, D, 1993: The stories we live by: personal myths and the making of the self. London: The Guildford Press.

MacDaniels, C. 2000: Renaming as an act of resistance. In Ritchie, J. and Wilson, D., editors, Teacher narrative as critical inquiry. New York: Teachers College Press,90–110.

McNamee, S. 1993: Research as conversation. Conference paper: Constructed realities: therapy, theory and research. Norway.

Miller, J. 1998: Autobiography as queer curriculum practice. In Pinar, W., editor, Queer theory in education. London: Lawrence Erlbaum, 365–75.

Morris, M. 1998: Unresting the curriculum: queer projects, queer imaginings. In Pinar, W., editor, Queer theory in education. London: Lawrence Erlbaum, 275–86.

Oates, S. 1999: Biography as history. Waco, TX: Mankaham Press Fund.

Polkinghorne, D. 1988: Narrative knowing and the human sciences. New York: Albany State University of New York Press.

Pollner, M. 1991: Left of ethnomethodology: the rise and decline of radical reflexivity. American Sociological Review 56, 370–80.

Probyn, E. 1996: Outside belongings. New York: Routledge.

Quinlivan, K. and Town, S. 1999: 'Queer as fuck? Exploring the potential of queer pedagogies in researching school experiences of lesbian and gay youth. In Epstein, D. and Sears, J., editors, A dangerous knowing: sexuality, pedagogy and popular culture, London: Cassell, 242–56.

Richardson, L. 1990: Writing strategies: reaching diverse audiences. London: Sage.

Ricoeur, P. 1984: Time and narrative (trans. K. McLaughlin and J. Costello). Toronto: University of Chicago Press.

Rosaldo, R. 1989: Culture and truth: the remaking of social analysis. Boston, MA: Beacon Press.

Said, E. 1989: Representing the colonized: anthropology's interlocutors. Critical Inquiry 15, 205–25.

Scott, J. 1992: Experience. In Butler, J. and Scott, J., editors, Feminists theorize the political, New York: Routledge, 20–40.

Sikes, P. 2001: Life history research in educational settings. Buckingham, UK: Open University Press.

Smith, S. and Watson, J. 2001: Reading autobiography: a guide for interpreting life narratives. London: University of Minnesota Press.

Sparkes, A. 2003: Bodies, identities, selves: autoethnographic fragments and reflections. In Denison, J. and Markula, P., editors, Moving writing: crafting movement in sport research. New York: Peter Lang, 51–76.

Summerhill School: <http://www.summerhillschool.co.uk.pages/schoolpolicies.htm>

Talburt, S. 1999: Open secrets and problems of queer ethnography: readings from a religious studies classroom. International Journal of Qualitative Studies in Education 12, 525–39.

Thomas, D. 1993: Treasonable or trustworthy text: reflections on teacher narrative studies. Journal of Education for Teaching 19, 214–21.

Tierney, W. 1993: The cedar closet. International Journal of Qualitative Studies in Education 6, 303–14.

——1997: Academic outlaws: queer theory and cultural studies in the academy. Thousand Oaks, CA: Sage.

——2000: Undaunted courage: life history and the postmodern challenge. In Denzin, N. and Lincoln, Y., editors, Handbook of qualitative research, secondedition, London: Sage, 537–54.

Vicars, M. 2003: 'Queer goings-on': An autoethnographic investigation into the experiences and practice of performing a Queer pedagogy. Unpublished MA dissertation, University of Sheffield, UK.

——2005: I have a feeling we're not in Kansas anymore: a British gay educator's reconstructed life-history account of school. Sex Education 5.

Whitehead, J. 1997: How have I engaged with the power relations in the academy in supporting self studies of practitioner researchers. Paper presented to the symposium on: How do we co-create and share our educational knowledge and theories through talking together in our self studies of out educational research and practices. AERA Conference, March 24–28, Chicago. <http://www.leeds.ac.uk.educol/documents000000342.htm>

Winterson, J. 1991: Oranges are not the only fruit. London: Vantage.

Wright, E. 1984: Psychoanalytic criticism. London: Methuen.

27

Turning Difficulties into Possibilities
Engaging Roma Families and Students in School through Dialogic Learning

Ramón Flecha and Marta Soler

The large-scale European Union-funded research INCLUD-ED, Strategies for Inclusion and Social Cohesion in Europe from Education (European Commission, FP6, 2006–2011) has identified Successful Educational Actions (SEAs) that have improved educational outcomes for many children and young people in Europe. These actions are characterised by reorganising the available resources in the school and the community to support all pupils' academic achievement, instead of segregating some of them according to ability or by lowering down their educational opportunities. SEAs derive from a rigorous analysis of the educational systems, theories and practices, particularly, from the successful actions identified in 27 case studies across the European Union of schools serving families from low socio- economic status where children achieve excellent results (Valls & Padrós, 2011). For instance, some SEAs studied through the INCLUD-ED Project are interactive groups, dialogic reading, after-school clubs and some family education programmes like the dialogic literary gatherings. As a result of implementing these SEAs, these schools have improved students' performance and enhanced social cohesion, providing all children with better learning opportunities to reduce social and educational inequalities (Flecha, García, Gómez, & Latorre, 2009). These are not isolated best practices that lead to good results in particular cases or contexts. Rather, they are actions which have resulted in school success in different countries and very different environments, as they contain universal components, transferable across con- texts. These SEAs were clarified in the INCLUD-ED Final Conference, held at the European Parliament's headquarters on 6 December 2011. Researchers, including Members of Parliament, and end-users–including Roma family members–presented together the actions that have evidenced improvements in schools and communities, regardless of children's ethnic background or socioeconomic status.

In order to achieve the inclusive growth currently aimed for Europe (European Commission, 2010), it is necessary to provide schools and communities with the actions that help citizens succeed in education, and consequently gain access to the labour market and to full participation in society. This is particularly important for the most vulnerable, such as the Roma.[1] INCLUD-ED has responded to these challenges by analysing the educational actions that contribute to social cohesion, pro-viding key elements and courses of action to improve educational and social policies. Since this is a multidimensional topic, it was addressed through six sub- projects. This article focuses on the results obtained from a four-year longitudinal case study conducted under one of the INCLUD-ED sub-projects (Project 6). We studied La Paz Primary School for four years, and identified and analysed a range of SEAs implemented there, assessing their impact on improving Roma children's learning outcomes and coexistence (Flecha, 2012). Among them, family participation in decision-making processes and in children's learning activities emerged as particularly important for increasing both Roma children's engagement in school and their academic success.

The case study: La Paz Primary School

La Paz Primary School is located in a very deprived neighbourhood of the city of Albacete, Spain, where the Roma constitute 90% of the population. Most families have limited literacy (i.e. around 50% have some basic education and 25% are illiterate) and with a highly precarious economic situation. Since the 1980s, the neighbourhood situation declined further, along with the primary school. The situation within the school was intolerable, with high rates of early school leaving, absentee- ism and conflicts in the classrooms, as well as conflicts between teachers and families (Padros, Garcia, de Mello, & Molina, 2011). Consequently, school enrolment decreased enormously, and around 300 students were lost over 10 years. By the academic year 2005–6, only 40 pupils were attending regularly.

According to the school internal evaluations, in 2006 children at the different grades had very low linguistic competence and low reading and writing skills, as compared to the average at their age. Mathematics abilities proved to be also poor across the different levels. Overall, hardly any child had an appropriate level of attainment, and conflicts among pupils and between them and teachers occurred every day. In this scenario, many Roma families removed their children from the school and no longer trusted the teachers, contrasting with the widespread myth about the Roma that they are not interested in education and dislike schools (Bhopal, 2011; Gómez & Vargas, 2003). According to Wilson (2003), ghetto schools provide low-quality education and low expectations. These schools often water down the curriculum and provide low academic levels, little stimulating material and less quality instrumental learning, as compared to other schools (Anyon, 1995; Darling-Hammond, 1996; Oakes, 1990). Conversely, improving the educational levels in these schools has been identified to make an important contribution to getting out of the ghetto (Wilson, 2003).

Looking for a real solution to this critical situation, local authorities and school administrators, in dialogue with INCLUD-ED researchers, decided to implement the *Dialogic Inclusion Contract*. This is a dialogical procedure in which researchers, families, children, teachers, community members, and policymakers recreate through egalitarian dialogue the SEAs previously identified through research, in order to transform the educational and the social context (Aubert, 2011). Together they decided to implement in the school the SEAs oriented to academic achievement, which challenged educational stereotypes about the Roma. To make that possible, the regional government closed the school and re-opened it again with new staff, who committed to being trained on the SEAs and implementing them. The children and families of the new school decided on a new name, and St. John Primary became La Paz (which means peace).

Once the SEAs were implemented, the children's learning outcomes improved significantly, as will be reflected in the section on results. Children now attend the school every day, far more enthusiastically than before. In this article we will see how SEAs transformed the school at different levels, reducing the traditional mismatch between the Roma students' and families' demands and the school. We will focus specifically on how dialogic learning which includes interactions between teachers, learners, and also family and community members in the school, leads to educational success and social cohesion in schools.

The dialogic approach to enhance Roma children's learning based on the participation of the community

Educating Roma children is still a challenge in Europe. Data from the Roma Education Fund (2010) show that about 75% of Roma people have completed less than a primary education, and that the percentage of Roma dropouts from primary school varies across different countries, from 15 to 69%. Roma schooling is also affected by high rates of absenteeism and by particular educational practices of segregation carried out in many schools (Greenberg, 2010).

In addition, the stereotypes and folk assumptions with regard to a 'natural' Roma disaffection with school have also contributed to the educational exclusion of the Roma. These stereotypes are linked to the idea that the Roma, in order to pre- serve their culture, exclude themselves from mainstream education. Roma researchers such as Hancock (1988) and Rose (1983) have questioned these assumptions, arguing that they are used by the non-Roma to keep them at the margins of society. Similarly, other analyses about the Roma children in mainstream schools have concluded that school disaffection can be explained by the ethnocentric perspective of educational systems (Gómez & Vargas, 2003). Therefore, mainstream schools do not consider engaging in dialogue with Roma families, who end up perceiving the school as an institution of the non-Roma world. According to Gómez and Vargas (2003), 'schools have been sites for assimilation, reproduction, and the perpetuation of social exclusion … when they include and value their culture and hear and recognize Romaní voices, Romà disaffection turns into passion' (p. 560).

Research has found that family involvement in schools improves children's achievement (Dearing, Kreider, Simpkins, & Weiss, 2006; Epstein, 1991). By getting involved in the school, parents improve their skills related to school activities, which allows them to better help their children; in addition, increased dialogue and communication between the family and the school helps resolve both behavioural and academic issues (Hill & Taylor, 2004; Sheldon & Epstein, 2005). The same is true in relation to Roma families. There are a number of studies that have explored the relationship between the Roma students and families and the non-Roma schools and teachers, and how it impacts on Roma children's engagement with education and on school performance. The Roma Education Fund (2010) highlights that engaging Roma parents in their children's education is an important way to increase students' educational opportunities, to help them do better in school and ensure their access to compulsory education. However, Bhopal (2004) identified that Roma families, despite the positive value they give to schooling, do not trust the educational institutions that have to care for their children. This constitutes an important barrier for Roma children's education. Along these lines, Derrington (2005) found that parents' prior experiences in education and held beliefs about schools had an influence on breaking down home–school relationships as well as on Roma students' disengagement with secondary school. There is, therefore, a 'cultural dissonance' (Derrington, 2007) between the families' and the schools' expectations, which is a factor impacting Roma students' retention in education. In this context, promoting dialogue with the Roma community has been identified as central to closing this gap and to transforming these situations (Bhopal, 2004). In addition, the commitment of the school staff to create inclusive schools has also been studied as an element of key importance for the inclusion of the Roma (Bhopal & Myers, 2009).

The role of dialogue in learning and development has been central in a number of learning theories and the object of an important body of research. Dialogue is the basis of cooperative situations of learning among students and between students and other community members. The dialogic learning approach includes all the many interactions with diverse people that support children's learning in the school and beyond. Some studies have highlighted the importance of enhancing such interactions. For instance, when children work in smaller groups they can develop higher levels of interaction (Galton, Hargreaves, & Pell, 2009). Teachers can create moments of dialogic inquiry in the classrooms (Wells, 1999) which involve looking for solutions through dialogue (through cooperative interactions mediated by language). Furthermore, the involvement of parents from different backgrounds in children's learning increases interaction opportunities (Rogoff, Goodman Turkanis, & Bartlett, 2001).

Dialogic learning considers learning interactions that occur among peers but also between children and significant adults, including teachers, relatives and other members of the community

(García, 2012). It entails the transformation of the learners' social context through multiplying learning interactions in the different spaces in which children act (i.e. classroom, school, after school, home). It also considers the importance of dialogue based on egalitarian relationships. That means that the interactions should be based on the validity of the arguments provided or the intentions to reach understanding and agreements, rather than power claims, or imposition (Habermas, 1984). Research shows that today's children learn more and better when learning is organised from the dialogic learning principles and includes interactions with adults other than teachers (Flecha, 2012). Roma children have been particularly affected by segregation practices, limited educational opportunities and the consequent high levels of school dropout (Greenberg, 2010). That is why the importance of engaging the Roma community in defining actions and policies has been emphasised. Greenfields and Ryder (2012) showed how research done 'with' and 'for' Roma rather than 'on' them contributed to their economic and social inclusion by including their voice. The transformation of schools into Learning Communities is an example. According to the European Commission (2010), 'Schools as Learning Communities' create favourable conditions that support students at risk of dropping out, by increasing the commitment of pupils, teachers, parents and other stakeholders in supporting school quality and development. These schools are implementing SEAs (evidence based) to create spaces for dialogic learning with the participation of all the community (Flecha et al., 2009). They are accounting for a wide range of knowledge, skills and learning levels to help reduce the disadvantaged situation of Roma students and improve the quality of their education (Tellado & Sava, 2010).

Engaging families and community in the transformation of the school through a dialogical approach

The implementation of SEAs in La Paz school followed a dialogic and participatory process in which the whole school community decided how the school had to be transformed to reverse the educational exclusion they were suffering. Involving the families in the process of transforming their reality and that of their children has been key to helping them develop a sense of belonging to the school and a belief in possibility, not only on an individual but also on a collective basis. Throughout the four years of the longitudinal case study, we followed the implementation of diverse SEAs and how they influenced children's attitudes and learning outcomes. In this section we will focus on two of these SEAs. First we will characterise each of them, alongside the participants' perceptions about their impact, to later discuss the sustainability of children's learning improvements across time.

A school where Roma dare to dream: participation in decision-making

The first stage of the school transformation was the 'Dream.' During this phase, the school organised activities for teachers, families and children in which they talked about the kind of school they would like, and expressed preferences and dreams related to learning and to the school. Everybody was encouraged to participate in the Dream. After the Dream, a Mixed Committee (of teachers, family members and pupils) classified all the dreams to make them visible to all the school community. They also proposed priorities for the school emerging from those dreams that were discussed and approved in the first General Assembly of La Paz Primary School. The Mixed Committees would meet periodically and the Assembly annually. Opening up the decision-making processes in the school to the community allowed, on the one hand, the raising up of Roma voices and the undermining of the idea that they felt their culture threatened in schools. On the other hand, the involvement of the community allowed the reformation of a mainstream school through dialogue with the Roma about the SEAs, the educational goals for their children, their own potential to support this education and the presence of the Roma identity, among other issues, in order to help develop a shared educational project. Maria's[2] words show how teachers spoke to the Roma families and used language to include them in the decision-making process by asking them for their opinions and desires. Teachers' interactions encouraged families, particularly Roma mothers like Maria, to participate and engage in dreaming the school:

'We are going to do this, we are going to completely change the school, and you will also contribute everything you want for the school.' The head teacher told us this and it has been a great change, and now the school is too much … and I hope that it carries on like this … They also count on us: 'What do you think? If we were going to do such and such, … what would you like most to do, this or that?' and they meet with us, we do many meetings, we meet once a week.

The teaching staff ensured that spaces and opportunities existed so that Roma families participated in the school, because they were aware of the positive impact this would have on the school performance. Assemblies were created as a means of encouraging the participation of families and members of the community in La Paz school. The whole community was invited to participate in these assemblies, which were held at least once a year, and everyone's voice was taken into consideration. Jose, the Inspector, attended one of these mass assemblies where almost all families of the pupils from the school participated. He explained:

When the first general school assembly was arranged, around 60 people attended it, that is, family members of all types, the full teaching staff and myself. No one could remember so many people getting together in school before … perhaps 80 or 90% of the families of the school were represented, as well as neighbourhood associations.

This evidence challenges unfounded perceptions that Roma families are not interested in school. In the same vein, Roma mothers like Carmen argue that when they see the value, they are eager to participate. She said:

Everything that is good for our children and for the school, we contribute. If there is a meeting and I cannot stay for half an hour … but even if it is only for five minutes I would go there, to see what they are talking about.

The Dream opened a space for dialogue in which Roma families brought interests and concerns about their children's education to the fore. One of the dreams was related to helping students to finish compulsory education. After finishing primary education in the neighbourhood school, the pupils from La Paz had to go to secondary schools in other parts of the city. This became a real barrier for Roma adolescents. On the one hand, the neighbourhood was physically separated by a road, which they had to cross; on the other hand, their neighbourhood was strongly stigmatised by the rest of the city. For this reason, many were at risk of dropping out and not completing secondary education. Increasing the educational provision in La Paz school was an initiative suggested by the families which was implemented by the teachers and the educational administration. Four years after the Dream, the school witnessed the first cohort of pupils graduating from secondary education.[3] In this case, attending the school they know, in their own neighbourhood, was crucial in reducing truancy and preventing early school leaving. Julio, as a Roma father and a member of a local Roma association, describes this situation:

Since they do the whole secondary school here, because they do it here, my children attend, my children will be here, because they are in their [own] neighbourhood, they are in their [own] environment. And they will complete it and they will get their education.

Thus, through a dialogical process where the community was taken into account in the decision-making processes, not only were education difficulties identified, but also the best way to tackle them. The dialogue between the teaching staff and the members of the community allowed the start of a process of transformation of the context which implied, in Freirian terms, turning difficulties into possibilities (Freire, 1997). Ultimately, the Roma community's participation in the school's Dream, the Assemblies and the Mixed Committees through a dialogic process helped to reduce the Roma children's exclusion from the educational system. These shared spaces between families and teachers also transformed families' and children's educational expectations, and changed difficulties into new opportunities never dreamed before. Julio continued:

> My older daughter is finishing the secondary school this year, now she is working very hard and doing better every day. Now she knows she can do it, she wants to go to college, she wants to be an educator and continue working hard for the children of this neighbourhood … and I want that too.

Transforming classroom interactions: family and community involvement in children's learning

One of the SEAs that La Paz school decided to implement was Interactive Groups. This is a form of organising classroom activity into small heterogeneous groups, with several adult guides, and based on dialogic learning. Family and community members participated in these groups as volunteers, and their role was to promote and encourage supportive learning interactions between pupils. All children were committed to completing their tasks and helping the others in their group, so that at the end of the session they had all finished the task successfully. Everyone was therefore accountable for the group's performance.

Before the transformation of the school, Roma families were not even allowed to cross the main entrance of the school door. This was partly because of the assumption that Roma relatives were not equipped to contribute to the children's learning. However, the teachers, the Principal and the Inspector rapidly observed important improvements in learning processes and achievement. Families' participation in the classroom increased the children's efforts and motivation for learning. For instance Luisa, a Roma mother who volunteers in the school, explains the effect her participation had on a particular boy in terms of the child's engagement in the learning activity. She realised how important her participation was for one particular child, and in turn, this became a very important reason for her to continue participating in the school.

> There are other children whose parents don't come, and when I come they [children] immediately say, 'come and help me', and maybe the day I don't come they do nothing. When I talk to the teacher she tells me so. But the day I do come, children do everything; I mean they work harder … I come almost every day because of that child, because when I come he is happier, he feels more like working … but the day I don't come, he falls asleep in the classroom, and does nothing, so … I come mostly because of that child, so that he can make progress.

Most teachers confirmed that the pupils became more motivated when Roma relatives and neighbours from the community interacted with them in the classroom: they put more effort into their own work and in helping their classmates; they increased engagement into class dynamics and improved their learning process. Nuria, a primary education teacher interviewed, described the effects of this participation on children's motivation as follows:

Specifically, the parents who participated in Interactive Groups … you could see that their daughter or son got involved, made an effort, became motivated, helped the others, incorporated into the dynamic … becoming very productive children.

In addition, they learned more because they could engage in more and different kinds of interactions, as there were four adult volunteers in each classroom. Lucía, a Roma girl, says that she appreciates how having more people in the classroom helped her and explains how engaging in dialogue with those adults enhanced her learning:

[How much do you learn when there are other people in the classroom?] A lot … because I'm not used to [having] lots of people there and when they explain things to me it stays in my head.

On the one hand, the knowledge stays in Lucía's head because she feels closer to these volunteers and it helps her to strengthen the meaning of schooling. On the other hand, their interaction is not based on 'expertise.' The fact that the participating mothers do not have academic credentials prevents one-way learning interactions in the classroom: with the adult explaining and the children listening. Esther, a teacher of eight-year-olds, illustrates how parents' participation in Interactive Groups does not require having a specific curricular knowledge but to be able to foster cooperation and dialogue:

Parents who participate in interactive groups, we know that it is not necessary for them to have any special pedagogical knowledge, they simply join the group, encourage the children to help each other, … I mean, although they might not know how to add or subtract on a paper … they can see that the children are adding and subtracting and how they do it and help each other. They also observe how the children internalise this knowledge, and … can still interact with the children through the strategies they themselves provide for the children.

The contributions of the Roma volunteers are based not on academic intelligence but on the cultural intelligence they have derived from their own experience and the cultural context they share with the children (Oliver & Gatt, 2010). As part of this cultural intelligence, Luisa knows how to deal with the different children in the group and how to foster their participation in knowledge construction. She knows the children well from the neighbourhood and, when she interacts with them, she takes into account that some of them are shy and others more talkative, and brilliantly manages the group to encourage a balance in their participation. All the children feel their contributions are important; and they all look at Luisa with respect. Because of this understanding, she succeeds in managing the children's interactions:

For example, Luis, who is very quiet, I try to talk to him so that he can give his opin- ion also, so that he will talk to me or describe something to me because, since I see that he's so quiet, when I do that it breaks the ice and then he starts … And once he starts speaking, he does not stop. But he is quieter. Juan is not. Sometimes I have to interrupt him or tell him to stop for a while and let his other classmates talk. I talk to him just as I do with Luis, but in a different way.

Luisa contributes to the interactions in a different manner from the teacher, thus enriching the learning process in the small group. With their non-expert background and language code, families' members like her contribute to the creation of a supportive learning environment, accounting for the different characteristics of the children. Although Verónica, a young Roma mother of six children, did not finish her primary school, her dialogue with Jaime promotes the boy's self-reflection and development of meta-cognitive strategies that help him to do better in his academic task. In her speech we notice that it is not only what she says, but also how she says it, the affectionate tone with which she talks to the child, her empathy and understanding:

> Jaime is a very restless child, for instance, I tell him, 'Jaime, listen to me dear, look, when you hurry, how do you do it? You do it badly and ugly, don't you? And when you go slowly, how do you do it? You do it very nice and very clean, right?' He wants to do it faster and I tell him 'Jaime, slowly dear' and then he goes slowly and so on, and I ask him 'how did you do it?' and he says 'very nice', and I tell him 'you see?'

When Roma families participate in education activities, like Interactive Groups, the transformation of learning goes beyond the school walls. The dialogic learning interactions promoted in the school context also transfer to other contexts that these adults and children share. As a result, the learning habits and activities in their homes changed, and children and families started to interact around learning in ways they never did before, as this teacher describes:

> The children are much more encouraged to learn. They take books home to read, because they are already reading with their father or mother, and [they have the idea of] 'I know how to read now' because before they did not know how to read because they [just] learned this year. So of course, because they are more motivated, they want to participate more.

Impact on the children's learning outcomes

The implementation of the SEAs in La Paz school has had an impact in the whole process of school change. Since the SEAs described above started to be implemented in 2006–7 pupils have improved their academic performance, as reflected in their higher scores on the national standardised tests (see Figure 1). Specifically, when the dialogic transformation process started building upon family involvement in educational activities, Roma children's engagement increased.

The results from the standardised tests conducted by the Department of Education show the pupils' improvements in specific subjects. In 2007–8, the eight-year-olds' classroom showed an improvement from the previous year from 1 to 2.5 (out of 5)[4] in all language skills evaluated: listening, speaking, talking, reading, writing and language use. The results obtained in subsequent standardised tests between 2008–9 and 2009–10 maintained the improvements in language skills as well as the rest of the skills evaluated. In the case of nine-year- old pupils, they improved in language from 2 to 3 (out of 5), and the same improvement was obtained in cultural and artistic skills, social and citizenship skills, learning to learn, autonomy, and emotional skills. Additionally, their score in mathematics increased from 1 to 3 (out of 5), and the score in knowledge and interaction with the physical world from 2 up to 4. It is particularly relevant that the pupils surpassed the scale mean score in all these areas.

Data from the questionnaires completed by the students about their perception of their learning improvement are consistent with the academic results obtained in the tests. Throughout the four-year period of the longitudinal study, the percentage of children perceiving that they had improved 'very much' in mathematics increased from 63.89% to 94.59%. The same is true for reading, which also improved from 58.33% to 89.04% according to the children's perception.

Finally, the rates of pupils' absenteeism were reduced considerably. While in 2006–7 there was a 30% rate of absenteeism, in 2007–8 this had been reduced to 10% and in 2008–9 absenteeism was just occasional. In the same period, the enrolment of new pupils in the school increased. In 2009–10 the percentage of pupils' enrolment grew 27.66% in relation to the previous year, and the 2010–11 enrolment grew an additional 10.56%.

According to the data presented above, children's academic outcomes have improved since the implementation of SEAs. The different types of data analysed–quantitative and qualitative–confirm the same trend, and particularly the quantitative data show that the improvement has been sustained throughout the studied period.

Discussion

Before the transformation of La Paz school, Roma children continuously experienced failure and had few opportunities to engage in actual learning. For example, they used not to work together with their classmates; they were expected to work individually, but just drawing and colouring. Learning activities had little meaning for them, as they did not offer any cognitive challenge. Parents had rarely been in the school and did not feel the school could help them to improve their educational level or to participate more fully in society. Many Roma children and families did not want to go to such a school. But La Paz school pupils have since then significantly improved their academic results, showing that it is possible to transform this situation and create the conditions for learning interactions that improve the performance of Roma children and increase their engagement.

The results presented here, based on the way learning is promoted at La Paz, are consistent with learning theories which state that interaction, dialogue and small-group work promote children's learning. These results show that pupils belonging to cultural minorities, and specifically Roma children, benefit from dialogic learning interactions. Importantly, dialogue-based learning interactions address the problems inherent in educational practices often aimed at students from minority groups, which minimise their possibilities for richer learning interactions and therefore their learning outcomes.

Importantly, La Paz school also shows that the power of learning through dialogue is enhanced when such dialogues include relatives and other members of the community who have historically been excluded from participation in educational activities, and actually from the school discourse. This is particularly crucial in a context like that of La Paz, where most of the families are Roma and only have a basic education or even less. The involvement of these families in the school's learning spaces creates bridges between the community and the school discourses and transforms the traditionally unequal relations between them–and also gives community context to the school curriculum.

In addition, when families take part in learning interactions they create the conditions for learning-related dialogue. These adults do not need to have an academic education to help their children learn. Indeed, the Roma women participating in La Paz classrooms do not have such knowledge. Instead, they apply the knowledge they have developed from their experience and their social context. This knowledge is crucial for managing the behaviour of children from minority groups, for supporting and motivating them, and for encouraging them to engage in peer support and reasoning, and in sharing learning strategies. Moreover, these women's engagement in learning activities makes it possible to transfer these in-school interactions between children and families to the home context and to other spaces in the neighbourhood. This makes it possible to extend the period of learning time beyond the time in school, which has proven to foster children's learning and achievement.

These results suggest how important it is for schools to create learning spaces where children and relatives can learn together and engage in interactions and dialogues that bring together the school, the community life, the curriculum and their identities. This is especially important for Roma students, as they are often pushed into practices that promote segregation, and their families and communities are seen as not interested in education and as incapable of contributing intellectually.

The case of La Paz exemplifies what Freire (1970) calls the 'untested feasibility.' Roma engagement and success in school had been an 'untested' reality that mainstream schools have usually not been able to establish, and for which the Roma themselves were blamed. But being 'untested' did not mean being 'unfeasible.' When educational actions are shaped and implemented in dialogue with the community, this 'untested' reality is imagined as possible and becomes a reality that can be created by transforming the existing reality. The success of La Paz, however, was not to 'test' a good idea but rather to implement SEAs which had already demonstrated, with evidence from research, that they worked. The SEAs were recreated in the context of La Paz which in turn constitutes more evidence of the transferability of these actions.

When schools offer such spaces for dialogic learning with community members, the school world and the Roma world no longer need to be separate and incompatible realities. Attending and succeeding at school does not mean giving up the Roma identity any more, as all the Roma families and children (like in La Paz) can take part in decision-making processes, including education and curriculum-related decisions, and can act as intellectual contributors in the classrooms and beyond, to eventually create a school that is helping the Roma children to succeed educationally. By recreating the pears. The case discussed in this article shows that when schools and communities dream together the school they want for their children, stereotyped folk assumptions are broken down and educational possibilities then emerge. Families worldwide want the best for their children but they need to know which are the successful actions and how they can contribute, having been so removed from schools for such a long time. In La Paz the dream came true through implementing SEAs based on dialogic learn- ing, which have proven equally successful in a range of other contexts. Luisa, like many Roma mothers in La Paz, expresses this well when she talks about her children:

> You see, last year … not a soul could get him to go there, and he would say 'the teacher yells at me, and the teacher scolds me', not a soul could get him into the school, and now it's 8 am and he is up, … which is incredible, and ready to learn. Indeed, there's been here a lot of improvement.

These social and educational consequences justify all the effort.

Notes

1. We acknowledge the common use of the term GRT [Gypsies, Roma and Travellers] in the UK. In this paper we use the term 'Roma' used at the Council of Europe. It refers to Roma, Sinti, Kale and related groups in Europe, Travellers and the Eastern Europe groups, and covers the wide diversity of the groups concerned, including persons who identify themselves as 'Gypsies'.
2. Secondary education refers to compulsory education from 12 to 16 years old in the Spanish educational system.
3. The standardised tests conducted by the regional government provide the results through a range score from 1 to 5.
4. The standardised tests conducted by the regional government provide the results through a range score from 1 to 5.

References

Anyon, J. (1995). Inner city school reform: Toward useful theory. *Urban Education, 30*, 56–70.
Aubert, A. (2011). Moving beyond social exclusion through dialogue. *International Studies in Sociology of Education, 21*, 63–75.
Bhopal, K. (2004). Gypsy travellers and education: Changing needs and changing perceptions. *British Journal of Educational Studies, 52*, 47–64.
Bhopal, K. (2011). 'This is a school, it's not a site': Teachers' attitudes towards Gypsy and Traveller pupils in schools in England, UK. *British Educational Research Journal, 37*, 465–83.
Bhopal, K., & Myers, M. (2009). Gypsy, Roma and Traveller pupils in schools in the UK: Inclusion and 'good practice'. *International Journal of Inclusive Education, 13*, 299–314.

Darling-Hammond, L. (1996). The right to learn and the advancement of teaching: Research, policy, and practice for democratic education. *Educational Researcher, 25*, 5–17.

Dearing, E., Kreider, H., Simpkins, S., & Weiss, H. B. (2006). Family involvement in school and low-income children's literacy: Longitudinal associations between and within fami- lies. *Journal of Educational Psychology, 98*, 653–64.

Derrington, C. (2005). Perceptions of behaviour and patterns of exclusion: Gypsy Traveller students in English secondary schools. *Journal of Research in Special Educational Needs, 5*, 55–61.

Derrington, C. (2007). Fight, flight and playing white: An examination of coping strategies adopted by Gypsy Traveller Adolescents in English secondary schools. *International Journal of Educational Research, 46*, 357–67.

Epstein, J. L. (1991). Effects on student achievement of teachers practices of parent involve- ment. *Advances in Reading/Language Research, 5*, 261–76.

European Commission. (2010). *Europe 2020. A strategy for smart, sustainable and inclusive growth*. Brussels: European Commission.

European Commission. (2011). *Tackling early school leaving: A key contribution to the Europe 2020 agenda*. Brussels: European Commission.

Flecha, A. (2012). Family Education Improve Student's Academic Performance: Contributions from European Research. *Multidisciplinary Journal of Educational Research, 3*, 301–21.

Flecha, A., García, R., Gómez, A., & Latorre, A. (2009). Participación en escuelas de éxito: Una investigación comunicativa del proyecto INCLUD-ED. *Cultura y Educación, 21*, 183–96.

Freire, P. (1970). *Pedagogy of the oppressed*. New York: Continuum.

Freire, P. (1997). *Pedagogy of the heart*. New York: Continuum.

Galton, M., Hargreaves, L., & Pell, T. (2009). Group work and whole-class teaching with 11 to 14 year-olds compared. *Cambridge Journal of Education, 39*, 119–40.

García, R. (2012). Out of the ghetto psychological basis of dialogic learning. *International Journal of Educational Psychology, 1*, 51–69.

Gómez, A., Racionero, S., & Sordé, T. (2010). Ten years of critical communicative methodology. *International Review of Qualitative Research, 3*, 17–43.

Gómez, J., & Vargas, J. (2003). Why Romà do not like mainstream schools: Voices of a people without territory. *Harvard Educational Review, 73*, 559–90.

Greenberg, J. (2010). Report on Roma education today: From slavery to segregation and beyond. *Columbia Law Review, 110*, 919–1001.

Greenfields, M., & Ryder, A. (2012). Research with and for Gypsies, Roma and Travellers: Combining policy, practice and community in action research. In J. Richardson & A. Tsang (Eds.), *Gypsies and Travellers* (pp. 151–67). Bristol: The Policy Press.

Habermas, J. (1984). *The theory of communicative action. V. 1. reason and the rationalization of society*. Boston: Beacon Press.

Hancock, I. (1988). Reunification and the role of international Romani union. *Roma, 29*, 9–19.

Hill, N. E., & Taylor, L. C. (2004). Parental school involvement and children's academic achieve- ment: Pragmatics and issues. *Current Directions in Psychological Science, 13*, 161–64.

Oakes, J. (1990). *Multiplying inequalities: The effects of race, social class, and tracking on opportunities to learn mathematics and science*. Santa Monica, CA: Rand Corp.

Oliver, E., & Gatt, S. (2010). De los actos comunicativos de poder a los actos comunicativos dialógicos en las aulas organizadas en grupos interactivos. *Signos, 43*, 279–94.

Padros, M., Garcia, R., de Mello, R., & Molina, S. (2011). Contrasting scientific knowledge with knowledge from the lifeworld: The dialogic inclusion contract. *Qualitative Inquiry, 17*, 304–12.

Puigvert, L., Christou, M., & Holford, J. (2012). Critical Communicative Methodology: including vulnerable voices in research through dialogue. *Cambridge Journal of Educa- tion, 42*, 513–26.

Rogoff, B., Goodman Turkanis, C., & Bartlett, L. (2001). *Learning together: Children and adults in a school community*. New York: Oxford University Press.

Roma Education Fund. (2010). *Annual report 2010*. Romania: Roma Education Fund.

Rose, R. (1983). Sinti and Roma in Germany. *Roma, 7*, 21–24.

Sheldon, S. B., & Epstein, J. L. (2005). Involvement counts: Family and community partnerships and mathematics achievement. *Journal of Educational Research, 98*, 196–206.

Tellado, I., & Sava, S. (2010). The role on non-expert adult guidance in the dialogic construction of knowledge. *Journal of Psychodidactics, 15*, 163–76.

Valls, R., & Padrós, M. (2011). Using dialogic research to overcome poverty: From principles to action. *European Journal of Education, 46*, 173–83.

Wells, G. (1999). *Dialogic Inquiry*. New York: Cambridge University Press.

Wilson, W. (2003). Race, class and urban poverty: A rejoinder. *Ethnic and Racial Studies, 26*, 1096–1114.

Further Readings

Section 6: Critical Pedagogy and the Classroom

Aksoy, H. (2013).'Özgürleştiren Öğretmen' (Liberating Teacher), *Öğretmen Dunyasi*, Year 3 (May), 37–40.

Altman, R., & De, M. (2010). 'Expanding Possibilities for Underserved and Marginalized Youth Using Freire's Critical Pedagogy of Active and Reflective Arts Practice: Three Case Studies from Bronx (USA), Coventry (UK), and New Delhi (India).' *UNESCO Observatory, Faculty of Architecture, Building and Planning, The University of Melbourne Refereed E-Journal, 1*(5). Retrieved from http://web.education. unimelb.edu.au/UNESCO/pdfs/ejournals/altman-paper.pdf.

Aparicio Guadas, P. (2012).*El hilo de la vocación: educarse y educar aún: consideraciones intempestivas de un maestro ignorante* (the Thread of One's Calling: untimely considerations of an ignorant school master), Xativa: Edicions del Crec.

Bissett, S. Z. (2012). 'Bala Ga Lili: Meeting Indigenous Learners Halfway.' *Australian Journal of Environmental Education, 28,* 78–91. doi:10.1017/aee.2013.2.

Borg, C., M. Cardona, and S. Caruana. 2009. *Letter to a Teacher. Lorenzo Milani's Contribution to Critical Citizenship.* Malta: Agenda.

Connolly, B. (2013). 'Theorising Creative Critical Pedagogy: the Art of Politicized Agency.' *Rizoma freireano, 14,* 1–15.

Darder, A. (2012). *Culture and Power in the Classroom.* Boulder, CO.: Paradigm.

El-Geretly, H. (2002). 'From Reaching in to Reaching Out: El-Warsha 1987–1999.' In J.-P. Hautecoeur (Ed.), *Ecological education in everyday life. ALPHA 2000* (71–81). Toronto, Buffalo & London: University of Toronto Press.

Enguita, M. (1999). *La profesión docente y la comunidad.* Madrid: Morata.

Fischman, G and Stromquist, N (2000). *Imagining Teachers,* Lanham, Maryland: Rowman & Littlefield.

FitzSimmons, R., & Uusiautti, S. (2013).' Critical Revolutionary Pedagogy Spiced by Pedagogical Love.' *Journal for Critical Education Policy Studies, 11*(3), 230–43. Retrieved from http://www.jceps.com/.

Flecha, R and Soler, M (2013).'Turning Difficulties into Possibilities. Engaging Roma Families and Students in School through Dialogic Learning,' *Cambridge Journal of Education* DOI: 10.1080/0305764X. 2013.819068.

Freire. P. (1995). The Progressive Teacher. In de Figueiredo-Cowen & D. Gastaldo (eds.). *Paulo Freire at the Institute* (17–24). London, UK: Institute of Education

Freire, P. (1998b). *Teachers and Cultural Workers: Letters to Those who Dare to Teach.* Boulder, CO: Westview Press.

King-Calnek, J. E. (2006). Education for citizenship: Interethnic pedagogy and formal education at Escola Criativa Olodum. *The Urban Review, 38*(2), 145–64. doi: 10.1007/s11256-06-028-4.

Latapí, P. (1988). 'Participatory Research. a New Research Paradigm?' *Alberta Journal of Educational Research, 43,* 310–19.

Mazawi, A. E. (2011). 'Education as Spaces of Community Engagement and a "Capacity to Aspire,"' in *Educators of the Mediterranean: Up Close and Personal,* Sultana, R.G. (ed.) Rotterdam, Taipei and Boston, Sense Publishers.

Nyirenda, J. E. (1996). 'The Relevance of Paulo Freire's Contributions to Education and Development in Present Day Africa,' *Africa Media Review, 10*, 1–20.

Phtiaka, H. (1997). *Special Kids For Special Treatment: How Special Do You Need To Be To Find Yourself In A Special School?,* Brighton: Falmer Press.

Sani, R. and Simeone, D. (eds.) *Don Lorenzo Milani la Scuola della Parola* (Don Lorenzo Milani and the School of the Word), Macerata: edizioni università di Macerata

Schoorman, D., Acosta, M. C., Sena, S. R., & Baxley, T. (2012). 'Critical Pedagogy in HIV-AIDS Education for a Maya Immigrant Community.' *Multicultural Perspectives, 14*(4), 194–200. http://dx.doi.org/10.10 80/15210960.2012.725317.

Scuola di Barbiana. 1996. *Lettera a Una Professoressa* (Letter to a Teacher). Florence: Libreria Editrice Fiorentina.

Singh, M. (2011). 'Transformative Knowledge Exchange and Critical Pedagogy: Internationalising Education through Intellectual Engagement.' In R. Tinning & K. Sirna (Eds.), Education, Social Justice and the Legacy of Deakin University: Reflections of the Deakin Diaspora. doi:10.1007/978-94-6091-639-7_13.

Section 7
Critical Higher Education and Activism

Always bear in mind that the people are not fighting for ideas, for the things in anyone's head. They are fighting to win material benefits, to live better and in peace, to see their lives go forward, to guarantee the future of their children.

Amilcar Cabral, *Revolution in Guinea* (1974)

Freedom is not something that one people can bestow on another as a gift.
They claim it as their own and none can keep it from them.

Kwame Nkrumah, *Former Prime Minister and President of Ghana*
& Lenin Peace Prize Speech (1963)

28

The University at a Crossroads

Boaventura de Sousa Santos

INTRODUCTION

When we consider the European university, or indeed the university worldwide, the present is a moment in which it is as important to look back as to look forward. In the case of Europe, we are now in the middle of the Bologna Process—named after the Bologna Declaration organized by the European Union education ministers in 1999 aimed at reforming higher education in Europe and creating the European Higher Education Area (EHEA)[1]. It is a period prone to intense fluctuations between positive and negative evaluations, between a sense that it is either too late or too early to achieve the intended results. In my view, such intense fluctuations in analysis and evaluation are a sign that everything remains open, that failure and success loom equally on the horizon, and that it is up to us to make one or the other happen. The great philosopher Ernst Bloch wrote that by each hope there is always a coffin: *Heil* and *Unheil*. Though it is our main objective to focus on the European university, it would be foolish not to think that the challenges facing the European university today are to be found in all continents, however different the reasons, the arguments, or the proposed solutions may be.

In general we can assert that the university is undergoing—as much as the rest of contemporary societies—a period of paradigmatic transition. This transition can be characterized in the following way: *we face modern problems for which there are no modern solutions*. Very succinctly, our modern problems are the fulfillment of the ideals of the French Revolution: *liberté, egalité, fraternité*. In the past two hundred years we have not been able to fulfill such objectives in Europe, let alone elsewhere. The solutions designed to fulfill them—I mean: scientific and technological progress; formal and instrumental rationality; the modern bureaucratic state; the recognition of class, race and gender divisions and discriminations; the institutionalization of social conflict raised by them through democratic processes, development of national cultures and national identities, secularism and laicism; and so on and so forth—have not been able to deliver the objectives so strenuously struggled for. The modern university, particularly from mid-19th century onwards, has been a key component of such solutions. It was actually in light of them that institutional autonomy, academic freedom and social responsibility were originally designed.

The generalized crisis of modern solutions has thereby brought with it the crisis of the university. After the Second World War, the early 1970s was a period of intense reformist impulses worldwide. In most cases, the student movements of the late 1960s and early 1970s were the motive behind them. In the past forty years, however, for different but convergent reasons, in

295

various parts of the world the university has become, rather than a solution for societal problems, an additional problem.

As far as the university is concerned, the problem may be formulated in this way: the university is being confronted with strong questions for which it has so far provided only weak answers. Strong questions are those questions that go to the roots of the historical identity and vocation of the university in order to question not so much the details of the future of the university but rather whether the university, as we know it, has indeed a future. They are, therefore, questions that arouse a particular kind of perplexity. Weak answers take the future of the university for granted. The reforms they call for end up being an invitation to immobilism. They fail to abate the perplexity caused by the strong questions and may, in fact, even increase it. Indeed, they assume that the perplexity is pointless.

As proposed and further investigated below, I submit that we must take up the strong question and transform the perplexity they cause into a positive energy both to deepen and to reorient the reformist movement. The perplexity results from the fact that we are before an open field of contradictions in which there is an unfinished and unregulated competition among different possibilities. Such possibilities open space for political and institutional innovation by showing the magnitude of what is at stake.

Strong Questions

Let me provide some samples of the strong questions facing the university at the beginning of the 21st century. Without claiming to be exhaustive, I select twelvesuch questions.

The first strong question is this: Given the fact that the university was part and parcel of the building of the modern nationstate—by training its elites and bureaucracy, and by providing the knowledge and ideology underlying the national project—how is the mission of the university to be refounded in a globalized world, a world in which state sovereignty is increasingly a shared sovereignty or simply a choice among different kinds of interdependence, and in which the very idea of a national project has become an obstacle to dominant conceptions of global development? Is the global university a possible answer? If so, how many such global universities are viable? What happens to the large number of the remaining ones? If global elites are to be trained in global universities, where can be found in society the allies and the social base for the non-global universities? Which kinds of relationships between global and nonglobal universities will there be? Will the focus on ranking contribute to the cohesion of the European higher education area or, on the contrary, to its segmentation through unfair competition and the rise of commercial internationalism?

A second strong question may be formulated as follows: The idea of a knowledge society implies that knowledge is everywhere; what is the impact of this idea on a modern university which was created on the premise that it was an island of knowledge in a society of ignorance? What is the place or the specificity of the university as a center of knowledge production and diffusion in a society with many other centers of production and diffusion of knowledge? Will academic review and refereeing practices continue to significantly determine scholarship evaluations and recruitment and promotional opportunities in universities world-wide? Will they go on doing that in such a way that it promotes narrowly defined, monoculturally generated conceptions of good scholarship, methodological rigor and theoretical soundness, as it happens, in general, today? Or, on the contrary, will the new technologies of production and dissemination of knowledge (internet / ebook / ejournal / elibraries, etc.) undermine the traditional, elitist practices of gate-keeping in scientific and academic journal and book publishing, making it possible to pursue new, creative, and more egalitarian, culturally sensitive, and paradigmatically open-minded practices of peer reviewing?

Third strong question: At its best, the modern university has been a locus of free and independent thinking and of celebration of diversity, even when subjected to the narrow boundaries of the disciplines, whether in the sciences or the humanities. Bearing in mind that for the past 30 years the tendency to transform the truth value of knowledge into the 'market truth' value of knowledge has become increasingly strong, could there be any future for nonconformist, critical, heterodox, nonmarketable knowledge, and for professors, researchers and students pursuing it? If yes, what will be its impact upon the criteria of excellence and inter-university competitiveness? If not, can we still call university an institution that only produces competent conformists and never competent rebels, and that only regards knowledge as a commodity and never as a public good?

Fourth strong question: The modern university has been from the beginning a transnational institution at the service of national societies. At its best, the modern university is an early model for international flows of ideas, teachers, students and books. We live in a globalized world but not in a homogeneously globalized world. Not only are there different logics moving globalized flows but also different power relations behind the distribution of the costs and benefits of globalization. There is transnational greed as there is transnational solidarity. Which side will the university be on? Will it become a transnational corporation or a transnational cooperative or non-profit organization? Is there a contradiction between our emphasis on cultural and social development and the emphasis of some European politicians and powerful think-tanks on economic development and the university's contribution to the global competitiveness of European businesses? Why have some major reform efforts outside Europe chosen the slogan: "Neither Bologna nor Harvard"?

Fifth strong question: In the long run, the idea of Europe is only sustainable as the Europe of ideas. Now, the university has historically been one of the main pillars of the Europe of ideas, however questionable such ideas may have been. This has been possible by granting to the university a degree of institutional autonomy unimaginable in any other state institution. The dark side of this autonomy has been social isolationism, lack of transparency, organizational inefficiency, social prestige disconnected from scholarly achievement. In its original design, the Bologna Process was to put an end to this dark side without significantly affecting the university's autonomy. Is this design being carried out without perverse results? Is the Bologna Process a break with the negative aspects of the traditional university, or is it a brilliant exercise in reshuffling inertias and recycling old vices? Is it possible to standardize procedures and criteria across such different university cultures without killing diversity and innovation? Is it possible to develop transparency, mobility and reciprocal recognition while preserving institutional and cultural diversity? Why are bureaucrats taking control of the good ideas and noble ideals so easily?

Sixth strong question: Job prestige goes together with job qualification and scarcity. The modern university has been at the core of the social production of high-powered job qualifications. If rankings manage to fragment the European and the future global university system, which jobs and which qualifications will be generated by which universities? The world system is built on an integrated hierarchy of core, peripheral and semi-peripheral countries. The current financial and economic crisis has shown that the same hierarchy holds in Europe and, as such, social cohesion is showing its dark side: it exists on the condition that the structural hierarchy not be affected, that countries remain as core, peripheral or semiperipheral, without moving either up or down in the hierarchy. Not necessarily coincident with location in the hierarchy of the countries in which they are located, are we going to have peripheral, semi-peripheral and central universities? Will the Bologna Process rigidify such hierarchies or make them more liquid? Depending on the geopolitical distribution of rankings, will hierarchy among universities contribute to accentuate or rather to attenuate the hierarchies among European countries?

Seventh strong question: As the university diversifies the degrees of qualification—first, second, third cycle and postdoctoral degrees—social illiteracy increases in the lower degrees, thus justifying the greater value of higher degrees. This is in fact a spiral movement. Has it exhausted its development potential? How many more cycles are we going to have in the future?

Are we creating endless illiteracy in the same process that we create endless knowledge? Will peripheral and semi-peripheral universities be charged with solving the illiteracy problem, while the core universities will have the monopoly of highly qualified knowledge?

Eighth strong question: Can the university retain its specificity and relative autonomy while being governed by market imperatives and employment demands? Given the highly problematic validity of cost-benefit analysis in the field of research and development, will the university be allowed to assume certain costs in the expectation of uncertain benefits, as it has always done in the past? What will happen to knowledge that has not and should not have market value? Regarding marketable knowledge which impact on it is to be expected if such knowledge is going to be valued exclusively according to its market value? What is the future of social responsibility if extension is reduced to an expedient or burden to raise financial resources? What will happen to the imperative of making the university relevant to the needs of society, taking for granted that such needs are not reducible to market needs and may actually contradict them?

Ninth strong question: The university (or at least the public university) has historically been embedded in the three pillars of modern social regulation—the state, the market and civil society; however, the balance of their presence in the structure and functioning of the university has varied in the course of time. Indeed, the modern European university started in Bologna as a civil society initiative. Later on, the state strengthened its presence, which became dominant from mid-19th century onwards, and in the colonies particularly after they became independent. In the last 30 years the market took the lead in structuring the university life. In a few decades the university went from producing knowledge and professionals for the market, to becoming itself a market, the market of tertiary education, and finally, at least according to powerful visionaries, to being run like a market organization, a business organization. Since then, civil society concerns have been easily confused with market imperatives or subordinated to them, and the state has very often used its coercive power to impose market imperatives to the reluctant universities. Is the Bologna Process a creative response to neoliberal, one-dimensional demands or, on the contrary, a way of imposing them through a transnational European process that neutralizes national resistance?

Tenth strong question: The European universities and many other universities around the world that followed their model were instrumental in disseminating a Eurocentric view of the world, a view powerful enough (in both intellectual and military terms) to claim universal validity. This claim did not involve ignoring the cultural, social and spiritual differences of the non-European world. On the contrary, it entailed knowing such differences, even though subjected to Eurocentric purposes, whether the romantic celebration of the Other or the colonial subjugation and destruction of the Other. In both cases, knowing the Other was at the service of showing the superiority and therefore the universality of European culture; a detailed, colonial or imperial knowledge of the Other was required. My university, for instance, the University of Coimbra, founded in 1290, contributed immensely to the development of knowledge committed to the colonial enterprise. The quality and intensity of the homework done by the missionaries before embarking overseas are astounding, all the more astounding when we compare them with the homework done by World Bank and International Monetary Fund (IMF) executives when they go around evangelizing the world with the neoliberal orthodoxy in their heads and pockets. Of their knowledge claims it cannot be said what the great leader of the African Liberation movements, Amilcar Cabral, said about colonial knowledge: "The search for such knowledge, in spite of its unilateral, subjective and very often unfair character, does contribute to enriching the human and social sciences in general."[2]

The eleventh question is this: Is the university prepared to recognize that the understanding of the world by far exceeds the Western understanding of the world? Is the university prepared to refound the idea of universalism on a new, intercultural basis? We live in a world of norms in conflict and many of them are resulting in war and violence. Cultural differences, new and old collective identities, antagonistic political, religious and moral conceptions and convictions are today more visible than ever, both outside and inside Europe. There is no alternative to violence other than readiness to accept the incompleteness of all cultures and identities, including our own, arduous negotiation, and credible intercultural dialogue. If Europe—against its own past— is to become a beacon of peace, respect for diversity and intercultural dialogue, the university will certainly have a central role to play. Are the European universities being reformed having such role in mind as a strategic objective of their future?

The twelfth question, probably the strongest of them all, is the following: Modern universities have been both a product and a producer of specific models of development. When the Bologna Process started there were more certainties about the European project of development than there are today. The compound effect of multiple crises—the financial and economic crisis, the environmental and energetic crisis, the crisis of the European social model, the migration crisis, the security crisis—points to a civilizatory crisis or paradigmatic change. The question is: In such a tumultuous time, is the university's serenity possible? And, if possible, is it desirable? Is the Bologna Process equipping the university to enter the debate on models of development and civilizatory paradigms, or rather to serve as acritically and as efficiently as possible the dominant model decided by the powers that be and evaluated by the new supervisors of the university output at their service? At the international level, given the conflict between local conceptions of autonomous development and the global development model imposed by the rules of the WTO, and given the fact that the European states are donor states, will the European university contribute to a dialogue among different models of development? Or will it rather provide intellectual legitimacy to unilateral impositions by the donor states, as in the colonial period?

The Present as the Future's Past

In my view, one decade after the beginning of the Bologna Process, we have so far been providing only weak answers to these strong questions.

The weakest of them all are the nonanswers, the silences, the taken-for-grantedness of the new common sense about the mission of the university. This is a situation that we should overcome as soon as possible. The danger is to convert really mediocre achievements into brilliant leaps forward, to disguise resignation under the mask of consensus, to orient the university towards a future in which there is no future for the university.

In my mind, we are at a juncture which our complexity scientists would characterize as a situation of bifurcation. Minimal movements in one or other direction may produce major and irreversible changes. Such is the magnitude of our responsibility. We all know that we never act upon the future; we act upon the present in light of our anticipations or visions of how the future will look like. The strong questions indicate that there is no single, consensual anticipation or vision to be taken for granted, and that is why the questions invite deep reflection.

I suggest that we are before two alternative visions and that their co-presence is the source of the tensions running through our university system today. They both invite two opposing imaginary visions of a retrospective evaluation of the reforms under way. That is, they look from the future at our present.

According to one of them, our reform efforts were indeed a true reform, as they succeeded in preparing the university to confront the challenges of the 21st century effectively—by diversifying its mission without giving away its authenticity, by strengthening institutional autonomy, academic freedom and social responsibility under the new and very complex conditions of Europe and of the world at large. Thus, the European university was able to rebuild its humanistic ideal in a new internationalist, solidary and intercultural way. According to the other, imaginary, retrospective vision, the Bologna Process was, on the contrary, a counterreformation, as it blocked the reforms that the universities in different European countries were undertaking individually, and each one according to its specific conditions to face the above-mentioned challenges; furthermore, the Bologna Process forced a convergence beyond a reasonable level. It did this with the purpose of disabling the university from the mechanisms that would allow it to resist against the business and market imperatives in the same manner as it resisted in the past against the imperatives of religion and later of the state.

In order not to end this essay on a pessimistic note, I will start by briefly detailing the second retrospective vision and then turning to the first one. The second vision, the vision of the counter-reformation, displays before us a dystopic scenario with the following features.

As we realize that the financial crisis has unveiled the dangers of creating a single currency without putting together public and fiscal policies and state budgets, it may well happen that, in the long run, the Bologna Process turns out to be the euro of European universities. Here are the foreseeable consequences: the principles of solidary university internationalism and respect for cultural diversity will be discarded in the name of the efficiency of the European university market and competition; the weaker universities (gathered in the weaker countries) will be dumped by the university rating agencies into the ranking garbage bin. Though claiming to be rigorous, university ranking will be, in a great measure, arbitrary and subjective. Most universities will suffer the consequences of fast decrease of public funding; many universities will be forced to close down.

As is happening in other levels of education, the wealthy students and their parents will search throughout many countries for the best quality / price ratio, as they are already doing in the commercial malls which universities are also becoming, while the poor students and their parents will be confined to the poor universities existing in their poor countries or neighbourhoods. The internal impact will be overwhelming: the relation between research and teaching, highly advertised by Bologna, will be a very paradise for the universities at the top of the ranking (a scarce minority) and perfect hell for the large majority of the universities and their scholars. The commodification criteria will reduce the value of the different areas of knowledge to their market price. Latin, poetry or philosophy will be kept only if some informatic macdonald recognizes in them any measure of usefulness. University administrators will be the first ones to internalize the classifying orgy, an orgy of objective maniacs and indicators maniacs; they will excel in creating income by expropriating the students' families or robbing the faculty of their personal lives and leisure. They will exert all their creativity to destroy university creativity and diversity, to standardize all that is standardizeable and to discredit or discard all that is not. The faculty will be proletarianized by the very means of educational production of which they are supposedly owners—that is, teaching, assessment, research. They will end up being zombies of forms, objectives, evaluations that are impeccable as to formal rigor but necessarily fraudulent in substance, *workpackages, deliverables, milestones,* bargains of mutual citation to improve the indices, evaluations of *where*-you-publish-*what*-I-couldn't-care-less, careers conceived of as exhilarating but flattened at the low positions in most situations. For the younger faculty the academic freedom will be a cruel joke. The students will be as masters of their learning as they will be slaves of their indebtedness for the rest of their lives. They will enjoy autonomy and free choice in curricular matters with no idea of the logic and limits of the choices presented to them, and will be guided, in personalized fashion, toward a mass alternative of professional employment or of professional unemployment. Tertiary education will be finally liberalized according to the rules of the World Trade Organization.

As I said, none of the above has to happen. There is another retrospective vision, and in our hearts and minds we very much hope that it will prevail. But for it to happen, we should start by recognizing and denouncing that the supposed new normalcy of the state of affairs in the above description is in fact a moral aberration and will entail the end of the university as we know it. Let us consider now the other retrospective vision, the vision which, looking from the future into our present, evaluates the Bologna Process as a true reform that changed the European university deeply and for the better. Such vision will emphasize the following features of our current undertakings.

First, the Bologna Process was able to identify and solve most of the problems that the pre-Bologna university was suffering and unable to confront, such as: established inertias that paralyzed any reformist effort; endogamic preferences that created aversion to innovation and challenge; institutional authoritarianism under the guise of scholarly authority; nepotism under the guise of merit; elitism under the guise of excellence; political control under the guise of democratic participation; neo-feudalism under the guise of department or school autonomy; fear of being evaluated under the guise of academic freedom; low scientific production justified as an heroic resistance to stupid terms of reference or comments by referees; generalized administrative inefficiency under the guise of respect for tradition.

Second, in so doing the Bologna Process, rather than discrediting and throwing overboard the self-evaluation and reformist efforts that were being undertaken by the most dedicated and innovative professors and administrators, provided them with a new framework and powerful institutional support, to the extent that the Bologna Process could become an endogenous energy rather than an outside imposition. In order to succeed in this, the Bologna Process managed to combine convergence with diversity and difference, and developed mechanisms of positive discrimination to allow for the different national university systems to cooperate and compete among themselves in fair terms.

Third, the Bologna Process never let itself be taken over by the so-called international tertiary education experts with the capacity of transforming subjective, arbitrary preferences into self-evident truths and inevitable public policies. It kept in sight two powerful intellectual views of the mission of the university produced in the early years of the past century and unequivocally took sides between the two.

One was formulated by Ortega y Gasset and Bertrand Russell, two intellectuals with very different political ideas, but who converged in denouncing the political instrumentalization of the university; the other, formulated by Martin Heidegger in his inaugural lecture as rector of Freiburg University in 1933, in which he invited the university to contribute to the preservation of the German strengths of soil and blood. The Bologna Process unequivocally adopted the first and refused the second.

Fourth, the reformists never confused the market with civil society or the community and urged the universities to keep a broad conception of social responsibility, encouraging action research as well as extension projects aimed at bettering the lives of the more vulnerable social groups trapped in systemic social inequality and discrimination, be they women, the unemployed, young and elderly people, migrant workers, ethnic and religious minorities, and so on.

Fifth, the reform Process made it very clear that universities are centers of production of knowledge in the broadest possible sense. Accordingly, it promoted interculturality, heterodoxy and critical engagement in the best liberal tradition which the pre-Bologna Process university had abandoned in the name of political or economic correctness. In the same vein, it encouraged internal scientific pluralism and, most importantly, granted equal dignity and importance to knowledge with market value and knowledge with no possible market value. Moreover, the reformists understood clearly all along that in thefield of research and development, cost-benefit analysis is a very crude instrument and may kill innovation instead of promoting it. In fact, the history of technology amply shows that the innovations with highest instrumental value were made possible with no attention to cost / benefit calculations.

Sixth, the Bologna Process managed to strengthen the relationship between teaching and research, and, while rewarding excellence, it made sure that the community of university teachers would not be divided between two stratified segments: a small group of first class university citizens with abundant money, light teaching loads and other good conditions to carry out research, on the one hand, and, on the other, a large group of second class university citizens enslaved by long hours of teaching and tutoring with little access to research funds only because they were employed by the wrong universities or were interested in supposedly wrong topics. It managed to combine higher selectivity in recruitment and strict accountability in the use of teaching time and research funds with a concern for really equal opportunities. It conceived of the rankings as the salt in food: too little makes it unpalatable; too much kills all the flavors. Moreover, at a given point it decided that what had happened in international rankings elsewhere could be applied to the university system as well. Accordingly, as the GDP index exists today side by side with the index of human development of the UNDP, the Bologna Process managed to insert internal plurality in the ranking systems.

Seventh, the Bologna Process ended up abandoning the once fashionable concept of human capital after concluding that the universities should form full human beings and full citizens and not just human capital subjected to market fluctuations like any other capital. This had a decisive impact on the curricula and on the evaluation of performances. Furthermore, the Bologna Process managed to convince the European Union and the European states that they should be financially more generous with the public universities not because of corporatist pressures but rather because the investment in an excellent public university system is probably the best way of investing in the future of a Europe of ideas, the only way for Europe to remain truly European.

Finally, the Bologna Process expanded exponentially the internationalization of the European university but took good care to promote other forms of internationalism than commercial internationalism. In this way, the European area of higher education ceased to be a threat to the academic freedom and intellectual autonomy of universities throughout the world to become a loyal and powerful ally in keeping the ideas of academic freedom, institutional autonomy and knowledge diversity well and alive in a world threatened by the *pensée unique* of market imperatives.

I have presented you with two alternative visions of our future. There is no doubt in my mind that all of us here wish that our future be molded by the retrospective vision I just described. It is in our hands to make that happen.

Notes

1. Please visit the following site for more in-formation: http://www.ond.vlaanderen.be/hogeronderwijs/bologna/
2. Cabral, Amílcar (1982), "The role of Culture in the Struggle for Independence," in Aquino de Bragança and Immanuel Wallerstein (eds.), *The African Liberation Reader*, 197–203.

29

Higher Education and Class
Production or Reproduction

Panagiotis Sotiris

Critical educational theory has always dealt with questions of social class. Treating education as a mechanism reproducing class division, hierarchy and inequality has been one of main motives behind most critical and radical writings on education. Questioning this role of education, and particularly Higher Education, in the reproduction of class relations has been not only a theoretical tenet but also a political position in struggles regarding access to education, funding and curricula – struggles that demanded reforms and changes in education that would undermine the reproduction of class divisions.

Marxist debates on social classes have been an important part of the broader theoretical discussion on class formation and reproduction. In the Marxist tradition social class is not simply a descriptive category registering the existence of social inequality and the emergence of collective identities and differential life-chances. It is also a strategic theoretical concept. For Marxism, history is defined as a history of class *struggles* and class antagonism is presented as being at the centre of the different historical modes of production (Marx – Engels 1970, pp. 30–31). Moreover, for Marxism social class is linked to social emancipation, since the working class is presented as being inherently anti-capitalist.

What is more important is that the Marxist conception of social class is not simply a theory of class antagonism. Class is linked to a theory of the social relations of production. In the case of the capitalist mode of production, what we see is not only the generalization of commodity circulation and exchange, but also a particular set of social relations of production leading to various forms of formal and real subsumption of labour to capital, as the result of relations of power and ownership within production. These have to do with the means of production and their use, the ability to buy labour power, the allocation of resources and the selling of the products of labour, the organization, rhythms and times of production, but also with coping with the various forms of resistance within capitalist production.

These social relations and practices are constantly reproduced within production and take the form of imperatives that the capitalists must comply with in order to gain a share in competitive markets through differentials of labour productivity. This process leads to the constant production and reproduction of specific roles, practices, positions, and subjectivities. Consequently, the line of demarcation between the owners of the means of production and workers is constantly being redrawn. That is why class in the Marxist tradition is always linked not to stratification of earnings, life chances, real and symbolic capital, but to *exploitation* (Wright 22004). Exploitation always implies and opens up some form of resistance to exploitation, even in the silent way of not fully conforming to the tasks or rhythms required. The centrality of exploitation as a structurally antagonistic relation implies a much more relational, dialectical – in the sense of mutual and reciprocal determination – and strategic-political conception of class antagonism than envisaged by non-Marxist theories of social stratification.

Class formation implies class reproduction, in terms of the ways classes, as collective sets of social agents, are reproduced and the practices and institutions that play a role in these processes. Education has been central in the theoretical discussion of such issues, in the sense of its role in the reproduction of hierarchies and divisions in society. Different educational trajectories lead to different class positions, and in schools, vocational colleges and universities or during apprenticeships we can see the acquisition of attitudes and identities, not only skills.

In the long history of the debates on social reproduction and education at least two theoretical dangers (and temptations) have emerged. One is *functionalism* in the sense of a conception of society as system able to foresee its needs and have specific institutions – such as education – fulfilling specific functions, in a certain teleological fashion. The other is *structuralism* not in the sense of a particular theoretical trend but in the more general sense of a theorization of society based upon the assumption that deep or latent structures are the substance of society and determine the functioning of particular institutions.

Contemporary debates about radical politics tend to avoid thinking in terms of class politics. This has been the result of an earlier emphasis on 'new social subjects' and more recently of thinking not in terms of social classes but more of collective subjects emerging through social and political demands. From the "Multitude" of the early 2000s (Hardt and Negri 2000), as the aggregation of all those opposing the capitalist 'Empire', to the current image of the '99%' as opposed to the '1%', we have metaphors which are powerful in terms of articulating a sense of collective anger and protest against global capital, but do not enable an actual theoretical analysis of social classes and alliances. However important politically and symbolically these notions are, as expressions of a new radicalism, we still need to reopen the debate on classes and class reproduction.

To reopen the debate on classes we must also deal with new theoretical propositions regarding the role of education in class formation. Radical theorists since the 1990s have pointed to the increased tendency towards the entrepreneurialization, commodification and commercialization of practices and institutions traditionally associated with social reproduction, including schools and universities. They use this as evidence that we must abandon the production/reproduction dividing line and instead understand education as a production site of social classes as well as knowledge. Consequently, struggles in Higher Education, can be seen as forms of the antagonism between living labour and capital. Therefore, the question whether higher education produces social classes or classes are produced outside of education and are reproduced within education, has a broader theoretical and political significance.

Current developments, especially in higher education, pose important theoretical challenges and must be incorporated in any critical theorization of Higher Education. Going back to the class reproduction theories of the 1970s cannot account for recent developments. Simply opting for a theory of cognitive capitalism and the production of immaterial labour in academia leaves many questions unanswered. In what follows I try to suggest an alternative to the production/reproduction dichotomy through a reading of Gramsci's conception of *hegemonic apparatuses*.

Hegemony and Hegemonic Apparatuses

The Gramscian concept of hegemony can offer us a way to theorize education in the context of a more dialectical conception of power. By this I do not refer to the well-known influence of Gramscian notions in critical education theory, regarding the importance of cultural elements, the role of intellectuals, the need to study consent along with coercion. I am referring to what we can gain from more critical and dialectical readings of Gramsci that stress the complexity of his conception of hegemony, the State and hegemonic apparatuses (Buci-Glucksmann 1980; Thomas 2009). Gramsci's prison writings (Gramsci 1971; Gramsci 1978–96) are not about the importance of culture or consent as a political strategy. They deal with the complex ways through which social power is turned into political power within societies. The complex articulation of civil society (everyday practices and transaction, economic, 'corporatist' and other), political society (political and ideological institutions) and the State, offers a more dialectical conception of the relations between economy, society and the State. It is what Gramsci describes as the 'Integral State', as "the entire complex of practical and theoretical activities with which the ruling class not only justifies and maintains its dominance, but manages to win the active consent of those over whom it rules" (Gramsci 1971, p. 244).

A Class is never simply situated through production and then ensures its domination through the State and its reproduction through education. Both its hegemony and its constitution, along with maintaining the subaltern position of the exploited classes, are constantly re-constituted through the apparatuses of the 'integral state', not excluding the factory, exemplified in Gramsci's insistence that in Fordism "hegemony is born in the factory"(Gramsci 1971, p.282). Moreover, Gramsci's conception of the hegemonic apparatus, which can be public or private, offers a much more complex way to incorporate the different 'functions' and practices that we generally describe as education, than the limitation of Althusser's conception of Ideological State Apparatuses. Specifically it helps us to stress how these apparatuses are conditioned by class strategies and form part of hegemonic and (counter) hegemonic projects, and consequently are the sites of constant struggles. In such a way we can incorporate Poulantzas' insight about state apparatuses being the condensation of social relations, not as a call 'to fight within the institutions' but more like an affirmation of the state's necessarily antagonistic, contradictory and conflict-ridden character.

In this sense higher educational institutions are indeed 'state apparatuses' in the sense described by Althusser: social sites where social force is transformed into power (Althusser 2006, pp.104–10), provided that we think of power as class strategy. But they are not simply ideological apparatuses, at least not in the normal sense of ideology and surely not in the sense that they do not include also economic and political and social imperatives. That's why they are better described as hegemonic apparatuses. This conception of state apparatuses as "machines transforming social force into power" should not be read as implying a static form. On the contrary, it must be combined with Poulantzas' insistence on a relational conception of state power, in the sense of apparatuses being the condensation of relations of power and consequently always transversed by social and political antagonisms.

This relational conception can help us better understand the hegemonic function of state apparatuses. It is not the result of some inherent structural determination, nor of conscious design, but of the articulation of singular practices and strategies. Thus, we can think the question of the new 'productive' or entrepreneurial practices within academia, not as the end of the distinction between social production and reproduction, but in terms of strategies that enable the shifts in the forms of social reproduction. It also enables us to think in terms of the articulation of singular practices, decisions, choices into class strategies, without resorting to some conception of 'structural' determination as a 'hidden' logic of things.

Of course, it is important to insist that class relations are produced primarily 'outside' the university although particular emphasis must be placed on the fact that this conception of a logical and causal priority, does not mean some sort of ontological hierarchy. Class is produced and reproduced simultaneously, the result, at the same time, of structural imperatives and singular strategies. The important thing is to insist that antagonistic social relations, embedded immanently within the very form of capitalist production, determine the existence of social classes.

Production, Reproduction and Struggle

It is in light of the above that we must rethink the notions of production/reproduction of class. This does not mean that we must abandon any distinction between production and social reproduction in favour of a diffuse social production embracing all aspects of society. But we must rethink the relations and mutual determinations between social production and reproduction. Instead of a simple distinction between production sites and reproduction sites charged with the task of reproducing the conditions of production, we must think capitalist power and exploitation, in terms of both command and enhanced productivity, as a much more complex set of processes and practices that encompass all of society.

However the question remains open: How can we still think of education in general and of universities in particular as sites of class reproduction? I think that we cannot answer this question simply by referring to reproduction as a "function" of education and as part of some teleology that works "behind the backs" of active social agents. Instead we must see the different class strategies around education, its planning, funding and management and how this determines the role of education in social reproduction. When we refer to class strategies this does not suggest only hegemonic capitalist strategies. We also refer to resistances, counter-strategies, counter-hegemonic projects, both in the 'narrow' sense of protests movements and demands within education – the collective action of the student and teaching personnel movements in favour of public education, better wages, better working prospects, better quality of campus life and against privatization, corporate control of research, deterioration of campus life – but also in the broad sense of social and political conflict regarding the position of the collective worker in contemporary capitalist societies, exemplified in the struggles against austerity and precariousness.

Higher education institutions do not produce class relations, nor do they define the practices, antagonisms, conflicting class strategies and class interests that lead to the formation of classes. But surely Higher Education is a terrain of class strategies. I am not referring only to those strategies that we more easily associate with social reproduction, namely decisions regarding the direction of the expansion of Higher Education, policies about tuition, legislative frameworks regarding the structure of courses and degrees. I am also referring to those strategies within Higher Education, at a more micro level, that have to do with entrepreneurial objectives, market decisions or an ideological preference for market practices, that also in the end, and through their outcomes, tend to be class strategies and lead to the reproduction of the conditions of the dominant capitalist strategy.

Such a perspective can help us study the current capitalist restructuring of Higher Education, the changes in university funding and management, and the changes in degree structures and how they relate to changes in capitalist production and class structure, especially if we take into consideration the current expansion of Higher Education and the tendency for increased access to Higher or Post – Secondary Education. We can no longer think of universities as providing the main class barrier or the main dividing line between the working class and the 'middle class' and the bourgeoisie, even though class barriers to access Higher Education continue to exist. Even the division between intellectual and manual labour, if we think of it not in terms of an opposition between those 'working with their hands' vs. those 'working with their brains' but of the distinction between those who design or manage and those who execute, does not coincide with the question of access to Higher Education, since one find university degree holders in many posts that are low in the job and decision hierarchy. In contemporary capitalism a large segment of the working class is "reproduced" within universities.

In light of the above, I think that we must focus on the new contradictions arising within capitalist production. Contemporary capitalist production has an increased need for highly qualified technical and scientific personnel both in manufacturing but also in the service sector and finance, exemplified in the importance of informational technology, new innovatory production process, increased reliance on data processing, new communication markets, and biosciences. If we describe these processes as if capitalists make plans and then demand that the educational sector produce the necessary personnel, then we are dangerously simplifying. On the other hand, it would be equally oversimplifying to say that we have the 'multitude' or some 'new cognitive proletariat', that has by itself, through some sort of intrinsic collective creative ability the necessary educational and cultural capital, and which is then violently subsumed by capital.

We need a more dialectical way to think of these processes and their consequences for Higher Education. What we have is the emergence of new forms of productive processes (and new areas for the accumulation and valorisation of capital) that require the application of scientific knowledge, new technologies and consequently the employment of a workforce with increased skills education. These skills do not 'pre-exist' the productive processes they are applied to, even though they demand a theoretical and technical formation that cannot be achieved on the spot: they emerge at the intersection between production, education and research. In this sense, new forms of production 'induce' the need for new educational practices, curricula, even degree structures, a process obviously facilitated by the new linkages between production, finance and academia. At the same time, the entrepreneurial shift in education leads to universities being oriented towards technological and organizational interventions, and consequently skills, degrees, study modules, that have a potential to be relevant to actual or potential productive processes. One could study the emergence of separate bioengineering courses and degrees as an example of such an interaction.

Moreover, the new forms of academic management and planning that insist on openness to markets also facilitate this interaction between the world of production and education. The result is that the needs of industry are more easily internalized within academic decision processes. This is evident in the ways the question of demand is discussed, especially in universities that rely on tuition. 'Demand' is not only a symptom of an increased commodification of Higher Education (as opposed to education serving knowledge and the common good); it is also one of the ways that tendencies in the labour market and capitalist economy in general are internalized within academic planning processes.

In this sense, certain choices within Universities, even if they are motivated by more 'short sighted' attempts to gain some niche of the educational market, or to compete for research funding, along with more strategic conceptions of educational planning - as expressed in general directions for European Union or State funding, in government 'white papers' and in deliberations about the allocation of resources – all these lead to Higher Education functioning indeed as a *hegemonic apparatus.* Higher Education as hegemonic apparatus helps the reproduction of class structures and the articulation of dominant class strategies, enhances capitalist accumulation and undermines the resistances of the subaltern classes. At the same time, movements and conflicts within Higher Education, as manifestations not only of specific student grievances but also of broader social demands and aspirations, also determine counter-hegemonic strategies in the evolution of Higher Education. Student movements, social movements and campaigns emerging in Higher Education (such as the anti-sweatshops campaigns), broad social and political movements with a strong base inside Higher education (from the anti-globalization movement to current forms of radicalism), all these have also been instrumental in the evolution of Higher Education, even in the sense of placing obstacles to its complete entrepreneurialisation.

The shift towards a more entrepreneurial higher Education is not limited to questions about degree structures, access and hierarchies, but also to the ideological and political balance of forces both within and outside academia. The emergence of an entrepreneurial higher education has been instrumental in answering a crucial challenge in contemporary capitalist society, namely the need to have a collective labour force that is at the same time more qualified, including the need for a larger segment having a higher education degree, but with less collective rights and aspirations – including its perception of a 'fair wage' – and more easily adjustable to a more oppressive, insecure, precarious and exploitative environment, to low pay and large intervals of unemployment. Apart from the changes in curricula, of particular importance is the change in the nature of the degree. The turn from 'strong' and broad degrees, covering a variety of potential forms of employment and corresponding to well defined positions in labour process hierarchies, to highly fragmented and individualized forms of 'qualifications portfolios' in permanent need of enrichment through life-long learning practices. Institutional changes such as the 'diploma supplement' introduced in European countries as part of the Bologna Process reforms, attest to the extent of these changes.

At the same time we see the recurring tendency of exactly these segments of the global workforce, in various struggles, from the student movements of the 2000s, to struggles against austerity, to the Indignados or Occupy movements, to insist on rights and justice, to struggle in order to have their increased expertise being translated into better employment conditions, salaries, and prospects, to resist the various forms of formal and real subsumption of their labour to the imperatives of capital, and to be much more aware of the potential for a non-exploitative form of cooperative production (traces of it already evident in the emergence of "new commons" such as open source software). The importance of this generation of well-educated and highly-trained young people in the global eruption of protest, contestation and even insurgency in the past years, offers ample evidence of this tendency, not only in advanced capitalist societies. The mass participation of college graduates in the 'Occupy movement' epitomizes this, but also the presence of educated youths in the Arab Spring (Solomon and Palmieri (eds.) 2011).

Conclusion

In a period of intense conflict and struggle regarding the future of education, theoretical debates on social production and reproduction are more than necessary and should not be considered a luxury. Marxist theories of class reproduction provided invaluable insight into the role of education in the reproduction of social classes and challenged dominant technocratic conceptions of the neutral or purely 'technical' character of educational policy. Recent theoretical works have enabled us to better understand the dynamics of the shift towards corporate and entrepreneurial higher education, but their ontology of cognitive labour falls short of providing an alternative to the dangers of a functionalist and teleological conception of educational apparatus. In contrast, by combining the emphasis on singularity and practice in recent radical social theory, with a more 'productive' conception of social power, along with a return to Gramsci's concept of hegemony, integral state, hegemonic apparatus, as a strategic-relational theory of power, we can arrive at a better understanding of today's transformation of higher education as the result of capitalist class strategies, but also at an awareness of the potential for resistance and change.

Therefore, entrepreneurial Higher Education is both a class strategy aiming at ensuring conditions for the reproduction of the conditions of capitalist accumulation (steady flow of qualified personnel, applicable scientific knowledge, product development) and a hegemonic project aiming at undermining the aspirations of the subaltern classes (as attempt towards inscribing precariousness in the form and hierarchy of degrees, reproducing neoliberal ideology, fragmenting collective aspirations and practices). It not only extends knowledge and skills but promotes the identities, habits and illusions of a particular kind of worker within neoliberal capitalism. Entrepreneurial Higher Education involves not only the transformation of university governance into more managerialist modes and structures but also a particular culture of knowledge, a particular view of knowledge acquisition and utilisation. It attempts to pre-emptively make sure that the expansion of higher education does not alter the balance of forces in the workplace and to guarantee capitalist hegemony in production. Consequently, the core contradictions in contemporary advanced capitalist societies are internalized to Higher Education. This is, of course, a particular manifestation of a broader social and political tendency, and higher education reforms form part of a broader capitalist hegemonic strategy that includes the production of new learner identities in schools, accountability frameworks for teachers, and new worker identities within new kinds of work-place disciplinary structures.

All these give to current struggles around Higher Education a strategic depth and importance, makes them part of a greater social mobilization against processes of capitalist restructuring and helps them connect more easily with other social movements. These struggles will not only determine the direction of Higher Education policy, but also the political and ideological practices and subjectivities (both individual and collective) of large segments of the global workforce, thus affecting the balance of forces between capital and labour.

References

Althusser, L. (2006). *Philosophy of the encounter. Later Writings 1978–1987*. London: Verso.

Buci-Glucksmann, C. (1980). *Gramsci and the State*. London: Lawrence and Wishart.

Gramsci, A. (1971). *Selections from Prison Notebooks*. London: Lawrence and Wishart.

Gramsci, A. (1978–1996). *Cahiers de Prison*. 5 vols. Paris: Gallimard.

Hardt, M. and A. Negri (2005). *Multitude. War and Democracy in an Age of Empire*. London: Hamish Hamilton.

Marx, K. and Fr. Engels (1970). *Manifesto of the Communist Party*.

Solomon, C. and T. Palmieri (eds) (2011). *Springtime. The New Student Rebellions*. London: Verso.

Thomas, P. D. (2009). *The Gramscian Moment. Philosophy, Hegemony and Marxism*. Leiden: Brill.

Wright, St. (2002). *Storming Heaven. Class composition and struggle in Italian Autonomist Marxism*. London: Pluto.

30

Local Struggles
Women in the Home and
Critical Feminist Pedagogy in Ireland

G. Honor Fagan

While writing this paper I am filled with the current reality of yesterday's possibilities. Ireland has just elected a new woman president, Mary Robinson, a Labour Party member who has consistently struggled for women's rights, for the unemployed, for the youth forced to immigrate from their home, and for all the underrepresented in my country.[1] The election of President Mary Robinson may or may not have a huge social impact, but it dramatizes the shifting ground of formal politics in Ireland. This development has come about, in part, through concrete political struggle, stemming from yesterday's dreams. These dreams were informed by critical education. Both the dreams and the practical developments were struggled over; they must still be struggled over in order that the changes are carried through to the point of bettering the lot of all people – in short, that they are or become radically democratic.

I want to draw attention to the necessarily pedagogical nature of struggle if it is to contribute to a new politics, to a politics that is new in that it achieves radical democracy. I believe that educators have played, and can continue to play, an important role in the social struggle for justice. Critical educators played a part in the political developments that just happened in Ireland. We must now work to insure that these developments be maintained and grow. This means that our practice must speak to a new politics of radical democracy.

Women-in-Waiting

In 1989, I worked, over a period of four years, with groups of women who came together in their local adult education centers to study and work for a diploma in social studies.[2] The courses that I worked on were organized by local community adult education committees, in conjunction with the Adult and Community Education Department based in St. Patrick's College, Maynooth, a national university of Ireland.[3] The courses were, and still are, run in the morning hours from ten to twelve clock, and they primarily attract women who are in the home. If no male unwaged person enrolls in the morning courses a situation arises in which, through the existing division of labor, women find themselves in a classroom with no men present. This happened in the vast majority of the courses taught, will address myself for the remainder of this paper to these all-women classrooms; they provided unique learning situations, with unique dynamics, for the women involved.

Let me draw a profile of the women in attendance. Almost without exception they are either married or widowed.[4] They have devoted their lives to the home and the family. Almost all of them gave up paid employment to work in the home either on getting married or just before the birth of their first child. They fall into two categories. The first consists of women who have just finished the nursery-level stage of rearing their children and who can now just about organize two hours for themselves one morning a week while the children are at primary school. Women at this stage are generally very short of free time. The second category consists of women aged between 45 and 60 who have reared their children and now find themselves with much spare time. They live in suburban housing estates, and their husbands usually hold nine-to-five jobs, though some of their husbands are unwaged.

Women in the first category, who have just left their children at primary school, talk about the change of roles they experienced on becoming married. They speak of their last few years with babies and toddlers, of their feelings of isolation in the home. Many of them say they have spoken baby talk for so many years that they fear they have lost the ability to socialize with adults. They have experienced a loss of their public selves. They speak of having changed from being workers who had weekly paychecks and a social life to being simply wives and mothers. They feel their most pressing requirement is to be reconnected with what they consider the "real world" again. They feel relief that their children are no longer dependent on them, and there is a definite sense of waking up to new possibilities.

Women in the second category, on the other hand, spent their entire married lives in the home.[5] They are older and believe their lives have taken a difficult turn because their families, whom they have serviced all their lives, are now independent of them in the practical sense. These women now feel useless; they feel that there is a vacuum in their lives. They will make comments such as "I've been put out to pasture "or in other ways suggest that their "functional" life is over and they have no direction.

All these women begin the program with a hunger for intellectual stimulation. They are searching for an unspecified development. They experience a strong drive for some sense of "progress" in their life or a sense of fulfillment which they have not quite found. This is particularly noticeable when I compare these women with third-level students, that is, students attending formal university in Ireland. The latter group is more likely to have a career-functionalist view of education, or else their interest in learning has been beaten down by the system. Despite their youth, third-level students express far more cynicism than the adult students. Central to the women's openness for learning and participation is an uneasy lack of assertiveness on their part regarding the worth of their work in the home. This is not to say that they lack a belief in, or loyalty to, their position in the home, but rather that they have internalized the public and private lack of interest shown in their lives and the low status given to their work. Strongest of all is the sense that the lives they live have nothing to offer to the sphere that is "academic;" "theoretical; 'or "philosophical;' yet they feel that "academia ' 'has something to offer them. They want to "open their minds; 'and "become part of the world again.

In general the women speak of a tiredness, not rebelliousness, with the servicing of their families. They all believe that their childrearing work is a good thing and has its genuine rewards, but they are confused by the low status they experience. All are seeking a place or a niche to fit into, since they feel that in the home they are dislocated and severed from the broader society. It is difficult for them to articulate exactly what they want in relation to the broader society. Their decision to come to the class usually came about through a struggle: a struggle over time, a struggle over resources, a struggle for hope and possibilities. Is it just contact, respect, status they need? Why do they decide to comeback to what they see as a form of schooling, and why social studies? From my point of view I have come to believe that they are seeking knowledge about society, and their own relation to it. I believe that their very interest in the course arises from a belief that they need knowledge, and a hope that knowledge is linked to power.

To these women family life is central, because they believe their only status is located within it. Some get on quite well with their husbands while others resent them and the perks that go along with being a husband and working outside the home. Some are in "unhappy" marriages and are bitter about their married life. Some are just worn out with very little spark left. These are women who have a huge burden of care -who are minding handicapped children, for example, or sick parents or parents-in-law, which is the case with about one third of the group. They come to the class because they need, very badly, to get out of the home, and because they are slowly but surely "going out of their minds!'

An Educational Process – Lifting the Lid

In Ireland the social weight of the caring role is ascribed to the woman in the home. Only those who understand the extent to which women in the home have internalized the caring role will understand the need these women feel to do something for themselves. When we break down the amount of time that they are not "on call" it adds up to zero. Coming to the class represents the first step to reclaim some of their time for themselves. This becomes a recurrent theme in the class because I consistently want them to take time. Perhaps this is a bias academia has given me, but in this context the women's reading and writing is a political issue. They need to sit down, think, and generate ideas. They need to write, both for themselves and for the other women in the group. Much more importantly they need to learn that the ideas they generate are as valuable as those of everyone else who writes. Politically, in fact, they are more valuable because women in the home have been the voiceless people.

At the beginning of each year we discuss what each of us wants from the year's course. Each woman talks about why she wants to attain a social studies diploma and describes what area of social studies she is interested in. Sometimes the social issues they want to discuss are topical issues they have heard being discussed on the radio or television - harmful food additives, third-world hunger, damage to the ozone layer, poverty, or unemployment. Always the social issues are fairly abstract, and the women express a careful objectivity toward the subject matter, an attitude they learned in school years earlier. They have a distant view of the social as something that is separate and disconnected from them. Other issues they list which they would like to discuss could be labeled as psychological, such as stress or bereavement. At this point I begin to describe my interests and areas of knowledge and the limitations of my knowledge. We eliminate areas on the basis of group interests and group knowledge.

I begin by pointing out that we have a unique vantage point from which we can study. I explain that this class will be like any other educational situation they have found themselves in. I put forward a radical philosophy of adult education and I present the methodology that we will use if it is acceptable to them. In this way I try to make sure that they are not afraid of conflicting with me as a figure of authority, and that our differences can be aired, listened to, and taken into account. To be more specific I tell them about five grounding principles that we can use as part of our methodology and style of learning if they understand and agree with them. Communicating these general ideas for learning, which they do not expect, usually receives their full enthusiasm and commitment. We take note in advance that we will probably clash on some issues because of our different politics.

A radical philosophy of adult education requires that my political interests be made explicit. I outline my politics using three concepts: critical, feminist, socialist; tell them that this is essential for them to know from the beginning. They usually think this is an interesting peculiarity and seem to welcome the novelty of these positions, rather than viewing them as a threat to their own worldviews. However, I observe through their silent rather than verbal reactions that it is primarily my position as a feminist that they distrust. I have to struggle in the beginning to convince them that my feminism will not be pedagogically threatening, because politically it has such repercussions for their affective investment in their everyday life. As a teacher I believe the success of the course depends on how I deal with and take into account their resistance to feminism. I usually have to deal with their discomfort straight away and so I start a discussion by expressing that our positions on feminism are polarized, that this is both a political and a personal difference, and that we will discuss these differences openly throughout the course. Their suspicions of feminism are considerable due, in part, to their personal difficulties with aspects of feminism, such as their association of feminism with abortion. Apart from this they are also afraid of feminist politics, since they have witnessed and lived through the severity of the political clashes which have occurred in Ireland over the past decade between feminists and the church, and between feminists and the state. Due to local circumstances of feminist political losses and the dominance of an antifeminist public discourse in Ireland, I find it necessary to assure them that while my politics might be threatening, I will do my best to ensure that my pedagogy will not be intimidating. In order that the focus and onus is not entirely on me in this discussion, I direct the discussion toward their own politics, although many of the women do not immediately acknowledge that they have a politics.

The following are some grounding statements I make in order to form the basis for, and direct, the pedagogical proceedings. These statements are opened up to discussion.

- All education is political. As I have said I outline my politics to the women by describing myself as being critical, socialist, and feminist. I will answer any questions that they care to ask me about this position. I also tell them that any education they have received to date had both a philosophy and a politics behind it, but that it cloaked its politics in a jargon of false objectivity. I assert that, for me, education is politically committed and that this will affect the course deeply.
- The shortest route to understanding society and how it works is to analyze how our individual selves have been shaped by social forces which have positioned us in our current social status. In other words, the focus of our study will be our social position; in moving toward an understanding of that, we can link up with an understanding of how society operates as a system and how society operates on us.
- The people in the course all have 20 to 40 years more experience than each woman is informed by her experience in the world and her exposure to the media. Throughout the year we will organize and critically analyze what they know.
- In class we will operate along communal lines as opposed to competitive lines, which means that we support each other in our efforts to learn. This means supporting the other women in the group. This does not necessarily mean, however, that we will always agree with one another. Ideas expressed will be viewed critically.
- We will engage in a group project that makes contact politically with some current social issues.

Course Content

Working with these general principles we examine and analyze several institutions, social issues, and social theories of change. Course content, as I mentioned already, is organized around group interest and group knowledge, under the very general subject matter of social studies. They are more comfortable with a format that reflects my formal knowledge and their interests, and they use me as the major resource person in the group. We examine areas not as if they are static, but from a point of view of transformative change. This reflects my politics and to an extent their politics, because it is clear that they are interested in change. Also, however, a focus on transformative change forces us to do more than receive information on how society works. We gain more knowledge and more power through participating in a process of analysis and in working on possibilities of change. We find this focus on change to be a beginning of empowerment. Typically we examine what might be unethical about the technological project and why societies are moving along a destructive route. We critically examine institutions in Ireland such as the educational system, the institution of the family, the prison system, the class system, and the legal system. We examine who runs the country and in the name of what or whom. We examine the social forces in Irish society, asking who has a social and political project and who has not. We ask which social project becomes implemented and why that particular project? Whom does it serve? We examine our country in relation to other countries, the development of first world countries and their underdevelopment of countries in the Southern hemisphere.

Throughout the course we help clarify some of the above questions by listening critically to current affairs programs on radio and television and by reading national newspapers. Throughout the analysis we use our position as women as a base point of critique. How are we as women involved in the social process? What role do we play? What needs to be changed? What changes do we need to make? What role can we play in bringing about that change? We also examine our varying class positions and ask where, from these subject positions, we can gain an entry into political processes?

Let me be more specific on this pedagogical process and the role-play in it by taking one institution – the educational system – and elaborating on how we tackle it, break it down, analyze it, critique it, and then develop our own ideas on alternatives. One week in advance I ask that we begin discussing education the next week. I ask that during the week, they think about their own education. I say I will ask at the next class that we all describe three of the best things about our own education and three of the worst. At the beginning of the next class each woman tells us of her schooling. This serves many purposes. Each woman tells part of her own story and each woman talks in front of a group of 20 people. This builds support among the group, because the telling of the personal story always demands a support structure and the women willingly give this. Secondly, it builds the women's confidence. This is important, since at least three quarters of the women who have come to the course have no confidence to speak in front of a group. Since they have never been given the authority to speak publicly, they have internalized a fear of doing so. Thirdly, it gives legitimacy to their personal experience as an entry into the understanding of society. This type of pedagogy is not necessarily needed in a privileged setting, but these women need it because they bear the mark of their status. This usually takes the form of being easily intimidated or "too shy" to speak up.

At the beginning of the class, some of the women are visibly nervous because they know they have to speak out and this is an ordeal for them. As the class progresses the stories and shared experiences take over; they forget their fears and talk publicly, many for the first time. They know they will be all right here, that it is safe to speak. This is an important breakthrough. Without first making sure that each woman has talked, there would be no point in continuing: in a class of women, and perhaps in every class, the individual who isn't "the teacher" has to claim her voice so that we are sure that voice will be given to all agreements and disagreements. Initially the women make body language contact with 'the teacher' 'if they disagree with a point rather than speaking out themselves. They expect these "vibes" to be picked up by the teacher and hope that "the teacher' 'will give voice to their disagreement. This is perhaps the most striking habit some women have formed, so as not to put their own voice at risk in the arena of argumentation. In the beginning of the course this has to be discussed openly so that they can see what they are doing and analyze why they are doing it. Once the group dynamic of openness, support, and critique is established, the course moves along very productive lines.

After we have given personal voice to our schooling experience we move away from personal, individual interpretations and on to a more social under standing of the various roles of schooling. In the stories the women tell, issues of gender and class oppression emerge.[6] We discuss curriulum and use their stories to uncover the social aspects of schooling. I use my sociological background to provide different sociological readings of schooling. Through a functionalist perspective we view schooling as fulfilling specific functions. Through a Marxist approach we view schooling as reproducing the class system and all its inequalities. We discuss and I clarify or elaborate on anything asked in relation to these theories. There is at this stage a palpable excitement in the classroom because this type of information is so new to them. They really have not looked on schooling in this light before. I ask them then if they would like to consider who benefits from the system and who does not. Enthusiastically the class agrees to continue examining these issues. It proves very difficult to get the balance right between giving input and allowing space for them to develop independently. Pressure is always exercised on me as the "authority:" even if that subject is the rearing of their own children. This is part of what must be blocked if they are to build their own confidence. The next week I present a class analysis of the educational system. We discuss this and I ask them to develop a gender analysis of schooling from their own knowledge.

Education as Production as Opposed to Description

Together they begin to understand and I increase my understanding of how social systems operate. We discuss the different axes of power, gender oppression, class oppression, and "first world/third world" oppression. On a national basis we have critically analyzed the formal party politics of our country and highlighted whose interests the parties serve. We have observed church involvement in state decisions and we have looked at the social forces in our state and whose social project is being implemented. We have addressed the conflict in Northern Ireland. We have developed our awareness of the structuring of poverty, crime, and punishment. In short, an under standing about society has unfolded.

One of the women's sons is a priest in Sao Paulo. He is there, she explains to us, working for the people in the shanty towns. She tells us this when the class is dealing with the organization of poverty in the Southern Hemisphere.

From watching her face as she relates what her son has told her, we can see (and we acknowledge) that he learned care and commitment, in part, from her. Such a loving face, but it also holds its marks. Where is her confidence I ask myself. I feel like shaking her into assertion and confidence. Slowly her hesitancy turns into a form of direction in the context of the group. She decided she wanted to do something with the Travellers.[7] She read and she found out as much as was possible in the peace of the library and through television and newspaper coverage. However, we began to see that she was too used to the shelter of her home. She never got the courage or confidence to talk to formal representatives of the Travellers, though I know she treated with respect and care the Travellers she did come into contact with.

On a more socially productive level, apart from a new social awareness they have developed, each woman has taken concrete actions. Each woman has talked out in front of a group of 20 women. Each one has developed or expressed her understanding of how she has been kept subordinate in the realms of family, community, academia, and politics. Each woman has worked in a cooperative effort to present a project. These projects have been on areas such as marriage separation, childcare, services for women in the home, and even women and mental illness.

We hold two formal evaluations each year, one in the middle of the year and one at the end, though usually evaluations are ongoing. The first evaluation gives us all a chance to discuss the areas in which the course could be improved, and their suggestions can be implemented before the end of the term. I usually ask them to take more time for themselves, to establish the right for maybe one or two hours in which their partner would cover their home duties so that they lay claim to their individual need for time in which to do some reading or writing for themselves. They speak as if the time we spend together as a group has opened their eyes. Their perspectives and their understandings have changed. Their confidence has grown and their sense of worth, self-esteem, and anger against oppression gives them a new sense of agency and direction. Sometimes, of course, there are problems with husbands, even to the extent that some want their wives to drop out of the class. None have. That should give some indication of the struggles being waged on the home front!

The final evaluation speaks to possibilities. As we progressed through each social and personal investigation of power, we tried to think of alternatives. For example, for education we spoke of future adult informal education. Yet we realized that the formal system of education is linked with all the other systems and structures and to the reproduction of a class/gender/subcultural oppression in our country. At the end of the year the group stays together. They as a group get involved in a practical struggle, for example, preschool facility development in the inner city. They form women's groups and meet with other women's groups. They support each other in political struggles in the home with the family. We have begun a process of education that is organized as a praxis of resistance, struggle, and change.

Conclusion

The productive educational process I describe in this paper conveys a sense of what the practice of critical feminist pedagogy can look like in a local context, and what can be achieved through its practice. In this adult education context the critical pedagogical practice recognizes itself as a political, social, and cultural process. It critiques inequities and forms of subordination and oppression, but with a view toward transformation. It is a form of transformative and engaged education, and operates as such by involving the students and teacher alike in an engaged practice of critique, liberation, and transformation.

A feminist critical pedagogy makes the gendered subjectivities of the teacher and students part of the text or the subject matter. A critical inquiry is grounded in gender subjectivity, using this concrete subjectivity as an example that allows the addressing of, and inquiry into, other axes of oppression such as class, race, and global positioning. The presence of gender difference and consequent gender oppression is a constant reminder of other forms of oppression. A critical feminist pedagogy focuses on pedagogy not merely of the informational kind but of the productive kind. The approach involves politics at a local level. What one learns is learned through a process of engagement. It does not allow for a lack of commitment. In moving along a process of personal conscientization, in conjunction with becoming critically aware of how society differentiates and segregates to oppress certain people, the combination of personal involvement with critical theorizing ensures pedagogy as productive. It is just such a pedagogy I have described in this paper.

Notes

1. Mary Robinson was elected president of Ireland in November of 1990.
2. Students seek this social studies diploma chiefly for its educational and academic prestige; it is not recognized as significant in the commercial sphere, though it may sometimes help in obtaining jobs with local government agencies.
3. Adult education is government-funded and fairly widespread in Ireland, but it does take many diverse forms. Local vocational education committees offer a wide variety of classes, ranging from carpentry and flower arrangement to academic subjects used for attaining formal academic qualifications, was employed by St. Patrick's College, County Kildare, to teach social studies in various local centers throughout County Kildare and County Dublin.
4. No single mothers seem to have the time to participate in a course like this. One did begin to attend a class, but due to her responsibilities she had to drop out.
5. In Ireland women were forced to give up employment in the public sector on marrying.
6. Race as such is not an issue in Ireland due to a fairly racially homogeneous population, though sectarianism is an issue, particularly in the North of Ireland. Also we have a distinctive subculture of navellers who are severely oppressed.
7. Travellers are a subculture in Ireland. They are people who were disinherited historically, who travel from place to place in Ireland living in caravans. They in large part live in poverty even though the "head" of the family is entitled to and receive social welfare. Our larger culture is prejudiced against their way of life and seems to try to assimilate them, but the Travellers are organizing to resist this threat.

31

Say You Want a Revolution
Suggestions for the Impossible Future of Critical Pedagogy

Gert J.J. Biesta

The question of the possibility of a critical pedagogy is immediately connected with the question of the possibility of education. What makes education possible, so I want to argue, is its impossibility. Hence, the only possible future for a critical pedagogy is an impossible future.

The Crisis in Critical Pedagogy?

Although critical pedagogy has many faces and histories, the varieties of critical pedagogy in general agree in their emphasis on the political character of education. Critical pedagogies claim that education is not a natural, ahistorical phenomenon but that it should be understood in its sociohistorical and political context. Moreover, critical pedagogies are in one way or another committed to the imperative of transforming the larger social order in the interest of justice, equality, democracy, and human freedom.

As a *critical theory of education* this emancipatory interest translates into a (critical) analysis of educational practices and theories meant to expose the way in which these practices and theories support unequal relationships. The central assumption here is that liberation can be brought about when people have an adequate understanding of their own situation. Critical pedagogies not only attempt to provide such understanding, but they also consider education to be one of the main practices in modern society through which people can develop their capacity for critical reflexivity.[1] As a *critical educational practice,* critical pedagogy is therefore also one of the central means in the struggle for justice and liberation.

Over the past decades critical pedagogy has come to flourish, especially in North America.[2] The history of the North American critical tradition goes back to the progressivism of John Dewey and the more radical efforts of social reconstructionism. In the 1970s, important impulses came from the "new sociology of education," which focused on the role of schooling in the reproduction of inequality. Around 1980 scholars such as Michael Apple and Henry Giroux pushed this debate one step further with their criticism of the deterministic character of the base-superstructure model of reproduction. They argued for a focus on the cultural *mediations* between the material conditions of an unequal society and the formation of the consciousness of individuals in that society. Critical scholarship during the 1980s revealed a growing concern with the possibilities of positive pedagogical action (for example, Giroux's call for a "language of possibility") and a shift from class as the only difference that makes a difference, to a recognition of the importance of race and gender.

In the last decade, critical pedagogy has shown an increased interest in questions of culture, both inside and outside the schools; in issues concerning identity and identity politics; and in multicultural education. On the theoretical plane the major development has been the engagement with feminist scholarship and with poststructural, postmodern, and postcolonial theories. It has also been during the last decade that critical pedagogy has itself become an object of critique. On the one hand, questions have been raised about the actual influence of critical pedagogy on classroom practice, and about the possibility of using critical pedagogy in the classroom. On the other hand, the possibility of the very project of a critical pedagogy has been challenged. To the extent to which critical pedagogy incorporates Enlightenment ideals – and the idea of emancipation through critical reflexivity is the central mission of Enlightenment – it has especially been the postmodern critique of the Enlightenment project that has raised fundamental questions about the possibility of critical pedagogy.

Although I think that it is an overstatement to say that critical pedagogy today is in a state of crisis, I do think that it is important to draw up the balance sheet and to decide upon the possible future for critical pedagogy – not in the least since its ambitions seem to go as far as the next millennium.[3] The essays by Peter McLaren and Ilan Gur-Ze'ev provide an excellent occasion for doing so, not only because they identify some crucial problems in the current state of critical pedagogy, but also because their solutions point in quite different directions.

In this essay I want to address some of their concerns. My aim is not to articulate a new program or a new direction for critical pedagogy. I only want to suggest a particular point of view – which focuses on the importance of the recognition of the *impossibility* of critical education (which is not what is *not* possible but what cannot be foreseen and calculated as a possibility but literally takes us by surprise) – from which I hope meaningful questions can be raised about the direction in which critical pedagogy is heading, and more specifically the direction in which McLaren and Gur-Ze'ev want critical pedagogy to go.

The Future of Critical Pedagogy

As I see it, McLaren's main question is whether the theoretical tools of contemporary critical pedagogy are still adequate to provide a critical analysis of the current state of education. He contends that this is not the case. McLaren argues that any analysis of the current state of education must pay attention to the effects of the "new capitalism" – which is a global and transnational capitalism – and of its "political bedfellow," neoliberalism. He shows how new capitalism has invaded, distorted, and deformed every sphere of life, including the sphere of education, by making capital the "paragon of all social relationships." McLaren argues that what is new about today's capitalism, namely, its global or transnational character, not only makes its predatory power unprecedented in history, but also has made it much more resistant to democratic control.

On one level McLaren blames the educational Left for having become so infatuated with "more conservative forms of *avant-garde* apostasy found in certain incarnations of French postmodernist theoretical advances" that it has more or less become blind to issues of class and economic inequality. The insertion of postmodernism has led to a preoccupation with questions of identity politics, primarily around the issues of gender and ethnicity. It has caused a retreat from historical materialism and metatheory as dated systems of intelligibility, so that class struggle is now seen as an outdated issue. McLaren concludes that the educational Left – insofar as it has been influenced by postmodern "nihilism" and "relativism" – is no longer able to address the most urgent issues concerning education in an age of global capitalism.

But the problem with postmodern critical pedagogy is not only that it has forgotten the question of class. McLaren also suggests that postmodern critical pedagogy, because of its emphasis on values such as diversity and inclusion, has become an ally of new capitalism and neoliberal educational policy, at least by offering a language that can easily be coopted by the new capitalism. Instead of being a critical device against the new capitalism, postmodern critical pedagogy in fact plays into its hands.

Against this background McLaren concludes that a renewed agenda for critical pedagogy must include strategies of addressing and redressing economic distribution, and that it must be centered around "the transformation of property relations and the creation of a just system of appropriation and distribution of social wealth." This, so he claims, requires that critical pedagogy return to a "historical materialist approach to educational reform" to serve as a point of departure for a politics of resistance and counter-hegemonic struggle.

Gur-Ze'ev's evaluation of the current state of critical pedagogy starts from a different angle. One of the main problems he sees with the critical pedagogy developed by Paulo Freire and Giroux is its inability to escape the normalizing character of traditional pedagogy. With respect to Freire, Gur-Ze'ev points to the dangerous implications of his "non-critical" preference for the self-evident knowledge of the oppressed to that of the oppressors. What guarantees, so he asks, that the self-evident knowledge of the marginalized and repressed is less false than that which their oppressors hold as valid? It is this "easy optimism," and the "positive utopianism" in which it is expressed, that makes Freire forget these questions. As a result his liberatory pedagogy turns into a potentially violent form of "counter totalitarianism."

Gur-Ze'ev's critique of Giroux's version of critical pedagogy concerns its "positive utopianism," its "hasty optimism," and its "arrogance as to the possibility of liberating the repressed and constituting a better world within current reality." He also criticizes the "modernistic attitudes" in Giroux's pedagogy, which not only manifest themselves in his ideas about the possibility of an alternative, dialogical relation between students and teachers, but, if I see it correctly, also are at stake in the patriarchal character of Giroux's own theorizing.

The interesting thing about Gur-Ze'ev's essay is his claim that there exists a part of critical theory – the part developed by Max Horkheimer and Theodor Adorno in their *Dialectic of Enlightenment* – that has problematized precisely this modern, instrumental dimension of critical pedagogy.[4] This part has, however, been overlooked by many supporters and opponents of critical pedagogy. Gur-Ze'ev argues that a critical pedagogy that wants to combat instrumental rationality by more instrumental rationality, remains part of the problem it wants to solve. As he puts it: "A pedagogy that overemphasizes the importance of the effectiveness of revolutionary praxis and whose yardstick is power is not to be counted as part of critical education or critical pedagogy." Although Gur-Ze'ev sees many similarities between the critical theory of Horkheimer and Adorno and the work of Michel Foucault, he argues that there remains one decisive difference in that critical theory still has a utopian dimension – albeit a negative utopianism – while the work of Foucault and other postmodernists, so he claims, is decisively anti-utopian.

Negative utopianism provides the starting point for Gur-Ze'ev's nonrepressive form of critical pedagogy called "counter-education". Counter-education radically differs from the conception of education of critical pedagogy, because it "refuses all versions of educational violence" and has no positive alternative to false conscious ness, such as the memory or knowledge of the marginalized and oppressed. Yet, if I see it correctly, counter-education also has a positive dimension, in that it wants "to educate to decipher reality," and wants to struggle for the development of the "reflective potential of human beings and their ability for articulation of their worlds as a realization of their reason." And, because its aim is to strive for conditions under which everyone will be able to become part of the human dialogue, to work toward the possibility that the human subject will be able to stand up and confront "the forgetfulness of being."

McLaren and Gur-Ze'ev present critical educators with two different options. McLaren wants to bring the critical project back to its Marxist roots because, so he claims, only such a perspective can provide "the proper level of abstraction" to grasp the situation we are in. Gur-Ze'ev, on the other hand, raises questions about the critical project itself and suggests that we should change the terms – though not the general direction – of the project. Rather than suggesting a simple way out, I want at this point to introduce some further considerations about the possibility and the possible future of critical pedagogy.

The Impossibility of Education

One of the most basic questions in any discussion about education – a question so basic that it is easily overlooked – is the question of the possibility of education. This question is especially important for critical pedagogy, not only since it has chosen education as the primary means for social change, but also because it explicitly wants to educate the educator.

Is education possible? According to Sigmund Freud it is not. In the last text he wrote, he refers to education as one of those "impossible professions" – the other two being analysis and government – "in which one can be sure beforehand of achieving unsatisfying results."[5] Freud is not alone in his opinion. Much educational research presumably still is driven by the wish to find the "secret formula" so that education can be made into a technique with a predictable, positive outcome. In this view, the fact that such a formula has not yet been found is simply seen as an indication that our knowledge is still incomplete.

Yet the impossibility of education, the fact that it cannot be conceived as a technique, that its outcome cannot be predicted, can also be seen as an essential characteristic of all human interaction, education included. This is, for example, the way in which Hannah Arendt conceives of human action and interaction. For Arendt, to act means to take an initiative, to begin. Action corresponds to the human condition of *natality*. With each birth, so she argues, something "uniquely new" comes into the world.[6] This new beginning "can make itself felt in the world … because the newcomer possesses the capacity of beginning something anew, that is, of acting.[7] Interaction is therefore a process in which we act "upon beings who are capable of their own actions."[8] This makes human interaction "boundless" and "inherently unpredictable."[9]

Arendt's understanding of human interaction brings to the fore that education can never be understood as a process where the teacher simply molds the student. Any account of education has to take into account that what is presented by the teacher is not passively taken in but actively "used" by the student. It is only because the student "uses" what is presented that education is possible. Yet, this use at the very same time introduces unpredictability and transformation. As Michel de Certeau puts it, it is through the use that an uncodeable difference insinuates itself into the happy relation the system would like to have with the operations it claims to administer."[10]

Seen from the side of the system, this uncodeable difference is what causes the system to fail. Seen from the point of view of education, however, this uncodeable difference can be seen as the very sign of someone –some one, a singular being – coming "intopresence."[11] For Arendt, this is the *raison d'être* of action. In acting and speaking, she argues, "men … reveal actively their unique personal identities and thus make their appearance in the human world."[12] This is not a process in which some predetermined identity is brought into the open. Arendt stresses that no one knows whom one reveals when one discloses one's self in word and deed. This only becomes clear in the sphere of action. The agent that is disclosed in the act is therefore, not an "author" or "producer," but a subject in the twofold sense of the word, namely, as one who began an action and as the one who suffers from its consequences.[13]

It is at this point that the impossibility of education becomes politically significant, because it is only when the temptation "to replace acting with making" is resisted, that the "risk of disclosure" remains possible.[14] The attempt to replace acting with making, which, according to Arendt, "is manifest in the whole body of argument against 'democracy,' is therefore an attempt to abolish "that space of appearance which is the public realm." In this sense it is an argument "against the essentials of politics" itself.[15]

If it is the case that the very possibility of education is sustained by its impossibility, then it follows that the idea of critical pedagogy as a positive program and project is problematic for two different reasons. First, because such a program can only be successful if it is able to control the "use" of what it tries to achieve. At this point I agree with Gur-Ze'ev's concern about the totalitarian tendencies of such an enterprise. Second, because such a program would eventually imply an erasure of the political realm, of the realm where the risk of disclosure is a possibility. This is the main danger implied in the normalizing tendency of critical pedagogy.

Although McLaren is clearly aware of the need for critical pedagogy to be critical of its own universal, patriarchal, and Eurocentric assumptions, this does not prevent him from enumerating a list of what *must* be done. Of course McLaren is right that many things must be done. But the heart of critical pedagogy does not lie in the execution of a program, as that would close the very space that critical pedagogy wants to open up. In the end the only consistent way for critical pedagogy to proceed – and at stake is not a theoretical consistency but a pedagogical and political one – is by a perpetual challenge of all claims to authority *including the claims to authority of critical pedagogy itself.*

This implies that such a challenge cannot be put in the name of some superior knowledge or privileged vision, not even, as Gur-Ze'ev correctly concludes, the knowledge or vision of the marginalized or oppressed. It can only proceed, so I want to suggest, on the basis of a fundamental *ignorance*. Such ignorance is neither naivete nor skepticism. It just is an ignorance that does not claim to know how the future will be or will have to be. It is an ignorance that does not show the way, but only issues an invitation to set out on the journey. It is an ignorance that does not say what to think of it, but only asks, "What do you think about it?"[16] In short, it is an ignorance that makes room for the possibility of disclosure. It is, therefore, an emancipatory ignorance.

The Impossibility of Demystification

The idea that ignorance should play a role in critical pedagogy seems to contradict a major idea of the critical tradition, which is that emancipation can be brought about when people have an adequate understanding of, if not simply the plain truth, about their own situation. This Enlightenment idea(l) occupies a central place in McLaren's essay as he argues that we need a specific perspective in order to be able to grasp the current state we are in; and we need to grasp that state in order not to be determined by it.

Although Gur-Ze'ev is profoundly critical of the project of critical pedagogy as far as it concerns its positive utopianism, in one respect he also stays remarkably close to the idea(l) of emancipation via reason. He argues, for example, that human beings are called "to decipher the current realm of self-evidence and to demystify the codes and manipulations of the powers constituting their conceptual possibilities, their life conditions, and their concrete limitations." It is the "reflective potential of human beings" which, if I understand Gur-Ze'ev correctly, makes a "transcendence" from the world possible.

Both McLaren and Gur-Ze'ev stress that knowledge is never neutral but that it is always contaminated by power. McLaren draws the most traditional conclusion from this insight, which is that criticalists need to reveal how relationships of subordination and domination are both expressed in and reproduced by specific knowledge formations. The assumption here is that knowledge can be used to illuminate how power works and, consequently, that it can be used to combat these operations of power.

The main question with respect to this strategy is, of course, whether there is any reason to believe that the knowledge produced by the criticalist is itself uncontaminated by the operations of power. The traditional answer, that is, the answer of the Western tradition, is to refer this question back to the nature of human beings, to their natural capacity of reflexivity (Aristotle's rational animal), thereby trying to safeguard the possibility for critique in an ontological way.[17]

McLaren sees the postmodern critique of this ontological safeguarding of critical reflexivity mainly as an "assault on the unified subject of the Enlightenment tradition," as a result of which too much ground is lost for the critical project. Gur Ze'ev is rnore aware of the problematic character of the idea of a subject disconnected from the games of power. He positions himself closer to Foucault and Martin Heidegger who, so he says, "enlighten the all-penetrating presence of powers and conditions that constitute the human being, the conditions of his/her production, his/her possibilities and limitations."

Yet I think that Gur-Ze'ev also misses the point of what Foucault has tried to express in the concept -which is perhaps better not to be understood as a concept of power/knowledge. He presents Foucault as one who has contributed to the Enlightenment task of demystification by revealing how knowledge is infatuated with power. To my understanding, however, power/knowledge is not the ultimate demystification, but a critique of the very possibility of demystification. It is basically a critique of the Manichean foundations of the Enlightenment project in that it puts a challenge to the idea that power and knowledge are (ontologically) separate entities that are in a constant struggle, and that Enlightenment consists in the victory of knowledge over power. Power/knowledge is not an attempt to show that, as McLaren points out, "power is everywhere and nowhere," but a critique of the very terms in which Enlightenment has been conceived. The task is, as Foucault puts it, to abandon "a whole tradition that allows us to imagine that knowledge can only exist where the power relations are suspended.[18]

The implication of this understanding of power/knowledge is that knowledge can no longer be used to combat power. This is not to say that change is no longer possible or that knowledge has become futile. It rather signifies the end of the "innocence" of knowledge as a critical instrument, and thus the end of the possibility of demystification. It urges us to recognize that we are always operating in a field of power/knowledge *against* power/knowledge.

Does the recognition of the impossibility of demystification mean that we have become eternal prisoners of the system? This question only makes sense as long as we believe that we can occupy a place outside the system from which the system can be viewed. Foucault urges us to move beyond the inside-outside alternative. It is true, he says, "that we have to give up hope of ever acceding to a point of view that could give us access to any complete and definitive knowledge of what may constitute our historical limits.[19] But this does not lead us to a limitless relativism. Foucault agrees that criticism "consists of analyzing and reflecting upon limits":

> But if the Kantian question was that of knowing what limits knowledge has to renounce transgressing, it seems to me that the critical question today has to be turned back mto a positive one: in what is given to us as universal, necessary, obligatory, what place is occupied by whatever is singular, contingent, and the product of arbitrary constraints?[20]

What Foucault is arguing for is a "practical critique that takes the form of a possible transgression.[21] The critical practice of transgression is not meant to overcome limits (not in the least because limits are not only constraining but always also enabling).[22] Transgression is the practical and experimental "illumination of limits."[23]

Against this background I am inclined to conclude that the impossibility of demystification opens up a whole domain in which critical pedagogy can operate at least a bit more positively than Gur-Ze'ev thinks possible – and perhaps as positively as McLaren hopes to be possible. The critical practice of transgression as the experimental illumination of limits can take the form of *counter-practice*. A counter-practice should not be designed out of an arrogance that it will be better (or that one claims to know that it will be better; once again: ignorance) than what exists. A counter-practice is only different. The critical task of a counter-practice can therefore only be to show (to prove, Foucault says) that the way things were was only one (limited) possibility. But this step is crucial, as it opens up the possibility "of no longer being, doing, or thinking what we are, do, or think." In this way, Foucault argues, "it is seeking to give a new impetus ... to the undefined work of freedom."[24] In this sense critical pedagogy as counter-practice can open up that "space of appearance" which is the political realm. It does not open up this realm in an unlimited way, it does not constitute a utopia, it does not provide the "great escape" of demystification. It only reveals one other possible power/knowledge constellation.

The Impossibility of Justice

One crucial question has not yet been dealt with. The problem is this: Although we do not want to restrict the possibility of disclosure beforehand, there is also no reason to assume that any disclosure is just as good as any other just for the reason that it is a disclosure. At this point I am inclined to agree with McLaren's observation that if postmodernism has nothing more to offer than an unqualified celebration of differences, it then creates a situation where other forces -like the forces of the new capitalism – can easily come in and take over. William Connolly puts the predicament as follows: "Without a set of standards ... there is no possibility of ethical discrimination, but the application of any such set ... also does violence to those to whom it is applied."[25] Does this mean, then, that what McLaren hints at – that a totalizing vision "remains as urgent today as it was thirty years ago," that critical pedagogy needs to be *grounded* (in a historical materialist approach), and that it needs to be informed by a "principled ethics of compassion and social justice" – is inevitable if we do not want to let politics slide down to mere chaos?[26] Does critical pedagogy need a set of standards, does it need a criterion, a normative referent, a utopia -even if it is only a provisional or a negative utopia?[27]

In a certain sense the answer to this question has to be an unqualified "yes." After all critical pedagogy, in any of its forms, is not politically neutral but has an explicit commitment. But what does it mean to be committed to something like justice (the term both McLaren and Gur-Ze'ev seem comfortable with)? I want to suggest – and here I will rely on Jacques Derrida, one of those "postmodernists" whom neither McLaren nor Gur-Ze'ev seems to think offers work with any ethical and political significance – that in the very name of justice, there has to be a commitment to the impossibility of justice.[28]

One way to understand Derrida's ideas about the impossibility of justice is by reading them as the claim that justice can never be *present.* Justice, in its shortest formula, is a concern for the other. It is a concern for the other as other, and hence for the otherness of the other, which for that reason cannot be foreseen. Justice, in short, "always addresses itself to singularity, to the singularity of the other."[29] But if this is so, then we are obliged in the very name of justice to keep the unforeseen possibility of the incoming of the other, the surprise of the "invention" of the other, open.[30] It is for this reason that Derrida argues that justice is "an experience of the impossible," where (and this is crucial) the impossible is not that which is not possible, but that which cannot be foreseen and calculated as a possibility, that which "exceeds calculation, rules, programs, anticipations and so forth."[31]

The implications of this insight are not restricted to the determination of whether a situation or a person is just –about which Derrida says that we can never say "this is just" or even less "I am just ...without immediately betraying justice"[32] – but extend to the very definition of justice itself. Here again, we can say that it is for the very sake of justice as a concern for what cannot be foreseen as a possibility, that we can never decide once and (literally) for all what justice is. Justice is therefore not a principle or a criterion (as this would mean that we would know right now what justice is), nor an ideal (as this would mean that we would now be able to describe the future situation of justice), not even a regulative ideal (or what McLaren calls a provisional utopia, as this would still require a decision on what justice is, although with the implication that the ideal is not expected to be present in some future). It belongs to the very "structure" of justice that it never can be present and therefore never will be present. It is by necessity, as Derrida would say, a justice to come, which means that it is *always* to come.[33]

The fact that justice is not a criterion or a principle means that it is not something that we can have knowledge about and that we only need to "apply" to concrete circumstances. Justice is not a matter of knowledge. Justice – "if it has to do with the other" – is always incalculable, because "once you relate to the other as the other, then something incalculable comes on the scene."[34] Justice, in short, requires *judgment*. But how, so it could be objected (and has been objected), can we judge if we do not know what justice *is*? How can we decide if, as Derrida claims, at the basis of our decisions lies a radical *undecidability* that "continues to inhabit the decision?"[35]

Derrida's response to this objection offers a way out of the predicament men tioned above, because it conceives of a possibility for "ethical discrimination" that is precisely *not* the application of a "set of standards." The point is that undecidability should be taken literally as "that condition from which no course of action necessarily follows."[36] It is, therefore, the very condition that makes a decision necessary in the first place. It is only here that "ethics, politics, and responsibility, *if there are any,*" will begin: "When the path is clear and given, when a certain knowledge opens up the way in advance, the decision is already made, it might as well be said that there is none to make; irresponsibly, and in good conscience, one simply applies or implements a program."[37] A critical pedagogy committed to justice will, therefore, have to articulate this commitment out of a recognition of the impossibility of justice. This implies that it cannot know in advance where the dividing line between the tolerable and the intolerable will be. It requires a decision, a decision which at the very same time is necessary (it can, for the sake of justice, not wait) and impossible (as it has no ground).

On the level of practice this means, once more, that a critical pedagogy cannot proceed by saying, "This is just, do as I do." The only thing it can do -and to my mind *must* do – is to invite a judgment by asking, "What do you think about it?"[38] This question (and here I tend to agree with Gur-Ze'ev) is nonrepressive in that it does not prescribe how to judge, but "simply" opens up the possibility for one's *own* judgment. Although the nonrepressive character of this act could be taken as a sign that this is an event of emancipation, I want to stress – and here I strongly disagree with Gur-Ze'ev – that this question is in the most profound sense a *violent* question.

Derrida refers to this violence as "transcendental violence," in order to express that this violence is a condition for the very possibility of the coming into presence of the subject.[39] While in this sense this violence is a necessary violence, it still *is* a violence because the subject which is summoned into existence will never have been able to "ask" for its own subjectivity. Here we touch upon a limit for all education.

Conclusion

In the preceding pages I have argued that a critical pedagogy that wants to be pedagogically and politically consistent will have to reckon with three impossibilities: the impossibility of education, the impossibility of demystification, and the impossibility of justice. In all cases "impossibility" does not denote what is *not* possible, but that which does not appear to be possible. Impossibility is therefore not the *opposite* of the possible: impossibility *releases* the possible.[40] The recognition of the impossibility of education releases the possibility of disclosure. The recognition of the impossibility of demystification releases the possibility of transgression. The impossibility of justice releases the possibility of the incoming of the other. From here, the only conclusion that can be drawn about the future of critical pedagogy is that it will be an impossible future. That will be the real revolution.[41]

Notes

1. Interestingly enough, phrases like "demystification" and "liberation from dogmatism" can be found in one of the founding documents of German critical pedagogy and in one of the most recent defenses of the North American version. See Klaus Mollenhauer, *Erziehung und Emanzipation* [Education and Emancipation] (1964: reprint, Milnchen: Juventa Verlag, 1976), 67; see also Peter McLaren, *Revolutionary Multiculturalism: Pedagogies of Dissent for the New Millennium* (Boulder, Colo.: Westview Press, 19971, 218.
2. I will confine myself in this essay to the North American tradition. With respect to European critical pedagogy, three general remarks can be made. First of all it should be noted that critical pedagogy in Europe has especially been developed in Germany. Second, the history of German critical pedagogy is closely related to the critical theory of the Frankfurt School, drawing its main inspiration from the work of Horkheimer, Adorno, and Habermas; see Helmut Peukert, "Kritische Theorie um! Pädagogik," *Zeitschrift für Pädagogik* 30, no. 2 (1983): 195–219. Third, although there arc still authors working in the critical tradition (partly inspired by North American critical pedagogy), German critical pedagogy had its heyday in the 1960s and 1970s.
3. See McLaren, *Revolutionary Multiculturalism.*
4. Max Horkheimer and Theodor Adorno, *Dialectic of Enlightenment,* trans. John Cumming (New York: Herder and Herder, 1972).
5. Sigmund Freud, quoted in James Donald, *Sentimental Education* (London: Verso, 1992), 1.
6. Hannah Arendt, *The Human Condition* (Chicago: The University of Chicago Press, 1958), 178.
7. Ibid., 9.
8. Ibid., 190.
9. Ibid., 190–91.
10. Michel de Certeau, *The Practice of Everyday Life,* Berkeley: University of California Press, 1984), 200. An interesting example of the educational significance of this insight can be found in Louis Miron, *The Social Construction of Urban Schooling* (Cresskill, N.J.: Hampton Press, 1996).
11. See Jean-Luc Nancy, "Introduction," in *Who Comes After the Subject,* ed. Eduardo Cadava, Peter Connor, and Jean-Luc Nancy (New York: Routledge, 1991), 7. I explore the pedagogical implications of this idea in more detail in Gert Biesta, "Where are you? Where am I? Identity, Intersubjectivity and the Question of Location," in *A Report on Identity: Questioning the Logic of Identity Within Educational Theory,* ed. Carl-Anders Salstrom I Rapporter friin Centrum for Didaktik, Intitutionen for Liirarutbildning, (Uppsala Universitet, 1998), 15–41.
12. Arendt, *The Human Condition,* 179.
13. Ibid., 184.
14. Ibid., 220.
15. Ibid.
16. I take the idea of the role of ignorance in emancipatory education and of the emancipatory potential of the question "What do you think about it?" from facques Ranciere, The Ignorant Schoolmaster: Five Lessons in Intellectual Emancipation (Stanford: Stanford University Press, 1991), 36. In a fascinating essay on education as problematization, Tan Masschelein has explored the pedagogical implications of this approach in much more detail, albeit from a slightly different angle. See Tan Masschelein, "In Defence of Education as Problematisation: Some Preliminary Remarks on a Strategy of Disarmament," in Adult Education and Social Responsibility, ed. Danny Wildemeersch, Matthias Finger, and Theo fansen (Frankfurt am Main: Peter Lang, 1998), 144.
17. See also Gert J.J. Biesta, "Pedagogy Without Humanism: Foucault and the Subject of Education," *Interchange* 29, no. l (1998): 1–16.
18. Michel Foucault, *Discipline and Punish: The Birth of the Prison* (New York: Vintage, 1975), 27.
19. Michel Foucault, "What is Enlightenment?" in *The Foucault Reader,* ed. Paul Rabinow (New York: Pantheon, 1984), 47.
20. Ibid., 45.
21. Ibid.
22. See Jon Simons, *Foucault and the Political* (New York: Routledge, 1995), 69.
23. Ibid. See also Michel Foucault, "A Preface to Transgression," in *Language. Counter-memory, Practice,* ed. Donald F. Bouchard (Ithaca: Cornell University Press, 1977), 33–38 and Roy Boyne, *Foucault and Derrida: The Other Side of Reason* (London: Routledge, 1990).
24. Foucault, "What is Enlightenment?" 46.
25. William Connolly, *Identity\Difference* (Ithaca: Cornell University Press, 1991), 12.
26. I have addressed this question in a more general way in Gert *T.T.* Biesta, "Postmodernism and the Repoliticization of Education," *Interchange* 26 (1995): 161–83.

27. McLaren, *Revolutionary Multiculturalism,* 232. I doubt whether Gur-Ze' ev's plea for "conditions under which everyone will be able to become part of the human dialogue" would still count as a negative utopia.

28. I deal with this in a more detailed way in Gert R.J. Biesta, "Deconstruction, Tustice, and the Question of Education," *Zeitschrift für Erziehungswissenschaft* I (1998): 395–411.

29. Jacques Derrida, "Force of Law: The Mystical Foundation of Authority," in *Deconstruction and the Possibility of Justice,* ed. Drucilla Cornell, Michel Rosenfeld, and David Gray Carlson (London: Routledge, 1992), 20.

30. See Jacques Derrida, "Psyche: Inventions of the Other," in *Reading de Man Reading,* ed. Lindsay Waters and Wlad Godzich (Minneapolis: University of Minnesota Press, 1989).

31. Derrida, "Force of Law," 27.

32. Ibid., 10.

33. Ibid., 27.

34. "The Villanova Roundtable. A Conversation with Jacques Derrida," in *Deconstruction in a Nutshell,* ed. John Caputo (New York: Fordham University Press, 1997), 17.

35. Jacques Derrida, "Remarks on Deconstruction and Pragmatism," in *Deconstruction and Pragmatism,* ed. Chantal Mouffe (London: Routledge, 1996), 87.

36. Ernesto Laclau, *Emancipation(s)* (London: Verso, 1996), 78.

37. Jacques Derrida, *The Other Heading: Reflections on Today's Europe* (Bloomington: Indiana University Press, 1992), 41.

38. See once more Masschelein, "In Defence of Education as Problematisation."

39. See for this notion Jacques Derrida, *Writing and Difference* (Chicago: University of Chicago Press, 1978), 79–153. I have discussed the question of the violent character of education in more detail in "Where Are You? Where Am !?" For a rather similar and quite inspiring approach of the question of the violence of architecture see Bernhard Tschumi, *Architecture and Disjunction* (Cambridge: MIT Press, 1994).

40. See Richard Beardsworth, *Derrida and the Political* (London: Routledge, 1996), 26.

41. Gert p. Biesta, "Revolutions that as yet have no Model: Performance Pedagogy and its Audience," in *Philosophy of Education 1997,* ed. Susan Laird (Urbana, Ill.: Philosophy of Education Society, 1998), 198–200.

Further Readings

Section 7: Critical Higher Education and Activism

Alvarez, Z., Calvete, M., & Sarasa, M. C. (2012). 'Integrating Critical Pedagogy Theory and Practice: Classroom Experiences in Argentinean EFL Teacher Education.' *Journal for Educators, Teachers and Trainers*, 3, 60–70. Retrieved from http://www.ugr.es/~jett/index.php.

Amsler, S., Canaan, J., Cowden, S., Motta, S., & Singh, G. (2010). *Why Critical Pedagogy and Popular Education Matter Today*. Birmingham: Centre for Sociology, Anthropology and Politics, Higher Education Academy.

Cutler, A. (2009). 'In the Age of Stupid: a Call for Popular Education and Critical Pedagogy Both Inside and Outside the University.' In S. Amsler, J. Canaan, S. Cowden, S. Motta & G. Singh (eds), *Why Critical Pedagogy and Popular Education Matter Today*. Birmingham: Centre for Sociology, Anthropology and Politics, Higher Education Academy.

De Vita, A e Piussi, A. M (2013). 'Social Creation' in Mayo, P. (ed.) *Learning with Adults. A Reader*, Rotterdam, Boston and Taipei: Sense Publishers.

Escobar, M., Fernandez, A., & Guevara-Niebla, D., with Freire, P. (1994). *Paulo Freire on Higher Education. A Dialogue at the National University of Mexico*. Albany: State University of New York Press.

Finger, M. (2005). 'Critical Theory.' In L.M. English (Ed.), *International Encyclopedia of Adult Education* (165–68). Basingstoke, UK & New York: Palgrave Macmillan.

Finger, M., & Asún, J.M. (2001). *Adult Education at the Crossroads. Learning Our Way Out.*' London & New York: Zed Books.

Forbes, C. (2005). 'Taking a critical pedagogical look at travel-study abroad: "A classroom with a view" in Cusco, Peru'. *American Sociological Association*, 33(2), 181–94. Retrieved from http://www.jstor.org/stable/4127523.

Gadotti, M. (2008). 'Educazione degli Adulti e Sviluppo delle Competenze: Una Visione basata sul Pensiero Critico' (Adult Education and the Development of Competences. A Vision based on Critical Thinking). In F. Batini & A. Surian (Eds.), *Competenze e diritto all'Apprendimento* (Competences and the right to learning). Massa, Italy: Transeuropa.

Gelpi, E. (1985). *Lifelong education and international relations*. London: Croom Helm.

Gelpi, E. (2002), *Lavoro Futuro. La formazione professionale come progetto politico* (Future Work. Vocational Education as a Political Project), Milan: Edizioni Angelo Guerini e Associati SpA.

Gravani, M. N., and Zarifis, G. K.(2013). 'Introduction – A critical response to the European area of lifelong learning.' In G.K. Zarifis & M. N. Gravani (Eds.). *Challenging the 'European area of lifelong learning' – A critical response*, Dordrecht: Springer.

Harris, A. (2011). 'Singing into language: Sudanese Australian young women create public pedagogy.' *Discourse: Studies in the Cultural Politics of Education*, 32(5), 729–43. http://dx.doi.org/10.1080/01596 306.2011.620755.

Huttunen, R and Suoranta, J (2006). 'Critical and Cultural Orientation in Radical Adult Education in Antikainen, A., Harinen, P. and Torres, C.A. (Eds.) *From the margins. Adult education, Work and Civil Society*, Rotterdam, Taipei and Boston: Sense Publishers.

Hickling-Hudson, A. (1999). 'Beyond schooling. Adult education in postcolonial societies.' In R.F. Arnove & C.A. Torres (Eds.), *Comparative Education. The Dialectic of the Global and the Local* (233–55). Lanham, MD: Rowman & Littlefield.

Kapoor, D. (2009). 'Globalization, Dispossession and Subaltern Social Movements (SSM). Learning in the South.' In A. Abdi and D. Kapoor (Eds.), *Global Perspectives on Adult Education* (71–92). London & New York: Palgrave Macmillan.

Kanu, Y. (2005). 'Tensions and Dilemmas of Cross-Cultural Transfer of Knowledge: Post-structural/ Postcolonial Reflections on an Innovative Teacher Education in Pakistan.' *International Journal of Educational Development,* 25, 493–513. Retrieved from www.elsevier.com/locate/ijedudev.

Ku, H. B., Yuan-Tsang, A. W. K., & Liu, H. C. (2009). 'Triple Capacity Building as Critical Pedagogy: A Rural Social Work Practicum in China.' *Journal of Transformative Education,* 7(2), 146–63. Retrieved from http://jtd.sagepub.com/content/7/2/146.

Kumar, R. (2012). 'The Charge of Neoliberal Brigade and Higher Education in India.' *Journal for Critical Education Policy Studies,* 10(2), 258–281. Retrieved from http://www.jceps.com/wp-content/uploads/ PDFs/10-2-09.pdf.

Ollis, T. (2011). 'Learning in Social Action: The Informal and Social Learning Dimensions of Circumstantial and Lifelong Activists.' *Australian Journal of Adult Learning,* 51, 248–68.

Pereira, Fátima (2013). 'Concepts, Policies and Practices of Teacher Education: an Analysis of Studies on Teacher Education in Portugal.' *Journal of Education for Teaching: International Research and Pedagogy,* 39(5), 474–91.

Piussi, A.M (2003). 'L'incerto crinale. Formazione e lavoro nell'esperienza femminile e nel lifelong learning' (the Unclear Crest. Education and Work in Women's Experience and in Lifelong Learning), *Studium Educationis,* 2, 404–16.

Schedler, P.E. (1996). 'Gay Emancipation and the Information Society.' *Studies in the Education of Adults,* 28(2), 280–91.

Semali, L. (2009). 'Cultural Perspectives in African Adult Education: Indigenous Ways of Knowing in Lifelong Learning.' In A. Abdi & D. Kapoor (Eds.), *Global Perspectives on Adult Education* (35–52). London & New York: Palgrave Macmillan.

Sotiris, P. (2013). 'Higher Education and Class: Production or Reproduction?' *Journal for Critical Education Policy Studies,* 11, 95–143.

Stromquist, N. (2004), 'The Educational Nature of Feminist Action,' in *Dimensions of Adult Learning. Adult Education and Training in a Global Era,* Foley, G. (Ed.), Sydney: Allen & Unwin, Berkshire: Open University Press-McGraw Hill.

Suoranta, J., & Moisio, O. (2006).'Critical Pedagogy as Collective Social Expertise in Higher Education.' *International Journal of Progressive Education,* 2(3).

Teodoro, A (ed.) *A Educação Superior No Espaço Iberoamericano. Do Elitismo á Trasnacionalização* (Higher Eucation in the Ibero-American Context. From Elitism to Transnationalisation) Lisbon: Edições Universitarias Lusófona, 2010.

Contributors

Co-Editors

Antonia Darder is an international critical education scholar who holds the Leavey Endowed Chair in Ethics and Moral Leadership at Loyola Marymount University and is Professor Emerita at the University of Illinois Urbana Champaign.

Peter Mayo is a professor in the Department of Education Studies at the University of Malta and member of the Collegio Docenti for the doctoral research program in Educational Sciences and Continuing Education at the Università degli Studi di Verona.

João Paraskeva, born in Maputo, Mozambique, is the chair of the department of Education Leadership and Director of the Program in Education Leadership and Policy Studies at the University of Massachusetts, Dartmouth.

Section 1. Critical Pedagogy and the Politics of Education

Ayman Abu-Shomar is Assistant Professor of English Literature and Cultural Studies in King Saud University (KSU), Riyadh, Saudi Arabia.

Inês Barbosa de Oliveira is Professor in the Faculty of Education and Graduate Studies in Education at the State University of Rio de Janeiro (UERJ).

Maria Luiza Süssekind serves as Adjunct Professor at the Federal University of Rio de Janeiro (UNIRIO) and Visiting Professor at the University of British Columbia, Canada.

Ana Sánchez Bello is an Assistant Professor in the Department of Pedagogy and Didactics at the University of Coruña, Spain.

Domenica Maviglia is a faculty of education researcher at the University of Messina in Sicily, Italy.

Tom G. Griffiths is a senior lecturer in comparative and international education at the University of Newcastle, New South Wales, Australia.

Jo Williams is a lecturer at the Victoria University of Melbourne, Victoria, Australia.

Section 2. Globalization, Democracy, and Education

George J. Sefa Dei is Professor of Sociology and Equity Studies, Ontario Institute for Studies in Education of the University of Toronto.

Dave Hill is Professor of Education Policy, University of Northampton, United Kingdom.

Ravi Kumar teaches in the Department of Sociology, Jamia Millia Islamia University, New Delhi, India.

Maria Nikolakaki is Assistant Professor of Pedagogy and Education at the University of Peloponnese, Tripoli, Greece.

Jerrold L. Kachur is Professor in the Department of Educational Policy Studies at the University of Alberta, Canada.

Section 3. History, Knowledge, and Power

Zygmunt Bauman is a Polish sociologist and Emeritus Professor at the University of Leeds, United Kingdom.

Maria Paula Meneses is a researcher at the Centre for Social Studies at the University of Coimbra, integrating core studies on Democracy, Citizenship and Law.

Walter D. Mignolo, an Argentine semiotician, is the William H. Wannamaker Professor of Literature and Director of the Center for Global Studies and the Humanities at Duke University.

Madina V. Tlostanova is professor in the Department of History of Philosophy at Peoples' Friendship University of Russia.

Nur Masalha is a Palestinian academic and Program Director of the M.A. in Religion, Politics, and Conflict Resolution at St. Mary's University, Twickenham, United Kingdom.

Keita Takayama is a senior lecturer of Contextual Studies in Education at the University of New England.

Section 4. Society, Politics, and Curriculum

Alicia de Alba is Professor at the National Autonomous University of Mexico in Mexico City.

Kemal İnal is an Associate Professor of Education at Gazi University in Turkey.

Güliz Akkaymak is a doctoral candidate from Turkey studying Sociology at the University of Western Ontario, Canada.

Deniz Yıldırım is Assistant Professor at Istanbul Technical University, Department of Electrical Engineering, Istanbul, Turkey.

Jurjo Torres Santomé is Professor of Curriculum Studies and Education Policy at the University of Coruña, Spain.

Padma M. Sarangapani is Associate Professor and Head, CHRD, the Institute for Social and Economic Change (ISEC), Bangalore, an all-India Institute of interdisciplinary research and training in social sciences.

Section 5. Critical Praxis and Literacy

Vanessa de Oliveira Andreotti is a Canada Research Chair in Race, Inequalities and Global Change at the University of British Columbia.

Kailash C. Baral is Director at the English and Foreign Languages University, Shillong Campus, Shillong.

Moshe Levy is a sociologist in the Ariel University Center of Samaria.

Yair Galily is an applied sociologist, mass media and management researcher and a lecturer at the Zinman College, Wingate Institute, and the Interdisciplinary Centre, Herzliyya.

Parvin Safari is a teacher educator in Teacher Education College of Yazd, Iran, and currently teaching English in Iranian schools in Kuwait.

Mohammad R. Pourhashemi is a teacher educator in Teacher Education College of Yazd, Iran, and currently teaching English in Iranian schools in Kuwait.

Hok Bun Ku is an associate professor in the department of Applied Social Sciences at The Hong Kong Polytechnic University.

Angelina W. K. Yuan-Tsang is an associate vice-president of The Hong Kong Polytechnic University. She is also a professor and chair in the department of Applied Social Sciences.

Hsiao Chun Liu is an assistant professor in the Department of Social Work at the Shih Chien University in Taiwan.

Section 6. Critical Pedagogy and the Classroom

Fátima Pereira is Assistant Professor in the Faculty of Psychology and Educational Sciences at the University of Porto, Portugal where she is also a member of the Ethical Commission, and Vice-Coordinator of the Continuing Education Service.

Anne Hickling-Hudson is in the professoriate at Australia's Queensland University of Technology (QUT), where she teaches and researches in cross-cultural and international education.

Mark Vicars is a teaching and research academic in the School of Education at Victoria University, Melbourne, Australia.

Ramón Flecha is professor of sociology at the University of Barcelona and the founder and former Director of CREA, the Center of Research on Theories and Practices that Overcome Inequalities.

Marta Soler is Professor of Sociology at the University of Barcelona and current Director of CREA.

Section 7. Critical Higher Education and Activism

Boaventura de Sousa Santos is Professor of Sociology, University of Coimbra (Portugal), and Distinguished Legal Scholar at the University of Wisconsin-Madison.

Panagiotis Sotiris is Adjunct Lecturer in Sociology at the University of the Aegean, Greece.

G. Honor Fagan is a Professor of Sociology at the National University of Ireland, Maynooth.

Gert J. J. Biesta is Professor of Educational Theory and Policy at the University of Luxembourg, former president of the Philosophy of Education Society USA, and editor-in-chief of the journal *Studies in Philosophy and Education*.

Permissions

Index

Titles of publications appear in *italics*.